World History from 1500

OTHER BOOKS IN THE HARPERCOLLINS COLLEGE OUTLINE SERIES

ART
History of Art 0-06-467131-3
Introduction to Art 0-06-467122-4

BUSINESS
Business Calculus 0-06-467136-4
Business Communications 0-06-467155-0
Introduction to Business 0-06-467104-6
Introduction to Management 0-06-467127-5
Introduction to Marketing 0-06-467130-5

CHEMISTRY
College Chemistry 0-06-467120-8
Organic Chemistry 0-06-467126-7

COMPUTERS
Computers and Information Processing 0-06-467176-3
Introduction to Computer Science and Programming
   0-06-467145-3
Understanding Computers 0-06-467163-1

ECONOMICS
Introduction to Economics 0-06-467113-5
Managerial Economics 0-06-467172-0

ENGLISH LANGUAGE AND LITERATURE
English Grammar 0-06-467109-7
English Literature From 1785 0-06-467150-X
English Literature To 1785 0-06-467114-3
Persuasive Writing 0-06-467175-5

FOREIGN LANGUAGE
French Grammar 0-06-467128-3
German Grammar 0-06-467159-3
Spanish Grammar 0-06-467129-1
Wheelock's Latin Grammar 0-06-467177-1
Workbook for Wheelock's Latin Grammar
   0-06-467171-2

HISTORY
Ancient History 0-06-467119-4
British History 0-06-467110-0
Modern European History 0-06-467112-7
Russian History 0-06-467117-8
20th Century United States History 0-06-467132-1
United States History From 1865 0-06-467100-3
United States History to 1877 0-06-467111-9
Western Civilization From 1500 0-06-467102-X

Western Civilization To 1500 0-06-467101-1
World History From 1500 0-06-467138-0
World History to 1648 0-06-467123-2

MATHEMATICS
Advanced Calculus 0-06-467139-9
Advanced Math for Engineers and Scientists
   0-06-467151-8
Applied Complex Variables 0-06-467152-6
Basic Mathematics 0-06-467143-7
Calculus with Analytic Geometry 0-06-467161-5
College Algebra 0-06-467140-2
Elementary Algebra 0-06-467118-6
Finite Mathematics with Calculus 0-06-467164-X
Intermediate Algebra 0-06-467137-2
Introduction to Calculus 0-06-467125-9
Introduction to Statistics 0-06-467134-8
Ordinary Differential Equations 0-06-467133-X
Precalculus Mathematics: Functions & Graphs
   0-06-467165-8
Survey of Mathematics 0-06-467135-6

MUSIC
Harmony and Voice Leading 0-06-467148-8
History of Western Music 0-06-467107-7
Introduction to Music 0-06-467108-9
Music Theory 0-06-467168-2

PHILOSOPHY
Ethics 0-06-467166-6
History of Philosophy 0-06-467142-9
Introduction to Philosophy 0-06-467124-0

POLITICAL SCIENCE
The Constitution of the United States 0-06-467105-4
Introduction to Government 0-06-467156-9

PSYCHOLOGY
Abnormal Psychology 0-06-467121-6
Child Development 0-06-467149-6
Introduction to Psychology 0-06-467103-8
Personality: Theories and Processes 0-06-467115-1
Social Psychology 0-06-467157-7

SOCIOLOGY
Introduction to Sociology 0-06-467106-2
Marriage and the Family 0-06-467147-X

Available at your local bookstore or directly from HarperCollins at 1-800-331-3761.

HARPERCOLLINS COLLEGE OUTLINE

World History from 1500

J. Michael Allen
Brigham Young University

James B. Allen
Brigham Young University

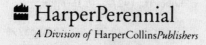
HarperPerennial
A Division of HarperCollins*Publishers*

To Kelli and Renée

An American BookWorks Corporation Production

Project Manager: Jonathon E. Brodman
Editor: Robert A. Weinstein

Library of Congress Cataloging-in-Publication Data

Allen, J. Michael, 1956–
    World history from 1500 / J. Michael Allen
        p.   cm.
    Includes bibliographical references and index.
    ISBN: 0-06-467138-0
    1. History, Modern.   I. Allen, James B., 1927–   . II. Title.
D208.A44   1993
909.08—dc20   92-53296

01 00 99 98 RRD 10 9 8 7

Contents

Preface

In presenting this short history of world civilizations since 1500, we have tried to do at least three things. First, we have tried to present an outline of the major events that have had worldwide consequences. Second, we have tried briefly to interpret those events in such a way as to suggest how they might contribute something to world understanding. Finally, we have from time to time added brief anecdotal illustrations in order to enrich the interpretation as well as to add interest.

We are the first to recognize that in a short work such as this all too much must be left unnoticed. But we owe you, the reader, at least passing mention of some things we have chosen not to include. Our hope is that you will find enough interest in world history that you will be motivated to read good books on all these topics.

First, and perhaps most glaring, is our omission of practically any discussion of the islands of the Pacific and the people who have inhabited them. Yet a growing body of literature outlines the history of these people, and we believe the student who takes time to search out their history will find some fascinating reading.

Next, we have not detailed historical development in many of the major nations of the Eastern and Western hemispheres. Again, the reason for this is that we had space to deal only with some of the major events and movements that, in the long run, became pivotal in the history of the world as a whole. We have sometimes incorporated considerable illustrative material, hoping that the reader will find it useful in understanding our interpretations.

Our final great omission is in the area of literature and the arts. Again, we urge you to read widely in these areas if you wish to round out your understanding of the world in which you live.

Our story, then, deals mainly with the great political and economic developments in the world since 1500 and the ideas that accompanied them. Sometimes ideology was the cause of a major event or long-range movement. At other times, the movement produced, or at least fed, new ideas. In any case, most such movements cannot be understood without an understanding of the ideology that accompanied them. We have tried to supply insight into some of these ideas.

We hope this book will be used in a variety of ways. First, it is intentionally short so that students reading it in a college class will have time to read some of the excellent detailed studies available for every topic we cover. We have suggested some of those studies at the end of each chapter. Next, we hope that readers who may not be in school will find it a useful guide to this era of history and that it will stimulate you to further study.

This book's coverage begins in approximately 1500, but obviously many of the events and movements we discuss have their origins before that date. For readers who wish to understand the background for many of the topics and regions discussed here, we would suggest consulting the first volume of this series, *World History to 1648*, by Jay Pascal Anglin and William J. Hamblin.

We owe a great debt to the many scholars whose detailed studies have provided us with valuable insights. We also thank Professor William J. Hamblin of Brigham Young University for sharing with us some of his material on the Middle East and permitting us to use it. To these and other people who have contributed so much, we offer our thanks.

In addition, we particularly wish to express our appreciation to our project manager, Jonathon Brodman, for his combination of exceptional patience and professional skill. Finally, our families deserve special thanks for their good humor and support throughout this project.

J. Michael Allen
James B. Allen

1

Western Europe: The Reformation Era

1509	*Praise of Folly* published
1517	Luther's ninety-five theses
1521	Diet of Worms
1524–1525	Peasants' Revolt in Germany
1533	Marriage of Henry VIII and Anne Boleyn
1540	Society of Jesus (Jesuits) approved by Pope Paul III (founded 1534)
1541	Theocracy established in Geneva under Calvin
1545–1563	Council of Trent
1553–1558	Restoration of Catholicism in England under Mary
1555	Peace of Augsburg
1588	Defeat of the Spanish Armada
1618	Beginning of Thirty Years' War
1648	Peace of Westphalia

By the end of the fifteenth century, the "new monarchies" of England, France, and Spain had developed national governments with strong, centralized authority that had effectively challenged the political power of both the nobility and the church. At the same time, the so-called "Holy Roman

Empire" was a diverse collection of hundreds of fiefs, ecclesiastical city-states, free cities, counties, and duchies that encompassed most of central Europe and northern Italy. Charles V (emperor from 1519 to 1556) felt it his obligation to preserve the power of the church in his domain, but his dream of a strong, unified empire was little more than a grand illusion.

Trade was expanding in Europe, wealth was growing, and the population was increasing. But there were also signs of tension, none of which had more possibility for disrupting society than the smoldering discontent within the church. The Protestant Reformation became the most shattering and far-reaching upheaval in centuries. It brought an end to a thousand years of Christian unity in the West, gave rise to new political and economic theories, and laid the foundation for ideological conflict and religious-political wars that continue to affect parts of the world even now. The Reformation brought about so much religious and political upheaval, in fact, that it is not inappropriate to call it the Protestant Revolution.

THE PROTESTANT REVOLUTION

Pressures for Reform

Martin Luther is usually thought of as the founder of the Reformation, but by the time he posted his famous ninety-five theses on the door of the church at Wittenberg Castle there was already a climate in Europe charged with religious discontent and highly conducive to change.

THE DECLINE OF PAPAL PRESTIGE

Dissatisfaction was aimed at all levels of the church hierarchy, beginning with the papacy, whose spiritual and political prestige had been waning for over two centuries. Most disturbing were the negative images bred by papal involvement in secular affairs. Rigid control over income-producing church lands; a military establishment; conduct of diplomacy on the same basis as any secular prince; fund raising, often through the buying and selling of ecclesiastical offices; elaborate courts; fortunes dispensed on patronage of the arts: all these things and more helped undermine the papacy's spiritual image. In addition, kings, princes, and people of wealth chafed at the political and economic power the pope could wield over them with the mere threat of excommunication.

OTHER REASONS FOR DISCONTENT

Abuses were seen at all levels. One of the most disturbing was the sale of indulgences, which involved relief from the earthly penalties of sin in return for financial contributions. The opportunity for exploitation was obvious. Critics were also dismayed that local parish priests were often in abject poverty, many were nearly illiterate, and the state of priestly morality was distressingly low. Clerical vows of celibacy were broken often; drunkenness, gambling, and other unacceptable behavior were not uncommon.

At a different level, many people seeking a more spiritually satisfying personal piety were vexed by the pomp and ceremony of church services, as well as the emphasis upon sacraments and the role of the priest. It all seemed to make salvation less a matter of personal faith than a matter of form, and it was not uncommon for dissatisfied individuals to seek fulfillment in other ways. Some looked for it in the Bible, and some found solace in lay religious fraternities dedicated to simple, pious living.

Technology and the arts also contributed significantly to the spread of discontent. The printing press had found its way into some 250 European cities by 1500; books, including the Bible, were becoming common. In addition, a profusion of satire, criticism of the clergy, and outrage at some church practices appeared with increasing frequency in printed matter as well as in the works of artists.

CHRISTIAN HUMANISM

The most important intellectual movement to help set the stage for religious reform was Christian Humanism, whose disciples anxiously probed the literature of early Christianity in their efforts to offer people a better guide to true Christian morality and spirituality. The greatest of the Humanists was the Dutchman Desiderius Erasmus, who told lay people that they should seek to live by "the philosophy of Christ," an inner piety that was not related to church routine and ceremonies. His most well-known book, *The Praise of Folly*, was a witty satire on all the weaknesses he saw in the society of his day. But more than that, it was also an appeal to his readers to go back to the simple Christian life. Scandalized at the thought that anyone should be kept from reading the scriptures, he tried to encourage the study of the Bible and published a new edition of the Greek New Testament. Erasmus was the most important intellectual forerunner of the Reformation but, ironically, as it progressed he was rejected by both sides: the church because he wanted to reform it, and the leaders of the Reformation because he refused to break with the church.

Martin Luther came on the scene at exactly the right time: intellectuals, rulers, churchmen, and lay people alike were ready for reform. Like the Humanists, Luther wanted it to come from within the church, but the circumstances of time and place moved reform in other directions.

The German Setting for the Reformation

There was no more likely place for reformation to occur than in the German states. Politically, the power of the emperor had long been in decline. But despite their desire for political independence, most of the German princes found it impossible to resist the church, with its rich, financially independent hierarchy and its hold on the minds of the people. City governments, too, resented the privileges and immunities enjoyed by clerics, such as the fact that priests, monks, and nuns were exempt from civic responsibilities and paid no taxes, even though religious orders held large amounts of urban property. People at all levels were resentful toward the church for many reasons, yet too divided to do anything about it.

Martin Luther and the Rise of Protestantism

THE INDULGENCE CONTROVERSY

The spark that finally ignited the smoldering conflict was the indulgence controversy. Indulgences were initially granted during the late eleventh century, at the time of the First Crusade, as a reward for those willing to fight to regain the Holy Land for the church. By the early sixteenth century the belief had developed that indulgences granted total pardon for all the penalties of sin—both in this life and after—and the sale of indulgences had become a common way of raising revenue for the church. In 1517, Pope Leo X (r. 1513–1521) revived an earlier indulgence proclaimed to raise funds for rebuilding St. Peter's Cathedral in Rome. The archbishop of Magdeburg, who badly needed funds to repay the debt he had incurred in order to hold more than one high ecclesiastical office, then hired the Dominican friar John Tetzel to sell indulgences throughout his territory. Tetzel's advertising campaign appealed especially to the ignorant, who were told that they could not only buy relief from the consequences of their own sins, but could also do the same for their deceased families and friends. "As soon as coin in coffer rings, the soul from purgatory springs," was reported to be one of his more melodramatic slogans. Such tactics brought phenomenal success to the campaign in Magdeburg, but they also stirred Martin Luther to action.

Martin Luther. Martin Luther began his clerical career in 1505 after being frightened in a thunderstorm and vowing to become a monk if he survived the ordeal. He was ordained a priest in 1507, and by 1512 was a professor of scripture at the University of Wittenberg. As a young friar he became deeply introspective, worrying constantly about salvation and living with a highly troubled personal conscience. He found little help in the sacraments and forms of the church. Only after he gained an insight that moved him in a new theological direction did he begin to find personal peace of mind.

Ninety-Five Theses. After intensive study of the writings of Paul, Luther concluded that the external forms of the church—elaborate ceremonies, formal liturgy, even penance—had nothing to do with salvation. Faith alone was the only way to receive God's grace, and this was a free gift that could not be earned. The indulgence campaign flew in the face of everything Luther believed. On October 31, 1517, he posted on the door of the church at Wittenberg Castle a list of ninety-five theses, or propositions, on indulgences. He raised searching questions also about papal wealth and other related topics.

Luther's intent was to stimulate public theological discussion, but the impact of his theses was much greater than he anticipated. Printed copies circulated widely, evoking discussions of even broader theological issues. The most crucial of these was that of authority: Did or did not the pope have the right to authorize indulgences at all? Luther said he did not, for indulgences were not sanctioned by scripture and therefore had no effect on salvation. His opponents argued that by questioning the authority of the pope such doctrine undermined the church itself. At first Leo X characterized the affair as merely a "squabble among monks," but eventually he issued a letter condemning some of Luther's propositions, ordering his books burned, and giving him two months to recant. Luther defiantly burned the letter in public and was excommunicated.

Charles V. It seemed impossible at that point for Emperor Charles V, who felt it his duty to protect the church, to remain aloof from the controversy. When he held his first imperial diet (an assembly of the empire's cities and princes) at Worms in April 1521, he summoned Luther to appear. Ordered to recant, Luther again refused, saying that he was bound by the scriptures and would be convinced by no other authority. The already excommunicated monk soon found himself also condemned and outlawed by the emperor. He went into hiding at the Wartburg castle, under the protection of Frederick the Wise, Elector of Saxony. He had little to fear, however, for even the princes who would remain Catholic were antagonistic enough to imperial power that they would not deliver to the emperor someone who promised to continue to erode that power.

LUTHER'S IDEOLOGY AND ITS APPEAL

Luther's most fundamental doctrine was that people were justified in the eyes of God by faith alone—not by good works or the sacraments of the church. Because of the depravity innate to humans, they were totally incapable of winning salvation through their own efforts. This hardly meant that a Christian could continue to sin, for faith in Christ compelled one to do good works, but in the end it was only faith that would be accepted by God and result in personal salvation.

A second issue was religious authority. In Luther's theology this authority rested solely with the Bible. All other forms of authority or channels of communication, including the pronouncements of the pope or of church councils, must be rejected. God's chosen faithful, Luther declared, constituted a "priesthood of all believers," thus eliminating any need for priests or popes. Luther also denied the efficacy of all the sacraments but the two he saw authorized in scripture: baptism and the Eucharist (the Lord's supper). In addition, the liturgy was simplified and services were conducted in the vernacular rather than in Latin.

The capstone to Luther's lifework was his monumental translation of the Bible into German, completed in 1534. It provided families with the opportunity to read the scriptures for themselves and actually stimulated literacy among both men and women.

The attraction of Lutheran teachings was obvious. Princes who had chafed at the rule of Rome welcomed a theology that subordinated the church to the state. Laymen saw in it the possibility for eliminating clerical abuse. The masses admired Luther's defiance of church authority, as well as his advocacy of a simpler, more personal religion, based on the spirit of early Christianity and the centrality of the scriptures.

CONSEQUENCES IN GERMANY

Luther did not anticipate most of the consequences of what he was doing, and he was stunned by some of those he lived to see. His teachings intensified social unrest among the peasants, for example, and in 1525 many angrily condemned their lay and ecclesiastical lords, who were imposing new economic burdens. Luther sympathized with them, but he also warned them against armed rebellion. Nevertheless, uprisings broke out in several states, with the peasants using slogans taken directly from Luther's writings. They were crushed after an estimated 75,000 people were killed.

Protestant Origins. As Luther urged the princes to confiscate ecclesiastical wealth and promote other church reforms, he also strengthened nationalistic feelings in the princes' domains—feelings that fed on opposition to the emperor and to his support of the church. Rulers throughout Germany took up Lutheranism, secularized church property (a means of bringing the church directly under their control, as opposed to that of the pope), and instituted simple, uncomplicated worship services. In 1529, however, at the Diet of Speyer, the emperor withdrew his policy of toleration. The Lutheran princes responded with their own declaration, "protesting" the emperor's decree. This was the origin of the term *Protestant*. Realizing that the emperor was not unwilling to resort to military force against them, in 1531 they formed a defensive alliance, known as the Schmalkaldic League, that effectively deterred him for over a decade. When war did break out even the Catholic princes refused to support the emperor. The result was the Peace of Augsburg in 1555, which formally recognized the right of each prince to determine the religion of his own state.

Protestantism was irreversibly established in Germany, and perhaps half the population of the empire was Lutheran. But the ink was hardly dry on the ninety-five theses before unorthodox teachings began to appear in many other places and in many forms.

Ulrich Zwingli and the Swiss Reformation

Switzerland was a patchwork of small, disunited states and cantons, one of which was Zurich. There, in 1518, came Ulrich Zwingli, a reformer who, like Luther, emphasized the primacy of scriptural authority and rejected the role of churchly forms. But he went further than Luther by rejecting all the sacraments, putting more emphasis on the role of the individual, and teaching that people are inherently good.

By 1529 Zurich and five other cantons had become Zwinglian. Two years later war broke out between them and the Catholic cantons. Zwingli's forces were defeated, and the reformer himself, serving as a chaplain, was killed in battle. Switzerland remained split, however, between Catholics and the reformers.

John Calvin and the Reformation

John Calvin was second only to Martin Luther in his importance to the Reformation. French by birth, Calvin devoted himself early to the study of theology. When, in 1534, he became identified with Lutheranism, he was forced to leave France. He found his way to Geneva where a friend, William Farel, was attempting to establish a reformed church. Farel persuaded Calvin that it was his obligation to God to stay and help.

CALVIN IN GENEVA

In 1537, the year after he was elected a preacher, Calvin's plan for church reform was accepted by the citizens of Geneva, but the following year he and Farel were exiled for making too many intrusions into political affairs. Three years later, however, the citizens invited Calvin to return. He soon instituted a powerful theocracy in Geneva patterned after his idea of the ideal Christian community. It was governed by two councils, the municipal council and a church consistory. The consistory, which had the authority to excommunicate, took upon itself the task of managing the moral as well as the religious life of Geneva. Eventually the majority were converted; those who remained Catholic were excommunicated and forced to leave.

The rules in Calvin's Geneva were strict, and the regimen was stern. People were regulated in the way they dressed, required to attend religious services, and forbidden to participate in such activities as card playing, dancing, and even trivial singing. Fines and punishments for the smallest offenses were severe enough, but the most serious offense, open heresy, was punishable by death.

CALVIN'S IDEOLOGY

Calvin's most important work was his *Institutes of the Christian Religion*. Like Luther, he emphasized the omnipotence of God and the total depravity of man. People could do nothing about their own salvation, but God had already predestined certain individuals, the "elect," to be saved. All the rest were predestined to be damned.

Hopeless as it may seem at first glance, this doctrine actually enhanced faith and piety among believers. While individuals could not know that they were among the elect, they were told to stop worrying about it and act as if they were. If, then, they lived according to God's will, including performing good works and attending services regularly, they could find communion with God, feel his grace in their hearts, and have reason to believe that they were among the elect.

Calvinism also helped give rise to modern capitalistic thought, for it justified wealth based on private property and individual effort, on the assumption that economic success was another sign of being among the elect. Thrift, industry, and hard work were among the highest values of the Calvinistic community.

THE SPREAD OF CALVINISM

Calvin founded an academy in Geneva and its students helped spread his ideology far and wide. By the time he died in 1564 there were more than 1 million Calvinists, called Huguenots, in France. In Scotland, meanwhile, John Knox founded the Presbyterian Church on Calvinist principles and persuaded the parliament to make it the state religion. In the Netherlands most of the population of the northern provinces joined the Calvinistic Dutch Reformed Church.

The English Reformation

In England, meanwhile, nascent Protestantism was surviving, though illegally, among the Lollards. The English Humanist William Tyndale, in Antwerp, began printing an English translation of the New Testament and sending copies to England with merchants. The Lollards eagerly distributed them, along with some of Luther's ideas. The monarch's support of the Catholic church, however, kept the pressures in check until the king himself decided it was time to throw off the remaining ties with Rome.

NATIONALIZING THE ENGLISH CHURCH

The spark that ignited the English reformation, however, had little to do with church reform and everything to do with the politics of the monarchy. King Henry VIII (r. 1509–1547) was married to Catherine of Aragon, who had given him six children but no surviving male heir. He fell in love, meanwhile, with Anne Boleyn, and decided he wanted to divorce Catherine and marry Anne. He sent a petition, therefore, to Pope Clement VII, asking for an annulment of his marriage. But Clement delayed, hoping that the problem would go away. To further complicate the matter, Emperor Charles V, who at the time held sway over Clement, was a nephew to Catherine. Henry was not to be denied, however; his personally appointed archbishop, Thomas Cranmer, granted the annulment. In 1533, Cranmer performed the marriage between the king and Anne Boleyn.

Henry soon decided to take the English church away from the jurisdiction of the pope. In 1534 parliament's Act of Supremacy declared Henry head of the Church of England. Certain prominent dissenters refused to recognize this act, including the humanist Thomas More, who resigned his lord chancellorship in protest. Some dissenters, including More, were beheaded for their opposition. Despite the apparent decisiveness of the break, however, under Henry the doctrines and practices of the church saw only minor change, though he dissolved the monasteries and confiscated their lands.

EDWARDIAN REFORM

Edward VI (r. 1547–1553) was the son of Jane Seymour, whom Henry had married after having Anne Boleyn beheaded because she did not produce a male child. During his reign several significant reforms were promoted. Clergymen were allowed to marry, the liturgy was simplified, and Archbishop Thomas Cranmer produced the *Book of Common Prayer*, to be used in all services in the Church of England. He also revised some doctrines and ceremonies to bring them more in line with reformed churches on the Continent. But when young Edward died the reforms stopped.

THE CATHOLIC RESTORATION

The new monarch was Mary Tudor (r. 1553–1558), Henry's daughter by his first wife. Determined to restore Catholicism, she earned herself the nickname "Bloody Mary" by having almost 300 Protestants burned at the stake. Her brief reign temporarily wiped out all Protestant reforms, but in another way it built support for Protestantism as it created hatred for Catholicism in the hearts of many English people.

ELIZABETH I AND THE ANGLICAN SETTLEMENT

When Mary died, the throne went to Elizabeth I (r. 1558–1603), the daughter of Anne Boleyn. Ruling as a Protestant, Elizabeth resisted pressures from some to conduct a ruthless anti-Catholic witch hunt. Nevertheless, everyone had to attend the Church of England; the *Book of Common Prayer* again became the basis for a uniform liturgy. The Thirty-Nine Articles, approved in 1563, outlined the doctrines of the Anglican church, but they were vague enough to satisfy a wide variety of people. This settlement was not universally accepted, however. In Ireland the Catholics bitterly resisted any effort to impose Anglicanism upon them. In addition, people known as Puritans (because they wanted to purify the church by eliminating more of its forms and modifying more of its doctrines) began to challenge the Anglican establishment.

Radical Protestantism: The Anabaptists

There were some similarities among all the reformers discussed so far, particularly their insistence that the church and state were linked, and their retention of some doctrines and practices, such as infant baptism. There were more radical reformers, however, who believed that in order to make the church more like early Christianity individuals must not be baptized until they were adults—old enough to be converted. Their enemies called them Anabaptists, "re-baptizers," for even though they had been baptized as infants they insisted on having this ceremony performed again.

Anabaptists rejected all forms of church authority but joined together in voluntary associations of adult believers. Some formed utopian communities where they abolished private property and shared everything in common. They also believed in the complete separation of church and state and in the ideal of religious liberty. These things, however, alarmed other Protestants as well as Catholics, all of whom insisted that church and state went hand in hand and that there was no room for religious dissent. As a result, Anabaptists were brutally persecuted from all sides. Tens of thousands were executed in northwestern and central Europe, while others fled to such places as Bohemia and Poland. They survived as Brethren, Hutterites, and Mennonites, and later some filtered back into Germany and, eventually, to North America.

THE CATHOLIC REFORMATION

The Roman Catholic Church was far from oblivious to the need for reform. Efforts to eliminate corruption and bring about change were taking place long before the Protestant Reformation erupted. The results were limited but, beginning with Pope Paul III, more effective and far-reaching reforms took place. Some were designed to eliminate abuses, others to clarify church doctrines and practices, and still others were intended to root out heresy and, if possible, reclaim the Protestants. The latter effort is sometimes called the Counter-Reformation.

Inadequate Early Efforts at Reform

Although there were some commendable efforts at reform early in the sixteenth century, they depended largely on the whims of individual popes. Julius II (r. 1503–1513) made a few moderate changes but his successor, Leo X, seemed too concerned with the secular splendor of the papacy to pay much attention to reform. Hadrian VI (r. 1522–1523) practically eliminated the luxurious papal court, cut back on the bureaucracy, halted the buying and selling of offices, and curtailed the lavish patronizing of the arts, but Clement VII (r. 1523–1534) had no interest in continuing the effort. Clement

VII also became absorbed in political conflict between France and the Holy Roman Empire that resulted, in May 1527, in the emperor's troops thoroughly sacking the city of Rome.

Paul III and the New Reformism

It remained for Paul III (r. 1534–1549) to lay the foundation for permanent internal reform. Determined to reassert papal authority throughout the church and to carry out whatever reforms were needed, in 1537 he appointed a committee to advise him. Its report was a frank, realistic assessment of abuses, and Paul immediately put into effect many of its proposals aimed at the hierarchy. He also decided to call a general church council for the purpose of reexamining church theology and, it was hoped, resolving some of the uncertainties that still plagued it. There was heavy resistance in Rome to such a move, however, and he was unable to convene the council for another ten years.

THE INQUISITION

Paul was determined also to root out heresy. In 1542 he founded the Sacred Congregation of the Holy Office, with jurisdiction over the Roman Inquisition. Composed of a committee of six cardinals, the Inquisition could impose both religious and secular penalties, and could even order executions. Under Paul III its activities were kept under control, but in later years its excesses became notorious. It accepted hearsay as evidence of heresy and other wrong-doing, felt no obligation to inform the accused of charges against them, applied torture, and often destroyed heretics themselves along with their heresies. The mere threat of being called before the Inquisition was a fearsome experience, and the atmosphere of suspicion, spying, and accusation it created seemed to some like a reign of terror. The Inquisition was most effective in the Papal States.

THE COUNCIL OF TRENT

Paul's general council finally assembled in Trent in 1545. Meeting only three times by 1563, it had a stormy history, characterized by rivalry and intense disagreement among various national factions. Most of the council's time was spent on doctrinal issues; in the end most people were amazed that it could agree on so many questions.

PAUL'S REFORMING LEGACY

Paul's achievements as a reformer set the stage for even more sweeping reforms to come. Realizing, however, that the permanency of reform depended upon his successors, he appointed to the College of Cardinals (which elected popes) men well known for their piety or learning (or both) who were also dedicated to reform. The result was a succession of popes who, by the early seventeenth century, had restored to the papacy and the church an image of spirituality and morality.

Emergence of New Religious Orders

Internal reform was strengthened also by the rise of several new religious orders, such as the Capucines, founded in 1528. This group became well known as missionaries and preachers. Their poverty, austerity, and simple preaching even convinced some Protestants to return to the Catholic fold. The Ursuline order of nuns, founded in 1535 and approved in 1544, focused on training young girls for their future roles as wives and mothers. The impact of none of these orders, however, could compare with that of the Society of Jesus, founded by the best-known figure of the Catholic Reformation, Ignatius Loyola (1491–1556).

THE SOCIETY OF JESUS

A Spanish soldier, Loyola received a serious wound in battle and, while recuperating, spent considerable time studying religious literature, especially the life of Jesus. He went through a period of deep personal soul-searching, and by the time he emerged from the hospital he had decided to devote the rest of his life to becoming a true soldier of Christ. Dressed in the plainest of clothing (some youngsters dubbed him "Father Sack"), he adopted a life of service and total austerity, wandered from place to place, and even traveled barefoot to Jerusalem and back. Eventually he decided to continue his studies in Paris, after which he recruited a small group of followers intent on accompanying him on a return to the Holy Land. They ended up in Rome, however, offering their unconditional services to the pope.

Loyola's most important publication, *Spiritual Exercises*, laid out a rigid spiritual regimen for a four-week period of retreat and study. Through such an exercise, those who joined found the spiritual strength to devote themselves to a new life of strict religious piety.

The Society of Jesus was approved by the pope in 1540, and it quickly attracted many recruits who proudly went by the name *Jesuits*. They took vows of poverty, chastity, and obedience, with special emphasis on obedience to the pope. They led lives of service, indifferent to personal discomfort and safety. They also founded schools that provided the best education available for children of both the rich and the poor.

As conscious tools of reform, the Jesuits were not above using any means necessary, including spying and persecution of heretics, to bring it about. They preferred to convert heretics rather than kill them, however. They spread rapidly throughout Europe, and their society became one of the most important instruments of the Catholic Reformation. They eventually took their message throughout much of the world.

Paul III's Successors

PAUL IV

For the most part, the fourteen popes who reigned between 1549 and 1621 were faithful in continuing the reforms begun by Paul III. Paul IV (r. 1555–1559) was particularly zealous. His nephew, Cardinal Carlo Cafra, pursued the Inquisition with unprecedented ruthlessness in Rome. Paul also attacked abuses at all levels, imposing heavy penalties on anyone who resisted or evaded his reforms. He tightened discipline among the cardinals themselves, drastically reduced the bureaucracy, and severely punished simony (the buying and selling of church offices), despite what all this did to reduce church revenue. In addition, the Holy Office published an *Index of Forbidden Books*, which banned Catholics from reading the listed books and pamphlets on the grounds that they contained heretical ideas. Books were burned by the thousands, and people were punished for possessing indexed works. Paul's excesses, however, shocked even his own cardinals and made him highly unpopular in Rome. Nevertheless, building on the foundation laid by Paul III, his reforms permanently changed the image of the papacy and enhanced the unity of the church.

THE DECREES OF THE COUNCIL OF TRENT

One symbol of this newfound unity was the fact that by the time the final session of the Council of Trent concluded in 1563, the delegates had fully agreed on all the questions of doctrine and reform that had been submitted to them. Moreover, the predominance of the pope over councils had been reasserted, and it was he who had the responsibility for confirming and executing its mandates.

The Council's most important decrees were those affirming the truth of all the doctrines Protestant reformers had rejected. It also reaffirmed the importance of the priest as well the elaborate ritual connected with worship services, insisted on sweeping clerical reforms, forbade the sale of indulgences, and required every diocese to establish a seminary where the clergy could be trained.

The first two popes to hold office after the council concluded, and particularly Pius V (r. 1566–1572), completed most of the internal reforms and expanded the work of the Inquisition. Another pope, Sixtus V (r. 1585–1590), completely reorganized the curia by fixing the number of cardinals at seventy and instituting fifteen permanent congregations to handle specific administrative and doctrinal matters. Reform was a gradual, sometimes difficult process, and it never succeeded in making reconciliation with Protestantism, but it added a new vitality to the church.

LEGACY OF VIOLENCE: WARS OF RELIGION

Background: Complexities of European Politics

Among Charles V's imperial problems was a series of wars with the Valois kings of France over certain Habsburg lands in Italy. These wars actually helped advance the cause of Protestantism when Charles, unable to keep control in Germany, signed the Peace of Augsburg in 1555. All his hopes had failed: the Protestant states were officially recognized, and his title of emperor carried with it little effective power.

In 1556 Charles abdicated, dividing his territories between his brother Ferdinand and his son Philip. Ferdinand received Austria and the empire, while Philip inherited Spain, the Low Countries (present-day Holland and Belgium), Milan, Sicily, and Spain's American possessions. As Philip II of Spain (r. 1556–1598), the new king continued the war with France and won in 1559. In England, meanwhile, Queen Elizabeth felt constantly threatened by the presence of Mary, Queen of Scots, a Catholic and legal heir to the throne who was a favorite of many of Elizabeth's opponents. These political intricacies, with religion as one of their most volatile elements, provided part of the complex and often confusing background for the tragic wars of religion that continued to plague Europe in the Reformation era.

Religious Conflict in France

By 1559 perhaps 10 percent of the population of France were Huguenots, but the weak French monarchy could do little to check their growth. Even French nobles became Protestants, which led to inevitable clashes with Catholic lords. Peasants, too, fought and killed each other. Protestants frequently attacked Catholic cathedrals, destroying statuary, stained-glass windows, and other sacred items that, to them, were symbols of idol worship. On August 24, 1572, in the infamous St. Bartholomew's Day massacre, 3,000 Huguenots were killed. At the end of three days, thousands more (variously estimated from 12,000 to 20,000) were slaughtered throughout the country.

The Catholic-Protestant struggle soon became intertwined with a three-sided rivalry for the throne that ended in 1589 with the assassination of Henry of Guise and King Henry III. A Protestant, Henry of Navarre, ascended the throne and reigned as Henry IV (r. 1589–1610). Henry believed that a strong monarchy was the only way to keep France from collapsing. Knowing that only by being part of the religious majority could he promote the cause of the monarchy as well as that of religious toleration, Henry compromised his religious principles and joined the Catholic church. On May 13, 1598, he proclaimed the famous Edict of Nantes, guaranteeing freedom of conscience to the Huguenots.

Philip II and the Revolt of the Netherlands

In the Netherlands, meanwhile, the Calvinist population was growing, especially in the north, and gaining the support of wealthy merchants who wanted independence anyway. The Protestants openly encouraged resistance to Catholic authority. Philip finally ordered the regent, his half-sister Margaret, to eliminate them. Her response was the Inquisition. She also raised taxes. In 1566 all these acts together resulted in a rash of anti-government and anti-Catholic violence. The response was brutal, as Philip's troops ruthlessly exterminated religious and political dissidents—1,500 on one day alone, March 3, 1568.

APPEAL TO ELIZABETH

Civil war continued to rage; in 1576 the provinces came together under William of Orange (called William the Silent). The ten southern provinces gradually fell to Philip's troops and remained Catholic. The other seven declared their independence as the United Provinces of the Netherlands in 1581 and became Protestant. They also begged Queen Elizabeth to come to their aid. Elizabeth, however, had no desire to offend Philip, either by executing Mary or by supporting the Dutch Protestants. But finally, convinced that if the Protestants lost Philip would invade anyway, and increasingly fearful of Mary's plots, she did both.

SPANISH ARMADA

Philip's response was to mount a vast armada of 130 ships to escort barges carrying an army of perhaps 30,000 invasion troops across the English Channel. The fleet sailed on May 30, 1588, but it was soundly defeated by 150 British ships. The war dragged on until 1609 when Philip III (r. 1598–1621) finally consented to a truce. Technically, at least, this recognized another Protestant state, the United Provinces of the Netherlands.

The Thirty Years' War

The most disastrous of all the religious wars of this period was the Thirty Years' War (1618–1648), which grew from religious and political struggles within the empire and surrounding states. As Protestant–Catholic tension continued to increase, two armed camps arose, the Protestant Union and the Catholic League. The fighting began in 1618 after a struggle relating to the throne of Bohemia. In the course of the war, characterized by a myriad of complex religious and political alliances, all the major powers of western Europe found themselves involved. In October 1648, the Peace of Westphalia finally brought an end to the war.

PEACE OF WESTPHALIA

The Peace of Westphalia marked what amounted to the end of any remaining power for the Holy Roman Empire, though the empire continued to exist in name, and with a politically impotent emperor, for another 150 years. Instead, there were over 300 independent German states, as well as hundreds of tiny semi-independent principalities. The ruler of each state had the right to determine the religion of that domain. The treaty reaffirmed the Peace of Augsburg, except that the princes could choose Calvinism, as well as Catholicism or Lutheranism.

The tragedy of the Thirty Years' War was in the devastation it wreaked on the people of Germany and Bohemia. Over a third of them died as disease, pestilence, and starvation followed the marauding armies. Economic devastation was also long-lasting, as the already dwindling trade and commerce of some areas were thoroughly destroyed. The war brought nothing but decline for most of the German population.

By 1648 the national states of Europe had been strengthened politically, and a few new national states, including the Netherlands, were on the rise. The political power of Rome had been broken, and the pattern for the development of modern political states had been set. The religious world had been shattered by the rise of Protestantism, and there was recognition of the right of each state to determine its own church. Most importantly, the church no longer controlled the state; rather, the secular authority controlled the church—with respect both to ecclesiastical appointees and church finances.

Some may have asked at the time whether it was all worth the price. The human race's capacity for inhumanity was nowhere better illustrated than in the persecution, thought control, torture, intrigue, execution, murder, and war all carried out in the name of religion. The contending faiths, however, were eventually forced to recognize that there can be no such thing as a universal church with total political and religious hegemony; such religious tyranny only binds the human mind and makes religion a matter of force or bias rather than faith or reason. This recognition was an important start toward the modern concept of free religious worship.

In the long run, the new religions, as well as the revitalized Catholic church, all made important spiritual and social contributions to the peoples of the world. The Bible could be enjoyed by all who could read, which led to their own greater spiritual development. Emphasis on Bible reading helped promote greater literacy, opening the doors of the mind to books and new ideas far outside the realms of traditional religion. For all its excesses, the Reformation helped create vital new opportunities of all sorts, along with important new ideas, for the people of the Western world.

Selected Readings

Bainton, Roland H. *Here I Stand: A Life of Martin Luther*. New York: Abingdon Press, 1950.

Bouwsma, William J. *John Calvin: A Sixteenth-Century Portrait*. New York: Oxford University Press, 1988.

Chadwick, Owen. *The Reformation*. Harmondsworth, England: Penguin, 1972.

Cheetham, Nicolas. *Keeper of the Keys: A History of the Popes from St. Peter to John Paul II*. New York: Charles Scribner's Sons, 1982.

Delumeau, Jean. *Catholicism between Luther and Voltaire*. Philadelphia: Westminster Press, 1977.

Dickens, A. G. *The English Reformation*. 2nd ed. London: Batsford, 1989.

Dunn, Richard Slator. *The Age of Religious Wars, 1559–1715*. New York: Norton, 1979.

Haile, H. G. *Luther: An Experiment in Biography*. Garden City, NY: Doubleday, 1980.

Harbison, E. Harris. *The Age of Reformation*. Ithaca, NY: Cornell University Press, 1955.

Jensen, De Lamar. *Reformation Europe: Age of Reform and Revolution*. Lexington, MA: D.C. Heath, 1981.

Kettelson, James M. *Luther the Reformer*. Minneapolis: Augsburg Publishing House, 1986.

McManners, John, ed. *The Oxford Illustrated History of Christianity*. New York: Oxford University Press, 1990.

Parker, Geoffrey, ed. *The Thirty Years' War*. Boston: Routledge & Kegan Paul, 1984.

Spitz, Lewis W. *The Protestant Reformation, 1517–1559*. New York: Harper & Row, 1985.

2

The Expansion of Western Europe: The Age of Exploration, Discovery, and Colonization (1492–1650)

1487	Bartholomew Diaz rounds Cape of Good Hope
1492	Columbus's first voyage
1494	Treaty of Tordesillas
1497–1499	Voyage of Vasco da Gama
1500	Pedro Alvares Cabral lands on Brazilian coast
1510	Goa comes under Portuguese control
1519	Magellan crosses straits from the Atlantic to the Pacific
1521	Aztecs surrender to Cortés's forces
1533	Ecuador seized by Spanish
1543	Portuguese reach Japan
1571	Spain conquers the Philippines
1588	Defeat of the Spanish Armada

1607   Founding of Virginia

1608   Establishment of Quebec

1620   Separatist "pilgrims" land at Plymouth

1636   Rhode Island founded by Roger Williams

*B*eginning about 1500 the history of the world became a history of European expansion. Unknown continents were discovered and great empires were established. The effects were myriad, and ran in both directions. European ideology, social customs, and religion were exported worldwide. Cultures of native peoples were forever changed, sometimes with devastating effects. European culture, too, was affected as the establishment of colonies brought new foods, new attitudes, and many new economic opportunities.

Five nations—Portugal, Spain, France, Holland, and England—were at the heart of this expansion. Understanding the reasons for and results of their expansionist impulses provides a framework for understanding the problems and accomplishments that followed.

THE EXPANSIONIST IMPULSE: BASIC INGREDIENTS

European expansionism was the result of a variety of motives, as well as some important technological advancements.

Motives

Incentives for expansion were economic, political, and religious in nature. The phrase "gold, God, and glory" seems to reflect the most powerful combination of motives.

ECONOMIC AND POLITICAL MOTIVES

Long before the sixteenth century the Crusades had introduced European people to the goods and luxuries of the East. Some goods, such as spices, became necessities, but they were becoming increasingly costly. They had to be transported over long and sometimes dangerous overland routes, and several middlemen each took their profits before the goods reached European merchants. What Europeans needed was a new, less costly route to Asia. Before the route was actually traversed, however, a new world was opened for conquest. This led to intense economic and political rivalry among the European powers to see who could first secure the prizes it offered and who could hold the others away.

Individuals went to the "new world" for many reasons, but most commonly to seek their fortunes. Young Spaniards expected to find new wealth in the mines. English settlers expected to get rich through ventures connected to the land and commerce. Indentured servants looked optimistically toward the end of their terms of service, when they could obtain land of their own and become independent.

RELIGIOUS MOTIVES

For rulers and common people alike, religion was also a powerful motive. Even though the Catholic rulers of Spain, Portugal, and France were bent on building empires and gaining wealth, they were also sincerely committed to converting the heathen peoples of the world. The Spanish conquerors in the New World were required to take priests with them on every expedition. The English and Dutch were just as committed to spreading the Protestant gospel, and actively encouraged missionary enterprise among native Americans. Some colonists went to America specifically to escape restrictions on their religious practices at home. They sought places where they could worship freely according to their own forms and consciences.

ADVENTURE AND MYTH

Love of adventure, curiosity, and a fascination with the possibility of locating peoples and places popularized in the mythology of the time were also factors. Some searched for Prester John, a legendary Christian king believed to rule somewhere in Africa. Others were fascinated by fables of exotic people—some with tails, others with no heads but with faces emerging from their chests. There were also tales of Amazon women on the mythical island of California, of a fountain of youth in Florida, of exotic plants and animals, and of the seven golden cities of Cibola. On a more realistic level, explorers also returned with accurate descriptions of plants, animals, and people. These reports captured the imagination, stimulating a desire to explore more far-off places.

Despite any other considerations and motives, however, the most important ingredient in the expansion of Europe was the quest for wealth.

Technology

Technological innovation contributed significantly to European expansion, for it finally made venturing farther out to sea more practical. Ships became faster and more maneuverable. By the fifteenth century the use of the magnetic compass had become widespread. Other important developments included the astrolabe, a device for observing the position of the sun and stars, and the quadrant, which measured the altitude of these heavenly bodies. Techniques for map making and charting the seas also continually improved.

THE PORTUGUESE AND SPANISH PHASE

Early Portuguese Discoveries

Portugal led the way, developing the first worldwide trading empire and dominating the sea routes to India and the Orient throughout the sixteenth century. It also had claims in South America.

PRINCE HENRY THE NAVIGATOR

The success of the Portuguese was due largely to the work of Prince Henry, a skilled and experienced navigator. Intrigued with stories of the Kingdom of Prester John, he hoped to discover the fabled Christian empire by sailing around Africa. As he laid plans for successive voyages he conducted considerable research on navigation and trained many young mariners.

EARLY EXPLORATIONS AND DISCOVERIES

In the late fifteenth century Portuguese seamen gradually moved down the coast of Africa, established stations, and brought back gold and slaves. In 1487, while on a voyage intended to locate the southern tip of Africa, Bartholomew Diaz and his ships were caught in a storm. When it subsided they found they had actually rounded the Cape of Good Hope, thus opening the way for later voyages to India. Vasco da Gama became the first European to reach India by sea during his voyage of 1497–1499. After that, Portuguese trading posts were quickly established in India.

SIGNIFICANCE OF THE CONTACT WITH INDIA

When da Gama entered Calicut harbor at the southern tip of India in May 1498, he was treated coolly by the Arab merchants who already had a monopoly on the Asian trade. They saw him, correctly, as a threat. He also discovered that the Indians were not particularly interested in the trinkets he brought from Europe. He was able to gather up a cargo of pepper and cinnamon, however. Upon his return to Portugal, da Gama found his cargo to be worth sixty times his initial investment. There was no turning back— the Portuguese were determined that the Indian and Asian trade would be theirs.

DISCOVERY OF BRAZIL

The Portuguese also made the first European contact with Brazil. The coastline was discovered in 1500 when Pedro Alvares Cabral, sailing toward

India, veered off course. Cabral claimed the territory he found for Portugal; later it was discovered that Brazil lay on the Portuguese side of the line drawn by the Treaty of Tordesillas (see below).

THE EAST ASIAN TRADING EMPIRE

The Portuguese were determined, first, to replace the Muslims in the Indian Ocean arena. The Muslims had controlled the spice trade there for too long. The Portuguese soon began seizing and destroying Muslim forts along the coast.

Extent of the Empire. Alfonso de Albuquerque, one of the great navigators of the age, was the architect of the vast Portuguese trading empire. Albuquerque, who was governor-general of the Portuguese colonies from 1509 to 1515, planned the strategy for expansion and carried it out. Earlier the Portuguese had established a colony in Calicut, on the southern tip of India. In 1510 they wrested Goa, farther north along the western coast, from the Muslims. They also took Malacca, on the Malayan peninsula, and then gradually extended their trading posts toward East Asia. In 1513 the Portuguese reached China. There, they obtained the right to establish a warehouse, and the East Asian operations proceeded; in 1543 they reached Japan.

By the early sixteenth century the Portuguese had laid claim to (though they did not fully control) most of the African coast and the west coast of India. They also dominated Ceylon and had established themselves in Madagascar, Malacca, Macao, Canton, and Java. As far as land mass was concerned, the Portuguese empire was small; however, their few island and coastal posts were so strategically located that they gave Portugal control of trade routes covering half the world. Portuguese fleets sailed annually around Africa and on to India and China, with Portuguese posts available to them all along the way. The Arab monopoly was broken.

Reasons for Success. The Portuguese were successful in their quest for commercial domination despite the fact that the countries they encountered were civilized, had far greater human resources, and did not particularly want many of the European trade goods the Portuguese originally brought with them. There were several possible reasons, besides the masterful planning and organization of Albuquerque. For one thing, they had superior naval power. In addition, Portugal eventually was able to take advantage of the silver, sugar, and other goods that poured in from South America and that were wanted by their Indian and Asian trading partners. At the same time, the people of India were having political problems and were not united, making it relatively simple for the Portuguese and other Europeans to overwhelm them even while ousting the Muslims.

Still Some Competition. The Arabs were not completely gone from the East-West trade, however. In some cases corrupt Portuguese officials accepted bribes to allow Arab shipping in the Red Sea and the Persian Gulf. Old overland routes remained in use; the Arabs and Venetians continued to compete successfully throughout the sixteenth century. In the following century, the Dutch and English helped change the nature of East-West trade permanently.

Spain and the "New" World

COLUMBUS AND THE QUEST FOR THE WESTERN ROUTE

In 1484 a Genoese mariner by the name of Christopher Columbus appeared before the king of Portugal asking for financial support to explore what he believed was the shortest route to India—across the Atlantic. The issue was not the shape of the earth (almost everyone knew it was round), but its size. Columbus believed it was only about 3,000 miles from the Portuguese coast to Japan. The Portuguese, however, were convinced that the world was much larger, and that the African route was still the shortest. They therefore rejected Columbus's plea. Two years later he was in Spain, where he won the support of Queen Isabella.

Spain's Advantage. One reason for Spain's ability to expand its economic interests was the consolidation of several kingdoms into a united Spain, under Isabella and Ferdinand, in the fifteenth century. With the increased political and financial strength of the monarchy, Spain could bear the costs of supporting exploration.

Pre-Columbian Contacts. Columbus was not the first to "discover" America. Norse explorations and conquests in the North Atlantic eventually took Leif Ericsson to Newfoundland about 1001. Over the next few years at least three different attempts at colonization were made by the Norsemen. Claims have been made for other explorers arriving even earlier. These voyages, however, had no lasting effects. No one was aware of them by 1492. The importance of Columbus's voyage is that it resulted in the first contact with America to have meaningful worldwide consequences.

Columbus's Motives. Columbus set sail for Asia on August 3, 1492, with three small ships. He was carrying a letter to the Great Khan of China and was armed with a commission that would make him governor of any lands he might discover. Columbus had visions of personal wealth, but he also dreamed of opening up opportunities to take the Christian gospel to the heathen. Nearly all the elements leading to exploration and colonization were bound in this one man: religious idealism, mythological geography, a search for personal glory, and strong economic motivation.

His Discoveries. In mid-October Columbus landed at the island of San Salvador, in what is now the American West Indies. He thought he had discovered the islands west of India, and that on another voyage he would find China or Japan. With the continuing support of the Spanish crown, he made three more voyages, believing until his death in 1506 that he had found the shortest route to India. He discovered all the major islands of the

Caribbean, including Haiti (originally called Hispaniola by the Spanish), San Salvador, Puerto Rico, Jamaica, and Cuba. Other hardy explorers followed. It soon became clear that what Columbus had actually found was a new world—new, at least, to Europeans.

Treaty of Tordesillas. As soon as Columbus publicized his claim to India, Portugal did the same. In order to resolve the conflict, the pope issued a proclamation in 1493 dividing the discoveries of the world between the two countries. The next year, however, Spain and Portugal signed an agreement, the Treaty of Tordesillas, that moved the line farther west. It was on the basis of this agreement that Portugal eventually claimed Brazil.

Later, Spain and Portugal made another agreement with respect to Asia. In a 1529 treaty the Spanish king gave up all claims to the Moluccas, or the Spice Islands, and a demarcation line was drawn to the east. The Spanish showed continuing interest in the Philippines, however, conquering them in 1571.

THE PEOPLE OF THE "NEW" WORLD

Uncertain Origins. Those who called America "new" did so from a European perspective, not stopping to observe that to well over 100 million people who were already there it was not new at all. They were descendants of ancient peoples who may have arrived from 10,000 to 30,000 years earlier. Many probably came via the land bridge that once occupied the Bering Straits, while others may have been involved in transoceanic voyages now lost to history. In any case, they covered the land from what is now northern Canada and Alaska to the tip of South America. Archeological evidence shows that various civilizations rose and fell and that those in South America reached the highest levels.

Lost Records. Unfortunately, many written records were destroyed by the Spanish, who were intent on wiping out any memory of heathen beliefs and practices. In 1562, for example, a Franciscan missionary named Diego de Landa, overzealous to stamp out heathenism, ordered that all the Maya manuscripts (written in elegant glyphs) in one town be burned. The result was the destruction of probably the greatest collection anywhere of Maya history and literature. To his credit, however, de Landa soon regretted his action. A few years later he laboriously wrote out a detailed account of the Maya he observed. He recorded their customs, religion, language, and other cultural traits as best he could.

Misunderstandings and Misnomers. Like civilizations elsewhere, the people of America were culturally diverse. They had had their dynasties, wars, and periods of feast and famine. When they first encountered Europeans, they had no idea what to expect from them or how to deal with them. Neither, it seems, did the Europeans know what to do with the original Americans. They called them Indians, a misnomer that became permanent.

Europeans generally made little effort to understand the native religious or cultural heritage. All too frequently they saw the natives either as objects of exploitation or as impediments to the advance of "civilization." At the same time, ironically, some Europeans mythologized the Native American as the "noble savage," a child of nature whose simple life and innocence could provide an appealing example to the world.

MAGELLAN

Columbus touched off a continuing scramble to find an alternate route to India. Voyages of discovery were conducted by Italian, Portuguese, Spanish, French, and English mariners. Ferdinand Magellan, a Spaniard, finally found the prize. Sailing from Seville with a fleet of five ships in September 1519, Magellan reached the straits that now bear his name in October. The seas were so rough that it took him a month to cross through to the Pacific. Reduced to three ships (one had been lost and another deserted), he continued his epic voyage to the Philippines where, in mid-March 1520, he and forty of his crew were killed. The survivors, in two remaining ships, went on to the Spice Islands, where they were attacked by the Portuguese. One ship was eventually captured but the other, the *Victoria*, damaged, leaking, and with a crew ravaged by hunger and stress, limped into the harbor at Seville on September 3, 1522. It had been a heroic voyage, and despite the tragedies some positive good had resulted. In addition to demonstrating that such a voyage was possible, the trip also demonstrated once again the economic value of the Asian trade. The single cargo of spices the *Victoria* had been able to obtain paid all the expenses of the entire two-and-a-half-year voyage.

The Spanish Empire in Latin America

The Spanish explored and conquered most of the Caribbean, killing, absorbing, or exploiting the labor of the native peoples. The area eventually provided sugar, coffee, spices, and tropical fruits for the tables of Europe, but as Spanish adventurers looked for greater fields to conquer the Caribbean islands became ports of supply for going to the mainland.

CONQUISTADORES

The most advanced and complex civilizations in Central and South America were the Aztecs and Mayas in the Yucatán peninsula and the Incas in Peru. These and other people were conquered for Spain by a number of conquistadores—adventurers and soldiers of fortune who were on a quest for wealth. During this quest, the conquistadores established the first great European empire overseas.

Cortés and Mexico. Hernando Cortés was the first to conquer a native civilization on the mainland. In 1519 he left Hispaniola leading an expedition of 600 men. They had with them seventeen horses, a cannon, and some muskets. He landed at present-day Vera Cruz, on the southeastern coast of the Yucatán peninsula, and scuttled his ships. His men had no choice but to conquer.

He moved toward the capital city, Tenochtitlán (now Mexico City), fighting and then making alliances with some of the tribes hostile to the Aztecs and their emperor, Montezuma. It may seem strange that Montezuma would allow this foreign force to enter the city peacefully, but apparently a few Aztec superstitions and religious traditions caused him to hesitate. In addition, the fact that some of their subjugated tribes were friendly to Cortés may have helped persuade the Aztec ruler to welcome the Spaniard into his capital city.

Treacherously, however, Cortés immediately took Montezuma captive. This, in turn, stirred the native priests into whipping up rebellion against the foreign intruders. During one uprising the Spaniards executed Montezuma in retaliation. Much of the Spanish force was lost; the rest had to leave the city. It was not long before they returned with about 800 more soldiers and 25,000 native allies. The great capital city was reduced to rubble. In August 1521 the Aztecs finally surrendered.

It took the Spanish somewhat longer to conquer the rest of Yucatán and northern Mexico, but by 1550 they had done so.

Pizarro and the Conquest of the Incas. If it seemed reckless for Cortés to think of conquering the Aztecs with 600 men, it was even more so for Francisco Pizarro to try to take the Inca empire in Peru with only 180 men, 27 horses, and 2 cannon. But the Incas, with 50,000 troops available, were overconfident. They had been told the white men's weapons were harmless, they had no basis for understanding Pizarro's real power, and they believed there were only a few of the invaders anyway. They had no idea that the Spaniards could be reinforced from the sea.

Pizarro set out in 1531, reaching the city of Cajamarcá on November 15, 1532. He found it deserted, for the Incas believed they could lure the Spanish into a trap and defeat them easily. The next day, however, believing he had little to fear, the ruler, Atahualpá, accepted Pizarro's invitation to ride into the city unarmed. Like Cortés, Pizarro then captured the Inca ruler and slaughtered many of his people. Atahualpá offered a huge ransom of gold and silver articles—piled seven feet high in a seventeen-by-twenty-two-foot room—for his freedom. Pizarro took the booty; then, with characteristic treachery, he executed the king. With the loss of its ruler the Inca empire fell apart. Pizarro made it easily to the capital, Cuzco, which he looted. The next year he moved on to the coast where he founded the city of Lima, which became Peru's permanent capital.

Expansion. The search for wealth led Spanish explorers and conquistadores into both American continents. They found nothing to compare with the treasure troves of the Aztecs and Incas, but the fact that such wealth had been discovered in one place gave them the incentive to follow almost every fabulous tale they heard. Ecuador was seized in 1533. Central Chile was conquered in 1540–1541. The Spaniards traversed the coast of most of South America and a large part of its interior—including tracing the Amazon River from the mountains of Peru to its mouth on the northeastern coast of Brazil.

They also expanded into North America. Juan Ponce de Leon, governor of Puerto Rico, explored the Florida coast in 1513 and tried unsuccessfully to establish a colony there in 1521. Other explorers went as far up the Atlantic coast as Newfoundland, while still others struggled overland from Texas to Mexico. Hernando de Soto went from Florida to North Carolina. In 1540 Francisco Vasquez de Coronado, compelled onward by rumors of gold and of the fabulous seven lost cities of Cibola, went from Mexico through New Mexico and as far east as Kansas. In response to a French threat, the Spanish established a short-lived colony on the coast of South Carolina in 1562. Three years later they established St. Augustine in Florida, the oldest permanent settlement in the present United States. In the 1580s missionary efforts began in New Mexico, followed by a drive for colonization; Santa Fe was founded about 1610. Eventually the Spanish claimed nearly two-thirds of the present United States, though they did not establish permanent settlements in Florida, Texas, and California until the eighteenth century.

STRUCTURE OF SPAIN'S AMERICAN EMPIRE

The conquistadores were not administrators. They soon lost their influence, to be replaced in the conquered provinces with what amounted to a Latin American feudal system. At the top were the royal administrators. Next came the encomenderos (roughly similar to feudal lords), who ruled over but presumably protected the laborers (comparable to serfs).

The Viceroyalties. General jurisdiction over colonial affairs was held by the Council of the Indies, located in Spain and under the supervision of the crown. At first the American empire was divided into two parts, New Spain, under a viceroy in Mexico City; and the viceroyalty of Peru, in Lima. Each was subdivided into smaller units, administered by audiencias, or courts, consisting of twelve to fifteen judges. By 1776 there were five viceroyalties: New Spain, New Granada, Brazil, Peru, and La Plata.

Mercantilism. The Spanish empire was the ultimate example of mercantilism—the idea that colonies existed for the benefit of the mother country. One-fifth of all the gold and silver mined in the colonies went to the crown. In addition, the colonies were discouraged from developing their own manufacturing and other industries, for manufactured goods were shipped to them by the Spanish. Mercantilist policy also forbade transporting goods in ships other than those of the mother country. This policy was also followed by other European colonial powers, particularly the English.

Early Economic Activity. About 200,000 Spanish immigrants arrived in South America in the sixteenth century. Many were former soldiers. Some developed large estates and imported sheep, cattle, and horses. They also created large sugar plantations to help feed the European appetite for this great luxury.

Native Exploitation. One major problem was that of exploiting native labor. At first, the encomenderos, or "protectors," were given the right to take tribute from native villages and to impose forced labor. Slavery was forbidden, but the encomienda system was open to abuse. It resulted in little more than legalized slavery. In 1520 the king (Charles I of Spain, or Emperor Charles V of the Holy Roman Empire) abolished it. His edict, however, did little good. Encomenderos simply refused to acknowledge the law and royal officials did little or nothing to enforce it. The king finally modified his orders. Meanwhile, many religious pleas came in behalf of the natives. The Catholic missionaries insisted that the Indians, too, had human rights. One famous Dominican, Bartolomé de Las Casas, had returned to Spain in 1515. He put continuous pressure on the crown. Las Casas also had the support of the pope, who issued an official document (known as a bull) in 1537 declaring that the Indians of America had souls, were capable of receiving the faith, and should be deprived of neither liberty nor property. In response, the king reversed his orders again, forbidding compulsory Indian labor and outlawing any further encomiendas. Once more, however, political pressure forced him to modify his rules. Nevertheless, the worst abuses of the system had been checked. After mid-century, the encomienda system waned. Replacing it was a system whereby government officials allotted workers for particular jobs, theoretically protecting their rights and wages more equitably than the old system. In reality, there were still abuses, and even though the worst offenses declined, traces of this kind of servitude remained for generations.

SOCIAL AND ECONOMIC IMPACT OF COLONIZATION

Changes in Society. It was inevitable that the coming of the conquerors would result in fundamental changes in native society. Immediately the Indians were placed under new forms of government, required to speak a new language, and were converted (usually by coercion) to a new religion. Their culture was practically destroyed, and they were exploited and brutalized by a new labor system.

The South American Slaughter. The greatest human tragedy accompanying Spanish colonialism was the death of millions of Indians during the first century. It is estimated that the native population of Peru dropped from 1.3 million in 1570 to 600,000 in 1620. In central Mexico, the population is said to have dropped from about 25.3 million when Cortés arrived to 1 million in 1605.

One reason was simply the murder and carnage that accompanied conquest and subjugation. Another was the fact that the native people were forced to work under conditions they had never experienced; they could not stand long hours either in the hot, sweltering sun as they slaved on plantations, or below ground working in unlit, dangerous mines. But the most important cause of the devastation was disease. As people were crowded together in labor camps, epidemics of various sorts set in and spread like wildfire. Smallpox was the worst of all.

Black Slavery. All this contributed to the introduction of another trade item in South America: African slaves. Beginning in the sixteenth century, native Africans were captured and shipped by the thousands in order to replace the native populations who were dying off in the mines and on the plantations.

The Economy of the Empire. The mainstay of the Spanish empire's economy was the gold and silver that native laborers or black slaves pulled from the mines of Mexico and Bolivia. It was all supposed to be stamped and registered; 18,600 tons of registered silver and 200 tons of registered gold had arrived in Spain by 1660. Additional amounts were smuggled in.

Latin America also had an important agricultural and stock-raising economy. Indian labor employed at the haciendas produced food for sale to cities and mining communities. Meanwhile, black slaves imported from Africa were employed on the huge plantations. Eventually sugar, tobacco, coffee, and cotton plantations dotted various parts of Latin America.

The Pacific Trade. The Spanish empire also developed a vigorous seaborne trade in the Pacific. It was centered in Manila, which served as a link between Spanish America and the Oriental trade. Annually a huge Spanish galleon sailed back and forth between the Mexican port of Acapulco and Manila, trading for Chinese silk and other items that had been brought to Manila by the Portuguese.

THE NORTHERN EUROPEAN PHASE

Challenge to Spanish Hegemony

Spain and Portugal reigned almost supreme in the Americas and in their Indian and Oriental trading empires throughout the sixteenth century. They were not unchallenged, however, as three other European powers became increasingly dependent upon developing their own trade and, eventually, colonies. At first they avoided intruding on the Spanish and Portuguese empires, turning instead to the North Atlantic. As early as 1496 John Cabot, sailing for England, discovered rich fishing waters off the coast of Newfoundland. In the long run the bounteous harvests reaped there proved to be of more long-lasting value than Spain's gold and silver from Central and South America. Eventually fish from this area became one of Europe's chief staples.

IN SEARCH OF THE NORTHWEST PASSAGE

Fish, however, could hardly satisfy the insatiable appetite for the potential wealth offered by the spice trade. Northern Europeans, therefore, anxiously extended their search for an alternate route—the legendary northwest passage that would take them through the American continent and on to the Orient. In 1524 an Italian, Giovanni da Verrazano, sailing for France, sailed along the North American coast from the Carolinas to Maine. His hopes were so high that at one point he looked across North Carolina's Outer Banks, saw Pamlico Sound, and deluded himself into believing it was the Pacific Ocean. Several English explorers conducted expeditions along the northeast coast and inland as far as rivers could carry them. They included Martin Frobisher (1576–1578), John Davis (1585–1587), Henry Hudson (1607–1611), and William Baffin (1615–1616). All were disappointed, but Hudson's discovery of Hudson Bay eventually resulted in opening up one of the richest fur-trading regions in America.

DIRECT CONFRONTATION: THE PRIVATEERS

The French and the Dutch. If a new route to India and Asia could not be discovered, then direct confrontation was the only way to undermine Spanish and Portuguese dominance. The first serious challenge came from France when, as early as 1524, a French privateer plundered a Spanish treasure ship in the Azores, in the North Atlantic. Next came the Dutch "Sea Beggars," whose activities grew directly from the protracted struggle by the Netherlands for independence from Spanish rule. The war ended in 1609, though the Spanish did not officially recognize the Dutch Republic until 1648. In the meantime, in the latter part of the sixteenth century Dutch privateers continually plundered Spanish ships in the Atlantic and conducted illegal trade with Spanish colonies—illegal because it violated the rules of Spanish mercantilism.

English Sea Dogs. Next came the English "Sea Dogs." Queen Elizabeth of England encouraged both Dutch and English privateers to engage in smuggling and piracy. The first great Sea Dog was John Hawkins, who in 1562 profitably smuggled African slaves into Hispaniola. He conducted a similar exploit two years later in Venezuela and Panama that netted him a cargo of silver that, it is said, made him the richest man in Europe. On his third voyage, however, from 1567 to 1568, he was caught by the Spanish at Vera Cruz. Three of his five ships were captured or destroyed. He escaped with his own ship and another commanded by his cousin, Francis Drake.

The exploits of Drake soon exceeded those of Hawkins. In 1577 he set out on his famous voyage around South America. Having abandoned any pretense of peaceful competition, he raided Spanish towns and plundered a Spanish treasure ship. He sailed north as far as California, then turned west and sailed the rest of the way around the world. After his triumphal return to England in 1580 he was knighted by the queen, who had secretly financed the expedition in the first place.

THE EFFECT OF POLITICAL RIVALRY IN EUROPE

In the meantime, the major states of Europe were squabbling both internally and with each other over a variety of issues that had both religious and political overtones (see chapter 1). These would have a direct effect on their rivalry for overseas empire. In the case of England and Spain, for example, the defeat of the Spanish Armada in 1588 helped bring about the independence of the Netherlands from Spain. In the following century the Dutch would become the first to challenge the commercial power of Portugal and Spain. Even though Spain eventually rebuilt and improved its fleet, the defeat of the Armada created a surge of national pride in England and signaled the beginning of England's eventual supremacy on the high seas.

The English as Colonizers

INCENTIVES FOR AMERICAN COLONIZATION, AND FIRST ATTEMPTS

Incentives. In their economic and political rivalry with France and Spain, the English hoped that America would yield gold. This proved to be a false hope, but they also took seriously the pleading of Richard Hakluyt, who was enthralled with the discoveries of the sixteenth century. He published books on them, and pleaded with the queen for the establishment of English colonies. The multiple benefits of a colonial venture, he argued, would include extending Protestantism, expanding trade (thereby increasing tax revenues), providing employment for England's "lustie youths," providing English ships with timber and other supplies, providing bases in the event of war with Spain, and enhancing the search for a northwest passage. He argued persuasively; in the end, many of his objectives were realized.

First Attempts. The first attempts at American colonization were disastrous. In 1578 Sir Humphrey Gilbert received a patent from the queen for colonization. In 1583 he led an expedition to Newfoundland, which he took possession of in the name of the queen. He lost some ships, however, and began to return home with the remaining two. His ship vanished and he was never heard of again. His half-brother, Sir Walter Raleigh, sponsored two unsuccessful attempts on Roanoake Island, between the Outer Banks and the mainland of North Carolina. The first group of colonists spent the winter of 1585–1586 on the island, but abandoned it the following summer because of trouble with the natives and a threat of a Spanish attack. The next year Raleigh tried again, sending 117 men, women, and children to the same location. The governor, John White, returned to England for supplies and was unable to get back to the colony, because of the war with Spain, until 1590. He found the settlement abandoned and in ruins. The colonists had vanished, leaving only one word, "Croatoan" (the name of a supposedly friendly Indian tribe), carved on a doorpost. Their fate remains a mystery.

THE ENGLISH COLONIES

Some Differences from the Spanish. In contrast to the experience of the Spanish, the English had no civilizations to conquer in the part of America where they chose to settle. There were scattered Native American tribes, some friendly and some hostile to the newcomers, but nothing like the great Aztec and Inca empires. The methods by which the colonies were established and governed were also different. While the Spanish operated under the direction of the crown, English colonies often were established by joint stock companies organized by private entrepreneurs who were willing to take risks in the expectation of reaping profits. They were granted charters by the crown, allowing them to settle and govern their respective colonies. In other cases, as in Pennsylvania, private individuals, known as proprietors, were granted such charters. In some cases the colonies were later taken over by the crown as royal colonies.

Virginia: The First Successful Colony. The first permanent English colony in America was Virginia, founded by the London Company in 1607. Unfortunately, the venture seemed ill-fated from the beginning; even though the colony survived, the stockholders made no profits. By 1622 the company had sent over 10,000 colonists to Virginia, yet at the end of that year fewer than 2,000 were still alive. There were several problems, including malaria, lack of survival skills on the part of the colonists who had initially hoped simply to go looking for gold, and poor management from the company. In its first year the colony survived only because the talented and strong-willed John Smith took over and forced the colonists to work instead of engage in speculative activities. The original settlers were practically all male; the only people who made any profits in the first few years were a group of enterprising entrepreneurs who brought volunteer women from England to be selected as wives (in exchange for a handsome fee, of course). In the end, Virginia's salvation came from a completely unexpected source. It was discovered that tobacco thrived there, and could be sold in England at a handsome profit.

New England. Religious concerns motivated the colonization of New England. The first permanent settlers were a group of separatists, dissenters from the Church of England who were looking for a place where they could promote their own faith without interference. Thrown off course from their original plan to settle in Virginia, they landed on a lonely Massachusetts shore in December 1620, named it Plymouth, and decided to stay. In contrast to the settlers in Virginia, they were hard-working, pious, and industrious. Although the colony did not become wealthy, it provided one of the more noteworthy stories of colonial success.

The Massachusetts Bay Company, meanwhile, was a purely commercial venture organized by a group of English Puritans—devout people who wanted to "purify" the Church of England from its elaborate forms and rituals and who emphasized the Calvinist doctrines of human depravity and salvation by election, or predestination. They were not separatists, but when they found it no longer possible for them to worship as they pleased in England they took their company, its charter, and almost 1,000 settlers to Massachusetts in 1630. Theirs was a unique combination of economic and religious motivation. It is unlikely that they would have made the move if they did not feel assured that they could do at least two things: make a profit (their Calvinist leanings persuaded them that the "elect" of God would be blessed with economic success) and establish a "City of Zion," or an ideal Christian community that would be a "light on a hill" to all the world. In trying to do the latter they attempted to establish a rigid, ordered society in which there was freedom to worship according to Puritan norms, but not according to any other pattern. Strict laws governed various aspects of public and private life and forbade any other religious groups to establish themselves or preach. The colony grew rapidly, eventually absorbing Plymouth and building an economy based on fishing, the fur trade, and shipbuilding.

Eventually other colonies spread outward from Massachusetts Bay. Rhode Island was founded in 1636 by Roger Williams, a Puritan dissenter who objected to the restrictions on religious consciences. In the 1630s and 1640s other such refugees established settlements in present-day Connecticut, New Hampshire, and Maine.

The economy of New England became basically one of small farms, commerce, and shipbuilding. It seems ironic to the modern mind that after the slave trade was introduced into the American colonies, Bible-toting New England shipmasters were the ones who plied the infamous but lucrative "triangular trade." In one form of the trade, they took American manufactured products to the West Indies and exchanged them for molasses, which they then transported to New England to be turned into rum. The rum not consumed in the colonies was taken to Africa, where it was exchanged for slaves who, in turn, were crammed into the ships with no room to move about and carried to the Indies in the nefarious and often deadly "middle passage." And so the cycle continued.

Later Colonies. Maryland was founded in 1632 as a proprietary colony, but after that, between 1642 and 1660, emigration to America slowed to a mere trickle because of civil conflict at home. When the Stuart kings were restored to the throne, however (see chapter 5), there was a new thrust. Wealthy friends and supporters of Charles II were given proprietorships in

Carolina. Two main centers of population emerged. Finally, in 1712, they were formally separated as North and South Carolina. In 1732 the king granted a proprietorship in Georgia to James Oglethorpe and a group of philanthropist-reformers. They turned the colony into a refuge for people imprisoned for debt. Spain continued to be outraged at these incursions into areas bordering on Florida, but by that time could do little about it. Economically, these colonies all became dependent upon large plantations and slavery. The growing of rice spread rapidly in the Carolinas and Georgia, though in later years cotton became increasingly important.

Farther north, meanwhile, the Dutch yielded to the English their New Amsterdam colony (see below), which became New York. New Jersey was later carved out as a separate colony. In 1681 William Penn was granted the proprietorship of what became the colony of Pennsylvania. This colony, benefiting from Penn's Quaker conscience, developed the most politically tolerant government of all the colonies. In 1701 the colony of Delaware was carved from Pennsylvania. Economically, these middle colonies generally subsisted on farming and the fur trade.

Thus the entire eastern seaboard was organized with English colonies by the end of the seventeenth century, with only Florida remaining as a viable Spanish claim. Immigration proceeded apace, and English domination of this portion of North America was assured. By 1688 there were over 300,000 English settlers concentrated along the Atlantic seaboard, as compared with about 20,000 French in Canada and the Mississippi Valley and little more than a handful of Spaniards in Florida.

The Dutch Empire in the Seventeenth Century

THE CARRYING TRADE

The Dutch took their initial steps into the rivalry for world power as carriers of commodities for the northern European powers. At first they shipped fish, preserved by new techniques, to various parts of Europe. They traded for corn, timber, and salt. Soon they were taking on cargoes of Spanish and Portuguese goods from their Latin American empires. The Dutch developed larger, slower, but more spacious ships, without cannon, that could carry more cargo than others. These ships helped them begin to dominate the carrying trade of the world. By 1600 their merchant marine, by far the largest in the world, numbered as many as 10,000 vessels. They developed a virtual monopoly on the Arctic whaling industry, competed successfully in the Russian area with the English Muscovy Company, and dominated the carrying trade in the Baltic region. One of their key advantages was the fact that they provided other maritime powers with naval stores (i.e., various items necessary to maintain a ship, such as tar, pitch, timber, hemp, and flax used for canvas sailcloth).

CHALLENGING THE PORTUGUESE

Dutch Fleets in the East Indies. In 1595 the Dutch sent their first fleet to the East Indies. The two-and-a-half-year voyage was costly: only 89 men returned out of the original 289 that went out. It was becoming almost common, however, for such expeditions to return with profits that outdistanced the economic losses. This one was no exception. The next expedition was even more lucrative, making a profit of 400 percent. Dutch fleets bound for the East Indies became larger and more frequent. In addition to the greater capacity of their ships, the Dutch soon found that they had several advantages over the Portuguese. These included superior seamanship as well as better and less expensive trade goods.

The East India Company. By 1602 all the private Dutch trading companies were brought together into one large organization, the Dutch East India Company. With the added strength of such unity, and with good administration, the company drove the Portuguese from the East Indies by 1629, from Malacca by 1641, and from Ceylon by 1658. It also compelled the English to withdraw to their posts in India. In addition to its trade between Asia and Europe, the company developed a huge inter-Asian trade that eventually controlled most of the commerce between China, Japan, and the Indies. Later the Dutch established a series of posts to administer and protect its monopoly, as well as a number of protectorates, which became part of a territorial empire in the eighteenth and nineteenth centuries. One of the company's most important trade products was coffee. The company began to grow coffee beans in the East Indies early in the century. Within a few years it was selling 12 million pounds annually to European coffee drinkers.

COLONIES

New Amsterdam. Besides its vast commercial empire, Holland also began to establish colonies in the seventeenth century. The first was in North America. The Dutch East India Company had hired an Englishman, Henry Hudson, to search for the illusive northwest passage. His contact with the Iroquois Indians in the Delaware Bay area resulted in a lasting trade relationship between them and the Dutch. In 1614 the Dutch West India Company established fur-trading posts on Manhattan Island. Ten years later it began a permanent settlement near there. The governor, Peter Minuit, soon purchased Manhattan from the Indians. This became the basis for the settlement of New Amsterdam, the capital of the colony of New Netherlands. The company's chief interest was the fur trade, though it also encouraged agriculture. In 1664, however, New Amsterdam fell to an English fleet. The English had been harassing Dutch shipping elsewhere, and as part of this intensifying international rivalry King Charles II of England simply granted the Dutch colony to his brother, the Duke of York. The Dutch were powerless to resist when the fleet sailed in.

South Africa. The most permanent Dutch colony was established by the East India Company in South Africa, on the Cape of Good Hope, in 1652. Its purpose was to be a provisioning port for ships bound for the Orient. It provided fresh fruit, meat, water, and other goods for Dutch ships, which helped prevent scurvy and saved thousands of seamen's lives and made a priceless contribution to Dutch commercial power in its "golden age." But the colony became more than a port of call. Former company employees and other settlers established farms in the area. Although they had some conflict with the native people, they nevertheless prospered and spread. In the process, as in every other European incursion into previously inhabited areas, they also changed the way of life of the native people.

DECLINE

In the eighteenth century, however, the Dutch trading empire gradually gave way to England and France. Both countries had larger populations, more natural resources, and other advantages that made it increasingly difficult for the Dutch to compete. The English built up their own merchant fleet, pursued their own mercantilist policies, and profited from the growing strength of their several overseas colonies, as opposed to Holland's single colony in South Africa.

French Expansionism

NEW FRANCE

The French claim to North America was established by the explorations of Jacques Cartier. In three different voyages between 1534 and 1542 he followed fanciful tales that led him to explore the Gulf of St. Lawrence and part of the St. Lawrence River. The first permanent French settlement was Quebec, established in 1608, the year after the English settled Virginia. Its founder was Samuel de Champlain, who then pushed French explorations out into the Great Lakes. His encounter with the Iroquois Indians, however, was less than friendly. Although the French got along reasonably well with other tribes, the Iroquois were always allied against them, acting as a kind of buffer between the French and the expanding English colonies.

Champlain was the first governor of New France, which became a great fur-trading empire. The colony's charter, however, stipulated that only French-speaking Catholics could settle—a provision that had important consequences in later years, especially after England took over the French possessions in America.

LOUISIANA

From the Great Lakes the French sent explorers in several directions. One was Robert Cavalier, sieur de la Salle, who paddled all the way down the Mississippi in 1682 and named the vast region Louisiana. The first settlement in that area was at Biloxi, Mississippi, in 1699. New Orleans was founded in 1718 and soon became the capital of Louisiana.

RELATIONS WITH THE ENGLISH

French and English rivalry became intense, yet until the French and Indian War (or the Seven Years' War; see chapter 5) there were no major hostilities. Each side had advantages. By the mid-eighteenth century England had some 1.5 million people inhabiting its colonies, while the French had no more than 80,000 in Canada and Louisiana. Nevertheless, the French generally got along better with the Indians, except for the Iroquois, offering them better trade goods and encroaching far less upon their lands. In addition, the French offered good markets for some colonial goods. Even in wartime, English colonists found the French trade too lucrative to pass up. They continued to provide foodstuffs and other supplies to French buyers.

French-English Colonial Rivalry Outside North America

THE WEST INDIES

The French and English both established colonies in the West Indies, where they traded with the Spanish and the Portuguese. This went against the grain of Spanish mercantilism, but with trade benefiting both parties the rules seem to have been relaxed. More importantly, the West Indian colonies produced sugar, tobacco, and indigo, all of which were important to the economies of the respective mother countries.

INDIA

By the end of the seventeenth century the two nations also faced each other in India. The English, who had fallen back to India after being driven from the East Indies by the Dutch, possessed Calcutta and Madras on the east coast as well as Surat and Bombay on the western side. The French held Chandarnagar, near Calcutta, and Pondichéry, near Madras. Both held on to these colonies at the behest of the Moghul empire. That would change, however, in the eighteenth century with the disintegration of that empire. The little colonies of the seventeenth century gave both countries the footholds necessary to become dominant political forces in India in the eighteenth century.

English, French, and Spanish Empires: A Few Comparisons

GOVERNMENT

In contrast to the French and Spanish colonies, the English colonies developed a high degree of self-government. For the most part the lower houses of the colonial legislatures were elected by property holders and had the right to pass all laws, including the levy of taxes, for their colonies.

Generations of experience with self-government prepared the English colonists well for independence when it came after 1776 (see chapter 7).

NATIVE AMERICANS

The English treatment of the Native Americans was a contrast to that of the Spanish, though it did not produce much better results. While the Spanish saw the Indians as a people to be exploited, and sometimes to be intermarried with, the English saw them as people who were in the way. The establishment of "civilization" simply meant that the "heathens" must be removed. Sometimes they made treaties with the resident tribes, not realizing that in the minds of the tribal chieftains a treaty meant little more than permission to live on the land—not permission to fence it and keep other people out. The result was a series of Indian wars, in which the Indians lost and were kept continually retreating away from the frontiers of English settlement. The French, on the other hand, looked at the Indians as trading partners. Because of their good relationships with the Native Americans, except for the Iroquois, the French were able to succeed in establishing their vast trading empire in Canada and the Mississippi Valley.

The sixteenth and seventeenth centuries brought great changes to many parts of the world, all related to the expansion of Europe. For the first time Europeans gained access to many parts of the world. A new continent was discovered in the process of trying to obtain better economic contact with an older one. Five nations wrestled with each other for commercial hegemony around the world. Each developed a vast world trading empire. All established colonies, and four became major colonial powers on the American continent. All this brought major economic changes to the world. It also brought tragic social changes into the lives of Native Americans, as well as Africans who were transported to the "new world" as slaves.

Selected Readings

Boxer, C. R. *Dutch Merchants and Mariners in Asia, 1602–1795*. London: Variorum Reprints, 1988.

———. *The Portuguese Seaborne Empire, 1415–1825*. London: Hutchinson, 1969.

Burkholder, Mark A., and Lyman L. Johnson. *Colonial Latin America*. New York: Oxford University Press, 1990.

Josephy, Alvin M. *The Indian Heritage of America*. New York: Knopf, 1973.

Morison, Samuel Eliot. *Admiral of the Ocean Sea: A Life of Christopher Columbus*. Boston: Northeastern University Press, 1983.

Nowell, Charles E. *The Great Discoveries and the First Colonial Empires*. Ithaca, NY: Cornell University Press, 1954, rev. 1965.

Parry, J. H. *The Age of Reconnaissance: Discovery, Exploration, and Settlement, 1450–1650*. Berkeley: University of California Press, 1981.

————. *The Spanish Seaborne Empire.* London: Hutchinson, New York: Knopf, 1966.

Phillips, William D., Jr., and Carla Rahn Phillips. *The Worlds of Christopher Columbus.* Cambridge, England: Cambridge University Press, 1992.

Reader's Digest. Mysteries of the Ancient Americas: The New World Before Columbus. Pleasantville, NY: The Reader's Digest Association, Inc., 1986.

3

East Asia: The Ming Dynasty in China and the Restructuring of Japan

1368	Founding of Ming dynasty
1368–1398	Reign of T'ai-tsu, first Ming emperor
1467–1477	Onin War; beginning of "warring states" period in Japan
1515	Portuguese traders arrive in Canton
1543	First Portuguese sailors land in Japan
1549	Francis Xavier reaches Japan
1587	Hideyoshi bans missionary work in Japan
1590	Reunification of Japan completed
1592	Hideyoshi's first invasion of Korea
1597	Hideyoshi's second invasion of Korea
1600	Battle of Sekigahara; Tokugawa Ieyasu victorious
1601	Matteo Ricci meets Chinese emperor
1644	Fall of Ming to rebel band; entry of Manchus into China

The expansionist urge did not affect every country equally. At the same time as European explorers were sailing to various parts of the globe, China did expand its borders. But except for a brief period in the early fifteenth century, the Chinese did not engage in overseas exploration. Instead, they turned their attention inward, recovering from a century of Mongol rule and recreating the ordered state and society that was always the objective of Chinese statecraft.

The sixteenth century in Japan was a time of warfare. When the country was finally unified late in the century, its new rulers sought first to limit Western influence, and eventually to eliminate it by closing the country.

MING CHINA (1368–1644)

Chinese history is characterized by a succession of dynasties, the first of which was established centuries before a comparable level of political organization was achieved in Europe. The Ming dynasty was the last truly Chinese dynasty. Though its successor, the Ch'ing dynasty (1644–1911), adopted many of the forms of Ming rule and much of Chinese culture, it was a conquest dynasty from the Manchu tribes of the north.

Perhaps this is one reason why the period of the Ming dynasty is considered one of the "golden ages" of China. But there are other reasons as well. It was a time of general peace, prosperity, and growth. It was also a time when literature and the arts continued to display impressive vitality.

The Ming and Ch'ing dynasties are often considered together because of the similarities in their approaches to statecraft and because many of the Ming cultural, economic, and social trends continued into the Ch'ing period. The years of the two dynasties, from the middle fourteenth century to the early twentieth century, might be thought of as "late-traditional" or "late-dynastic" China. Here we will discuss only the Ming dynasty, however, and save discussion of the Ch'ing for a time when East and West were being inexorably drawn closer together—and closer to conflict.

Recovery and Growth

DEMOGRAPHIC CHANGES

The population of China was vast by any standard, but it suffered severely during the century of Mongol rule that preceded the establishment of the Ming dynasty. Northern China bore the brunt of the Mongol invasions. Added to this was the impact of disease (including the bubonic plague, which was as devastating in China as it was in Europe) and occasional natural disasters. The population, estimated at perhaps 150 million or more on the eve of the Mongol invasions, had been reduced to perhaps 60 million by the time the Ming dynasty restored native Chinese rule.

During the nearly three centuries of Ming rule, China experienced steady population growth. Estimates of the increase range from 100 percent (from 60 million to around 125 million) to 300 percent or more (as high as 200 million) by the end of the dynasty in the seventeenth century. This was accompanied by an increase in food production that both fostered and resulted from the growth in population. The Ming government, particularly concerned about the recovery of the ravaged north, encouraged migration to depopulated areas. In addition, the government sponsored water projects (dikes and irrigation) and land reclamation to stimulate agricultural growth. Production was also aided by better strains of rice and new kinds of crops, including corn introduced from America late in the period.

ECONOMIC ACTIVITY

China's economy continued to be centered on farming, the occupation of the vast majority of the population. The Confucian ideology that characterized both statecraft and social relations had always emphasized the importance of agriculture, placing peasants at least theoretically in a position of respect, if not of wealth and power.

Commerce and Industry. But commerce and industry also grew during the Ming dynasty, along with the increase in population. Cash crops such as silk and cotton allowed many farmers, particularly in the Yangtze River valley, to augment their income or to obtain goods from other parts of China. From large cities to smaller market towns, commercial exchanges steadily increased. In the last century of Ming rule, silver further stimulated commercial activity. Much of it was mined in China's southwestern provinces, while much was imported from Japan and the Spanish colonies in exchange for Chinese silk and other goods. Ironworks, porcelain factories, and large-scale silk spinning enterprises attest both to the advanced nature of the Chinese economy and to a high level of organization.

Ming Government

The basic outline of Chinese administration had been set centuries earlier, in the bureaucratic organization of the Han dynasty (206 B.C.– A.D. 220). The Ming rulers consciously emulated the centralized government of the T'ang dynasty (616–906), but carried centralization to an even higher degree. Furthermore, the extensive bureaucracy of the Ming dynasty helped the government survive during periods of rule by weak emperors. It also eased the transition to a new, foreign dynasty when the Ming fell in the seventeenth century.

IMPERIAL DESPOTISM

The pattern for Ming politics was set by the dynasty's founder, the emperor known as T'ai-tsu. As capable as he was autocratic, T'ai-tsu attempted to concentrate as much power into his own hands as possible.

The "Mandate of Heaven." The theory behind Chinese emperorship allowed for this. Confucian ideology argued that, ideally at least, the emperor was the epitome of virtue and moral rectitude. He was the "son of heaven," the father of the national family, the guarantor of peace and stability. He and his dynasty ruled the country by virtue of the "Mandate of Heaven," the centuries-old idea that Heaven sanctions the rule of the regime in power as long as the country is governed wisely and humanely. This is not to be confused with the "divine right of kings," used to justify absolutism in Europe. The Mandate of Heaven implied no personal god passing judgment on the emperor or his subjects. Heaven was impersonal and nonanthropomorphic, but it could have a powerful impact on individual lives. The emperor's loss of the mandate could be manifested in dramatic ways; floods, famine, and widespread popular discontent could all be taken as signs of Heaven's displeasure.

Exercising Power. The emperor could be simply a figurehead, taken advantage of by ambitious bureaucrats and advisers. But depending on his personality and political will, he could also be a very real and powerful political actor. Though T'ai-tsu set a pattern of despotic, centralized rule, his successors were not always able or inclined to exercise such personal control. Into the fifteenth century, Chinese emperors continued to take a personal interest in government, ruling directly with the aid of trusted counselors. From about 1500 on, however, the Ming dynasty suffered from an absence of vigorous imperial leadership, though China continued to produce remarkable cultural achievements. During the later days of the Ming, emperors often could not be bothered with the business of government, frequently preferring instead to indulge themselves in some of the more immediate pleasures attendant to the position. Some of them found the hedonistic pleasures of the palace irresistible. The early seventeenth-century emperor Hsi-tsung even became an accomplished carpenter, though his abilities at statecraft did not match his expertise at making furniture.

Overthrow of the Ming. With the decline of competent imperial leadership, the Chinese government was plagued by maladministration and competing factions. The influence of eunuchs—who owed their position to the personal favor of the emperor and were despised by the official Confucian bureaucracy—increased, accompanied by palace intrigue and corruption. Attention to the problems of the provinces waned, resulting in widespread discontent. This was fertile ground for the rise of rebel bands, whose numbers swelled during the last days of the Ming dynasty. It was one of the most powerful of these, led by Li Tzu-ch'eng, that captured Peking in 1644. With the suicide of the Ming emperor, the dynasty came to an end.

THE BUREAUCRATIC STATE

The Chinese bureaucracy is one of the outstanding accomplishments of Chinese political history.

Administrative Structure. The emperor, at the apex of the state, had a vast army of officials under him. In addition to his personal advisers and the top administrative councils, the affairs of the nation were handled by six boards, or ministries: Personnel, Public Works, Finance, Punishment, Rites, and War. At the next level were provincial governors and district magistrates. The district magistrate was the lowest level official appointed directly from the central government. He was the crucial link between the imperial bureaucracy and the affairs of local society. Charged with the important responsibilities of keeping the peace and collecting tax revenues, this official could only perform well in his duties if he could gain the trust, or at least the cooperation, of the local aristocracy.

The Examination System. The Chinese bureaucracy also included military officials, but the most interesting aspect of Chinese government was the civil service. Chinese theories of government by no means allowed for popular participation, but the method of recruitment into the Chinese civil service did allow for occasional injections of new blood.

Government posts were given to men who had passed a grueling series of examinations based on classical Confucian literature. The theory behind this system was based on two premises. First, the Confucian classics contained the principles of good government and personal morality. Second, people could improve themselves through education. Combining these two premises led to the conclusion that a thorough education in the Confucian classics would produce literate men of virtue. And who would not want to be ruled by such people?

The Examination. In theory, the examination was open to almost any man, but in practice it was very difficult for anyone but members of the leisured upper classes to afford the time and tutors to adequately prepare. Most examination candidates did not make it past the first of the three examinations. Passing the examinations required a thorough knowledge both of the classics and of the most important commentaries on those books. It was expected that a candidate would not just be familiar in a general sense with the content of the books, but that he would have them memorized. And if that were not enough, the candidate was also graded on his ability to conform to certain set literary styles. It was a daunting task indeed! It is an indication of how attractive a career in government service was that so many men, young and old, studied for years to prepare for the examinations— some of them taking the test over and over again in the hope of passing. Many who failed to reach the highest levels of the examination system became local teachers. Others, unable to deal with the dashing of their cherished hopes, suffered breakdowns or even committed suicide.

Strengths and Weaknesses. The examination system had its advantages and disadvantages. The institution of the system, centuries before the Ming dynasty, was a conscious attempt to create a meritocracy—rule by those who had demonstrated their ability, rather than those who happened to be born into the right families or who gained the favor of the ruler by whatever means. At its best, the system produced a class of dedicated, highly educated officials. But it did not reward creativity, emphasizing instead orthodoxy and the maintenance of tradition. There were limited reforms in the procedure in the nineteenth century, but it was not eliminated until the first decade of the twentieth century.

Ming Society

Though urban areas grew steadily during the Ming dynasty, China remained a predominantly agricultural society, centered on the farming family.

THE SOCIAL ORDER

We have already mentioned the growth in commerce that changed the Chinese economy during the Ming period. Naturally, Chinese merchants benefited from this growth, as they were the ones who transported goods from one place to another and made them available for sale. In contrast with most of Europe, however, in China it was difficult to translate commercial success into political power or social prestige.

Peasants. Peasants were the most numerous group in China, and the elite scholar-official class recognized that the prosperity of the empire depended on peasant labor. Confucian statecraft required that the government be solicitous of the peasants' welfare, even while the peasants were expected to work hard and yield taxes to the government.

Artisans and Merchants. Ranking just below the peasants were artisans who, while they did not produce the staple crops on which everyone depended, nevertheless made objects of utility and value. Merchants, who were becoming increasingly important in the Chinese economy, were accorded very little social prestige. They were relegated to the bottom position in the official social hierarchy. Commercial activity was looked down on by the Confucian-educated rulers of China, who felt that a superior person did not engage in the base activity of making money. So even as merchants enriched themselves during the Ming commercial boom, they remained socially and politically inhibited.

The Farming Family. The basic unit of Chinese society, the farming family, was organized along patriarchal lines. Every family member was needed for work, especially at planting and harvest times. A large family could be a mixed blessing. It meant more mouths to feed, but it also meant more hands available for work and could be seen as a sign of prosperity. The rhythms of agricultural life were far different from the politics of the capital or the commotion of the growing trading centers—and more resistant to change.

A CONFUCIAN SOCIETY

Confucian Principles. Though it is often thought of primarily as a religion, Confucianism was originally a set of principles attributed to Confucius, the sage and would-be statesman of the sixth and fifth centuries B.C. These principles were designed to create a well-ordered society at a time when "China" was a collection of small states frequently at war with one another. Confucian principles emphasized virtue, benevolence, morality, and respect for hierarchy in government, society, and the family. By the time of the Ming dynasty, these principles were deeply ingrained in Chinese culture.

Social Order. Like the family, the entire social order was based on a hierarchy of gender and age, with men dominant and seniority respected. This was consistent with Confucian ideology, which encouraged each person to know his or her place in the family and society and to act in accordance with that position. This reached as high as the emperor himself, who was expected to be benevolent and concerned, and as low as the humblest peasant, who was expected to be obedient and hard working.

Filial Piety. The supreme virtue in Confucianism was filial piety. Parents—and especially the father—were to be accorded undying respect and obedience. This ideology fit well with the demands of the centralized Chinese state, as the emperor was depicted as the figurative father of the entire country. Just as the children in a family should honor and obey their father in exchange for his nourishing and protecting them, so all the subjects of the emperor should honor and obey him in exchange for his benevolence and wise rule.

Ming Culture

The Ming period is known for its accomplishments in scholarship, literature, and the visual arts. Building on work done by frustrated and officially suppressed scholars during the years of Mongol rule, Chinese writers also made contributions to the development of drama as both a theatrical and a literary form. The peace that prevailed during the Ming period provided an atmosphere conducive to all of these expressions.

SCHOLARSHIP

Partly for the reasons already discussed, China placed a very high value on education and scholarly achievement. Chinese scholarship tended to be inward-oriented, concentrating on further refining and explicating traditional Chinese ideas rather than on seeking out new ideas from abroad.

Neo-Confucianism. Confucian scholarship flourished during this period, but it was the body of learning and the methodology known as

"Neo-Confucianism," a combination of classical Confucianism and metaphysical speculation. Neo-Confucianism developed during the Sung dynasty (960–1279), and the interpretations that followed from the synthesis of the twelfth-century scholar Chu Hsi became orthodoxy for Chinese scholars and examination candidates.

Wang Yang-ming. One of the most important Ming thinkers was Wang Yang-ming. This philosopher and official had the same objective as all other Confucians: the discovery of historical, metaphysical, and moral truth. But Wang wrestled with the problem of how to incorporate the knowledge of truth into everyday life. Because everyone is born with the ability to live a morally good life, Wang argued, the responsibility of the individual is to overcome the obstacles to such a life that come from living in the real world. Not satisfied with much of the philosophical speculation of his day, Wang tended to deemphasize "book learning" as an end in itself in favor of practical application. His influence continued long after his death and spread to Korea and Japan as well.

LITERATURE

Though playwriting was important, the novel is perhaps the cultural achievement most often identified with the Ming period. Chinese writers produced a number of very important literary works, some of which not only rank high within the Chinese tradition, but deserve to be considered world classics as well.

The Romance of the Three Kingdoms, published in 1522, tells the story of the conflict between three states that emerged after the fall of the Han dynasty. The characters heroically depicted in its chapters formed the basis for Chinese images of valor, heroism, loyalty, and military strategy. Its popularity was not confined to China, but spread also to Korea and Japan.

Journey to the West, or *Monkey*, was published in the late sixteenth century. It centers around the trip of a Chinese Buddhist monk to India. Monkey is one of the monk's supernatural protectors and traveling companions. Possessed of fantastic powers, he also has a mischievous temperament. The novel is full of comedy and adventure.

The Water Margin (also known as *All Men Are Brothers*) is the tale of 108 Robin Hood–type bandits who strike out against corrupt officials and champion the cause of the oppressed. This novel was extremely popular, but its message of popular vengeance against corruption in high places led to its being banned by authorities of the Ch'ing dynasty.

The Golden Lotus, written during the late Ming period, is a novel about the pursuit of sexual pleasure by a wealthy merchant. It is quite explicit in its descriptions—so much so that when it was first translated into English, certain passages appeared only in Latin.

VISUAL ARTS

Calligraphy. Painting and calligraphy had long been highly prized in China. Scholars, in fact, were expected not only to be familiar with a large body of literature and to be able to compose essays that could stand as works of literature, but also to write with a good hand. This was a mark of character. In the sixteenth century, both painting and calligraphy flourished in Soochow, just south of Nanking on the Grand Canal linking the Yangtze River valley with northern China.

Porcelain. Another important visual art—both as an art form and as a trading item—was porcelain. Beautiful blue and white vases, plates, and other objects—known in the West simply as "china"—became valued possessions in Asia and Europe. This was not only an important channel of East-West contact; it also provided the major stimulus for the development of the pottery industry in Europe, where many early styles were attempts to copy Chinese patterns.

Ming Foreign Policy in East Asia

Early Ming emperors pursued a vigorous foreign policy, further extending the limits of the empire. The Ming dynasty arose with the expulsion of the Mongols, who had ruled China as the Yuan dynasty for nearly 100 years, but the Mongols continued to be a threat from the north throughout the sixteenth century.

The Tribute System. The Chinese preferred to either play off one foreign threat against another or to manage foreign affairs through the "tribute system." Under this arrangement, emissaries from foreign rulers would accept the nominal "superiority" of the Chinese emperor, in exchange for trading privileges, gifts, and the emperor's vestiture of authority for the king of the visiting ambassador. Given the costs of war, this could be a sensible foreign policy move for states wishing to deal with China. It also had the effect within China of confirming the official view of the emperor as the ruler of a civilization that was the epitome of cultural advancement.

Not all foreign states could be dealt with in this way, however. In the 1590s, the *de facto* ruler of Japan, Toyotomi Hideyoshi, twice invaded Korea on his way to conquer China for his emperor. The Korean government, which had accepted tributary status, appealed for help to China. The Chinese belatedly sent troops, but only after much of Korea was devastated by the Japanese invasion. The Japanese were driven back, largely through the instrumentality of Korean Admiral Yi Sun-sin's famous iron-clad "turtle boats," but the financial strain of Chinese participation weakened the Ming dynasty, which collapsed less than fifty years later.

Ming China and the West

The Portuguese. The first European inroads into China were made by Portuguese traders, who arrived in Canton in 1515. By mid-century the Portuguese had established themselves at Macao. Other European nations soon joined in, notably Spain and the Netherlands, purchasing such luxury goods as silk, spices, and porcelain. The balance of trade was decidedly in China's favor. Europeans had very little that interested the Chinese.

Jesuits. The traders were followed by Catholic missionaries, who were less interested in trade than in saving souls. The Jesuits (or Society of Jesus), the Catholic order that was at the forefront of the Counter-Reformation, were the most important early Westerners in China. They brought with them not only the message of Christianity, but impressive knowledge of Western science and technical skills. Highly disciplined and trained, the Jesuits were able to use their knowledge of astronomy, cartography, mathematics, and other fields to gain some influence with the emperor and the ruling class of scholars.

Matteo Ricci. The pioneer in this endeavor was Matteo Ricci. Ricci not only had an impressive command of Western learning, but he also applied himself to learning Chinese language and literature. In 1601, he became the first Jesuit to be granted an audience with the Chinese emperor himself. From this point on, Jesuit influence spread more rapidly in China, at least among the ruling class. The Ming emperor even appointed one of Ricci's successors director of the Bureau of Astronomy.

The Rites Controversy. The Jesuits ran into trouble, however, in the so-called "Rites Controversy." The Jesuits had a policy of accommodating themselves and their message to local culture and customs as much as possible. This brought them into conflict with other priestly orders, particularly the Dominicans, who felt that Jesuit accommodation diluted the purity of the Christian message.

The status of Confucius and the acceptability of Confucian rituals finally brought the conflict to a head, with the Jesuits arguing that Confucian ceremonies in honor of deceased ancestors were not worship but were social and family ceremonies that helped hold Chinese society together. Eventually, the debate had to be decided by the pope himself, who in the early eighteenth century decided against the Jesuits, spelling the effective end of early Catholic missionary work in China.

Impact on the West. It should be noted, however, that while Western influence on China during the Ming dynasty was minimal, Chinese influence on the West was more substantial. The impact of the Chinese porcelain industry has already been mentioned. This was part of a craze for things Chinese, and it would not be unusual to see aristocratic European homes decorated with Chinese art. The lavishly decorated "Chinese Room" of the Potsdam Palace in Dresden is one of the most famous examples of *chinoiserie*—the fascination with things Chinese. In addition, European Enlightenment philosophers were fascinated with the reports they received on China, which seemed to point to an idyllic society of peaceful splendor and enlightened government.

THE TRANSFORMATION OF JAPAN

Throughout the later fifteenth century and the sixteenth century, the island nation of Japan underwent decades of convulsions, disorder, and disunity. When European traders and missionaries arrived during this period, they saw a country that must have looked strikingly familiar to feudal Europe. Local rulers paid nominal allegiance to the emperor, but within their domains they were virtually autonomous. Warfare was endemic, as regional commanders sought to enlarge their lands and armies by conquest. By 1600, however, Japan had been reunified and a new political order had begun to take shape. This new order was accompanied by a renewed emphasis on a clearly defined social order. It also had economic implications, as Japan closed its doors to most outside trade and other foreign contacts and developed an internally oriented commercial economy. The merchant class became wealthy and, denied access to political participation, turned much of their wealth to artistic and hedonistic pursuits.

Warring States and Reunification (1467–1600)

In 1467 a dispute over succession to the office of *shogun* (the military strongman who ruled the country in the name of the emperor) led to a major power struggle. Known as the Onin War (1467–1477), this struggle was the beginning of a century of competition and war over land and political influence.

DISINTEGRATION

Fighting spread from Kyoto, the emperor's capital, to the provinces. As it did so, Japan disintegrated into a collection of principalities of varying size, each ruled by a local lord assisted by his army. The warriors who made up these armies were known as *samurai*. The samurai became the group most readily associated with the "warring states" period; an entire body of literature and mythology centers on the romanticized exploits of brave, loyal warriors.

The Japanese term *gekokujô* (those below overthrow those above) has been used to describe this period of warfare. The chaos implied by the term probably gives a fair indication of the precariousness of power and the fragility of the periods of peace that occasionally interrupted the fighting. Eventually, however, a group of 200 or so military lords emerged, known as *daimyo*, who were able to more effectively control their domains and their samurai armies. As the domains became more centrally organized, they appeared more and more like independent states.

Castle Towns. One important development during this period that had far-reaching implications for later Japanese history was the establishment of "castle towns" in the late sixteenth century. Dominated by an imposing citadel, these towns initially served two purposes: they gave the daimyo a strong defendable location from which to rule his domain, and they allowed him to gather his warriors in one place for better control.

In the long term, the castle towns were less important as strategic military locations than they were for several other reasons. With the warriors removed from the land to the castles, rural life became regulated largely by the peasants themselves, rather than by samurai overlords. The samurai lived on stipends paid to them by their lords, rather than on the income from land grants as had previously been the case. With a large number of samurai now settled in one place, a thriving merchant class came into being to serve their needs. Over the course of the Tokugawa period (1600–1868; see chapter 12), this merchant class became very wealthy, leading a social transformation that eventually had political consequences as well. The castle towns also accelerated urbanization in Japan, as more and more of the political, economic, and cultural life in any domain was concentrated in its castle town. Many of Japan's major cities started out as castle towns.

RESTORING STABILITY

Most of these developments took decades (or even centuries) to reach their full extent. More immediately, however, for the "warring states" of Japan, the emergence of castle towns symbolized a shift in momentum away from disorder toward order and reunification. They at least helped promote local stability and paved the way for the establishment of a stable political order, which took shape in the early seventeenth century.

Oda Nobunaga. It fell to three warlords in the late sixteenth century to finally end the century of war and decentralization. Oda Nobunaga started the process. Nobunaga was a skillful tactician, and even used firearms—recently introduced into Japan by the Portuguese—to good effect in the wars that accompanied Japanese unification. In 1568, Nobunaga entered Kyoto with his army. Controlling Kyoto was vital for any warlord with aspirations of ruling the entire country, since Kyoto was the seat of the emperor and the all-important symbolic center of the Japanese state and race.

Nobunaga was determined to eliminate challenges to his power, regardless of where he saw them. He could be ruthless in pursuit of his aims. As he saw it, restoring order in Japan included eliminating the political and economic influence of the large Buddhist monasteries outside of Kyoto. As part of this campaign, in 1571 Nobunaga destroyed the great Buddhist establishment on Mt. Hiei, both a center of Japanese Buddhism and a haven for "warrior-monks" who were virtually a law unto themselves.

Toyotomi Hideyoshi. Nobunaga was assassinated by one of his vassals in 1582. Toyotomi Hideyoshi, a foot soldier who had risen to become one of Nobunaga's leading generals, avenged his master's death and then resumed efforts to reunify the country. Through a combination of military conquest and political conciliation, Hideyoshi completed the task of unification by 1590. Ambitious enough to want the title of shogun, Hideyoshi had to settle for lesser titles because of his low birth. But he was clearly the supreme military power in Japan.

In the process of reunifying the country, Hideyoshi realized that the warfare of the preceding century had created an armed peasantry. This situation, he concluded, would be detrimental to any effort to create a stable political order. He therefore ordered that all peasants turn in their swords and other weapons. The resulting "sword hunt" brought in countless swords, spears, and other items. It appears to have been quite successful in creating a society in which the majority of the population were disarmed, ruled over by a small warrior elite who now had an absolute monopoly on the use of force.

census

Hideyoshi also conducted new land surveys to assess the productivity of agricultural land and the size of individual parcels. This became the basis for a new land tax that allowed for more systematic tax collection and greater predictability in tax revenues.

Ironically, considering his own humble birth, Hideyoshi also took steps to freeze Japanese social structure. The "sword hunt" was part of this process, as it created a distinction between warriors and everyone else. But there was also a fairly rigid distinction created between farmers and townspeople. Members of one social class rarely married into another class. Furthermore, each class was given different legal privileges and protection.

INVASION OF KOREA

Having reunified the country, Hideyoshi turned his eye to the mainland. Apparently hoping to add Korea and China to his conquests, he invaded Korea in 1592 and 1597. The invasions devastated much of Korea, though before Hideyoshi's troops could reach China, the Ming government had sent troops to assist the Koreans in driving them back. The cost of military involvement in Korea, in fact, is often cited as one of the reasons for the decline of the Ming dynasty in China. But the real hero for the Koreans was Admiral Yi Sun-sin, commander of a fleet of ships that operated in the island-dotted waters off the southern coast of Korea. Admiral Yi is credited with developing the world's first iron-clad ships, the so-called "turtle boats." Despite the Japanese troops' success on land, the Korean ships wreaked havoc with the Japanese navy. The Koreans turned back the Japanese invasion, but not before sustaining serious economic damage and loss of cultural treasures. Admiral Yi, who sustained a mortal wound while leading his fleet against Japan, has been enshrined as perhaps the greatest hero in Korean history.

ESTABLISHING TOKUGAWA RULE

Hideyoshi died in 1598, leaving only a child as his heir. The leading daimyo, who had paid at least lip service to Hideyoshi's succession wishes while he was alive, soon fell to fighting among themselves. A coalition of eastern daimyo, led by Tokugawa Ieyasu, emerged victorious in 1600 at the Battle of Sekigahara. Unlike Hideyoshi, Ieyasu was able to claim the title of shogun in 1603 by manipulation of his genealogy to show descent from the right medieval warrior family. Ieyasu established his family as the new hereditary rulers of Japan for the next 250 years. In addition, he took steps to create a stable political and social structure. The two and a half centuries of Tokugawa rule were a period of peace and prosperity. They were also a period of important social transformations, as will be discussed in chapter 12.

The Arrival of the Europeans

The Portuguese were the first Europeans to arrive in significant numbers in Japan. The first sailors arrived in 1543, landing on the island of Tanegashima after being blown off course. They were followed by traders and missionaries, initiating a period of regular contact that only ended when the Japanese government adopted a "closed-country" policy in the seventeenth century.

TRADERS

Japan was already trading regularly with China and Korea. The arrival of Western traders widened the scope of Japan's commercial contacts. The Portuguese were not the only Europeans interested in Japan; they were soon followed by Spanish, Dutch, and English ships. Most trade with Westerners was conducted in the port city of Nagasaki. During the Tokugawa period, Nagasaki was the only city open to European trade, and then only to the Dutch, whose traders were confined to the small island of Deshima, just off Nagasaki. Suspicious of Westerners, the Japanese government sought to strictly control foreign trade, both before and after the establishment of Tokugawa rule.

MISSIONARIES

With the traders came Catholic missionaries, particularly members of the Society of Jesus, known as Jesuits. In 1549, only nine years after the order was approved, one of its charter members, Francis Xavier, arrived in Japan. By the time he left two years later, Xavier had planted the seeds of a successful, if brief, Catholic missionary effort in Japan. His work was continued by other missionaries, most of whom met with considerable success. Thousands of Japanese became converted, and southern daimyo, anxious for trade with the Western nations from which the Jesuits came, generally did not discourage the missionaries' efforts. There were an estimated 150,000 Christian converts in Japan in 1580, a number which had doubled by 1600.

A blow to the missionary effort came in 1587, when the unpredictable Hideyoshi issued an edict ordering missionaries to leave Japan. Converts were generally not openly persecuted, however, as they would be in the early seventeenth century. In fact, Hideyoshi's edict was not strictly enforced, and more missionaries entered the country in the 1590s. After the beginning of rule by the Tokugawa family, however, persecution became more severe. An edict of 1614 banned Christianity. Active persecution of converts reached its peak in the Shimabara Rebellion (1637–1638), in which 30,000 to 40,000 converts lost their lives. What remained of the Christian religion in Japan was forced underground.

Japanese Culture

Despite the upheavals that characterized the century prior to Tokugawa rule, Japanese culture continued to display a high level of sophistication.

Historians of culture refer to the transition period between the "warring states" and reunification as the "Momoyama period," from the location of Hideyoshi's castle outside of Kyoto. Indeed, magnificent castles are one of the most lasting cultural legacies of this time. But the castles are not important only for their architecture. By decorating their castles with paintings, sculptures, screens, and other art objects, castle lords fostered a wide variety of arts.

VISUAL ARTS

The visual arts found a new subject for study with the arrival of Europeans in the sixteenth century. *Namban* ("Southern Barbarian") paintings showed the huge ships in which Westerners traveled to Japan. Japanese artists also depicted the Westerners themselves, emphasizing features which seemed particularly strange. A "typical" European in one of these paintings might be tall and awkward, with a long nose and red hair.

THE TEA CEREMONY

Japanese warriors were particularly attracted to the tea ceremony. In fact, there was no greater devotee than Hideyoshi himself. The actual drinking of tea was only one aspect of this highly stylized ritual, which was perfected during the Momoyama period. It had connections with Zen Buddhism, which emphasized austerity and contemplation rather than extensive iconography and textual study. The popularity of the tea ceremony also provided an impetus for the pottery industry, as finely crafted tea implements, many of them imported from Korea or showing Korean influence, became valued for both artistic and practical reasons.

*I*n China, the Ming dynasty was a period of recovery, economic growth, cultural brilliance, and stability. China was generally able to deal with outsiders on its own terms. A growing population was supported by an increase in agricultural productivity. The later years of the dynasty, however, were years of decline. As unrest increased in the countryside, the weakened central government found itself unable to deal with the combined problems of internal dissension and external pressure from Manchuria. The fall of the dynasty in 1644 opened the door for the conquest of China and the establishment of China's final dynasty.

During the same period, Japan moved from chaos and civil war to reunification under a centralized military government. But even the period of disunity was a time of important developments, such as the creation of numerous castle towns and the more rigid stratification of Japanese society. These developments eased the creation of a new political and social order under the leadership of the Tokugawa family.

Of particular note during this period is the contact between European and East Asian states. Cultural influence flowed in both directions, but China and Japan were generally able to dictate the pace and extent of Western contact. This early phase of East-West contact had relatively little lasting impact on East Asian societies. When we return to East Asia in chapter 12, however, it will be at a time when both societies were undergoing changes, and when Western pressure was both more insistent and more powerful.

Selected Readings

Boxer, C. R. *The Christian Century in Japan, 1549–1650.* Berkeley: University of California Press, 1951.

Fung Yu-lan. *A Short History of Chinese Philosophy.* Derk Bodde, ed. New York: The Free Press, 1948.

Gernet, Jacques. *A History of Chinese Civilization.* Cambridge: Cambridge University Press, 1982.

Hall, John Whitney, Nagahara Keiji, and Koso Yamamura, eds. *Japan Before Tokugawa: Political Consolidation and Economic Growth, 1500 to 1650.* Princeton, NJ: Princeton University Press, 1981.

Hane, Mikiso. *Premodern Japan: A Historical Survey.* Boulder, CO: Westview Press, 1991.

Huang, Ray. *1587, A Year of No Significance: The Ming Dynasty in Decline.* New Haven, CT: Yale University Press, 1981.

Hucker, Charles O. *China's Imperial Past.* Stanford, CA: Stanford University Press, 1975.

Keene, Donald, ed. *Anthology of Japanese Literature from the Earliest Era to the Mid-Nineteenth Century.* New York: Grove, 1955.

Mote, Frederick W., and Denis Twitchett, eds. *The Cambridge History of China. Volume 7: The Ming Dynasty, 1368–1644, Part I.* Cambridge: Cambridge University Press, 1988.

Sansom, George. *A History of Japan: 1334–1615*. Stanford, CA: Stanford University Press, 1961.

———. *Japan: A Short Cultural History*. Stanford, CA: Stanford University Press, 1978.

Schirokauer, Conrad. *A Brief History of Chinese and Japanese Civilizations*. New York: Harcourt Brace Jovanovich, 1978.

Totman, Conrad. *Japan Before Perry: A Short History*. Berkeley: University of California Press, 1981.

4

India and the Islamic World: Sixteenth Through Eighteenth Centuries

1729–1747   Nadir Shah rules Iran; military expansionism

1739   Sack of Delhi by Nadir Shah

1746   Beginning of Wahhabi fundamentalist movement in Arabia

1757   Battle of Plassey; British begin conquest of India

Historians have observed that by the middle of the sixteenth century the Ottoman empire was possibly the strongest military power in the world. The Ottoman state was one of three great Islamic empires that, collectively, dominated India, the Near East, southeastern Europe, and the northern coast of Africa. All secured their power in the sixteenth century, largely as a result of their use of important new developments in military technology. The Ottomans, however, spreading out from Turkey, became the most distinguished, not just militarily, but also in terms of culture. Literature, particularly poetry, flourished, as did the arts. Among the arts, ceramics, weaving, and architecture were especially important. In the same era that the Renaissance was reaching its height in Europe, Sinan was building some of the world's great mosques in Constantinople and elsewhere.

The Muslim empires were not just military-political states. They were also religious states—built and expanded, in part, as a Muslim crusade. In this chapter we will trace the rise of these three great states, examining briefly their strengths and weaknesses as well as the nature of their religion. We will also see how Western powers, in their quest for commercial expansion, began to influence and, eventually, dominate the weakening Islamic world.

THE MILITARY REVOLUTION IN ISLAM

Gunpowder Weapons

In the late fifteenth century a military revolution swept over the Islamic world, following much the same patterns as in the West. The development of effective gunpowder weapons—first artillery and later muskets—created new political and social power structures, which contributed to the disappearance of the older medieval order. Artillery greatly reduced the military effectiveness of castles and fortified cities, which in turn diminished the independence of decentralized feudal lords. This facilitated the rise of powerful centralized empires, which maintained their power by their relative superiority in artillery over regional warlords. Muskets further diminished the military power of the medieval mounted military aristocracy. Before muskets, the military aristocrat, with his superior training and equipment, generally had the capacity to defeat a poorly armed and trained peasant. With a musket, however, a partially trained peasant could kill the most highly trained and expensively armed mounted aristocratic warrior. Ultimately, the finest armor proved incapable of stopping a musket ball. Thus, in competition between various armies, those with the best and most numerous cannons and muskets generally proved able to defeat their enemies.

Results of the Military Revolution

In the Islamic world this new military situation led to four major developments. First, Islamic central governments were able to become increasingly centralized and autocratic. Second, small Islamic states and principalities proved unable to compete in new gunpowder technologies and were overwhelmed by their stronger and larger neighbors. Third, Islamic states with superior gunpowder technology were able to overwhelm non-Islamic neighbors in the Balkans, India, and parts of Africa. Fourth, the Central Eurasian nomads, whose military power depended on their skills at mounted archery, were eventually overwhelmed by musket-armed infantry. But in the end, although the Ottoman Turks were initially among the world leaders in the development and application of military gunpowder technology, the Muslim world slowly lost ground to the western Europeans, leading to the complete collapse of Islamic military power in the early eighteenth century. This inaugurated nearly two centuries of European domination over nearly all Muslim peoples.

THE GUNPOWDER EMPIRES

These developments led to the formation of three "Gunpowder Empires" in the Islamic world: the Mughals in India, the Safavids in Iran, and the Ottomans in the Near East and the Balkans.

Mughal India (1526–1756)

The fifteenth century in India was a period of extreme political fragmentation and conflict, with numerous small states, both Hindu and Muslim, struggling for the prize of the domination of India. In the end, an Afghanistan-based Islamic dynasty, using the latest gunpowder weapons, conquered the entire subcontinent.

BABUR (r. 1504–1530) AND THE RISE OF THE MUGHALS

Babur, the founder and one of the most remarkable rulers of the Mughal dynasty, was a descendant of two other famous conquerors—Timur and Chingiz Khan. A man of enormous energy and talent, Babur is noted for his scholarship (he wrote a massive autobiography), military genius, interest in natural science, and excellent artistic sense. Heir to the small principality of

Ferghana, he quickly rose to military dominance in Afghanistan. He modernized his army, mixing traditional central Asian horse-archer tactics with new gunpowder weapons and tactics derived from Ottoman Turkish mercenaries. With this powerful new military system, Babur invaded northern India in 1523. His campaign culminated in 1526 at the battle of Panipat, where Babur's powerful army crushed the more traditional Muslim army of the moribund sultanate of Delhi. By his death in 1530 Babur was master of most of northern India. He had founded the Mughal dynasty which would dominate India for the next two centuries.

AKBAR (r. 1542–1605)

Local Indian Muslim rulers took up arms against the Mughal invaders and nearly expelled them. But in the reign of Akbar, Mughal power was reasserted. In his sixty-three-year reign Akbar subdued all of northern India and Afghanistan and created a powerful centralized administration and modern army. A system of land reform provided peasants with fair taxes, laying the basis for agricultural prosperity. New wealth was derived from a rising class of artisans and merchants, and from international trade with the newly arriving Europeans.

Religious Views. Although raised a Muslim, Akbar took a great interest in all the religions of India, sponsoring a series of debates between the various denominations of his realm, including European Jesuits. In an attempt to unite his Hindu and Muslim subjects into a new society, he created his own religion, the Divine Faith, with himself as the high priest. His efforts were understandably accepted by neither Muslims nor Hindus.

ISLAMIC CULTURE IN MUGHAL INDIA

In the seventeenth century, Mughal Islamic culture reached its highest form in India. Nearly all of India was united into a single prosperous state, and Islamic arts flourished. The cultural achievements of Mughal India derive from two main sources of inspiration: Islamic Persian culture, and indigenous Hindu cultural forms adapted to the tastes and requirements of Islamic rulers.

Literature. Mughal literature was based on the models supplied by the courts of Islamic Persia. Numerous scholars and administrators from Persia were hired by the Mughal sultans and brought with them their Persian cultural heritage. Poetry and history writing in Persian especially flourished. Among the notable works of history in Islamic India are the *Baburnama*, an autobiography by the conqueror Babur, and the *Akbarnama*, a biography of Akbar. Some Sanskrit literature, most notably the *Mahabharata*, was translated into Persian for the entertainment of Mughal emperors.

Painting. The arts of Islamic India flourished in two major areas: painting and architecture. The Mughal emperors patronized a splendid school of painting combining influences from Persia, China, and India. Numerous large albums of miniatures and illuminated manuscripts depict details of Mughal court life and military campaigns.

Architecture. Indian Mughal architecture includes mosques, palaces, and tombs. Even the fortifications of Mughal India were often built with a style and beauty that renders them works of art. Among the best examples of the vibrant Mughal architecture is the palace complex at Fatipur Sikri. However, the most splendid building is the magnificent Taj Mahal. Built by the Mughal emperor Shah Jahan (r. 1627–1658) in 1634 as a tomb for his beloved wife Mumtaz Mahal, the Taj Mahal is considered by many to be the most beautiful building in the world.

DECAY

Aurangzeb (r. 1658–1707). The last half of the seventeenth century was dominated by the emperor Aurangzeb. A stern and autocratic man, he is noted for his military expeditions, tyranny, and oppressive taxes. A strict Muslim, Aurangzeb reversed the earlier Mughal policy of accommodation with his Hindu subjects, initiating a series of oppressive anti-Hindu laws. Although successful in his lifetime, his policies undermined the strength and unity of the Mughal state, ultimately leading to a precipitous decline in Mughal power.

The Maratha Rebellion and its Consequences. Aurangzeb's tyranny and anti-Hindu policies sparked massive rebellions of the Rajputs and Sikhs, but the most serious rebellion was that of the Hindu Marathas under their charismatic leader Shivaji. In a very real sense, Shivaji's rebellion represents the first stirring of resurgent Hindu nationalism and anti-Muslim sentiment, which would culminate in social problems in the twentieth century.

The Maratha rebellion was never fully subdued, and after Aurangzeb's death, Maratha Hindu warriors and other rebels increasingly undermined the Mughal state. Delhi was threatened, and Mughal military resources strained; ultimately the Iranian brigand-king Nadir Shah sacked Delhi in 1739. Although Mughal emperors remained on the throne, their empire vanished as various regional warlords and rebels declared independence. Thus, by the middle of the eighteenth century India was again in political chaos, with numerous warring petty Hindu and Muslim states ripe for eventual conquest by the British (see below). Mughal emperors continued to rule at Delhi as powerless puppets until the last ruler was finally deposed by the British in 1858.

Safavid Iran

ORIGINS

Following the collapse of the Timurid empire in Iran in the late fifteenth century, Iran was rent into numerous small, unstable principalities, constantly at war with each other. The political and social chaos of the age lent itself to apocalyptic religious fervor. In the mountains of Azerbaijan in north-western Iran, a small band of fanatical Shi'ite Sufis known as the Red Turbans (Qizilbash) were galvanized by their leader Ismail (r. 1501–1524). Proclaiming himself a quasi-messianic figure, Ismail led his troops to a sweeping conquest of Iran and Mesopotamia in the first decade of the sixteenth century. In spite of his defeat by the Ottoman army at the battle of Chaldiran in 1514, after which Mesopotamia was conquered by the Ottomans, the Safavids had become firmly established in Iran, which their dynasty would rule for the next two centuries.

THE SHI'ITE CONVERSION

Origins. Prior to the Safavid conquest, Iran had been largely a Sunni Muslim society, with only small non-Sunni minorities. Nonetheless, Iran had always served as a center of Sufism, esoteric Islamic thought, and heresy. Ismail had risen to power based on his claims to be an incarnation of the Twelfth Shi'ite Imam, a claim which aroused great excitement throughout Iran. Twelver Shi'ism was declared the official state religion, and a massive proselyting program was undertaken, both by conversion and by coercion. In the end, nearly all Iranians were converted to the Twelver branch of Shi'ism.

Significance. The conversion of Iran to Shi'ite Islam in the sixteenth century was to have important effects on world history. First, within Iran itself, Shi'ite culture, thought, mysticism, and philosophy became a fundamental element of Iranian society. Unlike the Sunni branch of Islam, Iranian Shi'ism developed a quasi clergy, in which the *ulama* (scholars) were organized into a regular hierarchy, and a great deal of social, legal, educational, economic, and political power eventually was usurped by the scholar class in Iran.

Shi'ite Fundamentalism. Finally, of course, the conversion of Iran to Shi'ism laid the foundation for the radical political revolution led by the Shi'ite Islamic fundamentalists, who overthrew Shah Mohammed Pahlavi in 1979 and transformed the balance of power in the Middle East in the late twentieth century. Today, the Iranian Shi'ite Islamic fundamentalist movement is still a major force in the Islamic world.

The Bahai. Another later offshoot of the conversion of Iran to Shi'ism was the development of Babism and Bahaism in Iran. Originating as a millennialistic and esoteric movement within Shi'ism, Babism derives from Mirza Ali's claim to be the Bab (gateway) to the Shi'ite "Hidden Imam." Bahaism derives from a disciple of the Bab, Baha'ullah, who saw himself as the prophet of a new age, striving for the unification of all religions and world peace. Bahaism today has increasingly distanced itself from its origins in the Shi'ite messianic fervor of the early nineteenth century and remains a small but worldwide religion.

THE GOLDEN AGE OF SHAH ABBAS I (r. 1588–1629)

Iran reached its political and cultural height during the reign of Shah Abbas I. A man of tremendous energy and brilliance, Abbas led Iran into perhaps its most glorious cultural age. Having established a strong military and efficient administration, Abbas set about making his capital at Isfahan one of the great centers of commerce and culture in the world. At its height the population of the city numbered over 1 million, making it one of the largest, wealthiest, and most splendid cities of the seventeenth century.

Persian Culture. Iranian art especially flourished in the age of Abbas. Iranian painting, architecture, tile working, carpets, tapestries, brocades, metalworking, and ceramics all became internationally renowned. The architectural masterpieces of the age are the Lutf Allah and Royal mosques. The cultural power of this golden age was felt throughout most of the Islamic world. Iranian models in poetry, literature, art, and architecture were adopted throughout the Ottoman and Mughal empires. Persian was the international language of culture and diplomacy in the Islamic world. The education of most Muslim gentlemen would include a healthy dose of Persian poetry, much as their contemporaries in Europe were gaining a classical education based on Greek and Roman models.

FALL OF THE SAFAVIDS

Nadir Shah (r. 1729–1747). Following the glorious reign of Abbas, the Safavid dynasty was led by a series of weak rulers. They squandered the power and wealth of the state, leaving it open to outside intervention. A general in the service of the last Safavids usurped all real authority, attempting to reestablish power and stability. A brilliant general, Nadir Shah defeated the Ottoman Turks, central Eurasian Turks, and the Mughals, sacking their capital at Delhi in 1739. However, he was a poor statesman, unable to come to grips with the social and economic crisis facing the Islamic world. He was assassinated in 1747, after which Iran entered a half century of political chaos.

Qajar Dynasty (1794–1925). Eventually one of the regional warlords established supremacy in Iran, initiating the Qajar dynasty, which ruled Iran throughout the nineteenth century. The Qajar rulers were never able to establish strong centralized government, faced numerous social problems, and were threatened by the expansionist Russians and British. By the beginning of World War I they were essentially under Russian hegemony.

THE OTTOMAN EMPIRE

The Rise of the Ottomans

ORIGINS

Various bands of Turkish nomads had settled in the Anatolian highlands following the great Turkish victory over the Byzantines at Manzikert in 1071. In the early fourteenth century these Turks were divided into numerous petty tribes, which vied with each other in attacking and plundering the collapsing Byzantine state. The most important and successful of the tribal warlords was Osman (r. 1281–1326), whose successors would rule Turkey for over 600 years as the Ottoman dynasty.

CONQUEST OF CONSTANTINOPLE

The Ottomans made steady military progress during the fourteenth and fifteenth centuries, conquering most of Anatolia from rival Muslim Turkish princes and conquering nearly all of the Christian Balkans as well. Constantinople, the capital of the Byzantine empire, with its massive walls, proved unconquerable until the Turks developed artillery. In 1453 Constantinople fell and was renamed Istanbul, the new capital of the Ottoman empire; the city was destined to become the greatest center of Islamic culture for the next several centuries.

CREATION OF THE EMPIRE

Ottoman military expansionism did not cease with the fall of Constantinople in 1453. During the next century and a half the Ottomans conquered most of modern Serbia, Croatia, Hungary, Romania, Moldavia, and southern Russia from the Europeans. Syria and Egypt were conquered from the Mamluks by 1517. Mesopotamia and much of Arabia were added by 1538. Most of North Africa was conquered by 1574. Throughout the sixteenth and early seventeenth centuries, the Ottomans were not only the most important Islamic empire, but the largest and most powerful European state as well.

The Golden Age

SULEIMAN THE MAGNIFICENT (r. 1520–1566)

The greatest ruler of the Ottoman empire was Suleiman the Magnificent. His policies and personality left a permanent stamp on all facets of Ottoman life. His early career was marked by his modernization of the Ottoman army, and by his great military conquests in the Balkans, eastern Mediterranean, and North Africa, creating a vast, prosperous, and secure empire. The political boundaries established by Suleiman remained essentially unchanged for the next century and a half.

ADMINISTRATION AND ARMY

Suleiman's second great contribution was the establishment of a sound Ottoman administrative system. Known in Turkish as Suleiman the "Lawgiver," he supervised the creation of an administrative and legal structure for the empire, under the legal genius Khoja Chelebi, which would last until the great Westernizing reforms of the nineteenth century. The early Ottoman empire was renowned in Europe for its powerful military, efficient bureaucracy, and autocratic imperial authority. Recruitment for the army and bureaucracy was based in part on the *devshirme*, a "tax" on young Christian boys who were taken in a state of quasi-slavery to the great palace university at Istanbul for a grueling training course in military and administrative skills. The elite soldiers who emerged from this training program, known as the Janissaries, were among the finest in the world. The success and longevity of the Ottoman empire is in large part due to its superb administration and army.

CULTURE

Finally, Suleiman presided over the golden age in Islamic culture. The crown of Ottoman culture was its architecture, created by a delightful and harmonious blend of Byzantine, Arab, and Persian styles. The master architect of Suleiman was Sinan, one of the greatest architects in world history. A product of the devshirme system, Sinan first served for nearly twenty years as a military engineer in the Janissary. His skills in engineering won him the position of royal architect in 1538; he designed over 300 buildings in the course of his fifty-year career. His masterpiece is the Selimiye mosque at Erdine, which surpasses the size of the great Byzantine dome of Hagia Sofia. The entire architectural "feel" of Istanbul is essentially the extension of the artistic vision of Sinan.

Other arts also flourished in the Ottoman empire. Following Persian models, painting and manuscript illustration became an important art form. Metalworking and tile working were also highly developed. The Ottomans developed a complex semiartificial literary language which was a mixture of Turkish, Persian, and Arabic; indeed, the educated Ottoman could speak all three languages fluently. Poetry was an integral part of Ottoman aristocratic society; historical writing also flourished.

CRISIS IN THE ISLAMIC WORLD

By the early eighteenth century, all the major Islamic empires were in a state of severe crisis with both internal and external dimensions. Internally, the Islamic states were faced with government corruption and incompetence, economic depression, intellectual stagnation, and decentralization. Externally, Islamic societies were unable to face the rising military and economic threat of western Europe.

Government Corruption

By the early eighteenth centuries, most Islamic governments had become incapable of governing. In part this was due to moral decadence of the leaders. Many rulers of Iran, Turkey, and India were alcoholics or drug addicts who had murdered their way to the throne, only to idle away their time and squander government resources in the pleasures of the harem. Rather than dealing with the important and difficult problems of governing, imperial courts became rife with corruption, intrigue, and murder.

TYRANNY

Tyranny became the norm in governments in the Islamic world. In the Ottoman empire, for example, a new ruler ascending the throne would frequently systematically murder all his brothers and other potential rivals. As polygamists, Ottoman sultans would normally have numerous sons, each of whom would realize that if he did not succeed his father, he would most likely be killed. The resulting factions, intrigues, murders, and coups created an environment in which an heir to the throne would likely be a murderous paranoid tyrant. Courtiers who dared to challenge such rulers often paid for their impudence with their lives. Under such circumstances, reform was extremely difficult. The resulting paralysis left rulers and governments incapable of dealing with the numerous serious problems facing the Islamic world.

Economic Depression

The Islamic world entered a period of relative economic depression in the eighteenth century. Warfare and internal disorder contributed to depopulation. Europe was beginning its industrial and economic revolution, increasingly gaining control of the trade routes of the world. Competition from European products and the usurpation of the trade routes by the Europeans led to the decline of Islamic industries and the loss of trade routes. For example, Isfahan, the capital of the Safavid dynasty, which had been one of the great trading and cultural centers of the world in the seventeenth century, had been reduced to one-fourth of its former population by the end of the eighteenth century.

Government incompetence, corruption, and squandering of resources, combined with the economic depression, meant that most governments in the Islamic world were in a continual state of bankruptcy. Unable to pay their soldiers, bureaucrats, or foreign loans, the governments attempted to increase taxes on an already impoverished peasant population. Such oppression led to widespread dissatisfaction with the imperial order.

Intellectual Stagnation

Continuing intellectual patterns which had begun in the Renaissance, the eighteenth century in Europe was a period of tremendous intellectual vitality and development. Along with new philosophies and ideas about democracy, new intellectual approaches to the natural and physical universe were developed, which culminated in the European Scientific Revolution. These changes gave the Europeans an increasing advantage in technology, providing greater agricultural and industrial capacity, more wealth, better ships and weapons, and superior armies.

A similar intellectual revolution was not forthcoming in the Islamic world. After many brilliant intellectual advances in technology, law, and sciences in the sixteenth century, Islamic thought became sterile and conservative, content with repeating the authoritative pronouncements of the past rather than attempting to break new ground. For example, printing was introduced in Europe in 1453; within a few decades every major city in Europe had its own printing presses. The first printing press in Istanbul was not introduced until 1727, nearly three centuries later. Thus the Islamic world participated in few of the tremendous intellectual changes which were transforming Europe. By the time Muslim intellectuals realized they were seriously behind Europeans, it was far too late to catch up. This technological and intellectual lag behind the West has plagued the Islamic world since the eighteenth century.

Decentralization

As the great empires decayed and became increasingly unable to govern, regional forces within their boundaries began to emerge. In some cases these revolts took the form of mere attempts by local warlords to assert their independence or to usurp the throne. In other cases, however, local oppressed Muslim peoples, or non-Muslims who sought independence, rebelled in hopes of seceding from the empire. Thus, the Christians in the Balkans, the nomads in Arabia and northeastern Iran, and the Hindu Marathas and Rajputs in India all rebelled against their respective central governments. At the same time, local governors and warlords, such as Muhammad Ali in Egypt, asserted their independence and created essentially independent states.

Military Inferiority

The greater economic strength, control of the seas, and superior military technology of the Europeans, combined with the decaying conditions in the Islamic empires, gave the Europeans an increasing military superiority over the governments in the Islamic world. In 1669 the Ottomans were able to conquer Crete from the Venetians, while in 1683 they besieged Vienna. Aurangzeb continued Mughal expansion in India, conquering Bijapur and Golkonda from 1686 to 1687. However, these were the last great conquests of any Islamic state in the world. Within a few decades Islamic military might had collapsed. Muslim armies have been continually on the defensive against European powers until the present.

Results. These problems created an enormous social, economic, and political crisis in the Islamic world. Although these problems developed over several decades, the result was the complete collapse of the Safavid and Mughal dynasties, the serious decline of the Ottomans, and imposition of European military domination over nearly all Islamic countries. The greatest political, economic, and intellectual problem facing the Muslim world became determining the proper response to European world domination.

THE AGE OF WESTERN DOMINATION (c. 1750–1870)

Western European competition with Islamic civilization dates back to the Middle Ages with early wars between Arabs and Byzantines and the Crusades. However, European explorations and mastery of the sea in the sixteenth century provided a new phase in this competition. Initiated by the Portuguese in the early sixteenth century, various levels of armed conflict between Europe and the Islamic world continued for several centuries in northwest Africa, west and east Africa, Arabia, India, the Balkan frontier, and central Asia.

However, it was only in the eighteenth century, when the social and political crisis in the Islamic world had reached its full proportions and European military technology had become substantially superior, that the Europeans began having a real potential for actual conquest and colonization. Aside from the failed attempts by the Spanish and Portuguese to conquer Morocco in the sixteenth century (which in a sense were the last vestiges of the Crusades rather than the first manifestations of the new mercantile and colonial European expansion), the first major European success was the British conquest of India.

The British in India

THE COMING OF THE EUROPEANS

The first European intervention in India involved the establishment of Portuguese trading colonies in 1498 and the Portuguese acquisition of the port of Goa in 1510. Thereafter, the Dutch conquered Ceylon (modern Sri Lanka), while the French and British also established control over important ports such as Madras, Bombay, and Calcutta.

THE EAST INDIA COMPANY

It was not until the collapse of the effective power of the Mughal emperors in the mid-eighteenth century that the Europeans became major players on the India scene. At first the Europeans simply represented one among many competing factions, which included Mughals, Afghans, Turks, Rajputs, Marathas, and other Hindus. Furthermore, the earliest British intervention in India was not an official government act, but an effort by the British East India Company, seeking purely economic gains. The goal of most Europeans was not military conquest, but the establishment of ports and the control of trade and industry. However, they were not averse to using military force and Indian mercenary armies to accomplish these goals. By the mid-eighteenth century, however, the increasing political chaos in India, coupled with superior European military technology and the growing importance of the India trade to European economies, caused the military rivalries in Europe itself to spill over into India.

BRITISH CONQUEST OF INDIA

From 1756 to 1763 the Europeans initiated what could be called the first "world war," as French and British forces clashed in Europe, North America, west Africa, and India. In India the British, with their Indian allies, met the French and their allies at the battle of Plassey in 1757. It ended in a decisive victory for the British, laying the foundation for creation of the British empire in India. Thereafter, the British increasingly adopted a policy of territorial expansion in India as the means to ensure their economic supremacy. During the next century, all of India was conquered or otherwise acquired by the British.

EFFECTS OF BRITISH RULE

British rule in India had mixed results. On the one hand, the British managed to bring political order and economic stability to the subcontinent. Sectarian and ethnic differences between Hindus and Muslims were temporarily ended as the British played the role of unbiased outsider in preserving peace. A great deal of modernization also occurred with the expansion of rail lines, telegraph systems, and other Western technologies. Many Indians received Western-style educations, which allowed them to adopt modern technologies for their country.

On the other hand, there were also numerous problems with British rule in India. In a sense the British became a new Indian "caste," occupying the most privileged and powerful positions in Indian society, while compelling the Hindu and Muslim Indians to serve as subordinates. Furthermore, although there was great internal economic and technological development in India, most of the economic benefits from British rule in India were gained by the British. Early dissatisfaction with British rule in India culminated in

1857 with the unsuccessful Indian (Sepoy) Rebellion. Similarly, the Afghans, one of the most independent-minded and warlike peoples on earth, refused to submit to British rule and successfully prevented the British from conquering their homeland in a series of Afghan Wars (1839–1880).

Despite the relative benevolence of British rule, it was still a case of a foreign power dominating local peoples. By the late nineteenth century, a new generation of Indian intellectuals, trained in modern schools but still loyal to their homeland and traditions, began the long process which would ultimately lead to independence by founding the first Indian National Congress in 1885.

OTHER ISLAMIC STRONGHOLDS: BRIEF OBSERVATIONS

Islam controlled or, for a time, dominated many other parts of the non-Western world. North of Iran, the Islamic state of Uzbek was founded by Muhammad Shaybani, a descendant of Chingiz Khan, in the fifteenth century. It continued for well over 200 years. Farther east, the Chaghatay Muslims ruled another state until the mid-seventeenth century. For most of that time, however, this group was dominated by a Sunni faction whose leaders claimed to be descendants of the prophet Mohammed himself. Though never rivaling the strength of the other Muslim empires, the Chaghatay Muslims were zealously committed to spreading Islam both as a religion and as a political power.

Islam also spread along the south Asian coast and into the Indies, following the rich trading possibilities that also attracted Europeans. There were small Muslim states on the Malay peninsula, in Sumatra and Java, and in the "Spice Islands" (the Moluccas). The most powerful of these states, Acheh, was on the island of Sumatra, south of the Malay peninsula. Founded in 1524, it remained an Islamic state until the twentieth century. Its rulers were in constant competition with the Portuguese, who also had strongholds on the island, but neither power was able to drive the other out. It was the Dutch who finally dislodged them in 1910.

Muslims extended their religion, their commercial activities, and their political influence into much of Africa. There they also soon came in contact with Europeans, bent on building their own commercial empires by dominating the coastal trade and later by taking over the entire continent. The story of Africa, with its numerous peoples and crosscurrents of Islamic and European imperialism, will be told in chapters 11 and 13.

*A*t the end of the fifteenth century, the major trade routes between Asia and Europe were under the control of the Muslims. In the next century Muslim empires, and particularly the Ottoman empire, reached the height of their grandeur and power. But after the discovery of a water route to Asia, European powers in quest of wealth gradually made inroads into Muslim hegemony. The next century would see the beginning of Western domination of the globe. By the end of the eighteenth century, even the mighty Ottoman empire was beginning to dwindle, partly because of its own internal weaknesses, in the face of the steady Western assault.

Selected Readings

Daniel, Norman. *Islam and the West: The Making of an Image*. Edinburgh: University Press, 1960.

Hodgson, Marshall G. S. *The Venture of Islam: Conscience and History in a World Civilization*. 3 vols. Chicago: University of Chicago Press, 1974.

Hourani, Albert. *A History of the Arab Peoples*. Cambridge, MA: Belknap Press of Harvard University Press, 1991.

Lapidus, Ira M. *A History of Islamic Societies*. Cambridge and New York: Cambridge University Press, 1988.

Robinson, Francis. *Atlas of the Islamic World Since 1500*. New York: Facts on File, 1982.

Savory, Roger. *Iran Under the Safavids*. Cambridge and New York: Cambridge University Press, 1980.

Shaw, Stanford J. *History of the Ottoman Empire and Modern Turkey*. 2 vols. New York: Cambridge University Press, 1976.

5

Absolutism and Constitutionalism: Europe in the Seventeenth and Eighteenth Centuries

1603–1625	Reign of James I, the first Stuart king
1618–1648	Thirty Years' War
1625–1649	Reign of Charles I of England
1640–1688	Frederick William, elector of Brandenburg
1643–1715	Reign of Louis XIV
1649–1660	Puritan commonwealth in England
1653–1658	Protectorate of Oliver Cromwell
1660–1685	Restoration of Stuart monarchy; reign of Charles II
1661	Louis XIV begins his personal rule
1682–1725	Reign of Peter the Great in Russia
1685	Edict of Nantes revoked
1688	Glorious Revolution
1689–1797	War of the League of Augsburg
1702–1714	War of the Spanish Succession

1711–1740	Reign of Charles VI of Austria
1714	Hanover kings begin to reign in England
1721–1742	Sir Robert Walpole heads English cabinet
1740–1748	War of the Austrian Succession
1740–1780	Reign of Maria Theresa of Austria
1740–1786	Reign of Frederick the Great of Prussia
1756–1763	Seven Years' War
1762–1796	Reign of Catherine the Great of Russia
1772	First partition of Poland
1780–1790	Reign of Joseph II of Austria
1793, 1795	Second and third partitions of Poland

Five major monarchies—France, Great Britain, Austria, Prussia, and Russia—dominated European politics in the seventeenth and eighteenth centuries. A sixth, Spain, had been a great power, but was in decline in the seventeenth century. Each monarchy took a different form, according to its unique internal circumstances, but all the rulers aspired to the "divine right" absolutism epitomized by Louis XIV of France. The Netherlands was also a dominant economic power, but it was not a monarchy.

In this chapter we will look at the rise of these six state systems. We will note especially the differences between absolutism and constitutionalism, and why one system developed in one place while another unfolded elsewhere. We will also comment on economic development, internal conflicts, and international tensions and wars. The European powers became highly competitive states, as each sought to maintain the kind of balance of power that would promote its own interests. England and France, in particular, vied not just for power on the continent but also for world empire. All this had important consequences for the future.

ABSOLUTISM AND CONSTITUTIONALISM: SOME DEFINITIONS

The nature of any government is partly determined by the way it defines sovereignty, or the location of ultimate political power. Does it reside in the person of the ruler, in the people, or in some combination of the two? Kings, queens, ministers, and political philosophers in the seventeenth and eighteenth centuries defined sovereignty in a variety of ways. Politically, France, Austria, Russia, and Prussia headed down the road of absolutism, while England, France, and Holland became constitutional states.

Theories of Absolutism

Under the modern concept of the rule of law, the powers of government are circumscribed by clear and unmistakable legal canons. By contrast, seventeenth- and eighteenth-century monarchs adhered to absolutism, or the rule of will—the belief that they were sovereign and their wills alone were law. There were, however, somewhat differing rationales for absolutism.

THOMAS HOBBES

Some definitions of sovereignty were concerned with the nature of man. In his most famous and controversial work, *Leviathan* (1651), the English political philosopher Thomas Hobbes held that it was the natural state of human beings to be at war with each other. Sovereignty, he reasoned, is located in the people but, out of self-interest and the need for peace and security, they delegate it to the state (i.e., to the monarch). The understanding between the people and the monarch, then, is a contract, something like Rousseau's "Social Contract" (see chapter 6); in return for protection the people owe the monarch their total loyalty. If they rebel, the monarch may punish them as he sees fit. Otherwise, Hobbes maintained, there could be no order, and humanity would return to its "nasty, brutish," disorderly state of nature.

FRENCH ABSOLUTISM

Powerful as it was as a rationale for absolutism, Hobbes's philosophy did not necessarily appeal to the rulers of his day. More attractive to most was the theory of absolutism that justified the rule of Louis XIV of France, the most powerful monarch of the age. It assumed, contrary to Hobbes, that sovereignty resided directly in the person of the monarch and that it was given by "divine right." Responsible only to God, the monarch's word was law. Even the church was subject to royal authority.

THE ABSOLUTIST STATE

In the ideal absolutist state, the monarch was the all-powerful head and all other authorities acted directly in his or her behalf. By necessity, absolutist states developed strong central bureaucracies staffed by professional civil servants. Above all, the means to tax and otherwise raise revenue was centrally controlled. The monarchs also had their own personal standing armies, as opposed to armies loyal only to local princes. Frequently the greatest threat to the absolute power of the monarch came from the nobility. This required some monarchs to curry the favor of the nobles in order to obtain their cooperation and support. In other cases they found ways to weaken the nobles by co-opting them or making them dependent upon the crown. In most absolutist states, however, the nobles and landed aristocracy remained relatively free from taxation. The heavy financial burden of supporting the bureaucracy and the military fell mostly on the workers and the peasants.

Enlightened Absolutism

One aspect of the Enlightenment (see chapter 6) was an emphasis upon rational, scientific approaches to government. Some Enlightenment philosophers stressed democratic forms of government. Others, however, believed that "enlightened absolutism" (or, as many have called it, "enlightened despotism") was the best way to achieve order in society as well as responsible government. Rational monarchs, they argued, would be humanitarians as well as absolutists. They would be concerned for the well-being of the people of the state and would promote reforms aimed at improving that well-being. Several monarchs called themselves "enlightened," though often their enlightenment was tempered by the realities of maintaining political and military power.

Constitution-alism

In contrast to an absolutist state, a constitutional state is one in which the power of the government is defined and limited by law. In constitutional monarchies a monarch is the head of state, but there are bounds beyond which he or she may not go. Constitutions defining those limits, as well as the power of the legislature, may be single written documents, or simply the embodiment of a historical series of legislative acts, judicial decisions, and traditional practices. The nature of the electorate may be defined variously, but the members of the electorate are sovereign and exercise power through their representatives. The legislature usually consists of two houses, with the lower house chosen by the electorate. In Britain this is the House of Commons. In the period under discussion, the British electorate was defined by rather severe property qualifications and consisted of only a small portion of the adult male population. The upper house represented the nobility and the bishops of the established church.

THE ASCENDANCY OF FRANCE: THE MODEL OF ABSOLUTISM

No monarch of Europe had a more magnificent court or exemplified the absolute power of the state any better than Louis XIV of France. Taught from his youth that the Bible proclaimed the "divine right of kings," Louis believed that he was answerable to no one but God. "I am the state," he allegedly declared, and whether he actually said it or not, he acted like it.

Background for Absolutism: Richelieu and Mazarin

The quest for absolute power in the French monarchy was not new with Louis XIV. The immediate groundwork for what he achieved, however, was laid by Cardinal Armand Jean du Plessis Richelieu, chief minister under Louis XIII.

RICHELIEU

Louis's grandfather, Henry IV, brought the monarchy several steps closer to absolutism before his assassination in 1610. He strengthened the bureaucracy and at the same time weakened the influence of the nobility and of the parliament. His son, Louis XIII, made his most important personal contribution to absolutism by appointing Cardinal Richelieu as chief of the royal council and, later, first minister. Richelieu spent the rest of his life trying to make France the leading power in Europe and, above all, to establish the undisputed authority of the crown. He was cunning, ruthless, and masterful at both administration and intrigue. He worked particularly hard at destroying the power of the nobility, the most serious threat to absolutism. One way of doing this was to refuse to call together the Estates General—the ancient deliberative and advisory body that generally represented the nobles. The nobles' influence in the provinces was sabotaged when he increased the power of royal *intendants* (administrative officials) over France's various administrative districts. Nevertheless, Richelieu was also shrewd enough to try to co-opt the nobility by giving them various military and diplomatic positions.

Richelieu did not hesitate to execute anyone caught in a conspiracy against the government, nor was he averse to taking action against Protestants if he thought it was in the interest of the state. Most notably, convinced that the Huguenots were disloyal, he used military force to destroy their political and military power. In 1628 their largest fortified city, La Rochelle, fell to Richelieu's forces after a fourteen-month siege.

MAZARIN AND YOUNG LOUIS XIV

Richelieu's hand-picked successor, Jules Mazarin, continued his program of strengthening the monarchy through centralization. When Louis XIV inherited the throne in 1643 at age five, his mother, Anne of Austria, became regent. Mazarin continued as chief minister, and the two led France together until Mazarin died in 1661. Meanwhile, young Louis was witness to all the challenges and intrigues affecting the monarchy, and he learned well at the feet of Mazarin. The minister's most serious challenge was a series of rebellions by discontented nobles and others, known as the Fronde. These sporadic civil wars went on from 1648 to 1653. During that time Mazarin even had to leave France twice. In the end, however, the Fronde was crushed. When Mazarin died in 1661, he left the most powerful kingdom in continental Europe in the hands of Louis XIV. During Louis's long reign, which lasted until his death in 1715, the strength and prestige of the French monarchy became the envy of all the crowns of Europe.

The Monarchy of Louis XIV: Absolutism in Its French Context

With Mazarin gone, one of Louis's first decisions was not to appoint another prime minister. From then on he ruled personally.

SOCIAL AND POLITICAL ASPECTS

At least on the surface, everything good seemed to happen to France in the time of Louis XIV. Literature and the arts, characterized by a revival of classical antiquity as well as glorification of the state, flourished under his patronage. For the first time in history, France was the dominant power in European politics. Through the grandeur of his court, his absolute power, and the brilliance of French culture, the "Sun King," as Louis was sometimes called, eclipsed all others. When Louis sneezed, it was said, all Europe caught cold.

The Significance of Versailles. About ten miles outside Paris, in the small town of Versailles, Louis XIII had built a royal hunting lodge. There Louis XIV created the grandest court of Europe. The elaborate art and architecture, together with the magnificent grounds and fountains, were deliberately and skillfully designed to overawe all who came. The nobility were required to live there for at least part of each year. What they did there, however, demonstrates the degraded state of their power even while they enjoyed the trappings of their position. They went to endless balls, parties, and musical productions. They played essential roles in the elaborate ceremonies that took place at the king's bedtime, when he arose, at mealtimes, and at state affairs. For all practical purposes, however, they became little more than ornaments of the court, enjoying the resplendence of Versailles but excluded from the king's councils and thus having no power at all.

Absolutist Government. Louis ruled through an extensive bureaucracy consisting of three main councils of state, several lesser administrative councils, and a host of civil servants. He personally attended all the sessions of the major councils. Royal *intendants* carried out their decisions. Thirteen regional *parliaments* took care of local affairs, but their power was extremely limited. With a military and civil establishment personally loyal to him, Louis seemingly held all power.

CHURCH AND STATE: THE HUGUENOTS

Louis believed that a unified state must have religious as well as political uniformity. Richelieu had been tolerant of the religious beliefs and practices of the Huguenots, even after destroying their military and political power. Louis, convinced that they were still a threat to both church and state, went further. He put several restrictions on them, including barring them from public offices. Then in 1685 he outlawed them by revoking the eighty-three-year-old Edict of Nantes, which had granted them religious liberty. One result was that over 200,000 Huguenots fled to England, Germany, Holland, and America.

MERCANTILISM AND THE ECONOMY

Outward appearances to the contrary, Louis never had enough money to support all he tried to do. In particular, his incessant wars drained the treasury and imposed increasingly heavy tax burdens on the people.

Jean-Baptise Colbert, controller-general of finances, tried to improve the economy by applying the principles of mercantilism—the philosophy that all economic activity must be regulated in way that promoted the interest of the state. He imposed tariffs to raise the prices of French goods and keep French industries alive. He also subsidized key industries, including textile manufacturers, and set up a rigid inspection system for quality control.

When Colbert died in 1683, France was beginning to enjoy a new era of prosperity, especially among the commercial classes. Before Louis died, however, the economy was in a shambles. Poor harvests, soaring grain prices, the costs of war, rising taxes, and several other factors all combined to bring new suffering, even starvation, to the peasants. Threats of rebellion were not uncommon, and many peasants emigrated elsewhere.

WAR, EXPANSIONISM, AND THE BALANCE OF POWER

Louis, nevertheless, gloried in war. It was necessary, he seemed to believe, to national unity as well as to demonstrate to the world the strength of his monarchy. It would also expand his domain. In 1667 and again in 1672, for example, he invaded the Netherlands, where he took over several Flemish towns. In 1681 he conquered the city of Strasbourg. One result of his expansionism was the formation of the League of Augsburg in an attempt to stop him. During the nine-year War of the League of Augsburg (1689–1697), Louis gained nothing.

War of the Spanish Succession. In 1700 Louis's grandson inherited the Spanish throne, reigning as Philip V. This seemingly propitious event delighted Louis. It dismayed other European powers, however, for the alliance of these two thrones meant nothing more than French hegemony in Europe and an upset in the balance of power. The result was a twelve-year dynastic war, the War of the Spanish Succession (1702–1714). Financially unprepared, and at a time when France was being torn apart internally, Louis marched into the Spanish Netherlands to protect his claims. He found himself facing the newly formed Grand Alliance of the Hague, consisting of the Netherlands, England, and the Holy Roman Empire. Like other wars, the War of the Spanish Succession extended itself beyond the European continent; fighting occurred both in India and in America. In the end, it was Louis who sued for peace.

Treaty of Utrecht. The war ended with the Treaty of Utrecht (1713–1714). The result was that Philip retained his throne, but only at the cost of Louis's most important objective. He had to agree that the French and Spanish crowns would never be united. The European powers had consciously put into operation the principle of balance of power and had set limits on how far one of their number could expand. A hundred years later, as a result of the Napoleonic wars, the same principle would be applied to France even more forcefully (see chapter 9).

FLAWS AND WEAKNESSES IN LOUIS'S SYSTEM

Clearly, despite outward appearances, there were serious imperfections in Louis XIV's absolutist state. The king was always in danger of antagonizing deeply entrenched vested interests. Much of his power came by compromise. The large number of councils led to administrative inefficiency. Bribery and other kinds of corruption in government ran rampant. There was also widespread misery and seething discontent in France, partly as a result of heavy taxation. The seemingly unending wars were not only unpopular but also too expensive. By the time Louis died, France was some 3 billion livres in debt.

Louis left an unenviable legacy for his successors. Louis XV, however, paid little attention to governing and left the affairs of state in even greater disarray than his father. From such seeds his son, Louis XVI, would reap the disastrous harvest of revolution (see chapter 7).

ABSOLUTISM IN CENTRAL AND EASTERN EUROPE: AUSTRIA, PRUSSIA, AND RUSSIA

In the seventeenth century strong rulers arose also within the Holy Roman Empire, though there were variations in the nature of their absolutism. Two major powers, Austria and Prussia, emerged as the empire itself decayed. At the same time, Russia became an important new power in European politics.

Habsburg Austria

In 1648, at the end of the Thirty Years' War, the Holy Roman Empire was hardly an empire at all. It was really a confederation of about 300 independent kingdoms only loosely united under a member of the Austrian Habsburg family who held the title of emperor. The Habsburgs, however, had little real power; what they did have came mainly through bargaining and compromise with local bishops and princes. Their hereditary lands included Bohemia, part of Hungary, Croatia, and Transylvania, but even

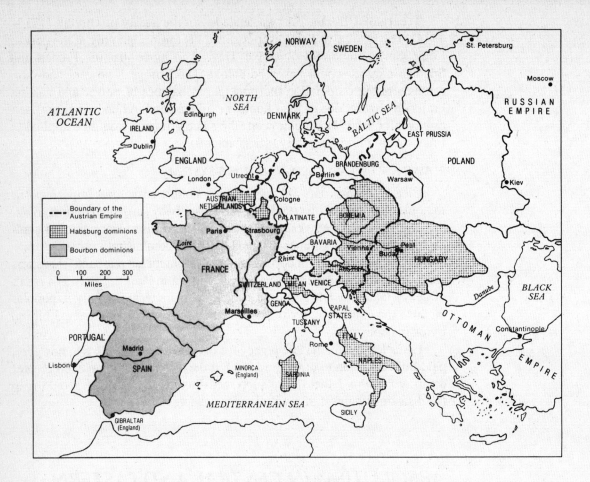

Fig. 5.1   Europe in 1714

there they needed the cooperation of the local nobility in order to exercise power. Their fondest goal was to create some kind of unified state that they could control. They were held back, however, not just by geography and local politics, but also by great diversity in languages and cultures—a problem that has persisted in the area to the present day.

STRENGTHENING THE MONARCHY

Leopold I, emperor from 1657 to 1705, made some important military moves toward strengthening the monarchy and bringing a sense of unity into the Habsburg possessions. He successfully repelled an invasion by the Turks. He conquered the remaining parts of Hungary and Transylvania that were not already firmly under his rule and extended his holdings into much of twentieth-century Yugoslavia. He also suppressed a rebellion of the Magyars, the dominant people of Hungary.

The *Pragmatic Sanctions*. The Habsburg monarchy faced a new crisis when Charles VI, emperor from 1711 to 1740, had no son. Since there was no precedent for a female ruler, Charles feared that after his death the Habsburg holdings would be divided up. His *Pragmatic Sanctions* was a legal document intended to ensure a single hereditary succession to Habsburg lands beginning with his daughter Maria Theresa. He thought the other powers had accepted the principle, and Maria Theresa duly succeeded her father. Within two months, however, her lands were invaded by Prussia.

The War of the Austrian Succession (1740–1748). Frederick II of Prussia (see below) saw Maria Theresa's succession as a chance to grab up the mineral-rich province of Silesia. He not only caught her off guard but surprised the other European powers as well. It was not long, however, before several traditional Habsburg rivals joined in the conquest. Finally, at the Treaty of Aix-la-Chapelle, the young empress gave up her claims to Silesia. In the meantime, the war expanded in scope far beyond the original intent of Frederick (see Overlapping Wars, below).

Maria Theresa and Habsburg Power. Despite the problems she encountered on her succession, Maria Theresa took some important steps toward strengthening Habsburg power. The sudden confrontation with the powers of Europe may, in fact, have acted as a catalyst in her determination to strengthen the central administration. She improved tax collection, even forcing the nobles and clergy to submit to at least minimal taxation. She created a more effective bureaucracy, centered in Vienna. Not considered an enlightened despot, she nevertheless expanded her reforms to provide some relief for overburdened and overtaxed peasants. The aristocracy was no longer able to require as much work from them.

Joseph II: Enlightened Absolutist. Fully supporting her in all these policies was her son Joseph II, co-ruler with her from 1765 until her death in 1780. Holding the throne for ten more years, Joseph went far beyond his mother in both strengthening the monarchy and attempting to reform Austrian society. His attitude, in fact, made him one of the most enlightened monarchs of the day. He did all he could to bring the monarchy closer to absolutism, but at the same time, he had a genuine feeling of responsibility toward his subjects. With respect to religion, for example, he extended religious freedom to Protestants, the Greek Orthodox, and Jews. He also severely curtailed the influence of the Roman Catholic Church. Among other things, he closed its monasteries and did away with its seminaries. He also continued his mother's work of improving the lot of the peasants. Unfortunately, some of these social reforms did not last. One tax reform, for example, was poorly received by nobles and peasants alike and led to a peasant revolt. Joseph's brother, who succeeded him as Leopold II, was finally forced to repeal several of Joseph's measures.

Hohenzollern Prussia

Austria thus emerged from the ruins of the crumbling Holy Roman Empire as one of the major states of Europe. So, too, did Prussia. The Holy Roman Empire still existed in theory, and emperors continued to be named. But one of the greatest clichés in history is also one of the most accurate—the empire was neither holy, nor Roman, nor an empire.

THE GREAT ELECTOR

Frederick William, a member of the Hohenzollern family, became elector of Brandenburg, one of the Prussian states, in 1640. The term "elector" referred to his right to help select the emperor. Eventually Frederick became known as the "Great Elector." The provinces ruled by his family were widely scattered, each dominated by its own legislature, or estate. It was Frederick William's challenge to turn them into a single, centralized state. Like all absolutists, he quickly set about strengthening his personal army. He also took taxing power away from the nobles (known as "Junkers"). He did not undermine their authority over the peasants, as some monarchs did, but he co-opted them by making them bureaucrats.

FREDERICK WILLIAM I AND THE PRUSSIAN KINGDOM

Frederick William's son, who succeeded his father in 1688, received a more tightly controlled state than any Prussian ruler yet. Then, in exchange for his support in the War of the Spanish Succession, the Holy Roman Emperor (Leopold I, a Habsburg) granted him the title "King of Prussia." He ruled as Frederick I. His son, Frederick William I, reigned from 1713 to 1740 and finally completed the work of consolidation begun by the Great Elector. He eliminated the estates, thus concentrating power into a central administration. His strong, effective bureaucracy was unusually free from corruption. He was hardly an enlightened despot, however, for he did nothing about the heavy burdens borne by the peasants. At the same time, he had a passionate love for the military. He built a large, highly disciplined, well-equipped army that became known as the best in Europe. Frederick William was wise enough to seldom use his army, however. It was a symbol of Prussian power, but not something to be thrown around at every whim.

FREDERICK THE GREAT

His son, Frederick II, who ruled from 1740 to 1786, thus came by his military proficiency quite naturally. He had spent much of his youth studying politics and war and became a brilliant military strategist. Almost his first act as king was to take over Silesia, touching off the War of the Austrian Succession. Later he demonstrated his exceptional talents in the Seven Years' War (see below), after which he came to be called Frederick the Great. In his continuing efforts to strengthen the kingdom, Frederick added to his territory by occupying most of West Prussia. He improved the bureaucracy by raising the standards of civil service and severely punishing corruption and inefficiency. Economically, like other rulers of his time, he promoted the principles of mercantilism. He also worked hard to rebuild industry and agriculture that had been ravaged during various wars.

Frederick's Enlightened Despotism. As a young man Frederick spent his leisure time engrossed in reading literature, studying philosophy, writing poetry, playing the flute, and carrying on correspondence with the intellectuals of the Enlightenment. He developed a particular affection for Voltaire and later entertained him at the Prussian court. Such interests no doubt helped stimulate Frederick's commitment to enlightened monarchy. His concern for the people was demonstrated in a variety of ways. He expanded freedom of speech and of the press and promoted education. The legal system and the courts were reformed during his reign. He also did away with torture, except for crimes such as murder or treason. He promoted religious toleration, even allowing Jesuits (members of a well-disciplined Catholic missionary order) into his Protestant kingdom. His toleration went only so far, however, for he would not allow the immigration of Jews. Neither did he range very far in the area of social reform on behalf of the peasants, who remained tied to the estates of the Junkers. Nevertheless, historians generally recognize him a model of enlightened despotism.

Frederick died in 1786. His son, Frederick William II, inherited a strong, financially sound, consolidated state.

Romanov Russia

As the kings of France, Austria, and Prussia were building their absolutist states, another actor stepped onto the stage of European politics. In Russia, the Romanov family created a dynasty that lasted from 1613 to 1917, longer than any of the others. It became a powerful new force for European powers to reckon with.

Prior to 1613, when Michael Romanov became tsar, anarchy and civil war dominated Russian politics. By the time Peter the Great appeared on the scene, however, the Romanovs had created a somewhat stable monarchy with a centralized bureaucracy. There were also various powerful groups that could cause problems. The *streltsy* (elite Russian guards) constituted a powerful class at court. The *boyars* (nobles) were proud and haughty and could change political loyalties at any time. Already the tsars had catered to them in various ways. The tsars had also created what amounted to a kind of feudalism by giving large land grants, along with serfs to work the land, to loyal civil and military officials. In addition, the Greek Orthodox church became increasingly political. There were also dissidents within the church, such as a group of "Old Believers" who objected to certain reforms in the liturgy. Some of them were members of the streltsy.

PETER THE GREAT

In 1682 a ten-year-old boy named Peter and his sickly brother Ivan found themselves in a most impractical situation. They were named dual monarchs, with their sister Sophia as regent. In 1689, however, Sophia was overthrown, and a few years later Ivan died. During the course of his reign, which lasted until 1725, Peter became known as Peter the Great.

Peter's Goals. Peter was convinced that he must make his position immune against intrigue. He was also determined to make Russia one of the major states of Europe. Fascinated with the West, in 1697 Peter traveled in disguise throughout western Europe. He became determined to imitate almost everything he saw in his effort to reform Russia and make it a first-rate military power. He also set about to undermine the power of the boyars and streltsy, control the church, strengthen the central authority, and improve the economy. Like other monarchs in quest of absolutism, he was not loathe to use ruthlessness and violence to achieve his ends.

The Military and the Civil Bureaucracy. Peter replaced the militia upon which his predecessors had depended with a strong, efficient, and professional military establishment. He also created an efficient, centralized bureaucracy that became more effective at collecting the taxes necessary to support his military machine. He personally dominated the government, however, delegating only minimal authority to his ministers. In doing all this, he also undermined the independence of the boyars and the streltsy. He incorporated the boyars into the establishment by requiring them to serve for life either in the army, as officers, or in government service. When the streltsy rebelled in 1698 he resorted to massive force, torture, and executions in order to discourage any further disloyalty. Nearly 1,200 were put to death, and it was said that he cut off many of their heads with his own hands.

The Church. In his effort to control the church, Peter secularized its administration in 1721. This was especially unpopular with the Old Believers, who correctly interpreted the move as a means of incorporating modern thought and practice into church teachings and policy. It was also a way to strengthen the state, for Peter saw the church not just as a religious institution but as a tool of the state.

Westernization. Peter encouraged the flow of Western ideas into Russia, primarily to strengthen the military and the bureaucracy. He encouraged his people to acquire Western-style technical and administrative skills to apply to the military as well as to business and industry. Peter urged more education, much of it based on Western learning, especially for the nobility. To facilitate this, he had many Western books translated into Russian. Western-style dress was also introduced. He received considerable opposition, however, when he required the boyars and others to shave their beards, for this flew in the face of long-standing religious tradition.

Expansionism. Russia, boasting a standing army of over 200,000 men, was in almost constant warfare throughout Peter's reign. One reason was Peter's effort to extend his territories. It was especially important to secure warm-water seaports so that Russia could trade more easily with the West and influence European affairs more fully. This goal was finally achieved in 1721, at the end of a war with Sweden; Russia acquired Estonia, Livonia, and part of Finland. This gave Peter considerable territory on the Baltic Sea and his cherished "window on the West."

St. Petersburg. Significantly, it was in this coastal territory that Peter founded his new capital city, St. Petersburg. It became a magnificent city, partly intended to do for Peter what Versailles did for Louis XIV. Nobles were compelled to live in St. Petersburg most of the year, and they paid for a major share of its construction. By 1782, during the reign of Catherine the Great, St. Petersburg boasted a population of nearly 300,000.

The Problem of Succession. Like most other absolute monarchies, Peter's had its weaknesses. One was related to the problem of hereditary succession. After his only son died, Peter claimed the right to name his successor himself. However, he failed to name one. This led to continual rivalries and intrigues as, for a time, the nobles and the military decided who would rule. Succeeding tsars were at best mediocre in their talents. It was nearly forty years before Russia had another who could match the distinction of Peter the Great.

CATHERINE THE GREAT

In 1762 the weak, unbalanced Peter III came to power. He had been married for seventeen years to an intelligent, shrewd German princess named Catherine. Already she had learned the secrets of palace intrigue, and it was possibly with her connivance that Peter was murdered only a few months later. She then succeeded to the throne. She reigned for thirty-four years, becoming known as Catherine the Great.

Catherine as an Enlightened Despot. Like most great despots of her time, Catherine was both able and ruthless. Nevertheless, she had drunk deeply at the well of the Enlightenment, and she was determined to become an enlightened despot. Far in advance of Peter the Great, who promoted Westernization largely because of what it would do for the military, she attempted to reform Russia for the sake of Russia itself. Among other things, she founded two hospitals, a college of medicine, a public library, and a girls' school. She brought in Western art, architecture, literature, music, and Western ideas of all sorts. She also limited the use of torture and extended religious freedom. For the sake of public health she advocated inoculation against smallpox, setting the example by being publicly inoculated herself.

Imperfect Absolutism. Nevertheless, Catherine soon discovered enlightened absolutism was not perfect, for too many liberal reforms would only undermine the monarchy. Ultimately she came down on the side of reaction. After a major peasant revolt, she granted absolute control of the serfs to the nobles. She also granted several other privileges to the nobles, including exemption from taxation, in order to court their continuing favor and strengthen their support of the state.

Expansionism. Economically, Catherine improved Russian trade, both internally and externally. At the same time, she kept alive the quest for warm-water ports, which led to war with the Ottoman empire between 1769 and 1774. She had long wished to drive the Turks from Europe anyway, and at the end of the war she had control of several Ottoman provinces along the Danube as well as an outlet to the Black Sea. In 1783 she annexed the Crimea. Significantly, it was also during Catherine's reign that Russia began to explore the northern American coastline, setting the stage for more direct imperialist activity in America in the nineteenth century.

Partition of Poland. One of the most important results of Catherine's expansionism was the partition of Poland, an enterprise that represented balance-of-power politics at its extreme. Her annexations of the provinces along the Danube had upset that balance. At the same time, the Polish monarchy was promoting certain reforms that, if extended, could threaten absolutism itself. Frederick the Great of Prussia, therefore, made a proposal that Catherine could hardly turn down. He suggested that Catherine return the Danubian provinces, but at the same time, Prussia, Austria, and Russia would each take over a large slice of Polish territory. Catherine thus gained a huge new addition to her empire that included nearly 2 million people. In two later partitions in 1793 and 1795, the three powers carved up the rest of Poland, which then disappeared from the map as an independent state until after World War I.

THE CONSTITUTIONAL ALTERNATIVE: GREAT BRITAIN AND HOLLAND

As most of the major European powers were centralizing and strengthening their monarchies, England and Holland were moving in different directions. The kings would have preferred absolutism, but the parliaments in both countries succeeded in limiting their power by constitutional means.

The British Monarchy

In 1603 a new line of rulers, the Stuarts, came to the English throne in the person of James I. There was great potential for conflict, however. The Stuarts longed for absolutism, yet Parliament was uneasy at the moves already taken in that direction. The Church of England was bitterly divided.

In the face of such friction, Stuart power gradually waned, even being temporarily eliminated between 1649 and 1660. By the end of the century, England had evolved into a model of limited monarchy.

THE EARLY STUARTS

The attempt of the early Stuarts to create an absolutist state proved disastrous. James I, for example, antagonized almost everyone. Parliament was especially resentful when he assumed the power to levy customs duties without its consent. Puritans were upset at his plan to strengthen the Anglican episcopacy (church hierarchy). In addition, his apparent pro-Catholic sentiment did not sit well with any English Protestants.

Charles I versus Parliament. His son Charles I, who came to power in 1625, acted much the same way, which resulted in a series of open confrontations with Parliament. When Charles went to Parliament for funds, it insisted that he sign a document that prohibited fund raising without its approval. It also forbade other things that tended to support absolutism, such as arbitrary imprisonment. Charles signed in order to get the money, but then in 1629 dissolved Parliament. He functioned independently until 1640. Meanwhile, religious tensions mounted over the efforts of Charles and Archbishop William Laud to impose Anglican uniformity on all the churches. When they tried to do it in Scotland, war broke out and Charles was forced to reconvene Parliament to ask for more funds. Parliament refused, and Charles dissolved it again. Later in the year, however, he called it together again. At that point, Parliament rebelled, passing laws that limited the power of the monarchy and made levying taxes without Parliamentary consent illegal. Archbishop Laud, meanwhile, was emphasizing the divine right of kings as well as trying to promote the power of the church hierarchy. In 1641 he was impeached and imprisoned, and four years later he was executed.

Civil War. Charles soon saw an opportunity to reassert himself, but his actions led to full-scale civil war. When a rebellion broke out in Ireland in 1641, Parliament was divided over whether to give the king an army to suppress it. Taking advantage of the stalemate, Charles raised an army and in January 1642 invaded Parliament. That body, however, had raised its own army, and the war that resulted lasted for seven years (1642–1649). Oliver Cromwell turned the Parliamentary army into a well-disciplined, highly motivated fighting machine. Charles was defeated. Parliament then executed him on January 30, 1649.

The Commonwealth. At that point Parliament declared that England was a commonwealth. It abolished the monarchy, the House of Lords, and Anglicanism as the state religion. Cromwell's army, meanwhile, conquered both Ireland and Scotland. A member of Parliament, Cromwell also called for various other reforms. When these reforms were not forthcoming, he marched in and disbanded Parliament in 1653.

Cromwell as Lord Protector. The following year a new assembly, controlled by Cromwell, named him Lord Protector. For the next five years he was virtually a military dictator. Some writers judge Cromwell's rule harshly. They point to his merciless suppression of the Catholics in Ireland, to other military adventures that were overwhelmingly expensive, to a decline in trade and commerce, and to the many rather harsh Puritan laws that were nobly inspired but also unpopular. He also censored the press and undermined other political liberties.

Cromwell's defenders view him as courageous, unselfish, and highly devoted to the cause of Puritanism. They also observe that he was genuinely reluctant to stay in office, though while there he used the office to promote measures that he felt could only improve the moral character of the people. The closing of theaters, gambling houses, and saloons were among those measures. He was generally tolerant toward religion; he allowed all Christians, except Catholics, to practice their faiths freely. Even Catholics were not as severely restricted as in earlier years. Cromwell also extended toleration to Jews and Quakers. But however he may be judged, by the time Cromwell died in 1658, the people generally were weary of military dictatorship. His son ruled ineffectively for a short period, but the army soon invited Parliament back into session.

THE STUART RESTORATION

In 1660, at the invitation of Parliament, the Stuart family again occupied the throne of England, this time in the person of Charles II. The Anglican church was again the established church. Charles hoped to achieve the absolutist goals of his predecessors. Yet even before he was officially restored, his position was weakened when he was forced to make specific promises with respect to sharing power with Parliament. Interpreting those promises led to bitter divisions and to the rise of the first permanent political parties in modern history. Religious issues were at the heart of much of the tension. The king's opponents, who included nonconforming Protestants, soon gained control of Parliament. They proposed an *Exclusion Bill* prohibiting Charles's brother James, a Catholic, from coming to the throne. Those favoring exclusion (and hence tending to oppose religious liberty) were called *Whigs*, while the others were dubbed *Tories*. The bill passed the House of Commons, but not the House of Lords.

THE GLORIOUS REVOLUTION AND THE
CONSTITUTIONAL LIMITATION OF ROYAL AUTHORITY

Charles's brother succeeded him as James II. He immediately came into direct conflict with Parliament over religious issues. He finally dissolved

Parliament and suspended all acts against Catholics and Anglican dissenters. In June 1688 James's Catholic wife gave birth to a son, raising the specter of a Catholic heir. This raised the religious question to such heights that Tories and Whigs joined in a Parliamentary coalition against the king. Just a month after the birth of his son, they invited James's daughter Mary and her husband William of Orange, *stadholder* of the Netherlands, to become joint monarchs of England. James was easily deposed, and this bloodless coup went down in history as the Glorious Revolution.

Constitutional Monarchy. The Glorious Revolution laid the foundation for a permanent constitutional monarchy. The new rulers agreed to several acts of Parliament that specifically limited their power. Citizens were given the right to petition the king for redress of grievances. In addition, it was declared that only Protestants could become king. Known in history as the English Bill of Rights, a group of such laws was approved in December 1689. Parliament also granted more religious toleration, at least to Protestants. This helped pave the way for England and Scotland to be officially joined together in 1707, becoming the united kingdom known as Great Britain.

Cabinet and Ministerial Government. After the Glorious Revolution the monarchs began to exercise what power they had through a council of Parliamentary leaders known officially as the Privy Council. Later it was called the cabinet (a term derived from the fact that initially they met in a small room called the cabinet). Its members were selected by the king or, later, his chief minister. In 1714 a new line of rulers, from the German house of Hanover, began to reign. This led to even less involvement by the king in the daily affairs of government, as George I allowed his ministers to exercise his power for him. The same was true with his son George II, under whom Sir Robert Walpole became chief minister. With the king's support, his own ability to control the House of Commons, and his effective use and control of government patronage, Walpole dominated the government from 1721 to 1742. Walpole exercised his office so skillfully that he has gone down in history as Britain's first prime minister, even though that office did not officially come into being until later.

The last British king to make any effort to reassert old monarchical prerogatives was George III, who began his sixty-year reign in 1760. He believed he was only reclaiming legitimate constitutional rights. In doing so, however, he not only antagonized many people at home, but also lost his American colonies (see chapter 7). In contrast to the rest of Europe, parliamentary government and constitutional monarchy was the established order in Britain.

The Netherlands

In the United Provinces of the Netherlands, meanwhile, an even more liberal form of constitutionalism appeared.

LOCALIZED POWER

The government of the Netherlands was distinguished from those of most other European states by the fact that its power was localized. There was a States General, or federal assembly, which met in The Hague. Nevertheless, real sovereignty centered in the provinces, where the estates (provincial legislatures) had to approve all the decisions of the Estates General.

Despite its decentralized nature, the Netherlands demonstrated considerable power. The States General controlled foreign affairs, and the provinces worked together well because it was in their common interest to do so. Even though, at times, they lost some land to foreign invaders, they also had some military success.

THE RISE OF THE HOUSE OF ORANGE

The governor of the Dutch confederation was called *stadholder*, a title conferred by the States General on William I of Orange as early as 1580. It remained hereditary in the Orange family. William led the revolt against Spain in 1568. His youngest son, Frederick Henry, led the republic during much of the Spanish effort at reconquest, even capturing some Spanish cities. The most famous member of the family became William III of England. In 1762 he successfully resisted an attempt by the Dutch republics to crush his family's political power. They were angered over his father's attempt to extend that power. That year, however, William was made captain general of the military and stadholder for life. At the same time, he was called upon to defend the Netherlands against attacks from England and France. At one point he effectively turned back the French by persuading the people to open the dikes, flooding the land through which the enemy was advancing. William not only repelled the invaders but also solidified the continuing political power of the Orange dynasty.

A "GOLDEN AGE"

The early part of the seventeenth century has been called the "golden age" of the Netherlands. Literature and the arts flourished, with painters such as Rembrandt producing some of the world's great masterpieces. The general religious orientation of the Dutch was Calvinistic, but they allowed greater religious freedom than any other state in Europe. It was also a period of expanding trade in which the Netherlands built its great commercial empire (see chapter 2). Though it began a decline in the early eighteenth century, the Netherlands remained financially strong; it even helped finance the American Revolution.

The Dutch republic came to an end in 1795, during the Napoleonic wars. After the Congress of Vienna in 1815, however, the provinces were reunited as the Kingdom of the Netherlands. Eventually it became a constitutional monarchy, with the House of Orange on the throne. The office of stadholder had been eliminated, but the kings were members of the Orange family. The dynasty continues today.

COMPETITIVE STATES AND COLONIAL RIVALRIES

As France, England, Austria, Prussia, and Russia each became powerful nation-states, they also became highly competitive; each sought a balance of political and economic power that would promote its own self-interest. By the mid-eighteenth century all of them, but particularly England and France, were engaged in an intense, worldwide commercial competition that was inextricably entwined with their political ambitions.

Overlapping Wars

Frequently that competition broke out in commercial wars; sometimes these wars overlapped, as in the case of the War of Jenkins' Ear and the War of the Austrian Succession.

In America, the French and the British were involved in intense rivalries in the West Indies. At the same time, mariners from both countries were anxious to open trade with the Spanish colonies on the mainland, but under Spanish mercantilist policies this was illegal. They became adept at smuggling, even though the Spanish maintained coastal patrols in an effort to stop such activity. In 1731 English sea captain Robert Jenkins's ship was boarded by a Spanish patrol searching for contraband. In a scuffle that followed, a Spaniard cut off Jenkins's ear. British merchants and West Indian financial interests pressed for retaliation, but nothing happened for seven years. In 1738, however, during a particularly intense debate in Parliament, Jenkins appeared in London displaying his preserved but withered ear in a move to reinforce the image of Spanish brutality. The following year Britain declared war on Spain.

What happened next demonstrates the broad scope of international rivalries in the mid-eighteenth century. When the War of the Austrian Succession broke out in 1740, France gave its support to Prussia. This, in turn, brought England, France's traditional rival, into the war on the side of Austria in an effort to maintain the balance of power. In 1744 France decided to expand the fighting to America, thus merging with Spain in the War of Jenkins's Ear. So far as England, France, and Spain were concerned, however, the war ended with things little different than they were before the fighting began.

The Great War for Empire

Peace, however, was only temporary. In 1754 war between France and England broke out again, this time in America. Known in American history as the French and Indian War, it went on for nine years. It became one element of the larger conflict that erupted on the European continent two years later and became known as the Seven Years' War (1756–1763). Historians have also rightly called it the Great War for Empire.

In America the fighting broke out over conflicting French and British colonial claims in the Ohio Valley. In Europe, meanwhile, the monarchies continued to compete for power and to shift alliances in whatever direction seemed most advantageous at the time. Great Britain and Prussia (only recently enemies in the War of the Austrian Succession) joined in a defensive alliance aimed at protecting German lands from invasion. Since Prussia and Austria were enemies, this had the effect of pitting Britain against Austria, even though these two states had long been allied in the wars of Louis XIV. Austria then made a defensive alliance with France.

Smoldering tensions broke into all-out war after Frederick II, suspecting a conspiracy against Prussia between Saxony, Austria, and France, sent troops to invade Saxony. It was not long before France, Austria, Sweden, Russia, and a number of smaller German states all were involved, intent on destroying Prussia. In 1762, however, Russia's new tsar, Peter III, made peace with Prussia. This, along with heavy financial assistance from Britain, enabled Frederick to hold his ground against the other powers. In a sense, the war ended in stalemate in Europe; no political boundaries were changed. In another sense, however, Prussia was the victor, for the plan to destroy it did not succeed.

In the conflict between Great Britain and France, meanwhile, William Pitt, who became Britain's prime minister in 1758, was determined to drive France from North America. The British soon gained the upper hand on the seas by practically demolishing the French fleet, thus preventing the French from sending reinforcements to America. The French, meanwhile, were aided in America by the initial neutrality of the five nations of Iroquois Indians. But that was not enough to keep British troops from overwhelming them in Canada. Before the war was over, most of the French West Indies had also fallen to the British. In India, the French were defeated at the Battle of Plassey in 1757.

The Great War for Empire was, in fact, the first world war. The major European powers fought with each other in North America and the Caribbean, on the Atlantic, on the European Continent, in the Mediterranean, in Africa, and in India. Ending with the Treaty of Paris in 1763, the war had momentous consequences for world history. The general balance of power was maintained on the European continent. France gave up most of North America, except for two fishing islands off Newfoundland and several sugar colonies in the Caribbean. It was also required to remove its troops from India, thus paving the way for the British conquest of that great subcontinent. England also got possession of Spanish-controlled Florida. Little did Britain realize, however, that its victory in America actually sowed the seeds for the dissolution of its American empire. Problems related to the war, and to the way Britain ruled its American possessions immediately after the war, led directly to the American Revolution.

Several themes characterized European history during the seventeenth and eighteenth centuries. One was the development of national monarchies, with each monarch dreaming of divine-right absolutism but none fully achieving it. Louis XIV of France came closest. Others attained varying degrees of absolutism, while the English crown was effectively limited by constitutional means.

A second theme was the intense competition between the European states. In pursuing their own self-interests, they kept Europe locked in almost continuous warfare. In the end, a worldwide war for empire changed the map of America and opened the way for both the expansion of England's global empire and the loss of its American colonies.

Meanwhile, Spanish prestige as a major world power began to decline. So, too, did the prestige of the old Holy Roman Empire, which was effectively replaced by two new monarchies, Austria and Prussia. In addition, a new power, Russia, emerged on the stage of world politics.

Another theme was the continuing Europeanization of the world. Russia adopted Western absolutist ideology as well as Western institutions, art, and literature. European trading activities increasingly dominated world economies. In addition, this was an era of changing world views, brought on by exciting new developments in Western scientific and political thought. The European Enlightenment affected science, government, religion, and almost every other aspect of Western thought, and eventually was felt around the world. The Enlightenment will be the topic of the following chapter.

Selected Readings

Anderson, M. S. *Historians and Eighteenth-Century Europe, 1715–1789*. New York: Oxford University Press, 1979.

————. *War and Society in Europe of the Old Regime, 1618–1789*. Leicester: Leicester University Press in association with Fontana Paperbacks, 1988.

Behrens, C. B. A. *Society, Government, and the Enlightenment: The Experiences of Eighteenth-Century France and Prussia*. New York: Harper & Row, 1985.

Campbell, Peter Robert. *The Ancien Regime in France*. Oxford: Blackwell, 1988.

Dukes, Paul. *The Making of Russian Absolutism, 1613–1801*. 2nd ed. London: Longman, 1990.

Parry, J. H. *Trade and Dominion: The European Overseas Empires in the Eighteenth Century.* New York: Praeger, 1971.

Plumb, J. H. *Sir Robert Walpole, the Making of a Statesman.* 2 vols. Boston: Houghton Mifflin, 1956, 1961.

Walton, Guy. *Louis XIV's Versailles.* Chicago: University of Chicago Press, 1986.

6

The Ascendancy of Reason: The Scientific Revolution and the Enlightenment

The seventeenth and eighteenth centuries brought about new developments in science and thought that were to have a revolutionary impact on Europe. New discoveries about the nature of the universe and the structure of nature led not only to a rejection of old models, but eventually to fundamental questions about the source of authority for ultimate truth. By the time of the Enlightenment, reason, science, and experience were used to explain the nature of the universe, the nature of God, and the nature of human social and political relations. In the minds of many, traditional answers were no longer satisfying.

THE SCIENTIFIC REVOLUTION

Background

In the sixteenth and seventeenth centuries a group of scientists emerged in Europe who looked for a greater understanding of the natural world in which they lived. Traditional thought, however, had answers to questions about the origin and shape of the cosmos and the place of the human race within it. When these beliefs were backed by the weighty authority of the Catholic church, it was extremely difficult for new concepts to gain a foothold. It could even be dangerous to propose ideas challenging inherited tradition, as such views could be interpreted as attacks on the church.

This is not to say that the sixteenth and seventeenth centuries were void of scientific learning. The ideas of the ancient astronomer Ptolemy and those of the brilliant philosopher Aristotle formed the basis for accepted views of the natural world. Their theories were studied closely, as were those of other ancient authorities, such as Archimedes, who offered an appealing explanation of the material world. Astrology—the notion that stars and planets have a direct impact on the everyday lives of men and women—was widely believed. While astrology did not offer a comprehensive explanation of the shape of the universe, it did stimulate interest in astronomy, one of the first fields of study that created the Scientific Revolution.

The Scientific Revolution was born not in a stagnant age, but in an age of considerable intellectual activity. What sets the Scientific Revolution apart from the preceding age is not just its intense investigation of the natural world, but the fact that the explanations it produced challenged traditional sources of authority and even the very notion of authority itself.

What we call the Scientific Revolution came in segments and took place over time, as each individual built on, rejected, or refined the work of others. Later, a number of philosophers tried to impose an overall structure on the new knowledge that had been acquired.

The Rejection of the Aristotelian World View: New Developments in Astronomy and Physics

Though other fields of study also received attention, developments in astronomy and physics began the Scientific Revolution. Innovations in these areas directly challenged traditional ideas and set the stage for the development of both a new world view and a new approach to investigation of the world.

COPERNICUS

Though he is usually credited with being the first pioneer of the new science, in many ways Nicolaus Copernicus was not a likely candidate. His understanding of astronomy was not based on observation—an approach that would gain ground only with the work of Brahe, Kepler, and Galileo. Rather, what Copernicus knew about astronomy and the structure of the universe was theoretical, based on his education in Italy. The prevailing opinion of the day, which Copernicus learned, came from the work of the second-century Alexandrian astronomer Ptolemy.

The Ptolemaic World View. Ptolemy had proposed that the earth was at the center of the universe, with the moon, sun, planets, and stars orbiting above the earth in crystalline spheres. This view was common enough that it found its way into one of the masterpieces of late medieval Christian literature, the fourteenth-century *Divine Comedy* by Dante Alighieri. Ptolemy even had a place for God and the angels at the outer reaches of the universe.

The Ptolemaic world view of the earth at the center of creation was not just theologically pleasing. It was also backed by theories of physics accepted since the time of Aristotle. According to Aristotelian physics, the earth was at the center of the universe because it was heavier than the other objects. The powerful combination of Ptolemaic cosmology, Aristotelian physics, and religious dogma created a view of the universe that was very hard to argue against.

Copernicus's Universe. Copernicus did not completely reject Ptolemy's views. In fact, he accepted much of the Ptolemaic system, with the sun replacing the earth as the center of the universe. This was an attempt to solve one of the major problems with Ptolemy's universe: the motion of the planets, which did not seem to be moving in circles, as Ptolemy proposed. Copernicus argued that placing the sun at the center, with the earth and other planets orbiting around it, would help solve this problem. Planetary orbits that seemed irregular could now be explained by the fact that the observers themselves were moving relative to both the sun and the planets.

Copernicus presented his theory in his book *On the Revolutions of the Heavenly Spheres*, published in 1543, the same year in which he died. In the long run, except for having the earth orbit around the sun, Copernicus was no more accurate than Ptolemy on questions of planetary location and orbit.

What he did do, however, was suggest that there was another way of looking at the universe. At the same time, he constructed a theory of the universe that opened up new possibilities for the application of mathematics to astronomical observation and prediction. When applied further by Copernicus's successors, mathematical models became the basis for all subsequent astronomy.

BRAHE AND KEPLER

Brahe. The next step toward a view of the universe with the sun at the center—a *solar* system, in other words—was taken by Tycho Brahe, a sixteenth-century Danish astronomer. Brahe himself did not believe the earth orbited around the sun; rather, he believed the sun and moon both revolved around the earth, while the other planets revolved around the sun.

Brahe did, however, conduct observations that eventually supported the heliocentric (sun-centered) theory. There were no sophisticated mechanical instruments available to Brahe, but his most important contribution was the record of his naked-eye observations. His German assistant, Johannes Kepler, later used the record of these observations to further refine the heliocentric theory.

Kepler. Kepler accepted Copernicus's placement of the sun at the center, but Brahe's detailed records and Kepler's own observations convinced him that the paths of the planets as they orbited around the sun were not circular. Rather, they were elliptical. The explanation for why they took this shape had to come later from a different source, but Kepler had demonstrated the importance of direct observation. He had also taken mathematics further than anyone before him in an attempt to explain the shape of the universe.

GALILEO

Kepler's *On the Motion of Mars* was published in 1609. In that same year, another event occurred which was to have much more far-reaching consequences for the development of science and a new view of the universe. Galileo Galilei, a university professor in Padua, Italy, used a telescope, only recently invented, to look into the heavens. Telescope-aided observation allowed Galileo to see things his predecessors had simply not known about. The complexity of the universe that quickly became apparent was in direct opposition to medieval views. Among other things, Galileo discovered that there were mountains on the moon, rings around Saturn, spots moving across the sun, and moons orbiting Jupiter.

In addition to his work in astronomy, the brilliant Galileo also made important contributions in physics. He discovered that objects fall at a predictable rate and worked out the mathematical formula to describe their acceleration. Galileo's work was an important step in the direction of one of the fundamental principles of modern physics: that *all* nature conforms to uniform laws that can be expressed mathematically.

Galileo and the Church. Galileo's work did not endear him to the church. It would be incorrect to suppose that the church constantly, heavy-handedly persecuted the scientists. Nevertheless, there were incidents when religious authorities saw scientific inquiry as a sufficient challenge to invite a response. In 1633, the year after he published *Dialogues on the Two Chief Systems of the World*, Galileo was condemned by the church and forced to recant his views. A public recantation, however, did not change Galileo's mind, nor did it diminish the influence of his work, though in the short term it may have discouraged some other scientists from continuing their investigations.

NEWTON

The developments discussed thus far culminated with Sir Isaac Newton, who was born in 1642, the same year Galileo died. Newton's studies ranged far and wide, including optics and laws of motion. But he is most noted for formulating the law of gravity. He published his findings in 1687 in one of the true landmark books in history, *Mathematical Principles of Natural Philosophy* (or *Principia Mathematica*).

Newton argued that there was one force that attracted every object in the universe to every other object. Furthermore, this force could be calculated mathematically. With the theory that *all* nature conforms to uniform laws that can be expressed mathematically, the universe became much more comprehensible and rational. And it filled in many of the gaps left by the achievements of the earlier scientific revolutionaries. Kepler, for example, had asserted that the planets followed elliptical rather than circular orbits. But Kepler's innovation lacked an explanation of *why* planetary orbits took that shape. Newton's work provided that explanation.

The Foundations of Modern Science

Discoveries in astronomy and physics were only part of a new way of looking at the world of nature—and the place of humanity within nature—that began to evolve in Europe in the sixteenth and seventeenth centuries. It was distinctive from the previous world view in its emphasis on experimentation and reason and in its unwillingness to rely on traditional sources of truth, including the authority of the church.

Known as the Scientific Revolution, this "tradition-shattering" development required, in the words of Thomas Kuhn, "the community's rejection of one time-honored scientific theory in favor of another incompatible with it."

THE EVOLUTION OF NEW SCIENTIFIC THINKING

Much of the new understanding of the world was arrived at through what we now term the "scientific method." Though the makers of the Scientific Revolution were separated from one another by many years and miles, their work combined not only to bring to light new information about the world, but also to produce a new *way* of looking at the world. In the long run, this new methodology was as revolutionary as the new factual information it revealed. Never again would traditional views based on religious doctrine or the acceptance of ancient authorities go unchallenged. The scientific method and the world view it supported are fundamental to modern Western thought.

PTOLEMY (2nd century A.D.)	– Traditional explanation of earth and heavens. – *Almagest* (A.D. 150).
NICOLAUS COPERNICUS (1473–1543) Polish	– Explanation of solar system with sun at the center. – Mathematically pleasing approach to astronomy. – Circular path of planets (as with Ptolemy). – *On the Revolutions of the Heavenly Spheres* (1543).
TYCHO BRAHE (1546–1601) Danish	– Naked-eye astronomical observations. – Most acccurate tables of observations in centuries. – Opponent of Copernicus.
JOHANNES KEPLER (1571–1630) German	– One-time assistant to Brahe. – Neoplatonist follower of Copernican theories. – *Elliptical* paths of planets. – *On the Motion of Mars* (1609).
GALILEO GALILEI (1564–1642) Italian	– Observations through telescope of moon and other planets. – Research into laws of falling objects. – Condemned by Church—forced recantation. – *Dialogues on the Two Chief Systems of the World* (1632).
ISAAC NEWTON (1642–1727) English	– Law of gravity. – Exploration of nature of light and laws of optics. – Redefinition of general laws of motion. – *Principia Mathematica* (1687).
FRANCIS BACON (1561–1626) English	– Ancient authority not the infallible source of truth. – Emphasis on empirical methods. – Optimistic view of future progress based on scientific examination of nature. – *The Advancement of Learning* (1605). – *Novum Organum* (1620).
RENÉ DESCARTES (1596–1650) French	– Truth guaranteed by rational understanding (even more than empirical observation). – "I think, therefore I am" (*"cogito ergo sum"*). – *Discourse on Method* (1637).

Table 6.1   Leaders of the Scientific Revolution

Though some of the pioneers of the Scientific Revolution lived earlier, the new scientific world view did not fully develop until the seventeenth century. Francis Bacon and René Descartes are the two most important figures in this evolution.

Francis Bacon and the Inductive Approach. A philosopher and English government official, Sir Francis Bacon is most important not for any particular invention or discovery, but for his philosophical stance toward the investigation of nature and the search for truth. His starting position was the fundamental rejection of ancient authority as the source of truth.

In his *Novum Organum*, published in 1620, Bacon championed the use of empirical methods of investigation—that is, the collection of data based on direct observation by the senses. Empiricism as a philosophical school—the doctrine that all knowledge is based on information provided by the senses—is sometimes traced as far back as Aristotle, but Bacon made it one of the fundamental elements of the emerging scientific method in the seventeenth century. Unlike many medieval thinkers (including Thomas Aquinas, to be discussed below), Bacon placed less emphasis on abstract logic. He argued that after collecting data through empirical methods, it would then be possible to use that data to arrive at general truths. This pattern of thinking, known as the "inductive" approach, was not new with Bacon, but he refined its use for the investigation of nature. The use of particular data to make general observations has been a hallmark of the scientific method ever since.

Descartes and Deduction. A different approach came from the work of the French mathematician René Descartes. Like Bacon, Descartes did not accept received authority as the source of truth. But he did not agree with Bacon that the inductive approach was the best course. Descartes was also interested in general laws of nature, but he felt that the process of observation, collection, and comparison of data was not as useful as reasoning from a set of self-evident propositions, or propositions based solely on reason (known as *a priori* knowledge). Descartes advocated the "deductive" approach, deriving specific truths from general observations.

Descartes was interested in finding an approach to understanding the truths of the universe that was as rational and clear as mathematics. He initially attempted to do this through inductive reasoning, but rejected the endeavor as unfruitful. He then determined to take as his starting point a fundamental fact that was absolutely irrefutable. The expression of that fact has become one of the most famous statements in the history of Western thought: *Cogito ergo sum* ("I think, therefore I am"). Descartes could not refute the proposition that since he was conscious and knew he was thinking, he must therefore exist. Acceptance of this proposition was the first step in a series of proofs. Descartes next argued for the existence of God, and from there for the existence of the world created by God.

Descartes's insistence on doubting ancient authority and relying instead on clear, rational propositions had a profound impact on the future of scientific thought. It became incorporated into the evolving scientific world view, providing a counterpoint to Bacon's emphasis on induction.

THE SCIENTIFIC METHOD

The combination of new information and new approaches to the discovery of truth resulted in an overall method used by future scientists to guide their study. The scientific method is one of the most prominent characteristics of Western thought and also one of its great achievements. It involves a combination of empiricism and mathematical reasoning. The scientist first formulates a hypothesis—a tentative conclusion, or even an "educated guess"—about the way in which some aspect of the natural world behaves. This hypothesis is formulated specifically for the purpose of testing it. The scientist then collects data relevant to the phenomenon under observation and uses that data to determine whether the original hypothesis should be accepted, modified and retested, or rejected. Once a hypothesis is conclusively supported by the results of tests against observable data, it is accepted as having been proved. In this sense, scientific "truth" is always subject to change as scientists discover more and more about the world and further refine their hypotheses and their testing procedures.

Science and Religion

Science and religion are often seen as competing sources of truth. Indeed, the two frequently are in competition, as in Galileo's trial or the rejection of traditional religious authority in the formulation of the scientific method. The Scientific Revolution was certainly an important step in the secularization of European society. If science could show that the church was wrong about the structure of the universe, then what did this say for other areas in which the church had made authoritative pronouncements? In other words, demonstrating the church's fallibility on *any* subject called into question its authority on *all* subjects. And if human intelligence could provide answers to problems of astronomy, physics, chemistry, and biology that were more satisfying than those the church had supported for centuries, then perhaps human intelligence was also sufficient authority for answers to other questions, including the question of the relationship between God and his creations or the even more fundamental question of the very origin of the human species.

DESCARTES AND THE CHURCH

But it would be wrong to see the pioneers of the Scientific Revolution as comrades-in-arms waging an all-out battle against the Roman Catholic Church. In fact, some of them were devout believers. Descartes, for example, was influenced by the church throughout his life, even changing his mind on his acceptance of the Copernican heliocentric system in response to the church's condemnation of that theory as heretical. And once he had established his own existence as the starting point for investigation of the world, Descartes's next step was to argue for the provability of the existence of God. From that truth flowed all others.

THOMAS AQUINAS

Nevertheless, the world view and methodology advocated by the scientists and philosophers considered in this chapter did mark a departure from tradition. In the sixteenth century, the world of philosophy in Europe was still dominated by the church, and particularly by the thought of the thirteenth-century theologian Thomas Aquinas, who was canonized in 1323.

Aquinas argued that truth revealed by God and truth discovered by human intelligence were really parts of one whole. Therefore, the two kinds of truth must be reconcilable. In his most important work, *Summa Theologica*, Aquinas sought to demonstrate that the theology of Christianity and the logic of Aristotle could be combined to produce a comprehensive, coherent view of truth. But ultimately, all of Aquinas's arguments were based on an appeal to authority, whether that authority was Aristotle or the Bible. Logic was then applied to authoritative statements in order to arrive at the answers to questions. Here was an important difference between Aquinas and Descartes. For Aquinas, God's existence—a truth of faith, or revelation—was the starting point for subsequent investigation. For Descartes, however, even that truth had to be based on the more fundamental, self-evident truth of his own existence.

GALILEO AND RELIGION

Galileo's trial by ecclesiastical authority is perhaps the most celebrated case of overt persecution of science by religion, though it was certainly not the only case in which the discoveries of science resulted in criticism by religious authorities. Such criticism goes back at least as far as Copernicus and his suggestion that the earth revolved around the sun. But years before Galileo's arrest by the Inquisition, he had argued that religious and scientific truth were compatible. One need not reject the Bible in order to accept the findings of science. In a now-famous letter written to the Grand Duchess Christina of Tuscany in 1615, Galileo wrote:

> I think that in discussions of physical problems we ought to begin not from the authority of scriptural passages, but from sense-experiences and necessary demonstrations. . . . Nothing physical which sense-experience sets before our eyes, or which necessary demonstrations prove to us, ought to be called in question (much less condemned) upon the testimony of biblical passages which may have some different meaning beneath their words.

AQUINAS AND GALILEO COMPARED

A comparison with Thomas Aquinas is most interesting. Aquinas *started* with the revealed truths of the Bible and sought to make all other truth conform to revelation. He was convinced that there was no necessary conflict between revealed and discovered truth, but revelation definitely had priority. Galileo also argued that the two kinds of truths were compatible, as long as the Bible was understood properly. But that is not so simple as it sounds. Who is to determine whether or not the Bible is properly understood? And how does one know when to favor one method of inquiry over another? While arguing for compatibility, in his letter Galileo came down firmly on the side of human reason. "I do not feel obliged," he wrote, "to believe that that same God who has endowed us with senses, reason, and intellect has intended to forgo their use and by some other means to give us knowledge which we can attain by them."

The Scientific Revolution did not completely eliminate older patterns of thinking, though it did lead to a flurry of new, more accurate knowledge about how the physical world operates. But it has also raised new questions and challenges for the religiously devout. Believers have sometimes accused scientists of being dangerous atheists, while some scientists have charged religious adherents with being superstitious and closed-minded. And just as discovery and scientific advancement continues today, so does discussion of whether science and religion are allies or foes.

Science and Technology

Advances in astronomy, physics, chemistry, biology, medicine, and other fields were important not only because they increased understanding of the world. Technology—the practical application of scientific knowledge—benefited from this new knowledge, changing forever the way in which people lived (see chapter 8).

Technology also had global consequences, enabling Western states to project their power to distant parts of the globe. The fact that much of modern world history is the story of European expansion and dominance is due in no small part to the ways in which Europeans used technology.

This is not to say that Europe had a monopoly on technological advancement. On the eve of the Scientific Revolution, there was probably no place on earth more advanced than China. Sir Francis Bacon, who felt that science provided the human race with a very optimistic future, argued that three revolutionary inventions were shaping the modern world (and modern states): the printing press, the magnetic compass, and gunpowder. Not one of these was initially invented in Europe. In fact, they were all developed first in East Asia.

How, then, does one account for the fact that modern science appears to be so closely identified with *Western* thought? This is one of the most intriguing questions raised by the Scientific Revolution. It is a question that still awaits a completely satisfying answer. Some other parts of the world certainly used plenty of *technology* to solve practical problems and increase the efficiency of human labor. And non-Europeans also considered at great length the structure of the universe and the behavior of the natural world. They often came up with detailed, comprehensive explanations that may not have been objectively accurate, but that were nevertheless coherent if one accepted the premises on which they were based. But a combination of factors—among them the humanistic emphasis of the Enlightenment, the European expansionist drive, the increasing secularization of European society, a social atmosphere conducive to the spread of ideas and interaction between scientists and other groups, and different assumptions about the role of knowledge in human societies—all seem to have created a European environment in which science flourished. The spread of Western scientific knowledge and methods to other parts of the world was perhaps one of the more salutary effects of European expansion.

THE ENLIGHTENMENT

The Scientific Revolution challenged traditional notions of authority and of truth about the natural world. The next step was to apply the same skepticism and some of the same methods to the study of human behavior and human society. This is one of the predominant features of the eighteenth-century movement known as the Enlightenment. Philosophers of the age felt that they lived in an enlightened age, free of the superstition, ignorance, and slavish acceptance of authority that characterized earlier eras. The Enlightenment produced some of the greatest minds in modern Western history, and some of its greatest artistic geniuses. It also produced ideas that would prove to have revolutionary potential.

Objectives of the Movement   Leaders of the Enlightenment were committed to the idea of progress—a future that was better than the past. This optimistic view was based in part on the scientific achievements discussed above, and in part on the conviction that human reason was capable of fully understanding human problems and offering solutions for them. More so even than the pioneers of the Scientific Revolution, the leaders of the Enlightenment wanted not to simply understand the world, but to actually create a new world governed by reason and intellect. They accepted the findings and the methodology developed during the Scientific Revolution. Now they wanted to take the same methods and apply them to the problems of human society.

The Fundamental Ideas of the Philosophes

Philosophes is the French term generally used to identify the thinkers who led the Enlightenment. The most famous of them was François Marie Arouet, known commonly as Voltaire. The philosophes were not scientists, nor were they philosophers in the strict sense of the word. Rather, they were thinkers who popularized their ideas and emphasized the need for social action as the result of gaining knowledge. Like Newton, the philosophes emphasized the value of sensory experience for gaining knowledge—not just about the physical world, but about the political and social worlds as well.

PROGRESS AND REASON

The philosophes operated on the basis of a number of fundamental assumptions. The first was the belief in progress, already mentioned above. The second was the belief that reason—the logical operation of the human intellect—was the key to solving the problems of human society, whether those problems were economic, political, religious, or social. Dedication to the principles of progress and reason led to the assumption that humanity was perfectible. It would take education, reason, and enlightened guidance to accomplish this goal, but it was attainable.

LIBERTY

The philosophes were also strong believers in liberty, which made them opponents of such practices as slavery. They also encouraged the maximum possible liberty in political and economic life. One of the most famous books produced during this period was Adam Smith's *An Inquiry into the Nature and Causes of the Wealth of Nations*, published in 1776. Smith called for as little government interference in economic life as possible. He reasoned that the national well-being is simply the aggregate of the well-being of all the individuals living within that nation. Since individuals are motivated by self-interest and since they know best what is in their self-interest, government should let the mechanism of self-interest operate to the benefit of the state.

FUNDAMENTAL FREEDOMS

Consistent with their emphasis on liberty, the philosophes favored the protection of fundamental freedoms, such as freedom of speech, religion, and the press, but this did not necessarily make them all democrats. In fact, the political philosophy of most of the philosophes has come to be known as "enlightened despotism." They hoped that an enlightened monarch would rule the people in accordance with natural law and the principle of reason, thereby guaranteeing happiness and order. Catherine the Great of Russia, Frederick the Great of Prussia, and the Austrian Joseph II (of the Habsburg empire) are the best known of the monarchs who attempted to apply Enlightenment ideas in one way or another within their realms.

LOCKE

Other fundamental ideas also were propounded by the philosophes or their immediate predecessors. John Locke laid out a theory of knowledge that was of great importance in Enlightenment thought. In his *Essay Concerning Human Understanding* (1690), Locke compared the human mind at birth to a blank slate, a *tabula rasa*, on which ideas are inscribed through experience. This empiricism was an essential aspect of the Enlightenment.

The ideas discussed above do not contain every element that characterized the Enlightenment, but taken as a whole the thought of the period can be summarized as a concern with progress, reason, and liberty. The philosophes felt that the extent to which these fundamental ideas were applied would determine the level of human happiness.

Deism versus Organized Religion

The philosophes' concern with liberty influenced their view of God and religion as well. The new information being publicized about the natural world made the universe seem more and more mechanical. This meant that it was not necessary for God to pay constant attention to the functioning of the universe. Many Enlightenment thinkers, therefore, began to see God less as a redeemer or a father and more as a rational creator, like a great watchmaker who built the mechanism and then left it to run on its own. This sort of theology left humanity with much more responsibility for its day-to-day affairs, but it also meant that the operation of human reason was enough to discover God and his attributes. Revelation was not needed, nor was organized religion. This belief in a rational but aloof creator is known as Deism.

THOMAS PAINE

One of the clearest statements of the Deist approach came from the pen of Thomas Paine. Paine was an Englishman who moved to America in 1774. His pamphlet *Common Sense* helped to galvanize American opinion in favor of independence from England in 1776. In 1794, in *The Age of Reason*, Paine wrote:

> I believe in one God, and no more; and I hope for happiness beyond this life.

> I believe in the equality of man; and I believe that religious duties consist in doing justice, loving mercy, and endeavoring to make our fellow creatures happy.

> But, lest it should be supposed that I believe many other things in addition to these, I shall, in the progress of this work, declare the things I do not believe, and my reasons for not believing them.

I do not believe in the creed professed by the Jewish church, by the Roman church, by the Greek church, by the Turkish church, by the Protestant church, nor by any church that I know of. My own mind is my own church.

Paine went on to state that he held no condemnation for those who did not believe as he did. While maintaining that everyone must be "mentally faithful to himself," Paine argued for tolerance in religion. This was a point Locke had made a century earlier in *An Essay on Toleration*, published in 1689, in which he argued for equal respect for all religions. Toleration was one of the qualities prized by Enlightenment thinkers.

ALEXANDER POPE

Deism could gain some inspiration from the attempt of the English essayist Alexander Pope to consider both belief in God and the complex and rational world that the Scientific Revolution was revealing. In *An Essay on Man* (1733–1734), Pope declared: "Know then thyself, presume not God to scan; the proper study of Mankind is Man." Pope believed in God and in a rational, ordered universe, but he took seriously the Old Testament admonition: "For my thoughts are not your thoughts, neither are your ways my ways, saith the Lord. For as the heavens are higher than the earth, so are my ways higher than your ways, and my thoughts than your thoughts" (Isaiah 55:8–9). To the extent that God could be known, he could be known through the operation of reason. But much more fruitful was the study of his universe and of humanity. The philosophes concentrated their efforts on such study.

The Indictment of Absolutism

One of the consequences of the philosophes' new concept of God—a being who was less a part of human history than earlier theologies had assumed—was that it delivered a blow to traditional European notions of divine-right absolutism. If God simply let the universe operate like a great clock and left human beings to work out their own problems, then it could hardly be argued that monarchs had direct divine sanction to justify their rule.

LOCKE

The Enlightenment attack on absolutism came from several quarters. In 1690 John Locke, an opponent of Charles II and James II, wrote his famous *Two Treatises of Government* partly to justify England's deposing of its king. Locke argued that governments had a certain obligation to those whom they governed; when governments fail to carry out their obligations (including the protection of life, liberty, and property), the people are justified in replacing the government with one that will protect the people's liberty. The revolutionary potential of such an idea is obvious; it was played out in revolutions in America and France late in the eighteenth century.

MONTESQUIEU

Other writers continued to undermine the philosophical foundations of absolutist rule. The Baron de Montesquieu, in *The Spirit of the Laws* (1748), argued that there were few absolutes when it came to forms of government. Rather, a government should respond to its environment. Montesquieu also called for a separation of powers in the government. This idea, like the ideas of Locke, had a great impact in the young American republic.

ROUSSEAU

In *The Social Contract* (1762), Jean Jacques Rousseau maintained that freedom and equality were essential for a just society. In order to promote freedom and equality, individuals must place the common good before their own personal interests. This is why individuals make laws once they organize themselves into communities. But because the people themselves make the laws, their obedience to those laws does not have to be coerced. Rousseau's ideal society was a self-regulating democracy, in which each individual subordinated his or her own interest to the general will and in which the general will of the community truly reflected the interests of the people who voluntarily comprised that community. There was no need for a separate class of rulers in such a community.

BECCARIA

Finally, on a less grand scale, penal reformer Cesare Bonesana, Marquis of Beccaria, undercut the arbitrariness of "justice" exercised in states under absolutist rule. *On Crimes and Punishments*, published in 1764, called for punishments to be meted out strictly in accordance with law, rather than for revenge or to satisfy a whim. Since the purpose of passing any laws in the first place was to bring happiness to the greatest possible number, Beccaria stated that "it is better to prevent crimes than to punish them." Liberty could best be preserved, justice could best be served, and happiness could best be guaranteed when society had as few laws as possible and when those who ran afoul of the law were punished predictably but not excessively.

Neoclassicism: The Arts, Letters, and Music

The Enlightenment was also an age of considerable literary and artistic achievement. Some of the greatest works of literature were the philosophical and social writings already referred to in this chapter. Novels such as Henry Fielding's *Tom Jones* (1749) and Daniel Defoe's *Robinson Crusoe* (1719) had a broader appeal than strictly philosophical works. But one of the most enduring examples of Enlightenment prose is Voltaire's *Candide*, published in 1759. This satirical view of society poked fun at everyone in a position of authority or privilege. It did not spare ecclesiastical authority; it was part of the trend toward secularization and criticism of the church which we have already discussed.

Greater than its prose achievements, however, were the achievements of the Enlightenment in music. The eighteenth century produced a group of composers who are still considered by many to be the undisputed masters of their art. Johann Sebastian Bach and George Friedrich Handel, both born in 1685, were two of the earliest. They were followed by Franz Joseph Haydn and Wolfgang Amadeus Mozart, who flourished in the late eighteenth century. Mozart produced such an array of compositions, some of them masterpieces that have become world favorites, that it is easy to forget that he lived only thirty-five years.

The Scientific Revolution and the Enlightenment created what might be called the "modern world view." This is an outlook based on reason and experience more than on theology, abstract philosophy, or faith. The universe that was revealed by the Scientific Revolution seemed to operate like a great machine, whose workings could be reduced to rational mathematical formulas. The philosophes of the Enlightenment took this one step further: if there are discoverable laws in the natural world, should there not also be discoverable laws governing human behavior? This offshoot of the Scientific Revolution led to the development of what we now call the social sciences.

One of the great twentieth-century philosophers of science, Alfred North Whitehead, described the seventeenth century as "the one century which consistently, and throughout the whole range of human activities, provided intellectual genius adequate for the greatness of its occasions." The philosophes of the Enlightenment built on the work of their scientist predecessors, extending the primacy of reason and experience into all realms of knowledge.

The Enlightenment's challenge to traditional theories of social and political organization laid the groundwork for more direct challenges to the status quo. Leaders and observers of revolutions in the late eighteenth century drew inspiration from the ideas of the philosophes. One such person, the Marquis de Condorcet, had observed the American Revolution from afar and found himself caught up in the French Revolution a few years later. Reflecting on what he had seen, Condorcet wrote, "the time will therefore come when the sun will shine only on free men who know no other master but their reason." This would be a time when the human race would "learn how to recognize and so to destroy, by force of reason, the first seeds of tyranny and superstition, should they ever dare to reappear amongst us." This optimism and faith in the future of humanity was typical of the Enlightenment.

Selected Readings

Berlin, Isaiah, ed. *The Age of Enlightenment: The 18th-Century Philosophers*. New York: New American Library, 1956.

Butterfield, Herbert. *The Origins of Modern Science: 1300–1800*. New York: Collier Books, 1962.

Cassirer, Ernst. *The Philosophy of the Enlightenment*. Princeton, NJ: Princeton University Press, 1979.

Darnton, Robert. *The Business of Enlightenment: A Publishing History of the Encyclopédie, 1775–1800*. Cambridge, MA: Harvard University Press, 1979.

De Santillana, Giorgio. *The Crime of Galileo*. Chicago: University of Chicago Press, 1955.

Drake, Stillman. *Galileo*. New York: Hill and Wang, 1980.

————, trans. *Discoveries and Opinions of Galileo*. New York: Doubleday, 1957.

Gay, Peter. *The Enlightenment: An Introduction*. 2 vols. New York: 1966, 1969.

Hampson, Norman. *Will and Circumstance: Montesquieu, Rousseau, and the French Revolution*. Norman: University of Oklahoma Press, 1983.

Hazard, Paul. *European Thought in the Eighteenth Century, from Montesquieu to Lessing*. London: Hollis and Carter, 1954.

Kuhn, Thomas S. *The Structure of Scientific Revolutions*. 2nd ed. Chicago: University of Chicago Press, 1970.

Palisca, Claude V. *Baroque Music*. 3rd ed. Englewood Cliffs, NJ: Prentice-Hall, 1991.

Pangle, Thomas L. *The Spirit of Modern Republicanism: The Moral Vision of the American Founders and the Philosophy of Locke*. Chicago: University of Chicago Press, 1988.

Shklar, Judith N. *Men and Citizens: A Study of Rousseau's Social Theory*. Cambridge: Cambridge University Press, 1985.

Westfall, Richard S. *Never at Rest: A Biography of Isaac Newton*. Cambridge: Cambridge University Press, 1980.

Whitehead, Alfred North. *Science and the Modern World*. New York: The Free Press, 1967.

7

Revolution in the West

1763   Seven Years' War ends

1776   American Declaration of Independence

1783   Treaty of Paris ends American revolutionary war

1787   American Constitution written

1789   Estates General meets in France

French National Assembly formed

Bastille in Paris stormed

Declaration of the Rights of Man

New American government in operation; George Washington as president

1791   Legislative Assembly meets in Paris

1792   Monarchy overthrown in France

1793   Louis XVI and Marie Antoinette beheaded

Reign of Terror begins under Robespierre

1794   The Thermidorian reaction against Robespierre

1799   Napoleon's rise to power begins

1800   Thomas Jefferson elected U.S. president

1804   Napoleon becomes Emperor of France

1814   Napoleon defeated, abdicates, and exiled

1815   Napoleon escapes from Elba, defeated, and exiled again

1816   Argentina becomes independent

1821 Peru and Mexico become independent

1822 Bolívar becomes president of Gran Colombia

Brazil becomes independent

The liberal political philosophy of the Enlightenment had its effect upon every element of European and American society. Even nobles, such as the Marquis de Lafayette of France, were convinced of the need for reforms that would place more power in the hands of the governed. Some enlightened despots and constitutional monarchs made significant reforms, but by 1775 there was still no national government established on the basis of liberal principles. By the end of the century, however, the smoldering pressures for reform had culminated in a revolution that forever changed the nature of Western government.

Historian R. R. Palmer called the last forty years of the eighteenth century the "Age of the Democratic Revolution." Though there were different manifestations of it, he said, all the revolutions of the era were part of one grand, essentially democratic movement. Palmer did not use the term "democratic" to imply the modern concept of universal suffrage, but rather to describe the movement "against the possession of government, or any public power, by any established, privileged, closed, or self-recruiting group of men." The political philosophy of the revolution "denied that any person could exercise coercive authority simply by his own right, or by right of his status, or by right of 'history.'"

The democratic revolution had its philosophical roots in classical liberalism. It took enough specific grievances, however, to provoke organized popular uprisings in order to bring about actual revolution and the demise of the old regimes. The American Revolution was the first such successful uprising. It was followed by the French Revolution. There were numerous differences between the two, but as part of the broader democratic revolution they gave pause to monarchs elsewhere. To some degree, they also helped stimulate the revolutions for national independence that opened the nineteenth century in Latin America.

THE AMERICAN REVOLUTION

The American Revolution was both conservative and radical. It was conservative in the sense that Americans believed they were fighting to maintain the traditional political system that they had enjoyed from the beginning, including the traditional "rights of Englishmen." On the international stage, however, it was radical, for it resulted in a new nation with a liberal government such as the world had never seen.

Causes of the American Revolution

While the immediate causes of the revolution stemmed directly from the Seven Years' War (see chapter 5), the long-range causes went as far back as the founding of the British colonies. As John Adams, one of the leading lights of the revolution, once said, "The Revolution was effected before the war commenced. The Revolution was in the minds and hearts of the people. . . . This radical change in the principles, opinions, sentiments, and affections of the people, was the real American Revolution."

TRADITION OF SELF-GOVERNMENT

Since the founding of the colonies the Americans had developed a tradition of self-government. This tradition included the all-important right to control their own property and consent to their own taxation. Theoretically the crown had full authority over the colonies, and Parliament could pass any kind of legislation, including taxes, affecting any part of the empire. From the beginning, however, there was little interference with the prerogatives of colonial legislatures, which usually represented all property holders in their respective colonies. Most importantly, these legislatures had the responsibility for paying most of their own governmental expenses and raising the money to do so. When, after 1763, British policy began to step on this tradition, the colonists asserted that their rights, which they had enjoyed for a century and a half, were being violated.

SALUTARY NEGLECT

A related element was a long period of what Edmund Burke later called "wise and salutary neglect." In an effort simply not to rock the boat, the British failed to execute their own navigation laws, which were designed to regulate the economy of the empire. American avoidance of the prohibitions against exporting certain manufactured goods or importing goods from other countries could hardly have been called smuggling, for the prohibitions were seldom enforced. Even during the Seven Years' War, trade with the French in Canada was almost commonplace. This traditional neglect helped create contempt for the system once the British revived it after 1763.

SOCIAL DISTINCTIONS

The American colonists also developed a social structure and social attitudes fundamentally different from those of the English. There were plenty of elites among them, but their elitism was based on wealth and, presumably, talent, not on noble birth or patronage. Except for the existence of slavery, mainly in the South, democratic attitudes rapidly developed. Psychologically, Americans were well prepared for Enlightenment ideals relating to the worth of the individual, the ability of the people to be self-governing, and natural rights.

IMMEDIATE CAUSES

After 1763, events moved rapidly toward confrontation and then toward separation. For Americans, the chief value of the recently concluded war lay in the elimination of the French from North America. Immediately after the war, however, the British government issued the Proclamation of 1763, which temporarily prohibited settlement west of the Appalachians. This could only anger traders, speculators, and prospective settlers, all of whom were anxious to take advantage of the opportunities offered by the elimination of the French threat.

Sugar Act. More irritating, however, was the effort to raise revenue in the colonies to help pay for the war and to support the increasing costs of defense. The Sugar Act was nothing more than a downward revision of duties imposed on molasses by an old navigation act, but this time it was to be enforced—not just as a means of regulating colonial manufacturing but primarily as a measure for raising colonial revenue.

The Stamp Act. The Stamp Act that followed was for the same purpose, and the colonists, determined that no taxes should be imposed on them without their consent, were irate. They responded with mass protests, boycotts, nonimportation agreements, mob activity against the home of the royal governor of Massachusetts, and tar-and-feather parties "honoring" hapless stamp masters. They also produced a flood of speeches, resolutions, and pamphlets, and the crisis mustered the first effective intercolonial organization. The Stamp Act Congress, which included delegates from nine colonies, met in October 1765 and sent its grievances to the king. The Stamp Act was soon repealed, though not without a statement from Parliament strongly affirming its right to make laws of any kind with respect to the colonies.

The Problem of Consent. In the course of the heated transoceanic debates, the colonists argued vigorously, often brilliantly, for the right to consent to their own taxation, which they could do only in their own representative assemblies. The British argued that, since the well-being of the whole empire was the basic concern of Parliament, everyone, whether actually represented or not, was *virtually* represented in its debates. To the Americans, this was nonsense.

Boston Massacre. In 1767 new taxes on imports were met with more protests, more boycotts, and eventually violence. The continuing presence of British soldiers, together with a law that required colonists to supply provisions and quarters for them (another form of tax in the minds of Americans), was still further provocation. When a few Boston rowdies threatened some of them in 1770, the soldiers fired on the mob and the

Boston Massacre, as American firebrands began to call it, soon fanned the flames of colonial discontent.

Intolerable Acts and American Response. In 1773 the government gave a monopoly on the tea trade to the hard-pressed East India Company, which resulted in the "Boston tea party," where tea chests were thrown into Boston harbor rather than allowed to be unloaded. In retribution, the British passed a series of Coercive Acts that closed the port of Boston, curtailed the judicial authority of the colonies, required colonists to quarter soldiers in their homes if necessary, limited Massachusetts's law enforcement powers, and curtailed town meetings. Americans labeled them the "Intolerable Acts," and from every colony came money and provisions to help beleaguered Boston. In September 1774, the First Continental Congress met in Philadelphia with representatives from twelve colonies. Its several resolutions reaffirmed colonial loyalty to the crown, but contained within them many seeds of revolutionary thought. They declared the Intolerable Acts null and void, called upon Massachusetts to arm itself for defense, and called for more boycotts against the British. A Declaration of American Rights specifically denied that Parliament had any authority with respect to internal colonial affairs. In effect, it was putting into practical words a theory long discussed: that the colonies were not subject to Parliament at all, but only to the crown, and that each, like England itself, was a separate realm, united with the other realms in their common loyalty to the crown and in their common interests.

Such liberal attitudes struck at the heart of the British theory of empire. Despite a few strong voices of reconciliation, therefore, Parliament punished the upstart Americans by declaring Massachusetts in rebellion, forbidding New England colonies to trade with any nation outside the empire, and excluding them from the North Atlantic fisheries.

The War for Independence

FIRST SHOTS

The "shots heard round the world" were fired at Lexington and Concord, Massachusetts, on April 19, 1775, when British troops attempted to capture arms and munitions being gathered by the colonists. The citizens, who were by that time calling themselves patriots, resisted with guns. The result was a British rout and a solidification of the revolution throughout the colonies. The Second Continental Congress assumed direction, named George Washington as commander-in-chief of a ragtag but determined Continental Army, and within a year debated the momentous question of independence.

THE DECLARATION OF INDEPENDENCE

Though most Americans were willing to fight for what they perceived to be their rights, there was no majority clearly in favor of independence. In January 1776, however, a pamphlet by the recently arrived British radical,

Thomas Paine, was published in Philadelphia. Entitled *Common Sense*, it was a fiery attack upon the monarchy and a compelling call for independence. Almost overnight it became a best-seller in the colonies, partly because it expressed so well their growing sense of separateness. Its influence was pivotal, and on July 2, with the consent of all the colonies, Congress voted for independence. On July 4 it officially adopted the Declaration of Independence, written by Thomas Jefferson of Virginia.

The Declaration proclaimed a rationale for revolution and a philosophy of government that became not just an American creed but also one of the most important summaries yet of the essence of Enlightenment thinking—and one that inspired liberals and revolutionaries everywhere. Its purpose was purely propagandistic—that is, to justify the revolution before the peoples of the world, and to gain their sympathy and support. Most of it was an attack upon the tyranny of the king, but three powerful sentences near the beginning were the embodiment of much of eighteenth-century liberal thought.

An initial reference to the "separate and equal station to which the Laws of Nature and of Nature's God" entitled the Americans was an indication that they simply accepted as fact the "natural rights" so long discussed by Enlightenment philosophers. "We hold these truths to be self-evident," it continued in that spirit, "that all men are created equal, that they are endowed by their Creator with certain unalienable rights, that among these are Life, Liberty, and the pursuit of Happiness." The next sentence was the death-blow to the idea of monarchy and the most concise statement possible of contemporary democratic thought. "That to secure these rights, Governments are instituted among men, deriving their just powers from the consent of the governed." Then followed the profound summary of John Locke's justification for revolution, written nearly ninety years earlier. "That whenever any Form of Government becomes destructive of these ends, it is the Right of the People to alter or abolish it, and to institute new Government, laying its foundation on such principles and organizing its powers in such form, as to them shall seem most likely to effect their Safety and Happiness."

THE WAR: INTERNAL AND EXTERNAL

The revolution was also a civil conflict, for many Americans, perhaps as many as 18 percent of the adult white males, remained loyal to the mother country. Loyalists, who tended to come from among the more wealthy populace, were harassed, their property was confiscated, and many of them simply returned to England.

Militarily, the war proceeded under the direction of Congress and was often discouraging. The Americans, who suffered from lack of money and supplies, sometimes held on only because the British did not follow through on their advantages. In other cases, such as at Saratoga in October 1777,

Americans won key and overwhelming victories. The Saratoga triumph, in fact, persuaded the French to join the war against the British. In October 1781 the combined actions of the French fleet and George Washington's army won a stunning victory at Yorktown. The war was over. When the Treaty of Paris was finally signed in 1783, Britain recognized American independence and ceded all its territory between the Appalachians and the Mississippi River. What had begun as the rebellion of thirteen colonies ended up as an American confederation that controlled half the continent.

INTERNATIONAL RAMIFICATIONS

Internationally, the Americans sought military and financial aid wherever they could, attempting to build on old European rivalries to help their own cause. France, Britain's historic enemy, sympathized with the Americans from the beginning; although they did not at first officially join the war, the French actually supplied a large portion of the guns and gunpowder used by American troops. French volunteers, too, came to fight, the most notable of whom was the Marquis de Lafayette, who soon became one of George Washington's must trusted generals. In 1779 and 1780, respectively, the Spanish and Dutch declared war on Britain, as allies of France. Russia, meanwhile, helped form the League of Armed Neutrality to help protect neutral shipping rights, and Britain found itself involved in a war against most of Europe. England also had colonies in India and the West Indies that had to be protected and defended in the continuing struggle of the European powers for empire.

It was perhaps these extended involvements that helped tip the scales in favor of ending the American war with as few losses as possible. This also explains why, at the Treaty of Paris, the British offered such favorable terms to the American negotiators. The French and the Spanish would not have allowed the vast western territory to be given to the Americans, but the British would rather have a weak American nation in the Mississippi Valley than a major European power. The American negotiators understood what was going on, wisely refused to tie themselves to the French negotiators, and actually conducted separate negotiations.

The New Republic

An important question remained after the conclusion of hostilities: What kind of nation had been created in America? Most of the colonies, which were actually small independent republics, wrote new constitutions, putting into effect the prevailing Enlightenment notions of social contract and popular sovereignty. Such liberal provisions as separation of powers to avoid abuses, bills of rights, and a powerful legislature with a limited executive characterized many of them. For the time being, however, the states hardly constituted a nation, for they each retained their complete sovereignty. After 1781 they were joined, but only loosely, under the Articles of Confederation.

THE AMERICAN CONSTITUTION

By 1787, various economic problems, clear weaknesses in their ability to negotiate on an international level, and the threat of serious internal disorders with no central authority to control them brought American leaders to a realization of the need for a stronger central government. During the Constitutional Convention of that year, delegates made the all-important decision to create a completely new kind of republic: one in which sovereignty was divided between two levels of government.

Federal Government. To the central (or federal) government, the Constitution granted the power to regulate foreign trade, levy taxes, conduct war, and carry out numerous other duties essential to the well-being of a united nation. It also had the power to enforce its laws. The Bill of Rights, added during the first year the new government went into effect, spelled out specific rights of the citizens that could not be violated by the federal government.

State Governments. The states, on the other hand, were each guaranteed their own republican form of government, and they retained all powers not specifically granted to the federal government. This included police power, control of local governments, and authority over education. Both the federal and the state governments had the power to levy taxes. American federalism was one of the distinctive features of the American contribution to the age of the democratic revolution.

American Democracy. From the standpoint of world movements, the American Constitution became the great example of liberal political philosophy put into practice. If the thrust of the age of the democratic revolution was the overthrow of absolutism and political power based on hereditary class and the establishment of representative self-government, the Constitution was the most effective liberal document of its day. All its lawmakers, as well as the chief executive, were elected officials who had to stand regularly for reelection. Thus, by the vote of the electorate, the government could be changed as often as the people were concerned enough to take action at the ballot box. Montesquieu's system of checks and balances was at the heart of the way the federal government operated, and the power of that government itself would be checked by the powers of the individual states. What was created in America was not democracy in the Greek sense of "one man, one vote," but a representative democracy, or a republic. This is not to say that Americans had created the ideal society, for vast inequalities, including slavery, continued to exist. But the ideal of equality before the law was stronger than it had ever been before.

THE REVOLUTION OF 1800

The new government began to function in 1789 under the auspicious leadership of George Washington, but opposition soon developed. Thomas Jefferson and other American liberals objected to such "Federalist" measures as the creation of a national bank, the encouragement of manufacturing, federal assumption of the revolutionary war debts of the states, and restrictions on the rights of certain immigrants. Such actions seemed designed not only to favor the rich and the well born but also to enhance the power of the central government at the expense of the states. "Democratic Republicans," as Jefferson's friends were called, objected strenuously, and in 1800 they were successful in getting Jefferson elected to the presidency. The election has been labeled the "revolution of 1800," for it transferred the reins of government to a new party with a political philosophy diametrically opposed to one already in power. In marked contrast to the violence that often accompanied such political change elsewhere, however, it had happened peacefully. In a sense, this nonviolent revolution was proof of the vitality of the new republic.

Impact and Significance of the American Revolution

The American Revolution was the first time an overseas possession had rebelled successfully against a European power. It also resulted in the first modern state to have a written constitution, and the first in which it was explicitly declared that the exercise of power was to be based on the consent of the governed, not on divine right. The revolution was significant, then, because it created a new and different type of state. In effect, it "changed the rules" of politics for much of the Western world.

The Declaration of Independence said that "all men are created equal," meaning "equal before the law," and Americans did all they could to make this a reality. They extended the franchise until all while males could vote (though property qualifications remained in effect in most states until after the revolutionary era). Many states passed laws forbidding importation of slaves. They also abolished established churches, and freedom of religion became the law of the land. In addition, all thirteen state constitutions included bills of rights, which guaranteed the natural rights of citizens.

Internally, the era of the American Revolution may not have been very revolutionary, for it resulted in nothing like the vast social and economic reorganization that later characterized the French and the Russian Revolutions. At the time, however, it had a profound impact on European observers. It meant that the ideas of the Enlightenment were more than interesting abstractions, for a new state had been established with a workable system of government based on the rights of the individual. To absolutists this spelled danger. For liberals, America became a symbol of freedom and opportunity.

THE FRENCH REVOLUTION

The American Revolution undoubtedly hastened the French Revolution, but it was the latter that opened the modern era of European politics. The French Revolution not only overthrew monarchy, it threw out the entire system of hereditary class and privilege, giving royalists, aristocrats, and other conservatives throughout Europe even more to think about than the revolution across the Atlantic.

Causes of the Revolution

SOCIAL STRUCTURE OF THE OLD REGIME

Historians are not agreed on the causes of the French Revolution, except that they were multiple and complex. One factor was France's increasingly unrealistic social structure.

The Three Estates. Legally, France's 25 million people were classified into three "estates." The first, the clergy, owned considerable land, paid practically no taxes, and was often characterized at the top levels by aristocratic, political appointees. The nobility, the second estate, owned one-fourth of the land, was not heavily taxed, and enjoyed a wide variety of privileges and immunities, including the right to tax the peasants. The third estate, the commoners, consisting of everyone else, comprised about 98 percent of the population. Members of this highly fragmented estate (merchants, doctors, artisans, but mostly workers and peasants) had little in common except for their opposition to the privileges of the two higher estates.

These orders, however, were not rigid. By the 1780s French society was actually based on wealth and economic achievement, and the more wealthy within the third estate had much in common with the nobility. Both groups opposed the claims of the monarchy to absolute authority and chafed under the economic bungling of the bureaucracy. Both were concerned with protecting private property and expanding their investments, and it was not uncommon for members of the third estate to attain noble status through government service or by purchasing offices that carried noble rank with them. Often the two estates were also linked by marriage.

WEAKNESS OF THE MONARCHY

Another factor was the weakness of the monarchy. Despite the king's claim to absolute authority, the clergy, the provinces, the towns, and various corporate bodies retained numerous rights and privileges. Furthermore, the nobility and influential commoners were frequently in a position to frustrate efforts of the crown to raise taxes and to do other things that worked against their economic interests.

ECONOMIC CHAOS

The most immediate problem was pure economic chaos, especially after the cost of participating in the American war for independence sent the national debt soaring to such heights that half of the continually burgeoning budget went to pay the interest. Essential government services were suffering, and there seemed to be no solution except to raise taxes. But the tax system itself was blatantly outmoded and unfair; it relied on taxing the already overburdened peasantry and on manorial dues, and it was impossible to obtain more revenue from either of these sources. Reforming the system, however, would affect the vested interests of every element of society, and the effort at reform sparked the move to change not just the economic system but the political and social system as well.

Phase I: The Establishment of a Limited Monarchy

THE RISE OF THE NATIONAL ASSEMBLY

In 1787 the economic crisis was so severe that Louis XVI and his ministers attempted to tax all landowners, regardless of status or legal privileges. In response, powerful nobles and high-ranking churchmen demanded that the king call together the Estates General, a body that represented all three estates but had not met since 1614. After considerable resistance and political turmoil, the king relented and called for it to meet in the spring of 1789.

Estates General. In the impassioned election campaign of 1788 to 1789, each estate elected representatives to the forthcoming assembly. Most of those elected were intent on making sweeping liberal reforms: the monarchy must be constitutionally limited, the Estates General must meet regularly and approve all laws and taxes, and individual liberties must be guaranteed.

National Assembly. The 1,200 delegates met at Versailles, just twelve miles outside Paris, in May 1789. Almost immediately they found themselves deadlocked over how they should transact business. The third estate, which represented the vast majority of the people, refused to meet separately, fearing that it would remain an inferior body that could be overpowered by the other two on every issue. Finally, on June 17 and after six weeks of wrangling, the third estate declared itself to be the National Assembly. On July 20, meeting in a large indoor tennis court, the delegates pledged themselves never to disband until they had written a new constitution.

In one sense this "Tennis Court Oath" was the real beginning of the French Revolution, because from that point, some kind of transformation of the government was virtually inevitable. On June 23 the king gave a conciliatory address, promising a constitution and other reforms, and then ordered the three estates to meet in their separate halls. Again the third estate refused. The king, in desperation, ordered the two privileged classes to meet with the National Assembly. The Estates General had been destroyed. The monarchy, however, was not quite dead, for the king ordered 20,000 troops to the area of Paris, planning to disband the Assembly with bayonets.

THE BASTILLE

Meanwhile, the French masses were caught in the grip of economic disaster, partly the result of a poor harvest in 1788. The price of bread was far beyond what the poor could afford; in Paris, one-fourth of the people were unemployed. Their outrage was only compounded when they heard rumors that the king's troops were about to sack the city, and they began to seize arms for defense. On July 14, 1789, hundreds of citizens stormed the Bastille, a medieval fortress long used as a prison, in search of gunpowder. In the melee ninety-eight people were killed, and the governor of the prison finally surrendered. The fury and spontaneous brutality of the masses was illustrated when both he and the mayor were butchered. Paris was no longer loyal to the king. He was forced to recall his troops, and the National Assembly in Versailles was saved. July 14, Bastille Day, eventually became France's most important national holiday.

RECONSTRUCTION OF THE OLD REGIME

Throughout the summer spontaneous popular insurrections spread across France. During the Great Fear, as it has been called, peasants looted homes of the lords, burned legal documents, seized lands and forests, and generally caused hysteria. At Versailles, the nobles got the message and agreed to eliminate all remaining vestiges of serfdom as well as to give up most of their exclusive privileges.

Living in Paris at the time was the Marquis de Lafayette, a delegate to the National Assembly whom the citizens had made commander of the city's armed forces after they stormed the Bastille. There, too, was his friend Thomas Jefferson, American ambassador to France. Lafayette, like many other nobles, was deeply concerned with the need for a declaration of rights, and he consulted with Jefferson on his own drafts of such a document. On August 27, 1789, the National Assembly issued its Declaration of the Rights of Man. Much shorter than the American Declaration of Independence, it nevertheless contained many of the same essential elements, including the ideals of equality before the law, representative government, and individual freedom. The next task was to draft a constitution, which the new National Assembly had vowed in June was its essential mission.

October Violence. At that point the revolution again turned violent, but this time the perpetrators were the working women of Paris, whose meager incomes were essential to their families. When the depression threw many of them out of work, their anger erupted into fury. On October 5, some 7,000 women marched from Paris to Versailles brandishing scythes, pikes, axes, guns, and sticks and demanding some kind of action that would bring them bread. Perhaps they despised no one more than the queen, Marie Antoinette. When they raided the royal apartments, hacking to death some of the royal bodyguards, they were breathing threats against her. Ultimately they forced the king and his family to move to Paris, where the king would be virtually imprisoned. The bizarre procession that paraded back to Paris on October 6 included the royal bodyguard, the king's carriage, and the mob eating and drinking and hurling insults at the queen. It was also chanting, symbolically, that it was bringing back "the baker, the baker's wife, and the baker's boy."

The Old Regime Restructured. Over the next two years the National Assembly, acting as a constituent (or people's) assembly, completely restructured the Old Regime. It abolished the nobility and created a constitutional monarchy. The constitution, completed in 1791, retained the king as head of state, but placed all legislative power in the hands of the Assembly. That body was elected by an indirect process, but those who could vote for electors, though limited by economic qualifications, included nearly two-thirds of the adult males. Civil rights eventually were extended to all people. Local government, too, was affected; the Assembly abolished the historic jumble of provinces, each with different systems, and replaced them with eighty-three departments of roughly the same size and with exactly the same governing institutions. The old judicial system, too, was swept away, being replaced with a system that included elected judges, trial by jury in all felony cases, and a new, liberal penal code. In addition, new paper currency was issued, backed up by former church property that had been nationalized.

Church Reform. The Catholic church was also the object of the National Assembly's reforming zeal. The church was nationalized, local priests were elected rather than simply appointed, and the clergy was required to take an oath of loyalty to the constitution. There was deep division within the clergy as well as among the laity. Many people resented a move that seemed impious, and were torn between loyalty to the revolution and loyalty to the priests who refused to take the oath. Some recalcitrant clergy even began to speak openly against the revolution itself. They were arrested, but in the long run the attack on the church was the Assembly's most serious mistake.

For the time being, however, the members of the National Assembly believed the revolution was over, and on September 30, 1791, they dissolved the Assembly and went home. In one way they were right, for the most constructive and permanent reforms of the revolution were in place. Politically, however, the worst was yet to come.

Phase II: The Radical Republic

Before the National Assembly dissolved itself, it provided for the election of a new representative body to be known as the Legislative Assembly. Because no member of the old Assembly could be elected to the new body, the Legislative Assembly that met in October 1791 was much different in character. The new legislators, sometimes known as "Jacobins" because of a political club they were associated with, were so ardent in their commitment to liberalism that they took the revolution far beyond the objectives of its founders.

THE END OF THE MONARCHY

Their first opportunity came from outside. The monarchs of Europe, spurred by French nobles who had fled their country (or emigrés), felt threatened themselves. They seriously contemplated invading France, restoring the monarchy, and, in the process, gaining some territory for themselves. The Jacobins actually welcomed this, not just as an opportunity to solidify their position with the masses, but also as an opportunity to export the revolution, "liberating" other peoples of Europe.

Jacobins Go to War. In April 1792 they went to war against Austria and Prussia, but the war began poorly. French troops fled at their first encounter; the enemy crossed French borders and began a drive toward Paris. At that point, however, fervent new nationalism seemed to inspire the masses. Army volunteers marched to battle singing a stirring song, "The Marseillaise," newly composed by one of their officers.

National Convention. When rumors spread that the king was in league with the enemy, angry patriots of Paris again mobilized themselves for action. On August 10 a mob captured the royal palace at the Tuileries, and the king and his family took refuge in the Legislative Assembly. Realizing that all hope for a constitutional monarchy was gone, and that its own existence no longer had legitimacy, the Assembly suspended the king, put him in custody, and prepared to dissolve itself. It also ordered the creation of a new legislative body, to be known as the National Convention and to be elected by universal male suffrage. Monarchy in France was dead. The monarch himself would soon follow.

RADICALIZATION OF THE REVOLUTION

Events moved rapidly toward even greater radicalization and toward an era in which violence and death were commonplace.

The Guillotine. In 1792 the National Assembly adopted a new instrument of execution: a beveled blade suspended between two upright supports that, when let drop, could quickly dispatch a person's head. Used previously in Scotland, it was urged on the Assembly by one of its members, Joseph Ignace Guillotin, a physician who believed that this uniform, presumably painless method was the only humane way to carry out executions. The guillotine, as it was soon called, became one of the horrors of the next few years and one of the most frightful symbols of the age.

The first wave of violence was the September Massacres in 1792. Enraged by stories that imprisoned counterrevolutionaries and aristocrats were in league with the invaders, Parisian crowds stormed the prisons, set up popular tribunals, and summarily executed over 1,000 prisoners.

The Republic Executes the Monarchs. The Convention, meanwhile, proclaimed France a republic. It also adopted a new calendar and a more informal style of address intended to carry the republic even further from the formal trappings of the aristocracy. It also agreed on the fate of the imprisoned Louis XVI. By a narrow majority, it found him guilty of treason. On January 21, 1793, stripped even of his kingly title, Louis Capet was executed. Marie Antoinette was taken to the guillotine in October.

Another War and Internal Division. The fortunes of the French armies temporarily improved, and in February 1793 the Convention declared war on Britain, Holland, and Spain. France was at war with nearly all of Europe. However, division began to appear at home as many peasants, encouraged by French Catholics and emigrés, resisted being drafted into the army. Guerrilla bands of Catholics and royalists occupied several cities and massacred patriots who still supported the revolution. The Convention was also bitterly divided between two factions. The Girondists and the Montagnards (the Mountain) were both determined to continue the war and to promote more internal reforms, but they mistrusted each other intensely.

Sans-Culottes. New pressures, meanwhile, were put on the Convention by the bitterly antiaristocratic masses (artisans, shopkeepers, and laborers). They were sometimes called the *sans-culottes* ("without breeches") for they wore trousers rather than the knee-breeches that characterized the dress of the aristocracy and the middle class. They also adopted other symbolic lifestyles intended to emphasize the virtue of their society and, by contrast, the decadence of their enemies. These included simplicity in dress and manners and the use of the word "citizen" as a form of address instead of titles such as "monsieur" or "madame." They became the driving political force in Paris. In the spring of 1793, after a poor harvest and a precipitous decline in the value of paper money spread scarcity and panic across the country, they demanded more radical political action in order to guarantee a steady supply of bread. The Montagnards joined with them. A popular uprising soon forced the Girondists out of power, giving the Montagnards complete control of the Convention.

Robespierre. One of the most effective leaders of the Montagnards was Maximilien de Robespierre, a fierce democrat who fully believed that the common people were the ultimate possessors of both goodness and good sense. In his enthusiasm, however, he also believed that ruthless force was necessary to achieve unanimity. To him, the survival of the revolution was the highest value. To achieve this survival, he felt the central government must be both powerful and efficient and must withstand every threat to its continued existence. If that ideal came into conflict with his democratic sympathies, Robespierre's loyalty to the revolution won out.

In the Convention, the more moderate Girondists thundered against what they called the tyranny of the sans-culottes. But on June 2, urged on by Robespierre, the Convention had thirty-one Girondists expelled and arrested. Ultimately they were tried for treason. Robespierre was elected to the Committee of Public Safety, which had dictatorial powers.

Meanwhile, a revolt against the Convention was growing in cities and provinces outside Paris. Soon only the area around Paris and the eastern front were under the control of the Convention. This triggered the most brutal period of the entire revolution: the Reign of Terror.

THE REIGN OF TERROR

Robespierre and the Committee of Public Safety, cooperating with the sans-culottes, attacked the crisis boldly. They instituted a kind of emergency socialism, with a planned economy such as Europe had never seen before. They tackled the problem of the bread supply with price controls, quality control, and rationing. They nationalized many small businesses, particularly those engaged in production of arms, munitions, and other things essential to the war effort, and they were not hesitant to obtain raw materials and military supplies simply through requisitioning.

Politically, the bloody Reign of Terror deserved its name. Anyone deemed to be an "enemy of the nation" was tried in newly created revolutionary courts. Some 40,000 men and women were executed or died in captivity. Another 300,000 were jammed into the overcrowded prisons. The rights of the accused were minimal at best. Execution was swift. In October 1793 the city of Lyons capitulated to the Convention's forces. The population was disarmed, the homes of many wealthy citizens were burned, and nearly 2,000 people were executed after hasty, on-the-spot courts-martial.

IN DEFENSE OF THE REPUBLIC

Despite the revolts outside Paris, Robespierre and the Committee of Public Safety successfully marshaled the patriotic fervor of those who accepted revolutionary ideals. Imbued with a new sense of national mission, they thought of the war as a national crusade. The armed forces grew to 1 million men. They were led by young generals who had come up from the ranks—a different breed than the aristocratic, politically appointed officers who formerly dominated the military. By the spring of 1794, the French were victorious everywhere; by July they held the Austrian Netherlands and the Rhinelands. At the same time, the Convention was pragmatic enough to realize that it could not mount a universal crusade to bring "freedom" to all people of Europe. It steadfastly refused the temptations to invade or become involved in revolutionary movements in Holland, Poland, and Italy.

Phase III: The Thermidorian Reaction

At home, the Committee of Public Safety continued its terror, supported by the "impartiality" of the guillotine, until finally it became too much. A coalition of moderates and radicals organized a conspiracy against Robespierre. On 9 Thermidor, year II, of the revolutionary calendar (July 27, 1794), the Convention declared him an outlaw. The following day he and his closest associates climbed the steps to the guillotine. As it had done before, the revolution was eating its own children.

The "Thermidorian reaction" changed the focus of the National Convention, as moderates reasserted their authority, abolished many economic controls, and placed severe restrictions on the sans-culottes' political organization. The result was inflation, shortages, and distress among the poor, contrasted with a seeming orgy of renewed ostentatious living among the rich. Early in 1795 the Parisians revolted again, but the government quickly suppressed them. Weary of struggle, the poor finally admitted defeat, and even the women called for peace.

THE DIRECTORY

The Convention wrote still another constitution. It provided for a five-man executive, the Directory, and a two-house Legislative Assembly. The new leaders, however, proved both ineffective and unprincipled. They kept up the war, but largely to keep men in the armies and thus reduce unemployment at home. The popular fervor for war was gone; in 1797 the disgusted voters elected several conservatives and monarchists. The Directory nullified the elections, however, and began its own dictatorial but ineffective rule.

THE RISE OF NAPOLEON

The time was ripe for the appearance of a popular hero who could muster political support in the belief that he could bring order out of chaos. Such a person could command almost unlimited power. The young General Napoleon Bonaparte turned out to be the man. Though of noble birth, Napoleon was a dedicated revolutionary and had won laurels for himself with brilliant victories in Italy. As news of his exploits reached France he became a national hero. He arrived back in France just in time to become part of a plot against the Directory by prominent members of the Legislative Assembly. On November 9, 1799, with soldiers present to ensure success, the conspirators forced the directors to resign. The following day Napoleon was appointed one of a new ruling triumvirate called the Consulate.

Named first consul, the charming, talented, and ambitious Napoleon dominated the Consulate. Another new constitution was overwhelmingly approved by a plebiscite in December and, for all practical purposes, Napoleon became a dictator.

Napoleonic Reforms. Napoleon brought civil strife to an end and instituted a series of domestic reforms that ultimately became his greatest permanent achievements. They also heightened his popularity with various classes. The Civil Code of 1804, renamed the Napoleonic Code in 1807, reasserted the equality of all citizens before the law and the sanctity of private property. Peasants were delighted when he reaffirmed their rights to lands they had been allowed to purchase even though confiscated from the church or the nobility. He perfected the centralization of the state, which not only improved administration in the provinces, but gave him the power to appoint mayors who, in turn, were naturally loyal to him. He appealed to the old nobility by granting amnesty to 100,000 emigrés, provided they take a loyalty oath.

Perhaps his greatest coup was healing the breach in the French Catholic church and, at the same time, gaining its loyalty. The Concordat of 1801, signed by Napoleon and Pope Pius VII, guaranteed religious freedom to Catholics; it also gave the government the right to nominate bishops and pay the clergy. Napoleon did not succeed in gaining universal support, but he placated most of France and thus solidified his position.

Emperor. At the same time, Napoleon undid some of the liberal reforms of the early revolution. Women's rights, for example, were rolled back. Penal and criminal procedures were tightened. In general, however, the French people felt both relief and new confidence in the future. Few seemed alarmed when, in 1802, Napoleon's ten-year consulship was converted into a lifetime position. It was only a short step from there to another constitutional revision that did away with the republic two years later. Napoleon was proclaimed emperor, with a hereditary title. On December 2, 1804, at a coronation ceremony presided over by the pope at the Cathedral of Notre Dame in Paris, the French hero crowned himself.

Phase IV: The Imperial Era

THE EMPIRE OF NAPOLEON

It was not just internal affairs that paved the way for Napoleon to gain the imperial title, but also the wartime atmosphere. Napoleon had an expansive dream of ruling an empire that covered all of Europe. Already his armies had taken Austria's Italian possessions and incorporated into France much of the German Rhinelands; he began to prepare for a cross-channel invasion of England. In October 1805, however, the French navy suffered near annihilation at the Battle of Trafalgar. Britain remained the only country in Europe not seriously threatened by Napoleon. In December his armies defeated the combined Austrian-Russian forces at Austerlitz, and the following year they overran several small German states. By Napoleon's personal decree, the Holy Roman Empire came to an end; a new German union, the German Confederation of the Rhine, came into existence. The French emperor was its "protector."

The Height of the Empire. By 1810 Napoleon's empire reached its height. French borders had been expanded to include Belgium, the old Austrian Netherlands, parts of northern Italy, and considerable German territory. There were also a number of satellite or dependent kingdoms, including northern Italy, Naples (southern Italy), Holland, the Grand Duchy of Warsaw, and Spain. In addition, Prussia, Austria, the Kingdom of Norway and Denmark, and Russia were Napoleonic allies. The satellite kingdoms were ruled by Napoleon's brothers or other close family members. Already, however, Spain was in revolt. In 1808, resentful of Napoleon's decision to depose the king and place his brother, Joseph Bonaparte, on the throne, various anti-Napoleonic elements resisted the French armies, took to the hills, and began a long, intense guerrilla war. Supported by British troops, the Spanish resistance sapped Napoleon's strength elsewhere.

Resentment of Napoleon's System. There was also resentment at Napoleon's "Continental System," which was aimed at bringing the undefeated England to its knees through economic warfare. With the Berlin and Milan decrees of 1806 and 1807, Napoleon attempted to exclude all British goods, including those carried in neutral ships, from the European continent. Britain responded with the Orders in Council, which threatened to seize neutral ships that did not stop at British ports; thereupon Napoleon threatened to seize any neutral ships that obeyed the Orders in Council. The mutual blockade had worldwide implications as both Britain and France were hurt and thousands of neutral ships, including many American ships, were seized each year. France and its satellites were hurt the most because of the scarcity of foreign goods and the resulting high prices of French goods; the whole affair only weakened Napoleon's position within his empire. Smuggling became rampant, for the emperor had created a system that was far beyond his power to enforce.

THE RUSSIAN CAMPAIGN

With rebellion brewing in Spain and elsewhere, and with economic ills beginning again to divide the French, it would seem that Napoleon would rein in his ambitions and try to gain more firm control of what he had. Instead, his aspirations became even more grandiose. On June 22, 1812, he declared war on Russia. The Russian czar, Alexander I, was a restive ally at best, and had withdrawn his support for the Continental System. Napoleon somehow became convinced that the success of his plans was dependent upon eliminating any possible military threat from Russia. That decision, however, proved to be the greatest blunder of his career.

Napoleon immediately invaded, but as his army of 600,000 men fought its way toward Moscow it overextended itself in the vast, unfriendly plain. When they reached the capital city in September, they found it deserted and mostly in ashes. Before evacuating, Alexander had ordered it burned, making

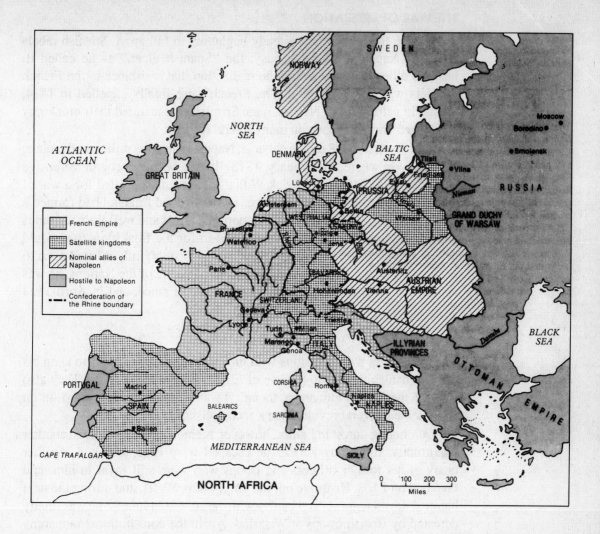

Fig. 7.1   Europe at the Height of the Napoleonic Empire, 1810

it useless as a winter headquarters for the French conqueror. Furthermore, contrary to Napoleon's expectations, Alexander simply refused to negotiate. After five weeks of waiting, Napoleon began his disastrous return to France. Short of food and supplies, his fleeing troops were constantly harassed and riddled by guerrillas from a Russian army that was still very much intact. Then came the freezing winter. By the time Napoleon's Grand Army struggled across the border into Prussia in mid-December, it was reduced to under 50,000 men. The hapless emperor returned to Paris, leaving behind a resentful remnant who felt he had deserted them. Worse, the Prussians deserted him, raising the specter of even more defections.

THE WAR OF LIBERATION

In fact, the empire was already beginning to fall apart. Spanish rebels had kept Napoleon's armies busy; the "Spanish ulcer," as he called it, inspired other Europeans with the realization that resistance to the French invaders was not impossible. The French were finally expelled in 1814, though in getting rid of Napoleon the Spanish also restored their monarchy and turned back the clock on many liberal reforms.

As a result of the Russian debacle, Napoleon lost his military advantage almost everywhere. In January 1813 Russia began a counteroffensive against him. In March Frederick William III of Prussia called for a war of liberation, and by June Russia, Prussia, Austria, and England had formed a new quadruple alliance. With the support of patriots and well-trained armies all over Europe, the alliance soon closed in for the final blow that would drive the invader from its territories. Napoleon stubbornly refused even to negotiate. Finally, in what has been called the Battle of the Nations, he was defeated at Leipzig. The alliance then invaded France, and in April 1814 Napoleon agreed to unconditional abdication.

FINAL DEFEAT AND EXILE

The victors were generous with the emperor, allowing him to keep his title but banishing him to the isle of Elba, off the coast of Italy. They also restored the French monarchy, though it was limited by a new constitution that retained several revolutionary accomplishments.

Continuing unrest in France, however, seemed to give Napoleon another opportunity. In February 1815 he escaped from Elba, gathered together many of his former officers and troops who were still loyal to him, and marched on Paris. He drove out the king, Louis XVIII, and during the next hundred days fought several battles with the allies. On June 18 he was finally defeated by British troops at Waterloo. Again the constitutional monarchy was restored. This time Napoleon was permanently exiled to the island of St. Helena, in the South Atlantic. There he wrote his memoirs, presenting himself as the great liberator and reformer of Europe whose work had been tragically undone by reactionary forces.

The French Revolution and Napoleon: Significance and Consequences

With Napoleon's downfall came the end of an era. What had begun as the establishment of a constitutional monarchy and the institution of numerous liberal reforms had gone through several stages. The monarchy had been overthrown, radical rule in the name of the people had become more tyrannical than the monarchy itself, and civil rights had been alternately promulgated and repressed. In the end, a new constitutional monarchy was in place. What, then, had been achieved, and to what degree was Napoleon either the savior or the betrayer of revolutionary values?

Although a monarch reigned, absolutism had been replaced by constitutionalism; the old nobility was forever gone. A decentralized state in
which special town charters and noble privileges allowed aristocrats and
others to rule in diverse ways had been replaced by a centralized state that
controlled not only police power but also an educational system, labor
relations, and a national banking system. Democratic participation in the
electoral process was not yet as widespread as in the United States, but the
rights of the citizens had been expanded and the right to own and control
property was more realistically available to all.

Napoleon promoted these and many other changes; the Napoleonic
Code guaranteed such basic freedoms as the right to receive equal treatment
before the law and religious freedom. On the other hand, Napoleon undid
other civil rights in the name of efficient government. Those who argue that
he was a betrayer of the values of the revolution can point to his dictatorial
regime, his suppression of civil rights, his grandiose plans for expansion of
an empire with a hereditary leadership, and the class-oriented structure that
characterized his administration. On the other hand, under his rule greater
social stability was achieved, and many of the social and economic ideals
of the revolution were permanently ensured.

THE WARS FOR INDEPENDENCE IN LATIN AMERICA

To some degree both the American and the French Revolutions helped
inspire revolutions in Latin America. The background causes differed in
many ways, but among the common elements were the ideas of Enlightenment philosophers that filtered into Latin America. These alone, however,
could hardly have fomented revolution—they could only help justify it. The
root causes were complex but included racial and social tensions, political
jealousies and rivalries, administrative restructuring of the colonies, a variety of economic grievances, and a desire to get out from under monarchy.

Background for Revolt

At the beginning of the nineteenth century Spanish claims in the Western
Hemisphere included all of the present United States west of the Mississippi,
and everything south to the tip of Cape Horn except Brazil, claimed by
Portugal.

ETHNIC GROUPS AND SOCIAL CLASSES

The revolutionary impulses in most places included not just efforts to
break away from Spanish rule but also, at times, internal conflict between

ethnic groups and social classes. Dominating economic and political life were the *peninsulares*, natives of Spain or Portugal who generally controlled economic activity. The *creoles*, white people of Spanish descent, were a little lower on the social scale and usually resentful of the power of the peninsulares. Subordinate to them were people of mixed native and European ancestry, or native and black ancestry, and lower still were the Indians and blacks. Indian laborers, whose economy was especially depressed, felt they had special cause for grievance as they worked for creoles on lands that had once been taken from their own ancestors. Blacks were still usually in bondage as slaves.

Racism and discrimination pervaded the colonies of Latin America, and it did not seem likely that the different classes could find much in common, let alone cooperate in a revolution. In some places, however, there was enough general dissatisfaction that the creole elite cooperated with the other groups in throwing out the Spanish. In other areas the creole elite wanted the Spanish out, but the Indians and blacks, fearing that the rule of the creoles would be more severe even than that of the peninsulares, sometimes cooperated with the Spanish rulers.

OTHER GRIEVANCES

In the last part of the eighteenth century the Bourbon government of Spain began an intensified effort to centralize colonial government, and in the process gradually replaced creoles with peninsulares. By 1790 only about a third of the bureaucracy were creoles, and, in an effort to avoid corruption, even they could not serve in their own provinces. To the creoles, this systematic elimination from government office meant loss of economic as well as political influence.

The colonies also experienced economic problems, despite the fact that a renewed Spanish mercantilism stimulated production of various raw products such as coffee, tobacco, sugar, hides, beef, and silver. Colonial manufacturing, however, slowed down as cheaper textiles and other goods from Europe and the United States flowed in. In addition, export taxes on manufactured goods antagonized the colonists. High intercolonial transportation costs raised the price of domestic products to the point that imported goods were often cheaper than those produced at home. In addition, the people resented the increased taxes levied by the crown in an effort to get them to pay a greater share of the costs of defending that part of the empire.

Early Setbacks

At first most creoles were not ready for revolution as such—they only wanted to bring about changes in the system. But when it appeared that independence might really be possible, many of them did not hesitate to join with the lower classes in an effort to bring it about.

A number of rebellions failed, however. In Peru, in 1779, Tupac Amaru led a bloody uprising against the Spanish regime but was finally captured and executed. Further north, in New Granada, rioting broke out in 1781 in response to new taxes on liquor and tobacco. It was not long before peasant armies led by creoles were marching on Bogotá, the capital city. Eventually, however, their leader, José Antonio Galan, was captured and executed. Another ill-fated rebellion came in 1806, when Francisco Miranda led an unsuccessful effort to throw off Spanish rule in Venezuela.

Two years later the actions of Napoleon set the stage for another round of rebellion in Latin America. When Napoleon deposed the Spanish emperor, creole elites saw this as an opportunity to seize political power for themselves. In 1810 Simón Bolívar, a gifted general who soon became the hero of Latin American independence, brought Miranda from London to lead another Venezuelan revolution, but this one, too, sputtered out as the creoles were divided among themselves. That same year an idealistic creole priest in Mexico, Miguel Hidalgo y Costilla, led the Indians in an uprising. In this case, the creoles and peninsulares collaborated to oppose him, and he was finally captured and placed before a firing squad. In 1813, however, there was a successful uprising in Paraguay that led to that country's independence.

Successful Revolution: San Martín and Bolívar

MARTÍN

The following year the Spanish monarchy was restored, but the harsh efforts of Ferdinand VII to restore absolutism prepared the ground for a second phase of revolution, this time successful. Argentina declared its independence in 1816, and one of its powerful military leaders, José de San Martín, realized that if the revolution were to be secure and permanent it must take place throughout the continent and not just in one state. Martín, therefore, led an army of Argentines and Chileans across the Andes in a dramatic assault on Chile. Within two years the entire southern part of the continent was independent. He then moved on to Peru where, in Lima in 1821, another independent state was declared.

BOLÍVAR

The following year Martín passed the revolutionary baton back to Bolívar, who had already led a successful revolution in Colombia and Venezuela and founded the Gran Colombia, which included the present states of Colombia, Venezuela, Ecuador (added in 1822), and Panama. He became its president in 1821. After his conference with Martín, Bolívar completed the liberation of Peru and then marched on to win independence for what became Bolivia. The last Spanish garrison in South America surrendered in 1826.

MEXICO

In Mexico, meanwhile, a liberal revolution in Spain, in which the king was forced to grant a constitution, convinced conservatives that they might be better off to break with the mother country. At that point Augustín de Iturbide, a distinguished military leader who had heretofore bitterly opposed the revolutionaries, came up with a plan that convinced most of the Mexican people to side with him in seeking independence. He promised constitutional government that appealed to the church by protecting its privileges and property rights, appealed to creoles by assuring their property and political offices, and appealed to the natives by promising them the same privileges as all other citizens. Mexican independence was achieved in 1821 as a united effort on the part of all classes. In July 1822 Iturbide was proclaimed Emperor Augustín I.

BRAZIL

Brazil's revolution was nonviolent. The king, a member of the royal Portuguese family who had fled to Brazil because of Napoleon's invasion, had introduced a number of reforms and was not disliked by his people. In 1820, however, a liberal revolution in Portugal made him return, but before he left he suggested to his son, Dom Pedro, that if there were a movement for independence in Brazil that he, Dom Pedro, become its leader. When Portugal tried to make Brazil more dependent and ordered Dom Pedro back to the mother country, he refused to go and the powerful economic interests rallied to his support. In September 1822, Dom Pedro declared Brazil an independent state, and he was proclaimed its first emperor.

There are important comparisons and contrasts to be made between the revolutions of this era. The American Revolution occurred in a land where there were no legal class distinctions; its liberal ideology was promoted by those who were attempting to preserve the system they were familiar with. The French Revolution was, in part, a revolt against the special privileges of the nobility, and an attempt to change the system altogether. The French Revolution became more radical and more violent in every way, and in the long run it also became more famous. In America, organized opposition became an accepted and legitimate part of the political system. In France, during much of the revolutionary era, opposition was not tolerated, and this fact did much to hasten the demise of the republic.

The American Revolution established a new government, based on liberal ideals as well as on "rights" Americans had long taken for granted, but it did not overthrow an entire system of government. The French Revolution overthrew a monarchy, completely changing the nature of the French political and social system. In the process, however, it went through four distinct phases in which liberalism and democracy at first seemed to thrive, then tended to disappear, and then came back in other forms. The era ended in 1815 with a constitutional monarchy in which power was centralized, but legalized class structure had disappeared and representative government and civil liberties were guaranteed. It also gave other monarchies more to think and worry about than even the American Revolution had.

Before their revolution, Americans were used to the idea and practice of self-government. The French were not. Americans were used to the idea of a loyal opposition; in 1800 they were able to pass through a revolution in which an opposition political party, with fundamentally different views on the role of the central government, took over peacefully. In France, until the accession of Napoleon, each time a new party took over it was through a coup, and the opposition was handed over to madame guillotine.

In Latin America there were separate national revolutions for independence, characterized by struggles over which revolutionary party would rule. Unlike those in France and North America, however, no central body directed the Latin American revolutions. Nor did any political document, such as the American or French declarations, set out a body of doctrine for all of Latin America. Nevertheless, some far-sighted leaders realized that independence in one area could not be permanent unless all the other areas became independent as well, and they worked toward that end. Simón Bolívar inspired Latin Americans everywhere and led the revolution in several areas.

Bolívar dreamed of a single continental state, but that dream was shattered. His own Gran Colombia disintegrated in 1830, the same year he resigned in disillusion. The Mexican republic lost control of Guatemala, El Salvador, Costa Rica, Honduras, and Nicaragua, which formed the short-lived Central American Federation in 1825 and then in 1838 became independent states. Eventually Mexico also lost its northern province of Texas. The new republics did not immediately achieve political stability, as continuing class divisions, disagreements over the nature of the new governments, and economic problems continued to plague most of them. By the end of the revolutionary period, however, fifteen independent nations had replaced the former Spanish colonial empire in America, and even though that was not Bolívar's vision, it was, in the end, his crowning achievement.

Selected Readings

Gipson, Lawrence Henry. *The Coming of the Revolution.* New York: Harper & Row, 1962.

Lefebvre, Georges. *The Coming of the French Revolution, 1789.* New York: Vintage Books, 1959.

Lynch, John. *The Spanish American Revolutions, 1808–1826.* New York: W.W. Norton, 1986.

Palmer, R. R. *The Age of the Democratic Revolution: A Political History of Europe and America.* 2 vols. Princeton, NJ: Princeton University Press, 1959–1964.

Thompson, J. M. *Robespierre*. New York: Blackwell, 1988.
———. *Napoleon Bonaparte*. Oxford, England: Blackwell, 1988.
Wood, Gordon S. *The Creation of the American Republic, 1776–1787*. New York: W.W. Norton, 1972.

8

The Impact of Industrialization

1760s	James Watt improves steam engine
1825	Railroad steam engine demonstrated
1830	Liverpool and Manchester Railway completed
1833	British factory legislation
1847–1931	Thomas Edison
1859	Publication of Charles Darwin's *On the Origin of Species*
1869	Suez Canal completed

When applied to broad, historical movements, the word "Revolution" does not always refer to sudden, almost precipitous change. We have seen, for example, that the American "Revolution" was really a change in attitudes and perspectives that took place over a period of more than 150 years. Nothing changed in 1776 so far as internal politics were concerned; the Americans succeeded mainly in retaining the pattern of home rule to which they had grown accustomed. Only with the writing of the Constitution of 1787 did they create an entirely new kind of political system. In France, on the other hand, the whole structure of monarchy and nobility was overthrown in one fell swoop, though the ideology of the revolution was partially undermined with the rise of Napoleon and the foundation of a new French empire. In both countries, however, an emphasis on such ideals as liberty and equality endured. These ideals became part of the long-term democratic revolution that eventually affected all of the West and much of the rest of world society.

At the same time, numerous other changes of far-reaching consequence were taking place in the West, including what is known as the Industrial Revolution. Its roots extended back into previous centuries, but beginning in England near the end of the eighteenth century a dynamic turn of events soon resulted in the creation of a mechanized factory system that produced vast new quantities of goods at dramatically lower prices. The masses could obtain products formerly available only to the upper classes, as well as new products never before available to anyone. As a result, the nature of world society was ultimately, and profoundly, transformed. Employment opportunities, social patterns, standards of living, political movements, and ideologies were all affected. So, too, was the international balance of power, as the Industrial Revolution produced new economic and technological tools that contributed to Western dominance in the world, Western imperialism, and a struggle for primacy among the Western powers themselves.

In the nineteenth century the West became dominant around most of the globe. Many interrelated elements contributed to Western dominance, but in this chapter we will focus on industry, science, technology, and some of the economic and social consequences of industrialism. In later chapters we will discuss in more detail the other events of the nineteenth century world and, in particular, the impact of Western imperialism.

BACKGROUND FOR THE INDUSTRIAL REVOLUTION

The Commercial Revolution

The Industrial Revolution had several roots, one of which was a commercial revolution that, beginning as far back as the sixteenth century, accompanied Europe's expansion overseas. Both exports and imports showed spectacular growth, particularly in England and France. An increasingly larger portion of the stepped-up commercial activity was the result of trade with overseas colonies. Imports included a variety of new beverages, spices, and foodstuffs. Turkeys, guinea fowl, and Newfoundland cod, for example, appeared on European tables with increasing frequency. At the same time, a growing export market took European textiles, hardware, firearms, ships, and ships' goods around the world and brought money flowing back. Europe's economic institutions, particularly those in England, were strong, had wealth available for new investment, and seemed almost to be waiting for some technological breakthrough that would expand their profit-making potential even more.

NATURAL ADVANTAGES

That breakthrough came in Great Britain, where several economic advantages created a climate especially favorable to the encouragement of new technology. One was its geographic location at the crossroads of international trade. Internally, Britain was endowed with easily navigable natural waterways, which helped its trade and communication with the world. Beginning in the 1770s, it enjoyed a boom in canal building, which helped make its domestic markets more accessible. Because water transportation was the cheapest means of carrying goods to market, canals reduced prices and thus increased consumer demand. Great Britain also had rich deposits of coal that fed the factories springing up in industrial areas and iron ore that provided the raw material for the manufacture of railroad equipment, tools, and a variety of industrial and consumer goods.

HUMAN AND POLITICAL POTENTIAL

Another advantage was Britain's large population of rural, agricultural wage earners, as well as cottage workers, who had the potential of being more mobile than peasants of some other countries. Eventually they found their way to the cities or mining communities and provided the human power upon which the Industrial Revolution was built. The British people were also consumers; the absence of internal tariffs, such as those that existed in France or Italy or between the German states, made Britain the largest free-trade area in Europe. Britain's relatively stable government also helped create an atmosphere conducive to industrial progress.

BRITISH ENTREPRENEURS

Great Britain's better-developed banking and credit system also helped speed the industrial process, as did the fact that it was the home of an impressive array of entrepreneurs and inventors. Among them were a large number of Protestant nonconformists, whose religious principles encouraged thrift and industry rather than luxurious living and who tended to pour their profits back into their businesses, thus providing the basis for continued expansion. Such a family was the three generations of Abraham Darbys, entrepreneurs in the iron industry. In the seventeenth century Abraham I developed new methods for casting iron. He was among the first to use coke instead of charcoal in the smelting process. His son, Abraham II, improved the procedure. Eventually coke smelting became the standard technique almost everywhere. In the late eighteenth century Abraham III built the first cast iron bridge, a 196-foot semi-arch that still spans the River Severn at the community of Ironbridge and is a major tourist attraction in Shropshire.

AGRICULTURAL REVOLUTION

A precursor to the Industrial Revolution was a revolution in agricultural techniques. Ideas about agricultural reform developed first in Holland where, as early as the mid-seventeenth century, such "modern" methods as crop rotation, heavy fertilization, and diversification were all in use. Dutch peasant farmers were known throughout Europe for their agricultural innovations; but as British markets and opportunities grew the English quickly learned from them. As early as the seventeenth century the Dutch were helping them drain marshes and fens where, with the help of advanced techniques, they grew new crops. By the mid-eighteenth century new agricultural methods as well as selective breeding of livestock had caught on throughout the country. One innovator was Jethro Tull, who promoted the use of drilling equipment to plant seeds. The long-range impact of such modernization is seen in the fact that between 1700 and 1870 food production increased by 300 percent.

THE ENCLOSURE MOVEMENT

Much of this increased production was consumed by Great Britain's burgeoning population, which between 1780 and 1851 grew from 9 million to nearly 21 million people. At the same time, people were moving to the city, partly because of the enclosure movement, that is, the fencing of common fields and pastures in order to provide more compact, efficient, privately held agricultural parcels that would produce more goods and greater profits. In the sixteenth century enclosures were usually used for creating sheep pastures, but by the eighteenth century new farming techniques made it advantageous for large landowners to seek enclosures in order to improve agricultural production. Between 1714 and 1820 over 6 million acres of English land were enclosed. As a result, many small, independent farmers were forced to sell out simply because they could not compete. Nonlandholding peasants and cottage workers, who worked for wages and grazed cows or pigs on the village common, were also hurt when the common was no longer available. It was such people who began to flock to the cities seeking employment and who found work in the factories that would transform the nation and, eventually, the world.

THE COURSE OF THE INDUSTRIAL REVOLUTION

These and other factors were all in the background, but the major impetus to the Industrial Revolution was changing technology. This was sparked by demand, for invention comes not just from necessity but also when it appears that there are profits to be made. Moreover, development of new technologies created chain reactions whereby one invention led to another which, in turn, stimulated more improvements in the first. As the economic potential became more clear, such inventions led to improvements in related technologies. The cycle went on in seemingly endless succession.

Cotton Textiles SIGNIFICANCE OF COTTON

The development of England's huge cotton mills in the late eighteenth and early nineteenth centuries was the first great achievement and the major symbol of England's Industrial Revolution. Eventually this industry seemed to dwarf all others. By 1831 it accounted for 22 percent of the nation's entire industrial production. It is worth noting that the production of more goods at cheaper prices also led to the more widespread use of those goods and thus many changes in living styles. Before the Industrial Revolution, for example, only the more wealthy could afford soft, comfortable cotton underwear. The masses often had nothing to wear under their rough outer clothing. But as cotton textiles became cheaper and more plentiful, larger numbers could afford them, and lifestyles related to clothing changed dramatically.

TECHNOLOGICAL INNOVATION

The Flying Shuttle and the Spinning Jenny. The revolution in the textile industry began in 1733 when John Kay, a British engineer and inventor, developed and patented the flying shuttle, which greatly sped up the weaving process. Previously, weavers strung a series of yarns (the warp) upright on a loom and passed the woof (filler) through, by hand, with a shuttle. Kay's invention sent the shuttle flying through the warp with the jerk of a cord, not only speeding up the process but also making it possible for one person to handle more cotton yarn at one time. It was about thirty years before the flying shuttle was used extensively. By then an uneducated but resourceful spinner and weaver in Lancashire, James Hargreaves, was working on a better and faster way to spin cotton thread. The prototype of his spinning jenny, built in 1764, had eight spindles. On later models one person could spin 8, then 16, and finally 120 threads at once. As with many technological breakthroughs, the spinning jenny was not welcomed enthusiastically by some people. It seemed to threaten the livelihood of hand spinners, some of whom destroyed Hargreaves's first machines because they feared the new technology would throw them out of work.

The Water Frame and the Spinning Mule. At about the same time another inventor, Richard Arkwright, was working on a different way to spin cotton thread faster. In 1769 he invented the water frame, so-called because it was water powered, which not only sped up the process, using rollers rather than spindles, but also produced tighter, stronger threads of any desired thickness that would make an even better warp. Then in 1779 Samuel Crompton, an English farmer and spinner, invented the spinning mule—so named because it was a hybrid that combined the best features of the spinning jenny and the water frame. Crompton had spent five years putting all his earnings into his project, but, ironically, he so disliked the fame it brought him that he voluntarily resigned all his rights to the machine.

Edmund Cartwright. The problem with all these inventions was that they were soon producing cotton thread in quantities far greater than the weavers could handle. It remained for Edmund Cartwright to restore the balance with the invention of the steam-powered loom, patented in 1787. Clearly it had the potential of revolutionizing the weaving industry but, like Hargreaves's spinning jenny, handweavers saw it as a threat to their livelihood. When the first power loom was installed in a Manchester mill, in fact, local handweavers burned the building and Cartwright was forced into bankruptcy. By the 1820s, however, the power loom had, for the most part, replaced handweavers in England's cotton textile industry.

The Problem of Power and the Impact of the Steam Engine

NEED FOR A NEW SOURCE OF POWER

The Industrial Revolution could not have happened, however, without a new, reliable source of power to drive the wheels of the new machinery, pump water from mines, and speed up transportation. Energy, in fact, was becoming a major problem in England in many ways. Wood, for example, was used for heating as well as for making charcoal to be used in producing iron, but England's great forests had long been used up. As a result, by the mid-eighteenth century the iron industry was suffering. England had great coal reserves, and coal had become the alternative to wood for heating homes and producing various products that required heat. But until the perfection of the steam engine coal could not be used to power machines. In addition, the coal-mining industry itself faced problems that only steam power could solve. As mines went deeper they constantly filled with water. Mechanical pumps, usually operated by horses or other animals walking around in circles, were the only answer. But these were expensive and inefficient to operate. In the long run, it was the steam engine that transformed not only the textile industry but other industries as well. It was also the steam engine more than any other invention that led to England's domination of the globe in the nineteenth century.

THE STEAM ENGINE

The first simple steam engines were invented by Thomas Savery and Thomas Newcomen in 1698 and 1705, respectively. Three decades later many English and Scottish mines had them in operation. About 1763 a brilliant young Scotsman, James Watt, discovered ways to improve the

Newcomen engine and make it more efficient. By 1800 some 500 of Watt's engines were in service throughout Great Britain, pumping water from mines and providing power to textile mills, iron furnaces, flour mills, and other industries.

MORE INNOVATION AND PRODUCTION

By this time invention upon invention was affecting every phase of British industry. The cotton mills and the steam engines required more iron, steel, and coal, which led to improved techniques in mining and metallurgy. As indicated earlier, the Darbys pioneered the method of substituting coke (made from coal) for charcoal in the smelting process. Henry Cort perfected the process further in the 1780s with his "puddling" method of removing impurities. He also developed steam-powered rolling mills that could produce finished iron in almost any form. In 1800 Great Britain was producing more coal and iron than the rest of the world combined: 12 million tons of coal and 130,000 tons of iron. Sixty-one years later these production figures were up to 57 million tons and 3.8 million tons, respectively. Cheap, plentiful, and finding all kinds of new uses, iron was one of the essential elements of the new industrial economy.

TRANSPORTATION NEEDS

Such growth in the textile, mining, and iron industries necessarily created a need for more and better transportation facilities, especially for shipping coal and iron. The canal boom, which provided England with 2,500 miles of canals by 1830, was one result, as was a period of intensive road building. In the last half of the eighteenth century John Metcalf, Thomas Telford, and John McAdam developed methods for constructing hard-surfaced roads that would bear traffic year-round, helping to speed up coach travel from four to eight or ten miles per hour. The most important contribution to the transportation revolution, however, came from the steam engine. This revolutionary source of power led to the development of the railroad and was harnessed for water transportation.

THE RAILROAD

Applying Steam Power. At first both American and British engineers attempted to apply steam power to cars capable of carrying passengers on the new hard-surfaced roads, but these proved impractical for many reasons, including the damage done to the roads. At the same time, the coal industry was moving its wagons on both planks and rails. By 1816 an iron rail capable of supporting a heavy locomotive had been developed. This immediately stimulated experiments with steam engines that could run on rails. In 1825 such an engine was successfully demonstrated by George Stephenson. Five years later the world's first major railroad, the Liverpool and Manchester

Railway, was completed; Stephenson's steam engine raced along the tracks at an amazing sixteen miles per hour. Significantly, Lancashire was the heart of industrial England; its largest city, Manchester, was the center of the textile industry, and Liverpool was the major port through which Britain was connected with the rest of the world.

Impact of the Railroad. The Liverpool and Manchester Railway was an immediate economic success and stimulated more private companies to build more lines. Railroads could move passengers and freight both faster and cheaper than canals or highways. Within twenty years some 6,600 miles of rail lines connected nearly all of England. By that time, too, the trains were traveling at an awesome fifty miles per hour. As in the case of so many other inventions, the railroad had a chain-reaction effect on other industries as well as on the society at large. By reducing the cost of shipping freight overland, it created larger markets which, in turn, encouraged the building of larger factories with even more powerful, more sophisticated machinery. Higher production at cheaper cost lowered prices, which stimulated the purchase of more goods by consumers but also helped drive traditional cottage workers, many urban artisans, and small manufacturers out of business. Employment patterns changed, both in England and elsewhere, as some of those thrown out of work, especially unskilled laborers, found themselves building railroads. Later they drifted into the cities and towns where they found work in factories, or in other urban occupations, becoming permanent parts of the rapidly growing urban population.

The Crystal Palace: Symbol of an Era

In 1851 the people of England were treated to a magnificent celebration of their nation's industrial triumphs. A grand exposition was held in the Crystal Palace, a huge building constructed of iron and glass that symbolized everything that had happened since the Industrial Revolution began. The technological advances proudly displayed by some 17,000 exhibitors demonstrated to Britons that their country was, indeed, the industrial leader of the world. By 1860 England was producing 20 percent of all the world's industrial goods, including half of its iron, half of its cotton, and two-thirds of its coal.

THE SPREAD OF INDUSTRIALISM

To the Continent and Elsewhere

WHY INDUSTRIALIZATION WAS SLOW ON THE CONTINENT

The spread of the Industrial Revolution to the Continent was slow and uneven. One factor in the delay was the Napoleonic wars, which inhibited contact with Britain and hence with its advancing technology until after

1815. Other reasons included political fragmentation on the Continent, economic rivalries, and a multiplicity of tariffs that restricted the flow of goods. In addition, entrepreneurship was less imaginative and versatile, partly because of the tradition of catering to the wealthy. Furthermore, continental banking and credit institutions were not as well developed as those of Britain. By mid-century, nevertheless, politicians and manufacturers on the Continent could readily see that British goods might well overwhelm them in the marketplace. They were ready to pay increasing attention to developing a greater industrial base.

BRITISH CONTRIBUTION

Great Britain, meanwhile, was not anxious to export its technology and the industrial advantage that technology brought. Before 1825, in fact, the law forbade skilled artisans and mechanics even to leave. It was also illegal until 1843 to export various kinds of manufacturing machinery. Such efforts to keep industrial secrets were unsuccessful, however. Despite the ban on leaving, it was often British workers themselves who shared industrial information. By 1825 no less than 2,000 skilled British workers were helping to advance industrialization throughout the Continent. They were not alone, however, for many continental entrepreneurs soon caught on and began to pour money and resources into industrial development.

BELGIUM

Belgium, which became independent from the Netherlands in 1831, became the first industrialized country on the Continent. Its advantages included rich deposits of iron and coal, efficient agriculture, and a strong tradition of textile manufacturing. It also had the aid of skilled British artisans. In 1799 William Cockerill began building cotton-spinning equipment in Belgium. Beginning in 1817 his son John built machinery, steam engines, and, eventually, railway locomotives. He also opened new coal mines and ironworks. Other skilled workmen came to work for the Cockerills; by 1830 the family operated one of the largest integrated manufacturing enterprises in Europe. It was the Cockerills, supported by Belgian banks, who set Belgium on the road toward industrialization, but other entrepreneurs followed. Soon the railroad industry expanded dramatically, for Belgium's strategic location made it a natural center for transportation in western Europe. In addition, the production of coal and iron, much of which was shipped to France and Germany, increased dramatically. By 1871 the majority of Belgium's people lived in cities and its economy was largely dependent on trade and industry.

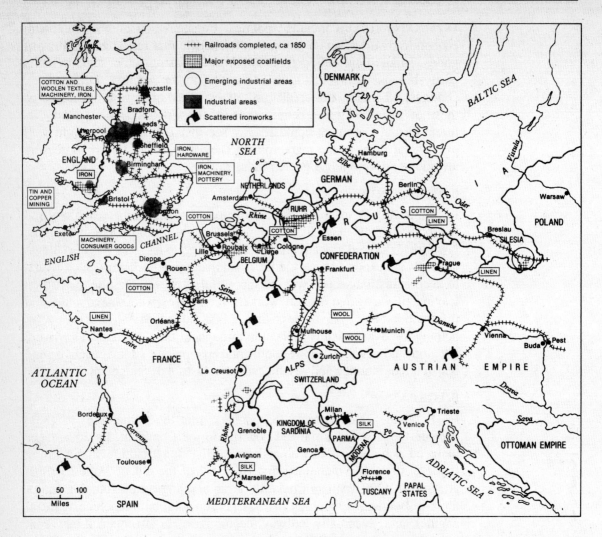

Fig. 8.1   European Industrialization, c. 1850

OTHER PARTS OF THE CONTINENT

Industrialization proceeded more slowly in the rest of the Continent, but by mid-century France, Germany, Austria-Hungary, Italy, and other areas at least were on the way. The most successful was Germany, where Fritz Harkort, a former Prussian army officer who had served in England, led the way. Fascinated by all he saw in England, Harkort was convinced that Germany must match its achievements as soon as possible. He set up a factory in an abandoned castle to build steam engines. He had numerous obstacles to overcome, not the least of which was lack of skilled labor. Harkort finally had to turn to expensive British mechanics. In addition, inadequate transportation facilities made marketing extremely difficult.

Eventually Harkort became famous for his steam engines, but in 1832, after sixteen years of operation, he was still sustaining financial losses and lost his company.

FURTHER SPREAD

In the last part of the century other European nations entered the industrial age. After Great Britain and France reduced their tariff barriers on timber in the 1860s, the Swedish timber industry boomed, paving the way for modernizing timber plants, building railroads, and developing other industries. Denmark and the Netherlands were farther behind because they lacked the mineral resources enjoyed by the early industrialized nations, but by the end of the century they had developed an industrial economy based on modern techniques for producing glass, porcelain, and alcoholic beverages. In other parts of Europe progress was still slower.

Industrialization also spread elsewhere, to the United States, the British Dominions and, finally, to Japan, though the results were uneven and varied. In 1860 the four great industrial nations, in order, were Great Britain, France, the United States, and Germany. The newer industrial nations, however, had the advantage of newer and more efficient factories; by 1900 the United States was the leading nation, followed in order by Germany, Great Britain, and France. In terms of the amount of industrial production *per capita*, Great Britain still led, followed by the United States, Germany, and Belgium. In terms of *total* industrial production, however, Great Britain had lost its primacy.

Other Economic Aspects of the Industrial Age

GOVERNMENT AND INDUSTRY

There were other economic consequences of industrialism. One was a new relationship between government and industry. On the Continent, especially, government support for industry became important. After 1815, for example, the French imposed tariff duties against English imports in an effort to protect their own manufacturers (who had hardly begun to achieve the technological capabilities of Britain). The government also began to build new roads and canals, and to help finance railroads, which could only promote the progress of industrialization. In Germany, Friedrich List, a prominent journalist and outspoken nationalist, urged the use of the tariff to promote industry. In 1834 his campaign finally led to the formation of a customs union, the *Zollverein*, which eliminated trade barriers (and hence promoted industry) among the various German states.

NEW FINANCIAL STRUCTURE

Banks also became increasingly important, more so in France and Germany than in Britain. Before about 1850 banks were traditionally private institutions, but about this time a new type of banking institution appeared—

the joint-stock bank. Such a bank had many stockholders and large financial resources. It thus had much more to lend to industrial corporations.

Besides such banks, there was also a growing number of business or industrial organizations with many stockholders. Investors were attracted because it gave them a chance to get in on the possibility of major profits at minimal risk. All they could lose was the value of their stock. Such corporations caught on especially in Great Britain, Germany, and Belgium, contributing significantly to continuing industrialization in those countries.

INDUSTRIALIZATION AND IMPERIALISM

Still another phenomenon connected with the Industrial Revolution was the new imperialism of the nineteenth century. This will be discussed in detail in chapter 13, but it is important to observe here that, as a result of industrialization, European countries competed even more intensely for markets. This was a prime factor in the imperialistic thrust. It led, in fact, to the perception of the need for "sheltered markets," or colonies, and the direct take-over of many areas. Surplus capital produced by the Industrial Revolution also contributed to the perceived need for colonies as outlets for new investment. Further, it increased the demand for raw materials to feed the never-ending hunger of the new machines, and many such products (i.e., rubber, petroleum, and various metals) came from underdeveloped parts of the globe. Such forces worked hand-in-hand with other incentives toward imperialism, and with the population pressures discussed above created a world of Western dominance by the end of the nineteenth century.

A WESTERN-DOMINATED WORLD ECONOMY

All this and more had a profound economic impact on both the volume and character of world trade and contributed to a more highly interrelated world economic system. By the 1880s, for example, Germany and the United States were producing all the coal, metals, and machinery they could use and were competing with Great Britain for the export market. In addition, France, the United States, and other countries had their own major textile industries. Because these countries erected tariff barriers against British textiles, British exports tended to be limited to the new markets developing in India and China. But the fact that those markets were developing at least was a step toward more international economic interdependence.

On the negative side was the fact that British imperialism also seriously undermined the local, nonindustrialized textile industry in such places. This was especially true in India, a British colony, for British mercantilistic policy specifically prohibited it from becoming industrialized and made it impossible for handweavers and small-scale manufacturers to compete with inexpensive British imports. Imperialism thus contributed to greater economic interdependence (i.e., the imperialistic nations depended on underdeveloped nations for much of their export market), even as it destroyed political and economic autonomy in much of the world.

At the same time, after 1850 Europeans began investing in other parts of the world by helping them develop local industries, such as railroads in Latin America, gold mines in South Africa, or rubber plantations in Malaya. They also invested in telegraph systems, mining, and light manufacturing. This had an important effect on developing economic interrelationships. As European investors made money, they could purchase more goods and services at home even as the overseas countries could develop export markets by selling to the Europeans, who had more money with which to buy their goods. Non-Europeans, in turn, had more money with which to buy products from Europe. The interrelated economic growth went on and on, though the greatest profits accrued to the more advanced Western powers. Huge earnings came not just through their sale of goods but also through their banking services and rapidly expanding shipping facilities. By the turn of the century the income per capita and general standard of living had risen significantly in Europe, Canada, the United States, and Japan. In the so-called Third World (Latin America, Africa, Asia outside Japan, and Oceania) these measures of prosperity remained about the same as they had been a century and a half before.

A TRANSPORTATION REVOLUTION

Expansion of the Railroad. Another revolution that both drew from and contributed to the Industrial Revolution came in transportation. In Great Britain, for example, by 1850 over 6,000 miles of railroad facilitated the transportation of goods within the nation and also carried some 73 million passengers annually. Twenty years later the railroad mileage had more than doubled, to 14,400 miles. Over the same period it grew from about 2,000 to nearly 11,000 miles in France, where Paris was the hub of a network that included good connections with Italy, Germany, and the Netherlands. In Germany railroad mileage grew from 3,600 to 12,000. In the United States it skyrocketed even more dramatically: from less than 35,000 miles in 1865 to 166,700 miles in 1900. The completion of the transcontinental railway in 1869 stimulated both internal and international trade, encouraged a stepped-up interior migration to the West, and enhanced economic opportunities for foreign immigrants.

The importance of the railroad lay in the fact that no other industry, not even cotton manufacturing in England, created as many new employment opportunities. It also opened new sources of raw materials, promoted new markets, and fostered the growth of new towns. Especially in Europe and North America in the nineteenth century, and later in other parts of the world, the railroad had a more visible effect on the economy and on the lives of the people than any other development of the age. Refrigerated railway cars, for example, improved living standards. The railroad also enhanced migration and promoted nationalism.

The Steamship. Complementing the railroad, and functioning in tandem with it in stimulating world trade, was the steamship, which began to replace sailing ships around 1860. Safer, for they were built of steel rather than wood or lumber, and able to carry more passengers and goods, steamships reduced the cost of shipping and ocean travel. Furthermore, after 1880 refrigerator ships made it possible for Argentine, American, Australian, and New Zealand beef to be shipped worldwide. In addition, raw products from Asia, Africa, and Latin America became increasingly affordable in the developed countries. A truly interconnected worldwide economy was developing, which seemed to be symbolized in 1869 by the completion of the 100-mile-long Suez Canal. Located at the crossroads of Asia, Europe, and Africa, the canal connected the Mediterranean with the Indian Ocean, via the Gulf of Suez and the Red Sea. It cut in half the time it took to transport goods between Europe and Asia. The Panama Canal, completed in 1914, had a similar effect on trade that previously had to go across or around the Americas.

THE CONTINUING SCIENTIFIC REVOLUTION: ITS UNITY WITH TECHNOLOGY AND INDUSTRIALISM

Industry, Science, and Technology: A Symbiotic Relationship

A continuing scientific revolution contributed to the Industrial Revolution. Like the other great transformations of this period, scientific developments were rooted far back in previous centuries but exploded in the late eighteenth and nineteenth centuries. Even though pure science was theoretical, speculative, and experimental in nature, in the new industrial age it also had some very practical and revolutionary consequences.

PHYSICS

Electricity. Discoveries in electromagnetism, for example, led to the telegraph. By 1866 a trans-Atlantic cable made possible instant communication between Europe and America. Other advances in electromagnetism, and particularly the work of Michael Faraday in the 1830s and 1840s, led to the development of huge machines called dynamos that used both steam engines and electromagnets. By 1870 they were providing the power for electric arc lights in many public places. By the end of the century, after the invention of the incandescent light bulb by Thomas Edison, electric lighting was rapidly replacing gas lighting in the cities of both America and Europe. The increasing availability of electricity also led to the development of electric motors and electric trams and railways. The first such railways began to operate in American cities in the 1880s, and in London the famous London Tube opened in 1890. Scientists and engineers harnessed water power to drive the huge dynamos. One of the most ambitious of such projects was at Niagara Falls. Electricity was first generated from there and transmitted to New York City in 1896.

Atomic Physics and Relativity. By the end of the nineteenth century the foundation had been laid for an even greater revolution in physics in the twentieth century. Physicists had discovered that atoms were not the solid, tiny spheres they had imagined but rather were themselves composed of even smaller, fast-moving particles. The experiments with radiation conducted by Nobel Prize–winning physicist Marie Curie and her husband, Pierre, demonstrated that radium does not have a constant atomic weight because it is always emitting subatomic particles. In 1900 a German physicist, Max Planck, originated modern quantum theory when he discovered that subatomic energy is emitted in uneven spurts, which he called "quanta." Suddenly the old distinction between matter and energy was blurred and, in effect, Newtonian physics was under attack. The universe was not quite as predictable as Newton had presumed. Then in 1905 Albert Einstein went even further when he postulated in his theory of special relativity that even time and space were not absolute. He also demonstrated that there was a relationship between mass and energy and that one could be transformed into the other. In his famous formula, $E=mc^2$, E represents energy, m represents mass, and c stands for the velocity of light. The validity of his formula was demonstrated over the years. Eventually this and his General Theory of Relativity were major factors in completely changing the scientific view of the nature of the universe from smallest subatomic particle to the endlessness of space.

The work of Einstein and other physicists had profound practical consequences for the modern world. The fact that the atom could actually be split was demonstrated by Ernst Rutherford in 1919, and in 1945 the unbelievably powerful atomic bomb was operative. On a more positive note, the postwar world also had hopes for the development of more peaceful and far less contaminating uses of atomic energy.

CHEMISTRY

Priestly and Lavoisier. Another revolution came in the field of chemistry, beginning with two men who laid the foundation for modern chemistry in the late eighteenth century. Joseph Priestly was fascinated with the discovery that ordinary air really consisted of many gases, or "airs." He set about to try to discover what they were and to separate them. His most famous discovery was what he called "dephlogisticated air," later named oxygen by Antoine Lavoisier. This discovery became the basis of a whole new system of chemistry. Carrying out numerous complex experiments with combustion, Lavoisier eventually laid down the principle of conservation of matter, which was as important to the future of chemistry as Newton's laws of gravity were to physics. In any chemical action, Lavoisier concluded, matter may alter its state, but its amount does not change. These and other experiments revolutionized chemistry so much that Lavoisier and some of his associates finally published a new table of chemical nomenclature that has remained largely intact ever since. Unfortunately, this famous French scientist, usually recognized as the father of modern chemistry, lived too close to another revolution. In 1794 his involvement in politics led to his execution by guillotine during the Reign of Terror.

Mendeleev. More discoveries followed. In 1808 John Dalton, a native of Manchester, published an early basis for modern atomic theory. About the same time the experiments of Humphrey Davey, who was working at the Royal Institution in London, extended Lavoisier's table of elements and also advanced the science of electrolysis. Throughout the early part of the century chemists worked hard at trying to measure atomic weights. In 1860 those who attended the first International Chemical Congress at Karlsruhe, Germany, made considerable progress toward agreement on this and on the chemical properties of the elements. One of those in attendance was a young Russian chemist, Dimitri Mendeleev, who later devised the idea of listing the elements in a table of increasing atomic weight that permanently systematized chemistry. The reason why his system worked in explaining the properties of the elements was not understood until the twentieth century, but Mendeleev was acclaimed everywhere except in Tsarist Russia, where his liberal political views got him into trouble. Today his periodic table still hangs on the walls of chemistry classrooms around the world.

Practical Applications. Many developments in chemistry contributed directly to the industrial and social revolutions taking place, and vice versa. Mining contributed to progress in chemistry because of the need to discover better ways to separate and refine ores; chemists were involved in the development of the coal gas and coal tar industries. A practical result of this combination of scientific discovery and technological innovation was that by 1816, only two years after the first coal gas light was installed in London, there were twenty-six miles of gas mains in the city. By 1823 gas was lighting the factories, streets, and homes of fifty-two English towns. With the development of coal tar, a liquid obtained after a distilling process, chemists had a veritable field day producing new dyes, drugs (aspirin, for example), perfumes, disinfectants, photographic chemicals, explosives, and many other practical consumer-oriented goods. The textile industry benefited from the development of synthetic dyes. Chemical fertilizers helped promote the continuing transformation in agriculture. Chemists devised powerful new explosives. One of these was Alfred Nobel of Sweden, who made a fortune from manufacturing dynamite, then left much of it to finance the international prizes that now bear his name. Engineers, moreover, profited greatly from the practical application of new chemical processes, one of which led Henry Bessemer in 1857 to develop a procedure for transforming iron ore into steel. The process was refined and perfected by others, and by the end of the century steel, which was lighter, harder, more malleable, cheaper, and longer lasting, was replacing iron in heavy construction and transportation.

BACTERIOLOGY AND MEDICINE

Progress in medicine and public health was also fostered in this new scientific age. About mid-century Louis Pasteur developed his famous germ theory of disease, which led to widespread purification by heat—pasteurization—of common beverages. It also led to the development and widespread use of vaccines to combat disease. Pioneers in this effort, beginning about 1865, were Robert Koch and other German researchers. An English surgeon, Joseph Lister, grasped some of the wider implications of Pasteur's work and developed a chemical disinfectant to combat the problem of infected wounds. His "antiseptic principle" seemed to work miracles, and it spread rapidly. German surgeons began the practice of sterilizing not just the patients' wounds but also their own clothing, hands, and instruments. The result of all this was a dramatic decline in death rates all over Europe in the last quarter of the century, especially in the cities.

Philosophical Implications of the Scientific Revolution

It was not just in relationship to commerce, industry, and social welfare, however, that the great scientific developments of the nineteenth century had an impact. By this time the perspectives of the Enlightenment had so affected both philosophy and science that the climate was more favorable than ever for asking totally new kinds of questions and for challenging old assumptions. The work of Kepler, Galileo, and others had completely shattered old concepts of astronomy and physics, and Newton's brilliant exposition of the laws of gravity demonstrated that the entire universe operated on the basis of certain natural laws. Such laws, many people believed, governed not only the relationships between physical bodies, but everything, including human development, social institutions, and political institutions. Moreover, these laws could be discovered. It was this exhilarating possibility that led not only to the great scientific discoveries of the nineteenth century but also to new economic and political philosophies, including those of Karl Marx.

GEOLOGY

One aspect of the continuing scientific revolution that had far-reaching philosophical, and even religious, implications was the work of the late eighteenth and early nineteenth centuries that laid the foundation for modern geology. The observation and classification of rocks by Abraham Werner, a professor of mineralogy in a German mining school in Freiburg, and James Hutton of Edinburgh, Scotland, presupposed a time scale that dwarfed the estimated age of 6,000 years that Biblical literalists sometimes claimed for the earth. Scientists observed that rocks and minerals were still being formed by extremely slow chemical and physical processes, and Hutton theorized that these processes had always been the same, which meant that the formation of the earth as mankind knew it had taken an incredibly long time. Such work was enhanced by an increasing fascination with observing and classifying fossils in the various strata of the earth.

This led to the development of a variety of theories relating to extinct species. In 1833 Charles Lyell published what became perhaps the most influential book in the history of geology: his three-volume *Principles of Geology*, which presented a rich abundance of evidence in support of Hutton's theory. He also classified rocks into different eras and used fossils to help identify the ages of various strata. All this clearly implied the appearance and disappearance of certain species, plus the appearance of new species. Significantly, Lyell's work was published just two years after Charles Darwin set out on his famous voyage aboard the *Beagle*. Eventually the principles of geology articulated by Lyell and others would play a major role in the development of Charles Darwin's theories of evolution.

DARWIN AND EVOLUTION

Darwin. The theory of biological evolution did not originate with Darwin, but it was Darwin who discovered the laws governing the evolution of species. He became the most influential of all nineteenth-century evolutionists. Beginning in 1831 he was the official naturalist on a five-year cruise to Latin America and the South Pacific, during which time he collected numerous specimens of many animal species. As he went from island to island he also observed significant variations between species of both flora and fauna. The matter haunted him, he said, for he could only conclude that somehow these species had been gradually modified. Later, influenced by all this as well as by his study of fossils and the work of Lyell, he concluded that life did not begin as a special creation, but rather all life evolved from a common ancestral origin. This meant that life forms are capable of change, that variations develop by a process of natural selection, and that in the struggle for survival it is the fittest of each species that survives. The details of Darwin's theory have been modified many times.

Scientists still disagree on numerous issues, but virtually all of them accept his general principles of evolution.

Darwinism and Its Consequences. The presentation of Darwin's theories had profound consequences for himself as well as for the religious and social perspectives of the world. His famous work, *On the Origin of Species*, was published in 1859, and it had immediate religious repercussions. Darwin himself did not believe that his theories undermined belief in God—in fact, he felt that his theory actually presented a grander view of life. He wrote in the last paragraph of his book:

> Thus, from the war of nature, the most exalted object which we are capable of conceiving, namely, the production of the higher animals, directly follows. There is grandeur in this view of life, with its several powers, having been originally breathed by the Creator into a few forms or into one, and that, whilst this planet has gone cycling on according to the fixed law of *gravity*, from so simple a beginning endless forms most beautiful and most wonderful have been, and are being, evolved.

For those who accepted his theories, nevertheless, Darwin had overthrown traditional arguments for the existence of God and traditional beliefs concerning the creation of man. He was almost immediately branded as an atheist and was received with open hostility by religious organizations as well as civic groups and local governments. In the United States, laws were passed against teaching evolution in the public schools, and churches were split over Darwinism and other modernizing forces. In some church-related colleges and universities teachers were fired for promoting such new and "dangerous" views. On the other hand, many people in America and Europe hailed Darwin as the "Newton of biology," and in the minds of many he reinforced the secular teachings of people such as Karl Marx.

In addition, a new school of social philosophy, dubbed "Social Darwinism" and led by the English philosopher Herbert Spencer, applied his principles of biological evolution to human institutions. Through the process of "survival of the fittest," they taught, the human race had progressed to ever greater heights, and certain races (the Anglo-Saxon race in particular) had surpassed them all. Both Darwin and Spencer were popular with the upper middle class, who saw themselves as the result of such evolution. Social Darwinism seemed to be a ready-made justification for both British and American imperialism in the nineteenth century. Spencer was also read widely in Japan as that state began its modern industrial development and later became an imperial power.

SOCIAL IMPACT OF THE INDUSTRIAL REVOLUTION

Science, technology, industrialization, urbanization, changes in financial institutions, and population growth were inextricably interrelated in the increasingly complex world of the nineteenth century (as they continue to be today) and had much to do with the social changes taking place at the same time. We will present here only a few aspects of those changes, but enough to demonstrate more fully the far-reaching social consequences of the age of industrialism.

Population and Migration

It cannot be said that the Industrial Revolution caused the dramatic population boom that was occurring at the same time, or vice versa, but certainly they were interrelated.

WORLD POPULATION

Between 1800 and 1900, world population increased by 71 percent, from an estimated 919 million to 1.571 billion. European population alone (including Asiatic Russia) jumped from 193 to 432 million or 120 percent. The population of North America jumped an astounding 1250 percent, from 6 to 81 million. Latin America saw a 174 percent growth (23 to 63 million), while Asia grew by 44 percent (595 to 857million).

GROWTH FACTORS

More significant than growth itself, however, were the reasons for it. In Europe, the most significant factor was not increasing birth rates—these, in fact went down—but the decreasing death rate. This, in turn, was a direct result of improvements in sanitation and other public health measures. Outside Europe, much of the growth was directly attributable to European influences. In Asia and Africa, for instance, European methods of hygiene and sanitation helped to decrease the death rate. In the Americas and Oceania, however, the major increase in population came directly from European migration. It has been estimated that in 1900 approximately 90 percent of the population of North America and Oceania was of European origin, as was 33 percent of the population of Central and South America.

INDUSTRIALIZATION AND MIGRATION

Industrialization was one of the prime reasons for the mass migrations of Europeans in the nineteenth century. At first rapid population growth created rising pressure on agricultural resources, especially in England. Some areas also experienced devastating natural disasters, such as the Irish potato famine in 1840, which increased the pressure for migration. In the 1820s about 145,000 people emigrated from Europe. Migration reached a peak of 9 million between 1900 and 1910.

In 1820 some 2,000 people left Great Britain, the center of the Industrial Revolution. By 1830 the number had jumped to over 50,000, and in the late 1840s and early 1850s over 250,000 subjects left Great Britain annually. Such emigration did not take away a large portion of the population, but some people considered it a kind of "safety valve" that at least helped siphon off the worst effects of the population boom and economic dislocation by holding out hope for greater opportunity on another economic frontier. It was, in fact, encouraged, and it was not uncommon for emigrants to leave singing such verses as:

> Brave men are we, and be it understood
> We left our country for our country's good,
> And none can doubt our emigration
> Was of great value to the British nation.

THE PESSIMISM OF MALTHUS

Rapid population growth resulted in considerable debate in Europe as to where it all might end. The most pessimistic assessment came as early as 1798 from economist Thomas Malthus. That year he published, anonymously, his provocative *Essay on the Principles of Population, as It Affects the Future Improvement of Society.* "The power of population is infinitely greater than the power of the earth to produce subsistence for man," he argued, which meant that unless population growth was checked by war, famine, or disease the food supply could not increase rapidly enough to compensate. Five years later he published a revised edition in which he also argued for "moral restraint" (i.e., late marriage and abstinence) as a means of limiting population growth.

Malthus was bitterly attacked by Enlightenment philosophers. Western society seemed to offer evidence to support both advocates and opponents of Malthusian theories. The population continued to grow but the food supply grew faster; by the end of the century living standards were generally higher. In the early nineteenth century, however, overcrowded conditions in the cities, together with urban poverty that became all too apparent, especially in Britain, may have convinced some observers that Malthus was right.

Social and Economic Conditions

As we have seen, along with industrialization came urbanization, and with urbanization came crowded living conditions, sanitation problems, and working conditions never before experienced by the migrants from the countryside. During the first half of the nineteenth century living and working conditions were especially harsh in England. They improved considerably during the last half of the century, but the conditions that characterized early industrialized society deserve mention.

WORKING CONDITIONS

Working conditions varied, but in the first half of the nineteenth century England's industrial centers received an especially bad reputation for what went on in their mills, mines, and factories. Former cottage workers were unused to the rigid schedule and long working hours demanded in the factories, which may have led them to exaggerate their complaints. It is true, nevertheless, that discipline was harsh, hours were long, and the factories were both unsafe and unsanitary. Women, moreover, received only half the wages of men, and children were paid only a quarter as much. Worst of all, workers had no security at all when it came to the possibility of compensation for injury, illness, unemployment, or old age.

CHILD LABOR

In the last part of the eighteenth century the factories were filled with orphaned and pauper children. They were usually overworked and were frequently mistreated. After such exploitation was outlawed in 1802, children still appeared in the mines and factories, but often as part of entire families who hired themselves out as a group. The whole family needed to work in order to survive, as well as to stay together. In a coal mine, for instance, a father might be found picking and shoveling the ore, the mother would be crawling on hands and knees through a tunnel hauling a carload of ore behind her, and the children would be working above sorting coal and tending the ventilation equipment. Children also found work, sometimes dangerous, in the cotton factories where their parents were employed.

EFFORTS AT REFORM

The report of an 1832 parliamentary investigation headed by reformer Michael Sadler graphically portrayed the long hours, miserable working conditions, and brutality of supervisors that characterized factory life. Especially damaging was the revelation of the numbers and ill-treatment of young children in the factories. Some improvement came after 1833 when Parliament prohibited the employment of children below the age of nine. It also limited the working day for those between nine and thirteen to eight hours and to twelve hours for anyone between fourteen and eighteen. Workers also attempted to form trade unions, though without much success. Many also actively participated in political movements aimed at further limiting working hours and alleviating some of the other distresses in the factories.

LIVING CONDITIONS

Living conditions in some of England's industrial towns were especially deplorable in the first part of the nineteenth century. In Manchester, for example, houses for factory workers were often built back-to-back, with only a narrow alley separating the two rows. They were poorly lighted, poorly ventilated, and had no running water or sanitation facilities. There were few outhouses and no sewers. The stench coming from garbage piled high in the alleys and narrow streets and from raw sewage running down the streets and finally into the River Ribble did not make the heart of industrial England a particularly pleasant place for a family of nine who might be living in a cellar or a two-room apartment. And neither was it very healthy, for residents in such areas were particularly vulnerable to epidemics of contagious disease.

PUBLIC HEALTH MEASURES

Such things were the unfortunate consequences of rapid economic change and development, but in their worst forms they did not last through the entire century. The great champion of reform in England was Edwin Chadwick, whose tireless activities finally convinced lawmakers that a filthy environment really was a cause of disease and that inexpensive iron pipes and tile drains—products of the industrial age—could be used to provide running water as well as sewage systems for entire towns. Largely due to Chadwick's work, the first public health law was passed in 1848. The idea quickly spread to other parts of Europe, as well as to the United States; by the 1870s at least those aspects of city dwelling were improving significantly. These measures, along with the great achievements in bacteriology and medicine mentioned above, dramatically reduced mortality rates of all ages. In the long run, it appears, despite the tragic conditions in some early nineteenth century cities, the age of industrialism profited the human race more than it hurt by extending both the length and quality of life.

INDUSTRIALISM AND SLAVERY

People of the time may not have thought much about it, but there was an interesting irony in the relationship between the development of the early British industrial system and what has happening in America. The textile factories were fed largely with cotton from the American South, where slavery was considered an economic necessity. Although slavery was becoming less economically viable toward the end of the eighteenth century, the expansion of the textile industry revived it. This led to increasing criticism of the institution and the rise of intense anti-slavery activism, which in turn brought about a counter-reaction in the South and the development of a class-oriented social philosophy that went so far as to justify slavery as a positive good. Ironically, the cheap cotton produced by

American slaves contributed, in turn, to the progress of what some people thought of as industrial slavery on the part of so many workers in England— the country that had just eliminated slavery and was calling on the rest of the world, particularly the United States, to do likewise.

By the end of the nineteenth century the effects of the Industrial Revolution that began in England toward the end of the eighteenth century were felt worldwide. Moreover, it is impossible to separate a discussion of this revolution from every other development in the nineteenth century in science, technology, medicine, public health, economic development, national and international politics, social philosophy, migration, imperialism, and religion. All were affected, and to some degree there was a kind of symbiotic relationship between them. Perhaps the long-range effect of what could be variously dubbed the industrial age, the machine age, or the age of the scientific revolution was best expressed by Henry Adams, an American, as he pondered what he had seen in the Great Exposition of 1900. He stood perplexed before the giant dynamo on display that exuded a potential for physical power that, to him, compared with the spiritual power of the Virgin at the Cathedral of Chartres. He did not understand the new power—he only knew that somehow it was going to make his America different. Awestruck in the face of what it could mean, he wrote:

> *The planet itself seemed less impressive, in its old-fashioned, deliberate, annual or daily revolution, than this huge wheel, revolving within arm's length at some vertiginous speed, and barely murmuring—scarcely humming an audible warning to stand a hair's breadth further for respect of power—while it would not wake the baby lying close against its frame. Before the end, one began to pray to it; inherited instinct taught the natural expression of man before silent and infinite force.*

Adams still believed the Virgin to be the most powerful, but his awe of the dynamo's "silent and infinite force" dramatically symbolized the profound changes that the machine and all its related developments were making in the nature of human society.

Selected Readings

Bowler, Peter J. *Evolution: The History of an Idea*. Rev. ed. Berkeley: University of California Press, 1989.

Briggs, Asa. *The Age of Improvements*. London: Longmans, Greens and Co., 1959.

Hamerow, Theodore S. *The Birth of a New Europe: State and Society in the Nineteenth Century*. Chapel Hill: University of North Carolina Press, 1983.

Headrick, Daniel R. *The Tools of Empire: Technology and European Imperialism in the Nineteenth Century*. New York: Oxford University Press, 1981.

Himmelfarb, Gertrude. *The Idea of Poverty: England in the Early Industrial Age.* New York: Knopf, 1984.

Hughes, Thomas Parke, ed. *Changing Attitudes Toward American Technology.* New York: Harper & Row, 1975.

Landes, David S. *The Unbound Prometheus: Technological Change and Industrial Development in Western Europe from 1750 to the Present.* London: Cambridge University Press, 1969.

Marks, John. *Science and the Making of the Modern World.* London: Heineman Educational Books Ltd., 1983.

Taylor, Philip A. M., ed. *The Industrial Revolution in Britain: Triumph or Disaster.* Lexington, MA: Heath, 1970.

9

Conservatism, Liberalism, and Nationalism: European Politics, 1815–1900

1814–1815	Congress of Vienna
1818	First meeting of Concert of Europe
1825	Nicholas I becomes tsar of Russia
1830	Charles X of France abdicates; Louis Philippe becomes a constitutional monarch
	Greece becomes independent
1830–1831	Belgium becomes an independent state
1832	Reform Act in Britain
1837	Queen Victoria begins 64-year reign in Britain
1846	Corn laws repealed in Britain
1848	*The Communist Manifesto* published
	Abortive liberal revolts spread from France to other parts of Europe
1854–1856	The Crimean War
1855	Alexander II becomes tsar of Russia
1861	Victor Emmanuel II becomes king of a united Italy
1867	Disraeli's first British prime ministry; another term, 1874–1880

1868	Gladstone begins first British prime ministry
1870	Third Republic proclaimed in France
1870–1871	Franco-Prussian War
1871	German Empire declared; Germany united
1881	Alexander II of Russia assassinated; Alexander III becomes tsar
1894	Alfred Dreyfus convicted by French military tribunal of passing secrets to Germany, touching off lengthy *cause célèbre*

*A*long with economic change in the nineteenth century came political change, though after the Napoleonic wars the great powers of Europe did everything within their collective power to halt the spread of liberalism and to return to their traditional political systems. In September 1814 the emperor of Austria opened the Congress of Vienna by hosting an unprecedented social affair at which he wined and dined over 200 heads of various European royal families. For them this was the social event of the century, but little did they realize that they were also celebrating the beginning of their own political decline.

The Congress was dominated by Britain, Austria, Russia, and Prussia. France, however, their former enemy, regained much of its lost prestige because of the skills of its artful minister Charles Maurice de Talleyrand-Périgord, who had made a career of surviving revolutions and political storms. In one sense their work was successful, for the political arrangements they made lasted for nearly forty years and there were no general, highly destructive wars for the rest of the century. But they left numerous issues unsettled, helping to make the period from 1815 to 1870 one of almost continuous internal unrest. Political liberalism sprouted everywhere. The vexing revolutions of the 1830s and 1840s were clear symptoms of irreversible challenges to the bastions of conservatism. By the 1870s the system they so carefully created was gone.

UNDERLYING IDEOLOGIES: CONSERVATISM, LIBERALISM, AND NATIONALISM

The political turmoil of the age represented a continuing struggle between seemingly well-entrenched conservative forces and the yearnings of an assortment of liberals and radicals who wanted to change the system in a variety of ways. Liberalism and nationalism sometimes went hand-in-hand in challenging the conservative establishment. In other instances, as in the case of German unification, nationalism became part of a conservative agenda. In still other cases, as conservatives realized they could not maintain the *status quo* forever, they compromised with and even absorbed part of the liberal agenda.

Nineteenth-Century Conservatism

Conservatives, such as Austria's Prince Klemens von Metternich, were bent on maintaining the sanctity of traditional political institutions, particularly the monarchy. It was also their goal to maintain a balance of power in Europe in order to ensure a permanent peace. Traditionally they were supported by vested interests, such as landowners, manufacturers, merchants, and the church (Catholic in France, Italy, and Spain, but Protestant elsewhere). Their economic and social policies, therefore, were usually affected by those interests. They seldom allowed freedom of the press or any serious political opposition, and were often brutal in suppressing dissent. Ruled by self-interest, they nevertheless sincerely believed that the peace and stability offered by the traditional regime was in the best interest of all the people.

Nineteenth-Century Liberalism

THE LIBERAL POLITICAL AGENDA

Liberalism was a curse to conservatives, for it seemed synonymous with revolution. Hostile to practically every conservative institution, liberals did all they could to undermine the prerogatives of the monarchy, the aristocracy, and the church. They promoted constitutionalism, the idea that government must be limited to specific powers by a written constitution. They also wanted representative, or parliamentarian, government; in that sense liberalism became synonymous with republicanism. This often led to demands for a constitutional monarchy as a first step toward a more satisfactory regime. Liberals also called for separation of powers among the legislative, executive, and judicial branches of government. Above all, they proclaimed the sanctity of the individual and promoted the protection of individual rights—including property rights and personal freedoms. But they also felt that the right to vote should be restricted by property qualifications. In practical terms this limited the vote to landowners and well-to-do businessmen and professionals. Liberalism thus became identified with the middle or upper classes, convincing the lower classes that it had little to offer.

LAISSEZ-FAIRE ECONOMICS

Early nineteenth-century liberals were adamantly opposed to government intervention in social and economic affairs. They believed that unrestricted private enterprise, an idea first advanced by Adam Smith in the eighteenth century, would result in greater productivity and greater income for everyone, not just the rich. As the century progressed, however, and as industrialism changed the nature of society, laissez-faire ("hands off") economics gradually became a tool of businessmen in their quest to remain unfettered by government.

At the same time, liberal concern for the individual brought a change in liberal attitudes toward government intervention. The industrial society had created conditions that seemed to destroy the dignity of the workers and that certainly did not require their masters to be concerned for their health or physical well-being. In the name of the individual, therefore, liberals began to advocate government intervention in the economy for the purpose of promoting individual dignity and freedom. Conservatives wrongly identified such liberalism with socialism.

UTILITARIANISM: BENTHAM AND MILL

Bentham. Liberalism took a turn toward utilitarianism, the belief that the goal of society should be to achieve the greatest happiness for the greatest number. English philosopher Jeremy Bentham described this belief in terms of pleasure and pain. The "utility" of any idea, he preached, should be determined by whether it provides more pleasure than pain, resulting in the happiness of the greatest number. Ethical and moral social decisions could be made scientifically—that is, on the basis of quantification rather than pure ideology.

Mill. John Stuart Mill built on the same theme, arguing that actions are right to the degree that they promote happiness and wrong if they produce the reverse of happiness. Also, one person's happiness must count for exactly as much as another's.

The Nature of Nineteenth-Century Nationalism

DEFINITION

Nationalism is a complex ideology; it has many diverse definitions and has been manifested in many ways. As it developed in the nineteenth century, it was based on the assumption that the peoples of a particular geographic area shared a cultural identity, as seen in their common history and, in particular, a common language. Nationalists attempted to make this cultural unity a political reality by defining state boundaries that coincided with the territory where each cultural group lived. This, of course, sounded good, but when empires such as Austria, Russia, and the Ottoman Empire controlled vastly diverse peoples, each of whom chafed under the rule of foreign kings, nationalism could become perplexing and explosive. Nationalism and liberalism were sometimes thought of as synonymous because of the liberal emphasis on freedom and self-government.

THE NEGATIVE SIDE

Unfortunately, some nationalists stressed differences between people to an extent that sowed the seeds of antagonism. The modern term "chauvinism" is related to one of Napoleon's soldiers, Nicolas Chauvin, who was known and later ridiculed for his excessive and belligerent patriotism. It was only a short step to a belief in national superiority. It was even a shorter step to theories of racial superiority and, from there, to justification of genocide, tragically exemplified a century later in German anti-Semitism and the Holocaust.

PHILOSOPHICAL AND POLITICAL ALTERNATIVES TO LIBERALISM

Nineteenth-century liberalism sought many political and social reforms, but except for the elimination of monarchy it was not aimed at drastically changing everything. Other, more radical philosophies were. Although they did not make as much headway in the nineteenth century, they must nevertheless be considered as part of the intricate fabric of the times.

Socialism

Early nineteenth-century socialism was the antitheses of liberalism, for instead of emphasizing individual rights it emphasized the well-being of the collective community. That goal, socialists believed, could be achieved only by planned, state-directed social change. Thus they were adamantly opposed to laissez-faire economics. In general, socialists called for state ownership of all means of production and distribution.

UTOPIAN SOCIALISM

One brand of socialism was concerned primarily with the development of model communities in which everything was owned collectively. This, Utopian socialists believed, would do away with the evils brought on by competition and the industrial society, for each community would produce just enough for its own needs. There would be no rich and no poor, for each member of the community would share equally in everything. Robert Owen in England and Charles Fourier of France were two of the most prominent leaders of Utopian thought. In a way Utopian socialists were impractical visionaries, for even though they and their followers established a number of small Utopian communities in Europe and the United States, they seemed to give little thought to how socialism could work or be implemented on a national scale. Most Utopian communities were short-lived. The Oneida

Community, which flourished in the United States from 1848 to 1881, was one of the longest-lasting.

CHRISTIAN SOCIALISM

Traditionally, Christianity and conservatism were allies, but in 1848 an English social reformer, F. D. Maurice, began to preach that socialism was the only logical result of true Christianity. As the movement grew, Christian socialists organized associations of skilled artisans, such as tailors, shoemakers, and builders. Such groups, which directed their own workshops, were successful only for a while. The movement was dead in England by the end of the 1850s, though it survived much longer in the United States.

FABIAN SOCIALISM

The most respected socialist group in England was the Fabian Society, founded in 1883. Adherents eventually included such prominent writers as George Bernard Shaw and H.G. Wells. Fabians rejected the Marxian idea (see below) that only violent class struggle would bring about the socialist revolution. Rather, they believed that if the people were properly informed about the problems of society, social reform would gradually come about. They did considerable research and publication and held public seminars. In 1889 they published the *Fabian Essays*, which helped them achieve more political influence in England than any of the other socialist groups.

MARXISM

Marx and Engels. Formulators of the most radical and "scientific" socialist perspective were Karl Marx and Friedrich Engels. Both came from middle-class German families; Engels's father owned a textile factory in Manchester, England. Marx became a radical agitator and was eventually driven from Germany. His exile took him to Paris, Brussels, and London.

In 1845 Engels published his now famous *The Condition of the Working Class in England*, which presented the most devastating critique of industrial life yet to appear. Marx, meanwhile, was an avid student of history, law, and philosophy. He was much influenced by Georg Wilhelm Friedrich Hegel, and particularly by his "dialectical" logic. Hegel taught that every idea, or "thesis," gives rise to an opposing idea, or "antithesis," and that the clash between them results in a new "synthesis." This, in turn, becomes a thesis that produces a new antithesis, and so on. Marx soon developed his own dialectical materialism, which maintained that reality was constantly changing (i.e., producing new syntheses), moving toward the inevitable goal of socialism.

Marx and Engels belonged to a secret, though short-lived, group that called itself the Communist League. The term *communist* was adopted because they wanted to clearly distinguish themselves from the less radical socialists. Communists wanted a complete reordering of society, including the abolition of all private property.

The Manifesto. Early in 1848 the two friends published *The Communist Manifesto*, a tract that had little immediate effect on European politics but eventually became the most significant political document to be produced in modern Europe. Using Hegelian-type logic, they argued that the history of humankind was the history of continuous class struggle. At each stage, however, the ruling class was replaced by a different class. Europe had already passed through three stages of rulers: kingly, aristocratic, and middle-class (bourgeoisie). The next step was for the propertyless proletariat to seize power. This must inevitably be accomplished by violence.

The Classless Society. In later writings, including his famous *Das Kapital*, Marx spelled out his economic and political philosophy more completely. The value of a product, he believed, was determined by the amount of labor that produced it. Laborers were thus the creators of value, not their masters, the capitalist factory owners. He predicted that in time all the means of production would fall into the hands of a few, making the poor even more numerous and eventually driving them to revolution. The ultimate achievement would be a classless society, in which there would be no such thing as private property and all people would share alike in the means and results of production.

Marxists also concluded that the achievement of a classless society would mean the end of the national state, for workers would be able to rule themselves. Marxist Communism thus became, in every way, the antithesis of conservatism, capitalism, liberalism, and nationalism—the major forces in Europe's nineteenth-century political struggles. It would have its chief political impact in the next century.

Anarchism

At first glance the ultimate goal of Marxism, the elimination of the national state, seems little different from the goal of another radical philosophy, anarchism. Anarchists believed that any and all restraints on freedom were detrimental to human development. They therefore opposed all organized government whatsoever. But they also decried the Marxist "dictatorship of the proletariat," for this implied some kind of continuing state. Anarchist ideologues had an optimistic but unrealistic faith in the ability of human beings, without governmental restraints, to live together in harmony. Once government was eliminated, the goodwill of the people themselves would give rise to the ideal society. The people would form their own grass-roots organizations for distributing goods and satisfying their various social needs. Anarchists made no effort to create specific plans for a future society, for they believed that if they attempted to help out in the process of creating it, they would only contribute to the creation of another form of government. Their main activities, therefore, were directed toward destroying the existing state.

IMPACT

Leading anarchists included Michael Bakunin and Prince Kropotkin of Russia and Pierre-Joseph Proudhon of France. Anarchism attracted disciples mainly in eastern and southern Europe, where reactionary governments were especially oppressive. It also had an effect on the French labor movement, as well as in Switzerland. Its influence was felt most strongly in Russia, especially in the agitation that resulted in the revolutionary movements around 1917.

The Trade Union Movement

Still another alternative to classical liberalism was trade unionism, which grew up in the last half of the nineteenth century. Trade unions were direct responses to the Industrial Revolution. Unionists believed that through organization workers could gain enough economic power to persuade employers that it was in their own self-interest to provide better wages and working conditions. The unionists used picketing, strikes, propaganda, and other presumably peaceful tools to try to achieve their ends, though at times they were associated in the public mind with radicals such as anarchists and communists.

Bitterly resisted at first by industrialists and conservative politicians, unions gradually became an accepted part of European social and economic life. They became legal in Great Britain in 1871. In France, troops were used to put down early union-inspired strikers, but in 1884 unions were legalized. They were accepted in Germany only after 1890.

Early unionists concentrated on organizing skilled workers according to their trades; thus the designation "trade union." By the end of the century they were also organizing industrial unions for the benefit of unskilled workers. Their numbers grew rapidly, though they did not attract a majority of the labor force. The mere fact of their existence by the end of the century, however, exemplified the vast economic and political changes that had taken place in less than a hundred years.

The Democratic Tradition

Finally, the most viable and far-reaching political development in the nineteenth century was the rise of democracy and more broadly based political parties. The modern democratic political tradition is a direct outgrowth of the changes made in the nineteenth century. Again, industrialization contributed, as the social and economic problems it created stirred the common people to demand more political influence. At least some degree of democracy existed in every state of Russia by 1900. Even the German Empire had a Reichstag, or lower legislative house, elected by universal manhood suffrage, though it had little real power. Elsewhere, as in England, the populace could speak reasonably well through its popularly elected representatives. In this respect the changes wrought over less than a century were greater than any seen in all previous world history.

We have covered some of the ideas that motivated monarchs, ministers, reformers, and the people in the streets during the rapidly changing, sometimes puzzling nineteenth century. We now turn to an overview of political life in Europe after the defeat of Napoleon, with an eye toward demonstrating the complex interrelationship between some of these ideas and how they helped underpin the fascinating transformations that occurred between 1815 and 1900.

THE METTERNICH SYSTEM

Making the World Safe for Autocracy: The Congress of Vienna and the Concert of Europe

After the defeat of France the four great powers of Europe—Britain, Austria, Russia, and Prussia—agreed to form a Quadruple Alliance for twenty years, for the purpose of guaranteeing whatever peace terms were arrived at and to deal with other problems. The details were worked out by the Congress of Vienna, which lasted from September 1814 to June 1815. The heads of state met only once, however, at the final and only full session, to ratify the agreements worked out by their ministers.

GOALS AND CHALLENGES

Motivated largely by self-interest, the great powers had several prime goals. One was to create a lasting peace. Another was to create a balance of military and political power in order to ensure their own security and to guarantee that neither France nor any other power would again dominate Europe. They also wanted to draw permanent, inviolable state boundaries in a way that would contribute to the balance of power. In addition, they meant to ensure the perpetuation of monarchy, the political system that was serving each of them so well.

Some issues, including the French boundary, had been decided earlier. France had relinquished all territory recently held on the banks of the Rhine, and its 1791 boundaries had been restored. But there were numerous problems to be solved, including what to do with the Duchy of Warsaw that had been created by Napoleon from Prussian territory. There was also the slippery question of whether old international rivalries really could be overcome in the interest of peace and stability. The eight-month series of meetings, intrigues, and debates reflected the efforts of each state to promote its own self-interest. They hardly trusted each other, but in the end they worked out a compromise system that seemed almost self-enforcing simply because it was in the self-interest of each of them to maintain it. The system revolved largely around three main ideas. The first was *legitimacy*, or the restoration of "legitimate" monarchies wherever possible. A second was territorial *compensation* to specific powers for various losses. There was also the principle of *containment*, the effort to ring France with strong states that would prevent any future French aggression. Ironically, the idea of containment has a strongly modern ring, though in the latter twentieth-century its presumed purpose was to preserve democracy, not monarchy.

LEGITIMACY

Legitimacy was imposed on France even before the treaty, with the restoration of the Bourbon monarchy and the enthronement of Louis XVIII. Legitimate monarchies were also restored in Spain, Portugal, the Italian states, and Holland; Great Britain was returned to the rule of the house of Hanover. There was no attempt to restore the defunct Holy Roman Empire, though a loose German Confederation of thirty-eight states was created.

COMPENSATION

In applying the principle of compensation, no internal territory was taken from France. But, almost as if they were creating a giant jigsaw puzzle, the powers redrew much of the rest of the map of Europe. Their settlements included the following: Prussia was given considerable disputed territory in the Rhineland, on France's eastern border. Most of the Duchy of Warsaw went to Russia, with other parts being given to Prussia and Austria. Prussia also received, in compensation for the loss of its Polish territory to Russia, Pomerania, two-fifths of Saxony, and the Rhineland territory. Sweden was compensated for its loss of Pomerania and Finland by being given Norway. The latter was taken from Denmark, which had supported France, but Denmark was partially compensated by receiving Lauenburg. The Habsburg rulers of Austria were compensated by receiving considerable territory in Italy.

CONTAINMENT

The containment of France was an integral part of some of these new territorial arrangements. Prussia, as a result of its Rhineland acquisitions, became the "sentinel on the Rhine" against further French aggression . The powers also created the Kingdom of the Netherlands, which included not just Holland, but also Belgium and Luxembourg. This new monarchy could oppose France more effectively than could Holland alone.

The Concert of Europe

Among the most influential architects of the settlement at Vienna was Klemens von Metternich, Austria's foreign minister. At his urging a new international peace-keeping organization, the Concert of Europe, was agreed upon. Sometimes called the Metternich System, the Concert met periodically to consider what to do about various challenges to the balance of power created in Vienna, thus making the European world safe for autocracy. In 1818, at the first meeting, even France was admitted. But eventually the Concert broke down, partly because of disagreement among the powers over when and where intervention was appropriate and partly because an increasing number of Europeans were beginning to demand a voice in their own political affairs. In addition, the twin forces of nationalism and liberalism were growing apace.

Cracks in the Armor

NATIONALISM AND THE REVOLUTIONS OF THE 1820s AND 1830s

Actually, the Concert began to break up shortly after the first meeting. Their will tested by revolutions in Naples, Spain, and Portugal in 1820, the great powers found themselves in serious disagreement over the question of intervening militarily to uphold "legitimate" governments. Russia, Austria, and Prussia believed they should, but France hesitated. Britain rejected the idea outright and gradually withdrew from the Concert, anticipating the possible need to eventually open trade relations with revolutionary governments. Meanwhile, nationalistic forces in all parts of Europe presented continuing challenges to the *status quo*.

Greece. One such challenge, the 1821 rebellion of Greece against the rule of the Ottoman Turkish Empire, was actually supported by members of the Concert, even though it violated the principle of legitimacy. The Russian interest was at least two-fold. The tsars considered themselves the legitimate protectors of Orthodox Christianity in Greece. Along with the heads of other European states, they were not pleased to see Greece remain in "captivity" to the Turks. Perhaps more compelling, however, was their continuing dream of imperial expansion, including the annexation of Constantinople. The British, too, supported the Greek nationalists, even loaning them money. In 1827 Great Britain and France offered to mediate, but when this failed, Russia intervened in behalf of the rebels. Greece finally gained its independence, but in the end the Concert of Europe made sure that it became a monarchy. In 1832 a Bavarian prince was crowned Otto I, but thirty years later he was overthrown during a military revolt. Before long, Greece had a democratic constitution and manhood suffrage, both of which would have been banes to the now-defunct Concert.

Belgium. In 1830 nationalists in Belgium rebelled against Holland. Numerous factors contributed, including differences in language, religious differences (Holland was mostly Protestant, while Belgium was Catholic), and conflicting economic interests (Dutch commercialism versus Belgium's manufacturing economy). With French and British support, an independent state was established in 1831. France and England came to the aid of the rebels, Austria and Prussia were unable to intervene, and an independent state was established in 1831.

Germany. Nationalist sentiments were also stirring in Germany, especially among liberal-minded university students, but under the leadership of Austria it was harshly suppressed. In July 1819 a conference of the principal states issued the "Carlsbad Decrees," imposing censorship on books and universities. A new commission was created to root out both liberalism and nationalism wherever they were found. In 1830 there was some liberalization of governments in a few states, but the two most powerful states, Austria and Prussia, successfully resisted any such reforms.

Italy. In 1831 a number of small revolutions broke out in various states of Italy. The Carbonari family attempted to overthrow the Habsburgs in Parma and Modena, but the expected French aid was never forthcoming, and Austria was able to put down the rebellion. The Papal States, which had been returned to the pope at the Congress of Vienna, also rebelled, but French intervention on the side of the pope nipped that effort in the bud. Both Austria and France maintained troops in Italy until 1838.

Poland. Rebellion also broke out in 1830 in the Russian section of Poland, but it was quickly crushed. In addition, the autocratic new tsar, Nicholas I, deprived the Poles of many freedoms previously granted by his predecessor. By this time, however, it was clear that France and England were no longer supporting the Concert of Europe, so in 1833 Russia and Prussia agreed to help each other in putting down such rebellions in their own territories.

THE LIBERAL CHALLENGE IN FRANCE

Louis XVIII. In France, the monarchy of Louis XVIII was moderate in tone. He allowed some liberal reforms, including a bicameral (two-chamber) legislature, a slight extension of the franchise, and greater freedom of the press. France also experienced some economic recovery, enabling it to pay its war indemnity. Numerous political factions sprang up, including republicans, who wanted to get rid of monarchy, ultraroyalists, who dreamed of restoring the absolutism of the Old Regime, and radical republicans, who were committed to socialism.

Charles X. Louis XVIII's successor, Charles X (r. 1824–1830), had been championed by the ultraroyalists and thought of himself as a monarch by divine right. Many of his early policies, such as indemnification of the aristocracy for land lost in the revolution, antagonized liberals. In the elections of 1828 a liberal majority was sent to the lower house. Charles moderated temporarily, but in July 1830 he dissolved the legislature, clamped down on freedom of the press, and restricted suffrage. In angry reaction, the populace of Paris took to the streets and erected barricades. Even the National Guard joined with the people in the demonstrations. The king called out the military; in the fighting over 1,800 people died. Deserted,

Charles abdicated and fled to England. The Bourbon monarchy was at an end.

The Citizen King. The Chamber of Deputies then chose Louis Philippe, known as the "citizen king," to take the throne as a constitutional monarch (r. 1830–1848). His July Monarchy, as it was called, was at first moderately liberal. It abolished censorship, for example, and extended the franchise somewhat, though still only about 250,000 people could vote.

THE ABORTIVE LIBERAL REVOLTS OF 1848

Nationalist uprisings were often accompanied by demands for liberal political reforms, though when they were crushed, conservative forces often reversed any gains that had been made. In other cases, however, liberalism slowly began to effect changes in the political systems. The revolutions of 1848 were the result of worsening economic conditions together with smoldering political discontent that had already touched off small outbreaks in Poland, Switzerland, and Austria. Under these conditions liberals were able to foment a series of revolutions throughout Europe in 1848. Only Britain and Russia remained untouched that year, but elsewhere governments fell, monarchs and ministers lost their power, and even Metternich resigned from office. In the end, however, the liberals were unable to gain the support of the masses. Without exception the revolutions of 1848 failed. Once again the old order, or at least a version of it that had been only slightly modified, held on.

Revolution of 1848 in France. Louis Philippe's government showed an interest in business development. The growth of industry brought economic prosperity to the upper middle class. Laborers, however, did not share the wealth; they sometimes listened to radical socialists who urged economically and socially planned societies. Early in 1848 many of the king's opponents met in a series of banquets, where they severely criticized the government and demanded parliamentary reform. When in February 1848 the government prohibited further banquets, crowds again took to the streets of Paris. After considerable violence, Louis, like Charles before him, abdicated and went to England.

Temporary Triumph of Conservatism in France. A provisional government was organized by the revolutionaries, who also set about drafting a constitution for the Second Republic. But there was profound disagreement within the coalition of liberals, radicals, and socialists. With unemployment high, socialists were demanding permanent government-sponsored cooperative workshops that would provide an alternative to capitalism and would eventually lead to a new social and economic order. Moderates rejected such a plan outright, but they compromised by allowing the establishment of a number of national workshops to provide temporary relief for unemployed laborers. In April, however, a new National Assembly was elected, dominated by moderates and conservatives who still had little sympathy for such measures. By June 120,000 people were enrolled in the workshops, with more pressing to join, but that month the new government dissolved all the workshops in Paris. Again Parisians took to the streets in protest. During the famous "June Days" of 1848 over 3,000 people died.

Conservative property owners, who still dominated political life, quickly set about trying to create a republican form of government that would satisfy all parties. The new constitution, completed late in June, provided for a strong president and a one-house legislative assembly elected by universal manhood suffrage. Late in the year Louis Napoleon Bonaparte, nephew of the great emperor, was elected as the first president of the Second Republic. It was not long, however, before he was quarreling with the National Assembly. In 1851, through a personal *coup d'état*, his term was extended to ten years. In a national vote over 7.5 million citizens supported his actions and only 600,000 disapproved. The following year he had himself declared Emperor Napoleon III. For the time being republicanism in France seemed to be held in check.

The Habsburg Empire. The 1848 French uprising touched off a series of uprisings all over Europe. Within the Austrian empire they began in Hungary, where nationalists demanded autonomy along with liberal political reforms. Though the emperor promised some reforms and actually abolished serfdom, his opponents were so divided that they did not maintain a strong coalition. In addition, minority groups in Hungary did not support unification. Nevertheless, Austria was unable to put down the rebellion until mid-1849, and then only with the help of Russian troops. A rebellion in Czechoslovakia, meanwhile, came to naught because Czech and German nationalists saw the question of autonomy differently and the monarchy was able to play one side against another. Austria's possessions in northern Italy also set up independent governments, but they were crushed by an Austrian army in July 1848. In October a rebellion of working-class radicals in Vienna was also crushed.

Italian nationalists, meanwhile, had not entirely given up hope. For a time they thought they might enlist the aid of the pope, who had reformed the administration of the Papal States and had a liberal reputation. Political problems in Rome, however, forced the pope into exile. A Roman republic was declared in February 1849. It was soon overthrown, however, by Austria. About the same time, France sent an army into Italy in order to prevent a unified state from emerging there. French troops remained in Rome protecting the pope until 1870.

Germany. In Germany, liberals forced Frederick William IV of Prussia to call a constituent assembly in 1848 and announce a new constitution, but a year later their power was so weak that the king could dissolve the assembly and promulgate a more conservative constitution. Various efforts to bring about German unification also failed, partly because liberals lost the support of German workers and artisans who wanted more radical reforms than they were willing to support. The liberals had established a parliament in Frankfurt. They even offered the crown of a united Germany to the king of Prussia, who refused it. They also differed among themselves over whether to include Austria in the projected German state. In 1849 the parliament dissolved.

Thus, by the end of the 1840s Metternich's system was still intact in Austria and elsewhere, even though its architect had resigned and fled his country. For the most part, European politics was still in the hands of the conservatives.

The Persistence of Conservatism: Spain and Russia

SPAIN: THE ILLIBERAL CONSTITUTIONAL MONARCHY

Spain and Russia, meanwhile, remained bastions of conservatism. Spanish liberals lacked the broad base of a well-developed middle class, but they made various efforts to bring about reform. In 1820 a group of army officers about to be sent to South America led a revolt against Ferdinand VII (r. 1814–1833). They forced him to submit to a written constitution, but three years later a French army came to his aid and brutally suppressed the rebellion. The torture and execution of the revolutionaries made this one of the most bloody examples of reactionary intervention during the century. Political tension continued and included an effort by the Cortés (parliament) between 1869 and 1874 to establish a liberal constitution. Finally, in 1875 another king from the house of Bourbon was placed on the throne as a constitutional monarch. The new government, however, was only slightly more liberal than earlier kings. Even the Cortés, theoretically based on universal suffrage, was controlled by political cliques. For the rest of the century Spain was ruled by a kind of coalition consisting of great land-owners, the church, and the army.

RUSSIA

Despite efforts by Peter I and Catherine II to Westernize Russia, that giant empire had generally remained aloof from Western European politics. The ambiguity continued in the nineteenth century, though the tsars involved themselves when it was in their self-interest to do so. Internally, they also vacillated between semblances of liberal reform and resurgence of conservatism, but by the end of the century autocracy still ruled. The Russian experience is a prime example of conservatism, nationalism, and religious orthodoxy all being part of the same package.

Alexander I: Pseudo-Liberal. At first it appeared that Alexander I was amenable at least to some liberal reforms, including relaxation of censorship, promotion of education, toleration of religion, and abolition of serfdom. The Napoleonic Wars, however, cut short any such pretensions. After the wars, the weakness of Alexander's commitment to liberalism was made apparent by the fact that even though he liberated serfs in the Baltic states, no land was given to them. They were thus still completely dependent on their masters. He also suppressed nationalism in the section of Poland that came under his rule.

Nicholas I: Autocrat. When Alexander died, his brothers disagreed over who should have the throne—each, ironically, wanting the other to take it. Constantine, however, was backed by a group of army officers who had been introduced to liberal ideas while fighting in Europe. They believed he would be more liberal. When Nicholas quickly took the throne as Nicholas I, therefore, he ruthlessly repressed these officers. Eventually he became the most extreme autocrat and reactionary in Europe. Among other things, the lower classes were kept out of institutions of higher education; in the primary schools, emphasis was placed on the ideals associated with Russian nationalism, orthodoxy, and autocracy. He even seemed to think of himself as the policeman responsible for preserving autocracy in the rest of Europe. He was ready and willing to provide troops to suppress liberal and nationalist movements anywhere. He also repressed Polish, Jewish, and Moslem minorities, even forcing Jewish children to be baptized into the Russian Orthodox Church.

The Crimean War Shatters the Concert. The Crimean War (1854–1856) marked a significant turning point, both for Russia and the Concert of Europe. It originated in two conflicts: Russia's long-standing desire to take over the Ottoman Empire's provinces along the Danube, and the conflicting claims of Russia and France as protectors of Christian shrines within the Ottoman Empire. Russia invaded the Danubian provinces in 1853, but the following year Britain and France came to the aid of the Ottomans in order to protect their own interests in the Mediterranean. The war was badly managed by both sides, but it ended with Russia giving up most of what it was fighting for. The significance of the war, however, lay not just in the embarrassment of Russia but also in the fact that it demonstrated the Concert of Europe no longer had the will to deal with issues relating to national boundaries. At least that part of Metternich's ideal was shattered, and a new era of instability and separate action in foreign affairs was ushered in.

Alexander II: Moderate Liberal. The reign of Alexander II (r. 1855–1881) began with a military defeat. At the same time, he recognized that some internal reforms must come. Alexander made a few concessions, such as easing censorship, in order to win liberal support. The most vexing problem, however, was the persistence of serfdom. The tsar finally decided that he must fully emancipate them. The process was long and complex, involving questions of compensation to masters as well as of how to make it possible for the peasants to purchase land. It also required some reforms in local government and in the judicial system. For the first time some principles of the Western legal system, including trial by jury, were incorporated. Alexander's reforms, however, did not satisfy many liberals, especially among students; in the 1870s violence and terrorism broke out. The revolutionaries did not have enough support for a wide-scale uprising, but the extremists among them decided that by assassinating the tsar they could at least call greater attention to their cause. On March 1, 1881, Alexander was killed by a bomb.

Alexander III: Reactionary. Alexander III (r. 1881–1894), duly impressed with the fate of his predecessor, became the consummate autocrat. Though he paid some attention to improvement of conditions in the factories, his generally reactionary policies were intended to roll back the clock. A strengthened central bureaucracy, more power to the secret police, increased censorship, and other policies restored the evils the revolutionaries were trying to eradicate. Only in the twentieth century would Alexander's son, Nicholas II, learn how powerful the continuing liberal undercurrents could become.

DIFFERENT PATHS TOWARD REPUBLICANISM: FRANCE AND ENGLAND

France: From Monarchy to Republicanism

NAPOLEON III: LATENT LIBERAL?

In France and England, meanwhile, liberalism and republicanism followed less difficult paths. In France, Napoleon III rejected laissez-faire, believing that government should intervene to promote economic growth and public welfare. His program included many public works, the completion of a national railway network, the formation of credit institutions, and a series of commercial treaties that helped promote French trade. At first he was a virtual dictator, keeping a tight reign on the legislature, controlling the press, and making life extremely difficult for liberals and other dissidents. Beginning in 1860, however, he gradually moved toward a moderate liberalism, transferring power to the legislature and promoting other reforms. In 1870 he granted a new constitution that provided for a democratic parliament, though the nation still had a hereditary monarch.

Disaster in Foreign Affairs. One factor in Napoleon's latent liberalism was an effort to mask, or compensate for, his foreign policy failures. These, in the long run, proved to be his undoing. He had won a victory over Russia in the Crimean War and had successfully intervened to put down nationalism in Italy, but the 1860s saw serious reverses. He failed in his effort to establish a Mexican empire under Maximilian, failed to stop Prussia's increase in power, and was defeated in the Franco-Prussian War (see further discussion

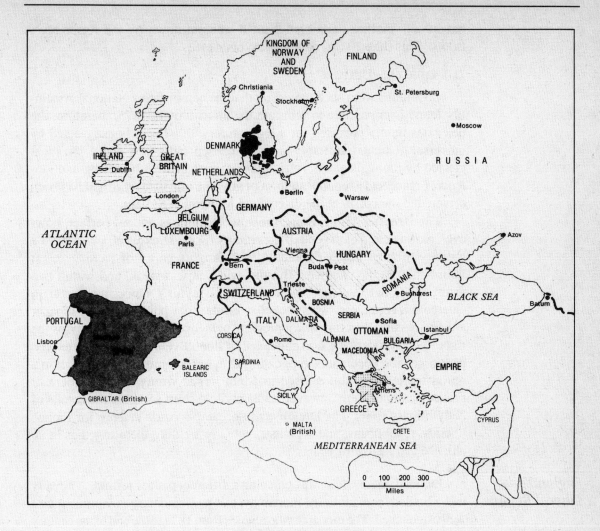

Fig. 9.1   Europe in 1871

below). He once remarked that public opinion always wins the last victory. But even though Napoleon tried to appease the public by promoting some liberal measures, by 1869 republicans, monarchists, and liberals all opposed him.

The Paris Commune. Napoleon surrendered to the Prussians on September 2, 1870. Two days later the republicans in Paris proclaimed the Third Republic, bringing his reign to an end. Peace negotiations were conducted by a new National Assembly, elected early in 1871. The settlement included the surrender of Alsace-Lorraine to Germany and the payment of a large indemnity. Parisians, in particular, objected; they soon elected a new municipal government, the Paris Commune, which was intended to govern the city independently from the rest of the country. It became a hotbed of radicalism, but in still another Paris bloodbath it was put down by the Assembly's troops. This time 20,000 people were butchered.

THE THIRD REPUBLIC

Conditions were such, however, that the conservative National Assembly found it impossible to reinstate the monarchy. In 1875, therefore, the delegates finally provided for a legislature with a lower house elected by universal manhood suffrage, a senate chosen indirectly, and a president elected by the legislature. Thus, after years of internal bickering and violence, France had a republican form of government. One more nail had been driven into the coffin of the discredited Metternich System.

The Dreyfus Affair. French republicanism was not yet perfect, however, as illustrated at the end of the century by the Dreyfus affair. In 1894 a military tribunal found Captain Alfred Dreyfus guilty of passing secret information to the Germans. But the evidence was weak, and within two years additional evidence demonstrating Dreyfus's innocence began to emerge. Nevertheless, when novelist Émile Zola published a newspaper article accusing the army of suppressing evidence and denying Dreyfus the right to due process, he was convicted of libel. Eventually the officer who had forged the documents implicating Dreyfus committed suicide, but in a retrial the military still refused to admit it was wrong. The president of France pardoned him, however, and a civilian court set aside the results of both military trials. The Dreyfus case became a *cause célèbre* for French liberals, republicans, and socialists, actually welding them together in an alliance that lasted for years.

England's Liberal Regime

England, meanwhile, was pursuing a different path of reform. It already had a limited, constitutional monarchy, and parliamentary government was well established. The monarch who reigned from 1837 to the end of the century was Queen Victoria (r. 1837–1901); she set the tone for the age not in terms of political power but in terms of religion, manners, and moral idealism.

There was still political discontent, however, and the depression and unemployment that followed the Napoleonic wars only added to demands for reform. All this was further exacerbated by the impact of the Industrial Revolution on urban life and poverty. Though revolution did not break out, in the early part of the century there were numerous public demonstrations, some of which led to violence and death. The response of the ruling Tory party, which was in the hands of the landed gentry, was to pass only mild reforms. It did, however, remove the prohibition on labor unions.

POLITICAL REFORM, 1830–1884

One of the pressures for parliamentary reform came from Ireland. It was represented in Parliament, but even though its population was overwhelmingly Catholic, only Protestants could be elected. In 1829, concerned that Irish protests would lead to more civil strife and perhaps even the loss of Ireland, Tories pushed through the Catholic Emancipation Act. This act, together with an earlier bill repealing political restrictions on Protestant Nonconformists, meant that no longer would the Church of England have a monopoly on political leadership.

The Reform Bill of 1832. Partly as an angry reaction to these changes, the Whig party was swept into power in 1830. The major issue it faced was reforming Parliament, including making it more representative of the growing number of middle-class industrialists and merchants. After a prolonged and bitter debate, the Reform Act of 1832 was passed. It redistributed seats in the House of Commons so that urban boroughs had more representation. This act was not democratic, however, for it also placed property qualifications on potential voters. It has been estimated that still only about 1.5 percent of England's 6 million men could qualify. Other reforms of the period included freeing slaves throughout the empire and prohibiting women and children from working underground in Britain's mines.

Chartism. Political protesters soon organized the Chartist movement, whose platform called for universal suffrage and other electoral reforms. The movement failed in its immediate objectives, though in later years most of its platform was adopted. In the 1830s the Tory party began to be called the Conservative party. During most of the next two decades it successfully resisted any further extension of the franchise. It was a surprise to almost everyone, then, when the Conservative ministry introduced a new reform bill in 1867. When it finally passed, it nearly doubled the number of voters by extending the franchise to most homeowners and renters, thus taking Britain a step closer to democracy.

Free Trade. Meanwhile, popular protest against high grain prices led to the formation the Anti–Corn Law League, which pushed for repeal of import duties on grain that kept prices up, thus benefiting the landed aristocracy but hurting the workingman. Repeal came in 1846, after the Conservative prime minister Sir Robert Peel was converted to the principle of free trade.

Reforms of Disraeli and Gladstone. Britain's two leading politicians in the latter part of the nineteenth century were Benjamin Disraeli and William Gladstone. Disraeli, a Conservative, is most well known for his contribution to the expansion of the empire, but he was also interested in gaining support from workingmen. He thus sponsored considerable social legislation and a number of political reforms. He was prime minister in 1867 and again from 1874 to 1880. Among his important domestic measures were the Public Health Act of 1875, which helped improve sanitation in industrial cities, and the Artisans Dwelling Act of 1875, whereby the government became directly involved in public housing for Britain's laboring class.

Gladstone formed the new British Liberal party from a combination of the Whigs and Radicals. He served as prime minister for fifteen out of the twenty-six years between 1868 and 1894. The liberal domestic programs promoted under his leadership were sweeping, responding to most of the serious complaints that had been smoldering for decades. Promotion to the highest military ranks, previously restricted to the upper classes, was opened to everyone. The civil service was reformed. Compulsory, free, public education was developed. Politically, Gladstone introduced the secret ballot in 1872. In the Reform Bill of 1884 most farm workers received the vote and parliamentary seats were again reapportioned to achieve more fair representation. By the end of Gladstone's ministry most of the old Chartist ambitions had been achieved.

THE IRISH QUESTION

One of Gladstone's most troublesome problems was the Irish question. Roman Catholics in Ireland chafed at paying taxes to support the Anglican church, and a powerful sentiment for home rule had developed. Charles Stewart Parnell, an Irish member of the House of Commons, organized other Irish members so that they frequently voted as a bloc and thus could gain more attention for the cause of home rule. Gladstone promoted two home rule bills, but neither was able to pass through the conservative House of Lords. Ireland presented thorny questions that still continue.

NATIONALISM TRIUMPHANT

Elsewhere in Europe, Metternich's dream of keeping nationalism and liberalism in check continued to rapidly dwindle away. In some cases nationalists were also monarchists, while in other cases they came to power in league with liberals and in the expectation of promoting more liberal reform.

Italian Unification

In Italy, nationalists had long wanted the small, autocratic principalities united into a single state such as had existed before the Lombard invasions of the sixth century, but many barriers stood in the way. They included sectional differences, the question of the role of the pope in a unified national state, and, after 1815, the new barriers erected by Congress of Vienna. The Papal States were restored to the pope, a Bourbon ruler was given Naples and Sicily, Austria received Lombardy, Venetia, and the Tyrol, and Habsburg monarchs were installed in other states.

CAVOUR AND GARIBALDI

Early attempts at unification, already noted above, failed. It remained for Count Camillo di Cavour, who became prime minister of Sardinia (Piedmont) in 1852, to achieve the goal. His success in improving economic conditions won him the admiration of other states. Cavour was not averse to using intrigue to create the possibility of uniting those states to Sardinia. During the Crimean War he joined the French and British in order to win their sympathies. Later he plotted with Napoleon III for a war against Austria. In 1859, at the end of that war, Sardinia received Lombardy. Later that year most of the rest of northern Italy chose also to unify with Sardinia.

The next year Giuseppi Garibaldi, who had participated in previous revolutions and was a thoroughgoing republican, used an outbreak in Sicily as an opportunity to invade with 1,000 red-shirted soldiers. With the secret support of Cavour he liberated both Sicily and Naples. He also planned to conquer the Papal States, but Cavour, fearing trouble with the pope, sent Sardinian forces to occupy them and to hold off Garibaldi. Cavour, a monarchist, was fearful also that Garibaldi would set up a republic in the south, so he quickly organized a vote whereby the southern territories chose to join with Sardinia in a united Italian republic. Garibaldi, fully committed to nationalism, went along. In February 1861 the king of Sardinia was crowned Victor Emmanuel II, King of Italy (r. 1861–1878). The Papal States were finally brought into the kingdom in 1870 as a result of the Franco-Prussian war. All the provisions of the Congress of Vienna for Italy had been completely overturned. In this case, monarchism and nationalism worked together to create a new member of the European family of nations.

The Unification of Germany

Perhaps the most important political development of all in the nineteenth century was the creation of a united Germany. In this case military idealism, conservative monarchical philosophy, and nationalism all worked together to create the most powerful single state in western Europe—one that would have a pivotal effect on the course of the next century.

BISMARCK

In 1862 the conservative king of Prussia, William I, and the liberal Parliament were deadlocked over taxes. The king turned for help to Otto von Bismarck, long a dedicated monarchist and reactionary. As soon as he became prime minister, Bismarck attacked Parliament, claiming that the constitution permitted collection of taxes even if Parliament did not vote for them. When a popular majority elected a new liberal Parliament, however, Bismarck saw the need to attract popular support away from the liberals. He did it by diverting public attention to foreign affairs. He went to war with Denmark over the northern duchies of Schleswig and Holstein. Austria joined in the war, and the two duchies soon came under the joint rule of both monarchies. In 1866, however, Bismarck picked a fight with Austria over the administration of the duchies. After a quick and decisive defeat the Habsburgs were excluded from German affairs. Prussia thus emerged as the only major power in the German Confederation.

The following year Bismarck incorporated three other states and the city of Frankfurt into Prussia. All the states north of the Main River became the North German Confederation. Prussia, the strongest state, was clearly the leader. The constitution gave the appearance of some liberalism, but the Reichstag (legislature) was limited in genuine power.

THE FRANCO-PRUSSIAN WAR AND ITS CONSEQUENCES

The opportunity for Bismarck to fulfill his dream of complete German unification came when it appeared that a relative of William I of Prussia might become king of Spain. This would antagonize the French, who did not want another German ruler on their borders. Bismarck believed that if France went to war with Prussia, the German princes would then not only support Prussia, but would also agree to German unity. Again Bismarck resorted to intrigue, this time by editing a press dispatch to make it appear that William I had insulted the French ambassador. As Bismarck hoped, this so piqued Napoleon III that he declared war on Prussia. True to their treaty commitments, and to Bismarck's plot, the southern German states supported Prussia. In the course of the war the princes of these states joined the North German Confederation in urging William I to accept the title of emperor. On January 18, 1871, the German Empire was declared in the Hall of Mirrors at Versailles. The German princes were heads of their own states within the empire, but Bismarck had achieved the goal of a united Germany. So far as France was concerned, its armies had been shattered, and it finally lost the military dominance in had enjoyed since the days of Louis XIV.

Nationalism in Ethnocentric Eastern Europe

In Austria, meanwhile, the various ethnic minorities were unable to create a solid front against the Habsburg rulers. After the unsuccessful revolts of the Czechs and Hungarians, the army was strengthened. New roads and railways were built in an effort to discourage any future revolts. In 1866, however, the Prussians defeated Austria, which gave new life to the Hungarian independence movement. A compromise was reached in 1867 whereby the Hungarians were given a separate parliament and constitution, though not a separate king. The dual monarchy of Austria-Hungary thus came into existence. Another bite had been taken from the Vienna settlement, and the Hungarians were temporarily satisfied. But the Slavic minorities in the empire were still clamoring for their own autonomy. Czechs, Ruthenians, Romanians, and Serbo-Croatians were all dismayed because German-speaking Austrians and Hungarian Magyars were allowed to dominate. Except for Hungary, both nationalism and any hope for constitutional government were dead in the Austrian empire.

The nineteenth century is often called the age of nation-states. It began with a few great monarchies in place. In 1815 they redrew much of the map of Europe in response to the Napoleonic wars. After the Congress of Vienna they believed they had created a system that would ensure continued peace as well as safety for the continuation of monarchies. Complex, underlying, and interrelated forces, however, gradually changed everything. As conservatism tried to preserve itself, it came in conflict with nationalist yearnings as well as with various liberal and radical philosophies that were affecting people everywhere. By 1871 the system so carefully worked out at Vienna had been shattered. By the end of the century several new national states had joined the European family of nations. Moreover, political liberalism had entrenched itself so deeply that the conservatives of the 1890s would seem radical if those of 1815 were to sit in on their deliberations.

The consequences of these changes were not entirely positive. Racism still characterized the attitudes of the majority in many national states. The power of the state was still used to repress various ethnic groups. In addition, the developments discussed here also set the stage for the conflict between the national states to be expanded worldwide. Imperialism, with both its positive and negative consequences, was a direct result of the increasing political and economic strength of the nation-states.

Finally, the rise and fall of Metternich's Concert of Europe is illuminating. The European powers had formed an international organization for the purpose of keeping the peace, preserving existing national boundaries, and making their world safe for autocracy. It failed on each count. A century later another international organization was formed at the end of another devastating war, this time designed to keep the peace, preserve national borders, and make the world safe for democracy. It, too, failed on each count. Exactly why these failures occurred is still a subject of intense historical discussion.

Selected Readings

Bentley, Michael. *Politics Without Democracy: Great Britain, 1815–1914: Perception and Preoccupation in British Government*. Totowa, NJ: Barnes & Noble, 1985, 1984.

Craig, Gordon A. *Germany, 1866–1945*. New York: Oxford University Press, 1978.

Hamerow, Theodore S. *The Birth of a New Europe: State and Society in the Nineteenth Century*. Chapel Hill: University of North Carolina Press, 1983.

Kissinger, Henry A. *A World Restored: Metternich, Castlereagh and the Problems of Peace, 1812–22*. Boston: Houghton Mifflin, 1957.

Mack Smith, Denis, comp. *The Making of Italy, 1796–1870*. New York: Walker, 1968. (Documentary History of Western Civilization.)

Rich, Norman. *The Age of Nationalism and Reform, 1850–1890*. 2d ed. New York: Norton, 1977.

Ulam, Adam B. *Russia's Failed Revolutions: From the Decembrists to the Dissidents*. New York: Basic Books, 1981.

10

The Americas and Australia: A Nineteenth-Century Overview

Nationalism was one of the most powerful forces of the nineteenth century. It spread not only across Europe, but throughout the non-European West as well, assuming diverse forms and leading to various consequences. The United States prepared to become a world power as it expanded its borders from coast to coast, but the spread of Euro-American civilization across the continent had tragic consequences for those who were already there. And the nation-building process was also accompanied by a disastrous civil war. Until World War I, the post-Napoleonic world saw no greater war than the U.S. Civil War.

For the British settlement colonies of Australia and Canada, the nineteenth century meant independence and parliamentary government. Latin American was a different story. This politically volatile region achieved some stability through unrepresentative dictatorships, but it also developed an economy dependent upon the United States and Europe.

EUROPEAN CULTURAL INFLUENCES

The Western world felt the continued influence of European culture, even after individual states became independent. North America, Australia, and New Zealand were dominated by populations with European backgrounds. The ethnic makeup of Latin America was somewhat more diverse, combining natives, immigrants, and those of mixed blood. Black slaves also accounted for a major portion of the population in both North and South America.

Spanish culture continued to dominate Latin America, with the exception of Portuguese Brazil. This influence could be seen in language, architecture, religion, social relations and practices, and other areas. In North America, British culture was dominant, except for the continuing presence of a strong pocket of French influence in eastern Canada. Though a number of important new religious movements began in the nineteenth century, religion in North America was largely imported from Europe, often undergoing considerable modification once it arrived. At least until the last half of the century, North American cultural life took many of its cues from Europe, though by the end of the century there was movement across the Atlantic in the other direction as well.

THE UNITED STATES IN THE NINETEENTH CENTURY

Eighteenth-century liberalism received concrete expression in the U.S. Constitution. At the same time, the United States maintained a political system in which power was shared between the central government and the states—a system known as federalism. But the Constitution left some questions unanswered. One of these—the question of the nature of federalism and the ability of the central government to enforce its authority in the states—was one of the causes of the Civil War. In the end, this question was answered in favor of enhanced central government power.

Politics, Religion, and Reform Before the Civil War

THE TWO-PARTY SYSTEM

The First New Party. The election of 1800 brought the Jeffersonian-Republican Party into power in the United States. This party had been formed by advocates of states' rights and others who feared being dominated by manufacturing and financial interests. Though the names of the parties and the issues that motivated them changed over time, in general a two-party system developed. This system and the rivalry between the two dominant parties have defined American politics since the nineteenth century.

The Parties: Internal Coalitions. By the 1820s, the Federalist Party of George Washington and John Adams was gone. By the 1830s, a new two-party rivalry was developing between the Democrats (followers of Andrew Jackson) and the Whigs (composed of anti-Jackson Republicans and former Federalists). In 1856, a new sectional, antislavery party was formed, known as the Republican Party. The Republican and Democratic parties remained the mainstream political parties after the Civil War, generally demonstrating enough flexibility to take over most popular issues and leave third parties with no special appeal. Instead of forming multiparty coalitions within a parliament, as in Europe, American political parties were each internal coalitions of diverse political interests.

REFORM: POLITICAL AND SOCIAL

Political Democracy. Some aspects of political democracy developed more quickly in the young American nation than in most others. Gender, property, and race qualifications were eliminated over the course of the nineteenth and early twentieth centuries, though changes in attitude did not always keep pace. Blacks were legally enfranchised in 1870, but various racist devices kept many of them from the polls for years to come.

Social Reform. Social reform accompanied political reform. By 1860 most states were well on the way toward making elementary education for all a reality, except for slave children in the South. Movements for prison and insane asylum reform were often headed by women, who were also active in the women's suffrage and antislavery movements. Other social causes, from temperance (abstinence from alcoholic beverages) to the elimination of dueling, also received popular support. As in Europe, Utopian idealism caught on among many people, including some religious groups, giving rise to short-lived Utopian communities.

Impressions of a European Observer. An interesting relationship between what was happening in the United States and the striving for democratic reform in France is seen in the life and writings of Alexis de Tocqueville, a young French aristocrat who toured the United States in 1831 and 1832. Profoundly impressed with what he saw, after his return to France he became a member of the Chamber of Deputies and worked for reform. In 1835 he published his famous two-volume work *Democracy in America*, which became the best analysis available of American political life. America, he told his countrymen, was a land of unlimited opportunity and of enviable political equality and wisdom. It had its weaknesses, including slavery and the way Native Americans were treated. Nevertheless, he believed, the American system was an ideal model for the kind of democracy and social equality he saw developing in Europe.

American Religion. De Tocqueville also reported that in the United States no religious doctrine displayed "the slightest hostility to democratic and republican institutions." Further, he proclaimed that there was "no country in the world where the Christian religion retains a greater influence over the souls of men than in America." These were somewhat idyllic assertions, though what was happening to American religion fit in well with the American democratic faith and the general spirit of reform.

The democratic emphasis was not just on personal ability but also on personal responsibility and participation. Such sentiments affected the attitude of frontiersmen and yeoman farmers toward religion. Seeking personal salvation, they were little attracted to the traditional Puritan emphasis on human depravity and predestination, nor to churches that stressed form and ritual. Rather, they seemed to be seeking a religious faith that emphasized the nobility of the individual, direct communication with the Divine, and a return to the simple teachings and practices of ancient Christianity. They flocked to the revivals that swept the country during the Second Great Awakening, beginning about 1800 and continuing for over two decades. They often joined one of the various new religious movements that sprang up, some of which placed emphasis on democratic, lay leadership. The most long-lasting of the new religions were the Disciples of Christ (forerunner of the present Churches of Christ) and the Mormons. Both claimed as the basis for their existence the restoration of primitive Christianity with its uncomplicated structure and teaching. The age was also characterized by a new surge of popular millennialism (a belief in the imminence of Christ's return and a period of universal peace) that reached its peak in the 1840s. Popular traveling preachers, lay ministers, religious philosophy adapted to the understanding and aspirations of the common person, and restorationism (the search for a restoration of an original, "pure" form of Christianity) were among the things that made the new American religion very much a part of the democratic spirit of the times.

NATIONALISM, AMERICAN STYLE

One kind of American nationalism was eloquently summed up by Andrew Jackson, who proclaimed that America should "go on elevating our people, perfecting our institutions, until democracy shall reach such a point of perfection that we can acclaim with truth that the voice of the people is the voice of God." This statement expressed the feeling that the United States had a destiny (many saw it as a divine destiny) to demonstrate to the world the nobility of its people and institutions and, in the process, to expand its borders.

Varieties of Nationalism. At least three different kinds of nationalism were expressed in early America. One was political and judicial—an effort to enhance the power of the national government as opposed to state governments. Another kind was pride in the country and its institutions, such as that expressed by Jackson. A third kind was expansionism.

Nationalism in Foreign Affairs. The young American nation came into dispute with several European powers, including an indecisive war with England in 1812 over the rights of neutral ships on the high seas. War resulted in a new surge of nationalism. Then, in 1823, President James Monroe issued what is known as the "Monroe Doctrine," stating that the Americas were no longer subject to colonization by European powers. The United States' own weakness might have made the Monroe Doctrine laughable had it not also been in England's interest to keep Spain from regaining its colonies.

Manifest Destiny. The American population was rapidly expanding westward. Many of the settlers were immigrants seeking new economic opportunities. Between 1845 and 1854 alone, 2.4 million people arrived in America from Europe. Good farmland east of the Mississippi was nearly all taken up. Both old and new Americans were looking beyond the river into the Louisiana Territory (purchased in 1803), Texas, the Mexican territory of California, and Oregon country. It was the nation's "manifest destiny," proclaimed magazine editor John L. O'Sullivan in 1845, "to overspread the continent allotted by Providence for the free development of our yearly multiplying millions."

Expansionism in Action. Most Americans believed him. They applauded a revolution in the Mexican state of Texas in 1836. Then, in 1845, they accepted Texas into the American union. That next year their expansionist president, James K. Polk, ended the agreement with Britain for joint occupation of Oregon. He also declared war on Mexico; the war ended in 1848 with the acquisition of practically all the remaining territory west of the Rocky Mountains. From the standpoint of territorial acquisition, the United States' first adventure in imperialism was a raging success. The vast new areas opened for settlement attracted hundreds of thousands of people, provided homes and economic opportunities for poverty-stricken immigrants from Europe, expanded American political institutions from coast to coast, enhanced America's economic growth. The transcontinental railroad, completed in 1869, sped up the settlement process and was the most important boon of the century to national business and commercial activity.

The Underside of Nationalism. The consequences of nationalism were not always positive. Judicial nationalism, which attempted to increase the authority of the central government, ultimately contributed to the political sectionalism that helped bring on civil war. Nationalistic pride brought on a high degree of antipluralism in a society that should have been able to accommodate a variety of ethnic, cultural, and religious differences. American "nativists" often looked askance at groups that were not Anglo-Saxon or Protestant, did not speak English, or seemed to be developing exclusive communities or secret organizations. Irish Catholics, German immigrants, Masons, Mormons, and other groups were all targets of political and economic persecution that often became violent.

Impact on Native Americans. In addition, territorial expansionism and western settlement were not a blessing to everyone. The American government never knew quite what to do with the Native Americans who were already on the land coveted by prospective settlers. Under the Indian Removal Policy of the 1820s and 1830s, many tribes were moved west of the Mississippi with the promise that they would be taught agricultural pursuits and never be required to move again. The promises were not kept. Later in the century the Native Americans on the great plains and further west continually resisted incursions on their hunting lands. Euro-Americans, however, could never understand their nomadic way of life; in addition to destroying the buffalo (their main source of food, clothing, and shelter), they also destroyed large numbers of the people themselves. Those who survived continued to resist white incursions until they were rounded up on reservations. There they carried out a valiant but pathetic effort to maintain a traditional way of life. In 1887 well-meaning reformers persuaded Congress to pass the Dawes Severalty Act, intended to encourage Native Americans to leave the reservations, take up farming, and become American citizens. Those who took up the offer, however, had no experience in private land ownership, and they did not know how to resist fraud. The tragic result was that much of the former reservation land ended up in the hands of white speculators. Land which was left to the Native Americans was largely unsuited for agriculture.

Sectionalism and Civil War

If there were strong nationalistic forces at work in the United States, there were equally strong sectionalist impulses. Unfortunately, sectionalism was sufficiently strong to lead to the tragedy of civil war.

ECONOMIC DIFFERENCES

Economic differences between North and South tended to divide the nation. The northern economy was based largely on family farming, commerce, and the New England textile industry. The North was also the center for banking and other business enterprises. The southern economy, on the other hand, was tied to large plantations, and particularly the production of cotton. It was dependent on slavery to provide the necessary labor. The two economies worked together; the South grew cotton, and the North shipped it or used it for domestic manufacturing.

POLITICAL SECTIONALISM AND WAR

Some Sectional Issues. Though the economic relationship between North and South worked reasonably well, political and economic issues could easily divide the two regions. The question of whether new states should be admitted as slave or free states was a volatile issue. An attempt was made to solve the problem by the drawing of a compromise line, north of which slavery would be prohibited. Economic policies could also be divisive. In 1830, South Carolina declared a national tariff null and void within its own borders, fearing that the tariff would be detrimental to its trading relationship with England. President Andrew Jackson declared the state in rebellion, and civil war was nearly the result.

A Sectional Party. At the same time, the movement to abolish slavery was becoming more militant. Southerners saw this movement as a threat to their way of life. In 1854, Stephen A. Douglas introduced a bill that included "popular sovereignty" as the means by which new states would decide whether or not to allow slavery. This angered northern abolitionists. The result was the formation of a new anti-slavery coalition known as the Republican Party.

Violence and Secession. Violence soon followed, as pro- and anti-slavery advocates clashed. Fuel was added to the fire with the Supreme Court's 1857 decision (in the Dred Scott case) that slaves, as property, were protected by the Constitution. In other words, Congress could not prohibit slavery in the territories. Then in 1860, the Republican Party nominated Abraham Lincoln, a known opponent of slavery, for president. Fearing that the election of such a man would lead to the elimination of slavery, South

Carolina seceded from the union, followed by the rest of the southern states. In 1861, they created the Confederate States of America.

The Constitutional Issue and War. The South argued that secession was a matter of states' rights. Abraham Lincoln, on the other hand, maintained that secession was illegal and the union could not be dissolved. Lincoln felt it was his duty under the Constitution to save the union, even if it meant civil war. And civil war was indeed the outcome of the two inflexible positions. In terms of loss of life, this four-year war was the most destructive war in which the United States has ever been engaged.

War's Legacy. Much of the South was devastated by the war. It took parts of the South a century or more to recover from the economic ruin. The heritage of bitterness between North and South was equally difficult to overcome. But one of the most important outcomes of the war—an outcome on which it is difficult to place a price—was the elimination of slavery.

Postwar America

CHANGING AMERICAN FEDERALISM

Postwar amendments to the Constitution prohibited slavery, prevented states from denying former slaves the right to vote, and defined citizenship in such a way that everyone, including former slaves, was recognized as a full-fledged citizen of the state in which he or she was born. But the Fourteenth Amendment also prevented states from depriving a person of life, liberty, or property without due process of law. In addition, states could not deny a person the equal protection of the laws. Federal courts could now review almost any state action, thus permanently changing the nature of American federalism.

RECONSTRUCTION

The reconstruction period following the war was dominated by a Republican-controlled Congress intent on establishing full citizenship for the freedmen. Some southern states passed their own laws restricting the activities of former slaves, but Congress responded by passing a series of Reconstruction Acts to govern the southern states. In addition, federal troops were stationed in the South to ensure compliance with government directives. The last of these troops were withdrawn in 1877.

Though the reconstruction governments in the states did much to help blacks become involved in politics, learn to read and write, and find employment, many southern whites were unable to adjust to the social implications of black freedom. Their reactions ranged from the organization of terrorist groups such as the Ku Klux Klan to the passage of discriminatory laws segregating public facilities or limiting voter participation through literacy tests, poll taxes, and other means.

ECONOMIC DEVELOPMENT

An Industrial Giant. The industrial economy of the United States after the Civil War was fueled primarily by the North. Fortunes were made in railroads, oil, steel, and finance. Entering the twentieth century, the United States surpassed all other countries of the world in steel production.

Urbanization. The period from 1860 to 1910 also saw the rise of the city. New opportunities for industrial employment attracted large numbers of people from the countryside to the cities. But despite the opportunities, urbanization was not all positive. Rapidly growing cities produced slums, disease, unemployment, and miserable living conditions for those who could afford to live only in crowded, dingy tenement dwellings.

This urban expansion was further aided by a wave of immigration around the turn of the century. From 1880 to 1910, between 17 and 18 million people flocked to the United States, many of them from southern and eastern Europe. They often faced prejudice and discrimination and were often seen as a threat to those looking for jobs in America's industrial economy.

DEMANDS FOR REFORM

There were growing demands for reform in the late nineteenth century in response to government corruption, agricultural difficulties, and the abuses of big business. Attempts to organize labor met with only limited success. Farmers also tried to organize in order to become more competitive. Many activist farmers joined the Populist Party and hoped to gain political influence through their support of William Jennings Bryan in his unsuccessful 1896 presidential bid.

CANADA

The Seven Years' War between France and Britain ended in 1763 with the signing of the Treaty of Paris. The former French colony of Canada now became a British colony. This was a shock to French Canadians, as they were now ruled by British governors and their economic life was dominated by English-speaking businesses and merchants.

British Legislation

Acquiring a colony in Canada created a complex political situation for Britain. British forms of government were unfamiliar to the former French colony. In addition, the Roman Catholic Church was very strong among the French-speaking population of Canada.

THE QUEBEC ACT

The Quebec Act was passed in 1774 partly to deal with these issues. Quebec had the largest French-speaking population in Canada and was therefore the center of French cultural influence and potentially the focus of the greatest difficulty for the colony's new British overlords. The Quebec Act gave Quebec an appointed governor and council and made the Roman Catholic Church the established religion there.

THE CANADA ACT OF 1791

The Quebec Act was designed to placate French Canadians. But especially during the war for American independence, more and more English loyalists moved to Canada. French-speaking Canadians felt they were being overwhelmed, while the English-speaking colonists wanted the kinds of representative assemblies to which they were accustomed. In an attempt to ward off further tension, the British Parliament passed the Canada Act in 1791. This act divided the colony into Upper Canada (mostly English-speaking) and Lower Canada (mostly French-speaking). Each half had its own legislature. Although the new political arrangement did help to diffuse some of the immediate tensions, in the long run Anglo-French antagonism continued to be a major feature of Canadian political, economic, and social life.

Self-Government: The Dominion of Canada

As Canada struggled to define its national identity, it also moved closer and closer to self-government and independence.

UNION ACT OF 1840

A variety of issues led to a series of insurrections in Canada in 1837. In America the British had already seen what could happen when colonies rebelled. Though they were able to suppress the rebellions in Canada, they realized that a long-term solution would require governmental reform rather than merely calling out the army. Lord Durham was therefore sent to Canada as governor. His 1839 *Report on the Affairs of British North America* became a landmark along the road to self-government. Durham's recommendation that Upper and Lower Canada be reunited with a single legislature, an appointed governor, and a greater degree of control over their own affairs formed the basis for the Union Act of 1840. London continued to control foreign affairs and some other matters, but Durham's report set a precedent on which the British Parliament could draw as it wrestled with the problem of self-government in its other English-speaking colonies in Australia, New Zealand, and South Africa.

NORTH AMERICA ACT OF 1867

The Union Act did not solve all of Canada's problems, however. Anglo-French rivalry continued, as did concern about possible domination by

Canada's neighbor to the south, the United States. In an attempt to create an even stronger union, in 1867 the British Parliament passed the North America Act after much debate. Under the terms of this act, the recently united Ontario and Quebec were once more divided into separate provinces. They joined New Brunswick and Nova Scotia in forming the Dominion of Canada, with Ottawa as the capital. A parliamentary form of government was adopted, the use of both English and French was guaranteed by law, and all matters except foreign affairs were left in the hands of the Canadians. The British government appointed a governor-general to be the head of state and maintain Canada's close ties with the mother country.

JOHN A. McDONALD

Canada's first prime minister under the new federation was John A. McDonald. The most important Canadian political figure in the last half of the nineteenth century, McDonald was determined to strengthen the Dominion further by expanding across the continent. By 1873 this had been accomplished in a number of ways. The Northwest Territories were purchased from the Hudson Bay Company in 1869. In 1870, the province of Manitoba was created from a portion of this purchase. British Columbia (on the Pacific Coast) joined the Dominion in 1871, followed two years later by Prince Edward Island.

Canadian Pacific Railway. McDonald and his government were convinced that the eastern and western portions of the Dominion had to be tied together by something more solid than the new political arrangements. McDonald had persuaded British Columbia to join the federation in part by promising a transcontinental railroad. Such a railroad seemed the best way to unite regions with diverse interests. The Canadian Pacific Railway was completed in 1887, and other lines followed.

Impact of the Railroad. In addition to linking Canada's eastern and western provinces, the railroad also spurred settlement along its path. As towns grew and people and goods moved along the lines, two more provinces—Alberta and Saskatchewan—were added to the Dominion in 1905. The railroad made it easier to move Canada's mining and timber resources. It also facilitated the westward movement of the wave of immigrants who made their way to Canada in the late nineteenth and early twentieth centuries.

Relations with the United States

The relationship between Canada and the United States continued to be marked by tension. The War of 1812 against the United States was one of the few events of the early nineteenth century that could unite Canadians. After the war, border conflicts and trade disputes continued. There was also a fear in Canada that its rapidly growing neighbor to the south might dominate Canada as well—economically and culturally if not politically.

These fears meant that even the Canadian transcontinental railroad had to be seen as a mixed blessing—it contributed to the growth of the Canadian economy, but it also helped link the Canadian economy to that of the United States.

Political and cultural links with England, a strong French presence in Quebec, and concern about its relationship with the United States made it difficult for Canadians to forge a distinct, clearly defined national identity.

AUSTRALIA

Claiming a New Land

In 1770, Captain James Cook "discovered" Australia and claimed it for King George. Such action was typical of both European and, later, American imperialism. National self-interest on the part of technologically advanced and economically powerful nations led them to simply take over other lands, regardless of the feelings or desires of the native peoples. The assumption seemed to be that less advanced people had no claim to an area if that area was necessary to the political and economic interests of the great Western nations. This was the price of "progress."

AUSTRALIAN ABORIGINES

The land that Cook claimed for his king was already inhabited by perhaps 300,000 aborigines spread across the vast continent. Their economy was a meager one, based largely on hunting, gathering, and fishing. They had been relatively undisturbed by outsiders before the arrival of Cook (though a Dutch navigator had landed on their shores 130 years earlier), but they became the first victims of European settlement in Australia.

The impact of British imperialism on the Australian aborigines was not much different from the impact of European imperialism on native peoples in the Americas or Africa. As the land was taken over by white intruders, the aborigines were unable to maintain either their traditional culture or their traditional economic activity. Disease, alcohol, dislocation, slaughter, and racial mixing led to a rapid decline in the aborigine population.

A Penal Colony

At the time of Cook's voyage, Britain was experiencing a serious problem with overcrowded prisons. Until the time of American independence, Britain had sent thousands of convicts to penal settlements in its colony of Georgia. With that option no longer available, Australia seemed to be the perfect substitute.

BOTANY BAY

Accordingly, in 1788 a fleet of British ships unloaded its cargo of convicts at Botany Bay. The expedition was headed by Captain Arthur Phillip, who had been appointed governor of the new penal colony. Conditions were extremely difficult, food was in short supply, and morale was very low. But though the early years were difficult, the colony survived and a number of settlements were established, including one at Port Jackson (modern-day Sydney).

Economic Development

To the first European settlers and explorers, Australia did not appear very hospitable. But although economic exploitation was not the primary reason for the settlement of Australia, the island's movement from colony to nation was facilitated by the settlers' ability to sustain a growing population.

SHEEP AND WHEAT

It was not Australia's fate to remain a penal colony. In addition to prisoners, free settlers began to immigrate during the early nineteenth century. Their immigration was encouraged by the availability of land, which also encouraged freed convicts and discharged prison guards to stay. But when Australia's terrain and climate proved to be conducive to sheep ranching and wheat farming, the island colony had discovered the products that would give its economy a significant boost. Convicts were even moved from prisons to sheep ranches to provide manpower.

THE AUSTRALIAN GOLD RUSH

In the 1850s, the discovery of another Australian resource—gold—not only brought a wave of immigration, but also fostered the settlement of new towns in the southeastern regions known as New South Wales and Victoria. Improvements in transportation, communications, and public institutions such as schools and libraries were also encouraged by the influx of settlers.

Political Development

Though it was dominated by British settlers, Australia was actually a number of separate colonies. Within a decade of the passage of the Australian Colonies Government Act of 1850, however, all of the colonies except Western Australia had adopted some form of representative self-government.

ESTABLISHMENT OF THE COMMONWEALTH

This development did not necessarily guarantee unity, however. In fact, each colony continued to go its own way, making it difficult to achieve any kind of unified economy or political system. Perhaps motivated by the recognition that division made them vulnerable to outside forces, by the turn of the century the separate colonies had agreed to form the Commonwealth of Australia. The new federation officially came into being on January 1, 1901. Ten years later, membership was expanded to include the Northern Territories.

"WHITE AUSTRALIA"

Rapid immigration to Australia gave rise to new settlements and paved the way for unification of the colonies, but it also led to racial tensions, emphasizing a theme that repeated itself often in various parts of the world. Asians flocked to Australian gold fields, as they did in North America. They were met with prejudice and hostility. Labor unions feared that the "yellow" immigrants would lower wages and decrease the standard of living. White settlers pressured the government to exclude Asians, Pacific Islanders, and other undesirables. The result was the passage of the Commonwealth Immigration Restriction Act of 1901. No more Asians could enter.

LATIN AMERICA

The colonization of Latin America led, by the end of the nineteenth century, to political and economic dependence on Europe and the United States. Though independence was gained for most Latin American countries, it did not always bring with it the kinds of political, economic, and social changes that would promote stability.

An Overview of the Nineteenth Century

Latin American republics took various directions after their wars of independence, though there were enough common experiences to allow a few broad generalizations.

DICTATORIAL REPUBLICS

Unlike the United States and Canada in the nineteenth century, the Latin American nations did not achieve a high degree of political stability. The new states called themselves republics, but the general populace had no experience with self-government. The revolutionary leaders, usually creoles, were also inexperienced in political leadership. Conditions were ripe for political or military strongmen to concentrate power in their own hands, rewriting or ignoring constitutions in the process. These strongmen, called *caudillos*, were usually military leaders or men with strong ties to the military. "Revolutions" occurred regularly, but they brought no significant changes. Power continued to be concentrated in the hands of a privileged few, who had no intentions of sharing it.

ECONOMIC LIFE

Latin American wars of independence freed the states from direct colonial control, but they also disrupted the economic life of most countries. Slavery was eliminated over the course of the nineteenth century, sometimes aided by the independence wars. Freedom did not automatically translate into economic opportunity for former slaves, but the possibility of assimilation and improved social status was generally better than in the United States.

Economic Colonialism. Economic conditions improved somewhat in the second half of the nineteenth century. Much of this improvement was due to exports and increased foreign investment. The tradeoff, however, was that both of these factors increased dependence on foreign economies. The economic subservience of Latin America was perhaps most dramatically demonstrated in cases of intervention by the United States and Britain in order to protect their economic interests in Latin American countries. Among the enterprises fostered by foreign investment were mining, railroads, and the production of sugar, rubber, bananas, and coffee.

The Land Problem. Another characteristic of the nineteenth century was the continuing concentration of land into the hands of a few. Sometimes this happened when large landowners appropriated the holdings of families who were unable to prove ownership of the land they were farming. Many natives were driven from their lands, while those who stayed were often barely able to keep alive. Debt and dissatisfaction spread among the native population.

Immigrants. Latin America also experienced the same influx of immigrants as the United States. And as in the United States, immigration was part of the larger economic development that led to industrialization and urbanization. In contrast to some other parts of the world, immigrants generally assimilated well into Latin American life. Blacks and Indians, however, remained at the bottom of the social scale, perennial victims of prejudice and attitudes of superiority.

Mexico

Mexico provides an example of some of the problems that plagued many Latin American states in the nineteenth century. In Mexico, most of the nineteenth century was a time of political instability and economic stagnation. The country was ruled by a series of autocratic caudillos, the strongest of which was Antonio López de Santa Ana. He was finally driven into exile in 1835. Mines, which could have provided a major economic boost, were not producing well. Furthermore, with a poor transportation system and scarce capital, much of the economic infrastructure of the country was in poor condition.

FOREIGN INTERVENTION

Mexico's political and economic instability made it susceptible to foreign intervention. American colonists in Texas declared their independence in 1835. In 1846, the United States and Mexico went to war over a border dispute. In the treaty ending the war, the United States gained most Mexican territory north of the present border. In one of the most audacious examples of intervention, French troops invaded Mexico in 1862 to support the claim of the Austrian Archduke Maximilian to be emperor of Mexico—a claim supported by the Roman Catholic Church. Maximilian was ousted by insurgents within five years.

APPARENT STABILITY

Like many other Latin American states, Mexico called itself a republic. But in fact, its presidents were dictators. In 1876, Porfirio Díaz played on popular discontent and led a revolt that made him president. His dictatorship lasted until 1911. Díaz curried the favor of the church, the landowners, and the army. He thus enforced a kind of stability on the country (which was attractive to foreign investors), but below the surface there was discontent, poverty, and hunger among farmers and workers.

Brazil

Brazil should also be mentioned because, unlike the other areas of Latin America, it was colonized by Portugal. Brazil retained the Portuguese language and cultural heritage after independence. It was also one of the most stable Latin American countries.

PEDRO II

As was the case in many Latin American countries, Brazil went through a period of initial political instability immediately after independence. But from 1840 until nearly the end of the century, it was relatively stable under the rule of Pedro II. In 1889, however, several factors contributed to the overthrow of his monarchy. Pedro lost the support of the church, the army, and the people generally. He was forced into exile in 1889, and a new Brazilian republic issued its first constitution in 1891.

ABOLITION OF SLAVERY

As in the United States, perhaps the most serious political and social problem in Brazil was the continuation of slavery. All the other republics had abolished it shortly after independence; the Civil War had settled the question in the United States. Brazil was therefore isolated on this issue. But the Brazilian economy depended on sugar and coffee production, both of which used slave labor. Pressure continued to grow for the abolition of slavery, however. This pressure finally bore fruit, as slavery was legally abolished in 1888.

*T*he United States, Canada, Australia, and Latin America had much in common in the nineteenth century, but also many differences. For each it was a period of nation building. Those areas that were not politically independent from Europe at the beginning of the century became so during the century. The United States and the Latin American states achieved their independence through war, while Canada and Australia were able to achieve self-governing status peacefully. England apparently had learned a lesson about the power of rising nationalism and found it in its own best interest to cooperate with rather than resist what was happening in its distant dominions. Liberal, democratic governments held sway in the English-speaking nations, while in Latin America dictatorships continued to rule.

Both North American nations spanned the continent by the end of the century, displacing Native Americans as they did so. In Latin America the native peoples did not have the same experience, but they did find themselves in economic bondage to the landed gentry and occupying the lowest level on the social scale.

The United States and Latin America both had economies dependent upon slavery at the beginning of the century, but shortly after mid-century slavery was eliminated—as the result of a war in the United States, more peacefully in Latin America. Blacks, however, found it difficult to combat the racial prejudice that continued to exist in both places. Economically, the English-speaking nations developed viable, independent economies, as the industrial revolution swept over the United States and Canada especially. The Latin American economy, left in a shambles as a result of the revolutions, was strengthened at the end of the century by investors from Europe and the United States who were promoting an effective economic colonialism.

Selected Readings

Foner, Eric. *Reconstruction: America's Unfinished Revolution, 1863–1877*. New York: Harper & Row, 1988.

Hatch, Nathan O. *The Democratization of American Christianity*. New Haven, CT: Yale University Press, 1989.

Keen, Benjamin, and Mark Wasserman. *A Short History of Latin America*. 2nd ed. Boston: Houghton Mifflin, 1984.

Kraut, Alan M. *The Huddled Masses: The Immigrant in American Society, 1880–1921*. Arlington Heights, IL: Harlan Davidson, 1982.

McNaught, Kenneth William Kirkpatrick. *The Pelican History of Canada*. Harmondsworth, England; Baltimore: Penguin Books, 1982.

McPherson, James M. *Battle Cry of Freedom: The Civil War Era*. Oxford: Oxford University Press, 1988.

Molony, John N. *The Penguin Bicentennial History of Australia: The Story of 200 years*. Ringwood, Victoria, Australia; New York: Viking, 1987.

Tindall, George Brown. *America: A Narrative History.* New York: W.W. Norton, 1988.

Tocqueville, Alexis de. *Democracy in America.* 2 vols., 1835. The Henry Reeve text as revised by Francis Bowen, now further corrected and edited by Phillips Bradley. New York: Vintage Books, 1958.

11

Africa and the Islamic World to the End of the Nineteenth Century

1415 First Portuguese foothold established in Morocco

1464 Sunni leader Ali founds Songhai

1591 Songhai defeated by Morocco

1633 Jesuits expelled from Ethiopia

1787 Sierra Leone founded

1788 First British exploration of Africa

1795 Baptist Missionary Society founded in England

1798 Napoleon invades Egypt

1805 Muhammad Ali becomes ruler of Egypt

1807 British outlaw slavery

1818 Shaka becomes Zulu ruler

1822 Liberia founded

1830 The French colonize Algeria

1881 Mahdist uprising in the Sudan

1887 Egypt becomes a British protectorate

1923 Turkey becomes a new state, after Ottoman empire ends

In chapter 4 we saw how Muslims extended their religion, commercial activities, and political influence into much of Africa. Later (see chapter 13) we will deal with the "great scramble" that by the end of the nineteenth century resulted in the wholesale partition of the African continent among the major powers of Europe. Prior to considering that episode, however, it is important to look briefly at some of the indigenous peoples of Africa and the outside forces that impinged on their cultures even before the scramble.

In addition, we will take another look at the Ottoman empire and the other Muslim states beyond Africa as they clashed with Western powers. Various inherent weaknesses made the Ottoman empire increasingly vulnerable. Attempts at reform did not succeed in stopping its deterioration. By the end of the century it had lost Egypt as well as other areas to European powers, and it was ripe for its own destruction. Other Muslim states, also, were the objects of European acquisitiveness. Meanwhile, Fundamentalist reform movements led to internal uprisings that foreshadowed tensions that still exist in modern Islam.

AFRICA BEFORE THE "GREAT SCRAMBLE"

Africa is the second most populous continent on the globe. It is characterized both historically and in modern times by wide political, economic, and cultural diversity. A glance at some aspects of this diversity provides an African perspective on the significance of the great European rush for territory that took place at the end of the nineteenth century.

Regions and Peoples: Some Generalizations   Africa consists of several distinctive geographic regions. A brief consideration of some of them will help in placing the peoples who will be described in later sections.

NORTHERN AND WESTERN AFRICA

The Maghreb (northwestern coastal area), with abundant rainfall, is particularly fertile. The economy of its ancient Berber (Caucasian) population was basically agricultural, but a merchant economy also developed. Because of this trading contact, the Berbers mixed readily with blacks who had migrated to the Sudan and West Africa.

South of the coastal region is the largest desert in the world, the Sahara, which spans nearly the entire continent. The southern Sahara merges into the Sudan—an area dominated by plains and grasslands. It was the home of such important early kingdoms as Ghana, Songhai, and Kanem-Bornu. West and south of the Sudan is the great tropical forest region, forming a somewhat narrow band along the West African coast. In the vicinity of the Congo

River it extends inland to the center of the continent. The important kingdoms to develop in this forest region included Ghana, Benin, and the Yoruba states.

EASTERN, CENTRAL, AND SOUTHERN AFRICA

In eastern Africa, the region of Ethiopia is an extremely rich, fertile highland. From there one of the major tributaries of the Nile flows northward, and the Nile itself flows across Egypt. Along the banks of the Nile is a narrow strip of especially fertile soil, which provided the agricultural base for one of the world's greatest ancient civilizations. East of the Ethiopian highlands, bordering on the sea, is a dry plain known as Somalia, which provides a bare livelihood for the nomadic herdsmen who still make up a large part of its economy.

Much of Africa south of Ethiopia consists of high, grassy plateaus. Also located there are the Zaire and Kasai river systems as well as the great lakes, Victoria, Tanganyika, Malawi, and others. In the region of Victoria and Tanganyika are heavy forested areas. More tropical rain forest forms a very thin line along the eastern coast from the equator south. Inland from this narrow strip are more high grasslands and steppes (areas with few trees), extending almost to the southern tip of Africa. Across the continent the lower western coast contains another desert, the Kalahari. The southern tip of Africa is known as the Cape of Good Hope.

The peoples of Africa are made up of numerous language and ethnic groups. Their origins are obscure, but many people in central and southern Africa are descended from ancient tribes who participated in a long series of interior migrations. As migrants settled in different regions, the cultures they developed varied greatly, as did their languages—hundreds of them. The languages seem to have a common origin, however, and those who speak them are often classified as Bantu-speaking peoples. The economies of all Africa's regions were basically agricultural, though important trading activities provided some economic ties centuries before the Europeans arrived. They also contributed to considerable ethnic mixing.

THE TRANS-SAHARA TRADE

Long before the sixteenth century, a thriving trans-Sahara trade grew up between the Sudan, northern Africa, and the people in the rain forests of West Africa. It developed most fully after the eighth century, when the camel came into use and revolutionized desert transportation. Agricultural products of all sorts were involved, but the most important commodities were gold and salt. Gold was produced in several places in West Africa, and became important not only as an export but also for ornamenting the elegant dress and furnishings of West African royalty. But salt was considered just as valuable, for it was in short supply in other parts of the Mediterranean world and in the Sudan. Often mined by slaves, it was found in rich abundance at several sites in the Sahara. Islam came to the Sudan partly as a result of the development of this trade.

Kingdoms Large and Small: A Few Examples

Before the nineteenth century Africa saw the rise and fall of numerous kingdoms, some large, some small. The most important, historically, was ancient Egypt. Some African states were ruled by powerful kings or princes with near-monarchical powers and centralized government; others might be described as confederations of tribes loosely bound together because they paid tribute to a common king. Some states as well as tribes were held together principally by family and kinship ties.

THE MAGHREB

Early in the Christian era the people of the Maghreb were under the domination of the Roman empire, which spread Christianity to the area. With the Arab conquests of the seventh century, however, the Muslim faith was established, entirely replacing Christianity. Eventually most of this area except Morocco was incorporated into the Ottoman empire.

AXUM, ETHIOPIA, AND CHRISTIANITY

One of the great ancient kingdoms in northeastern Africa was Axum. In the fourth century one of its most powerful kings, Ezana, converted to Christianity, and by the sixth century most of the kingdom was Christian. Characterized by strong Coptic (Egyptian) influences, this was the distinctive form of Christianity found there when European traders and missionaries intruded into Ethiopia over 1,000 years later. The kingdom of Ethiopia was composed, in part, of intermingled descendants of Axumites and Cushites. It was a powerful state at the beginning of the sixteenth century, but incursions from several sources created disorder and weakness. At one point Jesuit missionaries tried to establish Roman Catholicism, but they were expelled in 1633; Coptic Christianity remained the basic Ethiopian faith. In later years, Ethiopia was the only major African state to retain its independence from a European takeover, even though Italy had strong ambitions there.

KANEM-BORNU AND HAUSALAND

Another early kingdom, located in north central Africa in the region of Lake Chad, was Kanem, which flourished from about 800 to 1300. Kanem became a great Muslim state, with a commercial economy based largely on the slave trade. After its decline another kingdom, Bornu, rose on its heels and remained a powerful state through most of the seventeenth century.

Further west, meanwhile, the Fulani people were overrunning Hausaland, an area consisting of numerous small but powerful states. Constantly at odds with each other, these states were finally united by the

Fulani as the result of an Islamic *jihad* (religious war) early in the nineteenth century (see below).

GHANA AND MALI

On west coast of the Sudan, the kingdom of Ghana (not to be identified with the present state of Ghana) flourished from the eighth to the beginning of the thirteenth century. An extremely wealthy commercial empire, it traded in salt and gold (both produced elsewhere). Politically it was one of those strong confederations in which the tribal rulers paid tribute to the king. After the decline of Ghana, the kingdom of Mali took its place and expanded. Mali was ruled much like Ghana, except that a standing army was created to secure the power of the king.

SONGHAI

Mali went into decline in the fifteenth century, to be replaced by the rising kingdom of Songhai. This great commercial empire was in large part the creation of a member of the Sunni dynasty, Ali, who began his reign in 1464 and immediately set out on a conquest of the entire region. He captured the important commercial cities of Timbuktu and Jenne in 1468 and 1473, respectively. By the time of Ali's death in 1492, Songhai controlled all the great trading and cultural centers of the Sudan. His successor, the Muslim *askia* Muhammad Toure, strengthened the administration of the state by establishing a centralized government. He also divided the empire into regions, appointing administrators over each, and created a strong standing army. Under Muhammad Toure the city of Timbuktu gained increased stature as an important Islamic center of learning and faith. The city was also economically prosperous and the home of many artisans, craftsmen, and merchants.

Songhai slowly declined in the sixteenth century, however. One factor in the decline was the rise of European trade along the western coast, which began to interfere with the overland trade with Morocco. In 1591, therefore, the sultan of Morocco sent an army across the desert, that quickly defeated Songhai. After this defeat the area broke into numerous small tribal states, constantly at war with each other. In the process, they fed the rapidly growing slave trade along the Gold Coast, which soon became one of the great slave markets of the world.

THE FOREST KINGDOMS

A number of important kingdoms rose and fell in the West African forest region. One was a confederation of Yoruba states known as Oyo, which flourished between the fifteenth and late eighteenth centuries. At that time civil strife began to undermine whatever unity these states had, and the area was finally taken over by the British in the late nineteenth century.

Benin. East of Oyo, the well-known Edo kingdom of Benin reached the peak of its grandeur in the fifteenth and sixteenth centuries. Its culture was characterized by great art work, particularly in bronze and ivory. Among the first West African states to be influenced by European contacts, by the end of the fifteenth century it had begun to trade with the Portuguese. European influence, including Christianity, was not as great here as in some other places, but some of the Edo princes did study in Lisbon. A variety of internal weaknesses led to its decline and eventual absorption by the British in 1897.

Dahomey. Influenced much more profoundly by European incursions was Dahomey (west of Oyo), which arose in the seventeenth and eighteenth centuries. In 1730 it was conquered by Oyo and remained a tributary state until it regained its independence 100 years later. In the meantime, its leaders cooperated with the Europeans in promoting the slave trade, reluctantly at first but under the pressure of economic necessity. More than any other state, Dahomey eventually decimated its own interior population through slave raids. Its economy became almost dependent upon that ruthless form of human exploitation.

The Ashanti Union. Farther west, the Ashanti kingdom resulted from a union of smaller states in the late seventeenth century. It expanded in the next two centuries, extending over most of modern Ghana. At the same time, the Fante union was attempting to challenge the growth of Ashanti, but it never achieved the same unity. Ashanti eventually developed a powerful centralized state.

EASTERN AFRICA

In eastern Africa, many kingdoms had come and gone by the time the Europeans arrived. The most extensive, Mwena Mutapa, built by Bantu-speaking people who had migrated into the area centuries before, arose in the general area of modern Zimbabwe. A highly cultured, wealthy area, it declined in political power after Portuguese contact. It was soon taken over, however, by a new set of rulers, the Changamire, who remained strong until the 1830s.

European Influence and the Slave Trade

Before the fifteenth century the most direct outside influence on the African people came from Islam. Beginning early in that century, however, the European quest for wealth and a new route to Asia brought unsettling new influences that eventually had a profound effect on the continent's culture and political structure.

EUROPEANS IN SEARCH OF WEALTH

The Portuguese came first, establishing a foothold on the Moroccan coast in 1415. Gradually they moved down the west coast of Africa, established a few stations, rounded the Cape of Good Hope, and ranged up and down the east coast. Mozambique became the only permanent Portuguese foothold there, however. In the early sixteenth century they had established a great commercial empire in the East, with African stations as major supports. In the process, they also discovered that Africa had many riches for the taking—especially gold and slaves.

The Portuguese were soon followed by the Dutch (see chapter 2) and later by the English and French. The latter two groups were attracted by the slave trade, which became important to the development of their colonies in America. Eventually they took over much of the slave trade, except for the Portuguese foothold in Angola, in southwestern Africa.

EUROPEAN INFLUENCE

Throughout most of Africa, however, European contact was minimal until the nineteenth century. European incursions were, in fact, successfully resisted in many areas. But there were inevitable influences, especially along the Gold Coast of West Africa. Many small communities were transformed into active trading centers. In some cases this changed the political structure of the area by bringing to power new princes who gained economic strength through cooperation with the Europeans. These princes resisted European incursions into the interior, but they happily cooperated in coastal commerce.

Europeans also had an influence on the lives of some African peoples by introducing a number of new products into their diets and their trading systems. Maize and cassava (various tropical plants with edible roots), for example, became staples in some areas. Africans were also introduced to tobacco and alcohol by the Europeans. Other new products included jewelry of various sorts and firearms. In exchange, the Europeans took away gold, ivory, animal skins, spices, and slaves. Eventually the slave trade overshadowed all other economic attractions, even gold.

THE SLAVE TRADE

Even though Europeans were responsible for the evils of the transAtlantic slave trade, they did not introduce slavery as such to the Africans. In some areas it had existed since ancient times. Prisoners of war were sold into slavery. The early Muslim conquest contributed something to that process, for Islam justified the enslavement of infidels. Long before the Europeans came, many slaves were working in mines and on farms, though for the most part they were employed in households. In some cases they were even appointed as advisors to kings and thus enjoyed considerable prestige.

The Europeans, however, brought a new dimension to the slave trade. In some areas the trade had little effect, but in parts of West Africa whole populations were diminished to a mere fraction of their original strength.

Slavery also brought a new set of values—it was not just prisoners of war who would be enslaved, but one's own people or the people of neighboring tribes. In some cases new social classes arose, as powerful African families or trading houses began to dominate the trade.

It has been estimated that the total number of slaves exported from Africa, mostly to the Americas, between 1450 and 1900 exceeded 11 million. Perhaps the worst horror of the slave trade was the infamous "middle passage." Slave ships were designed for maximum efficiency, which meant that slaves were shackled and virtually crammed into tiny individual compartments with room only to lie down. They were seldom, if ever, taken on deck for air. It was a rare slave ship that made the trans-Atlantic voyage of several weeks without many deaths. Added to all this was the indignity of being branded and then auctioned off at an American slave market. The slave trade was humiliating and dehumanizing to the worst degree.

ATTEMPTS TO REPRESS THE SLAVE TRADE

Beginning with Great Britain, however, by the middle of the nineteenth century there was a strong movement toward the abolition of slavery. Among the most vigorous early agitators in Britain was a former African slave, Olaudah Equiano, also called Gustavus Vasa the African. In 1807 the British Parliament outlawed slavery, making it illegal for any British subject to participate in the practice. The following year the United States outlawed the slave trade, though not slavery itself. But the trade continued clandestinely as long as there was a profit to be made. Britain then set about putting pressure on other Western governments also to outlaw slavery. France made it illegal in 1815, and other nations began to put some restrictions on the trade. Their efforts, however, were largely ineffective.

Opposition to Abolition. Surprisingly, much of the opposition to abolition came from Africans themselves. There were a variety of reasons, but many had become accustomed to slavery as an economic fact of life. Efforts to persuade them to find alternative trade goods went largely unheeded, especially when it was clear that abolition could be an economic disaster not just for individuals but for whole states.

Slave Treaties. Late in the 1830s the British began to negotiate treaties with individual African chiefs. In return for subsidies the chiefs agreed to work for the abolition of the slave trade in their own areas. In addition, Christian missionaries and other traders began to work with interior peoples in an effort to move them toward agriculture and alternative trade.

SIERRA LEONE AND LIBERIA

All these efforts slowly began to reduce the number of Africans being enslaved and exported annually. In addition, two new African states were established with the idea of bringing freed slaves back to Africa from Europe and America. The first settlement at Sierra Leone, sponsored by a group of British humanitarians, began in 1787. The colony did not prosper at first, but ex-slaves from Britain and elsewhere continued to arrive. In 1808, however, the British government made Sierra Leone a crown colony, partly because it needed a naval base in Africa from which to carry out operations against the slave trade. It was not long before Sierra Leone's fortunes improved somewhat.

In the United States, the American Colonization Society was founded in 1818 for the purpose of colonizing former American slaves in Africa. After 1822 the little colony of Liberia slowly established itself south of Sierra Leone, but neither the American government nor the American Colonization Society provided much political help. Unlike Sierra Leone, after 1841 Liberia elected its own black government, so it became an experiment in self-government as well as colonization. Sierra Leone, however, attempted to dominate the colony, and there were continuing tensions between the two groups. Finally, in June 1847 Liberia proclaimed itself to be a sovereign republic and promulgated a constitution patterned after that of the United States.

Explorers and Missionaries

Although the slave trade, supplemented by gold and other trade goods, provided the incentive for most of the early European contact with Africa, beginning in the late eighteenth century Europeans broadened their interest. Scientific curiosity, economic motives, continuing interest in abolishing the slave trade, and religion were all important factors in the European penetration into the interior.

EUROPEAN EXPLORATION

The first British explorations were conducted under the auspices of the African Association, founded in 1788. This association sponsored Mungo Park, who in his expeditions of 1795 to 1796 and 1805 discovered the course of the Niger River. The French also sent expeditions into the interior in the early nineteenth century. Later in the century such explorations were stepped up. Their results will be commented on in chapter 13, in connection with the "great scramble" at the end of the century.

CHRISTIAN MISSIONS

Christian missionaries had found their way into some parts of Africa as early as the fifteenth century. Their efforts were renewed on a permanent basis early in the nineteenth century. The first society organized specifically to send missionaries to Africa was the Baptist Missionary Society, founded in 1795. Others followed, not only in Britain but also in France, the Netherlands, and the United States. At first they concentrated mostly on the coastal region of West Africa, but after they discovered that quinine could help combat the danger of malaria, they moved inland. In some areas there was considerable resistance; the missionaries had their greatest success only after European colonization.

Instruments of Change. Significantly, the missionaries were bent on changing the African people in more ways than simple conversion to Christianity. They also tried to stop such traditional practices as slavery, human sacrifice, polygamy, tattooing, secret societies, and even traditional forms of dance and dress. In short, they did everything they could to Europeanize as well as Christianize the African people. Education was all-important, and the missionaries were bent on teaching Africans how to read and write. At the same time, the missionaries conscientiously studied the African languages and reduced many of them to written languages.

The creation of an educated elite among the Africans had at least two long-range side effects. For one thing, it helped create new divisions and tensions among Africans themselves. In addition, it sowed seeds of division between Europeans and educated Africans when the latter discovered that some of their missionary-teachers supported eventual European takeover of their independent states. In the twentieth century, these same feelings would have their effect on the movement for decolonization.

Holy Wars and New African States

THE JIHADS

Religion played still another role in the nineteenth century, this one related to Muslim imperialism. Muslims were living peacefully beside Africans practicing their own native religions, but they were losing political power. In some cases they were also losing the right or ability to conform to certain Muslim standards. Reformers among the Muslims, therefore, became dismayed. This resulted in a series of violent jihads at the end of the eighteenth century and in the first half of the nineteenth century. The most successful occurred among the Fulani in Hausaland, beginning in 1804. Its leader, Usman dan Fodio, was a learned Muslim teacher who wanted to restore the pure principles and practices established in the days of the Prophet. By the time his successor, Muhammad Bello, died in 1837 the holy war had resulted in a new Muslim state that was still intact when the British later took over the area. There were other Sudanese jihads—one in Macina, west of Hausaland, that took place about the same time; another began nearby in 1851 and eventually came in conflict with and overwhelmed Macina. Similar uprisings took place elsewhere, some ending more successfully than others.

ZULU

Many other new states arose in Africa before the final onslaught of European colonialism. One was the great Zulu nation in southern Africa, formed by tribes of Bantu-speaking peoples as they came into conflict with each other in their expanding quest for land. Several of these tribes were united for the first time under a brilliant military strategist named Shaka, who ruled Zulu from 1818 to the time of his death in 1828. Shaka developed a highly disciplined military, even organizing women into fighting regiments. One of his great innovations was a short spear that his soldiers used for stabbing rather than throwing—that way they would not only be more accurate but would also not lose their weapons after one throw. Shaka's conquests, known as the *Mfecane*, affected Zulu people for thousands of miles around. They devastated many areas and set in motion mass migrations to other parts of the continent. Some of these groups wreaked havoc of their own as they marched across the territories of other people. The Zulu nation later came into direct conflict with the Boers after their Great Trek to the interior (see chapter 13.)

All this constitutes only a cursory sketch of the complex currents of religion, politics, and economic development within Africa before the European scramble to absorb it all at the end of the nineteenth century. Meanwhile, there were many other important developments within the major Islamic states of the Near East. Their early development has already been discussed in chapter 4. Here we will take their story through the nineteenth century.

THE NEAR EAST IN THE NINETEENTH CENTURY

The nineteenth century witnessed the total collapse of the old Islamic world order in the face of European economic and military imperialism. India was completely conquered and remained a British colony for nearly a century and a half. Iran remained independent but was reduced to economic and military impotence. Central Asian Islamic khanates were overwhelmed and conquered by the Russians. North Africa was colonized by the French, while Islamic societies in western and eastern Africa also became European colonies. Nearly all of the Balkan provinces of the Ottoman empire rebelled and obtained independence during the nineteenth century. Although the Ottoman empire survived, it too was reduced to military impotence and saw one of its prize provinces, Egypt, first become an independent state and later a British colony. By the end of the nineteenth century, most of the Islamic world was directly ruled by European elites, while those regions which remained independent, Iran, Afghanistan, and the core of the Ottoman empire, all came under European domination.

Challenges to the Ottoman Empire

THE WEST

Muslim leaders were able to ignore their deteriorating situation until Napoleon's invasion of the Ottoman province of Egypt in 1798. His quick defeat of the Egyptian army brought the military weakness of the Islamic world into sharp focus. This was no longer a case of European powers nibbling on the edges of the Islamic empires; Napoleon had struck at the heartland of the Islamic world. He was expelled only by an Ottoman alliance with England. Thereafter, the Ottomans increasingly became dependent on military aid and technology from Europeans.

INTERNAL REBELLIONS

The Ottoman empire also faced a series of internal rebellions. In the early nineteenth century, various Christian regions of the Balkans rebelled with European encouragement and achieved independence from the Ottoman empire (see chapter 13). In Arabia, a fundamentalist Islamic rebellion led by the Wahhabis united many of the bedouin tribes, winning several victories over the Ottomans and temporarily capturing the holy cities of Mecca and Medina. The Druze in Lebanon and the Armenians also revolted, leading eventually to a series of bloody massacres. The most serious threat to the Ottomans, however, came from the rebellion of Muhammad Ali in Egypt.

MUHAMMAD ALI AND EGYPT

Muhammad Ali was an Albanian Muslim mercenary in Ottoman service who emerged as the most powerful man in Egypt following the expulsion of the French in 1801. In 1805 the sultan appointed him as pasha (ruler or governor) of Egypt. In the following years he consolidated his power against his nominal Ottoman lords by suppressing rival bands of warriors and confiscating large estates, creating state monopolies on many of Egypt's most lucrative products.

Muhammad Ali, sometimes called the "father of modern Egypt," was the most successful of early modern Muslim reformers. He instituted land reform, a tax system, and government along European lines, laying the foundation both for prosperity and government finance. He brought Egypt into the world economy, making it one of the world's major producers of cotton. Modern printing presses and education systems were introduced. Finally, Muhammad Ali reformed the military along European lines, making Egypt the most powerful state in the Near East. During his reign Egyptian forces successfully campaigned in the Sudan, Arabia, Syria, and Anatolia. He was prevented from overthrowing the Ottoman Empire by French and British intervention. The French and British did, however, pressure the Ottomans into recognizing the hereditary right of Muhammad Ali's family to rule Egypt. In actuality, the Ottomans had practically no power at all left in Egypt.

THE BRITISH TAKE OVER EGYPT

At the death of Muhammad Ali in 1848 Egypt was the most powerful state in the Near East. A series of events over the next several years, however, led to the decline of Egyptian power and an eventual British takeover. Muhammad Ali's successors did not have his military and administrative genius; many proved to be incompetent. The completion of the Suez Canal in 1869 made Egypt of vital strategic importance to the British as a link to their colonies in India and Africa. But modernization, including the canal, proved to be very costly, which led to a major foreign debt. When the world cotton market collapsed following the reopening of the U.S. cotton trade to the world market after the American Civil War, Egypt's cotton industry collapsed, and Egypt was unable to pay its international debts. In 1875 it defaulted on its loans and the British took control of state finances and the Suez Canal. After putting down a nationalist uprising in 1882, Britain made Egypt a protectorate.

OTTOMAN ATTEMPTS AT REFORM

It soon became apparent to Ottoman leaders that their military, at least, required drastic reform. The first major reform efforts in the Ottoman empire were undertaken under the rule of Mahmud II (r. 1808–1839). Using European models and advisors, Mahmud attempted to reform the army and government. Powerful forces opposed to these reforms, such as the elite military group known as the Janissaries, were brutally crushed.

The European Model. In order to implement these reforms, many Turkish and Egyptian military officers were sent to Europe for education in the technologies and sciences necessary for a nineteenth-century military system. While in Europe, these officers learned European languages, gaining access to the culture and ideas current at the time. They thus returned to the Near East with a wide range of new ideas about government, democracy, religion, and the social order. Ironically, though these officers were sent to Europe to learn the technological skills needed to bolster faltering dynasties, they returned with ideas that put them among the chief avenues for the introduction of Westernization into the Near East. As a result, during the last half of the nineteenth century, many leading intellectuals in the Islamic world and India were agitating for the creation of European-style parliamentary governments and social reforms.

Success and Failure. Paradoxically, the nineteenth century reform movements were both a success and a failure. Successful agricultural reforms and the modernization of medicine increased life expectancy but created a massive population explosion, resulting in little real improvement in the standard of living for most people. The introduction of Western ideas on government and society led to pro-democratic political upheavals, revolutions, and social unrest. Most importantly, however, despite some remarkable successes of modernization in the Near East, Europeans always remained ahead, with their economies and technologies advancing exponentially faster than those in the Near East. Near Eastern peoples thus entered a period of a century and a half of playing unsuccessful "catch up" with the West.

The Nature of Colonialism and Imperialism: Generalizations

European colonialism and imperialism in the Islamic world followed a number of different patterns. In many cases intervention began as attempts to secure economic advantages, control of trade routes, and safe ports. As Asian trade began to play an increasing role in European economies, the security of the trade routes and ports became more important. Military intervention was thus justified. In order to defend the port cities, surrounding territory needed to be "secured." Each new acquisition of territory brought the Europeans in contact with new hostile powers, which again threatened security, thereby requiring further military intervention. By the early nineteenth century, many European leaders had decided that the only permanent solution to the problem was the establishment of protectorates or colonies in all strategic areas in the Near East.

More Incursions into Islam

As noted above, the British began territorial expansion in India in the eighteenth century. The Russians conquered much of Turkestan during the nineteenth century. Iran and Afghanistan remained semi-independent but became British or Russian protectorates with a "no man's land" between British India and Russian Central Eurasia. Coastal regions of Arabia, such as Aden, became British protectorates in order to secure ports and trade routes. The French intervened in Algeria by sending colonists in 1830; in 1848 it became part of France. France, Spain, and Germany quarreled over Morocco, but by 1912 most of it was under a French protectorate. France vied with Britain and Italy over Tunisia, but it became a French protectorate in 1881.

THE DEMISE OF THE OTTOMAN EMPIRE

By the end of the nineteenth century, only the Ottoman empire remained as an important independent Muslim state. Nonetheless, the Ottoman state was in a gravely weakened condition and retained its territory in the face of French, English, and Russian expansionist threats only through close military ties to Germany. Ottoman rule lasted in Libya until 1911, when Italy annexed it after declaring war on Turkey. In the end, continuing Ottoman efforts at reform proved too few and too late. In the twentieth century a group of liberals known as the "Young Turks" deposed their autocratic ruler and instituted more reforms. During World War I (see chapter 14), however, they made the mistake of joining on the side of Germany and Austria-Hungary. After the war the empire was broken up and occupied by foreign powers. From its ruins arose a new Islamic state, the Republic of Turkey. It was formally recognized in 1923.

Reaction to European Domination

The peoples of the Near East reacted to European domination in various ways.

WESTERNIZATION

Many Near Easterners attempted to copy the social, political, economic, and military structures of the West. Agriculture and industry were reformed based on European models; land was redistributed from landlords to peasants. Military, legal, and government systems were Westernized. Parliaments and European-style law codes were introduced. In many ways these reform efforts were of limited success, affecting only the educated elites. On the other hand, substantial advances in agricultural productivity, health care, and education were made. Government liberal and democratic reforms were frequently superficial, with military cliques holding the real core of power.

RESISTANCE

Some Muslims, while recognizing the value of Western technologies and social reforms, were unwilling to accept the European political and

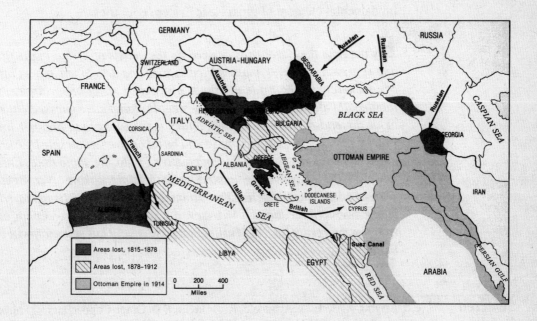

Fig. 11.1   The Decline of the Ottoman Empire

economic domination which often accompanied reform. Opposition to Europeans manifested itself on many different levels. Near Eastern governments had frequent wars with Europeans, which they invariably lost. Smoldering discontent would occasionally surface in anti-Western disturbances and riots. Nonetheless, the Europeans' superior technology and military power was sufficient to allow them to maintain control in the Near East.

Islamic Fundamentalism. Many see Islamic Fundamentalism as a recent development in the Near East, but much of the resistance to Western imperialism in the nineteenth century manifested itself as Islamic Fundamentalist movements. The most famous was the uprising in the Sudan under Muhammad Ahmad, who declared himself the long-awaited Mahdi (messiah) in 1881. The Mahdist state lasted until 1898, when it was overthrown by the British. Followers of this movement still play an important role in the politics of modern Sudan. The Wahhabi movement in Arabia (1746–1818) was initially directed against the Ottomans. In its later manifestations in the twentieth century, however, it culminated in the creation of the kingdom of Saudi Arabia. These and other related movements represent a trend toward radical anti-Westernism, which is still an important force in the Near East. Although most Muslims did not participate in these extremist movements, it is clear that the Islamic religion as a whole successfully withstood a century and a half of European imperialism. Few Muslims were converted to Christianity, and basic Islamic beliefs and practices remain a fundamental element of most Near Eastern countries.

By the time the Europeans arrived on the coasts of Africa in the fifteenth and sixteenth centuries, many African states had developed important paths of commerce, strong trade relations, and a number of important centers of intellectual and artistic activity. Few people would have guessed either then or at the end of the eighteenth century that in less than another hundred years nearly all these kingdoms would be taken over wholesale by European powers. That story will be told in chapter 13. At the same time, European powers were also making incursions into Islam, taking over Egypt and several other Muslim states. The Ottoman empire finally disappeared early in the twentieth century. It was never restored, but the twentieth century would see a resurgence of Muslim independence. That story too will be told in later chapters.

Selected Readings

Afigbo, A. E., E. A. Ayandele, R. J. Gavin, J. D. Omer-Copper, and R. Palmer. *The Making of Modern Africa. Volume 1. The Nineteenth Century.* Essex, England: Longman Group Limited, 1986.

Gailey, Harry A., Jr. *History of Africa. Volume II. From 1800 to Present.* Huntington, NY: Robert E. Krieger Publishing Company, 1981.

Hodgson, Marshall G. S. *The Century of Islam. Conscience and History in a World Civilization. Volume Three. The Gunpowder Empires and Modern Times.* Chicago and London: The University of Chicago Press, 1974.

July, Robert W. *A History of the African People.* New York: Charles Scribner's Sons, 1980.

Shaw, Stanford J. *History of the Ottoman Empire and Modern Turkey.* 2 vols. New York: Cambridge University Press, 1976.

12

Early Modern East Asia: China, Japan, and Korea

1600	Battle of Sekigahara, Tokugawa forces victorious
1614	Christianity banned in Japan
1644	Establishment of Ch'ing (Manchu) rule in China
1661-1722	Reign of K'ang-hsi emperor in China
1735–1796	Reign of Ch'ien-lung emperor in China
1793	McCartney mission to China
1839–1842	Opium War
1850–1864	Taiping Rebellion
1853	Commodore Perry arrives in Tokyo Bay
1860	Anglo-French march on Peking
1868	Meiji restoration
1871–1873	Iwakura mission
1876	Treaty of Kanghwa (Japan and Korea)
1884–1885	Sino-French War
1889	Meiji constitution promulgated
1890	Japanese Diet (assembly) convenes
1894	Tonghak Rebellion in Korea
1894–1895	Sino-Japanese War

1900	Boxer Rebellion
1904–1905	Russo-Japanese War
1910	Japanese annexation of Korea
1912	Abdication of last Manchu emperor of China

Early modern China, Japan, and Korea were all countries traditionally influenced by Confucian theories of statecraft and social relations. From the seventeenth century into the nineteenth century, they all enjoyed stable governments. And until the nineteenth century, all of them were able to dictate the pace and extent of their foreign contact.

But all of this changed dramatically beginning in the nineteenth century. A combination of internal and external pressure brought each of these states into the twentieth century in a different way. China spiraled toward disintegration. Japan pursued the goals of rapid industrialization and overseas expansion. Korea was caught up in the whirlpool of international politics, eventually to be absorbed by Japan.

CHINA: THE CH'ING DYNASTY TO 1800

The rise and fall of the Ch'ing dynasty (1644–1911) was the final turning of the "dynastic cycle" that to many Chinese seemed to be the pattern of their history. Like many previous dynasties, the Ch'ing dynasty rose vigorously, but eventually entered a period of decline that corresponded with pressure for concessions from outside powers. The end of the dynasty came not from external invasion as much as from the inability of the Chinese government to hold the loyalty of key segments of Chinese society. But the weakened state of the Ch'ing dynasty in the century before its demise should not cause us to ignore the fact that the Ch'ing period was a time of considerable vigor and accomplishment in Chinese political, economic, and cultural life.

Rise of Ch'ing

By 1644, the decline of the Ming dynasty had reached an advanced state. This made it relatively easy for Li Tzu-ch'eng's rebel band to take the capital of Peking, causing the suicide (by hanging) of the last Ming emperor. Li had little chance, however, to attempt to set up a dynasty of his own. In the area to the northeast now known as Manchuria, loose tribal groupings had evolved into a more centralized political and military structure by the early seventeenth century. In 1636, the ruler of this federation, Abahai, took the name Ch'ing for his dynasty. (This was the year after Abahai had adopted the name "Manchu" for his people. The Ch'ing dynasty is therefore sometimes referred to as the Manchu dynasty.) In the 1620s and 1630s the Manchus invaded Korea. They did not take over the government of that peninsular nation as they did in China, but they did force the Koreans to grudgingly accept a position of formal subordination to the Ch'ing state. Though relations eventually became predictable and smooth, many educated Koreans retained a sense of "Ming loyalty."

CHINA CONQUERED

Abahai himself hoped to conquer China, but he died in 1643 before being able to realize his dream. That task fell to Abahai's brother, Dorgon. In 1644, as Peking was in chaos due to Li Tzu-ch'eng's rebellion, Dorgon led an attack southward. The Chinese general in charge of border security, Wu San-kuei, threw in his lot with the Manchus rather than lend legitimacy to a traitorous rebel. Li's fate was thus sealed, and his followers fled. The Manchu army occupied the capital, and Dorgon installed Abahai's young son as the new emperor.

CONTINUITY WITH MING

Despite the fact that the Manchus ruled China by conquest, they maintained a considerable amount of continuity with the Ming dynasty they had replaced. This was done largely by design. China's Manchu conquerors realized that although they might be militarily superior to China, they were vastly outnumbered by the Chinese. In addition, the Chinese had a centuries-old tradition of centralized rule, while the Manchus had relatively little experience on which to draw. It made sense, therefore, to follow established patterns of statecraft that had already been proven both acceptable to the Chinese and effective in administering the affairs of such a vast realm.

The Bureaucracy. If they were to rule China successfully, the Manchus would have to win the support (if not initially the devotion) of the Confucian-educated elite. These were the people who staffed the Chinese bureaucracy. At the local level, those who did not make it all the way into the central government bureaucracy were the leaders of rural society. One of the ways in which China's new rulers attempted to win the support of this class was to point out that they had come to restore order—a cherished objective in Confucian thought. Wu San-kuei, the general whose acquiescence had facilitated the initial Manchu advance, had been persuaded to side with them at least in part because of their promise to punish the usurper Li Tzu-ch'eng and give the deceased emperor a decent Confucian burial. And this they did after entering Peking. It did not change the fact that the Ming dynasty was no more, but it was an important symbolic act which helped calm (though it did not eliminate) continuing Ming loyalism.

The Manchu leaders continued to staff the Ch'ing government with Chinese officials, both as a practical matter and for public relations purposes. Much of the structure of the Ming state was retained. There was no effort to replace Chinese culture with that of Manchuria. In fact, the Manchus continued a process of "sinification" of their own state that had begun even before the conquest of China. Because being "civilized" was traditionally more important in China than the place from which a person came, the Manchus' ability to adopt and continue traditional Chinese practices was a major reason that anti-Manchu sentiment was not a major issue during much of the Ch'ing period.

Ethnic Distinctions. This is not to say that the Manchus did not recognize differences between themselves and the Chinese. In order to preserve some cultural and ethnic distinctiveness, Chinese emigration to Manchuria was forbidden for most of the Ch'ing period, as was intermarriage between Chinese and Manchus. In addition, at least at the top levels of the government, the Manchus tried to create a balance between Manchu and Chinese officials. (Chinese officials continued to be predominant at all but the highest levels.) But for the most part, the Ch'ing period is marked by continuity with the Ming.

Structure of the State

The structure of the Ch'ing state reflected the Manchus' desire to create as little disruption as possible in the functioning of state machinery in China.

THE MANDATE OF HEAVEN

The emperor continued to reign from the capital at Peking. In theory, the emperor had absolute power in China. Confucian theories of statecraft stated that the ruling dynasty, and the reigning emperor in particular, possessed a "Mandate of Heaven" sanctioning their control. This is not to be confused with the idea of "divine right" that buttressed many absolutist monarchs in Europe. The Chinese concept of "heaven" was much more amorphous than the God of Christianity. Nevertheless, as the "Son of Heaven," the Chinese emperor was seen as the crucial link between the affairs of this world and whatever was beyond this world. But despite the fact that the emperor was theoretically absolute, in reality any emperor's ability to exert control depended on how well he was able to control the bureaucracy. There were always elements within the Chinese government anxious to act in the emperor's name if he did not have the personality or the political will to exert his own prerogatives.

ADMINISTRATION

Below the emperor, the Ch'ing government was organized into six boards (or ministries), again following the Ming pattern. These boards reflected the primary areas of government concern: Revenue, War, Rites,

Justice, Personnel, and Public Works. Provincial governors were dispatched throughout China from the central government. They were responsible for every aspect of life in the province to which they were assigned.

Magistrates. Below the governors were the district magistrates, the lowest level appointees from the central government. The magistrate was the real link between the central government and local society, but the typical magistrate was faced with an impossible task: to manage the affairs of an average of 250,000 people. In 1800 there were around 1,600 of these magistrates. There was no "official" government below them. Their responsibilities included collecting and forwarding taxes, maintaining order, administering the lowest level of the civil service examinations, taking care of social welfare, and solving any problems within their districts. Their salaries were not miserly, but their expenses were high and they were given no money for a staff. In addition, the "law of avoidance" stipulated that no district magistrate could serve within or near his home district. From the central government's perspective, this was done to ensure loyalty by making it difficult for a local official to build up any kind of power base from personal connections. (Governors and magistrates were also rotated regularly to achieve the same purpose.) But from the perspective of the local official, this meant that he might not know the local dialect, he was probably not aware of the specific pattern of local society in which he had to operate, and he could not automatically assume that he would be able to easily pursue his objectives just because he came with the prestige of an imperial appointment.

"Unofficial" Employees. The magistrates found that they had to rely on private secretaries and runners, recruited from the local population, if they were to have any hope of fulfilling their responsibilities. These "unofficial" employees were the ones who did much of the real work of local government. There might be several hundred of them in any given county. But because the magistrate had no budget for their salaries, they had to be paid by levying extra fees for their services.

A Top-Heavy Structure. The Chinese government was a top-heavy structure. For the most part, local society was self-governing, with a shell of central government over it. There were far more private secretaries and others carrying out government responsibilities in an unofficial way than there were actual officials of the central government. Furthermore, a large number of central government officials were in the capital, rather than in the provinces where the vast majority of the population lived.

Chinese Society

SOCIAL STRUCTURE

Ch'ing China was an overwhelmingly agricultural society. As discussed in chapter 3, Chinese social theory officially held to a social order in which peasants were esteemed just below the scholar-official class and above artisans and merchants. This hierarchy recognized that although the scholars might be the rulers, the peasants were the backbone of the state. The connection between the structure of the state and the actual functioning of local society was personified in the local magistrate, who was the state's representative but had to operate within the framework of local society. And in truth, though the "commoners" (below scholar-official rank) were classified into three broad groupings, none of these groups was homogeneous. Each could be further subdivided into smaller groups enjoying greater or lesser prestige, wielding greater or lesser local influence, and possessing greater or lesser wealth.

EXAMINATION SYSTEM

In theory, in China (unlike Japan) almost any male could potentially become a member of the civil service. Government service was still the preferred career objective for ambitious young men. And the examination system did provide for a certain amount of social mobility in China. But in practice the odds were against a peasant succeeding in the examinations. The incredible amount of study time needed to prepare for the examinations was the luxury of the wealthy, leisured class. For those who actually did succeed, the rewards could be considerable: prestige, tax exemptions, eligibility for government service, and possibly access to the corridors of power in Peking.

The Economy

The majority of China's population, then, continued to work the land. They were taxed on land holdings, but people of privilege found ways of winning exemptions from some taxes and having other taxes applied at a lower rate.

COMMERCE

There was also a considerable amount of commercial activity in China, which both contributed to and benefited from increasing urbanization. Trading took place over both land and water. Ships traveled not only along the Chinese coast, but along the internal waterways as well. The Yangtze River in particular, which can be navigated upstream for hundreds of miles, became the lifeline for growing commercial centers. The three-city complex known as Wuhan, for example, some 500 hundred miles from the coast up the Yangtze, became a national grain market.

LANDHOLDING

Landholding patterns changed somewhat during the Ch'ing period. During the seventeenth and eighteenth centuries the tenancy system became freer, resulting in more small landholders who rented land on a regular basis. By the end of the eighteenth century, there was much more freeholding than there had been in the first half of the Ch'ing period. Part of this change was

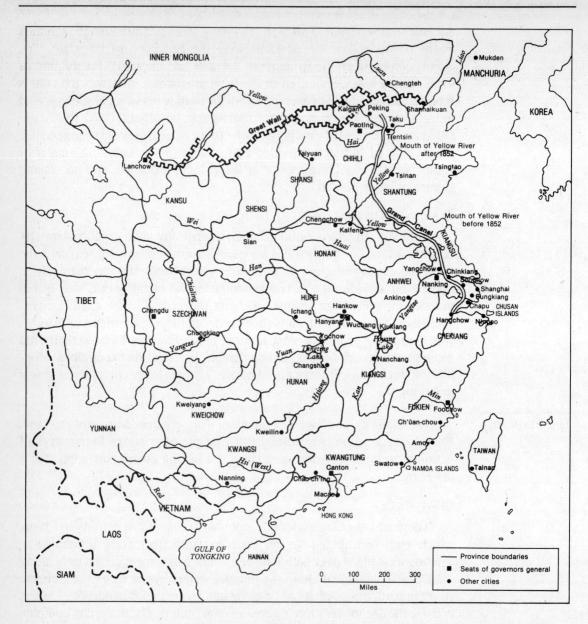

Fig. 12.1   China Under the Ch'ing

due to laws concerning the social status of peasants and to pressure brought to bear by the government as it tried to break up some of China's large hereditary estates.

The Middle Ch'ing Period

After the early years of consolidation and pacification, the Ch'ing dynasty settled into a period of prosperity, peace, and growth. China had a total of ten emperors during the 268 years of Ch'ing rule, but two emperors—

K'ang-hsi (the second emperor, reigned 1661 to 1722) and his grandson Ch'ien-lung (the fourth emperor, reigned 1735 to 1796)—accounted for 121 of those years. They were capable and effective rulers, preferring a hands-on approach to government affairs.

CH'IEN-LUNG

Ch'ien-lung was a great patron of scholarship and the arts. In one of the most remarkable scholarly undertakings in human history, he commissioned the compilation of a huge collection of classical Chinese literature, known as the *Complete Library of the Four Treasuries*. The work was begun in 1772 and took two decades to complete, resulting in 36,000 volumes. In addition to a catalog of over 10,000 titles (grouped into the four "treasuries" of classics, history, philosophy, and belles lettres), nearly 3,600 complete works were included in the collection, though in the course of the compilation possibly as many as 2,000 other books, considered dangerous or unorthodox, were destroyed. Ch'ien-lung also collected art works of all kinds. Ch'ien-lung retired from the throne in 1796, not desiring to offend standards of filial piety by ruling longer than his grandfather.

DECLINE OF CH'ING

Despite the fact that China had some vigorous emperors during the early and middle Ch'ing period, by the nineteenth century the emperor's position had seriously declined in importance, except as a symbol. Central government authority was increasingly in the hands of the Grand Council and other top insiders. The nineteenth century also saw another development that would hold even greater consequences for the future of the Ch'ing dynasty: a shift in the balance of power away from the center and toward the provinces. A combination of decay from within and pressure from without meant that by 1800, the Ch'ing dynasty's most vibrant days were behind it.

PRESSURE FROM THE WEST

The end of a period of vigorous imperial rule in China coincided with an increased desire on the part of Westerners to trade with China. Most trade to this point had been one-sided in favor of China. The Chinese had items the Europeans wanted to buy (spices, silk, porcelain, tea), but the Europeans could find nothing the Chinese were willing to buy in large quantities. As a result, European traders had a sizable trade deficit with China. But the persistent Westerners were determined to stay in China. They wanted not only the goods the Chinese produced, they wanted to penetrate the potentially huge Chinese market as well.

The Canton System and British Efforts to Change It

However, the Chinese lack of interest in what the West was bringing (whether missionaries or trading goods), combined with a cultural predisposition to look down on commercial activity, led Chinese leaders to place strict limits on the trade that was allowed. Westerners (primarily British and Dutch) could trade only at Canton, in southern China (safely away from Peking). And even in Canton they were subject to restrictions on mobility and lifestyle. This approach to foreign trade has become known as the "Canton system."

SIR GEORGE McCARTNEY

The British finally lost patience with this system and attempted to change it. In 1793 King George III sent Sir George McCartney at the head of a mission to try to establish "normal" diplomatic relations with China. The British emissary never really had a chance to present his case, however. The fiasco is an indication of just how far apart the two sides were in their assumptions about dealings between countries. For centuries, the Chinese had considered foreign representatives to be bearers of tribute from their home countries. From the Chinese perspective, the payment of tribute was the price willingly paid for access to the higher civilization that emanated from China. Lord McCartney, also bearing gifts, looked for all the world like another tribute-bearing foreign envoy. McCartney, however, had no such thoughts. As the personal representative of his king, he was not about to perform the ritual of prostrating himself before the emperor three times and knocking his head on the floor as a sign of submission, which was required of all foreign emissaries (a ritual popularly known in English as "kowtow").

MATTERS OF FORM

There was no office specifically concerned with foreign affairs until very late in the Ch'ing period. Rather, relations with other states were dealt with through the Board of Rites. In other words, they were to some extent matters of ritual. It would not be entirely accurate to say that in foreign affairs the Chinese were more concerned with form than substance. For China's rulers, at least, form *was* substance in many areas of life. Lord McCartney's refusal to conform to matters of form meant that he was never able to get to the matters at the heart of his mission. Another mission in 1816, led by Lord Amherst, had a similarly unfruitful ending.

Tea and Opium

THE VALUE OF TEA

The main item the British were interested in buying from China was tea. Tea was in many ways a more attractive commodity than were luxury goods because nearly everyone in Britain drank it; it was affordable by a majority of the population. British traders also supplied Chinese tea to British colonies overseas. The main trader in tea, the East India Company, found in tea a lucrative trading item back home, but also a necessary one. The Company's conquest of India in the mid-eighteenth century had been financed by the crown, and profits from the tea trade were used to pay back the debt. And the government had its own interest in the tea trade beyond repayment of loans: it levied a 100 percent duty on imported tea.

TEA AND COTTON

The difficulty for the British was that they had no item that the Chinese would buy in sufficient quantities to keep the trade going. Initially, the British traded Indian cotton from their plantations there, but British demand for tea was such that the merchants had to supplement Indian cotton with cash payments in silver, creating a negative balance of trade. Two developments in the late eighteenth century increased the problems for the British. First, the American Revolution ended England's easy access to New World silver. Second, the Chinese began shipping their own raw cotton from the north, along the China coast, to Canton, where it could be sold at a lower price than Indian cotton. More than ever before, the British needed to find a product that could replace not only Indian cotton in the tea trade, but silver as well.

THE OPIUM TRADE AND ITS CONSEQUENCES

It turned out that India was well suited for the growing and refining of opium, a highly addictive drug that had been used medicinally in China for hundreds of years. This seemed like the perfect answer to Britain's trade dilemma. Their Indian colony was put to good use producing opium, there seemed to be a large market for the drug in China (and the practice of giving out free samples did not hurt business), and the East India Company was able to get all the tea they could transport by this means. In fact, so popular did opium use become in China that the balance of trade was quickly reversed. Now silver was flowing out of China in large quantities.

Opium and the Economy. Opium smoking was prohibited in China, but this did not prevent the British and their employees from continuing to sell it. In effect, the British craving for tea was satisfied by drug smuggling. By the 1830s the opium trade amounted to millions of silver dollars and hundreds of tons of opium annually. In addition to its debilitating effects on users themselves, the opium trade had a serious negative impact on the peasant economy, which was the basis of the entire national economy. There were two currencies in China, copper and silver. Farmers used copper for most small transactions, but taxes had to be paid in silver. This meant that a farmer had to exchange copper for silver in order to pay taxes. Currency exchange, like other economic transactions, follows the law of supply and demand. As silver flowed out of China, it became more expensive for farmers to obtain the needed silver to pay their taxes. Because tax rates did not vary with the rate of exchange between copper and silver, the opium trade resulted in sudden, steep tax increases on China's peasants.

The government finally decided that forceful action was necessary. The emperor appointed Lin Tse-hsu to go to Canton and resolve the problem. A capable bureaucrat, Lin was determined to take whatever steps were necessary to put an end to the traffic in opium. He was quite successful, in fact, in shutting down the internal supply network and rounding up Chinese drug dealers, but he wanted to go further and attack the problem at its roots. This meant demanding that the British merchants agree not to continue bringing the drug into the country. Lin's efforts fell short here. Though they did turn over some 21,000 chests of opium (which they had not been able to sell anyway due to Lin's crackdown), the British merchants refused to sign an agreement that they would end the opium trade permanently.

The Opium War. At this point, the dispute went beyond words and legal arguments, resulting in what is known as the Opium War (1839–1842). The Chinese were ill-prepared to take on the force of British firepower and were plagued by tactical mistakes. After a series of one-sided battles, the Chinese were forced to accept British surrender terms. The Treaty of Nanking, signed in 1842, was supplemented and elaborated upon by later treaties. Key provisions of the treaties included the opening of several Chinese ports to foreign trade, the ceding of Hong Kong to the British, the establishment of a low tariff on Western goods, the right of foreign nationals to be tried by courts of their own country rather than by Chinese courts (a practice known as "extraterritoriality"), and most-favored-nation rights for Western nations (guaranteeing that China could not grant a concession to one country without granting it to all). All of these terms had the effect of limiting Chinese sovereignty. For this reason, the treaties signed with the British and other Western powers have come to be known as "unequal treaties." They were not so much negotiated as they were dictated by the victors. The Opium War settlement set the pattern for Chinese foreign relations through the nineteenth century and into the twentieth.

The Opium War as a Clash of Cultures. The Opium War (and another round of fighting and treaties in the years between 1856 and 1860) was as much a clash of cultures as it was a clash of arms. The Chinese, content with what their culture and economy had to offer them and comfortable in centuries-old patterns of foreign relations that kept them at the center of their world, were not prepared to change their assumptions about how the world operated just because the Westerners wanted them to. England, on the other hand, was building an overseas empire in an age when political and economic competition would not allow them to back down—both for reasons of national pride and for fear that some other country would replace them in the China market. The Chinese were accustomed to dealing with other states as tributaries; the British were unwilling to accept inferior status, insisting instead on having their diplomats accepted as the equals of Chinese officials and their sovereign as the equal of the Chinese emperor, the Son of Heaven. Finally, the Opium War dramatically demonstrated some of the early effects of the Industrial Revolution on the history of the world. Europeans could now forcefully project their power around the globe, enabling them to build political and commercial empires unheard of before. Despite China's millennia-old tradition of cultural brilliance and technological sophistication, it was not prepared to deal with this new threat from the West. Much of China's history during the 150 years following the Opium War is a story of struggle to shake off the yoke of imperialism and regain its position at the forefront of the world's civilizations.

Dynastic Weakness, Reform, and Decline

The final seventy years of Manchu rule in China were marked by continued Western pressure, internal rebellion, and efforts at reform and strengthening. Following the signing of treaties opening Chinese ports to foreign trade and later treaties that specifically included the right of missionaries to propagate their faith, Westerners were much more of a presence in China than ever before. The British were the predominant presence, but they were joined by the French and other foreigners. The Opium War had not ended the opium trade. Foreigners continued to export tea and silk from China and to import opium and other goods. By the end of the nineteenth century, Chinese tea had declined in importance as a trade item with the increase in production of Indian tea.

THE TAIPING REBELLION

In the middle of the nineteenth century, the Chinese government had to face a threat more immediate and serious than Western pressure. The Taiping Rebellion was the most serious rebellion of the Ch'ing period and came close to toppling the dynasty. A frustrated civil service aspirant named Hung Hsiu-ch'uan had gathered around himself a band of followers, initially from disadvantaged or marginal elements of Chinese society. They were originally a religious group, called the Society of God Worshipers. Claiming to have received visions from God, Hung fashioned a theology and social ideology that combined elements of Christianity with classical Chinese ideas. By 1850, the Ch'ing government saw Hung's burgeoning group as a threat, with its call for ousting the Manchus and establishing a "Heavenly Kingdom of Great Peace" (*T'ai-p'ing t'ien-kuo*, from which is derived the name "Taiping Rebellion"). Imperial forces were dispatched to suppress the movement, but they were unable to defeat the tenacious Taiping rebels. The central government finally had to call on regional commanders to organize armies to fight the rebels. In the process, the government granted numerous concessions to these regional armies. But it was these forces that finally defeated the

Taiping Rebellion in 1864, at great cost. Estimates of loss of life over the course of the rebellion range as high as 40 million. In addition, much of the important lower Yangtze River valley, where the Taipings held out in the city of Nanking beginning in 1853, was devastated. The Ch'ing dynasty was saved, but at the expense of a considerable amount of central government authority. The balance of power in China now shifted to the provinces, the domains of the regional commanders who defeated the rebellions that plagued China in the mid-nineteenth century.

FAILURE OF REFORM

The Chinese made several efforts at reform in the last half of the nineteenth century. While these reform efforts indicated that there was still life and some flexibility left in the dynasty, none of them seemed able to reverse dynastic decline. There were, in fact, some very creative minds at work in China, trying to find solutions to China's problems. Their quest for answers took them from ancient Chinese tradition to new Western ideas and everywhere in between. But one of the biggest problems with reform efforts was that the government itself was not united around reform objectives. As a result, the reformers, the most important of whom were not palace officials, were never able to count on the support of the government. While some of China's political, economic, and military reforms may have helped the dynasty survive as long as it did, in the end they did not create a strong, unified state.

THE IMPACT OF FOREIGN IMPERIALISM

The last decade or so of the nineteenth century was the heyday of imperialism in China, as in many parts of the world. China was involved in disputes with one foreign power after another during these years. A territorial dispute with Russia ended with the signing of a treaty in 1881, but this was a rare case of a potential conflict being settled by negotiation. There was a different outcome in Indochina (Vietnam). In 1884 and 1885, China and France went to war over the issue of French dominance in an area that had traditionally been in China's sphere of influence. The French won the war, winning reparations, greater commercial rights, and recognition of their position in Indochina.

But the conflict that really demonstrated China's weakness was not against a Western power, but against Japan. China's defeat in the Sino-Japanese War of 1894 and 1895 not only demonstrated the power of an invigorated Japan, but it also undermined any confidence Western powers had in China as a result of earlier reform efforts. The foreigners thus began to divide China up into spheres of influence—a process that has sometimes been likened to "carving China up like a melon." Increased foreign pressure led to a variety of reactions, ranging from intellectual movements to violence.

The Boxer Rebellion. The last angry reaction against the foreign presence in China came in 1900, when a group of rebels known as Boxers (because they had initially organized as martial arts groups) laid siege to the foreign legation quarters in Peking. The siege was lifted by a multinational force, which then rounded up and executed many Boxer leaders. It was not the first time Western forces had marched on Peking (a combined British and French contingent had done so in 1860), but a new element was added, foreshadowing things to come. This time, the foreign force included Japanese soldiers.

THE FALL OF THE CH'ING DYNASTY

Sun Yat-sen. By 1911 the Ch'ing dynasty was weak, life was getting harder in the countryside, radical ideas were becoming more widespread, and China's semicolonial status was as apparent as ever. Sun Yat-sen, a farmer's son who was educated in Hawaii and Hong Kong, made several unsuccessful attempts to lead revolts that would overthrow the government. He was more successful at fund raising and organizing than at revolution, however. Throughout the first decade of the twentieth century the number of adherents of Sun's "Revolutionary Alliance" grew to around 10,000.

The Dynasty Toppled. Though Sun is often credited with being the "father" of the movement that finally toppled the Ch'ing government, the dynasty's fall is not attributable solely to Sun's organization, personality, or ideas. A combination of radical youths, disaffected soldiers, angry peasants, and indifferent officials, united less by common objectives than by the accident of timing, proved too much for the weakened dynasty to bear. This was demonstrated convincingly by a provincial rebellion that began in Wuhan in October 1911. In February 1912 the last Manchu emperor, the young boy Pu-yi, abdicated, clearing the way for the establishment of a republican government.

Aftermath. But while a republic was indeed established in China, first under the presidency of Yuan Shih-k'ai and later under Chiang Kai-shek, the new government was unable to unite the disparate elements in Chinese society. Instead of a peaceful transition to republican rule, China slipped toward chaos. In the absence of an effective central government, regional power fell into the hands of warlords. Chinese history from the fall of the Ch'ing dynasty to the victory of the Chinese Communist Party in 1949 is largely a record of struggle to recreate order and unity, with the continual threat (and sometimes the reality) of both civil war and external invasion.

THE TOKUGAWA PERIOD IN JAPAN (1600–1868)

The two and a half centuries during which Japan was ruled by the Tokugawa family was a time of general peace, but below the surface there were important social, political, and economic changes at work. These changes came to the surface in the nineteenth century, just as the West began to pay renewed attention to Japan.

The Tokugawa Settlement

When Tokugawa Ieyasu defeated his foes at the Battle of Sekigahara in 1600 (see chapter 3), he emerged as the preeminent military figure in Japan. He was awarded the title of *shogun* in 1603. The shogun was the man who, in the name of the emperor, was responsible for running the affairs of the country. His government, generally known as the shogunate or *bakufu* (military government), was the actual center of political power, while the emperor reigned above the political fray in his traditional capital of Kyoto. Tokugawa Ieyasu's base of operations in Edo (now called Tokyo) became the seat of his government and the *de facto* political capital of Japan. But because the victory at Sekigahara had not resulted in the complete extinction of their enemies, the Tokugawa family had to find ways to control potential threats to their position.

Controlling the Daimyo

THE PROBLEM

Tokugawa Ieyasu's most immediate problem was how to control the *daimyo*, lords of large domains that covered the majority of the country. All of them officially pledged loyalty to the Tokugawa family, but the Tokugawa family's position was not so unassailable that they could rely simply on pledges. The Tokugawa even classified daimyo according to their supposed loyalty, distinguishing between those who had been allies prior to 1600 and those who pledged their loyalty only after Sekigahara. There was also a small group of daimyo who were related to the Tokugawa family. Some of the so-called "outer" (*tozama*) daimyo—those whose loyalty was the most suspect—happened to possess some of the largest domains.

CONTROL MEASURES

The Tokugawa instituted various measures designed to control the daimyo and thus maintain stable rule for their family. The most important of these was the so-called "alternate attendance" system. Each daimyo was required to spend half his time in Edo and half in his domain. This served several purposes. The most obvious is that it gave the Tokugawa a chance to keep close watch on the daimyo while they were in Edo (normally every other year, though the specific arrangements could vary). But there were other aspects to this system as well. When the daimyo left Edo to return to his domain, he had to leave his wife and his heir behind, in effect "hostages" to the shogun to ensure the daimyo's good behavior. In addition, the expense involved in maintaining large households both in Edo and in their domains and in making the regular trips between the two places (during which the daimyo would be accompanied by a large number of retainers) was a serious drain on daimyo finances. This was part of the intention behind the system, since a daimyo spending large sums of time and money traveling to and from Edo would have less of both to devote to building an army or plotting against the government.

Other control measures included government inspection of castle repairs and regulations on marriages between daimyo families; the Tokugawa also retained the right to move daimyo from one domain to another in order to make Japan's strategic layout more pleasing to them.

Foreign Policy: The Closed Country

The Tokugawa government also instituted an official "closed country" foreign policy. This policy was adopted in part to prevent coastal daimyo from benefiting by foreign contact. But the government was also worried about the possibility that Christianity might undermine social order. The first half of the seventeenth century was a time of severe persecution of Christians, with tens of thousands losing their lives.

THE DUTCH EXCEPTION

Foreign travel was outlawed, and foreign trade was severely curtailed. Although trade with China and Korea continued, Western trade was cut off with the exception of the Dutch. The Tokugawa concluded that of all Europeans, the Dutch were the least interested in spreading Christianity. They were therefore allowed limited trading privileges at the island of Deshima, off Nagasaki. Because these Dutch traders were the only regular contact between Japan and Europe for centuries, so-called "Dutch scholars" (*rangakusha*) became an important source for the limited knowledge of the Western world that entered Japan.

Because Japan is an island nation, the policy of seclusion was generally enforceable. As a consequence, Japan experienced both the advantages and the disadvantages of developing in isolation from the outside world.

Economic Changes

The Tokugawa economy was based on intensive agriculture. The village was the basic administrative and economic unit in the country. The village as a unit paid taxes, contracted for water rights, and took responsibility for the behavior of its residents; villages tended to be semi self-sufficient.

COMMERCE

One of the most important economic changes during the Tokugawa period was the increasing commercialization of the Japanese economy. This was spurred by the growth of cities, many of them based on castle towns. The concentration of population in cities meant that markets were available for farmers who could produce more than they needed. Eventually, individual farmers and even entire villages began to produce specialized, market-oriented goods. Regional trade led to a network of larger trading centers.

STANDARD OF LIVING

Though economic development was uneven, there was a general rise in the standard of living during the Tokugawa period. There were a number of reasons for this. One was the fact that more land was being brought under cultivation through reclamation and assarting (clearing out trees or bushes in order to make land arable). Because peasants knew that taxation was regular and predictable, they had an incentive to produce a surplus to keep for themselves or sell. In addition, technical improvements (tools, fertilizer, and draft animals), better water control, and new crops all resulted in an overall increase in agricultural production during the Tokugawa period. During the first half of the Tokugawa period, cultivated land may have doubled in productivity. Population also increased in the early Tokugawa period, but it apparently leveled off sometime in the eighteenth century and may even have been on the decline by the end of the period.

THE NEW MERCHANT CLASS AND URBAN CULTURE

The increasing diversification and specialization of the Japanese economy led to the growth of a merchant class that moved goods from one part of the country to another and sold them. Looked down upon in the official Confucian ideology, merchants were nevertheless a vital part of the Tokugawa economy. And with the increasing commercialization of the economy, many merchants became very wealthy. But they had few opportunities to use this wealth, as they were effectively cut off from direct political influence and the government passed sumptuary laws that limited other ways in which they might spend their money. As a result, concurrent with the rise of cities as commercial centers, there was the development of a rich urban culture, fueled by the money of the merchants. Beginning in the late seventeenth century there was an explosion of art, literature, theater, and pleasure seeking, drawing themes from what the Japanese referred to as the "floating world" (*ukiyo*)—a world that was as much psychological and emotional as physical. "Eat, drink, and be merry" might have been the watchwords of the new urban culture.

Strains in the System

But the very changes that led to cultural and economic growth during the Tokugawa also led to problems. In spite of economic development, the shogunate and many daimyo found that they were in economic difficulty. They were spending more than they brought in. There were few options for solving this problem, none of them especially attractive. They could raise taxes, but they then ran the risk of inciting peasant protests. The growing merchant economy was not taxed as rapidly as it grew, which left more money available for merchants to spend on the pursuit of pleasure, but also added to their frustration with a system that left them wealthy but lacking in power and prestige commensurate with their wealth. The government tried to deal with its financial shortfall through such methods as cutting the stipends of bureaucrats and acquiring loans (forced or otherwise) from the wealthy merchant houses, but there was a limit to how far such measures could be taken.

SOCIAL PROBLEMS

There were also social problems in the late Tokugawa period, including the growth and rearrangement of class distinctions. The gap between the weathy peasants and the rest of the farming population grew. And despite an official social ideology that placed the warriors (samurai) at the top of the social order and the merchants at the bottom, the merchants with their great wealth slowly began to encroach on some areas of samurai privilege. This was demoralizing to many samurai (who, as a group, had already been reduced from actual fighting warriors to bureaucrats in Japan's peacetime government), who saw in this an indication that the system that had supported them for centuries was breaking down. There were many peasant rebellions during the Tokugawa period for a variety of reasons, but their number increased dramatically in the nineteenth century. As strains in the old social and political system increased, the major groups in Japanese society—samurai, peasants, and merchants—found that they had less of a stake in the continuation of that system.

EFFORTS AT REFORM

The Tokugawa government and individual domain governments were not blind to the problems that plagued the country, and they attempted various kinds of reforms to address those problems. Kenneth Pyle has offered a useful generalization of these reform efforts as being either "fundamentalist" or "realist" in their approach. The "fundamentalist" approach sought to "restore the fundamental or 'purer' conditions of the early Tokugawa Period. Idealizing a purely agrarian economy, this approach sought in various ways to suppress or at least restrain the growing power of the merchant class. It stressed retrenchment in government and revival of the moral values of simplicity, austerity, and frugality." The "realist" approach, on the other hand, "accepted the growing commercialization of the economy and urged the authorities to adjust to it, not deny it." The fundamentalist approach was the dominant one, but in the end all reform efforts fell short of solving the many problems plaguing the government.

The End of the Closed-Country Policy

COMMODORE PERRY

In July 1853 an American naval officer, Commodore Matthew C. Perry, sailed into Tokyo Bay at the head of a small squadron of ships. He bore a letter from President Millard Fillmore requesting trade and diplomatic relations with Japan. It is important to note that this expedition was headed by a military officer; Perry was prepared to back up his demands with force, if necessary.

RESPONSE TO THE WEST

The arrival of Perry, though expected, caused a crisis in Japan. Many in Japan wished to continue the traditional policy of seclusion. But the Japanese knew of the Chinese experience with the British and did not have to experience Western military might firsthand to know that they were up against a formidable force. The Chinese experience also showed what defeat in war would mean for Japan: the same kind of humiliation that China had suffered at the hands of a Western power. The Tokugawa government finally gave in to Perry's demands; in 1858 a treaty was signed with the United States, the first of a series of treaties with Western nations. These treaties contained many of the provisions that were part of the "unequal treaties" signed with China, including the opening of ports and extraterritoriality.

The Meiji Restoration

Shogunate authority continued to decline in Japan, as the government proved incapable of making a strong stand one way or the other in the face of the foreign crisis. Resentment toward the government only increased after the signing of the treaties. With the shogunate no longer able to command the loyalty of the daimyo, the emperor reemerged as the only symbol capable of uniting the country. Ironically, the Tokugawa government had paved the way for this development by taking the extraordinary step of soliciting the emperor's opinion on how to deal with the insistent foreigners.

SATSUMA-CHOSHU ALLIANCE

Disaffection from the government was especially potent in the two domains of Satsuma and Choshu. Traditionally antagonistic toward the Tokugawa, these two domains were also among the largest, strongest, and most financially healthy of all the domains in Japan. When they formed an alliance against the Tokugawa government and were joined by samurai activists from other domains, the days of Tokugawa rule were numbered.

THE EMPEROR RESTORED

In January 1868 the leading anti-shogunate daimyo, now in control of the imperial palace in Kyoto, issued a declaration in the name of the young emperor stating that Tokugawa rule was at an end. In theory, at least, the Meiji emperor (as he came to be known) was restored to a position of both reigning and ruling in Japan. This event, the "Meiji restoration," was symbolized by the emperor moving from Kyoto to Edo—renamed Tokyo—and taking up residence in the shogun's former palace.

Foreign pressure in Japan had not necessarily created the conditions for the Meiji restoration. There was plenty of resentment and need for reform without the added element of the foreign crisis. But the Western presence did act as a catalyst, accelerating the crisis within Japan brought on by all of the social and economic changes of the Tokugawa period and the inability of the central government to respond adequately to those changes.

THE MEIJI PERIOD (1868–1912)

The reign of the Meiji emperor was a time of swift change in Japan. It was the time when Japan emerged as a rapidly industrializing power. It was also the time when Japan began to flex its new muscles overseas, as it began building an empire in Asia that would grow until Japan's defeat in World War II.

Political and Social Changes

The Meiji Restoration was followed by a period of rapid reform. Some would even call the period a political and social revolution. Thomas C. Smith refers to the Meiji Restoration and its aftermath as "Japan's aristocratic revolution." In one of the most remarkable episodes of political reform in history, members of Japan's traditional ruling class—the samurai who had carried out the restoration—systematically eliminated the exclusive privileges of their own class in order to release the energies of the nation and build a nation that was united on a stronger basis than before.

The changes were far-reaching. In 1869 all legal class distinctions were abolished. Now no one was limited to certain privileges or occupational pursuits simply because of birth. By 1871 the domains were eliminated, many of them becoming provinces tied to the new central government. In some cases, former daimyo were appointed provincial governors, easing their transition into the new order. Universal male military conscription replaced the hereditary warrior class in 1873.

ROLE OF THE EMPEROR

All of these changes were carried out in the name of the emperor. It is important, however, to understand the crucial difference between the position of the emperor in Japan and China. In China, the emperor was actually a political player. As has been discussed, while it was possible for a Chinese emperor to remove himself from regular involvement in government affairs, many Chinese emperors were very active, preferring to handle as much state business as possible. The fact that the emperor was closely involved in politics and was therefore in some sense responsible for the success or failure of state policies is probably one reason why the Chinese emperor was unable to survive the upheaval of the early twentieth century. In Japan, on the other hand, the emperor's primary importance lay in his symbolic power. The emperor had not consistently been an active political decision-maker for centuries before the Tokugawa period. The emperor was the symbol of the nation, the link between the Japanese people and their mythical past, and as such he remained aloof from the political fray. It was in large part this aloofness that allowed the position of the emperor in Japan to survive not only the end of Tokugawa rule in 1868, but also Japan's destruction and defeat in World War II.

WESTERNIZATION

The leaders of Japan's new Meiji government were determined to create a strong, unified nation that was the equal of the Western powers. Learning from the experience of China, they wanted to keep the West at bay by adopting the very tools that made the West powerful. They were agreed, therefore, that Japan needed to adapt to the West and, especially, undergo major technological reform in order to create a powerful industrialized nation. Ultimately, the Japanese leadership was determined to achieve reform of the unequal treaties as soon as possible. Until this was accomplished, Japan would never be seen as the equal of the West.

Studying the West: The Iwakura Mission. Japan's leaders therefore determined that they must study everything about the West. In 1871 a good portion of the new government embarked on an overseas mission, under the leadership of Iwakura Tomomi, to study Western societies. Those who went abroad became convinced that Japan must institute changes even more far-reaching than those already implemented. The Iwakura mission was a powerful impetus for institutional change; the Japanese fashioned much of their new social, economic, and political structure after what they saw in Europe and the United States.

THE MEIJI CONSTITUTION

Finally, in 1889 the new Meiji constitution was promulgated, with the two-house national assembly (Diet) convening for the first time the following year. Apparently these reforms satisfied observers in the West. The first round in the process of revising the unequal treaties came in 1894, the same year in which Japan began its acquisition of overseas territory as a result of a war in Korea against China.

INDUSTRIALIZATION

The other major priority of the Japanese leadership was industrialization, which was carried out with great success at the same time as the Meiji political reforms. The government again took the lead, actively fostering industrial development. Rapid industrialization and overseas expansion went hand-in-hand. Their significance in world history will be discussed in the next chapter.

KOREA

Korea is a peninsular nation tucked between China and Japan. Though independent for many centuries, it has traditionally served as a bridge between the mainland and Japan for the transmission of culture, ideas, and soldiers. Especially beginning in the nineteenth century, Korea became a hotbed of international power politics because of its strategic location, which was of interest to China, Japan, Russia, the United States, and various European powers. In the end, Korea was made a victim of imperialism in a more direct sense than either China or Japan, as it was absorbed into the Japanese empire in the early twentieth century. The country's geopolitical position has led Koreans to sometimes refer to their country as "a shrimp among whales."

The Korean State

Korea has a history of long, relatively stable dynastic rule. From 668 until 1910, Korea was ruled by only three different dynasties. The longest-lasting of these, the Chosôn dynasty under the Yi family, was in place from 1392 until 1910. This half-millennium was not always tranquil, however. Korea was invaded twice by Hideyoshi's Japanese troops in the 1590s, and by the Manchus in the 1620s and 1630s. Through all this, the Koreans managed to maintain their independence as a state.

THE NATURE OF THE STATE

The King and the Bureaucracy. Korea was a Confucian state, with power concentrated in the hands of a king and bureaucracy. In accordance with Confucian theory, the king was absolute. In reality, however, he had to share power with an entrenched aristocracy that owed its position not just to royal favor but to a combination of landed wealth, traditional family prestige, and a pedigree dotted with people who held positions of importance in the government. This elite group controlled the bureaucracy and used it as a check on royal authority.

Farmers. As in China and Japan, Korea's population was predominantly farmers. They provided not only the food on which everyone lived, but the taxes that kept the machinery of government in operation. They were dominated by the same large landholding class that had a monopoly on high bureaucratic positions.

Korea and China. For centuries, Korea was a "tribute state" of the Chinese empire. In other words, the Koreans agreed to send regular missions to China, bearing gifts for the emperor and trade goods to exchange along the way. The Chinese emperor in turn invested the Korean king with his seal of authority. The relationship was one of overt inequality, but it was acceptable to both sides. The prestige of the Chinese emperor was enhanced, the Chinese were confirmed in their China-centered world view, and they gained an acquiescent state on their border. The Korean king gained an added measure of legitimation, and the tribute system kept the avenues of trade open. In addition, accepting tributary status was better than worrying about the possibility of Chinese invasion to enforce its terms on Korea. And it made for good foreign policy, as well. As long as the Koreans kept to the forms of the tribute relationship, the Chinese were content to leave them alone.

Korea in Nineteenth-Century International Politics

At least until the late nineteenth century, then, Korea's foreign policy was based on its relationship with China. This was suddenly changed as a result of China's weakness, Japan's strength, and the fact that Korea was again caught in the middle. In the nineteenth century internal social unrest, infighting in court politics, and external pressure combined to weaken Korea and create conditions ripe for colonization—conditions which an expanding Japan was quick to use to its advantage. A brief summary of events in the late nineteenth and early twentieth centuries will be helpful in understanding the way in which Korea was pulled into international politics and the consequences for Korea of the rivalries between larger powers.

TREATY OF KANGHWA

In 1876 Japan, having learned about "gunboat diplomacy" from its experience with the United States two decades earlier, forced the signing of the Treaty of Kanghwa, Korea's first modern treaty. Among other results, the signing of this treaty brought Korea out of the exclusive sphere of Chinese influence. The establishment of a Japanese legation in their traditional sphere of influence disturbed the Chinese, however, and they dispatched their own representative to Seoul as well. (For a time, this representative was Yuan Shih-k'ai, who, as we have seen, later became the first president of the Chinese republic following the fall of the Ch'ing dynasty.)

INTERNATIONAL CONFLICT IN KOREA

Beginning in 1882, a series of treaties were signed between Korea and Western states. The United States was the first of the Western powers to establish treaty relations with Korea, but other nations quickly followed suit. The increased visibility of foreign interests in Korea inevitably led to international competition. The rivalry between Japan and Russia was particularly intense. These two states—both neighbors of Korea—saw their influence on the peninsula as vital to their national security. In 1884, an attempted coup d'etat by a group of young aristocratic reformers, many of them inspired by Japanese reforms, nearly led to war in Korea between Japan and China. Fighting was averted, and each side agreed that neither would introduce troops into Korea without notifying the other.

JAPAN TAKES OVER

The Tonghak Rebellion. A test of this agreement was not long in coming. Poor social conditions had combined with increasing foreign influence to create a great deal of popular unrest. In 1894, this anger exploded into the Tonghak Rebellion. The Korean court asked for help in quelling the rebellion from its traditional ally China, which sent a contingent of troops. Japan also sent troops, but the rebels had dispersed before the foreign troops were in a position to deal with them. Instead, Japanese and Chinese soldiers ended up fighting against each other, sparking the Sino-Japanese War of 1894 and 1895.

Korea Extinguished. With Japan's victory and the signing of the Treaty of Shimonoseki, Korea was officially declared an independent sovereign state. What this meant, of course, was that anyone was free to establish any kind of relationship the Koreans would allow. Japan's defeat of Russia in 1905 eliminated Japan's major rival for dominance in East Asia. Agreements with the United States that same year acknowledged Japan's special interest in Korea (in exchange for Japanese recognition of America's special interest in the Philippines). Japan wasted no time in taking advantage of these agreements. In 1905 it established a "protectorate" in Korea. Five years later Japan annexed Korea outright, extinguishing its status as an independent, sovereign state and absorbing it into the Japanese empire.

Japanese Rule: Benefit or Disaster? Japan ruled Korea from 1910 until it was defeated in World War II in 1945. Historians and others still debate the question of whether the colonial period was a benefit or a disaster for Korea. On the one hand, the Japanese did contribute to Korea's industrial and infrastructural development. But on the other hand, Japan's frequently heavy-handed methods of control, its attempts to extinguish Korean language and separate national identity, and the fact that it oriented all Korean development toward Japanese rather than Korean needs created a great deal of resentment among the colonized population. Certainly one of the most important effects of Japanese rule in Korea was that it galvanized national sentiment. Nationalists of all kinds were able to unite around their opposition to Japanese control. This strong "us versus them" nationalism, tinged with an awareness of injustices done to them, is a strong element in twentieth-century Korean perceptions of the world.

Early modern China, Japan, and Korea provide some valuable perspectives on world historical developments. Particularly striking are the differences in China's and Japan's responses to Western pressure. China tended to rely on traditional approaches to foreign relations, even though the international political environment had changed. In addition, China's government was not in agreement on reform objectives, leading to weakness, paralysis, and eventually the demise of the old political order. Japan, on the other hand, was able to learn from China's experience. It was also able to draw on a long history of cultural borrowing and adaptation. Added to this was the fact that the new, young leaders of the Meiji government were generally united in their objectives and had the political will to pursue them.

While the Chinese state fell into dynastic decay and eventual disintegration, the Japanese began to build a strong industrialized state. Japan's defeat of China in 1895 signaled the fact that the balance of power in Asia had clearly shifted in favor of Japan. But as we shall see, the result of Japan's political changes and rapid industrialization was not only prosperity, but also expansion and, eventually, a war that would bring Japan its first defeat and first occupation by a foreign power.

As for Korea, this ancient country became the victim both of international power politics in East Asia and of Japan's expansionist impulse in the late nineteenth and early twentieth centuries. Annexation by Japan brought Korea's dynastic history to an end. When Korea emerged from under Japanese rule in 1945, it was still unable to attain true autonomy, as it became a focal point for the new Cold War realities that dominated international relations.

Selected Readings

Beasley, W. G. *The Rise of Modern Japan.* New York: St. Martin's, 1990.

Eckert, Carter J., et al. *Korea Old and New: A History.* Seoul: Ilchokak Publishers (for the Korea Institute, Harvard University), 1990.

Guy, R. Kent. *The Emperor's Four Treasuries: Scholars and the State in the Late Ch'ien-lung Era.* Cambridge, MA: Council on East Asian Studies, Harvard University, 1987.

Kim, Key-Hiuk. *The Last Phase of the East Asian World Order: Korea, Japan, and the Chinese Empire, 1860–1882.* Berkeley: University of California Press, 1980.

Palais, James B. *Politics and Policy in Traditional Korea.* Cambridge, MA: Harvard University Press, 1975.

Pyle, Kenneth B. *The Making of Modern Japan*. Lexington, MA: D. C. Heath and Company, 1978.

Smith, Richard J. *China's Cultural Heritage: The Ch'ing Dynasty, 1644–1912*. Boulder, CO: Westview Press, 1983.

Smith, Thomas C. *The Agrarian Origins of Modern Japan*. Stanford, CA: Stanford University Press, 1959.

———. Japan's Aristocratic Revolution. *Yale Review* 50 (1961): 370–383.

Spence, Jonathan D. *The Search for Modern China*. New York: W. W. Norton, 1990.

Totman, Conrad. *Japan Before Perry: A Short History*. Berkeley: University of California Press, 1981.

Wakeman, Frederic, Jr. *The Fall of Imperial China*. New York: The Free Press, 1975.

———. *The Great Enterprise: The Manchu Reconstruction of Imperial Order in Seventeenth-Century China*. Berkeley: University of California Press, 1985.

13

The West and the White Man's Burden: Empire Building Around the World

1839–1842	Opium War; unequal treaties and "most favored nation" concessions follow
1840	European powers intervene to stop Egyptian expansion
1848	Algeria annexed by France
1850	British East India Company controls most of India
1852	South African Republic established by Boers
1853	Commodore Matthew Perry arrives in Japan
1854	Orange Free State established by Boers
1856–1860	Second Opium War
1858–1864	David Livingston makes his most famous explorations of Africa
1878	Congress of Berlin
	Henry Stanley completes investigation of Congo River system
1880	French establish protectorate in area north of the Congo
1882	Britain declares Egypt a British protectorate
1884–1885	International conference in Berlin agrees to carve up Africa
1886	British take Burma
1887	French Indochina formed

Tripartite protectorate established in Samoa

1894–1895 Sino-Japanese War

1898 British conquest of the Sudan

Hong Kong area leased to Great Britain

U.S. annexes Hawaii

Spanish-American War

1898–1900 Boxer Rebellion

1899 "Open Door" policy announced

1903 Panama rebels, recognized by U.S; treaty for U.S. occupation negotiated

1904 U.S. President Roosevelt's "corollary" to the Monroe Doctrine

1904–1905 Russo-Japanese War

1907 Britain and Russia divide Iran into spheres of influence; Russia controls by 1912

1914 Panama Canal opened

A*s the nineteenth century came to a close, a new wave of expansionism, often called the "new imperialism," caught hold of the major Western powers. It became a rush for territorial acquisition worldwide. If that could not be accomplished, then carving out and maintaining spheres of economic influence was the prime objective.*

The economic philosophy behind European imperialism included free trade—primarily because it was in the interest of the imperialistic nations to promote it. Free trade worked well for countries anxious and able to sell their goods abroad, especially when their military might allowed them to move handily into other lands and when their mercantilist policies prohibited their colonies from manufacturing competing goods. On the other hand, it was a detriment to countries like India, which was not allowed to develop manufacturing, or China, which was unable to compete with the influx of cheap foreign goods.

In this chapter we will trace the rise of the new imperialism and its impact around the world. We will see how it expanded trade and improved the economic well-being of some nations while it hurt others. The new imperialism also created new tensions among competing states, caused wars, put millions of nonwhites under white rule or economic influence, changed political boundaries, expanded the economic influence of imperialist nations even where they did not have direct political control, and profoundly affected many traditional cultures.

THE NEW IMPERIALISM:
AN INTERPRETATION

Motives and
Justification

The imperialist push was motivated by economic incentives, vested interests, ideology, and other factors. Imperialism was the most relentless, however, when a combination of these motives was involved.

ECONOMIC MOTIVATION

The chief motive for the new imperialism was economic self-interest, and it was directly connected to the spread of the Industrial Revolution (see chapter 8). Great Britain, for example, feared the possibility that France and Germany would raise tariff barriers in their colonies, thus hurting British trade. New colonies were seen as ways to expand markets, as well as hedges against the expansion of competing powers. They also contributed to national security, military power, and international prestige. In addition, colonies provided the naval bases and provisioning stations necessary to protect the worldwide trade upon which the economies of the imperial powers were being built.

VESTED INTERESTS

Those who promoted colonial expansion included vested interests of all sorts. Manufacturers, bankers, and other financial interests saw expanding markets as economic necessities. Shipping companies stood to make large profits. White settlers needed more protection, missionaries were in search of more souls to save, and humanitarians were concerned with improving the lot of underprivileged humans worldwide. Explorers sought adventure, and military men sought excitement and, perhaps, advancement.

SOCIAL DARWINISM AND OTHER JUSTIFICATIONS

Social Darwinism and the White Man's Burden. Social Darwinism, although perhaps not the most important initial motive for imperialism, was a powerful tool for those who wished to rationalize and justify it. From Darwin's theories of natural selection and survival of the fittest, social theorists devised the ideology that human societies, too, evolved and that the white races of European stock had become inherently superior to other peoples. Imperialists argued that the Anglo-Saxon race was the superior race and thus had a great moral obligation to spread the blessings of its superior "civilization" to underprivileged peoples everywhere. Taking over their countries, dominating their economic development, teaching them "superior" political doctrines, and Christianizing them was all part of the "white man's burden."

The British imperialist ideal could hardly be suggested more clearly than on the dedication page of a book on East Asia published in 1894:

TO THOSE
WHO BELIEVE THAT THE BRITISH EMPIRE
IS, UNDER PROVIDENCE, THE GREATEST INSTRUMENT FOR
GOOD
THAT THE WORLD HAS SEEN
AND WHO HOLD, WITH THE WRITER, THAT
ITS WORK IN THE FAR EAST IS NOT YET ACCOMPLISHED
THIS BOOK IS INSCRIBED

In 1899 Great Britain's Rudyard Kipling wrote his famous poem "The White Man's Burden" in an effort to urge the United States to follow Britain's lead in taking up the course of empire.

Alfred Thayer Mahan and Sea Power. America, too, had its Social Darwinists and imperialist propagandists. Perhaps the most persuasive practical argument for American expansionism came from Captain Alfred Thayer Mahan, prominent naval historian and for many years president of the Naval War College at Newport, Rhode Island. In his book *The Influence of Sea Power Upon History* and in speeches around the country and in popular journals, he argued that national greatness and economic prosperity were dependent upon sea power. A large navy, a strong merchant marine, foreign commerce, colonies, and naval bases were all essential to economic development. It was America's destiny, he preached, to control the Caribbean, build a canal across the isthmus of Panama, and spread Western civilization throughout the Pacific.

Critics of Imperialism

People were by no means united in their attitudes toward imperialism. In England, J.A. Hobson argued in Marxist fashion that imperialism was the tool of the rich to find outlets for surplus capital, but that colonial possessions did not pay off economically for the country as a whole. More persuasively, Hobson and others condemned imperialism as brutal and immoral. They denounced Social Darwinism as merely a crude justification for allowing the strong to prey on the weak. Furthermore, critics complained that in building their overseas empires the European powers were being deceptive. Even while promoting representative government and personal liberties at home, they were imposing authoritarian rule and other forms of tyranny on native peoples of other countries.

In America, the American Anti-Imperialist League was formed in 1899. It included many prominent politicians, educators, and writers. One of their number, Mark Twain, addressed an essay "To the Person Sitting in Darkness," by whom he meant President William McKinley. In order to match American policies, he suggested, the flag should have "the white stripes painted black and the stars replaced by the skull and cross bones."

The Unequal Exchange

The truth about imperialism probably lay somewhere in between the claims of the advocates and the critics. However, even if there were reciprocal benefits, it was an unequal exchange. Imperialist states improved their economic and political power, opened markets, improved the standard of living at home, spread Christianity (which had both positive and negative consequences), improved the health and well- being of people in many areas, and brought order out of chaos in some of the underdeveloped regions in which they intervened. At the same time, the peoples of Africa and Asia found their traditional values, including the most positive aspects of their native religious values, threatened. Secular ideologies imported from the West sometimes had a devastating influence on traditional culture. At first the intruders were challenged, but eventually native peoples were forced to accept foreign rule. Later came a resurgence of anti-imperialism, leading to revolts and sometimes brutal repression, as native peoples groped for independence and racial dignity.

THE CLASH BETWEEN EUROPE AND THE ISLAMIC WORLD

An early form of the new imperialism was seen in the European encroachment on the Ottoman Empire and other Islamic states in the eighteenth and nineteenth centuries. This has already been discussed in chapter 11, but a few additional comments are appropriate here.

Breakup of the Ottoman Empire

At the peak of its power in the sixteenth century the Ottoman empire controlled most of North Africa, much of Arabia, the Balkans, and other parts of eastern Europe. In the seventeenth and eighteenth centuries, however, European powers whittled away at Ottoman holdings. It would not be long before the Ottoman state would be broken up.

THE BALKANS

Contributing to this breakup was a surge of nationalism throughout the Balkans, which played right into the hands of the western European powers. Serbia rebelled in 1804, gaining a limited independence by 1815. During a Greek rebellion that began in 1821 the European powers refused to support Turkey against the rebels. Eventually England, France, and Russia put pressure on the Ottomans to accept Greek independence, which finally came in 1830. From 1854 to 1856 the Crimean War made it further evident that the European powers were no longer willing to work together to maintain existing borders, as agreed at the Congress of Vienna. Later the Ottomans lost Serbia, Moldavia, and Walachia (the latter two becoming Romania in 1861).

THE "SICK MAN OF EUROPE"

The significance of all this was not just the breakup of Ottoman power but also the fact that it was opening the door to further European incursions into what was once a Muslim stronghold. Western powers, in fact, were becoming increasingly troubled with the Ottomans. In addition to its problems with nationalistic rebellions, Turkey was characterized by financial mismanagement, administrative incompetence, and lack of reform. By the late nineteenth century the sultanate was becoming known as the "Sick Man of Europe." European diplomats had their eyes on the "sick man's" territories, but the problem of how to take them over without coming to blows among themselves was complex. If one power obtained too much or too little, it would surely upset the delicate balance of power that they still theoretically supported. Actually, however, they were already going against the principles of the Congress of Vienna, and in the long run they would have few scruples about carving up the territory of either of the "sick man" or of anyone else.

Iran

As outlined in chapter 11, the Ottomans soon lost Egypt to the British. Other Muslim states in North Africa and elsewhere also came under the domination of European expansionists. Iran (Persia) did not fall, but late in the nineteenth century the shah found himself attempting to ward off threats from the European powers, including Russia. His effort to pit one against another by the way he dispensed favors angered Moslem fundamentalists, however. They soon began to preach government reform and a return to pure Islamic principles. A 1906 revolt failed, and the following year Iran was carved into spheres of influence by Britain and Russia. By 1912 Russia controlled the country.

THE EUROPEAN DIVISION OF SUB-SAHARAN AFRICA

As the major powers of Europe were participating in the breakup of the Ottoman Empire in southern Europe and northern Africa, they were also expanding their imperial interests in sub-Saharan Africa. The eventual result was a complete carving up of Africa among them.

Explorations into the East African Hinterlands

After mid-century the exploration of the African interior, especially by English, French, and German explorers, stepped up dramatically. Some were interested in opening up new fields for missionary work. Others, including the missionaries, were part of the larger British effort to eradicate the slave trade. Still others hoped to find the sources of Africa's great rivers and to open up trading possibilities. No matter what the motives, however, they all had imperialistic overtones.

LIVINGSTON AND STANLEY

The two most famous explorers were David Livingston and Henry Stanley. Livingston was vitally interested in opening the interior for missionary work. His speeches and published reports not only enthralled Europe but also, as he hoped, resulted in the organization of missions. His work also led to the discovery of many new places and popularized Africa throughout the Western world. Henry Stanley, an American newspaper reporter, was commissioned in 1871 to try to find Livingston, who had not been heard from for some time because Arab slavers failed to deliver his letters to the British consul in Zanzibar. He discovered the missionary-explorer, conducted still further explorations with him, and then returned to the coast. He soon convinced both *The New York Daily Herald* and the *London Daily Telegraph* to sponsor further expeditions. Eventually Stanley became the most important African explorer of the age.

THE MISSIONARY ENTERPRISE

Both Catholic and Protestant missionaries eagerly included Africa in their goals for spiritual conquest. Although they misinterpreted, or misconstrued, much of Africa's so-called "degraded" religion and culture, they also helped focus more interest and attention on the continent. They translated the scriptures, conducted schools, brought literacy to many people, and provided much-needed medical attention. Most were tireless, sincere, and totally devoted to their work, and many gave their lives, as a result of tropical disease, to their cause.

By 1890 the hinterlands of Africa were no longer mysterious or isolated. The region was mapped, traversed by Europeans, and open to economic exploitation. It was also being rapidly carved up by the Europeans in what has been aptly called the "great scramble" for Africa.

The Great Scramble

Beyond French-held Algeria, some Portuguese possessions in Angola and Mozambique, and a few European trading posts elsewhere, there was little European control in Africa until after 1880. Then the great scramble began, and within twenty years nearly the entire continent had been carved up and distributed among Britain, France, Germany, Italy, Portugal, Belgium, and Spain. Only Ethiopia, in eastern Africa, and Liberia, in West Africa, remained as independent states.

SOUTH AFRICA

During the Napoleonic Wars, Cape Colony, the Dutch settlement in South Africa, was taken over by the British. Many disgruntled Boers (Dutch farmers and cattlemen) responded in what is known as the Great Trek. Beginning informally earlier but proceeding seriously in 1836, they put all their possessions into ox-drawn wagons and marched into the interior. There they successfully fought native tribes, particularly the Zulu, for control of land. About 4,000 people had left Cape Colony by the end of 1837. For a time the Boers remained under British control, but in 1852 and 1854, respectively, they established their own independent republics—the South African Republic and the Orange Free State. At the end of the century they were defeated by the British in the Boer War, and soon afterwards all the South African colonies became the Union of South Africa, with British dominion status.

THE CONGO

At the heart of Africa was the Congo, where King Leopold II of Belgium decided to carve out a foothold. In the late 1870s he formed an organization to promote his aims and made Henry Stanley its agent. Stanley made alliances with tribal chiefs, set up trading posts, and eventually gained control of what became the Congo Free State. The French, unsettled by Belgium's sudden expansiveness, sent their own expedition into the area in 1880 and established a French protectorate north of the Congo. It was just at this time that the British were taking over Egypt in North Africa.

READY FOR CARVING

Like a raging land rush, the race for territory was on, but the major powers of Europe did not see Africa as a place for direct military confrontation with each other. If they could achieve their imperialist goals without shedding European blood, it was so much the better. As a result of such concerns, and sparked by some immediate disagreements between the major powers, French premier Jules Ferry and Otto von Bismarck, chancellor of the recently united German Republic, set up an international conference. Meeting in Berlin, the conference began in October 1884 and went on for three months. The European colonial powers and the United States were all there, mainly to establish rules for a partitioning process that was already well along. Gaining the most immediate benefit was Leopold II. In a treaty negotiated outside the regular meetings, the Congo Free State, and Leopold's personal sovereignty over it, was recognized. In effect, the new state became Leopold's personal fiefdom, for he considered it his private property and ruled it as such in order to obtain as much commercial benefit as possible. At the end of the conference the powers signed the Berlin Act, in which they agreed that if any power planned any further annexation or protectorate, it would first notify the others and would guarantee "effective occupation" of the area in question. What this amounted to was an open invitation for European states to press from all sides and establish effective claims. The conference also agreed to work toward eliminating both the slave trade and slavery in Africa.

GERMANY AND FRANCE

Germany began to play a role in Africa after Bismarck had a sudden conversion to the advantages of acquiring colonies. In 1884 and 1885 Germany took over Togoland, Camaroons, and German Southwest Africa as protectorates. The French gained control of Somalia and Tunisia before the Berlin conference. Later they moved south from Algeria, across the western and central Sudan, and into Guinea, the Ivory Coast, Dahomey, and the kingdom of the Samori. They also moved into the Lake Chad region and occupied a large area north and west of the Belgian Congo. In all this Bismarck supported France if it came in conflict with British interests.

BRITAIN AND THE SUDAN

The British, meanwhile, pushed northward from Cape Colony and also from their long-held island of Zanzibar, partly to protect themselves from the moves of Belgium, Portugal, and Italy. In order to maintain its position in Egypt, Britain knew that it must also control the access to Egypt through the valley of the upper Nile. When it appeared that the French were preparing to invade the Sudan, the British became alarmed and planned an expedition of their own into the area, under the command of General Horatio H. Kitchener. They built a railroad in order to supply arms and reinforcements and slowly moved up the Nile. In 1898, fervently nationalistic Muslims attempted to block their progress. The most brutal battle occurred near Obdurmann, where Muslim defenders charged the British in wave after wave, only to be cut down by machine guns—newcomers in modern arsenals. Eleven thousand Muslims died, at a loss of only twenty-eight British soldiers. The British were then confronted by a small French force under Major J. B. Marchand at Fashoda. Marchand, however, decided to withdraw rather than fight; as a result of the "Fashoda incident" an Anglo-French war was averted. The British conquest of the Sudan was complete.

Impact of Imperialism on African Tribal Culture

The impact of imperialism on traditional African culture was somewhat similar to the impact of European expansion on the native cultures of the Americas. Traditional economies, political structures, and ways of life all inevitably were changed. Western political rule was imposed, and many natives were destroyed in the process. Tribal religions survived, though often in modified form, and at the same time numerous Africans accepted one of the various forms of Christianity introduced among them. Eventually they became dependent upon trade with the Westerners, but they also received the benefits of humanitarian aid, particularly medical care and education. In addition, some mission schools eventually became seed-grounds for nationalism and rejection of European rule.

THE JEWEL IN THE CROWN: BRITISH INDIA

In the great contest for world empire, Great Britain eventually won India, the most important European colonial possession in the Afro-Asian world. It is sometimes called the "jewel" in Britain's imperial crown. The British presence in India started when the East India Company established its first foothold in 1608. After defeating the French in the Seven Years' War that ended in 1763, the British gradually extended their control until in the mid-nineteenth century the East India Company controlled fully three-fifths of India.

Impact of British Control

BRITISH POLICIES AND THEIR CONSEQUENCES

British policies, however, were not designed to create much love on the part of the Indians. People of Indian origin were excluded from high government posts. The social and economic gap between British settlers and Indians widened. The British refused to allow large-scale industrial development (a mercantilist policy intended to promote British manufacturing), which only exacerbated the already appalling problem of large-scale poverty. In addition, the British seemed insensitive to Indian social and religious traditions. Indian resentment finally broke out in the Sepoy Rebellion of 1857, which was crushed within a year. Afterward, the crown took over most of the functions of the East India Company, thus finalizing imperial rule. But feelings of mistrust only intensified, especially as the disparity between British wealth and Indian poverty became increasingly apparent.

GOVERNING INDIA

After 1858 India's 300 million people were governed by an elite British civil service. This administrative core was supported by a military force consisting of British officers and Indian troops. Indians were not allowed to hold top posts in the government or commissions in the military. British rulers tended to believe in their own inherent superiority. Such elitism and racism was hardly conducive to warm relations.

SOME ADVANTAGES FOR INDIANS

There were, nevertheless, some positive results of British rule. A number of reforms were introduced among the people, including educational reforms. Many Indians developed administrative and other skills by serving in various second-level military and government positions. In addition, India again became a unified state. Nevertheless, the advantages of British rule were not enough to nip in the bud the rise of nationalism.

INDIAN NATIONALISM

It was inevitable that nationalist sentiments should find expression in India, though they were expressed in different ways. The Indian National Congress, founded in 1885, expressed faith in the ability of the Indians to work with the British in a gradual process of reform leading toward self-government. The more militant nationalists, led by B. G. Tilak, were not only anti-British but also anti-Muslim. In addition to self-government, they stressed a return to Indian languages and to Hindu culture. Finally, a distinctive form of nationalism evolved among the Muslims. Members of the Muslim League, founded in 1906, became increasingly dissatisfied with Hindu dominance of the Indian National Congress, as the Hindu-Muslim rift deepened in the twentieth century.

IMPERIALISM IN SOUTHEAST ASIA

British Expansion in Southeast Asia

It soon became important for Great Britain to connect its Indian possessions with those in Burma, an important source of rice. In 1886 British troops took northern Burma. Britain already held Singapore and was thus in a strategic position to affect trade between the Indian Ocean and the China Sea. Siam (modern Thailand), on the other hand, was in a good position to be a buffer state between French Indochina and English Burma. Britain and France signed an agreement in 1907 guaranteeing the independence of Siam, but making sure that the kingdom was divided into two separate "spheres of influence."

French Colonization of Indochina

After France lost India to England in 1757, it shifted its interests to the Indochinese peninsula. In the 1840s the government of Vietnam began to suppress Christianity. Thousands of people were killed, including priests. In response, in 1859 the French seized Saigon as well as three surrounding provinces. It set up a protectorate over Cambodia in 1864 and seized Hanoi in 1882. China responded by sending troops in 1883, but after two years of fighting, the French forced China to abandon any of its claims to Vietnam.

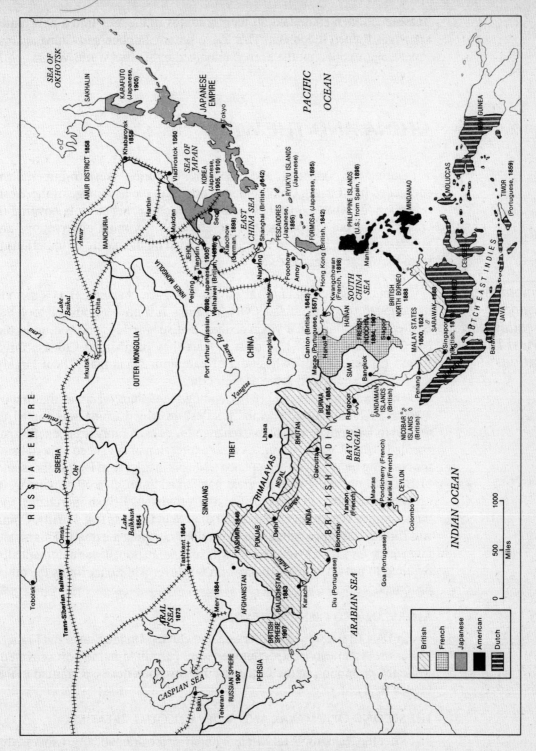

Fig. 13.1   Colonial Empires in Asia

The French then combined all their holdings in the area into a new entity known as French Indochina. This led to bitter complaints in China against French aggression, but the French remained until after World War II.

CHINA AND THE WEST

During the eighteenth and nineteenth centuries, Western imperialism succeeded in affecting Chinese trade policies to the advantage of the West, regardless of what the Chinese wanted. Much of this story is covered in chapter 12, from the perspective of China. A few more observations are appropriate here, however, in order to expand on the nature of imperialism from the Western perspective.

Opium Wars, Unequal Treaties, and "Most Favored Nations"

Britain saw the Opium War (1839–1842, see chapter 12) as a serious threat to all its commercial activity in China. Just how seriously it took the challenge was illustrated when sixteen British warships showed up in the harbor of Canton in 1840. For two years they bombarded Chinese forts, fought Chinese troops (whose out-of-date armaments made them largely ineffective), and seized some of their cities.

The Treaty of Nanking (1842), ending the Opium War, was the first of a series of humiliating "unequal treaties" in which China was forced to accede to Western demands in exchange for considerably less benefit than accrued to the Western powers. A clear expression of advanced imperialism, the Nanking treaty not only reopened trade but also gave to Britain the island of Hong Kong, along with its great port. In addition, five other ports were opened, and under an extraterritoriality provision, British merchants and their families were subject to British rather than Chinese law. Finally, China was forced to accept a "most favored nation" clause in the treaty. This meant that whenever China made a treaty with another nation, it was automatically required to provide Great Britain with whatever additional rights the other nation gained.

AMERICAN AND FRENCH TREATIES

In 1844 China signed similar treaties with the United States and France. Under the American treaty, churches were permitted in the ports covered, while the promotion of the Catholic faith was specifically permitted in the French treaty.

THE SECOND OPIUM WAR AND MORE UNEQUAL TREATIES

After the Nanking Treaty, opium imports rose dramatically. Other trade, however, grew more slowly, causing Western merchants to complain that the Chinese were not honoring their trade agreements. They were right, for the Chinese were finding various ways to circumvent incursions. The Westerners were also expressing complaints on several other issues. In 1856 another war broke out. This time the French and British joined together to defeat the Chinese. The result was more unequal treaties. In the Treaties of Tientsin, finally ratified in 1860, China agreed to open eleven more ports, to permit foreigners to travel to the interior, and to admit Christian missionaries to any part of China. The opium trade was also legalized. Other such unequal treaties were signed later in the century.

In the long run, these treaties and the ports they opened benefited the imperial powers greatly but had a generally negative impact on the Chinese economy. Some important native industries, for example, almost disappeared, for low import duties made it difficult for them to compete. Some Chinese merchants who settled at the ports profited, however, as did the Manchu government that upheld the treaties and was appropriately rewarded for doing so.

RUSSIAN ENCROACHMENT

China also found it impossible to resist Russian encroachments from the North. Russia planted a colony along the Amur River in the 1850s. In an 1858 treaty, it gained control of the whole north bank of the river. Two years later Russia obtained additional territory in the area between the Ussuri River and the Pacific. This region has been a subject of dispute ever since.

SPHERES OF INFLUENCE

Japan's victory over China in the Sino-Japanese war (1894–1895) demonstrated to Western powers how vulnerable China still was. This led them to carve up China, though not as they did in Africa. Rather, they began to define "spheres of influence," areas where each of them had special leasing and commercial privileges. Russia obtained the right to build a railroad across Manchuria and to control the Liaotung Peninsula, including Port Arthur. Germany got Shantung, while the French received Kwangchow Bay. Britain obtained control of Wei-hai-wei, on the Shantung Peninsula, and also extended its holdings in the Hong Kong area, which eventually became its major port of entry to the Chinese trade. After the second Opium War, the peninsula of Kowloon, on the mainland, was added to the British colony; later other territories were added. In 1898, all of these territories were combined and leased to Great Britain for ninety-nine years.

THE OPEN DOOR POLICY

The United States, meanwhile, was busy acquiring its Pacific empire but had no sphere of influence in China. In 1899, therefore, Secretary of State John Hay called upon the other imperialist powers to support an "Open

Door" policy by which Chinese trade would be kept open to all countries on an equal basis. In effect, Hay recognized their spheres of influence; but he asked them not to interfere with any treaty port or other vested interest within those spheres, to permit Chinese officials to collect tariffs on an equal basis, and to refrain from showing favoritism to their own nationals with respect to harbor dues and railroad charges. This was a little bit like asking everyone who opposed sin to stand up—no country would admit that it disagreed with such noble-sounding principles, but what it actually did might be another matter. In the end, Britain announced its support of the policy, but other countries gave less firm assurances.

SIGNIFICANCE OF THE BOXER REBELLION TO IMPERIALISTS

As a result of the Boxer Rebellion (see chapter 12), China was required to accede to several new demands. One was the right of the imperial powers to station troops in Peking and along the route to the sea. The consequence for the imperial powers was a strengthening of their positions in China. At the same time, even conservatives within China were finally convinced that clinging to the old ways was futile. The result was a powerful reform movement in which the conservative empress dowager herself was half-heartedly involved.

ESCAPE FROM THE EUROPEAN YOKE: THE MODERNIZATION OF JAPAN

Opening Japan to the West

The Tokugawa ruled Japan for over 250 years, and only toward the end of that time did Western ideas begin slowly to make their way into the country. The only foreign settlement allowed in Japan, in fact, was a small Dutch trading post on an island in Nagasaki harbor.

Early in the nineteenth century England, Russia, and the United States all began urging Japan to reopen its doors, but few in Japan had any interest. The issue intensified for the United States when shipwrecked sailors reported being treated badly by the Japanese. Americans also wanted to use a Japanese port for refueling and restocking ships. In 1853, therefore, the United States sent Commodore Matthew Perry steaming with his fleet of "black ships" into Edo harbor. This was the first step in opening Japan to the West (see chapter 12).

Westernization: Impact of the Meiji Restoration

Part of the significance of the Meiji Restoration in 1868 (see chapter 12) was that it brought to power a group of reformers who believed that it was in the best interest of Japan to study Western ways, adopt the best things they found there, and catch up. Their response to the Western threat was just the opposite of that of China, and by the end of the century they had made Japan the first modernized state in Asia. Under these reformers, the modernization of Japan proceeded rapidly. In the end, Japan succeeded not only in throwing off the Western yoke but also in becoming an industrialized and imperial power itself. In 1871, about half of the most important Meiji leaders took a year and a half to travel to the West. Their purpose was to study and learn, though for home consumption they said they were going to revise the unequal treaties.

ECONOMIC REFORM AND INDUSTRIALIZATION

The Meiji government created a powerful modern army and navy that not only crushed internal rebellion but also helped push Japan's imperialism at the end of the century. It also instituted sweeping economic reforms, beginning with a program of industrialization. It recognized that if Japan were to compete with the West at all, it would have to develop the same kind of economic base. At first the government itself developed new industries and built new factories, to act as models and training grounds for what would come later. It also developed a variety of other essential institutions, modeled after Western examples, such as schools, banks, post offices, and a government university. In the 1880s and 1890s, with government encouragement, private entrepreneurs invested in a variety of enterprises such as silk and cotton textiles, railroads, building materials, and chemicals. The new industrial oligarchy showed remarkable talent, creating huge economic empires within Japan comparable to those being created by many American entrepreneurs. By the end of the century Japan's successful economic development provided a stark contrast with that of China.

CONSEQUENCES OF WESTERNIZATION

The significance of the Meiji Restoration can be seen in the fact that in the first quarter-century after 1868 more changes took place in Japanese life than had occurred in perhaps the previous 600 or 700 years. No other country was modernized so thoroughly and so quickly.

Modernization meant Westernization, which had an important impact on many aspects of Japanese life. Japanese artists were influenced by Western romanticism; architects produced Western-style buildings. Western dress did not totally replace Japanese dress but was readily accepted and adopted by political and industrial leaders. Christianity was legalized, after 300 years of being suppressed. The significance of this move lay not just in conversions but also in the establishment of mission schools that eventually provided many Japanese with a good, high-level education. The Japanese also discovered Western literature of all sorts. Among other things, some read Herbert Spencer, the founder of Social Darwinist thought, and applied his imperialist philosophy to themselves.

Foreign Relations: Japan as an Imperial Power

The fact that Japan had become so thoroughly Westernized is aptly symbolized by the fact that it, too, was becoming an imperial power by the end of the century. Japan had a long-standing interest in Korea; in the 1870s it forced Korea to open its doors to Japanese trade. In addition, the Japanese were not above cultivating a Korean political faction friendly to their interests. Japan also had vital interest in China. As a result of the Sino-Japanese war (1894–1895), it obtained Taiwan, the Pescadores Islands, and the Liaotung Peninsula in Manchuria. It also got an indemnity and a most favored nation treaty with China. Later, however, imperialist Russia was able to use French and German support to force Japan to give up Liaotung, and then took it for itself. Japan was part of the international force that put down the Boxer Rebellion in China.

FULL-BLOWN IMPERIALISTS

Japan's new status was soon recognized by other nations. Beginning with Britain in 1894, the old humiliating treaties requiring extraterritoriality rights were rescinded. Japan's full-blown imperialist adventure began immediately. In 1894 it went to war with China over influence in Korea. In 1902 Japan and England joined in an alliance intended to check Russian expansion. Then in 1904 and 1905 came the Russo-Japanese War, the result of continuing disagreement over Chinese territory. In a convincing display of its new military might, Japan drove the Russians from Port Arthur and seized Mukden. Then, in a decisive two-day naval battle in May 1905, Japan almost completely destroyed the Russian fleet of thirty-six ships. The two countries accepted American president Theodore Roosevelt's offer of arbitration. In the Treaty of Portsmouth Japan received back the Liaotung Peninsula. Russia also gave up its southern Manchurian railway, the southern half of Sakhalin Island, and its own sphere of influence in Korea. In 1910 Japan annexed Korea outright.

IMPERIALIST AMERICA

The American westward movement and "Manifest Destiny," early forms of American imperialism, have already been noted in chapter 10. Expansionism reasserted itself immediately after the Civil War, when Secretary of State William Seward took the controversial step of purchasing Alaska from

Russia for $7.2 million, thus ending Russian colonialism in the Western Hemisphere. Later, American economic intervention in Latin America, its expansion in the Pacific, and its involvement in opening the doors of Asia demonstrated full-blown American imperialism in action.

The Beginning of a Pacific Empire

SAMOA

As American shipping in the Pacific increased after the Civil War, its interest in two important island groups became increasingly intense. Both Samoa and Hawaii had major harbors, and both could be important fueling and provisioning stations for the American navy and merchant fleet. In Samoa, the Americans negotiated a treaty in 1878 that gave the United States a naval station at Pago Pago, as well as extraterritorial rights. Other powers negotiated similar treaties. After a civil war broke out in Samoa in 1887, however, Germany, the United States, and Great Britain established a tripartite protectorate.

HAWAII

American interests in Hawaii were more vital. In particular, American sugar growers had attained important economic status and had forced their way into dominating the government. Then in 1891 Queen Liliuokalani began her heroic but ultimately hopeless campaign to minimize foreign influence and preserve "Hawaii for the Hawaiians." The result was a coup by American settlers, supported by the American minister in Hawaii, in which the queen was deposed and an independent government set up. Immediately the American minister recognized that government, which then sent a delegation to Washington asking for annexation. After a bitter four-year debate that pitted expansionists against anti-imperialists, Congress approved the annexation in July 1898. One of the most convincing arguments was simply that if the United States did not annex it, another power—possibly Great Britain or Japan—would.

War with Spain Enlarges the Pacific Empire

Spain, meanwhile, was mismanaging the Island of Cuba. A series of Cuban uprisings resulted in ruthless suppression by the Spanish. Newspaper reports created great sympathy in the United States for the Cubans. New civil strife broke out in January 1898, and to protect American citizens, President William McKinley sent the battleship *Maine* into Havana harbor. In the midst of increasing anger, the *Maine* was blown up. No one knew exactly what happened, but American newspapers fanned the angry flames in the United States, accusing the Spanish of the deed. Under extreme internal pressure, the president finally declared war on Spain.

THE PHILIPPINES, CUBA, AND PUERTO RICO

The chief American benefit from the war with Spain was the acquisition of an enlarged Pacific empire. Weeks before war broke out, an expansionist assistant secretary of state, Theodore Roosevelt, had alerted Commodore George Dewey, commander of the U.S. Asiatic Squadron, to move against the Spanish at Manila if war came. Dewey acted promptly, and before the war was barely begun, the Spanish fleet in Manila harbor was destroyed; the Philippines had been taken. The Spanish-American War was over in less than a year. Spain agreed to leave Cuba and to cede both Puerto Rico and the Philippines to the United States. An American protectorate was established over Cuba, though an independent government took over in 1902 under a constitution approved by the United States. However, the new constitution contained a clause authorizing the United States to intervene whenever necessary to preserve Cuban independence or to maintain a government adequate to protect life, liberty, and property.

Latin America and the Evolution of the Monroe Doctrine

Meanwhile, the United States believed it had adequate reason for intervening in the affairs of Latin America. In the process, it expanded on the Monroe Doctrine much further than its originator probably would have intended. Instead of a simple declaration that the Americas were no longer areas for European colonization, the Monroe Doctrine became a justification for intervention by the United States whenever its own interests seemed threatened.

THE OLNEY NOTE

There were several areas of tension between the United States and Latin American countries. One concerned the boundary between Venezuela and British Guiana. The United States took Venezuela's side. After Great Britain occupied the disputed territory, the American secretary of state, Richard Olney, sent an angry note to the British telling them that they were in violation of the Monroe Doctrine. This statement was an exaggeration when compared with Monroe's original intent, but it was consistent with the way Americans were thinking. "Today the United States is practically sovereign on this continent," declared Olney, "and its fiat is law upon the subjects to which it confines its interposition." In the end Britain backed down, but the incident only added to a growing and dangerous feeling on the part of Americans that their nation could get almost whatever it wanted, whenever it wanted.

THE ROOSEVELT COROLLARY

In the early twentieth century the United States intervened in Latin American affairs on several occasions. In the Dominican Republic, for example, it took over the customs service in order to force that country to use the funds to pay its foreign debt. Other nations were already threatening to intervene. In the spirit of the advancing interpretation of the Monroe Doctrine, President Theodore Roosevelt announced his own corollary. "Chronic wrongdoing," he said in 1904, might require outside intervention. Since no other nation could intervene, it was the role of the United States to exercise an "international police power" in this area. The policy worked well for a time but in the long run caused resentment and nationalistic foreboding in Latin America about its neighbor to the north.

DOLLAR DIPLOMACY

A relatively mild form of economic imperialism was intensified in later years, especially under the administration of William Howard Taft. In a policy often referred to as "dollar diplomacy," Taft encouraged American bankers to invest in the Caribbean region in order to prop up faltering governments. Americans were persuaded to invest in the Bank of Haiti. Through treaty arrangements, Americans loaned money to the governments of Nicaragua and Honduras. These nations were to ensure repayment by installing Americans as collectors of customs. The Senate did not ratify these treaties, but the administration continued to encourage such agreements. In 1912 the president of Nicaragua asked for help in putting down internal disorders, and American marines intervened. American collectors of customs were then installed; they put the government on a monthly allowance. American forces remained there, with only a one-year interlude, until 1933. There were similar interventions in Haiti in 1915 and the Dominican Republic in 1916.

PANAMA CANAL

The major issue in the Caribbean was the problem of constructing and controlling a canal across the isthmus of Panama. Such a canal was necessary to improve America's shipping as well as to enhance its naval power. After years of international squabbling over who would build the canal, where it would be built, and how it would be financed, President Roosevelt again took matters into his own hands. Early in November 1903, with the connivance of the United States, conspirators in the Columbian province of Panama staged a revolt. When Columbian troops tried to land at the port of Colón, they found American ships blocking the way. Like the revolt in Hawaii, the Panamanian revolt was over in a few days, its government was recognized by Washington, and an ambassador appeared in Washington on November 13. The result was a treaty in which the United States agreed to pay $10 million down and $250,000 a year for the right to occupy and control the canal zone perpetually. When asked to justify his action, Roosevelt only commented that if he did not act, Congress would be debating still. The canal was opened in 1914.

*I*mperialism was the child of industrialism. The growth of manufacturing spawned the need for markets. For the industrial nations this created a need for economic control which, in turn, often led to political control. At the beginning of the nineteenth century the influence of Western powers was felt in many parts of the world. By the end of the century, the industrialized powers, and only they, had built new world empires. The United States had joined them as an industrial leader as well as a dominant power in the Pacific. In addition, two non-Western nations, Russia and especially Japan, were well on the road to industrialization, and both were imperialist powers.

So far, even though military force had been used to take over weaker areas, the imperialist nations had avoided outright war with each other. Unfortunately, it could not be averted for long. Although industrialization and the kind of imperialism we have discussed were not alone to blame, they nevertheless were important elements in the background of two world conflagrations and numerous regional military showdowns in the twentieth century.

Selected Readings

Bettes, Raymond F., ed. *The "Scramble" for Africa: Causes and Dimensions of Empire*. Boston: Heath, 1966. (Problems in European Civilization series.)

Curzon, George N. *Problems of the Far East: Japan—Korea—China*. London: Longman, Green, and Co., 1984. (The quotation on p. 253 is from this book.)

Fieldhouse, David K. *Colonialism, 1870–1945: An Introduction*. London: Weidenfeld and Nicolson, 1981.

LaFeber, Walter. *The New Empire: An Interpretation of American Expansionism, 1860–1898*. Ithaca, NY: Cornell University Press, 1963.

Langer, William L. *The Diplomacy of Imperialism: 1890–1902*. 2d. ed. New York: Knopf, 1960.

Panikkar, K. M. *Asia and Western Dominance*. New York: Collier Books, 1969.

Paterson, Thomas G., ed. *American Imperialism and Anti-Imperialism*. New York: Crowell, 1973. (Problem Studies in American History.)

Smith, Tony. *The Pattern of Imperialism: The United States, Great Britain, and the Late-Industrializing World Since 1815*. Cambridge: Cambridge University Press, 1981.

Wright, Harrison M., ed. *The "New Imperialism": Analysis of Late-Nineteenth-Century Expansion*. 2d. ed. Lexington, MA: Heath, 1976. (Problems in European Civilization series.)

14

The Crisis of the West: The War to End All Wars

1882	Triple Alliance (Germany, Austria, and Italy)
1890	Bismarck resigns as German chancellor
1894	Franco-Russian Alliance
1897	Socialist Party founded in United States
1898	Russian Social Democratic Party founded
1904	Entente Cordial (Britain and France)
1905	Massacre of workers in St. Petersburg; peasant and worker strikes and revolts throughout Russia
1905–1906	First Moroccan crisis
1907	Triple Entente formed (Russia, France, and Great Britain)
1911	Second Moroccan crisis
1911–1913	Balkan wars
1914	Austrian Archduke Francis Ferdinand assassinated; chain reaction brings war to all of Europe
	Liberal Party comes to power in Great Britain
1915	*Lusitania* sunk by German submarine
	Rebellion and riots in Russia; tsar abdicates
1917	United States enters the war
	Bolsheviks take over in Russia; Russia withdraws from the war

1918   Russian tsar executed

Central Powers collapse; armistice signed

1919   Paris peace conference; Treaty of Versailles

Several elements in the political, social, and economic life of Europe and America in the early twentieth century tended to foreshadow much of the history of the next hundred years. Changes wrought by the Industrial Revolution continued to present challenges to the existing order. Territorial expansion ended, but it also presaged more Western economic and social dominance. International rivalries and alliances led to a war of worldwide magnitude, the most disastrous war the world had yet seen. Western leaders hoped they could make it the war to end all wars, but the tragic legacy of their peace settlement was another world war a generation later.

In this chapter we will consider a few of the challenges that affected the Western world in the years preceding World War I. We will also consider the causes and results of the war itself. In addition, we will examine a major political revolution that occurred in Russia at the height of the war. All these events made that era a major turning point in the history of the world.

ON THE EVE OF WAR: LIBERALISM AND LABOR TO 1914

Many domestic issues that stood out in the Western world were related to continuing efforts at liberal reform in the urban, industrial society that had emerged by the beginning of the twentieth century.

Women and Feminism

Working-class women in both Europe and America were still employed in large numbers in textile and garment manufacturing. Among those who were better educated, teaching and nursing remained important. There were also many new jobs connected with the technological and industrial revolutions, including secretarial work, clerical work, and sales. Wages in all such employment, however, remained low.

DOMESTICITY

Most working women were unmarried, and when they married they tended to quit work and remain in the home. More so than a century earlier, middle-class values dictated a predominant role for women in the home and constituted the so-called cult of domesticity. The "ideal woman" was a model of religious piety, the exemplar and protector of virtue, the teacher in the home, and submissive to the needs and directions of her husband.

WOMAN SUFFRAGE

There were, however, persistent reformers. The quest for woman suffrage garnered considerable support, especially in Great Britain and the United States. In Britain, Emmeline Pankhurst and her daughters founded the Women's Social and Political Union in 1903. The suffragettes, as members were called, campaigned vigorously for the vote, even resorting to civil disobedience and violence. Among American women leading the fight for suffrage were Susan B. Anthony and Elizabeth Cady Stanton. Theirs and a rival organization merged in 1890 to form the National American Woman Suffrage Association. Nine western states adopted woman suffrage before the war. With the coming of the war, however, women in both countries turned their energies to supporting the war effort. By 1915 only six nations (New Zealand in 1893, Australia in 1902, Finland in 1906, Norway in 1913, and Denmark and Iceland in 1915) had adopted woman suffrage.

General Extension of Suffrage and Growth of Labor-Oriented Parties

Universal manhood suffrage had been obtained in most major Western nations, except those of Latin America, by the early twentieth century. One result, in Europe, was the growth of organized political parties that appealed to the masses, much like those that already existed in the United States. The spread of political democracy in Europe gave rise to numerous factions and coalitions in the legislatures. It also gave various radical political movements, such as the British Labour Party, the opportunity to promote their ideologies more widely and vie more effectively for political support.

Growth of Socialism

As movements for economic and political reform gained ground, so did the appeal of various forms of socialism.

SOCIALISM IN EUROPE

Socialism, and particularly Marxism, did not catch on as readily in Britain as in other places. In France, however, the Socialist Party became popular before the outbreak of World War I, becoming a major party in the Chamber of Deputies (the popularly elected lower legislative house). There were also strong Marxian socialist parties in Belgium and Austria-Hungary. In Germany, Bismarck's failure to destroy the German Social Democratic Party (SPD) through repressive legislation helped goad him into proposing a program of social welfare legislation designed to woo laborers away from socialist propaganda. Health and accident insurance, disability benefits, and a system of social security for the aged were among the measures that marked the beginnings of the welfare state in Germany. After Bismarck resigned in 1890, however, the SPD continued to grow.

AMERICAN SOCIALISM

In the United States, the most successful socialist organization was the Social Democratic Party, founded in 1897 by Eugene V. Debs. The party's perpetual candidate for U.S. president, Debs ran five times. In 1912 he garnered nearly 900,000 popular votes, 6 percent of the total.

NON-REVOLUTIONARY SOCIALISM

Most socialist parties did not adopt the fervor for violent revolution that characterized the Bolsheviks in Russia. Rather, like the German SPD, they became content with revisionism. After all, the people they relied on most for support, the workers, were becoming less militant as unionization and social welfare legislation tended to alleviate the worst causes for complaint. In addition, most socialist parties were clearly national parties, not particularly concerned with worldwide revolution. Almost without exception, when the war came they remained loyal to the governments of their individual nations. Those that did not practically disappeared.

Unionism

Another continuing movement for social reform was trade unionism. Unions became legal in Great Britain, France, and Germany during the last half of the nineteenth century. At first, union organization took place mostly among skilled workers, but it had extended to other workers by the end of the century. Unionism's goal was to improve working conditions and wages, and its activities included sometimes long and violent strikes. Highly unpopular with employers, unions were never able to attract a majority of the workers in this era. Unions became stronger in Germany, however, than in any other country of Europe; between 1895 and 1912 membership jumped from 270,000 to about 3 million. Philosophically, German socialists generally resisted the temptation to identify themselves with pure socialism. Instead, they advocated collective bargaining—anathema to revolutionary socialists because it meant working within the system rather than trying to overthrow it.

THE UNITED STATES

In the United States the American Federation of Labor also continued to work within the system. Membership in this union, which emphasized the organization of skilled workers rather than striving for the solidarity of all labor, was over 1 million at the beginning of the twentieth century. A number of violent strikes, however, demonstrated the increasingly tense relationship between capital and labor and did not help the public image of unionism in general. A more radical movement, bent on completely overthrowing the system, was the Industrial Workers of the World, founded in 1903. The

Wobblies, as its members were called, engaged in numerous strikes and considerable outright violence. Any influence they may have had was effectively destroyed during World War I.

The Beginnings of the Welfare State

Governmental responses to the demands of working people resulted in the beginnings of what became known later as the welfare state.

DEFINITION

In contrast to pure socialism, which by definition means collective ownership and control of all means of production and distribution, the term *welfare state* refers simply to acceptance by the state of responsibility for the economic and social well-being of its people. Movement toward the welfare state generally began with the alleviation of hardship resulting from unemployment, disability, or old age. From there it could broaden to the point that government was providing health care and other extended services for all, regardless of financial status, as well as postretirement income.

SIGNIFICANCE AND DEVELOPMENT

The development of the welfare state followed the rise of industrialism, which created such complex new economic and social relationships that the abilities of individuals, families, and communities to provide all human needs were gradually, and often drastically, diminished. By the time of World War I governments almost everywhere in the Western world were at least beginning to recognize a need for some kind of involvement in providing for the needs of the people in general.

Germany and England. In Germany, the move began with Bismarck's reforms in the 1880s. In Great Britain, a flurry of social welfare measures were passed between 1906, when the Liberal Party came to power, and 1914. These included higher taxes on the rich in order to help finance such things as national health insurance, national unemployment insurance, and old age pensions.

The United States. In the United States, social welfare legislation was part of the so-called Progressive Movement of the early twentieth century. The movement began at the state level and resulted in state laws banning child labor, limiting the hours older children could work, limiting women to ten hours a day, limiting the hours of mining and smelter workers, and requiring employers to provide workmen's compensation for losses due to accidents. In addition, state governments became more fully involved in such public activities as schools, public health and welfare, caring for the handicapped, and loans to farmers. Little direct social welfare legislation was carried out at the national level before the war, though the government did provide workmen's compensation for federal employees, legislate an eight-hour day for railroad employees, and establish national farm loans and other aid to agriculture.

The Leninist Challenge

Some socialists saw in the welfare state a move toward their ideal, but such gradualism, or revisionism, was not an option for Russian socialists.

RUSSIA'S ECONOMIC PROGRESS

In the closing years of the nineteenth century Russia developed much of its industrial potential and demonstrated impressive economic progress. There were serious grievances, however, at every level. Working and living conditions among the laboring classes and peasants remained poor, business and professional people longed for political representation, and nationalist movements were creating problems in Poland, the Ukraine, and elsewhere. Moreover, Russia's humiliation in the Russo-Japanese War (see chapter 12) only intensified internal political unrest.

LENIN

The Russian Social Democratic Party, fully Marxist, was organized in 1898, but it was outlawed by the government and had to operate underground or in exile. One brilliant young lawyer, Vladimir Lenin, was exiled to Siberia in 1895. In 1900 he went to Switzerland, from where he conducted revolutionary activities for the next seventeen years.

Lenin and Bolshevism. Lenin soon parted company with those who relied on the ideal of peaceful revolution. Gradualism, he believed, would only postpone what really had to happen. Capitalism must be overthrown by violent revolution, which could be achieved only by a party of highly disciplined workers, led by an elite corps of intellectuals and full-time revolutionaries. In 1903 Lenin and his followers won a slim majority in the London Congress of the Russian Social Democratic Party. They called themselves *Bolsheviks*, meaning "majority." Nine years later, they organized a separate party.

THE REVOLUTION OF 1905

"Bloody Sunday." Lenin had little directly to do, however, with the ill-fated revolution of 1905. It grew out of a large but peaceful demonstration of workers marching toward Tsar Nicholas II's winter palace in St. Petersburg on a Sunday in January. They were attempting to present a petition for improved working conditions, but suddenly they were fired upon by the tsar's troops; perhaps 100 were killed.

The October Manifesto and Its Results. This massacre reverberated throughout Russia in the form of strikes, mutinies, and violence that lasted for the next ten months. The tsar finally capitulated; in an "October Manifesto" he promised full civil rights to the people as well as the establishment of a Duma (parliament) to be elected by popular franchise. Technically he made good on his promise, although the new constitution preserved several of his traditional powers, including the veto. The first Duma, however, began to demand liberal reforms unacceptable to the tsar, who dissolved it. For the same reason, and acting on the advice of his premier, Peter Stolypin, the tsar also dissolved the second Duma. Stolypin then engineered a change in election laws that allowed the next meeting of the Duma to be dominated by landholders loyal to the government. Conservatism still reigned, but by the time World War I broke out, Russia's constitutional monarchy ruled uneasily over a growing undercurrent of radical discontent. In Switzerland, meanwhile, Lenin was biding his time, waiting for the moment when enough social unrest could bring on the real revolution.

THE COLLAPSE OF EUROPEAN ORDER, AND WORLD WAR I

In 1914 a war broke out that was destined to affect many of the movements noted above as well as the economic and political structure of much of the world. More than in almost any previous conflict, the warring governments had genuine popular support, clearly reflecting the nationalism that had solidified many people in the late nineteenth century (see chapter 9).

Origins of the Great War

The underlying causes of the war were highly complex. They included imperialism, entangling alliances, and chauvinistic nationalism. While the relationship between these and other causal factors will continue to be discussed at length by scholars, the immediate chain of events that led to the outbreak of war is clear.

THE ALLIANCE SYSTEM

One result of the continuing political tensions among the European powers was a series of changing commitments and alliances that, in the long run, had unintended consequences.

Bismarck's Alliances. In Germany, Bismarck was concerned with maintaining peace, preserving the balance of power, and stemming both the tide of political liberalism and the possibility that France might try to regain some of the prestige and territory it lost in the Franco-Prussian War. He became the guiding light behind a new system of alliances intended to deal with such problems. One was the Three Emperors' League, formed in 1873, which brought together Germany, Russia, and Austria. In 1879, after Russia withdrew from the league, Bismarck signed a defensive treaty with Austria forming the Dual Alliance. Russia, in turn, sought reconciliation with Germany, and the Three Emperors' League was renewed in 1881. It lapsed again in 1887, but Bismarck negotiated a Reinsurance Treaty with Russia, whereby each power promised to remain neutral if the other were attacked. Meanwhile, with the addition of Italy in 1882, the Dual Alliance became the Triple Alliance.

Bismarck Undermined. With these defensive alliances in place, and with no territorial ambitions for Germany, Bismarck believed he had achieved a balance of power that would, indeed, keep the peace. In 1888, however, William II became *kaiser* (emperor), and his plans for Germany ran counter to those of the chancellor. Bismarck was forced to resign in 1890. Almost immediately most of his alliance system disintegrated. Only the Triple Alliance remained, and Italy was a weak and wavering partner.

Franco-Russian Alliance and the Entente Cordial. A new system of alliances soon appeared. The first was the 1894 Franco-Russian alliance against Germany—a practical arrangement for both countries since the kaiser refused to renew the Reinsurance Treaty with Russia, while France was seeking both an escape from its isolation and security from any possible German threat. By the end of the century Great Britain, too, was becoming suspicious of Germany, partly because it was building a new navy that could threaten Britain's overseas empire. In 1902 Britain entered into an alliance with Japan against Russian expansionism. Then in 1904 Britain concluded a series of agreements, known as the Entente Cordial, with France. This paved the way for England and France, traditional enemies, to become allies against Germany.

The First Moroccan Crisis and the Triple Entente. Bringing England and France together under the same roof had seemed impossible only a few years earlier. It was not long, however, before German ambition threw them into each other's arms. In March 1905 Germany invaded the French protectorate of Morocco and then called for an international conference to settle the dispute. The conference was held at Algeciras, Spain, in 1906. There, to Germany's chagrin, Spain, Italy, the United States, and Great Britain all supported France. In preparation for a possible German attack on France, the general staffs of Britain and France began to meet together in strategy sessions. The next step brought Russia, still allied with France, into this unlikely family. A 1907 agreement between Britain and Russia thus informally, at least, tied France and Britain together in what is known as the Triple Entente. Bismarck's alliances, well designed to keep the peace, had been replaced by a different system that had the potential for explosion.

TENSIONS IN THE BALKANS AND ELSEWHERE

The explosion was fermenting in the Balkans, where some states came under the rule of the weak Ottoman Empire, some were practically independent, and others were part of Austria-Hungary. The activities of the Young Turks (see chapter 11) threatened to give new life to the Ottoman Empire, however, which worried the major powers and resulted in a series of crises that eventually erupted in war.

Crisis in Bosnia and Morocco. The first crisis arose in 1908. In private negations Russia agreed to support Austrian annexation of Bosnia-Herzegovina in return for Austria's support for opening the Dardanelles (Turkish Straits) to the Russian navy. These agreements were supposed to be made publicly, at a forthcoming international conference. When Austria went ahead with the annexation before the conference, however, Russia was highly offended. It was further humiliated when it got no support at the conference from Britain and France (its allies in the Triple Entente) for its own demands. At the same time, Germany was affronted by Austria's action, but could do nothing because it felt dependent upon Austria (its partner in the Dual Alliance) in case of other problems. The Bosnian crisis thus strained, though it did not destroy, both alliance systems.

The next crisis came in Morocco, where France intervened to put down a rebellion in 1911. Germany sent a gunboat into a Moroccan port to protect its own interests, which more fully convinced both France and Britain of Germany's greater potential threat. The security of the two former enemies seemed more inextricably linked than ever.

The Arms and Propaganda Race. European anxieties inevitably led to an arms race. The first Moroccan crisis persuaded many people in Britain, France, Russia, and the United States that Germany had ambitions to dominate all of Europe. German leaders, on the other hand, pictured other European countries as involved in a villainous plot to encircle their country and stop its expansion. As such paranoia grew, Germany continued to expand its already powerful navy. Britain followed suit. Propagandists in each camp threw bitter epithets at the other; by the time war broke out, many Britons were convinced that Germany was deliberately preparing to destroy their empire.

The Balkan Wars. The European tinder box became more volatile in 1911 after Italy attacked the Ottoman Empire and took Libya and the Dodecanese Islands. Thus softened up, the empire was vulnerable to a successful attack the following year from the combined forces of Bulgaria, Greece, Montenegro, and Serbia. The result was that the Ottoman Empire ceded most of its remaining territory to the Balkan states in 1913. The victors were soon at each other's throats over the disposition of the spoils, however. That same year a second Balkan war broke out, with Greece, Romania, Turkey, and Serbia allied against Bulgaria. Austria, determined to stop the expansion of Serbia, soon intervened. The Serbs were stopped, and the emergence of the independent kingdom of Albania kept them from an outlet to the Adriatic Sea.

WAR ENGULFS EUROPE

These multifarious alliances and tensions created a ready-made situation in which the right incident could produce a chain reaction that could then explode into an all-engulfing inferno. That incident was another crisis in the Balkans.

The Assassination and Its Impact. On June 28, 1914, the heir to the Austro-Hungarian throne, Archduke Francis Ferdinand, and his wife were assassinated in the Bosnian capital of Sarajevo. It was widely (and correctly) believed that members of the Serbian government were involved in the plot; the reaction of the Austrians was predictable. They urged an immediate attack, but Hungarians within the empire insisted upon an appeal to their German ally. The kaiser answered with what is often referred to as a "blank check." It gave the Austrians the go-ahead to declare war on Serbia, promising to keep Russia, sympathetic with the Slavic people, out of any war that might follow. On July 24 Austria delivered an ultimatum to Serbia. It deliberately made at least one demand that was more than Serbia could accept—that Austrians be allowed to participate in the investigation of the assassination and the punishment of its perpetrators. The Serbs rejected the ultimatum, albeit in conciliatory language. On July 28 Austria declared war.

Chain Reaction. With that the dominoes began to fall. Russia began to mobilize in support of Serbia. Britain attempted to call an international conference to settle the issues, but Austria refused any such suggestion. Austria prepared for war against Russia, Russia stepped up its pace of mobilization, and Germany, recognizing that France inevitably would be drawn in, began its own massive mobilization. Germany declared war on Russia on August 1 and on France on August 3. It immediately implemented the Schlieffen Plan, which had been in place since 1905, and invaded France by marching through tiny Luxembourg and then Belgium. Great Britain, fulfilling its obligation to France as well as a long-standing guarantee of Belgian neutrality, declared war on Germany on August 4. Two days later Austria-Hungary declared war on Russia.

A War of Attrition

Neither side anticipated a long, drawn-out war, for both expected to win quickly. As the months and years dragged on, however, neither gained a major advantage, and both suffered devastating losses. The Triple Entente became known as the Allies, and Germany and Austria as the Central Powers.

STALEMATE ON THE WESTERN FRONT

Most of the fighting took place along Germany's western front, an area extending through Belgium and into France and from the North Sea through Alsace-Lorraine. The German war plan contemplated sweeping around the French defenses by attacking through Belgium, moving on to the English

Channel, and then making a big sweep to the South to complete the conquest of France. Then troops would be free to fight on the eastern front.

After the initial German drive the French began a series of counteroffensives, but French troops were unable to withstand Germany's overwhelming numbers and its machine guns. Soon, however, the French and the British joined forces and stopped the German advance at the Battle of the Marne in September 1914. At that point the war became a stalemate. Both sides dug in with trenches, barbed wire, and machine-gun nests. Massive attacks, supported by huge artillery barrages, were unable to make any permanent breakthroughs. Men were killed or wounded by the tens of thousands, reserves were continually brought up to replace them, and neither side achieved any permanent breakthrough. The fighting simply dragged on.

THE EASTERN FRONT

The war in the east initially went worse for the Central Powers, as heavy losses were inflicted by the Russians advancing into Austrian territory. Before long, however, superior German forces turned them back, inflicting over 2 million casualties in the process. They also gained new allies as Turkey and Bulgaria joined the Central Powers. After the Allies secretly agreed to deliver certain coveted territories after the war, Italy joined with them and began fighting Austrian armies. Other Allies included Serbia, Albania, Romania and Greece, while the Ottoman Empire (Turkey) and Bulgaria lined up with the Central Powers.

The Ottoman Empire. In 1915 the British attempted to break the deadlock by attacking the Central Powers through the Dardanelles, capturing Constantinople, and knocking the weakened Ottoman Empire out of the war. The plan was abandoned, however, after the Allies lost nearly 150,000 troops. In 1917 the British were more successful when Colonel T. E. Lawrence, soon to be known as Lawrence of Arabia, led an Arab revolt against the Turks. The following year the British finally destroyed the Ottoman Empire.

TOTAL WAR

Seldom, if ever, had European civilians been so totally involved in a war effort as they became in this one. As the war dragged on and shortages increased, it became clear to both sides that nothing short of total mobilization could avoid disaster. This led to a degree of governmental economic planning and control that would have been unthinkable only a short time before. The fact that governments on both sides succeeded in managing their wartime economies so well had the unintended side effect of strengthening the cause of socialism in some countries. Germany went farthest in the direction of a planned economy, even passing a compulsory labor law in 1916. Rationing was imposed in Great Britain, and all the nation's effort was poured into war production. A similar all-out mobilization took place in the United States once it declared war.

TECHNOLOGY AND WORLD WAR I

The technology of World War I increased mankind's potential for killing more than that of any previous era in history. Except for the atomic bomb, all the most important instruments of death employed in World War II and afterward were only improvements on the weapons used in World War I. The airplane, for example, had only minimal influence on the outcome of the war, but pilots on both sides pioneered tactics and theories that proved effective a generation later. Submarines were devastating when first used by the Germans. The armored tank, introduced by the British in 1917, became an important force in the ground war. The machine gun saw considerable improvement in the war and was a major killer in the stalemate along the western front. Important innovations in artillery included rapid-firing, accurate field guns and high-explosive shells that could spray destructive shrapnel. The telephone became a military weapon by which spotters could help gunners hit targets they could not even see. Radio, too, made its wartime debut in World War I. Finally, poison gas perhaps inspired more terror in the hearts of soldiers and civilians alike than any of the death-dealing wonders of the age. Countermeasures were developed, however, that largely blunted its effectiveness.

OVERSEAS

In a way, the term "World War I" is a misnomer, for there was relatively little fighting of great consequence outside Europe. The exception was East Asia, where Japan, honoring its 1902 alliance with Britain, quickly gobbled up the German colonies in China and the Pacific. Japan thus improved its position against China, where it already had imperial interests. On the other hand, the involvement of several other overseas nations did make the political scope of the war, if not the military action, a global one. Japan, China, British-controlled India, Cuba, Brazil, Nicaragua, Liberia, the United States, and several smaller nations all joined the Allies.

THE SEA WAR

Control of the sea was important to both sides. The German navy, however, did not play a significant role in the war, mainly because it could not break out of the blockade, enhanced by mines, that kept it bottled up in the North Sea. Its submarine fleet, however, was a different matter. After the British imposed a blockade on all shipping to Germany, intent on starving out its enemy, Germany responded with submarine warfare, intending to starve out the British. Not even neutral ships were safe in the area around Great Britain identified by Germany as a war zone. Neutral nations were irate at both countries. But since Germany actually sank a number of neutral ships, its offense seemed the greatest.

The *Lusitania*. The issue came to a head in 1915 after the Germans sank the *Lusitania*, a British liner carrying munitions as well as passengers. Twelve hundred people, mostly civilians, were drowned, including 118 Americans. President Woodrow Wilson quickly issued a stern warning that a repeat offense would not be tolerated. The Germans backed off for about two years.

AMERICAN ENTRY

In January 1917, however, Germany decided to resume submarine warfare and knock out the Allies quickly before America had time to become involved. Wilson immediately broke off diplomatic relations with Germany.

Wilson's Agony. Wilson agonized long and hard over the decision to go to war. He could not bring himself to send American troops to be slaughtered without some moral purpose greater than victory or revenge. In January he told the U.S. Senate that the United States was seeking "peace without victory" and "peace among equals," for this was the only kind of peace that could endure. Further, it must be based on freedom of the seas, disarmament, and a league of nations that would make any future war impossible. It was on the basis of such high motives that the conscience-torn American president finally rationalized American entry. Justifying it to the American people was made easier by two events.

Zimmermann Note. In February, Wilson received word from the British that they had intercepted a note from German Foreign Secretary Alfred Zimmermann to his ambassador in Mexico. It told the envoy to offer money, an alliance, and former Mexican territory in the United States to the Mexican government in return for its declaring war on the United States. Wilson made the news public on March 1, which immediately aroused Americans to a fever pitch, demanding action against Germany.

America Declares War. Wilson hoped the war could be turned into a crusade to make the world "safe for democracy," but the fact that tsarist Russia was among the Allies made this seem impossible. However, the overthrow of the tsar in March gave Americans at least the temporary illusion that the Allies were all fighting to maintain democracy. On April 6, 1917, the United States declared war on the Central Powers.

COLLAPSE OF GERMANY

With the collapse of Russian involvement in the war (see below), Germany was free to concentrate its efforts on the western front. It may well have achieved a victory had it not been for American intervention.

The Last Offensive. In 1918 the Germans decided to put all their efforts into one last drive to Paris. But their reserves were running out, the nation was totally exhausted, and fresh troops from America reinforced the Allies enough that the Germans were stopped again at the Marne. The Allies then began a counteroffensive that demonstrated not only the vitality of the American fighting forces but also the almost total exhaustion and disillusionment of the German troops. There were massive surrenders. In at least one instance German soldiers ready to surrender were heard to call out to their reinforcements that they should go home for they were only prolonging the war. Austrian forces, also, were exhausted, and their fronts in the Balkans and Italy collapsed.

Surrender. The kaiser formed a new government and began suing for peace. But negotiations dragged on while everything else simply fell apart for the Central Powers. Bulgaria signed an armistice on September 29. Turkey did the same on October 30. Austria-Hungary surrendered on November 3 and immediately dissolved into several national states. Finally, early in November, military mutinies and political rebellion among workers at home brought the government to a crisis. On November 9 Kaiser William II abdicated. A new government led by the Social Democratic Party asked for an immediate peace based on the Fourteen Points announced by Wilson as America's war aims. It signed an armistice on November 11.

Significance of the Social Democratic Party. The fact that the Social Democratic Party came to power when it did probably prevented a bloody civil war and obtained for Germany the best peace possible. Significantly, its coming to power also amounted to a revolution, for the old monarchy so carefully fostered by Bismarck was finally overthrown. The German Social Democrats, however, were more moderate than the Leninists in Russia; they were willing to accept both political democracy and gradualism. They were supported by the military and the populace, and as soon as they took over, general morale improved.

The Russian Revolution

In Russia, meanwhile, a revolution of major proportions helped change not only the course of the war but also the history of both Russia and the world.

COLLAPSE OF THE OLD ORDER

Disillusionment. The Russians were quickly disillusioned with the war. Their poorly equipped armies suffered terrible losses; the tsar, Nicholas II, was ineffective as a leader. The Duma as well as the people in general became increasingly critical. In the summer of 1915 demands in the Duma for a new, more democratic government reached explosive new heights.

Revolution. The tsar's answer was simply to dismiss the Duma and depart to the front, where he hoped to rally the troops. The leadership void in Petrograd (as St. Petersburg had been renamed) was immediately filled by his wife, but unrest continued. In March 1917 riots spread throughout the city. The tsar sent orders to fire on the rioters, but even the troops mutinied and refused to do so. Everyone had lost confidence in Nicholas II. On March 12 the Duma declared a provisional government, and on March 15 the Tsar abdicated.

THE RULE OF THE MODERATES

The provisional government, consisting largely of moderates called Constitutional Democrats, responded quickly with a program of liberal reform. It failed, however, to respond to demands for land reform. In the meantime, socialist groups began organizing workers into soviets, or workers' councils, which gradually became estranged from the government. Their disaffection was only exacerbated by food shortages, demands for land reform, and continuing disillusionment with the war.

Bolsheviks and Lenin. At the same time, the new government was determined to continue the war. As early as March 14, therefore, almost before the provisional government could do anything, the Bolshevik-dominated Petrograd Soviet (Council of Workers and Soldiers' Deputies) defied it by issuing the notorious "Order No. 1." This incredible order actually stripped military authority from officers and placed it in the hands of committees elected by common soldiers. The result, anticipated by the Bolsheviks, was the complete collapse of discipline and mass desertions. In addition, the Germans halted their Russian offensive so as not to encourage the Russians to reunite. They also smuggled Vladimir Lenin, along with other Bolshevik activists, from his exile in Switzerland to Petrograd, hoping he would create more internal difficulty in Russia.

THE BOLSHEVIK REVOLUTION

Despite all the internal strife and chaos, in May the provisional government launched another offensive against the Germans, which totally failed. At the same time, all over Russia peasants were expropriating land, and peasant-soldiers were deserting and returning home. In the cities, shortages led to factory closures, which in turn led angry workers to take over the factories in an effort to keep them running. A vast social upheaval was sweeping the country; Lenin and the Bolsheviks sensed that the time was ripe for revolution. Lenin's attempted July coup failed. In fear for his life, Lenin went into hiding and then into a self-imposed exile in Finland. But the next month a right-wing attempt to seize power also failed. The popularity of the Bolsheviks rose precipitously. Still in Finland, Lenin heard and believed a false rumor that the Germans and the British were about to make a separate peace. Fearing that they would then join together and invade Russia in order to destroy any vestige of revolution, he instructed his followers that the time was right to begin the insurrection. "History will not forgive us if we do not assume power now, he wrote. "We will win *absolutely* and *unquestionably*."

Trotsky and the November Revolution. Lenin's brilliant collaborator Leon Trotsky engineered the successful Bolshevik revolution. First he seized military power in Petrograd. Then, on the night of November 6, his forces seized the government and invaded the Congress of Soviets, whose meeting had extended into the early hours of the morning. Those opposed to the Bolsheviks left the hall. The remaining delegates immediately declared the Soviets in power, with Lenin, who had secretly returned to Petrograd, as the new head of state.

Abandoning the War. One of the new regime's first acts was to abandon the war effort. In December 1917, a truce was signed with Germany. The price for peace, however, was high. At the Treaty of Brest-Litovsk in March 1918 Russia was forced to give up all its western territories, which included almost a third of its population. It also had to pay a heavy indemnity to Germany. But Lenin and the Bolsheviks were free to pursue their goal of building a new kind of society under the absolute control of a single party.

THE BOLSHEVIK STATE

Though many doubted that the revolution would be permanent, Lenin, with the aid of Trotsky, remained in power. The two eagerly began the task of building a socialist society on the ruins of monarchy, aristocracy, and a short-lived attempt at political democracy.

Beginning the Transition. In moving toward a state-controlled economy, Lenin continued the policy of taking land from aristocratic landholders and granting it to the peasants. He also supported workers' demands that they be given direct control of factories. With these things accomplished, the peasants and the workers at least thought they had control of property and therefore had a stake in the revolution. In the long run, however, they had little or no personal control.

The problem of securing Bolshevik power was another matter. Free elections were held, but the Bolsheviks won only a minority of the delegates to the new Constituent Assembly, which met in January 1918. Lenin's response, with the use of Bolshevik soldiers, was to permanently disband the assembly after only one day—a portentous step toward one-party rule.

Civil War. The immediate consequence was more civil war. Old vested interests and army officers organized the "Whites" in opposition to the "Reds," as the Bolsheviks were called. At least eighteen regions proclaimed their independence, and the war went on for three years. The Bolsheviks, renamed Communists, were more united, however, and had a superior army under the harsh but effective leadership of Trotsky. They also resorted to terrorist tactics, executing thousands of people who were even suspected of favoring the opposition. Among the victims were the deposed tsar and his family, who were executed on the night of July 16, 1918.

Lenin Triumphant. Red fighting forces gradually wore down White armies. The Allies attempted to intervene in behalf of the old order, but their seemingly halfhearted efforts did little except help the Communists by provoking a nationalistic response. The revolution ended in permanent triumph for Lenin and the Bolsheviks. In 1924, after the death of Lenin, Petrograd was renamed Leningrad.

A DICTATED PEACE AND THE AFTERMATH OF WAR

The peace conference, meanwhile, opened officially in Paris on January 18, 1919. Seventy delegates attended, representing twenty-seven victorious allied powers. The Central Powers were not represented, and neither was Russia. The principle actors were the so-called "Big Four"—President Woodrow Wilson of the United States, Prime Minister David Lloyd George of Great Britain, Premier Georges Clemenceau of France, and Prime Minister Vittorio Orlando of Italy.

Wilson's Fourteen Points

A year earlier Wilson had presented to a joint session of Congress his own formula for peace, the famous Fourteen Points. The list included an insistence that there should be no secret diplomacy connected with the peace treaty. It called for freedom of the seas, lower trade barriers, arms reduction, and a revamping of the colonial system to take into account the interests of native peoples. It also included plans for redrawing European boundaries in order to give various peoples their choice of who should govern them (self-determination). The fourteenth point was the capstone of Wilson's utopian hope for the postwar world. It called for the formation of "a general association of nations . . . for the purpose of affording mutual guarantees of political independence and territorial integrity to great and small states alike."

Though most of these ideals were never fully achieved, the Fourteen Points initially provided people everywhere with high hopes for a fair peace. When he arrived in Europe, and briefly toured England, France, and Italy, Wilson was warmly greeted by enthusiastic crowds almost like a messiah. When it came down to practical negotiations, however, idealism gave way to national self-interest, secret treaties already in place, and the determination of the European allies to make Germany pay for the war.

The Reordering of Europe

Diverse interests and perspectives among the Big Four became apparent immediately. Wilson sought nothing but to implement his Fourteen Points. Clemenceau was determined both to make Germany suffer and to make sure it would never wage war again. Lloyd George, too, was determined to punish Germany and to make sure that nothing in Wilson's program would interfere with Britain's own policies. Orlando pushed mainly for the territorial awards Italy had been promised before coming into the war.

They argued for three and a half months, compromising on all the issues. Wilson did most of the compromising in order to keep his greatest dream, the League of Nations, intact. The final peace settlement consisted of five separate treaties. The major one, the Treaty of Versailles, was ready to present to Germany on May 6, and was signed in June. Separate treaties were signed with the other Central Powers.

GERMAN TERRITORY AND DISARMAMENT

Germany was required to cede the long-disputed Alsace-Lorraine to France. Much of Germany along the Rhine was demilitarized and was to be occupied by allied troops for fifteen years. Germany was also restricted to an army of 100,000 soldiers whose service was long term, thus thwarting the possibility of training a large reserve. In addition, Germany was forbidden to have a significant navy, submarines, war planes, tanks, heavy artillery, or poison gas. Overseas, Germany lost its African possessions to Britain, France, and South Africa, while its Pacific possessions were divided among Australia, New Zealand, and Japan.

SELF-DETERMINATION

Territorial realignments were made also in other parts of Europe. Silesia, Prussia, and other eastern territories were cut off from Germany. Poland was made an independent state for the first time since 1795 (see chapter 5), with an all-important corridor to the sea. Austria-Hungary was eliminated in favor of a number of smaller states and ostensibly in accord with the principle of self-determination. The same principle presumably led to the creation of Czechoslovakia, though there were still questions as to whether its government really represented the various nationalities within it. The same was true of Yugoslavia.

The old Ottoman Empire also disappeared, and a new, considerably smaller republic of Turkey was declared in 1923. Palestine and Iraq, formerly parts of the Ottoman Empire, were placed under British control, while Syria and Lebanon went to France. These areas, plus the former German colonies in Africa and the Pacific, were actually "mandates" of the League of Nations; eventually they were to be nurtured by their protectors for independence. The plan did not work, however; by the time of World War II, European colonialism had not disappeared.

THE LEAGUE COVENANT

The Treaty of Versailles included the Covenant of the League of Nations. In its broadest sense, the new organization was intended to be a deliberative body, where members would consult in their common interest, especially in the event of aggression or threat of war. Members agreed to submit their differences to arbitration. If a nation refused to abide by its agreement, it was subject to sanctions, including military ones. It sounded good on paper, but in practical terms there was no way, ultimately, to enforce the decisions of the league.

The league covenant also called for the eventual independence of European colonies elsewhere in the world, but again there was no strength in this provision. The long-range effect, however, was to raise hopes in colonial areas, and thus intensify nationalistic movements.

AMERICA AND THE LEAGUE

The league had several problems but none quite so ironic or serious as the fact that the United States, whose president was almost single-handedly responsible for creating it, refused to join. Conservative Republicans, arguing that the covenant undermined American sovereignty, persuaded the Senate to place reservations on America's acceptance of the treaty. Wilson refused to accept the conditions. As a result, the United States was never a signatory to the Treaty of Versailles and never part of the League of Nations.

Germany: The Costs of Defeat

For Germany, the most difficult parts of the treaty had to do with war guilt and reparations.

GUILT BY DECREE

The treaty specifically stated that Germany was responsible for the war and accepted responsibility for all losses and damages accruing to the Allies as a result. Being forced to accept such full-scale responsibility was a heavy burden indeed, but in the dictated peace the German representatives at Versailles had no choice.

REPARATIONS

The reparations were more frustrating than the guilt clause. No fixed amount was set at the conference, but Germany was to pay $5 billion annually until 1921, after which it would have thirty more years to pay whatever final figure was determined. The German government finally signed the treaty, but only under protest. The German people also protested, and as a result, they began to loose some confidence in the newly established government. They thought they had been betrayed.

A TURNING POINT IN WORLD HISTORY

As the war drew to an end, people everywhere expressed high hopes that the postwar world would bring great changes. One was W. E. B. Du Bois, the most able spokesman for American blacks of the era. In 1918 he expressed his hope for blacks and other races worldwide as he predicted what the new age would bring:

> This war is an End and, also, a Beginning. Never again will darker people of the world occupy just the place they had before. Out of this war will rise, soon or late, an independent China, a self-governing India, an Egypt with representative institutions, an Africa for the Africans, and not merely for business exploitation. Out of this war will rise, too, an American Negro with the right to vote and the right to work and the right to live without insult.

The dream ultimately came true, but not as soon as Du Bois so fervently hoped. Self-determination for most colonial states did not become a reality until after the next world war. Neither did Du Bois's hope for equality for the American blacks. Nevertheless, the war was a major turning point in world history. It had important immediate results as well as significant long-range consequences.

Immediate Human and Material Costs

The human and material costs were overwhelming. The human slaughter, especially, left deep, long-lasting scars in the souls of nations that would take much more time to heal than the bombed-out cities and devastated countryside that stood like pockmarks on the face of Europe.

HUMAN COSTS

Russia paid the heaviest price in military loss of life—1,700,000. Its wounded amounted to 4,950,000, which brought its total casualties to roughly 55 percent of the 12,000,000 ultimately mobilized for war. Germany came second in this grisly toll, with 1,808,546 killed and 4,247,143 wounded. Total military casualties amounted to 4,888,891 killed and 12,809,280 wounded among the Allies and 3,131,889 killed and 8,419,533 wounded on the side of the Central Powers. The Allies also lost 3,157,633 civilians, compared with 3,485,000 among the Central Powers.

THE COST IN DOLLARS

Economically, the heaviest cost of the war fell upon the Germans—an estimated $58,027,000,000 of a total cost of $86,238,000,000 was born by the Central Powers. The total economic burden born by the Allies was $193,899,000,000, with the British and French governments carrying the lion's share of $51,975,000,000 and $49,877,000,000, respectively. The United States spent $32,320,000,000.

Political and Social Consequences

The war provided a boost to many transformations already taking place in world society and was a catalyst for other changes.

WEAKENING EUROPEAN DOMINANCE

Economically, Europe was devastated, while the United States actually gained new financial strength. By 1930 it became the world's greatest creditor nation. The same was true with industrial production—by 1930 the United States, whose factories were stimulated and built up during the war, produced 42.2 percent of the world's industrial output. World economic leadership had crossed the Atlantic.

Superficially, Europe's global hegemony seemed more powerful than ever before. In addition to their prewar colonies, Britain and France controlled a number of former Ottoman areas in the Middle East. But their political power was not as secure as the map might make it seem. The postwar world would bring new tensions between them and their colonies as native peoples, teased by talk of self-determination, would look forward to independence, only to be disappointed.

THE IDEAL OF SELF-DETERMINATION

Two monarchies (those of Germany and Russia) were wiped out during the war, and two great empires (Austria-Hungary and the Ottoman Empire) disappeared. The breakup of these empires was an apparent triumph of self-determination for the several new national states that arose. The very existence of this ideal, however, continued to create discontent and civil strife within some of these states, as well as in the old states where substantial ethnic minorities still had nationalistic yearnings.

RUSSIAN COMMUNISM

In Russia, capitalism as well as monarchy had been destroyed, replaced by a communist state. Ostensibly designed to benefit the masses, the Bolshevik government also destroyed any vestige of democracy that had emerged under the old regime. Instead, it instituted stern, one-party rule. It also began to preach and plan for exporting the communist revolution worldwide.

SOCIALISM AND THE WELFARE STATE

While Lenin's brand of Marxism took hold in Russia, more moderate socialism received a boost in other European countries, such as England and Germany. The governments of these countries continued to move toward the welfare state, which probably acted as a hedge against communism. It helped to blunt the cries of those who were demanding that government pay more attention to social welfare and who could have been attracted to more extreme forms of socialism. The story was different in the United States, however, where socialists were the object of suspicion and the denial of civil liberties both during and after the war.

WOMAN SUFFRAGE

The movement for woman suffrage, generally put on hold during the war, revived with fervor afterward. Many European powers were quick to grant it. In Great Britain women over thirty received the right to vote in 1918, though not until twenty years later were they granted suffrage on the same basis as men. Woman suffrage was achieved in several other European states, including Austria and Germany, before 1920. Suffrage in federal elections in Canada came in 1918, and most of the provinces had already granted it by that time. It was achieved in 1920 in the United States. Before World War II numerous other nations around the world had granted it.

INTELLECTUAL DOUBT OF WESTERN VALUES

In terms of political philosophy, traditional European political institutions and ideas no longer seemed as viable to many people. The workers of Europe, especially, questioned the old order in their demand for a whole new approach to social and economic justice. Political winds blowing from Russia sounded impressive to some, though they seemed ominous to others who saw Bolshevism as the next great threat to world order.

Asians, too, began to take Communist ideology as seriously as they had once taken traditional Western liberalism. In China, for instance, where the Communist Party was founded in 1921, even non-Communists were impressed by what was happening in Russia and by the fact that Russia demonstrated support for their own nationalistic struggles. Dr. Sun Yat-sen, father of the 1911 revolution and also an ardent nationalist, once declared that "We no longer look to the West. Our faces are turned to Russia."

The world would never be the same because of the changes either generated or facilitated by World War I. What began in 1914 as still another Balkan war ended up involving the major nations of the world. Old dynasties were swept away in Germany, Russia, Austria-Hungary, and the Ottoman Empire, to be replaced by new leaders, institutions, and ideologies. Asians viewed the war as a European civil war in which they became involved only because Europe had extended so much of its influence in Asia. But they also saw in it a possible way to begin escaping from under the thumb of European powers.

The scars left by the war, both human and physical, would last for generations. Those left on the German people included the memory of horrendous numbers of dead, a heavy reparation debt that they felt they did not deserve, inability to pay the debt, dissatisfaction with their own govern-ment, belief that both the Social Democrats and the Allies had betrayed them, and a mood of understandable anger and disillusionment.

The peace was little more than a long armistice. In less than twenty years conditions created by the war and by the dictated peace led to a renewal of the fighting and, eventually, its escalation into an even more devastating world conflagration. World War II was, in large part, a continuation of what idealists once called the war to end all wars.

Selected Readings

Albrecht-Carrie, Rene. *The Meaning of the First World War*. Englewood Cliffs, NJ: Prentice-Hall, 1965.

Bailey, Thomas A. *Woodrow Wilson and the Lost Peace*. New York: Macmillan, 1944.

Carr, Edward H. *The Bolshevik Revolution: 1917–1923*. Harmondsworth: Penguin, 1966.

Dupuy, R. Ernest, and Trevor N. Dupuy. *The Encyclopedia of Military History*. 2nd ed. New York: Harper & Row, 1986.

Emerson, Ruppert, and Martin Rilson. "The American Dilemma in a Changing World: The Rise of Africa and the Negro American." *Daedalus* 94 (1965), pp. 1055–1084. (The quotation from W. E. B. Du Bois, used in the text, is taken from this source.)

Fischer, Fritz. *Germany's Aims in the First World War*. New York: W. W. Norton, 1967.

Hale, Oron J. *The Great Illusion, 1900–1914*. New York: Harper & Row, 1971.

Joll, James. *The Origins of the First World War*. 2nd ed. London, New York: Longman, 1992.

Kennan, George F. *The Fateful Alliance: France, Russia, and the Coming of the First World War*. New York: Pantheon Books, 1984.

Lafore, Laurence Davis. *The Long Fuse: An Interpretation of the Origins of World War I*. 2nd ed. Philadelphia: Lippincott, 1971.

Levin, N. Gordon, Jr. *Woodrow Wilson and the Paris Peace Conference*. 2nd ed. Lexington: Heath, 1972.

Lieven, D. C. B. *Russia and the Origins of the First World War*. London: Macmillan, 1983.

Marks, Gary W. *Unions in Politics: Britain, Germany, and the United States in the Nineteenth and Early Twentieth Centuries*. Princeton, NJ: Princeton University Press, 1989.

Payne, Robert. *The Life and Death of Lenin*. New York: Simon and Schuster, 1964.

Remak, Joachim. *The Origins of World War I, 1871–1914*. New York: Holt, Rinehart and Winston, 1967.

Remarque, Erich Maria. *All Quiet on the Western Front*. Boston: Little, Brown, 1975.

Tuchman, Barbara W. *The Guns of August*. New York: Macmillan, 1962.

Vicinus, Martha, ed. *A Widening Sphere: Changing Roles of Victorian Women*. Bloomington: Indiana University Press, 1977.

15

The Retreat of Democracy and the Rise of Totalitarianism

Labour Party and J. Ramsay MacDonald come to power in Britain

France begins building the Maginot Line

1930 Iraq given independence by Britain

1931 The British Commonwealth of Nations founded

Japan takes over Manchuria

1932 Franklin D. Roosevelt elected in the United States

Second Five-Year Plan in Russia

1933 Hitler becomes chancellor of Germany

New Deal programs begin in the United States

1936 Franco leads revolution in Spain

1937 Military rule established in Japan

1939 Franco's revolution succeeds in Spain, establishes a dictatorship

In the immediate aftermath of World War I, at least the Western world, with the exception of Russia, seemed safe for democracies. Western governments had high hopes of creating a stable international order and recovering economically from the ravages of war. New, democratic regimes dotted Europe. Democratic governments were in place in Germany, France, England, and the United States. Beneath the surface, however, there was considerable discontent caused by economic dislocation, seething nationalism among various ethnic groups in Europe, and dissatisfaction in Germany with the Treaty of Versailles.

Ironically, even though the United States almost completely withdrew from world leadership and from any international commitments, it had a profound effect on world affairs. It had changed from a debtor nation to a creditor nation, and its exports went to people worldwide. Its economic policies, especially those related to the Great Depression, had a direct effect on the rest of the world. American economic structure and methods were readily adopted in Europe.

Then came the Great Depression, which spread worldwide. Political responses led some Western powers toward the establishment of new authoritarian regimes, shattering the ideals and institutions of Western liberalism. Totalitarianism had already taken over in Italy, and during the depression it took over in Germany. Totalitarian communism was solidified in Russia. Political instability characterized the nations of eastern Europe, usually ending in totalitarian takeovers. The democratic governments of Britain and France moved their nations closer to the welfare state. So, too, did that of the United States, where democracy and capitalism were preserved but at the cost of a greatly increased role of the federal government in the lives of the people. In eastern Asia, meanwhile, Japan moved from several years of democratic, parliamentary government to a period of military control. In the meantime, Germany, Italy, and Japan all developed new expansionist aims. They also marched out of the League of Nations. The implications for world peace were foreboding.

TRANSITION TO PEACETIME POLITICS AND ECONOMICS

A few developments seemed to provide some hope for a long period of international peace. In 1925 European leaders signed a treaty at Locarno, Switzerland. Germany and France agreed upon a common border, while Britain and Italy agreed to intervene militarily if either Germany or France invaded the other. The treaty also dealt with boundary disputes between Poland and Czechoslovakia. In 1926 Germany became a member of the League of Nations. Two years later fifteen nations signed the Kellogg-Briand pact, which "condemned and denounced war as an instrument of national policy." The noble spirit of that agreement was seldom followed, but for the time being it provided another small ray of hope to a war-weary world.

The Western Democracies: Some Generalizations   Politically, the efforts of Western nations to maintain democracy seemed to offer continuing hope, though there were serious problems beneath the surface. Among them were chronic unemployment in some areas, unstable economies, and continuing political unrest.

THE WEIMAR REPUBLIC

In Germany, a new republic was established in 1919, called the Weimar Republic after the city in which its democratic constitution was adopted. That government came close to collapse during the French occupation of the Ruhr (see below). The nation also faced serious economic problems that only brought continuing political unrest. At the heart of these problems was its heavy reparation and war debt payments (see below). Sharp political divisions continued, with most of the working classes seemingly attracted to the Social Democrats.

FRANCE

France had similar political division, as both Communists and Socialists made appeals to the workers. Government, however, remained in the hands of coalitions, which included business interests. Though some inflation was present, and taxes were increased, by 1929 there was still general confidence in the future.

Quest for Security. Among France's chief postwar concerns was security. Still distrustful of Germany, the French were determined to strengthen themselves so as to ensure victory should war come again. France continued to draft young men into military service. It became involved in various kinds of alliances with Belgium, Poland, Czechoslovakia, Yugoslavia, and Romania in the 1920s. It also resumed diplomatic relations with Russia in an effort to forestall a new Russo-German alliance. The Locarno Pact became an additional safeguard. In 1929 France began building the imposing Maginot Line, a system of fortifications along its eastern border designed to keep out any invader. Ten years later France had 5 million trained soldiers as well as its impressive line of fortifications. The next year, however, it suffered the very thing it had so long been trying to prepare against—defeat at the hands of a newly vitalized German military establishment (see chapter 17). Democracy was still floundering in France, having provided no effective leadership against any of the crises of the age.

Financial Affairs. Financially, France was heavily in debt and suffering from inflation. It hoped to recoup its war losses through German reparations. When Germany defaulted on its promise to deliver coal and timber, Prime Minister Raymond Poincaré decided to take drastic action and occupy the Ruhr valley (see below). That debacle ended with the overthrow of Poincaré in 1924, though he was brought back to power two years later after a coalition government failed to stabilize the economy. Poincaré finally stabilized the franc, though at about 20 percent of its prewar value, bringing gradual new prosperity. Industrial production and exports rose, reparation payments began to flow in from Germany, and agriculture prospered.

GREAT BRITAIN

In Britain, unemployment became the most serious postwar problem. It reached a high of 23 percent of the labor force in 1921. State unemployment benefits as well as other social programs warded off the most severe tensions and paved the way for the eventual establishment of Britain's welfare state. It was during this time that the Labour party rose to prominence. Committed to the gradual adoption of socialism, Labour ran the country in 1924 with J. Ramsay MacDonald as prime minister. MacDonald extended the nation's unemployment relief programs and opened trade with Germany and Russia. He also extended diplomatic recognition to Russia, concluded a commercial treaty, and provided the Russians with a loan. This was too much for the Conservatives, who called for a vote of censure. MacDonald, however, called for an election, which was held in the fall of 1924. The Conservatives achieved an overwhelming majority.

Unemployment continued to grow, particularly in mining, which led to a crisis in 1926. Certain industrialists recommended reducing miners' wages in order to lower export prices and thus improve the market, whereupon the Trades Union Congress called a general nationwide sympathy strike. After only nine days, however, Prime Minister Stanley Baldwin's government convinced the union that it should call off the strike. The result was total defeat for the unions, lower wages for miners, and increasing alienation of the working classes from the Conservative party.

THE NEW NATIONS OF EUROPE

The new European states that emerged at the end of the war looked forward to maintaining peaceful and prosperous independence. Created as a result of the Allied commitment to self-determination, most of them had democratic constitutions that provided liberal suffrage qualifications and protected civil rights. In nearly every case, however, continuing ethnic differences and peasant unrest led to internal strife. Economically, most of these states had tremendous difficulties. Only Austria and Czechoslovakia were industrialized enough to compete in the European market.

War Debts and Reparations

At the heart of the problem of maintaining a lasting peace was Germany. While Germans chafed under the terms of the Versailles treaty, particularly the heavy reparation payments, France and Great Britain disagreed over its enforcement. France demanded strict implementation, not only to improve its own economy but also to keep Germany weak. The British, on the other hand, had reason for wanting a more prosperous Germany, for German trade was important to their economy. Many followed the lead of economist John Maynard Keynes in denouncing the treaty and demanding its revision.

The shaky Weimar republic made its first reparations payment in 1921, but in 1922 it could pay no more and asked for a three-year moratorium. Britain was willing to accept. France was not.

OCCUPATION OF THE RUHR

France's response, early in 1923, was to occupy Germany's Ruhr valley, rich in the production of coal and steel, in order to ensure reparation payments. The beleaguered Weimar government, in turn, called for what amounted to a general strike in the area. The French took over the mines and railroads themselves.

The occupation benefited no one. In Germany it resulted in runaway inflation, as the government printed paper money to pay its bills and support its people in the Ruhr. The inflation only deepened the resentment of businessmen and workers alike. It would not take a much greater crisis to persuade them to follow the most radical of leaders. The occupation was incredibly expensive for France. It also had no support from Britain or the

United States. In 1923 the German government called off the strike, agreeing in principle to make payments but asking for a reexamination of Germany's ability to do so. France agreed.

RECOVERY AND MORATORIUM

At that point the United States stepped in. France, England, and Germany all accepted the "Dawes Plan" of 1924, hammered out by an international committee headed by Charles G. Dawes, an American banker. Reparations were reduced, and annual payments were placed on a sliding scale based on the annual performance of the German economy. The United States also began to provide low-cost loans to Germany, enabling it to pay reparations (often in kind) to England and France. These countries, in turn, were able to make payments on the huge debts owed to the United States. Some economists have observed, however, that even though this cycle of loans, reparation payments, and war debt repayment seemed to work, it was actually a long-range mistake. It did little to create investment in long-term European economic growth.

For a time, nevertheless, this innovative plan stimulated a major economic recovery in Germany and allowed it begin making reparation payments. These were further reduced by the "Young Plan" of 1929. By this time there had been enough of an economic recovery worldwide that leaders breathed a sigh of relief. Unfortunately, the sigh was premature. The crash of the American stock market in October 1929 precipitated an economic nosedive that brought national economies around the world to the point of near collapse. It also ended any further efforts to continue the interdependent cycle of loans, reparations, and war debt payments. In 1931 the European nations accepted U.S. President Herbert Hoover's proposal for a one-year moratorium on reparations as well as war debt payments. By default, the moratorium became permanent.

Agriculture

One of the weak spots in the economy of the 1920s was agriculture. Improved agricultural technology stimulated great increases in production, but sent prices plummeting to record lows. At the same time, industrial wages were rising, making manufactured goods essential to farmers and peasants increasingly expensive. Unable to pay their debts, many farmers listened more readily to critics who were promoting various radical changes. In Germany, for example, farmers provided a major source of support for the Nazi party.

Various attempts at self-help or government aid were not highly successful. In the United States, farmer's co-ops helped in some areas. The government provided some storage, help in exporting, and bank loans. It also sought higher tariffs in order to raise the price of imported agricultural goods, such as sugar. Nothing solved the problem, however, which made many farmers listen with glee to a plan for dumping farm surpluses on the world market in order to raise prices at home and thus achieve "parity"—that is, prices that would give farmers the same purchasing power they had between 1909 and 1914. Legislation to implement such a plan was vetoed twice by President Calvin Coolidge.

THE GREAT DEPRESSION

In 1925 the world seemed on the road toward peace and prosperity. Seven years later it was in the midst of the Great Depression. No one at the time could really explain it, but it had created worldwide economic chaos, eliminated any possibility of further war debt or reparation payments, fostered tariff wars between nations, and created more general international tension than had existed since the Great War. Little wonder that people were confused.

Factors Contributing to the Great Depression

Economic historians will probably never fully agree on the causes of the Great Depression. Among the contributing factors, however, was a serious economic imbalance within the United States, related directly to the fact that productivity rose much faster than wages. At the same time, falling agricultural prices reduced the real income of farmers. In addition, wealth was rapidly being concentrated into the hands of a few. A disproportionate amount of wealth was being fed into the production of capital goods (i.e., the means of production), but such capital investment could not be sustained for long. In June 1929, industrial production began to fall.

Agricultural weaknesses continued in most countries. Various commodities, including wheat, sugar, coffee, rubber, wool, and lard, glutted world markets. When prices dropped so low that farmers no longer had effective purchasing power, world credit and markets collapsed. The flow of coal, iron, and textiles slowed precipitously, and unemployment in those industries skyrocketed. Efforts by governments to economize, and thus reduce spending, only weakened domestic buying power.

Nevertheless, people with money could hardly resist the temptation to invest it in further industrial expansion or in the stock market, creating the most "bullish" market in American history. American optimism was seldom higher than at the beginning of 1929; stock prices soared to unprecedented heights. The potential problem was only aggravated by the dangerous practice of buying stocks "on margin"—that is, paying only a fraction of the cost and borrowing the rest from one's stockbroker. When prices fell, people who probably should not have been investing were forced to sell in order to pay their brokers. The result was financial panic. In a matter of days paper fortunes resulting from such risky, overconfident investment by countless speculators were wiped out.

Crash and Spread

The great crash began in September 1929. By 1933, in a horrendous chain reaction, some 11,000 banks (44 percent of the total in 1929) failed, wiping out approximately $2 billion in savings. As purchasing power plummeted, so did industrial production, prices (including farm prices), and, inevitably, employment.

Contributing to the severity of the crash was the nature of the American banking system. Many banks, operating with minimal regulation, had few cash reserves with which to meet depositor demands. As depositors rushed to salvage their savings, many banks simply could not service them and were required to close their doors.

Worldwide Effects

At that point it became clear how much the United States was really involved in the economy of the globe. American financial institutions stopped making loans abroad and then began to call in their short-term foreign loans. The result was disaster in Europe. In 1931 major banks in Austria and Germany closed. World prices collapsed, resulting in a scramble by businesses around the world to dump manufactured goods and agricultural products in a frenzied effort to obtain cash. In an attempt to make its goods more salable on the world market, Great Britain went off the gold standard in 1931. Two years later nearly every major country, including the United States, did the same.

TARIFFS

One approach that clearly miscarried was a resort to protective tariffs. In the United States the Hawley-Smoot tariff act of 1930 raised duties to their highest levels ever. This attempt to protect domestic producers, however, only backfired, for nations around the world quickly retaliated with their own protective tariffs. Rather than dealing with the real causes of the depression (which no one could fully fathom anyway), the tariff merely served to intensify it.

SOCIAL EFFECTS

As industrial production declined, worldwide employment hit disastrous new lows. The resulting social dislocation and reduced standard of living was something never seen before in the United States. Bread lines sprang up everywhere. Once-prosperous workers and self-employed businessmen found themselves selling apples and pencils on the streets and even begging. The problem was also social. The loss of dignity, the disruption of homes and traditional ways of life, the increase in suicide and mental illness—all this and more was the result of sudden poverty. A political, economic, and social time bomb was ticking as farmers, peasants, and industrial workers around the world saw their societies being ground down in the mire of poverty, unemployment, and hopelessness.

EFFECTS IN JAPAN

In eastern Asia, Japan had been struggling with its own depression since 1926, and when the depression of 1929 struck, the result was catastrophic. Between 1929 and 1931 exports were cut in half, worker income dropped disastrously, and unemployment rose to about 3 million. The worst effects were felt in rural Japan where, as in the Western world, farm families suffered even amid a bumper crop of rice. When a 12 percent crop increase was predicted on October 2, 1930, the price immediately fell to 16 yen per unit (five bushels)—1 yen below the cost of production. By October 10 it was down to 10 yen. By the mid-1930s the income of peasants, which was always close to mere subsistence levels anyway, was down by 33 percent. In their text *East Asia: The Modern Transformation*, Fairbank, Reischauer, and Craig have drawn a pathetic image of the results: ". . . children begging for food outside the dining cars of trains, starving peasants stripping off the tender inner bark of pine trees or digging for the roots of wild plants, the agents for city brothels bargaining with farmers who had nothing left to sell but their daughters."

RESPONSES: THE DECLINE OF TRADITIONAL LIBERALISM

As the downward spiral continued, governments were either unable or unwilling to adopt effective "counter-cyclical" policies such as those prescribed by John Maynard Keynes. Instead of cutting budgets, Keynes declared, government should resort to deficit spending in times of depression in order to stimulate their economies. In times of inflation, higher taxes could then restore the balance as well as control the inflation itself. After World War II such economic sense became commonplace, but in 1930 it was anathema to economists and politicians alike.

Nevertheless, in every major nation the Great Depression had an impact on the way people perceived the role of government in society. In most cases it was also the catalyst for a pivotal change in that role. Keynesian practices, along with more liberal political-economic philosophy, became increasingly evident.

The American Response: The New Deal and the Changing Nature of Liberalism

In the United States, the Great Depression helped bring about a change from old-style liberalism to a new liberalism that brought the government more directly into the everyday lives of the people. The change probably would have come sooner or later anyway, with massive population increases, urbanism, new developments in transportation and communication, and the resulting social and economic pressures of the latter twentieth century. The Great Depression, however, hastened it and affected the form it would take.

THE CHANGING NATURE OF LIBERALISM: THE AMERICAN EXAMPLE

Traditional liberalism, with its emphasis on individual freedom, sought to expand civil liberties and limit the authority of the state. In the nineteenth century it moved toward utilitarianism, or a concern for the interests of society in general (see chapter 9). In that sense, even before the Great Depression many American liberals were convinced that the government must take a more positive role in society. Few, however, were willing to go as far as the New Deal eventually went. By the 1930s things had changed; Western liberals were proclaiming that government could best promote freedom and individual well-being only by more direct intervention (i.e., establishing a true welfare state). They promoted increased taxation (especially on the more wealthy), social security, more effective antitrust legislation, minimum wage laws, consumer protection legislation, and a host of other social welfare measures. As the new liberalism evolved, the old free-market liberalism of Adam Smith and John Stuart Mill became the new conservatism. The classic example of this change was the United States, where the Great Depression became a major turning point.

THE NEW DEAL

Elected in 1928, Herbert Hoover was president of the United States when the great crash came in 1929. Wrongly blamed by political opponents for the depression, he was nevertheless philosophically unable to promote any effective measures to alleviate it. The nearest he came was a bill for providing government loans to banks and other financial institutions, on the theory that prosperity would then "trickle down" to the masses. By 1932, however, conditions were so bad he had no chance of political survival. Instead, Americans were captivated by Franklin Delano Roosevelt, who won their confidence and promised them a "New Deal for the forgotten man." Elected by a landslide, Roosevelt was willing to experiment with almost anything short of socialism in order to preserve American capitalism.

Roosevelt's Attitude. Already large numbers of people were listening more seriously to radical share-the-wealth ideas. Some historians have observed, in fact, that many Americans were ready for drastic economic and/or political revolution. Only the New Deal, they suggest, prevented something akin to a socialist revolution. At the time, however, conservatives accused the New Deal either of being socialist or moving the nation toward socialism. In Franklin D. Roosevelt's mind, he was doing just the opposite—modifying capitalism in order to save it.

Roosevelt was willing not only to experiment but also to take advice. He never fully accepted Keynesian economic theories, however, and in the early days of the New Deal attempted to avoid massive deficits. In the end, nevertheless, he at least partially adopted the Keynesian approach—or, at least, the part that justified government spending.

New Deal Programs. The programs were myriad. Some worked, some did not. Some were declared unconstitutional. Some were popular, others were unpopular. Roosevelt's sharp attacks on big business and massive wealth alienated many capitalists, but the New Deal inspired confidence in the American people generally. It put them back to work and probably staved off pressures for even more drastic reforms. Equally important, many of its measures became permanent American fixtures, forever changing the expectations of Americans with respect to the role of government in the economy and in their personal lives.

During his first 100 days in office, Roosevelt had the complete cooperation of Congress. Almost his first act was to declare a national bank holiday. Before the banks reopened, Congress had reformed the system enough that only those with a hope of solvency were allowed to renew operations. This, however, included most of them, and with the help of new regulations and the breathing spell provided by the holiday, confidence in the system was restored. Congress also established the Federal Deposit Insurance Corporation that would guarantee bank deposits. These were among the permanent contributions of the New Deal to the new relationship between the economy and the federal government.

Perhaps the most ambitious New Deal program was the National Recovery Administration (NRA), which attempted to establish ways to fix prices and wages, thus reducing cutthroat competition, for the benefit of everyone. The key provisions of the act establishing it, however, were declared unconstitutional in 1935.

There were many other programs. The Agricultural Adjustment Act placed restrictions on agricultural production in an effort to boost prices to "parity." The Civilian Conservation Corps (CCC) provided jobs for young men in reforestation and other conservation projects. The Tennessee Valley Authority brought the government directly into business, with the establishment of a hydroelectric plant to provide power as well as nitrates for fertilizer. Eventually it improved the standard of living for millions of people in the Tennessee River valley. Under the Federal Emergency Recovery Administration (FERA) and Civil Works Administration (CWA) in 1933 and 1934, millions of people were put to work on public buildings and roads, teaching schools, or using their specialized skills for such things as painting murals in post offices—the first time the federal government had ever intervened so directly in providing employment. The Works Progress Administration (WPA), established in 1935, continued the same principle. A welcome and enormously popular program, it was one of those that helped curb the threat of social revolution. The Social Security Act of 1935 established a permanent program of old-age pensions and other benefits. The National Labor Relations Act that same year guaranteed the right of collective bargaining. The Rural Electrification Administration (REA), also established in 1935, provided low cost-loans for extending electricity into rural areas. It became permanent the following year.

Critics. Nevertheless, the New Deal did not cure the depression. Despite periods of recovery, at the end of the 1930s the nation was again plagued by falling production and rising unemployment. Roosevelt, meanwhile, was increasingly attacked from all sides. Some critics felt his spending did not go far enough. Roosevelt, however, was still concerned with at least attempting to achieve a balanced budget. In addition, he did not want wages on government work projects to compete with those in private industry. Critics on the right, including former President Hoover, castigated the New Deal as a gross violation of American tradition, sound economics, and the Constitution.

Unfortunately, only the shift to preparation for potential entry into a new world war (see chapter 17) brought about a more permanent recovery.

The Conservative Response in Great Britain

Britain's response to the Great Depression was more conservative than that of the United States, but it was also slightly more successful.

THE LABOUR PARTY, MacDONALD, AND THE NATIONAL GOVERNMENT

In the election of 1929 the Labour party and J. Ramsay MacDonald were returned to power, just in time to face the depression. Exports were dropping, business was declining, income was going down, and tax revenue was falling off. By this time, however, MacDonald's commitment to socialism had practically disappeared. Determined to maintain a balanced budget, he proposed no new programs.

The National Government. In 1931 the government requested loans from New York and Paris banks. The bankers delayed their decisions, however, asking Britain first to cut expenditures. This meant reducing benefits for the unemployed, and the Labour party would have none of that. MacDonald offered to resign. The king, however, asked him to form a new government, to be known as the National Government, made up of a coalition of the three major parties. MacDonald agreed, which enraged Labour leaders so much that they expelled him from the party. Nevertheless, he headed the coalition government until his resignation in June 1935.

Economic Programs. The new government took relatively conservative steps. These included cuts in military and civil service pay in order to economize. It also raised income and excise taxes. Like the United States, it resorted to protective tariffs in order to stimulate home production, though the results were not dramatic. It also lowered interest rates, making credit easier and providing some stimulus to business. These and other measures contributed to a gradual economic recovery after 1932, but they clearly did not solve the problems of unemployment and low income.

Beginnings of Retreat from Imperialism. While all this was going on, Great Britain began a gradual retreat from its worldwide empire. It started to withdraw from Egypt in 1922, remaining only in the Sudan and Suez after 1936. That same year, closer to home, it granted full autonomy to southern Ireland, thus removing a domestic issue that had been festering since long before the Great War. It recognized the independence of Iraq in 1930. Meanwhile, the British Dominions of Canada, Australia, New Zealand, and South Africa had all achieved internal self-government, and everyone recognized that it was time for them to become independent. Their autonomous status was recognized by Parliament in 1931. This gave rise to the British Commonwealth of Nations, a confederation bound together only by common allegiance to the crown.

Indecision in France

Though France was the last of the industrial nations to feel the pinch, the Great Depression hit with tremendous force in 1932. Much more than in England or the United States, however, political division over what to do about it kept much from being done. By the mid-1930s parliamentary government was in a turmoil as Fascists, Socialists, and Communists all vied for power. In 1936 socialist groups, with communist support, joined together to form the "Popular Front" and won a national election. The new prime minister was socialist Léon Blum.

Almost immediately 1 million workers nationwide went out on strike, in an effort to force major reforms. Blum placated them by negotiating a wage increase. He also worked for more social legislation, tried to stabilize farm prices, and devalued the franc in an effort to increase exports. Devaluation, however, only helped increase the cost of living. Other measures included removing banks from the control of wealthy families and nationalizing the arms industry. But workers were not satisfied with Blum's moderate accomplishments. A new wave of strikes swept France in 1937, and the Popular Front fell. The next governments were no more effective.

THE RISE OF FASCISM AND THE EMERGENCE OF THE TOTALITARIAN STATE

It will always remain a question as to whether the United States, by joining the League of Nations and otherwise participating more actively in world affairs, could have helped fulfill Wilson's dream of making the world safe for democracy and maintaining the integrity of national states. In any case, the dream was dead in less than twenty years after Versailles. All across the continent of Europe totalitarian states arose, civil liberties were done away with, and eventually small states were gobbled up by the major powers. It was history repeating itself, only in the guise of more modern state systems and new kinds of absolutist theories. The same was true in Japan, where military dictatorship and political centralization, only with a Japanese twist, took over.

Totalitarianism: Some Definitions

While totalitarianism may seem to be much like the ideal of absolutism described earlier, there are some essential differences. Absolutist states were dominated by hereditary monarchs and often promoted by the theory of divine right. Modern totalitarian states are usually dominated by a party. An individual is usually dominant, for a time, but there is no hereditary right to succession, nor is there any assumption that anything but the ideology of the party is important. Much more than under the old monarchies, it is the nature of totalitarian states to control every aspect of national life—religious, political, social, youth organizations, sports, the press, and anything else that could in any way affect the perpetuation of the party's ideology. Totalitarian regimes are especially notable for their effective use of propaganda to marshal the continuing support, or obedience, of the people. Control of all the public media, as well as control of the arts, is essential to the continuing success of totalitarian regimes.

There are, to be sure, varieties of totalitarianism. On the left is communism, which usually arises in economically underdeveloped countries and establishes a communist state through violent revolution. Communists are usually bent on completely overthrowing the existing order and establishing a classless society. Their support generally comes from workers and the lower classes. On the right are Nazism and fascism, which often draw their support from the middle classes and financial interests who are fearful of a social revolution that would destroy their privileges and status. The societies in which they arise are relatively advanced. Sometimes, as in the case of Hitler, they come to power peacefully. At other times, like Franco in Spain, they may take over violently after another government has left the country in economic and political chaos. Like communists, they resort to terror, violence, and secret police. But in order to fully maintain their power, they must also rely on the continuing support of the financial classes and cater to their needs. Both Italian Fascism and German Nazism amounted, in fact, to a system of state capitalism.

Regardless of the differences, for the common people the end result is the same. A totalitarian regime controls and regiments the whole of society. There is no assumption of personal or natural rights—only an assumption that in the interest of the people as a whole the state can do anything. What that really means, of course, is that in the interest of the state the people can be coerced into doing anything.

Mussolini's Fascist State: Italy in the 1920s and 1930s

Italy was a constitutional monarchy, with a king, a parliament, and a prime minister appointed by the king. The government, however, was weak—too weak to deal effectively with the economic distress and political chaos that followed World War I. By 1922, in fact, it was in general disrepute. One reason was its refusal to support the actions of Gabriel D'Annunzio, who had raised a private army and seized the port of Fiume, located in northwestern Yugoslavia. Nationalists considered this an affront, for they believed the port should have been returned to Italy at the end of the war. More important was the government's inability to deal with the unstable economy and to calm the factions, particularly members of the Socialist party, who were demanding various reforms. Unemployment was rampant, living costs were rising, and general discontent among the lower classes was rife. The Socialists, combined with the Catholic Populars (a Christian Socialist party), became a parliamentary majority, but the prime minister elected in 1921 refused to consider any of the economic and social reforms they demanded. He resigned the same year, but his successors were no more successful.

Meanwhile, financial interests and other conservative groups became increasingly fearful that a Socialist government would undermine their property and bring about a totally unacceptable economic and social revolution. Similar stories have been told over and over in the history of the world, but again the time was right for the rise of a strong leader who seemed to hold out the promise of actually being able to bring order out of chaos.

THE RISE OF MUSSOLINI

Benito Mussolini stepped onto the stage at just the right moment. A masterful opportunist, he had a history of switching sides whenever it suited his personal ends. Among other things, he was once a Socialist. After the election of 1919, however, he began to woo the conservatives. He could gain the power he wanted, he realized, only by gaining the support of financial interests, the military, and other conservative groups. That same year he founded the Fascist party. He soon set its terrorist squads, uniformed in black shirts, about the task of destroying the Socialist party. They went on a rampage, disrupting party meetings, destroying property, and attacking strikers and dissident farm workers. Conservatives turned their backs on such lawlessness, for it played into their own political agenda, and the government refused to try to stop it. Finally, in October 1922 the Fascists marched on Rome. On October 29, still in his newspaper office in Milan, Mussolini received a telegram from the king inviting him to become prime minister. The next day he arrived in Rome by train in time to greet his cheering followers as they marched into the city.

It was a short though gradual step from there to a complete takeover. When he became prime minister, Mussolini's party was only a small minority in the legislature. After manipulating the election laws, however, he obtained a Fascist cabinet in 1925 and was able to have all other political parties outlawed. Such action is one of the primary marks of a totalitarian state. He soon gained the support of industrialists and workers alike, who believed he would bring a new era of prosperity. His became the ideal example of right-wing totalitarianism.

EARLY ACCOMPLISHMENTS: THE LATERAN TREATY

Mussolini's accomplishments in the 1920s were impressive. Among other things, he established law and order (though at the price of continuing intimidation by his Fascist terrorists), suppressed the Mafia, and improved agricultural production. He also made an important political agreement with the Roman Catholic Church. Since 1870 the pope had been deprived of his historical sovereignty over Rome, and there had been little but hostility between the church and the Italian government. In the Lateran Treaty of 1929, however, Mussolini granted sovereignty to the Vatican over a small piece of land immediately surrounding St. Peter's. The treaty also established diplomatic relations with the Vatican. In addition, by making the church exempt from taxation and giving it certain other privileges, the treaty made it the religion of the state.

By 1938 Mussolini's totalitarianism had entered into almost every aspect of public and private life. Even public manners became more harsh and militaristic in nature, as exemplified by the required public greeting—not a handshake, but an arm outstretched in the manner of the ancient Romans.

THE DEPRESSION

The government of *Il Duce*, as Mussolini loved to be called, was severely tested during the Great Depression. Italy had all the same problems as the other nations of the world. It was partly for this reason that Mussolini inaugurated Italian imperialism in 1935 and invaded Ethiopia (see chapter 17). Such a move, he hoped, would open new markets, bring in new raw materials, and take the people's minds off their economic problems. At the same time, he did little to bring about basic reforms that might have improved the nation's economy generally. It seems almost surprising that, on the eve of Italy's entry into World War II, his regime still generated so much enthusiasm. Perhaps the eager, regimented, and spirited youth groups, a hallmark of successful totalitarian states, had something to do with it.

Hitler's Nazi Germany

In Germany, meanwhile, the Weimar Republic was unable to meet the multiple challenges of the postwar world. Those challenges paved the way for a takeover by a dictator whose aims were totally at odds with the agreements that brought the government into being in the first place.

WEAKNESS OF THE WEIMAR REPUBLIC

The Weimar Republic, named after the city in which its constitution was written, was based on a liberal, democratic constitution, but had within it a number of weaknesses. The technicalities of the system of representation encouraged the rise of a number of small parties, so that it was difficult for the chancellor, appointed by the president, to have a majority. More importantly, the government was never popular with the people. Many still believed they had been betrayed at Versailles. The French invasion of the Ruhr caused economic problems that made the government look even worse. Though it had weathered a few attempted coups, when the Great Depression came, it had no chance at all of gaining popular support.

HITLER'S RISE TO POWER

Adolph Hitler was born in Germany, but spent much of his youth in Vienna, Austria. There he picked up many of the radical biases that later became part of the ideological foundations of Nazism. He served as a corporal in the German army during World War I, where his intense nationalism was only intensified. By 1921 he had gained control of the National Socialist German Workers', or Nazi, party. After leading an abortive coup in 1923, Hitler spent several months in jail, where two important things happened. First, he wrote *Mein Kampf* ("My Struggle"), which soon became the guide to the future for all committed Nazis. He also made up his mind that he could not take over Germany through violence—he had to do it legally, from within.

By the mid-1920s the Nazis had what amounted to a private army, the SA (*Sturm Abteilung*, or storm troopers). Uniformed in brown shirts, they became instruments of intimidation and violence as the party carried out a campaign against communists, Social Democrats, Jews, and others. By 1933 they had almost 1 million members. Through massive political rallies and effective propaganda, Hitler's appeal grew. People of property, who were fearful of Social Democrats and communists anyway, found themselves listening to him seriously. The Great Depression played into his hands perfectly. With unemployment at over 6 million in 1930 (more than double what it was only two years earlier), Hitler could raise the fervor of workers and businesspeople alike as he promised that his party would stop reparation payments (which only drained German resources), create jobs, stimulate business, and rearm the nation. People were attracted in droves. In 1932 the Nazis dominated the Reichstag (the popularly elected lower house in the Weimar Republic). By then it was obvious that the existing government, even though it had begun to rule by decree, was powerless to deal with the deepening economic crisis. Hitler cultivated influential people in government, business, and the military who mistakenly believed they could control him. With their support he finally manipulated his own appointment as chancellor on January 30, 1933. His bloodless coup was completely legal, but it had tremendous portents for the future. Within the year, for example, Hitler had taken Germany out of the League of Nations. He would simply ignore it as he changed the nature of the government, built up the economy, and created a military machine capable of carrying out his expansionist ideology.

THE IDEOLOGICAL FOUNDATIONS OF NAZISM

Several themes, most of them dealt with in *Mein Kampf*, provided the ideological underpinning for the Nazi movement under Hitler. One was anti-Semitism, based in part on the assumption that the Jews were involved in an international economic conspiracy against the German people. Closely related was a nationalistic racism. Hitler preached that the Germanic, or "Aryan," people were truly superior to all other races—that they were, in fact, a master race. This menacing theory was justified in Nazi propaganda on the basis of certain nineteenth-century biological theories. Even though largely outmoded, they were marshaled in defense of what became some unbelievable policies of the state. Hitler's racism was also related to his expansionism; he wanted to bring all the Germanic peoples together as one great nation. This meant taking over the regions where they were. The expression he used was *lebensraum* ("living room"), suggesting the need for space in which the German nation could grow. The Slavs and other "lesser" races would occupy an inferior, almost servile position. To achieve all these ends, according to Nazi doctrine, the state must be headed by an all-powerful dictator (*führer*); Adolph Hitler was that person.

The goals of the party also included a number of pragmatic internal reforms, such as bringing major business concerns under the administration of the state and reforming land and agricultural policy. Although the Nazis did not think of doing away with private enterprise, they believed that all such activity should be both controlled and protected by the state. They were also committed to repudiating the hated Versailles treaty as well as uniting Germany and Austria under one head.

HITLER'S NAZI STATE

As soon a Hitler was appointed chancellor, he moved quickly to make his power both stronger and more permanent.

Control of the Government. Within a year and a half, Hitler was able to establish an absolute dictatorship. In March 1933 he was given the right to rule by decree for a period of four years. He made Germany a one-party state by outlawing the Communists and all other parties. He also outlawed labor unions. Nazis were installed at all levels of the bureaucracy.

Germany became a police state. Hitler even purged his own storm troopers, the SA, when it became clear that they stood in the way of his gaining control of the army; the generals considered them rivals. He had several hundred of them summarily shot, along with other "undesirables," on the night of June 30, 1934, paving the way for the generals to swear allegiance to him. The executioners on that infamous "night of the long knives" were members of Hitler's elite personal guard, the SS (*Schutzstaffel*). This ruthless group, led by Heinrich Himmler, together with the *Gestapo* (political police) became the dreaded enforcers of the *führer's* will.

Racism and War on the Jews. The Jews were objects of special attention. Doctors, lawyers, and other professionals lost their jobs or were not allowed to practice. Synagogues, homes, and businesses were destroyed. Marriage between Jews and Germans was prohibited. Jews were even stripped of their citizenship and forbidden to display the national flag. Perhaps a quarter of the 500,000 Jews who lived in Germany emigrated; others simply found themselves unable to do so. All this, however, was only preliminary to the horrifying Holocaust that took place at the height of the coming war.

Economic Policy and Rearmament. One reason Hitler retained popular support was that his government actually did something about the depression; German economic life turned around. A massive public works program, stepped-up food production, and rearmament eventually eliminated unemployment and stimulated business. The army, too, was never in better shape. By the time Hitler began his aggressions against other nations he had a highly disciplined, well-equipped fighting machine with which to carry out his aims.

Culture, Religion, and Education. As in fascist Italy, Nazi regulation reached into every aspect of German life. Art, literature, and the theater were all pressed into the service of the state. School textbooks were rewritten to exclude "subversive" references (e.g., to Jews and Bolsheviks), and to promote Nazi ideals. Youth organizations marched, sang, and played together under the auspices of Nazi leaders, and in the process absorbed the most convincing propaganda the system could produce.

Propaganda, in fact, was essential to continued Nazi popularity. Under the hand of Joseph Goebbels, the idea of truth lost all meaning. Instead, the public media were used to justify in the most glowing terms every illegal, unethical, or immoral act perpetrated by the party.

Religion too, and especially Protestantism, suffered under Hitler's regime. No one was safe who did not support his racism or the other policies. One group of 800 dissident Protestants was sent to concentration camps in 1937. Catholic schools and youth groups eventually were destroyed, though the churches remained intact. Worship services saw little interference, so long as they were not used to oppose the ideals of the Nazi state.

Hitler had his opponents, but they were never unified enough to provide effective political opposition. In general, rising prosperity and the pride they had not felt since World War I ingratiated him in the hearts of the German people.

The Retreat of Democracy in Eastern Europe and Spain

EASTERN EUROPE

In a sense the cards were stacked against the twelve small countries of eastern Europe. Their quest for self-determination and democratic government ended almost as it had begun. By the mid-1930s nearly all of them had succumbed to authoritarian regimes. By the end of the 1930s Hitler had imposed his totalitarian regime on most; Russia had taken over Lithuania, Estonia, and Latvia.

Economic Problems. The problems of these small countries were myriad. Their national economies, never as well developed as the larger countries of Europe, continued in a generally depressed state. Agricultural reform was not forthcoming. The lack of investment capital limited the development of industry. Like the other countries of the world, they also adopted what proved to be an untimely protective tariff policy that only stifled instead of promoting trade. These smaller countries, however, were even less well prepared than their larger neighbors to withstand the consequences.

Ethnic Nationalism. At the same time, they were being torn apart internally by a continuation of the long-standing ethnic nationalism that had been causing political tensions for centuries. In Czechoslovakia, the Czechs and the Slovaks were at best uncomfortable in their political union, each wanting autonomy or independence. This was only complicated by the fact that large German and Hungarian minorities chafed under Czech and Slovak rule. In Yugoslavia, dominated politically by the Serbs, the Slovenes and Croats harbored smoldering discontent. There were also ethnic minorities in Poland, Hungary, and Romania. Even more ominous, however, was the growing anti-Semitism that characterized not only Germany but the eastern European countries as well, especially Poland, Hungary, and Romania.

Dictatorial Regimes Take Over. Economic unrest, ethnic hostility, and the fact that these areas had little prior experience with democratic forms of government, all combined to make their postwar governments highly unstable. As a result, democracy retreated there as elsewhere in Europe, and they succumbed to dictatorial regimes even before they were absorbed by Hitler's Third Reich.

Hungary was the first to fall. Nicolaus Horthy set up a military regime in 1919, in reaction to the failure of postwar socialist and communist regimes. In 1926 Joseph Pilsudski set up a thinly disguised dictatorship in Poland. Lithuania's government became a dictatorship after a coup d'etat the same year. Also in 1926 power was seized in politically unstable Albania by Ahmud Zag, who then declared that country a monarchy in 1928. Yugoslavia, originally called the Kingdom of the Serbs, Croats, and Slovenes, was a constitutional monarchy from the beginning, dominated by the Serbs. In 1929 King Alexander (a Serb) established a royal dictatorship, but he was assassinated in 1934. The country remained torn by factions until Hitler's armies marched in. Austria became a dictatorship, supported by Mussolini, in 1933. The following year three more countries succumbed: Estonia, Latvia, and Bulgaria. Greece remained a republic until 1936, when a right-wing dictatorship took over. Romania became a royal dictatorship in 1938.

Czechoslovakia. Of all the eastern European states, only Czechoslovakia maintained a democratic government until it was overwhelmed by Hitler's expansionism. Several factors helped account for this stability. Economic conditions were better there than elsewhere. The people were more literate. Also, despite their ethnic differences, the tensions between people were not as great during those years as those experienced in other places, such as Yugoslavia. In addition, the political leaders were more ready to promote the kinds of social and economic reforms that would help alleviate popular discontent. Ethnic tensions, however, remained as the major weak spot.

SPAIN

In Spain, the economic and political instability that followed World War I led to the establishment of a military dictatorship. It was overthrown by a republican revolution in 1931, but remained politically unsteady. It seemed to alternate between liberal and conservative leadership, though elements of both were attempting to maintain some kind of republican government. By 1936, however, conditions were so bad that leaders of both left and right were ready to establish some kind of dictatorial regime. Political confusion reigned.

Franco and the Revolution of 1936. In July an army officer, General Francisco Franco, led a revolt that resulted in a bloody, three-year civil war in which close to 1 million lives were lost. But it became more than an internal struggle, as the nations of Europe took sides, according to their own political self-interests. Internally, those who supported the government included republicans, communists, and anarchists. They were supported from the outside by Russia. On the other side were Catholics (religion was a major issue in the continuing political struggle in Spain), monarchists, and Fascists. They were supported from the outside by Germany and Italy. Franco's forces won in 1939, but Spain remained a divided, poverty-stricken nation. Franco quickly set up a dictatorial regime that operated much like the Fascist governments of Germany and Italy. Actually a tool of conservative interests (including the church), Franco put down the labor movement, censored the press, and used terrorist tactics to promote order.

Stalin's Soviet Union

In Russia, meanwhile, the Bolsheviks were busily engaged in solidifying their revolution. They dissolved the Constituent Assembly in 1918, and thereafter the government was run by the Communist party. Its executive committee, the *Politburo*, determined policy. As a symbol of a complete break with tsarist past, the capital was moved from Petrograd to Moscow. In 1922 Russia was divided into four republics, known collectively as the Union of Soviet Socialist Republics. Later these republics were further broken up, and others were added. Each had its own government, or Soviet, but in reality all came under the domination of central party rule.

THE NEP

In the meantime, an economic crisis arose. The Bolsheviks had seized the banks, begun to print inflationary paper money, and prohibited private foreign trade. Complete regulation of farms and factories, moreover, simply did not work. By 1921 the economy was in a shambles, which led Lenin, flexible enough to face reality, to announce the New Economic Policy (NEP). This was actually a step back toward capitalism, as some industries were returned to private ownership and foreign investment was once more allowed.

STALIN'S RISE TO POWER

Lenin died in 1924, leaving a party riddled with factionalism. A four-way struggle for power soon evolved into a contest between Trotsky and Joseph Stalin, a member of the Politburo since 1919 and, since 1922, secretary of the party. Using all the tactics of behind-the-scenes intrigue at his disposal, Stalin formed an anti-Trotsky coalition among the leaders and also gained the support of rank-and-file party members. Many of Stalin's supporters, along with Stalin himself, disagreed with Trotsky's continuing pressure for immediate world revolution. Rather, they thought it more prudent to strengthen communism at home first. By 1927 Stalin had won, whereupon the party expelled Trotsky, exiled him to Siberia, and eventually banished him from the country. In 1940, in Mexico, he was murdered—perhaps, some say, on Stalin's orders.

Stalin's Purges. Such action taken against the man who, next to Lenin, was the most responsible for the success of the revolution only suggests the political callousness to which a totalitarian state must often stoop. It did not stop there. Even though his position was relatively secure, in the 1930s Stalin conducted a series of purges against anyone considered even slightly disloyal. Among the victims was one of his own close friends, Sergi Kirov, who was eliminated through outright murder. In other cases purge victims at least received trials, sometimes public and sometimes not, though the legality of the proceedings was often questionable. People were often hounded into making public"confessions" of error, after which they were quickly convicted and executed. In 1936, in the first trial to be held in public, 117 people were condemned to death for plotting Stalin's murder. In the end, nearly everyone who had helped establish the revolution was gone, and the party was firmly in the hands of Stalin and the "New Bolsheviks." Stalin was now the strong man of Russia, and would remain so until his demise in 1953.

THE ECONOMY: FIVE-YEAR PLANS

The economy, meanwhile, gradually turned around as a result of the NEP, but in 1927 economic policy was reversed again. Stalin and his associates believed that the new Soviet Union had to become a strong, industrialized nation. They again took direction of all industrial production and announced the First Five-Year Plan. It was designed primarily to promote basic industry. Quotas and goals were set, with special emphasis on mining, heavy industrial production, and electrification. At the end of 1932 the party announced that the goals had been reached early. It also announced another five-year plan, this time placing more emphasis on the production of consumer goods.

At the same time, the party again took complete control of agriculture and collectivized it. Like industry, farms were regimented in an effort to increase production. Peasants who resisted this reversal of their hope for land ownership were consigned to labor camps for the purpose of "reeducation."

SOCIETY UNDER STALIN

Life in Stalin's totalitarian state was not unlike life in Mussolini's Italy or Hitler's Germany. Every aspect was regulated, and no dissent was allowed. Mass purges and arrests at the hands of secret police were almost commonplace. Censorship was imposed. History was rewritten to suit the needs of the state. Propaganda blared at everyone from radios, newspapers, and movies. It was little different in kind from German and Italian propaganda, except that it praised communism instead of Nazism or fascism. Writers and artists of all sorts found themselves rewarded to the degree that their work promoted the glories of the socialist state and often punished to the degree that they did not.

On the other hand, while the standard of living in Italy and Germany went up, in Stalin's Soviet Union it did not. High taxes, food shortages, and housing shortages all continued to plague the people. At the same time, most people were at least employed, and state socialism provided for them all the benefits of the welfare state, such as health care, education, and old-age benefits.

FOREIGN POLICY

Even though Stalin had opposed Trotsky's plan for immediate world-wide revolution, he also became concerned with the implications of world affairs for the future of communism. In particular, the Japanese invasion of Manchuria in 1931 and Hitler's rearmament of Germany troubled him. One response was to join the League of Nations. Another was to foster the establishment of "popular fronts" around the world. These groups would do what they could, even allying themselves with other parties when practical, to fight fascism and other right-wing movements. It was not long before such action evolved into instruments of subversion.

Japan

In East Asia, meanwhile, Japan was the only country to approach the West in terms of industrial development. It was also more like the West in its nationalism, in political development, and in the fact that it had developed its own form of imperialism. In the interwar period, Japan continued its economic development, as well (at first) as its stride toward democratic government. Comparable to what happened in Germany and Italy, however, in the 1930s it moved away from effective parliamentary government and closer to a military dictatorship.

JAPANESE LIBERALISM

The Meiji constitution, promulgated in 1889, provided for a two-house Diet (parliament), a prime minister responsible directly to the emperor, and a cabinet. The premier and his cabinet did not necessarily represent the same parties, however, nor was their selection necessarily related to the parties in power in the Diet. For a number of years there was continuing tension between the Diet and the prime minister. That would only change with the rise of effective party government. Meanwhile, Japan continued to be influenced by liberal Western political models. Some romanticists even envisioned a day when individualism would dominate the entire culture. One writer, Mushakoji Saneatsu, in a passage mildly comparable to America's Thoreau a hundred years earlier, even said that "only a country without authorities is livable." Not many were that extreme, but there was mounting pressure for universal suffrage. A 1919 law finally allowed all men age twenty-five and over to vote if they paid 3 yen or more in taxes. The economic requirement was dropped in 1925. The working classes now had the right to vote. It is also significant that, as in parts of Europe, many young intellectuals turned toward Marxism.

Party Government. The years 1918 to 1931 are known as the years of party government. That is, a number of political parties were viable, elections to the Diet were held regularly, and the prime minister and his cabinet represented the majority party or the majority coalition. In 1918 Hara Kei, leader of the Seiyukai party, became prime minister. Hara was the first commoner to become prime minister. His was also the first administration in which most of the cabinet and the prime minister were from the same party. Throughout the 1920s such party rule would dominate. It seemed to reach its peak under Kato Komei, a member of the more liberal Kenseikai party, who ruled from 1924 to 1926. Under his premiership the electorate was quadrupled, to 12 million, with the passage of the universal manhood suffrage bill in 1925. He also promoted considerable social legislation.

THE RISE OF MILITARY GOVERNMENT

Just as party government seemed secure, however, the Great Depression hit Japan with an effect as devastating as anywhere in Europe. One consequence was the decline of party government in favor of militarism, leading to a military dictatorship that took Japan through the next world war. It was not just the depression, however, that caused the move, for party government had been able to begin an economic recovery. But it came too late to stop the decline in political party power. At the same time, the example set by European totalitarianism, as well as a new round of expansionism helped lay the groundwork for the rise in the power of the military.

The Manchurian Incident and Its Consequences. The incident that eventually led to a military takeover took place in Manchuria in 1931. Japan had heavy investments in Manchuria, as well as thriving trade relations. When it appeared that Japanese influence and economic control might be challenged by a rising Chinese nationalist movement in the 1920s, there were many discussions in Japan as to what to do about it. The army, which still maintained some independence from the Diet and the prime minister, was particularly interested in establishing more firm control. Late in 1931 some army officers provoked an incident by blowing up some tracks on a Japanese railroad and then blaming it on the Chinese. The army, with the reluctant support of the government and claiming "self-defense," immediately marched into Manchuria. The government was embarrassed, but could not stop the continuing advance. In September 1932, Manchuria, or "Manchukuo," was recognized as an independent state by the Japanese and made a protectorate (not unlike American actions in the nineteenth century in fomenting revolutions and then recognizing the newly "independent" states and annexing them, as in Florida, Texas, and Hawaii). The League of

Nations condemned the action, whereupon Japan simply resigned from the League.

The Manchurian incident was the death knell of party government. The cabinet was split over whether or not to support the army. A new prime minister, Inukai Tsuyoshi, was particularly irate at what he considered the army's usurpation of authority, but he was assassinated in May 1932. A number of young army officers, however, soon joined with other ultra-nationalists in a series of attempted coups. Their final defeat in 1936 was followed by a number of purges and executions that restored discipline in the army. At the same time, the government also began to attack extreme liberals, including communists, in order to demonstrate its own continuing nationalism. During the next year the power of the army over the government only increased. In the meantime, pressures were mounting for the occupation of China, which only added to the ability of the army to control the government, no matter who was prime minister. For all practical purposes, by the end of 1937 Japan was under military rule. It was also already at war with China. The stage was set for its entry into World War II.

*T*he world Woodrow Wilson hoped was safe for democracy prospered for a while, then seemed to fall apart. The worst, most long-lasting depression yet had worldwide consequences. Totalitarian regimes came to power in Italy, Germany, Spain, and Japan. Eastern Europe saw the emergence of a conglomeration of small-country dictatorships, weak both economically and politically and ripe for plucking by the continent's new superpower. Other European nations moved toward a new kind of liberalism that brought them closer to the welfare state. In the United States, Franklin D. Roosevelt's New Deal imposed important new programs of governmental regulation and intervention in an effort to save both capitalism and democracy; the result was a modified capitalism and the preservation of a stable republican government.

The events of these years also set the stage for a continuation of the war that only ostensibly ended in 1919. Real peace-keeping machinery was not in place. The punishments imposed on Germany backfired, helping to bring Hitler to power with his far-reaching aims for European conquest. Problems in East Asia in connection with Japanese expansionism sowed seeds of conflict with the United States. The period from 1919 to 1939 was only an intermission. The curtain was about to rise on act two. The Western democracies tried to keep it from happening, but as we will see in chapter 17, they were incapable of doing so.

Selected Readings

Berger, Gordon. *Parties Out of Power in Japan, 1931–1941*. Princeton, NJ: Princeton University Press, 1977.

Bullock, Alan. *Hitler and Stalin: Parallel Lives*. New York: Knopf, 1992.

Deutscher, Isaac. *The Great Purges*. Oxford, New York: Blackwell, 1984.

Fairbank, John K., Edwin O. Reischauer, and Albert M. Craig. *East Asia: The Modern Transformation*. Boston: Houghton Mifflin, 1965.

Galbraith, John Kenneth. *The Great Crash, 1929*. Boston: Houghton Mifflin, 1988.

Johnson, Paul. *Modern Times: The World from the Twenties to the Eighties*. New York: Harper & Row, 1983.

Kindleberger, Charles P. *The World in Depression, 1929–1939*. Berkeley: University of California Press, 1986.

Leuchtenburg, William E. *Franklin D. Roosevelt and the New Deal, 1932–1940*. New York: Harper & Row, 1963.

———. *The Perils of Prosperity, 1914–32*. Chicago: University of Chicago Press, 1958.

Mack Smith, Denis. *Mussolini's Roman Empire*. New York: Viking Press, 1976.

McElvaine, Robert S. *The Great Depression: America, 1929–1941*. New York: Times Books, 1984.

Orwell, George. *The Road to Wigan Pier*. New York: Harcourt Brace Jovanovich, 1958.

Pomper, Philip. *Lenin, Trotsky, and Stalin: The Intelligentsia and Power*. New York: Columbia University Press, 1990.

Pyle, Kenneth B. *The Making of Modern Japan*. Lexington, MA: D. C. Heath & Co., 1978.

Schoenbaum, David. *Hitler's Social Revolution: Class and Status in Nazi Germany, 1933–1939*. New York: Norton, 1980.

Snellgrove, Laurence E. *Franco and the Spanish Civil War*. New York: McGraw-Hill, 1968.

Sontag, Raymond J. *A Broken World, 1919–1939*. New York: Harper & Row, 1971.

16

The Quest for Self-Determination: Aspects of the Non-Western World to 1945

1857–1858	Sepoy Rebellion; British crown assumes direct control of India
1881	French occupy Tunisia
1882	British occupy Egypt
1890–1897	Armenian revolt against Turkey
1900	Boxer Rebellion
1905	Massacre of Armenians by Turks
	First Iranian revolution; parliament and constitution created
1908–1909	Young Turk rebellion and reforms in Turkey
1911–1912	Fall of the Ch'ing Dynasty
1912	Italy conquers Libya
1914–1918	World War I
1916	McMahon Agreement granting Palestine to the Arabs
1917	Balfour Declaration supporting a Jewish homeland

1919	Treaty of Versailles
	"May Fourth Movement" begins in China
	Amritsar Massacre in India
	First pan-African congress
1921	First meeting of Chinese Communist Party
1922	Ottoman sultan deposed; Turkey becomes secular state
1930–1931	"Cocoa holdups" in Gold Coast; farmers refuse to sell to British
1934–1935	The Long March
1937	Japanese invasion of China
1940–1943	World War II in North Africa
1947	Indian independence

The first half of the twentieth century was a time of great change throughout the world. The challenges faced by many regions were different from those faced in the industrialized West. In this chapter, we will briefly examine a few regions of the world, looking both at internal problems and at the impact of foreign powers on those regions. It should be kept in mind, however, that these are only examples of some of the kinds of problems and changes that characterized this period.

THE LAST DECADE OF CH'ING RULE

The Ch'ing (Manchu) dynasty in China had one decade of life left after the Boxer Rebellion was crushed by a multinational army in 1900. The Boxer Protocol, which set the terms for the satisfaction of the foreign powers whose legations were attacked by the Boxers, was signed in September 1901. Among other provisions, the agreement required China to pay an enormous indemnity over the next forty years, totaling over $700 million (including interest) by the exchange rates of the time. The major burden of the debt, of course, fell on Chinese peasant taxpayers, making a hard life even harder.

The Dynasty in Decline   China's Manchu rulers did make an attempt in the first decade of the twentieth century to reform the government and increase popular support for the dynasty, but most of their efforts fell short of what was necessary either for dynastic survival or for the building of a modern state.

At the same time, many young Chinese began to be exposed to foreign ideas. Some of them traveled abroad to study in Europe or the United States, but increasingly China's treaty ports—particularly Shanghai—became centers for new ideas, foreign contact, and the expression of dissatisfaction with China's situation. The slow pace of reform, China's semicolonization by foreign powers, and the seeming inability of the state to modernize were aggravating to Chinese who had seen developments in other parts of the world.

LATE CH'ING REFORMS

But China's rulers did make one last effort. In 1901, the Empress Dowager, the most powerful figure in Chinese politics (and now newly converted to the necessity of reform), appointed a reform commission. Many of the reforms that were instituted did not have a chance to fully take hold, but there were some noteworthy changes.

Administrative Reforms. For the first time, a government office was created exclusively for the management of foreign affairs. Some old bureaucratic positions that amounted to little more than sinecures were eliminated in an effort at streamlining the government. There were also military and educational reforms.

The Examination System. The reform that was perhaps most symbolic of the sweeping changes China was about to undergo was the elimination in 1905 of the traditional civil service examination system. For centuries, this system—based upon knowledge of the Confucian classics—had been the primary method for recruiting able men into the Chinese government. Its abolition was a recognition of the fact that a modern Chinese state would have to be based on a different kind of knowledge and experience.

The Constitutionalist Movement. At the same time that these reforms were being attempted, a constitutionalist movement was underway in China, leading to the election of provincial assemblies in February 1909. The Ch'ing rulers did not intend for these assemblies to be a challenge to dynastic authority. Rather, they would help keep local society in line, and perhaps even provide a show of national unity. But the establishment of provincial assemblies did not lead to true representative government. Only the educated, propertied class was effectively enfranchised, meaning that the same group that formerly provided officials by means of the examination system now had a monopoly on the new assemblies.

The 1911 Revolution

By 1911 there was sufficient dissatisfaction with the Manchu government that it did not take much to topple it. The "revolution" of that year was not so much a well-planned insurrection as it was the unforeseen coalescence of peasants, radical activists, students, and disaffected landowners.

SUN YAT-SEN

Sun Yat-sen is generally credited with being the "father" of the Chinese republic. Born in Canton and educated in Hong Kong and Hawaii, Sun returned to China in 1894 and began trying to foment uprisings to overthrow the dynasty and establish a more "modern" state in its place. He attempted numerous uprisings over the next fifteen years, all of which failed in their grand objectives. But if Sun was unspectacular as an insurrectionist, he was better as an organizer and fund raiser. He established a following among Chinese residents both in Japan and in the United States. In addition to organizing groups dedicated to the cause of revolution, Sun's other important contribution to the establishment of the Chinese republic was his enunciation of the so-called "Three Principles of the People": nationalism (of an anti-imperialist type), democracy, and socialism. Expanded upon by later leaders, these ideas became the official state ideology after the downfall of the dynasty.

THE FALL OF THE DYNASTY

The actual fall from power of the Manchus was not a grand revolution. In October 1911 a small group of activists accidentally exploded a bomb in the Yangtze River city of Hankow. This led to a general insurrection in the area around Hankow, including taking over the local military garrison. When the central government proved incapable of putting down this localized rebellion, alliances of soldiers and landholders in other provinces began to secede from China. The Ch'ing government called on Yuan Shih-k'ai to bring his powerful army to their aid, but the revolutionaries were eventually able to persuade Yuan to side with them, in exchange for a promise that he would be president of a new Chinese republic. Their military support thus pulled out from under them, the Manchus had little hope of maintaining power. On February 12, 1912, the last Manchu emperor formally abdicated.

REPUBLICAN CHINA

Yuan Shih-k'ai

Although both sides had turned to Yuan Shih-k'ai in 1911 as the answer to their problems, in fact there was little Yuan could do to solve China's real problems. Yuan (now the president of the Republic of China) and his militarist allies quickly came into conflict with the constitutionalists in China's new government. Disgruntled revolutionaries, as well as some moderates, responded by forming a political party called the *Kuomintang* (Nationalist Party) to serve as their vehicle for political activity.

Casting about for a way to increase his own power and build a more powerful, centralized state, Yuan in 1915 attempted to proclaim himself emperor of a new dynasty. The response was immediate. Having just ousted one dynasty, China's provincial leaders were not about to welcome in a new, unpopular one. The southern provinces began to secede once again, and Yuan was forced to abandon the attempt to restore monarchy to China. What could have turned into a prolonged struggle between Yuan and the Kuomintang was averted when Yuan died in 1916.

<table>
<tr><td>

The Disintegration of the State

</td><td>

WARLORDS

Yuan's death ended the facade of unity that had existed under the nascent republic. There ensued a power struggle not only within Yuan's army, but throughout the nation. An era began in which there was no central government that was truly effective. Instead, China was ruled by regional warlords, each with a private army and little inclination to restrain his own ambition in the name of national unity.

CONTINUING IMPERIALISM

In addition to the gradual disintegration of the state, China still had the problem of foreign economic and political encroachment to deal with. China's weakened position in the world was convincingly demonstrated at the Versailles peace conference after World War I. China had hoped that the delegates to the conference would return German holdings in the Shantung peninsula to Chinese control, now that Germany had been defeated. But Japan had also been a participant in the war on the side of the allies and, as one of the victors, staked its own claim to the former German possessions. Recognizing that the balance of power in Asia had clearly shifted to Japan and feeling that, if a choice had to be made, it was better to offend the weakened Chinese than the rapidly modernizing Japanese, the Versailles delegates confirmed Japanese possession of the former German holdings in Shantung. American president Woodrow Wilson's idealistic call for self-determination after the war did not help the Chinese.

</td></tr>
<tr><td>

The May Fourth Movement

</td><td>

THE VERSAILLES DECISION

When word of the Versailles decision reached China, stunned Chinese reacted in shock and anger at yet another example of the depths to which the international standing of this proud culture had sunk. The news sparked a nationwide series of demonstrations, beginning in Peking on May 4, 1919. Chinese expressed their anger at the world, and also at the Chinese delegates who had failed to regain Chinese territory. There was massive public support for the demonstrations, which moved beyond shouting and marching to boycotts of Japanese goods. But despite China's anger, the Versailles decision stood. Japan quickly became the most despised imperialist nation in China.

</td></tr>
</table>

CULTURAL FERMENT

The term "May Fourth Movement" is used to describe not only the demonstrations that took place in Peking and other Chinese cities. It also has a broader meaning when used to describe a period of great intellectual and cultural questioning and ferment. Many educated Chinese, searching for a solution to China's problems and wondering how things had gone so wrong, began to look at the centuries of Chinese tradition as a hindrance to modernization. As a result, a general reassessment of Chinese culture gained momentum, beginning in the second decade of the twentieth century.

This reassessment took many forms. There was a movement for language reform, to make the language of education and literature the same as the spoken language, rather than the arcane classical language that had made higher education the province of a privileged few. Others hailed "democracy" and "science" as the solutions to China's problems, arguing that tradition had fettered individual expression and that science could be a means for breaking down traditional, superstitious ideas. There were radicals and pragmatists, thinkers and activists, and for a time the intellectual and cultural atmosphere in China was such that all of them could voice their opinions and advocate their programs.

MARXISM

The Appeal of Marxism. One of the ideas that formed part of this intellectual unrest was Marxism. It gained momentum after the Russian Revolution of 1917 demonstrated that a revolution based on Marxist principles could work. But its initial appeal was still limited largely to intellectuals who saw in Marxist doctrine an answer to many of the problems plaguing China. Lenin, in applying Marxism to Russia, had argued that imperialism was the last stage of capitalism. This theory offered some solace to Chinese intellectuals who saw their country struggling under the weight of imperialism. China's plight was now partially explained. But an equally important contribution of Lenin's to Marxist theory was his argument about the role of a small party as the "vanguard" of revolution.

The Chinese Communist Party. The Chinese Communist Party (CCP) held its first meeting in 1921, in the French section of Shanghai. Only a small group of intellectuals met at first. Following standard Marxist ideology (and under the guidance of advisors from Moscow), the party initially concentrated its efforts on organizing urban industrial workers. The difficulty here was that China did not have a large urban proletariat—certainly not sizable enough to bring about revolution in a country the size of China. It was not until Mao Tse-tung, who eventually became party general secretary, was able to shift the focus of the party to China's vast peasantry that communism began to spread rapidly.

KMT-CCP Cooperation and Rivalry

In the early 1920s, particularly with the Communist Party still small and with warlords still a menace, the Nationalist Party (Kuomintang or KMT, now under the leadership of Chiang Kai-shek) and the Communist Party found common cause. Their primary joint objective was to rid China of warlords and imperialists. It was always a marriage of convenience, however, as Chiang was vehemently opposed to communism. Unlike the Communists—who drew their initial support from intellectuals and urban workers, and their later support from the peasantry—Chiang's power was backed by China's capitalists and industrialists.

THE PURGE OF COMMUNISTS

By 1927, even before the joint KMT-CCP campaign against China's warlords had been completed, Chiang could tolerate cooperation with the Communists no longer. In April 1927, his forces conducted a lightning purge of workers and Communist Party members. Within a day, hundreds had been killed, and the CCP was severely damaged. Unburdened of the Communists, Chiang then set up a Nationalist government with its capital at Nanking.

THE LONG MARCH

The Communists, meanwhile, began to regroup, this time concentrating on rural organizing in Kiangsi province, in southeastern China. Chiang was driven in his determination to rid China of communism once and for all. He therefore sent a series of "extermination campaigns" south to the areas of CCP strength. The fifth of these campaigns (1933–1934) was nearly successful, but the Communists managed to break through Chiang's lines. Thus began the famous Long March. Starting out with around 100,000 people, the Communists spent a year marching 6,000 miles, over terrain that was often treacherous and in weather for which they were ill prepared. Perhaps 10,000 finally reached the destination of Yenan in Shensi province, far to the northwest of Nanking and Chiang's capital.

The Long March was important for a number of reasons. First, it established the Communists in a base that was farther away from the KMT stronghold of Nanking, allowing them to reorganize and plan strategy. Second, it brought Mao Tse-tung into increasing prominence in the Communist Party. Third, it solidified a core of dedicated followers who had passed through the terrible ordeal together. Many of them later held important positions in China's communist government. And finally, the Long March continued to serve as a source of inspiration for decades after its completion.

WAR WITH JAPAN

Japanese Invasion. While Chiang Kai-shek was devoting much of his attention to the Communists, another serious problem was facing China. In 1931, imperial Japan, already in control of Korea since 1910, seized

Manchuria. The KMT government was now faced with both an internal threat and an even more menacing external one. Japan launched a full-scale invasion of China in 1937, plunging the two nations into a war that became part of the larger world conflict later that decade. The CCP and the KMT formed a united front against Japan in 1937, but it was never a cozy relationship. Both "allies" seemed to sense that the war with Japan was to some extent a prelude to their own showdown.

United Front. But the united front against Japan did have some important benefits for both the Communists and the Nationalists. The KMT leader, Chiang Kai-shek, enjoyed enhanced international prestige as the leader of China's forces fighting the imperial Japanese war machine. He also gained American financial and military aid in carrying out the war. The Communists, on the other hand, gained access to more weapons than they otherwise would have had. More important, their resistance to the Japanese invaders won them many sympathizers among China's peasants.

Effects of the War. World War II—or, more precisely, the war with Japan—was terribly destructive for China. Many areas were devastated in the fighting, notably places like Nanking where, during the infamous "Rape of Nanking" in 1937, Japanese soldiers killed, looted, and raped indiscriminately. In addition, the war severely weakened Chiang's Kuomintang, since the destruction of some of China's major cities also meant the elimination of his base of support.

Communist Activity. The Communists were active fighting the war against Japan, but they also concentrated on organizing the peasantry in the countryside as they passed through. They won many adherents by confiscating land from landlords and redistributing it to the farmers. They also advanced their social program in other ways, with the result that millions of peasants were prepared to help them achieve political dominance as well once the Japanese aggressors had been defeated.

INDIA UNDER THE BRITISH CROWN

Following the Sepoy Rebellion of 1857–1858 (see chapter 13), administration of India by the East India Company was replaced by direct British crown rule. India was the "jewel in the crown" of Queen Victoria, who even took the title "Empress of India" in 1877.

British Administration	**THE CIVIL SERVICE**

The British government staffed its government in India with an elite group of civil servants, many of whom were trained specifically for service in India. Eventually an entire British society developed in India, served by Indians whose affairs the British were there to administer and who were excluded from active participation in the most important matters affecting their own future.

DEVELOPMENT UNDER BRITISH RULE

India's British rulers did promote advancements in education, transportation, agriculture, and other areas. Railroads soon crisscrossed the nation, facilitating the easy movement of both people and goods. (This railway system remains as one of the positive legacies of British rule.) But although the railroad made British rule and economic exploitation easier, mercantilist economic policies did not allow the development of native Indian industry that might compete with British industry.

Indians fared unevenly under British rule. Most remained poor, a problem exacerbated by the importation of cheap British manufactured goods and factory-produced cotton, with which native products could not compete. There were other Indians who went to work for the British. While the upper levels of the civil service were reserved for the British, there was a vast bureaucracy below those levels largely staffed by Indians. And while the "white man's burden" made the British feel obligated to take "civilization" and enlightenment to all parts of their empire, there were Indians who left the subcontinent for a time to partake of British civilization at its source. As will be seen, those educated in Britain included some of the most important leaders of India's nationalist movement and the government of independent India.

The Rise of Nationalism in India

One of the obstacles in the way of any kind of India-wide nationalism is the fact that India was (and is) a diverse mix of religious, linguistic, and ethnic groups. Though not all Indians chafed under British rule—some seem to have found it quite pleasing—more and more began to find common cause in their desire for greater independence. To some, this meant complete independence, while others had more modest hopes for a greater Indian voice in government.

THE INDIAN NATIONAL CONGRESS

The formation of the Indian National Congress in 1885 provided a focus for individuals and groups who sought to work toward independence largely within the existing framework of British rule. Jawaharlal Nehru, the first prime minister of independent India, and Mohandas K. Gandhi were involved in Congress politics. So, for a time, was Muhammad Ali Jinnah, later the president of the Muslim League and eventually the "father" of Pakistan. It is one of the ironies of Indian history that all three of these nationalists were educated in the land of their colonial overlords and then returned to

India to advocate severing the colonial bond. Other important early national-ists were the moderate G. K. Gokhale (who was also affiliated with the Congress) and the militant B. G. Tilak.

WORLD WAR I

A turning point for Indian resistance to British rule came after World War I. Having supported the British war effort with a very large force, and having suffered heavy casualties while hopes of independence were delayed by the war, many Indians looked with great anticipation to the end of the war and the possibility of greater self-government. Disillusionment with the lack of change after the war made many Indians more willing to openly oppose British rule.

GANDHI

The new leader of the resistance was Mohandas K. Gandhi. Educated in law in London, Gandhi became an unceasing critic of British policy. He led a series of protest actions against colonial rule, always emphasizing that resistance must be nonviolent.

Unfortunately, not everyone shared Gandhi's commitment to non-violence. Beginning in 1907, Parliament repeatedly gave assurances that Britain intended to grant India its independence. But Indian disillusionment after World War I and further British repression made the road to inde-pendence a rocky one. One of the worst incidents occurred in Amritsar in 1919, when a contingent of British-led Indian troops fired on a peaceful, unarmed Indian crowd, killing 400 and wounding over 1,000.

MOVEMENT TOWARD INDEPENDENCE

Independence for India did remain the official objective of the British government, however slow the actual pace of change. Gandhi continued to lead a nonviolent resistance and civil disobedience campaign throughout the 1930s and early 1940s. But it took an election in Britain to finally open the way for independence. The determined wartime prime minister, Winston Churchill, was most unsympathetic to the idea of the breakup of the British empire. But in 1945, Churchill was replaced by Clement Attlee, whose Labour Party was victorious in elections that year. Attlee quickly announced a timetable for full Indian independence (see chapter 20).

THE MIDDLE EAST

The Height of Colonial Power, 1870–1914

EUROPEAN IMPERIALISM

Colonial power in the Middle East was based on a combination of military and economic supremacy. Europe's vastly superior military technology, organization, and resources meant that, outside of difficult terrain like the mountains or the deserts, armed resistance against European powers was essentially hopeless. Those Middle Eastern states that were able to resist European conquest did so because of military alliance with another European power. Thus, the Ottoman empire's alliance with Germany effectively prevented French or British conquest for several decades. Iran and Afghanistan maintained tenuous semi-independence because they were used as pawns in the balance of power and conflicting spheres of influence between Russian Central Eurasia and British India. Thus the political and economic struggles between European states began to be played out in part in the Middle East as the "Eastern Question," with Germans backing Turks, Russians backing Iranians, and British backing Arabs. The indigenous struggles of Europe and the Middle East became globalized.

MIDDLE EASTERN REACTION

Internally, the period of European colonialism and domination in the Middle East created a tremendous intellectual crisis among Muslims. Middle Easterners faced numerous serious social and political problems. Poverty, economic underproduction, poor communication and travel systems, illiteracy, factionalism, and social unrest plagued most Middle Eastern countries in the late nineteenth and early twentieth centuries.

Many modernist reformers sought to solve the problems of the Middle East by adopting the social structure of the Europeans in order to imitate their successes. Reformers called for new Western-style legal systems to replace Islamic law (*shari'a*), parliamentary government systems, and reforms in education and social law. Others saw the return to traditional Islamic values and legal systems as the mechanism by which peace, prosperity, and independence could be restored. But whatever disagreements there were among Middle Easterners concerning the best methods to solve the many problems of their region, all were agreed that one key element was independence from European political and economic control.

MODERNIZATION

European rule brought with it a great deal of modernization in the Middle East. The first printing presses, telegraphs, railways, and the Suez Canal were all built using European technology; European medical knowledge saved the lives of thousands. The discovery and exploitation of oil and other natural resources was undertaken by Western geologists. But despite these very important benefits, Europeans fundamentally used the Middle East as a region to be economically exploited, and as a chessboard for their own national rivalries. The peoples of the Middle East became mere pawns in the "game" of global domination.

World War I and Its Aftermath

WORLD WAR I

The complex system of rivalries, alliances, and patronage in Europe culminated in August 1914 with World War I. In the Middle East, the Ottoman Turkish empire was allied with the Germans and therefore entered the war against the British. The Turkish-German strategy centered around capturing Egypt and cutting the Suez Canal, Britain's important link to its Indian and African colonies. Ultimately, after unsuccessful campaigns in Iraq and at the Dardanelles, the British, allied with Arabian tribesmen, defeated the Turks on the Palestine front in 1917, capturing Jerusalem and Damascus. Turkish resistance collapsed shortly thereafter. By the end of the war in 1918, the British and French had conquered the Ottoman empire.

PEACE AND THE MANDATES

In order to defeat the Turks, the French and the British had made a number of conflicting promises and secret treaties. On the one hand, they promised their Arab allies that they would establish independent Arab kingdoms in the ethnically Arab-speaking parts of the former Ottoman empire (McMahon Agreement, 1916). On the other hand, they had also promised important European Jews that the British government would support the establishment of a Jewish homeland in the former Ottoman province of Palestine (Balfour Declaration, 1917). However, the real policy of the British and French was spelled out in the Sykes-Picot Agreement (1916), which agreed to divide the entire Middle East into French and British zones of influence.

The final working out of these conflicting Arab, Jewish, British, and French goals and interests created the boundaries of the modern Middle East and laid the foundation for many of the political and military problems that have plagued the region since the end of World War I. The basic elements of the final agreement divided the Middle East into two spheres of influence, the French in Syria and Lebanon, and the British in Kuwait, Iraq, Jordan, and Palestine. The British established members of the Hussein royal family of Arabia as their client kings in each of their countries. Continued Jewish immigration to Palestine was permitted, but limited.

THE CREATION OF MODERN TURKEY

The Ottoman empire, stripped of all its provinces by the British and French victory in the war, was left with essentially the territory of the modern state of Turkey. In the years following the World War I, Turkey fought wars with Greece, overthrew the moribund Sultan, and created the new nation of modern Turkey. The architect of the new Turkey was Kemal Attaturk (r. 1923–1938), who initiated a radical program of modernization, secularization, and Westernization. The Islamic script was abandoned in favor of the Roman alphabet, Islamic control over education and law was eliminated, while strong ties to the West were established. By World War II, Turkey had emerged as one of the most modernized countries in the Middle East. Their subsequent strong involvement in NATO has further strengthened their ties to the West.

World War II and Its Aftermath

BETWEEN THE WARS

Throughout the 1920s and 1930s, France and England retained strong control over most of the Arab-speaking world. The Arabs, for their part, grew increasingly discontented with European domination. Intellectuals arose in the Middle East who were of the third generation of colonial rule. They had often been educated in European-style schools and were able to agitate for self-rule in a wide variety of ways. Newspapers and journals were established that continually pointed out the inadequacies and injustices of European rule. Parliamentary organizations were established that slowly gained some measure of self-rule. Middle Easterners began to play an increasing role in the policing, defending, and day-to-day operation of European colonial governments. Step by step they gained the modern skills and training required to allow them to ultimately govern themselves. Nonetheless, real political power and independence still eluded them, and came about only because of the global crisis of World War II.

WORLD WAR II

North Africa was the scene of several important campaigns during World War II. The neutrality of Turkey prevented Hitler from attacking French and British Middle Eastern provinces from the north. Instead, using Italy and Sicily as a springboard, the German and Italian armies conquered nearly all of North Africa, eventually pushing to within seventy miles of Alexandria before being stopped at the battle of El Alamein in 1942. Thereafter the British from the east and the Americans from the west in Morocco drove the Germans from North Africa, invading Italy itself in 1943. Thus, by the end of the war, the American, French, and British allies were still in control of the entire Middle East.

SUB-SAHARAN AFRICA

During the first half of the twentieth century, sub-Saharan Africa—by now thoroughly colonized by European powers—experienced stirrings of nationalism. It was not until several years after World War II, however, that the movement toward independence bore significant fruit.

Africa Under Colonial Rule

After the "scramble" for Africa in the late nineteenth century, Britain and France had the most extensive empires on the continent. This was especially true after World War I, when German holdings were mandated by the United Nations to Britain and France. Colonial governments were better at exploiting the economic potential of their African possessions than they were at providing services or developing modern economies that could handle the challenges of independence. Of course, it was primarily for economic reasons that European powers had colonized Africa in the first place; both political and economic development within any region was tailored to the needs of the European power administering it. Mining (iron, copper, diamonds) and agricultural exports (coffee, peanuts, cocoa) were the primary areas of economic development.

TRANSPORTATION

Economic exploitation required infrastructural development. European powers therefore built railways and road systems. These were particularly important for linking coastal and interior towns, but they also facilitated greater colonial control, enabling government administrators to more easily travel between branch offices. As in India, the railway system is one of the major lasting legacies of European rule in Africa.

ADMINISTRATION

Maintaining order within the colonies was a high priority for European administrators, but training large numbers of Africans in administrative skills was not. Native Africans were needed to staff lower levels of the civil service, but the upper reaches of administration were kept beyond their reach. Some black Africans did go to Britain or France for higher education. They were among the leaders in nationalist and independence movements in some African countries. But the absence of a large corps of people trained in administration would present challenges for many of the newly independent African states after World War II.

Christianity in Black Africa

In the first half of the twentieth century, Christian missionary work continued to expand in black Africa. It spread quite rapidly in some areas, though conflicts developed between Christian teachings and native culture.

CHRISTIANITY AND NATIVE CULTURE

European missionaries were particularly troubled by the practice of polygamy and required their converts to forswear the practice—even to the point of forcing male converts with plural wives to give up all of their wives but one. Many Africans were willing to accept the missionaries' message. They were prompted by a variety of motivations, from sincere spiritual conversion to the desire to accommodate white Christian culture and be as close as possible to its benefits.

NATIVE CHURCHES

One way of attempting to make Christianity fit African needs and at the same time remove it from European domination was the development of so-called "Ethiopian" churches. These were churches which emphasized the Old Testament message, while at the same time attempting to preserve and extol the virtues of African cultures.

IMPACT

The impact of Christianity in Africa must be seen as mixed. Zealous Christian missionaries, eager to bring salvation to the masses of Africans, often pursued their mission with such vigor that they were insensitive to native culture, customs, and beliefs. This could have subtle but profound consequences for native society. One of the Ibo villagers in Nigerian writer Chinua Achebe's powerful novel *Things Fall Apart* expresses it this way:

> It is already too late. . . . Our own men and our sons have joined the ranks of the stranger. . . . How do you think we can fight when our own brothers have turned against us? The white man is very clever. He came quietly and peaceably with his religion. We were amused at his foolishness and allowed him to stay. Now he has won our brothers, and our clan can no longer act like one. He has put a knife on the things that held us together and we have fallen apart.

On the other hand, the native Christian churches did try to preserve elements of traditional culture, and the mission schools associated with European Christian churches provided an education for many Africans. They also produced a number of the leaders of the later nationalist movements.

Gradual Nationalist Stirrings

OBSTACLES

A number of obstacles slowed the development of nationalism in black Africa. One of these obstacles was the fact that ethnic or tribal identity tended to be more important than "national" identity. There was also the question of who would lead any potential broad-based nationalist movement. A "pan-African" movement did develop in the second and third decades of the twentieth century, though it was largely inspired by American or West Indian blacks, or by Africans educated in Britain or France.

SENGHOR AND *NÉGRITUDE*

One example of this development was the poet Léopold Senghor of Senegal. Senghor was one of the creators and leading proponents of the idea of *Négritude*. This concept—that African culture was valuable in its own right—was designed to transcend tribal or other differences and unite all black Africans.

African nationalism did not fully develop until after World War II. But many of the seeds were sown in the years prior to that conflict, as Africans became increasingly impatient with colonial rule and an increasing number of Africans began to desire their own states independent of white Europeans.

Though they did not all fall under the direct rule of Western states, all of the regions discussed in this chapter in one way or another had to deal with the spreading influence of Western power. Internal developments combined with the presence of the West to create nationalist movements throughout the world, though more slowly in some places than in others. The old colonial empires were about to break apart, however, as the changes following World War II created new or newly independent nations in many parts of the world.

Selected Readings

Dirlik, Arif. *The Origins of Chinese Communism*. New York and Oxford: Oxford University Press, 1989.

Fromkin, David. *A Peace to End All Peace: Creating the Modern Middle East, 1914–1922*. New York: H. Holt, 1989.

Gailey, Harry A., Jr. *History of Africa, Volume II: From 1800 to Present*. Huntington, NY: Robert E. Krieger Publishing Co., 1981.

Hourani, Albert. *A History of the Arab Peoples*. Cambridge, MA: The Belknap Press of Harvard University Press, 1991.

July, Robert W. *A History of the African People*. 3rd ed. New York: Charles Scribner's Sons, 1980.

Meisner, Maurice. *Li Ta-chao and the Origins of Chinese Marxism*. New York: Atheneum, 1982. (Originally published by Harvard University Press.)

Sheridan, James E. *China in Disintegration: The Republican Era in Chinese History, 1912–1949*. New York: The Free Press, 1975.

Spence, Jonathan D. *The Search for Modern China*. New York: Norton, 1990.

Wakeman, Frederic, Jr. *The Fall of Imperial China*. New York: The Free Press, 1975.

Wolpert, Stanley. *A New History of India*. 3rd ed. New York and Oxford: Oxford University Press, 1989.

17

World War II and the Rise of the Superpowers, 1931–1950

1935	Italy invades Ethiopia
	America passes the first of several neutrality laws
1936	Rhineland remilitarized
	Rome-Berlin Axis formed
1937	Beginning of a new Sino-Japanese war
1938	Germany takes over Austria
1939	Germany takes over Czechoslovakia
	Germany takes over Poland
	England and France declare war on Germany
1939–1940	Russo-Finnish War
1940	America's lend-lease program
	Fall of France
	Italy invades Egypt and Greece
	Battle of Britain
1941	Hitler invades the Soviet Union
	Japanese attack on Pearl Harbor brings America into the war

1942   Allies invade North Africa

1943   Allies invade Italy

1944   Allies invade France

1945   Yalta conference

Potsdam conference

United Nations formed

World War II ends

1947   Truman Doctrine announced

Marshall Plan

1948   Berlin blockade and airlift

1949   NATO formed

*N**ot long after the end of World War I the security arrangements by which the victorious powers hoped to avoid another war began to fall apart. Japan's takeover of Manchuria was only the first of a series of crises that would demonstrate the weakness of the League of Nations and the irresolution of the Western powers. The League of Nations condemned Japan, but that was all it could do. President Herbert Hoover denounced the action as a violation of the Kellogg-Briand treaty, but he also refused to authorize military intervention, arguing that this would be a breach of the same pact.*

By 1939 the stage was set for another war. German and Italian aggression pitted those two countries against England and France. Soviet interests in eastern Europe at first led to an alliance with Berlin and Rome. Later, however, Germany turned against the Soviet Union, which then became a British ally. Japanese expansionism, compatible with that of Germany, brought that country into the Rome-Berlin Axis. That same expansionism conflicted with Western interests in Asia, and particularly those of the United States. In 1941 this resulted in Japan's attack on Pearl Harbor, which then brought America into the war.

What caused the war? We have suggested that one factor was the Versailles treaty itself, which imposed such heavy burdens on Germany that under Hitler it finally saw fit to violate every provision. Another may have been Hitler himself and his plans for European domination. But if blame goes to Hitler, at least some must also go to Italy's Mussolini, Russia's Stalin, and Japan's Tojo, each of whom was also an aggressor. On the other hand, it could be said that the failure of the League of Nations to take decisive action against aggressors and the policies of neutrality and appeasement followed by the Western democracies were equally to blame. But whatever the case, these and other factors were all related, in some way, to the unfinished business of World War I. Sadly, almost immediately after the new war was over, the world was divided into two ideologically hostile armed camps. Genuine peace seemed as illusive as ever.

BACKGROUND FOR WAR

Weapons of Destruction

Technological progress during the interlude between the wars brought the world's war machines to new heights of destructive power. Fighter planes, dive bombers, long-range tactical bombers, and parachute troops changed the nature of war itself by making the air a field of battle. Highly improved and more heavily armored tanks made warfare on the ground more lethal, as did improved weaponry of all sorts. On the seas, battleships with their vastly improved long-range guns, aircraft carriers, destroyers, and modern submarines all had greater destructive power than anything seen before. In addition, sophisticated electronic devices, such as radio, radar, sonar, and code-breaking machines, all became essential to the conduct of war. Finally, the atomic bomb, conceived long before the war and developed in top-secret facilities during the war, was unleashed in 1945 to end the conflict.

Undermining Versailles in Europe

Several important events led to the outbreak of war. Among them were various aggressive acts by the new dictatorships, followed by weak reactions from Western democracies, all of which undermined the intent of Versailles and the League of Nations.

REACTION TO GERMAN REARMAMENT

When Hitler announced his intent to rearm Germany in 1935, Britain, France, and Italy immediately condemned the action. They did little about it, however, though Britain and France agreed to assist each other in case of German aggression. France also signed a pact with Russia against German aggression, even as Russia was making similar agreements with eastern European countries. None of these accords, however, influenced Germany, which continued to rearm.

ITALY'S INVASION OF ETHIOPIA

In Italy, Mussolini was dreaming of creating his own empire, starting with Ethiopia in northeastern Africa. He invaded in October 1935, correctly expecting little opposition from other European powers. By May his armies had taken over. The League of Nations condemned the aggression, imposing sanctions against Italy, but the sanctions were ineffective.

REMILITARIZING THE RHINELAND

In March 1936 Germany sent troops into the Rhineland, which was supposed to remain demilitarized. Again Britain and France did nothing but protest. Belgium soon withdrew from its military alliance with France, convinced that a reticent France would not protect it from German aggression anyway.

THE ROME-BERLIN-TOKYO AXIS

In October Germany and Italy signed an agreement creating the "Rome-Berlin Axis." Both countries were then free to pursue their expansionist aims without fear of interference from the other. The next month Germany and Japan announced a new agreement, known as the Anti-Comintern Pact. Ostensibly for the purpose of fighting the expansion of communism, the pact was also a way to protect German and Japanese expansionism. Italy joined the pact a year later. The world's three main aggressive imperialist powers were thus linked in mutually compatible goals that were opposed to everything that the League of Nations and the Western democracies seemed to stand for.

BRITISH AND FRENCH IRRESOLUTION: SOME OBSERVATIONS

By 1936 Hitler had broken practically every restriction imposed on Germany at Versailles. France and Britain, however, continually refused to act against him. Fearful of a new war, they even, at times, seemed to acquiesce. Hitler justified remilitarizing the Rhineland, for example, with the excuse that he was only obtaining firm control over land that was Germany's anyway. The other powers seemed to accept the argument. Hindsight suggests that Hitler's ultimate aims should have been clear, for they were implied if not specifically spelled out in all he had previously written and said. At the time, however, British and French statesmen thought they were doing what was best for peace; they were unwilling to take a military risk. Everyone hoped that each aggressive act would be the last, but it was not.

"PEACEFUL" AGGRESSION AND APPEASEMENT

So far, Hitler had not taken over any new territory. That changed in 1938, with the takeover of Austria and of Czechoslovakia. Both acts were technically "peaceful," and the other European powers seemingly remained powerless to do anything.

Anschluss. Hitler had long dreamed of unification between the two German-speaking nations, Austria and Germany. By 1938 he had cultivated considerable support for the Nazis in Austria. On March 12 his forces marched in—yet another violation of the Versailles treaty. In April a presumably popular Austrian plebiscite unified the two countries. The plebiscite did not represent the tens of thousands of anti-Nazis and Jews who had been treated to a diet of persecution and violence, but the world saw only images of cheering crowds and popular support for the *Anschluss* (unification).

Czechoslovakia. Hitler next turned to Czechoslovakia, where 3 million Germans lived in the border area called the Sudetenland. At Hitler's urging, these ethnic Germans began to demand autonomy, whereupon Hitler threatened to intervene in their behalf. Czechoslovakia mobilized for war, but then, prodded by Britain and France, Czech leaders finally gave in. Hitler's support for autonomy, however, was only a ruse—his ultimate goal was to take over all of Czechoslovakia. He therefore quickly instructed his people to make even harsher demands. Hitler was aware that an invasion of Czechoslovakia could result in war with France and Britain. He also believed that, despite their treaty arrangements, they simply did not want to go to war over that issue. He was right.

Appeasement. Great Britain and France began to seek some kind of compromise. The British prime minister, Neville Chamberlain, eventually took matters into his own hands. The result was a series of appeasements (though he probably negotiated as well as he could, given the overwhelming British sentiment against going to war). In a mid-September meeting he accepted Hitler's demands that the Sudetenland be transferred to Germany, on the basis of "self-determination." After persuading both the British and the French governments to agree, he met a second time with the German dictator only to find that Hitler's demands had changed again. Changing situations, Hitler claimed, required immediate military intervention. He agreed, however, to Benito Mussolini's suggestion that one more meeting be held to try to settle the matter peacefully. The meeting took place in Munich on September 30, 1938. There Chamberlain, French premier Edouard Daladier, Hitler, and Mussolini agreed to a whittling away at Czechoslovakia. Germany could have the Sudetenland, Poland and Hungary could claim certain territories in the eastern part of the country, and Germany and Italy would guarantee the territorial integrity of what remained. Chamberlain and Daladier were received home with all the laurels of conquering heroes. They had achieved "peace in our time."

Results of Appeasement. The meeting at Munich, however, has gone down in history as the ultimate example of the perils of appeasement. The Czechoslovakian state, reduced by territorial acquisitions on all sides, was simply unable to maintain political stability. Six months later, in March 1939, Hitler marched into Prague, declaring that intervention was needed to restore order. He then set up the puppet state of Slovakia and declared the remaining area a German protectorate. Stunned, Chamberlain still found justification for not responding militarily. Czechoslovakia's political disintegration was not caused by external aggression, he rationalized, so there was no legal reason for Britain or France to go to war.

Background for War in Asia

On the other side of the world, meanwhile, the Japanese military government moved steadily in the direction of the new imperialism. The armed forces, including the navy, were strengthened and modernized. Business and industrial leaders were won over to the idea that expansion was in the best interest of the nation, as well as in their own self-interest. Leaders of large industrial conglomerates such as Mitsui, Mitsubishi, Sumitomo, and Yasuda joined forces with the military in promoting industrial production and imperialism.

THE CHINA INCIDENT

In July 1937 a border clash between Japanese and Chinese patrols near Peking resulted in a Sino-Japanese war that eventually became part of World War II. Japan quickly turned the incident into an excuse for a major sweep southward, and by the end of 1938 it had captured Nanking, Shanghai, Hankow, and much of China's most populated area.

AMERICAN RESPONSE

Among the Western powers, the United States seemed most concerned with what was happening in Asia. American sympathies were with China, but President Franklin D. Roosevelt knew that invoking the American neutrality law would cut off the flow of arms and supplies and hurt China more than Japan. He did not, therefore, officially recognize the "China Incident" as a war. On October 5 he denounced the "reign of terror and international lawlessness" being conducted by aggressor nations and called for an international "quarantine" against nations "creating a state of international anarchy and instability from which there is no escape through mere isolation or neutrality." American isolationist sentiment, however, forced him quickly to abandon any further thoughts of intervention.

American Isolationism

The American response to Japan only emphasized the isolationist mood that characterized the people of the United States during the 1930s. The most serious problem, after all, seemed to be the Great Depression. Partly for this reason Roosevelt extended diplomatic recognition to the Soviet Union—a move that was criticized by anti-Communists for decades afterward. American diplomats had somewhat unrealistic visions of expanding markets through such recognition. They also realized that America and the Soviet Union had a common interest in opposing Japanese expansion.

NEUTRALITY LAWS

In general, however, the United States retreated further into its isolationist cocoon. A 1935 law prohibited the sale of arms and munitions to belligerents anywhere. In 1936 Congress forbade loans to belligerents. In January 1937 it extended the neutrality laws to civil wars. Later that year it forbade Americans from travel on belligerent ships and made it illegal to arm merchant ships trading with nations at war. The same law extended the embargo on arms, though it gave the president discretionary power to sell other goods to belligerents on a cash-and-carry basis. A Gallup poll that year revealed that 94 percent of the American people felt that efforts to *avoid* war were preferable to attempts to *prevent* war.

MOVING AWAY FROM NEUTRALITY

Nevertheless, Roosevelt and other leaders recognized that it might be impossible for the United States to remain permanently uninvolved, and they began to lay plans accordingly. In July 1936 the United States terminated a long-standing commercial treaty with Japan, making it possible to place an embargo on goods of war. When Germany attacked Poland in 1939, Roosevelt affirmed American official neutrality but told the American people that they need not remain neutral in thought. Later that year a new neutrality act allowed belligerents to buy anything—including arms and munitions—from the United States on a cash-and-carry basis. This easing of restrictions on arms sales was clearly intended to help the Allies, for at that point they controlled the seas.

As the war heated up in Europe, Roosevelt took still more preparatory actions. He committed funds to a secret atomic energy program that eventually resulted in the atomic bomb. He secretly, and illegally, sold surplus goods to Britain and France. In 1940, through an innovative "lend-lease" program, he loaned fifty overage destroyers to Britain in return for the lease of six naval bases in the Caribbean. In the fall Congress passed a draft law that brought 1.2 million new recruits into the military, and at the same time called 800,000 reservists into active duty. By December 1941, even though there was still a general hope for remaining uninvolved, America was committed to helping the Allies and to building up its own military forces.

THE GLOBAL WAR

Everything the Versailles treaty anticipated had disappeared. Hitler and his Third Reich had been strengthened, while Britain and France had lost respect and prestige throughout the rest of Europe. Japan, meanwhile, seemed to be having its own way in Asia.

War in Europe, 1939–1941

Up to this point most of Hitler's aggressions had been rationalized on the assumption that he was merely trying to unite German-speaking people. The takeover of Czechoslovakia, however, was a giant step beyond that.

THE DISAPPEARANCE OF POLAND

Britain and France could not so easily dismiss the next onslaught. They quickly gave Poland their assurance that in case of further aggression they would defend Polish independence. Similar promises were given to Romania, Greece, and Turkey after Mussolini invaded and annexed Albania in April 1939. But Hitler was secretly preparing to take over Poland, even though he had only recently courted that country's friendship in order to ease his conquest of Czechoslovakia.

Non-Aggression Pact. Hitler doubted that France and England would honor their commitments to Poland. Before invading, however, he assured himself that there would be no opposition from the Soviet Union. He negotiated a nonaggression pact, signed on August 23, 1939. This gave him free reign to move into Poland, while Stalin would have no opposition from Hitler with respect to his plans for the Baltic states of Estonia, Latvia, and Lithuania. In addition, it was agreed that Germany and Russia would divide Poland between them.

Blitzkrieg. On September 1 Hitler's troops and aircraft invaded Poland. The German *blitzkrieg* provided Europe with the first taste of what modern warfare could mean. First came the Luftwaffe. Its bombers and dive bombers quickly destroyed Polish airfields and most of its warplanes. They also wreaked havoc with the army and civilians alike. Then came the tanks, or panzer units, followed by lighter mechanized units and then by foot soldiers—a total in all these units of a million men. Poland fell in less than a month and disappeared from the map.

The Takeover of Europe

Two days after the invasion of Poland, England and France honored their commitments and declared war on Germany. At first, the British and Germans conducted a sea war. The French occupied the Maginot line, but did little more than wait for a German attack. Hitler, meanwhile, marched on other parts of Europe.

THE RUSSO-FINNISH WAR

First, however, it was Stalin's turn to take over someone else's territory. In November 1939, intent on strengthening its position in the Baltic, the Soviet Union invaded Finland. Unlike the other Baltic states, Finland had refused to give the Soviets the right to establish military bases on its territory. It was finally defeated in March 1940 and forced to give up the Karelian Isthmus (the connecting bridge between Finland and Russia). Also in 1940 Russia annexed Estonia, Latvia, and Lithuania.

HITLER ON THE MARCH

By that time Hitler's forces were on the march again. In April they moved into Norway and Denmark, conquering those two countries almost immediately. During one week in May they overwhelmed the Netherlands. In another two weeks they took Belgium. These two lowland countries were key to Hitler's plan for invading both France and England. In Britain, the discredited Neville Chamberlain resigned as prime minister, to be replaced by Winston Churchill. "I have nothing to offer you but blood, toil, tears, and sweat," Churchill realistically told the British people.

The Fall of France. It soon became clear that France's long-standing reliance on the Maginot Line was misplaced. The Germans simply swept around it on the north. By June 14, 1940, they were in Paris. The French premier, Marshal Henri Philippe Pétain, decided that it was wiser to give in to the German demands than to fight. He signed an armistice on June 22, turning over most of France to Germany. After that he headed a puppet government, operating out of Vichy.

NORTH AFRICA AND THE BALKANS

At that point Mussolini, emboldened by Hitler's success, got into the war, hoping to gain territories around the Mediterranean. In September 1940 his forces invaded Egypt but were driven back by the British. The Germans soon came to the rescue, however, and the Axis powers were in Egypt by April 1941. In another venture, Italy invaded Greece in October 1940, though it also took German troops finally to bring that country into the Axis orbit. In the meantime, the Germans, with the help of Bulgarian and Hungarian troops, overran Yugoslavia. Russia was also active in the Balkans and gained some border territories from Romania.

BATTLE OF BRITAIN

In the meantime, an air war, commonly called the Battle of Britain, raged between Germany and Britain. At first Hitler had no plans for invading the British Isles. With France gone, he assumed that Britain would simply see no point in further prosecuting the war. When this proved false, however, he developed plans for "Operation Sea Lion," an invasion across the English Channel. He began by trying to soften up Britain with a series of massive air strikes. Beginning in August 1940, the Luftwaffe bombed British airfields, harbors, and other key installations. In September it started raining bombs on London and other cities. The destruction was nearly overwhelming, but the British and the Royal Air Force (RAF) held out, spurred on by the courage and determination of their new prime minister. The Luftwaffe, in fact, suffered heavy losses—1,733 aircraft as opposed to 915 British fighters. In October Hitler decided to postpone Operation Sea Lion indefinitely. The air strikes, however, continued until June, when Hitler's attention was diverted to Russia.

THE SEA WAR

Meanwhile, British shipping was badly damaged by Germany's submarines, as "wolf packs" stalked the North Atlantic. Some of Britain's warships were also sunk. The attacks were countered in part by a convoy system, in which the United States cooperated. The British also sank two great German battleships, the *Admiral Graf Spee* in 1939 and the *Bismarck* in 1941. The tragic ironies of war, meanwhile, were illustrated in 1940 when Churchill was forced to make the "hateful decision" to keep the French fleet from falling into German hands. On his orders, British warships bombarded and immobilized French naval units in ports of Algeria and French West Africa.

HITLER'S RUSSIAN CAMPAIGN

By 1941 Hitler's relations with Stalin, never very cordial, were deteriorating. Among other problems, they had conflicting interests in the Balkans. Besides, Hitler believed that defeating the Soviet Union would further discourage Britain. On June 22, therefore, he turned on his ally in perhaps the most ambitious campaign since Napoleon did the same thing 129 years earlier. After some initial success, however, Hitler's armies soon found themselves facing the same kind of problems that Napoleon's had: cold weather, determined Soviet fighters, and the impossibly long lines of supply that accompanied deeper penetration. Early in 1943 the most ferocious battle of the campaign, the Battle of Stalingrad, ended in disaster for the Germans. In February the German commander surrendered, after 500,000 Axis soldiers had been killed, wounded, or captured. In the spring the Soviets opened a counteroffensive, and before the end of the year most of the territory held by the Germans had been retaken.

Pearl Harbor and the War in the Pacific, 1941–1942

Japan, meanwhile, continued its economic and territorial expansion in Asia, taking advantage of the fact that the European powers were preoccupied with German aggression closer to home.

JAPANESE-AMERICAN TENSION

Japan obtained important concessions on oil exports from the Dutch East Indies. In September 1940 it occupied much of French Indochina. It also signed a Tripartite Pact with Germany and Italy, hoping this would protect its almost unlimited objectives in Asia. The United States responded by placing an embargo on aviation fuel and scrap metals. Japan, however, encouraged by Hitler's continuing success against the Allies, was bent on systematically driving all Western powers from Asia and establishing its own hegemony everywhere on the continent. It would thus gain control of rich sources of strategic goods, such as rubber, oil, and tin. By July 1941 it had moved into the rest of Indochina.

American Responses. The takeover of Indochina brought a quick response from the United States that, for all practical purposes, ended trade between the two countries. Roosevelt froze all Japanese assets in America and placed an embargo on high-octane fuel. He also made the armed forces of the Philippines part of the American army, with General Douglas Mac-Arthur as commander of all American forces in the Far East. Americans generally were becoming increasingly sympathetic with the embattled Chinese. Beginning as early as 1937, one group of mercenaries, known as the "Flying Tigers," helped the Chinese air force considerably. In addition, the American government loaned money to the Chinese and in October 1941 sent an American military mission to advise the Chinese government.

PEARL HARBOR

So far as Japan was concerned, its relations with the United States had reached an impasse. It was not willing to give up anything in Asia, yet unless it did so the United States would not lift its embargo on badly needed oil. Negotiations with Washington were not succeeding. Under these conditions Japan's new prime minister, General Tojo, ordered an air strike on the headquarters of the American Pacific Fleet at Pearl Harbor, Hawaii. This brilliantly planned attack occurred without warning on the morning of Sunday, December 7, 1941. The results were devastating. Eight battleships were in the harbor; three went to the bottom, one was grounded, and the others were badly damaged. Several other ships were also destroyed or damaged, as were most of the airplanes at Hickam Field and other airfields. In addition, over 2,400 people were killed and nearly 1,200 were wounded. The Japanese lost less than thirty planes. Fortunately for the United States, however, the aircraft carriers stationed at Pearl Harbor were out on maneuvers. On the same day, Japan also attacked other American and British positions in Asia and the Pacific.

AMERICA ENTERS THE WAR

Pearl Harbor galvanized American feelings as nothing else could have done. On December 8 Congress declared war on Japan. Three days later Germany and Italy declared war on the United States.

THE PACIFIC WAR, 1941–1942

Japan's objective was to weaken the Western powers so badly that its hegemony in Asia and the Pacific would be secure. During the next year it seemed as if Japan would succeed. Three days after Pearl Harbor, for example, two British battleships were sunk off the coast of Malaya. The dim outlook for the region that December was poignantly recalled by Winston

Churchill in his memoirs. "There were no British or American capital ships in the Indian Ocean or the Pacific except for the American survivors of Pearl Harbor, who were hastening back to California. Over all this vast expanse of waters Japan was supreme, and we everywhere were weak and naked."

Japan's Pacific Empire. Shortly after Pearl Harbor, Japan took over American positions in Guam and Wake Island. Early in 1942 it took the Philippines. The Japanese also overran the Dutch East Indies, the Malay Peninsula, and Burma. By May Japan's new Pacific empire included practically everything east of India and north of Australia. More importantly, the area was rich in all the strategic materials, including oil, needed by Japan to sustain its economic independence.

Stopping the Spread. The United States fought back with a vengeance, as it repaired the damage done at Pearl Harbor and began to rebuild its navy. American aircraft carriers continually harassed Japanese outposts. On April 18, 1942, a group of bombers took off from the deck of the aircraft carrier *Hornet*, bombed Tokyo, and flew on to China. This daring raid did little damage but, as intended, it demonstrated American resolve and built up American morale. In June the American navy stopped the Japanese westward thrust at the Battle of Midway Island. In August a stand at Guadalcanal put a halt to Japan's southern progress. Not until the next year, however, did the United States gain supremacy in the Pacific.

The Allies on the Initiative, 1942–1945

Even before the attack on Pearl Harbor, American leaders had decided that in case of war they would not divide Allied efforts. Instead, they would concentrate on defeating Germany first, then go on to the Pacific. Meanwhile, during most of 1942, Germany and Italy seemed to be winning everywhere.

NORTH AFRICA AND ITALY

Beginning in November 1942 the Allies seized the initiative. American troops under General Dwight D. Eisenhower saw their first action in a combined operation in North Africa. It ended in May 1943 with the Allies in firm control of all of North Africa. In the summer they moved on to Sicily, and then in September they invaded the Italian mainland. By that time Mussolini had been overthrown. The new government asked for an armistice and then, cooperating with the conquerors, declared war on Germany. Germany, in turn, drove into Italy from the north, and fighting went on until the end of the war. This commitment, however, only weakened Germany, for it increased the number of fronts on which German forces had to fight.

ASSAULT ON "FORTRESS EUROPE"

The stage was now set for the final assault on Hitler's "Fortress Europe." After some disagreement as to whether to attack from the Balkans or across

France, the latter view, advocated by the Americans, prevailed. General Eisenhower was made the supreme Allied commander.

The Air War. American and British air forces began a long and devastating air war over Germany, intent on softening it up for invasion and destroying the Luftwaffe. At first Hitler was able to replace lost aircraft quickly, but by the end of March 1944 enough aircraft factories and other strategic installations had been destroyed that the air war was effectively won. By the end of the year there was practically no Luftwaffe left. The German army, however, was as yet by no means defeated.

Invasion. June 6, 1944, "D Day," was the day set for the invasion of France. American, British, and Canadian troops landed in massive numbers on the coast of Normandy. They met powerful opposition, but slowly worked their way inland. After another invasion in southern France, that country was finally liberated by the beginning of September.

Battle of the Bulge. The march toward Germany went well until December. That month, during Christmas week, the Germans launched a massive counterattack on the Belgian front, known as the Battle of the Bulge because they were able to drive so far into Allied lines. For a while the Allies were stopped, though with tremendous losses on both sides. The short-term victory turned out to be the last for the German army, however. The Allies quickly regained the initiative and in March 1945 crossed the Rhine.

Victory in Europe. Soviet troops, meanwhile, swept relentlessly toward Berlin from the east. With the German army falling apart on both fronts, it was only a matter of time before a final Allied victory. Hitler committed suicide on May 1, 1945. On May 7 the German military accepted Allied demands for unconditional surrender and signed a surrender document. The next day was proclaimed V-E Day—the day of victory in Europe.

WAR IN THE PACIFIC, 1943–1945

In the Pacific, American forces also gained the initiative in 1943. Beginning at Guadalcanal, one of the Solomon Islands, island after island was taken in a drive toward the Japanese homeland. Bombing raids on Japan itself began in June 1944, crippling Japanese industry as well as the navy. In October General MacArthur began reconquering the Philippines. The British, meanwhile, supported by the Americans, were back in Burma. Like Hitler, however, the Japanese government stubbornly refused to surrender.

Decision to Drop the Bomb. President Roosevelt died on April 12, 1945. This left the new American president, Harry S Truman, to make the most controversial and awesome decision of the entire war—whether or not to drop the fearful atomic bomb that had just been perfected. Truman was persuaded by several things, among them the fact that Japan clearly would not surrender until it was invaded and conquered. His military advisors calculated that such an invasion would result in 1 million American casualties and even greater numbers for the Japanese. The cost was too high. On August 25, while attending the Potsdam conference (see below), Truman made his fateful decision and issued orders to drop the bomb if Japan did not surrender before August 3. The next day, in what has been called the "Potsdam Declaration," the governments of the United States, Britain, and China warned Japan to surrender or face "utter and complete destruction."

War's End. The deadline passed without a surrender, as Japanese leadership was still divided on how to respond. Two cities were targeted for the bomb, and leaflets were dropped on both of them warning the inhabitants of what was about to happen. On August 6 the first bomb was dropped on Hiroshima, killing over 70,000 people. Russia entered the war against Japan two days later. On August 9 a bomb was dropped on Nagasaki, killing tens of thousands more. Even then the Japanese cabinet resisted surrender. Only the intervention of the emperor, Hirohito (something quite unprecedented), persuaded the government to give in. On August 14 (V-J Day) Japan surrendered. On September 2, 1945, formal documents were signed aboard the American battleship *Missouri* in Tokyo Bay. Accepting surrender on behalf of the United States was General Douglas MacArthur, who would be in charge of Japan's postwar political reconstruction.

Effects of the War

It was only after the war that the extent and implications of Hitler's "New Order" for Europe, and especially for the Jews, became fully known. Though the loss of life and property elsewhere was horrendous, this was the most appalling aspect of all that happened during the six years of all-out war.

HITLER'S NEW ORDER

Hitler's imperialistic plans represented the worst extreme in the history of modern racism. Conquered areas would provide *lebensraum* (living room). In many places the population had been decimated by war or by exporting people to become forced laborers in German factories (more than 7 million suffered this fate). Ethnic Germans would colonize these areas in order to begin the process of Germanization. Peoples related racially to the Germans, like the Scandinavians, were to be absorbed and receive preferential treatment. Others, the "inferior" races, were to be exploited and, depending upon their status, practically enslaved. Slavs were considered *untermenschen* (subhumans), good for little more than slavery. Many were simply worked to death in slave labor camps.

HOLOCAUST

The worst fate of all was reserved for the Jews. Even before war broke out Hitler was having them placed in concentration camps. After taking over Poland, he separated Polish Jews from other people and persecuted them ruthlessly. During the invasion of Russia, special strike squads sought out

Russian Jews; thousands were simply machine-gunned. By 1941, the SS was implementing Hitler's "final solution," the ultimate extermination of the Jews. In extermination camps located in both Germany and Poland, men, women, and children were mercilessly put to death in gas chambers only superficially disguised as shower rooms. It has been reported that at Auschwitz, in Poland, up to 12,000 per day were killed. By 1945 over 6 million Jews had been slaughtered in what has rightly come to be known as the Holocaust—the ultimate example of how monstrous man's inhumanity to man can become.

HUMAN AND MATERIAL COSTS

Beyond the massacre of the Jews, the cost of the war in human lives was greater than any war in history. The best estimates suggest that between 15 and 20 million military personnel were killed in action. Of these, perhaps 7.5 million were Soviet, 3.5 million were German, 2.2 million were Chinese, 1.5 million were Japanese, 300,000 were British, 292,000 were American, and 210,000 were French. The war also cost approximately 25 million civilian lives, including 10 million Soviets, 6 million Chinese, 400,000 French citizens, 65,000 British subjects, and 6,000 Americans. Total military expenditures amounted to at least $1.154 trillion, in addition to untold costs in property damages. The United States spent the largest amount, $300 billion, and Germany spent about $231 billion.

PEACE CONFERENCES AND THE ELUSIVE QUEST FOR GLOBAL UNITY

During the early years of the war seemingly little specific planning was devoted to the nature of the peace and the shape of the postwar world. A number of wartime conferences dealt with military strategy and general objectives, but only toward the end, at Yalta and then at Potsdam, did the Allies begin to spell out specific details for peace. In each case fundamental differences between the Western powers and the Soviet Union began to appear.

Yalta

In February 1945 Roosevelt, Churchill, and Stalin—the "Big Three"—met at Yalta, on the southern Crimean coast. They made several important agreements. One concerned the postwar organization to be known as the United Nations. Most of the details had already been worked out in previous diplomatic meetings, but agreements at Yalta on the nature of the veto power as well as the UN Assembly assured that the organization actually would come into existence. In deciding what to do with Germany, the Big Three assumed unconditional surrender and agreed to divide it into four zones of occupation (including a French zone). With respect to Poland, they agreed on its postwar boundaries, but Roosevelt and Churchill gave in to Stalin's demands for a border that left much of Poland's original eastern territory in Soviet hands. They also agreed that the new provisional government would be drawn from a Soviet-supported national liberation group, though Russia promised subsequent "free elections." The latter proved to be a farce. The same pattern was followed with respect to other eastern European countries.

Already the seeds of the upcoming cold war were sprouting. The fact that Russia had a different agenda for Europe than that of the United States and Britain had been clear for some time, but at Yalta it became a major point for discussion. With respect to East Asia, Russia agreed to join the war on Japan, but only if it received large territorial concessions, most of which took back what Russia lost in the Russo-Japanese War (1904–1905). In later years some Americans posthumously criticized Roosevelt for "giving away" eastern Europe and part of China to the Communists. At the time, however, Roosevelt and Churchill had little choice. The Polish area in question was already occupied by Russia, and it would have taken another war to change that. So far as China was concerned, it appeared that the war in the Pacific could go on indefinitely, and Russia's participation was deemed essential.

The United Nations

On April 25, 1945, delegates from fifty nations met in San Francisco for the purpose of drawing up the charter of the United Nations. Like its predecessor, the League of Nations, it was designed as a means for keeping the peace. The task would be difficult, for it had little power to enforce its resolutions beyond the willingness of member nations to follow them. The Security Council, the strongest arm of the United Nations, was composed of the United States, Great Britain, the Soviet Union, France, and China. Each had veto power over any resolution.

World political differences over the years have hampered its effectiveness, but the United Nations still remains as an important vehicle through which international disputes may be discussed and often dealt with. It also does considerable humanitarian work throughout the world.

Potsdam

By July 1945 Harry Truman had replaced Roosevelt as president of the United States and Clement Attlee had replaced British Prime Minister Winston Churchill. These two met with Stalin at Potsdam, Germany, in the final wartime conference of the Big Three. Again there were some fundamental differences, but they reached some important agreements. Nazi leaders would be tried as war criminals. In addition to dividing Germany into four zones (as agreed at Yalta), they would also divide Berlin, located well within the Russian zone, into four sectors. When it came to discussing political arrangements in eastern Europe, Stalin forthrightly refused Truman's demand for free elections. They could only result in governments unfriendly to the Soviet Union, he reminded the American president, and that simply was not acceptable. Even more than at Yalta, the beginnings of the incipient Cold War were apparent. Stalin was determined to have his way in eastern Europe. This flew in the face of Western idealism, but it was clear that nothing short of another war could change it. Few people in the West were prepared for that.

ORIGINS OF THE COLD WAR

Ideological issues dividing the Soviet Union and the West led to increasing suspicions and tensions. Russia was determined to maintain its dominance in eastern Europe; in various treaties and international agreements following the war it succeeded in doing just that.

A Divided Germany

The problem of what to do with Germany led to the first major confrontation. It had been agreed at Potsdam that the four zones of occupation would be treated as a "single economic unit." Stalin ultimately refused to go along with this, which meant that the Soviet zone soon became separate entirely from the economically integrated zones of Britain, France, and the United States. The long-range result was the permanent division of Germany into East and West German states, as well as the division of Berlin between East and West. This situation, a powerfully visible symbol of the cold war, would last for nearly half a century.

Ideology and the Iron Curtain

Many in the West were both dismayed and disgusted at what seemed like either unreasonable paranoia on the part of the Soviets or a quest for spreading totalitarian communism. In general, the Western democracies had no territorial ambitions, nor did they care to impose a political system, by force, on any country. The thing that mattered was getting about the business of peace. The conflict, however, was ideological, and the Soviets had little trust for the West and capitalism. The Western democracies were enemies, Stalin frequently declared, and simply could not be trusted. Peace with capitalism was impossible. The West received a warning in a speech by Winston Churchill on March 5, 1946, at Westminster College in Fulton, Missouri. "From Stettin in the Baltic to Triest in the Adriatic," he declared, "an iron curtain has descended across the continent." The image of the iron curtain grabbed the public imagination. For over forty years it was the standard metaphor for describing the relations between the Soviet Union and its satellites and the West.

Atomic Energy

The lack of ability to cooperate was demonstrated in November 1945 when the UN began to discuss control of atomic energy and created an Atomic Energy Commission. The American commissioner, Bernard Baruch, proposed outlawing atomic weapons and giving UN inspectors unrestricted, veto-proof rights to conduct investigations anywhere. With such a system in place, Baruch promised, the United States would destroy all its weapons. To the surprise of the Americans, however, the Soviets refused. The United States, in turn, refused Russia's demand that its remaining bombs be destroyed at once. The UN was at an impasse over the issue. In 1949 Russia set off its own atomic bomb. The incredible atomic arms race was on, and it lasted throughout the Cold War.

Korea

There were many potential trouble spots around the world where the Cold War had possibilities of becoming hot. One was Korea. As a result of various conferences before the end of the war, there was a general understanding that both the United States and the Soviet Union would have a postwar interest in this strategically important East Asian country. A final decision had not been reached, however, before the Japanese surrender. At that point it was quickly decided to divide Korea into American and Russian zones of occupations, at the 38th parallel. The capital city, Seoul, was in the American zone. The same ideological conflict affecting divided Germany as well as other countries would break out in open hostilities in Korea in 1950 (see chapter 19).

Containment

Meanwhile, communism gradually spread throughout eastern Europe, where, under Soviet guidance, "people's democracies" were established in several of its satellite countries. Consisting basically of one-party governments, these "democracies" were all either Communist or pro-Communist in their makeup. Americans were concerned by what they viewed as creeping communism bent on overwhelming the world. At that point the United States adopted a policy first clearly enunciated by American diplomat George F. Kennan. Kennan believed that communism contained the seeds of its own decay and that, given time, it would destroy itself. In the meantime, the United States should follow a policy of "long-term, patient but firm and vigilant containment of Russian expansive tendencies."

The Truman Doctrine. The first opportunity to implement the idea of containment came in Greece, where in 1947 a Communist insurrection was under way. The insurgents were clearly supported by the Soviets, with Britain supplying aid to the government. But that year Britain announced that it could no longer supply such aid, whereupon President Truman took up the challenge. In his March 12 announcement, however, he made the issue larger than Greece. "I believe," he declared, "that it must be the policy of the United States to support free peoples who are resisting attempted subjugation by armed minorities or by outside pressures." Further, he said, by helping freed and independent people maintain their freedom, the United States would be promoting the aims of the United Nations charter. The United States quickly provided economic assistance, military equipment, and advisors to both Greece and Turkey. By 1949 both countries had turned back the Communist threat.

Marshall Plan. In June 1947 another new plan was announced by U.S. Secretary of State George C. Marshall. Realizing that all European countries devastated by war were in need of economic aid, Marshall offered it to them, with no strings attached except that they use it for recovery. Marshall publicly declared that American aid was "directed not against country or doctrine, but against hunger, poverty, desperation, and chaos." Nevertheless, Marshall and Truman believed that by fighting poverty they were also fighting communism; their assessment generally proved to be correct. Under the Marshall Plan huge amounts of food and other provisions were poured into the countries of western Europe, helping them to forestall the growth of communism and establish firm democratic governments. The eastern European countries, however, were forbidden by the Soviets from accepting any aid at all—presumably because Stalin feared that it would take these countries out of his orbit and draw them toward capitalism and democracy. Instead, he cracked down even harder on opposition parties. The most dramatic example was in Czechoslovakia in 1948, where a Soviet-supported coup placed the Communist party in power.

Berlin Blockade and Airlift. That same year, the Soviets attempted to drive the Western powers from Berlin by closing off all railroads and highways between that city and West Germany. This threatened to starve the people of West Berlin. The Western powers responded to the blockade, however, with a massive airlift. For nearly a year they flew goods of all sorts into the beleaguered city. The Soviets finally backed down, and the West had won at least one Cold War skirmish.

NATO. The quest for security in the postwar world also sparked a new round of regional defensive alliances, authorized under the United Nations charter. The first such alliance was the Rio Pact, signed in September 1947. It committed the nations of the Western Hemisphere to come to each other's aid in case one were attacked; an attack on one was to be considered as an attack upon all. In 1948 the Treaty of Brussels brought together five European nations: Britain, France, Belgium, the Netherlands, and Luxembourg. The need for collective security against a possible Soviet threat seemed to require a broader coalition, however. In 1949, therefore, these countries along with four other European nations (Denmark, Norway, Portugal, and Iceland) joined with the United States and Canada in the formation of the North Atlantic Treaty Organization (NATO), patterned after the Rio Pact. Greece, Turkey, and West Germany later joined. In 1950 an integrated

defense force was created; the following year General Dwight D. Eisenhower, recalled to active duty, was placed in command.

Soviet Response: The Warsaw Pact. The Soviet Union countered with
its own collective defense system. In 1955 eight nations (Albania, Bulgaria,
Czechoslovakia, East Germany, Hungary, Poland, Romania, and the Soviet
Union) signed a mutual defense treaty known as the Warsaw Pact. The pact
became as much an instrument for political domination by the Soviets as it
was an alliance against NATO.

By 1955 the Cold War had resulted in the formation of two hostile blocs,
each armed to counter any attack and each fearful that the other would find
reason to attack first. The most destructive war in the history of the world
was over, but the people of the world seemed not much more comfortable
in their security than they had been twenty years earlier.

*B*etween 1931 and 1950 world politics changed again. The 1930s saw the
*rise of totalitarian regimes in Europe, but by 1950 West Germany and Italy
were democratic regimes with more chance of survival as such than they
had at the end of World War I. In eastern Europe, the Soviet Union had
strengthened its Communist government and dominated the governments of
several satellite states. In Asia, Japan was also becoming a viable democracy, under the tutelage of the United States. China, however, had been
taken over by a Communist regime that would outlast even that of the Soviet
Union. Some Asian countries maintained their traditional governments,
while some were highly volatile and unstable. Two, Korea and Indochina
(Vietnam), were divided ideologically and politically, much like Germany.
The United States, meanwhile, had completely abandoned its traditional
isolationism and had become an active participant in world economics and
politics. It was also the dominant superpower in one of two ideologically
hostile camps that would spar with each other and take part in a frightening
nuclear arms race for the next forty years. The other camp was dominated
by the other superpower, the Soviet Union.*

*But something else had happened. The world had grown smaller. Rev-
olutions in transportation and communication made it possible for world
leaders to know instantly what was happening anywhere else around the
globe and, if necessary, to be almost anywhere within twenty-four hours.
The world had never been closer in terms of opportunity for communication,
understanding, and economic and political interaction. Partly for that
reason, during the last half of the twentieth century even small nations who
previously had played relatively insignificant roles in world affairs would
suddenly appear as major actors on television screens and in political
debates around the world. Their problems became world problems, even
affecting the relationships of the superpowers. More than ever before, it
would be impossible to think of world history as the history of particular*

nations or regions. By the same token, it would be impossible to deal with regions without also dealing more fully with the world.

In the next five chapters we will consider five major regions of the world in an effort to balance our perspective of the world as a whole. In each case, however, we will consider not only the internal affairs of that region but also its symbiotic relationship to the world around it.

Selected Readings

Dawidowicz, Lucy S. *The War Against the Jews, 1933–1945*. New York: Bantam Books, 1976.

Eisenhower, Dwight D. *Crusade in Europe*. Garden City, NY: Doubleday, 1948.

The Encyclopedia of the Holocaust. New York: Macmillan, 1990.

Feis, Herbert. *The Atomic Bomb and the End of World War II*. Princeton, NJ: Princeton University Press, 1966.

Keegan, John. *The Second World War*. London: Hutchinson, 1989.

Keylor, William R. *The Twentieth-Century World: An International History*. New York and Oxford: Oxford University Press, 1992.

Mayer, Arno J. *Why Did the Heavens not Darken?: The "Final Solution" in History*. New York: Pantheon Books, 1988.

Nish, Ian. *Japanese Foreign Policy, 1869–1942*. London and Boston: Routledge and Kegan Paul, 1977.

Shirer, William L. *The Rise and Fall of the Third Reich: A History of Nazi Germany*. New York: Simon and Schuster, 1960.

Thomas, Hugh. *Armed Truce: The Beginnings of the Cold War, 1945–46*. London: H. Hamilton, 1986.

Toland, John. *The Last 100 Days*. New York: Random House, 1966.

Winterbotham, F. W. *The Ultra Secret*. New York: Dell, 1981.

Wright, Gordon. *The Ordeal of Total War, 1939–1945*. New York: Harper & Row, 1968.

Yergin, Daniel. *Shattered Peace: The Origins of the Cold War and the National Security State*. Boston: Houghton Mifflin, 1977.

18

The West Since 1945

1948 State of Israel founded

1949 Communists complete takeover of China

1950 Korean War begins

1953 Korean armistice

1957 EEC founded

Sputnik I launched

1960 Russia puts the first man in space

1961 The Berlin Wall erected

1962 Cuban missile crisis

1963 U.S. President John F. Kennedy assassinated

Nuclear Test Ban Treaty

1964 Far-reaching U.S. Civil Rights Act passed

1968 Martin Luther King assassinated

1969 The first man walks on the moon

1972, 1974 SALT Treaties

1972 Nixon visits China

1973 American troops leave Vietnam

1974 Nixon resigns as U.S. President

1975 Helsinki Accords

1977 Panama Canal Treaty

1982 Falkland Islands War

1990 Berlin Wall falls

1991 Germany reunited

Persian Gulf War

Soviet Union disappears

At the end of World War II the world was as a complex, contradictory, and not-yet-peaceful place to live. The United Nations was dedicated to keeping peace, but soon the major world powers would be locked in an ideological "Cold War" that would continue for forty years. Its protagonists constituted two armed camps, each possessing awesome nuclear weapons capable of destroying the other. The Cold War turned hot in China where, in 1949, the Communists took over. It heated up again in Korea in 1950, in Vietnam in the 1960s, and in other places around the world, though the superpowers avoided confronting each other directly and nuclear warheads were never unleashed.

Scores of other wars, revolutions, military coups, and civil conflicts caused death and misery around the world in the last half of the century. Among them was the bitter conflict between the state of Israel, founded in 1948, and the Arab world around it. In Asia and Africa, meanwhile, one of the great turning points in world history came with the end of European colonialism. It was not long before the former colonies found new ties, mostly economic in nature, with their prior rulers as well as with other world powers. But decolonization also sparked continuing political conflict and violence within many newly independent nations. Latin American nations, too, saw civil conflict in these years, usually as an ideological struggle between democracy on the one hand and communism or some other form of authoritarianism on the other. Whatever the cause, post-World War II political alignments failed to create a truly peaceful world.

Neither did the postwar world find solutions to wide economic disparity. Western Europe, parts of Asia, and North America saw rapid and amazing economic growth in these years. Even though there were distressing pockets of poverty in each of these areas, the general standard of living soared. But in the emerging nations of Asia and Africa, life remained difficult and poverty continued to abound. Efforts at industrialization and modernization resulted in considerable economic growth, but burgeoning populations almost negated the impact; the contrast in living standards between these and other nations seemed only to become more apparent. The United Nations, churches, and other charitable groups stepped up their efforts to help, especially in times of famine and other disasters, but in general poverty remained.

The world, however, was smaller and closer together than ever before. Jet airplanes made it possible for people to get almost anywhere within twenty-four hours. Improved telephone, radio, and television, especially after space technology put satellite systems in place, made instant communication commonplace. For the people of the industrialized nations, the problems as well as the pleasures of the rest of the world were right next door. In this chapter we will deal with some of the world's major problems as experienced by Western nations in the period from 1945 to about 1990. In the next four chapters we will deal the world as seen through the experiences of four different regions. While reading, however, bear in mind that none of these regions or developments was isolated from others—they are handled this way only for organizational convenience. The real world was not so simple.

THE COLD WAR CONTINUES

Though the roots of the Cold War extended back to the origins of communism itself, the implications of the ideological conflict hardly dawned on world consciousness until immediately after the war.

MUTUAL SUSPICION

The Soviets were determined to expand communism in as many places worldwide as possible. It was not long before they controlled every country in eastern Europe but Yugoslavia. But they were convinced that the West (especially the United States) would do anything, even to the point of aggression, to undermine or destroy communism. In both countries, in fact, a few extremists were advocating drastic measures, including a preemptory "first strike." American extremism was epitomized by the activities of Wisconsin's Senator Joseph R. McCarthy. In the 1950s, on the basis of totally unsubstantiated charges, he seemed to accuse almost everyone of communist sympathies or collaboration. But even among those who were not so extreme there was a general public hostility to communism and a conviction that it posed both a political and a military threat to American security. The policy of "containment" was widely supported.

THE 1950s

The United Nations. Many Cold War battles were fought within the United Nations. They often ended in stalemate, when one or the other superpower simply vetoed a resolution. Only when they agreed was very much accomplished. One notable example was the creation of the independent state of Israel in 1948.

Japan and China. The Soviets won out politically in eastern Europe, but the United States was in a better position to score a major Cold War victory, and make at least one new ally, in East Asia (see chapter 19). Under the careful tutelage of General Douglas MacArthur, Japan became not just a democracy but a strong economic partner. In 1951 it again became independent, and it immediately became a powerful ally. Mainland China, however, was taken over by the communists (who by 1960 became unfriendly with the Soviets), leaving only the island of Taiwan with a government friendly to the West.

Korea. The Cold War also turned hot in Korea, when an ideological civil war evolved into a struggle between the superpowers in 1950. The United States and the Soviet Union again avoided direct military confrontation, but international forces, acting under a United Nations mandate, kept the Soviet-supported Communist forces from overrunning South Korea. The Korean War caused deep political division within the United States when the government refused to authorize American troops in Korea to cross into China, a source of supplies and reinforcements for North Korean troops. Had it done so, however, there was a high likelihood that not only China but also Russia would have come into the war, perhaps touching off World War III and a nuclear holocaust. The war was actually a military victory for neither side, though the West believed it had achieved a moral victory by keeping South Korea from being overrun. Nevertheless, the continuing artificial division of Korea into northern and southern nations still remains as an unfortunate legacy of the worldwide ideological conflict between totalitarian communism and Western-style democracy.

German Rearmament. The Cold War led the United States into still more international alliances, including the Southeast Asia Treaty Organization (SEATO) and the Central Treaty Organization (CTO) in the Middle East. In addition, the Western powers consented to the rearming of West Germany in 1955, in response to the fact that the Soviets were providing military training for East Germans.

THE BRINK OF WAR

For a while, in 1955, it appeared as if there might be a thaw in the Cold War (though diehards on both sides never accepted peaceful coexistence as a viable possibility). In Geneva world leaders met in the first summit meeting since World War II. The meetings were cordial, but nothing of permanent significance happened. Instead, a series of incidents over the next seven years took the powers to the very brink of another hot war.

The Suez. In 1956 Egypt nationalized the Suez Canal, leading to an invasion by England, France, and Israel. They finally withdrew, at United Nations insistence, whereupon the Soviet Union began to pour massive amounts of increased financial aid into Egypt.

Hungary. Things became even warmer that year in Hungary, where a popular uprising ousted the Soviet-supported government as well as Soviet troops. The Hungarian "freedom fighters" were shattered when the aid they thought they had been promised by the United States simply did not materialize. The United States had made implied promises as part of the propaganda war, but when it came to a showdown the United States was afraid that military action would result in a major shooting war with the Soviet Union. The Soviets invaded and smashed the revolution. The only conclusion the Hungarians, and other East Europeans, could come to was that the United States simply was not willing to back them.

Berlin and the Wall. In two other instances, however, the United States did not back down. In 1958, concerned over the flow of people out of East Berlin into prosperous West Berlin, the Soviet government demanded that the Western powers evacuate Berlin. The allies refused, and after John F. Kennedy became president of the United States in 1961, he made it clear that he was willing to go to war rather than accede to such illegal demands. Russia's Khrushchev backed down but at the same time approved construction of a stone wall separating East and West Berlin. For the next three decades that wall was a visible and ugly symbol of the equally ugly tension that continued.

Cuban Missile Crisis. In 1962 Khrushchev sent nuclear missiles to Cuba, where a revolution under Fidel Castro had established a communist regime in 1959. Kennedy had already been embarrassed by the failure of the ill-planned Bay of Pigs invasion, intended to overthrow Castro. He was not going to stand, however, for a nuclear threat to be aimed at the United States from ninety miles away. He ordered a naval blockade and threatened whatever action was necessary, including nuclear war, if the missiles were not removed. Khrushchev backed down again, but the tensions continued. A year earlier, however, the United States had begun an attempt to diffuse Castro's efforts to export communism to the rest of Latin America. It promised members of the Organization of American States $10 billion in aid over the next ten years in an inter-American "Alliance for Progress."

LATER DEVELOPMENTS

The aftermath of the missile crisis saw at least a temporary thaw in the Cold War. A Nuclear Test Ban Treaty in 1963 demonstrated the willingness of both sides at least to try to put an end to the costly arms race. The treaty was not fully observed, and the arms race continued, but at least it represented a cooling off of tempers.

Vietnam and China. The continuing conflict in Vietnam (see chapter 19), meanwhile, was another case in which a country involved in civil war became a major pawn in the Cold War. After the South Vietnamese refused to accept communist rule, America first sent in "advisors" to help. Gradually, however the aid escalated to military involvement and 500,000 men. President Richard Nixon, elected in 1968, began a gradual withdrawal of American troops. In 1972, just before the next election, he also achieved the most impressive foreign policy coup of any recent president: a reconciliation with China that paved the way for the restoration of full diplomatic relations. This was possible partly because of the increasing distance between China and the Soviet Union. Bringing communist China closer to the United States was thus an ironic diplomatic victory in the Cold War. The United States had also finally faced up to political reality by dropping its opposition to Chinese membership in the United Nations, much to the chagrin of the Nationalist Chinese in Taiwan. Nixon's next act was to reach an agreement with North Vietnam and withdraw all American troops. The United States "won one (China) and lost one (Vietnam)" in the seemingly never-ending ideological struggle with the Soviets.

Détente. Far from being just a slap at Russia, however, the accord with China was a symbol of a new and hopeful phase of the Cold War—détente, or the effort to gradually relax tensions. Another was the completion of the long-sought Strategic Arms Limitation Treaties (SALT) of 1972 and 1974, slowing the arms race. In 1975 the U.S., Canada, and nearly every nation of Europe signed the Helsinki Accords, agreeing to the maintenance of existing European boundaries (recognizing, in effect, the areas of Soviet control).

Failure of Détente. By the end of the decade, however, détente had faded. The United States was so disgusted with the Soviet invasion of Afghanistan in 1979 that it boycotted the 1980 Olympic games in Moscow and placed an embargo on American grain shipments to the USSR. In addition, the Senate refused to ratify the SALT II agreement of 1979, fearing that the Soviets might take advantage of American arms reduction and develop a first-strike potential. New rounds of disarmament talks failed in the early 1980s, and the United States began to deploy more missiles in Europe. The Cold War was also fueled by conflicts of interest in such disparate places as Lebanon and Nicaragua.

The Cold War and Space. Even space became a factor in the Cold War, as the "space race" seemed to parallel the arms race. In the fall of 1957 the USSR launched *Sputnik I*, the first man-made satellite ever to orbit the earth. People worldwide stood in awe as they watched it moving slowly across the sky, the sun's reflection making it visible to the naked eye. But Americans wondered what this meant so far as rocket power was concerned, and why their country was not ahead in the development of engines that could not only put up satellites but also deliver missiles. The next year America launched its own satellite, and in 1960 the Soviet Union put the first man in space. In 1961 President John F. Kennedy challenged American engineers to put a man on the moon before the end of the decade. That goal was achieved in 1969. America was finally seen as being ahead in a race that was presumably peaceful but that everyone knew had ominous military overtones.

By the time American and Soviet negotiators renewed their discussions on nuclear arms limitations in 1985, a new factor had entered the mix. The United States was attempting to develop its controversial Strategic Defense Initiative, popularly known as "star wars," a laser weapon system controlled from surveillance satellites that could knock out nuclear missiles as they were launched. The Soviets, however, saw this as a violation of existing treaty limitations on antiballistic missiles as well as a possible threat of new kinds of offensive space weapons. They initially refused to negotiate until "star wars" was dropped, and America refused to drop it.

THE SUDDEN END OF THE COLD WAR

Desire for Accord. Within six years the Cold War was suddenly over. By 1985 the arms race was taking such a crippling bite from the economies of both the Soviet Union and the United States that both countries were anxious for an accord. Added to this was the attitude of the new Soviet Premier, Mikhail Gorbachev, who not only began a series of major internal reforms but also showed more willingness than any previous Soviet leader to disengage from confrontation with the West.

Ideological and Political Revolution. All this was accompanied by spectacular ideological and political revolutions all across eastern Europe. In 1990 the hated Berlin Wall, the most visible symbol of the Cold War in Europe, tumbled. In 1991 the two Germanies were reunited. That same year the old Soviet Union ceased to exist—broken up into its several independent states. The largest and most powerful was Russia. Ideological conflicts with the West virtually disappeared, as Russia and other republics attempted to move toward democracy and a form of free enterprise. In June 1992, Boris Yeltsin, president of the Russian republic, visited the United States. Among other things, he signed a historic agreement by which each nation committed itself to far-reaching cuts in its nuclear arsenal. Actually, both were already engaged in dismantling and removing some of their most threatening weapons, and the process would continue. The Cold War was over.

NATIONS OF THE WEST: OTHER INTERRELATED DEVELOPMENTS

Whether to include the Soviet Union in a discussion of Western nations presents an interesting puzzle. Geographically, most of it is part of Asia. Historically, we have discussed the Cold War as an East-West struggle, with the Soviets dominating the Eastern bloc and the United States as the major Western power. Nevertheless, for the purposes of the following discussion the Soviet Union is tied more closely to Europe than to the East Asian or Middle Eastern nations. These will be discussed in chapters 19 and 20.

Interdependence: Some Generalizations

Within a few short years after World War II it would be impossible to observe almost any part of the world, especially the West, without also observing the growing interdependence between the nations. In a sense, the theme of world interdependence that was emerging at the beginning of the sixteenth century was practically mature 500 years later. It is impossible here to go into great detail, but a few illustrations will suffice.

In western Europe, the development of the Common Market (see below), together with its dependence on other world markets, was one example. The Soviet Union developed a similar interdependence among itself and its satellites and also developed markets in other parts of the world. The United States and Canada developed economic ties with the Common Market, Japan, Latin American countries, and other parts of the world. The elimination of any one of these trading partners could have created chaos in one or more sectors of the economy. But until the 1970s the exchange rates in the international monetary system were based on a fixed rate of exchange of the U.S. dollar for gold. In 1971 that changed, however, after the United States decided it could no longer exchange its dollars for gold. From that point on international exchange rates fluctuated, depending upon a variety of factors in the world economy.

OIL FROM THE MIDDLE EAST

OPEC. One of the factors was the price of oil. World demand for petroleum products skyrocketed in the late twentieth century, as use for military needs, civilian transportation, and other needs and wants constantly increased. Much of the world was at least partially dependent upon oil supplies from the Arab countries, most of which belonged to the Organization of Petroleum Exporting Countries (OPEC). The United States, for example, imported about half its oil, and nearly half of that came from OPEC countries. In 1971, the same year as the monetary crisis, OPEC placed an embargo on oil exports, partly in connection with the Arab-Israeli war and partly in an effort to boost falling prices brought on by overproduction. Crude oil prices quadrupled, sending an economic shock throughout the Western world. The Eastern bloc had its own supply of oil, but Western nations were suddenly made painfully conscious of at least two realities. One was their own dependence on foreign oil, and the fact that the supply could be cut off at any time. The other was the fact that the world's oil reserves were not inexhaustible. Environmentalists had a field day, and many people paid increased attention to conservation, at least for a time.

Kuwait. Two decades later another oil-related crisis led to all-out war. In 1990 Iraq invaded and annexed oil-rich Kuwait, after several disagreements and demands with respect to disputed oil regions. Immediately, under the auspices of a United Nations resolution, military forces, mostly American, were sent to the Persian Gulf. In January and February 1991 they drove the Iraqis out and restored Kuwait's independence. American President George Bush justified the war on the basis of the need to protect national independence everywhere. Critics and others wondered, however, if America would have been so anxious to go to war if such an important source of oil had not been threatened. The conflict illustrated once again the interdependence of the world.

Building Toward a European Community

Even as the Cold War disappeared, in 1992 a long-term quest for a new kind of European unity seemed on the verge of becoming a reality.

THE COOPERATIVE SPIRIT AND THE EEC

Perhaps the most important undertaking for each European country after the war was economic recovery. The Marshall Plan helped, but each country was also concerned with reestablishing trade, rebuilding its vital industries, and developing a viable internal economy. It soon became apparent that this could not be done bilaterally. Some form of European cooperation was necessary.

The Organization Develops. The first step was the creation, at the suggestion of French foreign minister Robert Schuman, of the European Coal and Steel Community (ECSC) in 1952. France, West Germany, Italy, Belgium, the Netherlands, and Luxembourg formed a single market for the coal- and iron-producing sectors of their economies. It operated without tariff or other restrictions. In 1957 these six nations formed the European Atomic Energy Community (EURATOM) and the European Economic Community (EEC), better known as the Common Market. Tariff walls, quotas, and other impediments to trade disappeared as free trade was extended to nearly every part of each country's economy. In 1967 the EEC established a number of cooperative political institutions—a Council of Ministers, the European Commission, the European Parliament, the Court of Justice, and the European Council. Although these did not override national institutions, they provided a place for further discussion and cooperation. Some people were even talking about something akin to a United States of Europe, though most thought such talk was premature. Economically, however, the Common Market was a major success for the nations involved. They still had their individual economic difficulties, but cooperation saved them from even worse problems.

The Question of New Members. The question of increasing membership became complicated, and here old nationalistic feelings continued to create tension. By the 1960s Great Britain wanted to join, but it was opposed by France, especially President Charles de Gaulle. He felt that Britain's ties to the United States constituted a conflicting interest. In 1973, however, Britain, Ireland, and Denmark were accepted into the community. By 1986 Greece, Spain, and Portugal had also entered, bringing membership in the organization, now simply called the European Community, to twelve.

The Quest for Greater Unity. Beginning in 1987, the powers of the European Parliament were increased, and the European Community began to look forward to eliminating all remaining economic barriers of any sort, as well as any barriers to the free movement of people across national boundaries, by 1992. At the same time, other countries were applying for membership.

There was, of course, considerable opposition within some of the countries, especially Great Britain and France, to such total unity. Most Britons, however, remained committed. In 1992 a particularly emotional election campaign reflected the rising concerns of many French citizens. But in September, by a very narrow margin, they returned to power a government still committed to European unity.

MORE GOALS AND ACCOMPLISHMENTS

In light of the historic nationalism that had so often set the countries of Europe against each other before World War II, the extent to which they created a unified Europe was remarkable. They established common policies with respect to most economic activities, including transportation, foreign trade, and fiscal and monetary affairs. In 1979 a European Monetary System was created, which went a long way toward establishing stable exchange rates (though in 1992 this began to fall apart). The goal became to establish a common currency by 1999.

The European Community became the world's largest and most powerful trading power, accounting in 1992 for 20 percent of the world's trade. It also participated, as a community, in promoting economic development in underdeveloped and Third World countries. After the unification of Germany, for example, it immediately invested in the development of what was once East Germany. It also developed free trade arrangements with numerous countries in Africa, the Caribbean, the Pacific, and the Mediterranean area. In addition, the new realities of world trade made the United States and the European Community interdependent, and the two entities developed an important cooperative relationship.

Decolonization

Before the war Great Britain, France, the Netherlands, Belgium, Italy, and Portugal all held overseas colonies. In the postwar world they lost practically all of them. Most became part of a new, though loosely defined, political bloc often referred to as the Third World.

PRESSURES FOR DECOLONIZATION

The reasons for decolonization were varied, but one factor was the Cold War itself. Sensing the nationalism inherent among colonial peoples, the Soviet Union used the latent (and sometimes not-so-latent) discontent associated with colonialism as a means of encouraging demands for independence. In most instances, however, it did not take the Soviets to push nationalism. Many people within the colonies had been educated in Europe and quickly saw the dichotomy between democratic European political ideologies and colonialism. They were among the leaders of the rebellions and other independence movements. For them, decolonization was a quest not only for self-rule but also for dignity as a people and for equality. Sometimes their demands resulted in violence and civil war.

ATTITUDES AND PERSPECTIVES

For some Europeans, decolonization was not the traumatic loss that it would have been at the beginning of the century. They were not unhappy to rid themselves of the problems of colonial administration. Nevertheless, the loss of colonies also meant the loss of markets and trading partners. For Britain this was serious. The Common Market, however, began to heal that wound as the European Community developed mutually profitable economic relationships with Third World countries, especially in Africa. The only problem with that, so far as some Africans were concerned, was a feeling that the new economic relationship amounted to neocolonialism—that is, a continuing system of economic domination by their former colonial masters.

Britain and the Falklands. In 1982 Argentina laid claim to the Falkland Islands, a long-held British possession just off the Argentine coast. The British were incensed; Prime Minister Margaret Thatcher's action in sending the military to save the islands was one of the most popular moves of her career. The campaign succeeded, though it was tremendously expensive and only contributed to the worsening of Britain's economic woes. Some observers wondered if it was worth it, suggesting that what it really amounted to was the proud last gasp of an empire that had already disappeared.

Western Europe

These were only some of the major patterns in Western history in the last half of the twentieth century. At the same time, a few domestic developments also had significance from a global perspective.

GREAT BRITAIN

In Great Britain, the Labour government that took over after the war greatly extended social welfare benefits. It also nationalized several basic industries as well as the Bank of England. The liberal trend toward the welfare state, begun before World War I, continued, despite the fact that the Conservative party ruled from 1951 to 1964. In the 1980s a new Conservative government under Margaret Thatcher, Britain's first woman prime minister, attempted to reverse the process. Many industries were returned to private control, but cutting government expenditures also caused cuts in some welfare services. This, in turn, contributed to increasing distress among the working classes. Riots among the working classes and strikes by coal miners led to a series of crises in the 1980s. From the standpoint of world trends, the continuing conflict between modern conservatism and free enterprise on the one hand and modern liberalism and the welfare state on the other was but one example of similar kinds of internal conflicts taking place around the globe.

FRANCE

Influence of de Gaulle. France's Fourth Republic, established at the end of the war, was characterized by a series of weak and ineffective ministries. As in the case of Britain, the French government nationalized banks and certain industries and expanded social welfare legislation. However, it was continually attacked from the left by Communists and from the right by hard-line conservatives led by Charles de Gaulle. In the midst of a crisis over the impending secession of Algeria, de Gaulle came to power in 1958. He immediately created the Fifth Republic, approved in a popular referendum, giving himself, as president, extraordinary powers. With this new strength, he let Algeria go in 1962, even in the face of strong internal opposition.

De Gaulle led France for ten years, promoting conservative domestic policies and nationalistic foreign policies designed to boost France's prestige. In addition to keeping Britain out of the EEC, he withdrew France from NATO. He improved French relations with Germany and drew closer to China than most other Western powers. Wanting to develop French nuclear capability, he kept France from becoming a party to the Nuclear Test Ban Treaty of 1963. So far as the Cold War was concerned, he tried to maintain a neutral policy; he was never particularly friendly toward the United States. He resigned in 1968.

Moderation. French political leaders were generally moderate in their economic policies until 1980, when the Socialist party came to power. Though Communists, too, were included in the government, it was anti-Soviet in its orientation, maintained strong ties with the United States, and renewed French participation in NATO. More industries were nationalized, and there was more social reform, but by the end of the 1980s the government was pursuing a generally middle-of-the-road policy. The big question would be whether France would see fit to continue working toward the goal of full European unity.

GERMANY

Beginning in 1949 there were two Germanies. England, France, and the United States allowed their sectors to form the independent Federal Republic of Germany (West Germany), but the Soviet Union would not allow its sector to became a part of it. Instead, it established and dominated the German Democratic Republic, or East Germany.

West Germany. Under the initial authoritarian guidance of chancellor Konrad Adenauer (1949–1963), West Germany developed close ties with the Western powers and became a member of NATO. It also achieved what seemed to be a near-miraculous rebuilding and economic recovery, based on capitalism but supported by very high taxes. In addition, in response to the fact that the Soviets were remilitarizing East Germany, the West allowed a limited rearmament of West Germany. Some apprehension over the wisdom of this move continued in Western circles, however.

In 1969 the Social Democratic Party (SPD) again came to power, but by then it had given up its Marxist economic leanings. The new chancellor, Willy Brandt, maintained friendship with the West, but also reduced tensions with Poland and the USSR. As a result of his new policy, called *Ostpolitik*, treaties were signed with those two nations and economic agreements were made with others in eastern Europe. Brandt also initiated diplomatic relations with China. In addition, he signed a treaty with East Germany whereby each state officially recognized the other—a step that Adenauer never would have taken but one that, in the long run, helped pave the way for German reunification. Similar policies continued through the 1980s.

East Germany. East Germany, under Soviet domination, was not so fortunate. The economy languished, the puppet government was highly unpopular, and the people longed for unity with the rest of Germany. Popular uprisings were put down by Soviet occupation forces. By 1961 thousands of people were fleeing. This led to the erection of the hated Berlin Wall, protected by a no-man's-land behind barbed wire and guarded by soldiers and dogs. This only made many East Germans feel more like prisoners. Over the next three decades numerous escapes took place—some of a most dramatic nature. Other attempts, however, ended with East German citizens being either recaptured or shot to death.

Reunification. By 1989 the situation changed; even the Soviet Union looked the other way when about 200,000 East Germans emigrated to the West via Czechoslovakia and Hungary. There was nothing more the East German government could do. The wall finally came down in November. Negotiations for reunification began. On October 3, 1990, the two states officially became one. The economic contrast was severe, but the remarkable economic prosperity of West Germany provided the basis for survival. So, too, did the determination of the German people as a whole to be a united people. For East Germany, this was the first time it had known free government since the rise of Hitler in 1933. The people still living to enjoy it, however, were mostly the children and grandchildren of those who lost their freedom nearly sixty years earlier.

ITALY

Italy, too, with massive economic assistance from the United States, underwent a remarkable economic recovery after the war. Its monarchical government was replaced by a republic, and it experienced the same tensions between liberal and conservative political parties as other nations of Europe. The economy suffered in the 1970s, leading to labor unrest, violence, and the murder of a former premier, Aldo Moro, in 1978. Political turbulence characterized most of the 1980s.

SCANDINAVIA

The Scandinavian countries recovered slowly from the war, but exports of furniture and other home furnishings, especially, helped stimulate their economy. Norway became a major oil-producing nation, with the development of great deposits under the North Sea. As elsewhere, socialists on the one hand and more conservative politicians on the other continually vied for power in Scandinavia. In the 1980s Finland and Sweden had socialist governments, while Norway, Denmark, and Iceland were more conservative. All the Scandinavian countries, however, provided liberal health care and other social welfare programs. By the 1990s these programs were the cause of considerable political dissent, as they were in other welfare states, because of the increasingly heavy financial burdens they were imposing on the people.

Scandinavia's relationship to other world power blocs was mixed. Sweden remained neutral during the Cold War, but Finland, close to the Soviet border, was sometimes influenced by Soviet policy. In 1970, for example, Soviet pressure on Finland kept a proposed Scandinavian economic community from becoming a reality. In 1972 Denmark joined the EEC, and Sweden applied for membership in 1991.

USSR and Eastern Europe

THE POSTWAR YEARS, TO 1985

In the Soviet Union, the brutal regime of Joseph Stalin ended with his death in 1953. After considerable infighting over the next few years, Nikita Khrushchev emerged as leader, though not with the complete dictatorial power of Stalin. In fact, he denounced Stalin and his methods. The next few years became a period of "de-Stalinization." This did not mean a reversal of Communist goals, but only a slightly softer way of dealing with dissent.

Economically, the USSR continued to grow in productive capacity. Consumer goods increased, and the general standard of living improved somewhat. The improvement, nevertheless, seemed meager compared to what it might have been. Military expenditures and the space program were eating up too much of the budget. In addition, Soviet agriculture continued to suffer.

Khrushchev was ousted in 1964, largely because of the failure of his economic programs but also because of reversals in foreign policy, such as the Cuban missile crisis. In 1977 the Soviets changed their system, combining the office of Communist Party secretary and president of the USSR. Leonid Brezhnev, already party secretary, thus assumed both positions. Under Brezhnev the government reverted to more oppressive measures with respect to dissenters. World-famous writer Alexander Solzhenitsyn, for example, was exiled, and physicist Andrei Sakharov, a Nobel Prize winner, was arrested. Russia's image in the world seemed to be one of a return to Stalinism. Economic growth during this period remained slow.

GORBACHEV AND THE END OF THE USSR

Dramatic changes came to both the USSR and the world after the rise to power of Mikhail Gorbachev in 1985. Immediately he began an internal policy known as *glasnost*, or openness, which meant a relaxation of censorship and new freedom in political debate. He also announced a policy of *perestroika*, or economic restructuring. He hoped to revitalize the economy by allowing more freedom of enterprise. At the same time, he renewed détente, which eventually ended the Cold War.

Economic Problems. Gorbachev's economic policies, however, were no panacea, and it took a great deal of will to continue with them. They resulted in falling production, food shortages, and high prices—the natural results of an effort to make such a sudden, massive change in the economic structure of such a huge entity as the Soviet Union. Gorbachev found himself in deep political trouble. In August 1991 he was placed under house arrest, his opponents declaring that he had been deposed. The military, however, refused to support the rebels, and within a few days Gorbachev was back in power.

USSR Disbands. By this time the Soviet Union was beginning to fall apart. Gorbachev realized what was coming and resigned on August 24, urging the Communist Party itself to disband. Republic after republic quickly declared its independence. By the end of the year the USSR was a thing of the past.

The Challenge of the New Order. This did not mean that all was well. The economies of the newly independent republics were in disarray. Bitter ethnic divisions within the republics were causing civil strife. It would take considerable healing before the new nations were economically and politically viable. In December 1991 eleven republics formed a loose confederation known as the Commonwealth of Independent States (CIS). They needed to deal with such issues as command of the former Soviet military, nuclear weapons, and state property, but they failed to reach agreement. Russia, under Yeltsin, took over the nuclear weapons and most of the military. Hope for a brightened economic future came on April 1, 1992, when seven major nations (the United States, Japan, Germany, Great Britain, France, Italy, and Canada) announced that they were creating a $24 billion aid package for the new confederation.

THE SATELLITES

The USSR's hope for a ring of satellites that would remain firmly and obediently under its domination did not materialize; it frequently had to use force to put down the unrest in other East European countries. A revolt in Hungary was brutally repressed in 1956. A peaceful revolution in Czechoslovakia in 1968 resulted in a new government and a period of democratic reform. But the USSR intervened militarily, toppled the new regime, and reestablished its own hegemony.

Poland. Poland became the most troublesome satellite, but by the time the most serious threat to communist rule occurred the Soviets were not in a position, nor did they have the will, to intervene. In 1980 a labor union, Solidarity, demanded democratic reforms and promoted strikes in shipyards at Gdansk. With Soviet approval, though not intervention, the union was driven underground. In 1988, however, in the midst of severe economic problems, Solidarity renewed its public activity. This time, with the consent of the USSR, it was legalized and thus became the first legal independent party within a communist state. In 1989 Poland's first free elections were held. Solidarity candidates were overwhelmingly elected to the parliament. Lech Walesa, leader of Solidarity, was asked to form the new government. The following year, in Poland's first direct presidential election, Walesa was elected.

North America

The United States and Canada had no serious problem of economic recovery after the war. The war, in fact, was good to the American economy. Moreover, for the first time in the history of the United States there was no postwar recession. There were other problems in both countries, and later in the century economic problems caught up with them as they did with the rest of the world.

CANADA

Economic development in Canada after the war was unprecedented, with the gross national product rising from $12 billion to $61 billion between 1946 and 1966. Contributing to this was the discovery of rich oil and gas deposits in Alberta in 1946. In addition, the development of iron ore deposits led to a joint project with the United States—the St. Lawrence Seaway, completed in 1959.

Canada became one of the world's leading industrial nations. One of the reasons, however, was heavy investment from the United States, resulting in what many Canadians resentfully believed was too much American influence.

For most of the period Canadian politics was dominated by the Liberal Party. After the Liberal government signed a free trade agreement with the United States in 1988, however, it was thrown out of power in the general election that fall and replaced by the Conservatives.

Separatism. One of Canada's most serious internal problems was the desire of French-speaking Canada—Quebec—for greater autonomy, even independence. Quebec residents saw themselves as a "distinct society" within Canada and felt that they were not fairly represented in the federal government and did not receive adequate benefits from continuing membership in the federal union. In 1987 Canadian premier Brian Mulroney hammered out a compromise by obtaining an amendment to the 1982 Constitution Act that would have recognized Quebec's distinct status and given it a great deal more autonomy. The amendment required unanimous approval by all the provinces by 1990, however, and that was not achieved. In 1922, another constitutional package that would have recognized Quebec's "distinct society" and enacted other reforms failed in a nationwide referendum. The future status of Quebec was still in doubt.

THE UNITED STATES

In contrast to its position before World War II, the United States became, in effect, the colossus of the West. Completely abandoning its former isolationism, it built the most powerful war machine in the world. This machine was based not just on numbers of personnel, airplanes, ships, submarines, and military vehicles of all sorts but also on nuclear power and the capability to deliver it. The United States signed treaties with nations around the globe, recognizing the need for mutual defense pacts in order to help contain communism as well as protect its growing worldwide investments and markets. At the same time, it did not escape a series of crucial domestic problems, some of which had significance in the context of major world developments.

The Domestic Cold War. The Cold War gave rise to some of these problems. Many Americans listened too readily to extremists among the anti-Communists in the 1950s and early 1960s, who seemed to see a Communist conspiracy in almost anything the government did. During the Korean War conservatives were dismayed when President Truman refused to let General Douglas MacArthur carry the war into China. When MacArthur publicly criticized the president, Truman had no alternative but to relieve him of his command. The outcry cost the Democrats the election in 1952. The popular new president, Dwight D. Eisenhower, became only more popular when he concluded the war in 1953 with a Korean armistice. The most divisive war in American history, however, was the Vietnam War, which began a decade later. As the hopelessness of the war became all too apparent, more and more American "doves" began to demand withdrawal. They became the objects of brutal verbal attacks by "hawks," who advocated doing whatever was necessary to achieve a complete military victory. "Doves" often replied in kind, though many of them simply slipped away to Canada or elsewhere in order to keep from being forced to fight in a war they considered irresponsible and unjust. Recriminations went back and forth, but eventually most Americans wearied of the war. Only in the 1980s did some of the remaining wounds begin to heal, symbolized by the erection of a sensitive and deeply moving monument in Washington, D.C., in memory of those Americans killed in Vietnam.

Civil Rights. One of the most important revolutions to take place in postwar America was the civil rights revolution. Despite the fact that American blacks had been free for nearly a century, had fought in American wars, had made important contributions to literature and the arts, and had held important public and private positions of all sorts, they were still not accorded the full rights of citizenship across the country. There were still segregated schools, segregated restaurants and public facilities, and many other forms of prejudice and discrimination.

One of the first victories for blacks seeking more equal treatment was the pivotal Supreme Court case of *Brown* v. *Board of Education of Topeka*, in 1954. There the court declared school segregation unconstitutional. Southern states vowed to fight the decision, but in 1957 and 1958 President Eisenhower demonstrated the government's determination to uphold the law. He sent federal troops to Little Rock, Arkansas, to enforce desegregation in a high school.

Martin Luther King, Jr. But achieving desegregation and civil rights generally was a long, drawn-out process. One of the most charismatic leaders of the fight was the Reverend Martin Luther King, Jr., who advocated passive resistance, but at the same time set up training grounds in order to teach potential protest marchers how to react in the face of police dogs, clubs, fire hoses, mobs, and other such violence. King was assassinated in 1968.

The Violence of the 1960s. The decade of the 1960s was one of terrible racial violence in America, but also one of progress. Sitting down in "white" sections of segregated restaurants, boycotting buses and segregated businesses, protest marches, and many other nonviolent means were used by blacks and their white supporters to dramatize the unjustness and unconstitutionality of continuing segregation. They were usually met with violence. In 1964 a sweeping Civil Rights Act was passed by Congress and signed by President Lyndon B. Johnson. The most far-reaching law of its kind ever enacted, it outlawed desegregation in all public accommodations, limited the nature of state-imposed literacy tests (often used simply as a device to eliminate blacks from the voting booth), and established an Equal Opportunity Commission to administer a ban on job discrimination. Later Reverend King promoted massive black voter registration. Despite these achievements, racial violence continued through the decade. By the 1990s, however, even though there were still apparent problems of racial bias and misunderstanding, blacks and other minorities had achieved a new level of acceptance in all aspects of American society.

Assassinations. The 1960s was also a period of violence in other respects. America's youngest president, the popular John F. Kennedy, was assassinated in 1963. The reasons for it are still shrouded in mystery. His assassin was also assassinated. The following year Malcolm X, charismatic leader of a "black power" movement, was murdered. Kennedy's brother Robert F. Kennedy, former U.S. Attorney General and then a candidate for the Democratic presidential nomination, was gunned down in 1968, the same year as Martin Luther King, Jr. It was a decade that few Americans would easily forget.

Foreign Affairs: Nixon and China. In 1972 President Richard Nixon made a particularly important contribution to the process of easing world tensions. This was his visit to mainland China, engineered by his brilliant Secretary of State, Henry Kissinger. The visit not only eased tensions but also paved the way for opening permanent relations with China—something long overdue. It was generally conceded that this was something a Democratic president never could have done, at least not at that time. American conservatives, supporters of Nixon, were so suspicious of the possible left-wing, "communist dupe," or fellow-traveler tendencies on the part of any Democrat that they simply would not have supported any contact with China. But they trusted Nixon, who then achieved everything the Democrats would like to have achieved. The accord with China so delighted the American people that they returned the president overwhelmingly in that fall's election.

Watergate and the Fall of a President. Perhaps the United States' most disconcerting political crisis came in 1973–1974, with the revelations of the "Watergate Affair." It was discovered, and publicized in the press, that during the 1972 Presidential election campaign, Nixon had covered up White House involvement in illegal entry into Democratic offices at the Watergate Hotel. At first the president denied the accusations, but more evidence came to light and eventually a congressional impeachment hearing got under way. Finally, on August 9, 1974, Nixon resigned—the first American president ever to take such action.

Toward the Welfare State. Also politically significant in postwar America was the fact that there was no retreat from the social welfare and other regulatory legislation so castigated by conservatives during the New Deal. Republican presidents and Congresses accepted all of it and even built upon it. By 1992 the United States was close to becoming a genuine welfare state. Social Security, Medicare (old age medical benefits), and other social welfare programs, however, were raising havoc with the national budget, and the government was going further into debt every year. At the same time, costs of health care had skyrocketed beyond anyone's ability to pay if they did not have insurance or were not among the wealthy. Yet 36 million Americans were in just that position, and even those with health insurance were alarmed at the rising premiums.

One of the most controversial issues in the November 1992 election was health care and how to pay for it. Hanging like a cloud over any proposal, however, was the national debt—$3.9 trillion in 1992 and growing daily. Every recent presidential and congressional candidate had promised to reduce it, but none had made even a dent—the political costs of raising taxes or reducing spending, and hence benefits to constituents, were too high. All major candidates promised sweeping, government-supported health care programs, but neither made it clear how he expected to pay for it without increasing the debt even further.

Other Problems and Accomplishments. Americans also faced problems of rising unemployment, rising use of drugs, deteriorating educational achievements, rising crime rates, changing family and personal values, and the continuing deterioration of the environment. But these were also world problems, and each of them represented, in some way, the growing inter-relationship between all the peoples of the globe.

Nevertheless, despite its problems, America had achieved some notable successes. On the diplomatic front, besides those already mentioned in connection with the Cold War, was President Jimmy Carter's remarkable achievement in attaining an accord between Israel and Egypt in 1980, resulting in the return of the Sinai Peninsula to Egypt. Carter also negotiated a treaty with Panama, whereby the United States returned ownership of the canal to that small country but protected the vital interests of America and other nations. The treaty was controversial at home, but it improved international relations tremendously.

There were other important developments. America continued to provide humanitarian aid regularly and generously to underdeveloped regions around the world. Women were playing a more prominent role in all aspects of American public life in 1992 than they were in 1945. Technology revolutionized the average American's way of life (as it also did for people in other industrialized countries). The computer, especially, was representative of that change. By the 1990s it was becoming a necessity not only in the office and in the classrooms but even in homes—especially those where students lived. Finally, most young Americans seemed far removed from the times of their grandparents so far as religious, ethnic, and gender biases were concerned. The transformation was by no means complete, but the signs were healthy.

The world changed dramatically between 1945 and 1992, and the changes were reflected in the history of the West. The Cold War kept nations on edge for four decades, but was suddenly gone in 1991. The Soviet Union no longer existed, and the former Soviet satellites were independent states. Unfortunately, some things did not change, for bloody civil strife, based largely on ethnic divisions, raged in places—a prime example being the breakup of what was once Yugoslavia in the early 1990s, and the war that accompanied its dissolution.

The former colonial powers in the West lost their colonies in the postwar world. But decolonization was taking place as the quest for a new kind of European community was also taking place. Very quickly the European Economic Community brought new economic strength to the region, and by the 1990s it showed signs of leading toward an even greater spirit of both political and economic unity among the participating nations. But it was not independent of other nations; the economic and political success of the European Community was only one element in the larger picture of growing interdependence among the nations of the world.

In other developments, most Western nations continued the move toward becoming welfare states. Rapid increases in population, along with changing social and economic circumstances, seemed to demand it. For some countries it worked well, but for all countries it also helped create complex economic problems. In the United States, most major social legislation had always been anathema to conservatives, who labeled it as a stepping stone toward communism. It was a bit ironic, then, that while Russia and other former Soviet republics were trying to adopt free enterprise, the United States was moving closer toward becoming a welfare state and conservatives were helping to lead the way.

Selected Readings

Acheson, Dean. *Present at the Creation: My Years in the State Department.* New York: Norton, 1969.

Jenkins, Peter. *Mrs. Thatcher's Revolution: The Ending of the Socialist Era.* Cambridge, MA: Harvard University Press, 1988.

Johnson, Paul. *Modern Times: The World from the Twenties to the Eighties.* New York: Harper & Row, 1983.

LaFeber, Walter. *America, Russia, and the Cold War, 1945–1984.* 5th ed. New York: Knopf, 1985.

Leuchtenburg, William E. *In the Shadow of FDR: From Harry Truman to Ronald Reagan.* Rev. and updated. Ithaca, NY: Cornell University Press, 1989.

Nugent, Neill. *The Government and Politics of the European Community*. Durham, NC: Duke University Press, 1991.

Smith, Hedrick. *The New Russians*. New York: Random House, 1990.

Turner, Henry Ashby. *The Two Germanies Since 1945*. New Haven, CT: Yale University Press, 1987.

19

East Asia Since 1945

1945	Japanese surrender; end of World War II
	Division of Korea
1946	New constitution approved for Japan
	Philippines granted independence
1946–1949	Chinese civil war
1946–1948	Establishment of separate regimes in North and South Korea
1948	Burma becomes independent
1949	Establishment of People's Republic of China
	Indonesian independence
1950–1953	Korean War
1950	China joins Korean War on North Korean side
1951	U.S.-Japan peace treaty signed in San Francisco
1952	End of American occupation of Japan
1954	French forces defeated at Dien Bien Phu
1955	Creation of Japanese Liberal Democratic Party (LDP)
1958	Beginning of "Great Leap Forward" in China
1959	Sino-Soviet split
1961	Malayan independence
1965	Creation of largely Chinese city-state of Singapore
1966	Beginning of China's "Cultural Revolution"

1972   Normalization of Japan-China relations

1973   Paris accords on ending the war in Vietnam

1975   Last American forces leave Vietnam; North and South Vietnam reunified when North Vietnam takes Saigon

1979   U.S.-Chinese diplomatic relations restored

1984   Anglo-Chinese accord gives China control of Hong Kong in 1997

1986   Corazon Aquino becomes president in Philippines after "People Power" revolution

1989   Democracy movement in Peking; forceful repression by Chinese government

The years since the end of World War II have been a time of great turmoil and great changes in East Asia. The end of the war meant different things for different countries. For Japan, it meant occupation; for China, civil war; for Korea, division; for the former Indochina, a difficult process of war and independence; and for the other countries of Southeast Asia, liberation and the trials of nation building.

East Asia also became a Cold War battleground, as the United States and the Soviet Union sought to improve their own positions in the region at the expense of the other. The Cold War turned hot in Korea in 1950, with a civil war quickly turning into an international conflict. The contradictory themes of independence and outside involvement make the history of East Asia since 1945 a rocky and fascinating story.

JAPAN

World War II was devastating for Japan. Many of its cities were destroyed. The last months of the war were a nightmare for Japanese citizens, as American incendiary and conventional bombs laid waste to city after city. In one fire-bombing raid alone, in March 1945, over 100,000 people were killed in Tokyo. And the atomic bombing of Hiroshima and Nagasaki not only flattened those two cities, claiming hundreds of thousands of lives, but also left deep emotional scars that still affect Japan.

American Occupation   The war was followed by an occupation that was technically under the jurisdiction of the Allies, but was in fact carried out largely by the Americans, with General Douglas MacArthur as Supreme Commander for the Allied Powers, or SCAP—a term which came to refer to the whole bureaucracy of the occupation.

DEMILITARIZATION

According to documents outlining postsurrender American policy in Japan, the goal of the occupation was to "insure that Japan will not again become a menace to the peace and security of the world." This required, first of all, the demilitarization of Japan. This meant not only dismantling military equipment and organization, but also punishing those deemed responsible for Japan's wartime activities.

DEMOCRATIZATION

Constitutional Revision. The second step in the restructuring of Japan was to put in place democratic institutions. The Americans felt that this was the best way to ensure that Japan would not return to the days of anti-democratic military rule. Constitutional revision was immediately begun by a Japanese committee, but MacArthur soon became convinced that such a process would be too slow and that nothing further could be done until constitutional revision was completed. He therefore stepped in and directed a SCAP committee to draft a new constitution. This document was approved by the Japanese cabinet and formally issued in March 1946. Among its provisions was the famous Article 9, under which "the Japanese people forever renounce war as a sovereign right." It also dictated that "land, sea, and air forces . . . will never be maintained." Japan was allowed to maintain forces necessary for its own defense, known as the Self-Defense Forces, but the highly controversial Article 9 increasingly came into question as Japan's economic and political role in the world expanded.

The Emperor. Among its other provisions, the constitution of 1946 also stated that the emperor was nothing more than a "symbol of the state and of the unity of the people." Earlier that year, the emperor had publicly renounced any claims to divinity. The Japanese emperor continued to be an important symbol, however; the formal rites of accession for Emperor Akihito in 1989 were the occasion for great ceremony and visits by representatives of many foreign governments. But under the new constitution, sovereignty, which under the constitution of 1889 had resided in the person of the emperor, was now placed in the Japanese people as a whole, who were also given such protections as freedom of the press, freedom of assembly, and equality of the sexes.

Social Reforms. The occupation authorities also imposed certain social reforms on Japan, believing that the more deeply rooted their reforms were, the less likely Japan was to return to prewar patterns. Policy makers reformed Japan's education system along American lines, with an aim toward using it as an ally in instilling democratic principles. They were also quite concerned about the legal status of women—particularly about their right to vote. Women voted for the first time in Japan in parliamentary elections in April 1946.

Economic Reforms. Finally, SCAP instituted economic reforms in Japan. As with the political and social reforms, economic reforms were carried out with the idea of promoting democracy. SCAP promoted labor rights and the formation of labor unions. Land reform was an extremely important area of activity. Many former tenants now were able to own land themselves rather than working someone else's land. Occupation authorities also took steps to break up some of Japan's biggest business conglomerates; this was seen as a necessary step in the diffusion of economic power and the success of other democratic reforms.

The End of the Occupation

Japan responded very well to U.S.-imposed reforms, and the two recent enemies began to develop a friendly relationship. Though the American forces entered Japan as conquerors determined to reorganize the Japanese state and society, rapid changes in the postwar world also brought about changes in the way Japan was treated. The wartime alliance between the United States and the Soviet Union rapidly fell apart after the end of World War II. The strain in the relationship was showing even before the war came to a close; although the Soviet Union finally entered the war against Japan shortly before Japan's surrender, the United States effectively prevented active Soviet participation in the occupation. But the United States could not prevent Soviet involvement in the postwar administration of nearby Korea—the scene of the emerging Cold War's first hot flash. With U.S.-Japan relations turning friendly and U.S.-Soviet relations moving in the opposite direction—especially after the outbreak of war in Korea in 1950— American authorities were especially concerned that Japan become a strong American ally, linked to a world political order and economy dominated by the United States. The symbol of the new U.S.-Japan relationship was the signing of a peace treaty in San Francisco in September 1951; the occupation officially ended in April 1952. In a separate treaty, however, the United States agreed to continue to provide military protection to Japan, in exchange for which Japan granted the U.S. access to bases and other facilities in Japan. The treaty met with opposition on both sides of the Pacific from time to time, but the United States continued to provide a protective umbrella for Japan.

Economic and Political Recovery

Japan's postwar leaders—in particular, Prime Minister Yoshida Shigeru—made a conscious decision that the nation's first priority must be economic reconstruction. A corollary of this policy was that involvement in international politics must clearly be a matter of lower priority.

INVESTMENT AND TRADE

One of the effects of U.S. military protection was that Japan had to spend relatively little on defense—certainly far less than other leading industrial nations. This allowed Japan to invest heavily in economic development, leading to impressive economic growth rates and Japan's position as an international economic superpower. A combination of new technology, large-scale investment, and an able work force has propelled Japan into a leading position in an increasingly interdependent world economy. Japan's success was also due in part to a close relationship between business and government. The Ministry of International Trade and Industry (MITI) was instrumental in channeling resources and guiding export policy. The co-operation of business and government was such that outside observers often referred to Japan as "Japan, Inc."

The standard of living in Japan has soared since World War II; in 1991 Japan's Gross National Product (GNP) was over $2 trillion, with a per capita GNP of roughly $17,000. But like anywhere else, this growth was not accompanied by full social equality. Rapid economic growth was also accompanied by other problems. Much of Japan's economic success has been based on exports. Japan regularly has a large trade surplus, amounting to $52 billion in 1990. Within the space of a generation, "made in Japan" changed from a derogatory label to an indication of high quality. But Japan's rapid success has caused trade friction with numerous countries, sometimes leading to protectionist sentiment and even policies aimed at reducing trade deficits with Japan.

BUREAUCRATIC CONTINUITY

One of SCAP's political reforms during the 1940s was to carry out a purge of Japan's prewar and wartime political leaders. In the absence of the former leadership, Japan's extensive bureaucracy became increasingly important in the management of government agencies. Party politics was restored to Japan, with a large number of parties emerging to compete for power. The Socialist Party gained power in 1947, but their ascendancy did not last long. The Liberal Party and the Democratic Party (both of them conservative parties) merged in 1955, creating the Liberal Democratic Party (LDP), which has dominated Japanese politics ever since. Its long tenure in office could give the impression, however, that the LDP is a strongly unified party. In fact, it is a coalition of factions that compete for power and divide top government positions among their members. This arrangement has created a political system in which the veneer of one-party dominance masks much of the real competition and bargaining that goes on behind the scenes.

Japan in the Contemporary World

Japan's role in the contemporary world has been dominated by its economic power, not by its active involvement in world politics. It has resumed diplomatic relations with its former nearby opponents. Ties were restored with the Soviet Union in 1956 and with China in 1972. In addition, Japan has also normalized relations with its former colony in Korea. Obviously, Japan would like to have its neighbors think of it as a trading partner rather than a former aggressor. For countries like China and Korea (both North and South), however, this is not always easy. One highly publicized indication of the difficulties involved was the Japanese government's revision of history textbooks to be used in schools. The revisions tended to soften descriptions of Japan's actions in World War II, leading to loud protests from China and Korea.

Many nations, seeing Japan's economic success, have become frustrated at Japan's reluctance to take a more active role in international politics. This is often coupled with resentment at the fact that U.S. protection eliminates the need for Japan to spend as much on defense as other countries. There are signs that the Japanese government is willing to accept heavier international responsibilities, however. It contributed a large sum of money, though no soldiers, to the multinational force involved in the 1990–1991 Persian Gulf War. And in a more dramatic move, in 1992 Japan contributed military personnel to a United Nations peacekeeping force. Some see developments like these as ominous signs of a possible "remilitarization" of Japan, while others view them as indications that Japan is now willing to accept an international political role commensurate with its economic role.

THE PEOPLE'S REPUBLIC OF CHINA

In 1945, though Japanese aggression had been brought to an end, peace did not immediately come to China. The international conflict of World War II had simply postponed the resolution of an internal conflict between the Kuomintang ("Nationalist") government and a growing communist movement. During the war, the two parties had temporarily made peace with one another in the name of fighting a common enemy. But in 1945, the reasons that held the united front together no longer existed.

Communist Revolution in China

IDEOLOGICAL SHIFT

Over the course of the 1930s and early 1940s, communism in China underwent a shift of focus. The official ideology of the Chinese Communist Party (CCP), initially under tutelage from Moscow, had advocated a revolution based on an urban proletariat. The problem was that China did not have such a group with sufficient numbers to form the backbone of a nationwide revolution. The emerging leader of the CCP, Mao Tse-tung, did accept Lenin's idea that a small party would be the vanguard of a successful revolution. Mao, however, urged the CCP to concentrate its efforts on winning the support of China's rural masses. This rural emphasis was both facilitated and necessitated when the Nationalist government forced the communist movement into China's hinterland (see chapter 16). From this point on, as the communists organized rural areas and carried out land reform that put land in the hands of its tillers, the movement gained momentum.

A NEW NATION

At war's end, there was a short-lived effort on the part of the United States to broker a coalition between the Kuomintang government of Chiang Kai-shek and the CCP, led by Mao. This effort ultimately failed, and China was plunged into civil war. The communists' perfecting of guerrilla techniques during the war with Japan served them well, as did their rural organizing and the support they had gained as defenders of China during the fight against Japanese invaders. The United States supported the Kuomintang, but the CCP enjoyed increasing support from the people of China. The Communists swept to victory, with Mao proclaiming the establishment of the People's Republic of China from Peking on October 1, 1949. After a generation of disintegration dating back to the destruction of the Ch'ing dynasty, China was once again unified. Within about a year, Chinese armies had also gained control of Tibet, Inner Mongolia, and the northwestern frontier. A strong centralized government was organized in Peking, and China began the process of reconstruction and economic recovery.

Mao's China

The new People's Republic of China (PRC) was initially similar in structure to the Soviet Union. Power was concentrated at the top. The Chinese Communist Party was supreme, with Mao Tse-tung the most powerful leader in the land (though he was not without his detractors and opponents). China's increasing alienation from the United States caused the country to establish a closer relationship with the Soviet Union, although China and the Soviet Union had numerous disagreements that would eventually lead to a split.

CHINA AND THE KOREAN WAR

Chinese-U.S. antagonism was confirmed and hardened during the Korean War (1950–1953; see below), China's first major venture into the international arena since the establishment of the People's Republic. Mao and some other members of the Chinese leadership were fearful of the possibility of a Korean peninsula dominated by the United States, and of the speed with which United Nations forces were heading toward the Korea-

China border. Late in 1950, therefore, China joined the conflict on the side of North Korea, putting its soldiers into the field directly against U.S. soldiers, who dominated the United Nations force that had intervened on the side of South Korea. The war gave a boost to China's self-esteem and to CCP leadership, as Chinese forces proved capable of standing up to the United States. But the war was costly for China as well. Estimates of the number of Chinese soldiers killed, wounded, or missing range as high as 1 million. And the damage to U.S.-China relations would not begin to be repaired for nearly twenty years after the end of the war.

THE "GREAT LEAP FORWARD"

One of the appeals of the communist program in China before 1949 and in the early years after the establishment of the PRC was "land to the tiller." By the late 1950s, however, Mao had determined that a new approach was needed in order to increase the speed of China's economic development. The result was a campaign begun in 1958, known as the "Great Leap Forward," designed to rapidly increase both agricultural and industrial productivity. Land that had only a decade earlier been turned over to peasants was now collectivized on a massive scale. Rural China was organized into communes, with land worked collectively. Factories were organized along communal lines also.

But the Great Leap was a disaster for China. Backyard steel furnaces, which had been established throughout the country to involve everyone in heavy industrial production, produced only low-quality iron and steel. Crops failed in many areas, partly because so much labor was expended on the doomed backyard furnace project. China was also hit by natural calamities. Crop failures, natural disasters, and bureaucratic inefficiency led to scarcity and famine. Tens of millions of Chinese died as a result.

CULTURAL REVOLUTION

The disastrous policies that had brought about the Great Leap and its failure were replaced by more moderate policies to try to bring about an economic recovery. At the same time, Mao Tse-tung, though he remained General Secretary of the Communist Party, was surpassed in influence by more moderate leaders. By the mid-1960s, Mao was convinced not only that China had sufficiently recovered, but that the nation was lagging in revolutionary fervor and was slipping into "bureaucratism," "careerist" complacency, and "revisionism."

In response, in 1966 Mao inspired a new nationwide movement to purge the party and the nation of these undesirable tendencies and to return himself to a position of preeminence in the party. Known as the Great Proletarian Cultural Revolution, this ten-year convulsion became an attack on anything identified with traditional culture, foreign influence, and "bourgeois liberalism." Intellectuals and artists (as well as many white-collar workers) were sent to work in the countryside in order to "rectify" their attitudes, offensive books were banned and existing copies destroyed, cultural treasures were destroyed, and anyone suspected of insufficient revolutionary zeal or ideological purity became a potential target of the youthful Red Guards or other groups that swept across China. Mao's image was resurrected and enhanced to an unprecedented degree, and copies of his sayings, the so-called "Little Red Book," were seen everywhere. The Cultural Revolution affected all parts of China. Many people died during this decade of cultural and political chaos, and many more were beaten, publicly humiliated, or thrown out of their jobs.

Foreign Affairs

THE SINO-SOVIET SPLIT

Throughout the 1950s, relations between China and the Soviet Union steadily deteriorated. Mao had disagreed with Soviet views on the pace and direction of revolution even before the CCP victory in 1949, and the tensions increased after an initial period of cooperation following the establishment of the People's Republic. The Soviet Union had sent advisers to assist in China's economic modernization, but these were withdrawn in 1959 along with all Soviet aid. Border disputes and ideological arguments deepened the rift between the two communist giants.

THE UNITED STATES AND THE UNITED NATIONS

China's international position was enhanced in 1971, however, when the United Nations voted to accept China as a member, at the same time expelling Taiwan. From that point, China embarked on a road of increasing international respectability, initially led by the indefatigable pragmatist Chou En-lai. The most dramatic change in China's foreign affairs came in February 1972, when U.S. President Richard Nixon went to China and opened the way for enhanced relations between the two countries. Full diplomatic relations between the U.S. and China were not completed until 1979, but in the meantime many other countries established diplomatic relations with China, usually at the expense of relations with Taiwan.

Post-Mao China

Mao Tse-tung, who had brought China through the communist revolution and attempted to mold the huge nation along the lines of his revolutionary vision, died in 1976. His more radical supporters, including his widow, were arrested not long after Mao's death, bringing to the party and the nation a new, more moderate leadership, initially under Hua Kuo-feng but eventually under Teng Hsiao-p'ing. Teng had been purged during the Maoist era, but he returned to power in 1981 and led China through a period of modernization and restructuring.

PRAGMATISM AND ECONOMIC REFORM

China's new outlook was reflected in its rapprochement with the West. Teng and other Chinese leaders traveled to Western nations, looking for friendly relations and advanced industrial technology. The new leadership also began a process of dismantling Mao's image, influence, and policies. This was a difficult matter, as Mao was not only responsible for some of the excesses of the past but was also the founder of the People's Republic and the leader of the revolution. But over the course of several years, China's leadership steadily reversed many of Mao's policies.

China's new approach was most obvious in the economy. The post-Mao leadership gradually moved away from strict central planning to the incorporation of some elements of a market economy. Collectivization was reversed, with individual households responsible for agricultural production. Similarly, managers of local industrial enterprises were given more decision-making responsibility. The result was an increase in production, especially in agriculture. As of 1991, China had a Gross National Product of $413 billion ($370 per capita, according to World Bank estimates), with a growth rate of 5 percent. China carries on active trade with Hong Kong, the United States, Japan, Russia, and other countries, and in 1991 ran a trade surplus of roughly 9 billion.

COMMUNIST PARTY AUTHORITARIANISM

At the same time, the Communist Party was unwilling to jeopardize its control of China. It continued to resort to occasional crackdowns and policy reversals whenever it sensed the need to purge China of undesirable elements. A dramatic example of this occurred in 1989. Students and others, angered by government corruption and insensitivity and hoping to achieve a greater measure of political and economic freedom, carried out a series of demonstrations in Peking and other cities. They eventually occupied Peking's central Tiananmen Square, erecting a "Goddess of Democracy" statue reminiscent of the American Statue of Liberty and carrying out hunger strikes and other protest actions. At times, the crowd in the square numbered over 1 million people. By the night of June 3, the government had had enough. Elements of the People's Liberation Army were sent into the square in the early morning hours. With guns and tanks they crushed the demonstration—and many of the demonstrators themselves. Estimates of the number of people killed ranged from several hundred to as high as 3,000.

The massacre shocked the world, and for a time many nations pulled back from their previously cordial relations with China. The world's most populous country (nearly 1.2 billion people in 1991) was still going through the turmoil of trying to achieve economic modernization and international respectability. But the country's leaders were clearly not willing to sacrifice centralized party control to achieve it.

Greater China:
The Matter of
Taiwan and
Hong Kong

Two areas on China's periphery, Taiwan and Hong Kong, shared much of China's cultural heritage but developed in quite different ways in the twentieth century.

TAIWAN

When they were defeated by Mao's communist forces in 1949, the Kuomintang forces fled to the island of Taiwan, off the coast of China's Fukien province. There, still under the leadership of Chiang Kai-shek, they established a government over the island's inhabitants and the fleeing mainlanders. With American aid, the Republic of China (as the new government on Taiwan described itself) built a strong industrial economy. One of the continuing themes of contemporary Chinese history has been the ongoing rivalry between the two governments (island and mainland) and their competing claims to be the legitimate government of all of China.

Taiwan became a propaganda tool during the Cold War, providing a capitalistic counterexample to the mainland's communist system. American aid slowed considerably in the early 1960s, but the economy of Taiwan continued to develop on its own. The Kuomintang remained in control but gradually recognized the need for more involvement by Taiwanese, rather than continuing control by mainlanders. This island nation of roughly 21 million inhabitants (1991) has experienced remarkable economic development, with average annual growth rates averaging around 9 percent since the early 1960s.

HONG KONG

The island of Hong Kong first came under British control as a result of the treaty ending the Opium War in 1842 (see chapter 12). A treaty in 1860 ceded the southern part of Kowloon peninsula, just across from the island on the mainland. Later, the Convention of Peking in 1898 leased the rest of Kowloon and the adjacent "New Territories" to the British for ninety-nine years. The British colony grew until by the late twentieth century it was one of the world's leading financial centers. With a free market economy and very few trade barriers, it became a thriving international port, trading center, and tourist attraction. It had $80 billion worth of exports in 1990, mostly to China, Japan, and Western industrial nations.

The ninety-nine-year lease on part of Hong Kong had an expiration date of 1997. A 1984 agreement between the British and Chinese governments declared that in 1997 all of Hong Kong—not just the portions leased in 1898—would revert to Chinese rule. The joint declaration stipulated that China would not disturb Hong Kong's economy and social system for a minimum of fifty years after Chinese rule was restored. The crushing of the demonstrations in Peking and elsewhere in 1989, and a subsequent crackdown and tightening of government controls in China generally, led to considerable concern in Hong Kong and throughout the world about how reliable China's promises regarding Hong Kong would be. For the small colony's 6 million inhabitants, the future held only uncertainty.

KOREA

The last half of the twentieth century was a trying time for Korea. The peninsula went through the turmoil of civil war, which still leaves its mark on the divided country. Since then, the two Koreas have concentrated on economic development.

Liberation and Division

The end of World War II meant a variety of things for Korea. First, it meant liberation from Japanese colonial rule. After the Japanese annexed the peninsula in 1910 they established a harsh rule over Korea, suppressing dissent and tailoring Korean economic development to serve the needs of the Japanese economy. Upper-level positions in both government and industry were held by Japanese, though some Korean entrepreneurs were favored by the Japanese colonial government and were allowed to establish a variety of enterprises. Especially toward the end of its rule in Korea, Japan began a process of rapid, forced industrialization, creating new social pressures within Korea.

But if the end of the war meant liberation from Japan, it did not mean autonomy for Korea. During the war, the Allies had agreed to divide the administration of postwar Korea between the Soviet Union and the United States (see chapter 17). Accordingly, Korea was split into northern and southern occupation zones, with a dividing line at the 38th parallel. A plan for nationwide UN-sponsored elections fell apart, and by 1948 two separate states had been established (though in fact they emerged within a year of the end of World War II): the Democratic People's Republic of Korea ("North Korea") under Kim Il-sung, and the Republic of Korea ("South Korea") under Syngman Rhee. Each state had its superpower ally, but neither one was simply a puppet of its larger sponsor.

The Korean War

The social and ideological tensions that had built up during the period of Japanese occupation now combined with separate political regimes having very different ideologies to produce an explosive situation.

THE OUTBREAK OF WAR

As pressure increased along the dividing line, both sides prepared their military forces for war. On June 25, 1950, North Korea launched a massive invasion across the 38th parallel, quickly taking the southern capital of Seoul

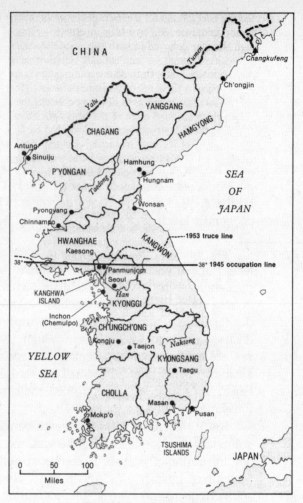

Fig. 19.1   Modern Korea

and pushing South Korean forces to the southeastern part of the peninsula. The United States, whose forces had previously withdrawn from the south, urged the United Nations to come to the aid of South Korea. A Soviet boycott of the United Nations Security Council allowed the measure to pass. The United States quickly sent troops from Japan. Eventually a United Nations force from seventeen nations as diverse as Colombia, Turkey, Luxembourg, and Canada joined forces on the side of South Korea, though the United States had by far the largest contingent and did the bulk of the UN fighting. Despite the fact that the war started as a Korean civil war arising from tensions that had been increasing for years, the emerging Cold War conflict between the two superpowers was soon superimposed on the peninsula. From the perspective of the United States, the war was the first real showdown between communism and freedom.

ARMISTICE

The tides of war took the opposing armies up and down the length of Korea more than once, causing great physical destruction in addition to the human costs. The war reached a stalemate while negotiations dragged on. In 1953, an armistice was finally reached, though a formal peace treaty has yet to be signed. The demarcation line in 1953 was little changed from the 1945 line dividing north from south, but the scale of the destruction in reaching that point was staggering. City after city was laid waste. The two capitals of Pyongyang and Seoul were reduced to rubble. Over 3 million Koreans died, and countless families were left homeless, separated, or both.

Korea After the War

Following the war, both sides began to rebuild their economic and political systems, the north still under the leadership of Kim and the Korean Workers' Party, the south under the rule of Syngman Rhee until he was forced from office in 1960. Rhee was followed briefly by an effort at representative government that was cut short by a military takeover in 1961 and a succession of former generals serving as president.

ECONOMIC GROWTH

Into the 1960s, North Korean economic growth outpaced that of the south. After that time, with strong direction from the government and considerable U.S. aid, the South Korean export-led economy began to show impressive growth. Beginning in the mid-1960s, South Korean growth was among the highest in the world. At the same time, growth of the North Korean command economy slowed. North Korea, however, tried to emphasize self-reliance both politically and economically, particularly as the breakup of the Soviet Union and China's increasingly important economic and political ties with South Korea deprived the north of its two closest potential allies.

Both states recovered remarkably well from the war, though based on completely different systems. South Korea today has twice the population of North Korea, though government campaigns to limit population growth have led to a population growth rate in the south that is about half that of the north. Economic development and standard of living provide a clear contrast. In 1990, estimated per capita GNP in South Korea was $5,600 with a growth rate of 9 percent, while in North Korea it was $1,390, with a growth rate of 2 percent. It is likely, however, that social problems resulting from growth have been less pronounced in the north than in the south, which has experienced frequent labor unrest.

THE QUESTION OF REUNIFICATION

In addition to history, language, and culture, if there is one thing which unites Koreans it is the desire for reunification. Progress on this issue has come in fits and starts, and there have been as many setbacks as there have been breakthroughs. It continues to be a highly emotional issue in Korea. It is also an issue of great international concern, as all countries in the region hope for a more stable political situation on this peninsula strategically nestled among China, Russia, and Japan.

VIETNAM, LAOS, AND CAMBODIA

Liberation and War

The countries of Vietnam, Laos, and Cambodia (Kampuchea) make up what was formerly the French colony of Indochina. Liberation from colonial rule did not come with the end of World War II.

THE ANTICOLONIAL WAR WITH FRANCE

The leader of the independence movement in Indochina was Ho Chi Minh, the Vietnamese communist leader, who declared independence for all of Indochina in 1945. Thus began a long war of independence from France that ended with a French defeat at Dien Bien Phu in 1954. At an international conference in Geneva, Vietnam was divided and Laos and Cambodia were declared independent. Ho Chi Minh led a northern Vietnamese government, while Ngo Dinh Diem, with American support, set up a competing government in the south. As was the case with Korea after World War II, the division was supposed to be temporary, with elections held in short order to reunify the country. But again as in Korea, this optimistic view of the possibility of peaceful reunification after a temporary division proved to be unattainable.

THE WAR OF THE TWO VIETNAMS

The Republic of Vietnam government in the south became the target of northern-supplied guerrilla warfare. American involvement was initially limited to sending advisers to its client state, but during the 1960s the scale of American involvement steadily increased to the point where the conflict in Vietnam became the major American foreign and domestic policy concern. Half a million American soldiers were eventually committed to the war by the time they gradually began to be withdrawn in 1969 (the same year in which Ho Chi Minh died).

AMERICAN INVOLVEMENT

The war became increasingly unpopular in the United States, particularly after it was revealed that President Richard Nixon had secretly extended the war to Cambodia and Laos by ordering bombing raids on communist bases and supply lines in those countries in 1969. In 1973, a peace agreement was signed in Paris; in 1975, Saigon, the capital of South Vietnam, fell to

North Vietnamese forces shortly after the last Americans left. The cost of the war was horrible: nearly 2 million Vietnamese dead, twice that many wounded, and 57,000 Americans dead. But Vietnam was finally liberated and united, bringing to an end the war of liberation begun against France thirty years earlier.

CAMBODIA AND REGIONAL PROBLEMS

In Cambodia, after the end of the war in Vietnam, a civil war resulted in the seizure of power by Pol Pot and his Khmer Rouge forces. They instituted a brutal reign of terror in the late 1970s, resulting in millions of deaths—by some estimates as much as one-third of the country's population. An invasion by Vietnam ousted Pol Pot's regime, but did not destroy his forces completely. And because Cold War logic compelled the United States to continue to see Soviet-supported Vietnam as its enemy, the United States gave support to Pol Pot's exiled forces. Much of the shifting political situation in the former Indochina was determined by the Cold War rivalry between the superpowers, but with the breakup of the Soviet Union and the decrease in the American military presence throughout Asia, there may be hope for a new direction.

SOUTHEAST ASIAN STATES

Finally, some mention should be made of the emerging Southeast Asian states and the challenges they have faced since the end of World War II.

THE PHILIPPINES

A new republic was created in the Philippines following independence from the United States in 1946. American influence remained strong, however, as did an American military presence until the early 1990s. Ferdinand Marcos became president in 1965 and proceeded to rule with an iron fist, declaring martial law in 1972. Increasingly unpopular and facing a growing communist insurgency, Marcos was forced out of office by a "people power" revolution and landslide electoral defeat in 1986. He spent his final years in exile in Hawaii until his death in 1989. His successor, Corazon Aquino (whose husband, also a Marcos opponent, had been murdered, presumably by Marcos supporters), was faced with the daunting task of unifying a country plagued by insurgency, political turmoil, and a weakening economy. But the rousing display of democracy in 1986 continued to be a source of encouragement.

INDONESIA

Indonesia, formerly Netherlands East Indies, won its independence from Dutch rule in 1949. The leader of the independence movement, Achmed Sukarno, became the first president of the newly independent country. Sukarno led the country by means of a so-called "guided democracy," which really meant the pretense but not the practice of democracy. General Suharto came to power in 1966 and set Indonesia on the path toward a somewhat greater degree of political stability. But there was no widespread political participation, and the fragile state of the Indonesian economy meant that the future of this heavily populated country remained uncertain.

MALAYSIA AND SINGAPORE

Malaysia (known as Malaya prior to 1965), plagued by a communist guerrilla insurgency since 1948, did not win self-government from Britain until 1957, becoming independent in 1961. But rivalry and bitterness between the Malays and Chinese immigrants continued. In 1965, therefore, the independent city-state of Singapore was created, populated primarily by Chinese. They turned their tiny state into a major international port and prosperous trading center that has become the hub of much of Southeast Asia's economic activity.

THAILAND

Thailand is unique among Southeast Asian nations in having remained free from colonial rule. The country is a constitutional monarchy. The king has little real political power, but the possibility of royal involvement in politics was dramatically demonstrated in the summer of 1992 when the king stepped in to help defuse a serious political crisis. Thailand has undergone some degree of industrialization and has benefited by its closeness to the commercial center of Southeast Asia in Singapore. Despite difficulties, Thailand has been one of the more stable Southeast Asian nations.

BURMA

Burma (now officially known as Myanmar) became independent from British rule in 1948 and has had a very rocky history since then. It has tended to be relatively closed to the outside world, hindering its ability to develop trading partners and thereby raise its standard of living. Periods of insurgency and political repression have plagued development of a stable state. In 1988 the military State Law and Order Restoration Committee took power. Military authorities did allow elections to be held in 1991 but ignored the results when the National League for Democracy won an overwhelming victory. The National League's leader, Aung San Suu Kyi, held under military house arrest, was awarded the 1991 Nobel Peace Prize for her "non-violent struggle for democracy and human rights."

*T*he world went through great changes after World War II. Nowhere was this more obvious than in East Asia. Japan quickly recovered both politically and economically to become one of the world's leading industrialized countries. China traveled a different road into the late twentieth century, emerging from civil war as a communist giant that went through both economic and political convulsions before it could concentrate its resources on economic modernization. Korea suffered the tragedy of national division, producing two states that competed to achieve economic prosperity at home and respectability abroad.

The states of Southeast Asia, with the exception of Thailand, spent the immediate postwar years achieving independence from their colonial masters. In some places, such as the Philippines, this immediate task was completed rather easily (though colonial influence remained visible). In other places, most notably Vietnam, it was accomplished only after protracted struggle and enormous loss of life. The colonial legacy and the experience of national birth from the matrix of colonialism has had a continuing influence on Southeast Asia.

The world economy has also played an important role in shaping modern East Asia, both north and south. Japan's success at finding a place in this economy is obvious, but every Asian state's development has to some extent been affected by the world's increasingly interdependent economy. The "four tigers" or "minidragons" of East Asia—South Korea, Taiwan, Singapore, and Hong Kong—are often hailed as examples of the next generation of world economic powers. The continuing challenge for all the states of East Asia will be to find the mix of economic and political development that will satisfy their people in an age of increasing democratic aspirations.

Selected Readings

Borthwick, Mark. *Pacific Century: The Emergence of Modern Pacific Asia.* Boulder, CO: Westview Press, 1992.

Bresnan, John, ed. *Crisis in the Philippines: The Marcos Era and Beyond.* Princeton, NJ: Princeton University Press, 1986.

Chanda, Nayan. *Brother Enemy: The War After the War.* New York: Harcourt Brace Jovanovich, 1986.

Cumings, Bruce. *The Two Koreas.* Foreign Policy Association "Headline Series," Number 269. New York: Foreign Policy Association, 1984.

Diamond, Larry, et al., eds. *Democracy in Developing Countries: Asia.* Boulder, CO: Lynne Rienner Publishers, 1989.

Dietrich, Craig. *People's China: A Brief History.* New York: Oxford University Press, 1986.

Eckert, Carter J., et al. *Korea Old and New: A History.* Seoul: Ilchokak Publishers (for the Korea Institute, Harvard University), 1990.

Gluck, Carol, and Stephen R. Graubard, eds. *Showa: The Japan of Hirohito.* New York: Norton, 1992.

Halliday, Jon and Bruce Cumings. *Korea: The Unknown War*. New York: Pantheon, 1988.

Johnson, Chalmers. *MITI and the Japanese Miracle: The Growth of Industrial Policy, 1925–1975*. Stanford: Stanford University Press, 1982.

MacDonald, Donald Stone. *The Koreans: Contemporary Politics and Society*. 2d ed. Boulder, CO: Westview Press, 1990.

MacFarquhar, Roderick, and John K. Fairbank, eds. *The Cambridge History of China, Volume 14. The People's Republic, Part I: The Emergence of Revolutionary China, 1949–1965*. Cambridge: Cambridge University Press, 1987.

Meisner, Maurice. *Mao's China and After: A History of the People's Republic*. New York: Free Press, 1986.

Pyle, Kenneth B. *The Making of Modern Japan*. Lexington, MA: D. C. Heath and Company, 1978.

Robinson, Thomas W. *Democracy and Development in East Asia: Taiwan, South Korea, and the Philippines*. Washington: AEI Press, 1991.

Schell, Orville. *To Get Rich Is Glorious: China in the 80s*. New York: Pantheon, 1984.

Spence, Jonathan D. *The Search for Modern China*. New York: Norton, 1990.

20

India and the Middle East

1945	End of World War II
1946	Jordan, Syria, and Lebanon become independent
1947	Mountbatten's mission to India
	Independence of India
	Creation of Pakistan
	Kashmir dispute
1948	Partition of Palestine; Israel becomes a state; Arab-Israeli war
	Death of Mahatma Gandhi
1951	Libya becomes independent monarchy
1951–1953	Oil crisis and failed revolution in Iran
1952	Egyptian revolution; rise of Nasser
1954–1962	Algerian war of independence against France
1956	Suez crisis
	Morocco becomes independent monarchy
1957	Tunisia becomes independent
1958	Military coup in Iraq overthrows monarchy
	Lebanon crisis
1962	Border clash between India and China
1962–1965	Civil war in Yemen; country splits in two
1966	Indira Gandhi elected prime minister of India

1967	Arab-Israeli war (Six Days' War)
1969	Coup in Libya by Gaddafi
1971	Bangladesh created from former East Pakistan
	Friendship treaty between India and Soviet Union
1973	Arab-Israeli war
	Arab oil embargo
1974	India successfully tests nuclear device
1979	Camp David peace accord between Egypt and Israel
	Iranian Islamic revolution
1980–1988	Iran-Iraq War
1982–1985	Israeli invasion of Lebanon
1984	Occupation of Golden Temple in Amritsar
	Indira Gandhi assassinated
1990–1991	Gulf War; beginning of Arab-Israeli peace talks

India after World War II faced a host of problems. Though it achieved independence from Britain within two years of the end of the war, absence of British rule did not mean an absence of challenges. Partition, border conflicts, religious strife, and a burgeoning population have presented formidable obstacles to the attainment of the full promise of independence.

In the Middle East, the last half of the twentieth century was a time of tremendous transformation. Politically, the region was transformed from European colonies to independent states. Economically, oil has brought great wealth and strategic importance to a previously impoverished region. The wealth from control of a large portion of the world's oil resources has resulted in increasing political and economic power on a global level for the oil-rich Middle Eastern states. The population and urban explosion, combined with vastly unequal distribution of the wealth from oil, has contributed to serious economic inequality between the oil-rich and oil-poor states in the region, and between the poor and rich inside each country. Superpower competition over access to the region's oil resources, combined with the region's internal instability and military conflict, led to the extensive militarization of the Middle East; these internal and external tensions resulted in numerous wars.

INDIA

Independence and Partition

In India, the most pressing problem at the end of the Second World War was the question of Indian independence. A corollary to this question, somewhat muted until 1945, now became unavoidable. India's Muslims, fearing Hindu domination in a new, independent state, began voicing a strong desire for a separate Muslim state, carved out of part of the British-ruled subcontinent.

THE MUSLIM LEAGUE

The Muslim League was the primary voice for those advocating a separate Muslim state. The League was founded in Dacca (now the capital of Bangladesh) late in 1906 to give Muslims a united voice amid all the other voices competing for a say in the future of India. When the debates regarding the partition of India began in earnest in 1946, the Muslim League's president was Muhammad Ali Jinnah. Jinnah had studied law in London as a young man and had initially become involved in Indian politics not through the Muslim League but through the Congress Party. By 1946, however, Jinnah had despaired of the possibility for adequate representation of Muslim interests in a Hindu-dominated India. At a league council meeting in July of that year, Jinnah called for "direct action."

The immediate result of this call was the unleashing of all the bitterness, hate, and distrust that had previously been held at least partially in check by the common desire for independence from Britain. Across India, Hindus and Muslims murdered each other in a convulsion of violence that claimed thousands of lives and compounded the difficulties for the British in their final year of rule.

MOUNTBATTEN'S MISSION

With plenty of problems besetting it at home, the British government, under Labour Party Prime Minister Clement Attlee, was prepared to grant India its independence. Early in 1947, Attlee announced that the transfer of power to Indians would take place by mid-1948. But the matter of partition was an extremely sticky one that would require the utmost diplomatic skill. The task of working out the terms of independence and settling the question of partition was given to Lord Louis Mountbatten. Having distinguished himself as the commander of Allied forces in Southeast Asia during World War II, Mountbatten was appointed viceroy of India in 1947—the last person to hold that post. His charge was, in effect, to eliminate his job in as swift and peaceful a manner as possible.

INDEPENDENCE

Within a month of his arrival in India, Mountbatten concluded that the partition of India and the creation of a separate Muslim state was inevitable. This decision was officially announced in the British House of Commons on July 15, 1947, setting a timetable of exactly one month, at the end of which two separate dominions—India and Pakistan—would come into being. Consequently, precisely at midnight on August 14, 1947, India was once again independent, and Pakistan was created. The predominantly Muslim northwest, as well as eastern Bengal, separated by hundreds of miles, became the two parts of Pakistan. (In 1971, East Pakistan became the independent nation of Bangladesh.) Muhammad Ali Jinnah realized his dream of being the leader of an independent Muslim state, while Jawaharlal Nehru (an associate of Gandhi) became India's first prime minister. Independence did not bring peace, however. In the first year, a massive migration brought refugees streaming across the new borders in both directions, hoping to live in the state most compatible with their religious tradition. As many as 10 million people moved, though moving was itself fraught with danger. An estimated 1 million of the refugees were murdered along the way, as Muslims attacked Sikhs and Hindus, and Sikhs and Hindus killed Muslims heading west to Pakistan.

Dispute over Kashmir. Even the formal partition of India did not settle all territorial questions. A dispute quickly erupted in 1947 over the territory of Kashmir, directly between India and Pakistan. Fighting eventually gave way to a cease-fire and a settlement under which Kashmir was divided. The division, however, provided a continuing source of tension between India and Pakistan.

Gandhi's Reaction and Death. The spiritual leader of India's nationalist movement, Mohandas K. ("Mahatma") Gandhi, was never comfortable with the idea of the partition of India, and hoped instead for a state in which Hindus and Muslims could live together in peace. Unfortunately for the Mahatma, his dream was overwhelmed by the reality of religious and political strife. Pained at the partition, Gandhi continued to call for tolerance toward Muslims in India. But on January 30, 1948, just a few months after one of Gandhi's dreams—Indian independence—had been realized, and when it was increasingly obvious that his other dream—Hindu-Muslim cooperation—would not be so easily achieved, Gandhi was gunned down by a religious fanatic. "The light has gone out of our lives," Nehru announced to the nation, "and there is darkness everywhere."

The Republic of India

In 1947, India embarked on a new phase of its history. The long-awaited dream of independence had been realized, but independence alone did not solve all the problems of the new nation.

CHALLENGES FOR THE NEW STATE

Urban Growth. As the first prime minister of the newly liberated Republic of India, Jawaharlal Nehru presided over a period of agricultural and industrial growth, much of it financed by aid from abroad. The country was beset with many of the problems of development, however, including rapid migration from rural areas to the cities. The capital city of New Delhi, as well as Bombay on the west coast and Calcutta in the east near the border with modern-day Bangladesh, experienced particularly rapid population growth. The rise in population outpaced the growth of services and jobs, however, leading to poverty and squalor for many urban residents.

Foreign Affairs. In addition to domestic problems, Nehru faced a number of foreign policy challenges. Both because of its location and because of its dependence on foreign aid, India under Nehru generally adopted a "nonaligned" foreign policy, leaning closely neither to the West, from which it had recently been liberated, nor to the communist world. This stance did not save India from disputes with other nations, however. The disagreement with Pakistan over Kashmir has already been mentioned. In 1962, India and China clashed over territory in the Himalaya mountains, between India and Chinese-occupied Tibet. To this day, border disputes continue between India and Pakistan, Bangladesh, and China.

INDIRA GANDHI

Nehru died on May 27, 1964, having led India continuously since the establishment of the republic. The popular prime minister was cremated at the same site where his mentor Mahatma Gandhi had been cremated in the early days of Indian independence. Nehru's immediate successor, Lal Bahadur Shastri, died less than two years later, just after signing an agreement regarding Kashmir with Pakistani leader Muhammad Ayub Khan. The viability of India's democratic institutions was tested in the aftermath of Shastri's death in 1966. The ruling Congress Party was divided between two candidates, but after a drawn-out balloting process in the Parliament, Nehru's daughter, Indira Gandhi (no relation to the late Mahatma), emerged victorious. She was defeated in 1977, but was elected prime minister again in 1980, serving from then until her death.

The "Green Revolution." In the early years of Prime Minister Gandhi's tenure, India experienced a "Green Revolution," resulting in dramatically increased agricultural production. Agricultural growth was accompanied by growth in India's industrial base, giving reason for optimism in the late 1960s that the new prime minister might help to alleviate some of the economic problems brought about by a rapidly growing population. Growth was uneven, however, and the benefits were not equally shared. Population growth and other problems continued to plague India's economy.

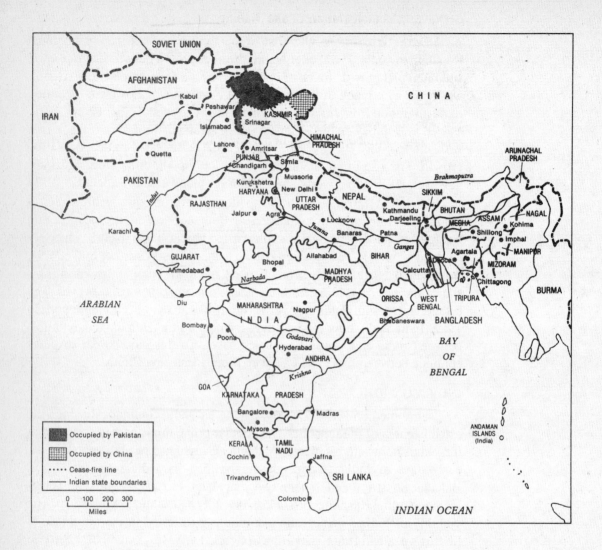

Fig. 20.1   South Asia in 1990

India and the World. In the 1970s, India's politics and its role in the world became increasingly unpredictable. In foreign affairs, the signing of a friendship treaty with the Soviet Union in 1971 marked a departure from India's traditional policy of nonalignment. India successfully exploded an atomic bomb in 1974, signaling the further spread of the world's most dangerous weapons and causing great apprehension in Pakistan, which also sought nuclear weapons technology.

Domestic Politics. In domestic politics, Prime Minister Gandhi became increasingly heavy-handed, even to the point of suspending civil rights. When she finally allowed elections in 1977, she was defeated. It was a convincing demonstration of the viability of Indian democracy. But this same democratic system brought Mrs. Gandhi back to power in the elections of 1980.

INDIA'S SIKHS

One of the continuing problems in Indian political, economic, and social life was the country's ethnic, linguistic, and religious minorities. India's Sikhs, concentrated in Punjab in the north, had started out as an offshoot of Hinduism in the fifteenth century. They accounted for perhaps 2 percent of India's population, but they were a highly visible minority; one of their number, Gyani Zail Singh, was elected president in 1982. Some Sikhs, feeling politically and economically disadvantaged under Mrs. Gandhi's rule, began to agitate for their own autonomous state. They pushed this demand in 1984 by occupying the sacred Golden Temple in Amritsar. Meanwhile, Hindus and Sikhs began killing one another as Mrs. Gandhi's government seemed unable to do anything to resolve the stalemate. But in June 1984, firm but tragic action was taken. The Indian Army was ordered into the temple grounds, and a battle raged for two days in the Sikhs' most sacred spot. Thousands of Sikhs were killed, and part of the temple compound was burned.

ASSASSINATION OF INDIRA GANDHI

Terrorist violence continued, and in this atmosphere Mrs. Gandhi became increasingly intolerant and suspicious. The prime minister herself finally became a victim of the violence. On October 31, 1984, less than five months after she had ordered the attack on the Golden Temple, Mrs. Gandhi was assassinated by two of her Sikh bodyguards. Many Hindus immediately went on a rampage, murdering Sikhs and destroying their property. In the chaos that reigned in India for several days after Mrs. Gandhi's murder, thousands of Sikhs became victims of India's turbulent religious politics.

RAJIV GANDHI

Mrs. Gandhi's son Rajiv, an airline pilot and relative newcomer to active participation in politics, was quickly sworn in as the new prime minister. He called for elections to be held that December, in which his Congress Party won a landslide victory. The new prime minister instituted a number of reforms and attempted to settle, or at least mitigate, some of India's internal rivalries, and in some areas he was successful.

Sri Lanka. During Rajiv Gandhi's tenure as prime minister, India's relations with Sri Lanka (formerly Ceylon) were a source of considerable concern. Despite its proximity to the Indian mainland, this 65,000-square-kilometer island, twenty-nine kilometers off the southern coast of India, has an ethnic and religious mix different from that found in India. The dominant religion is Buddhism, with fewer than 20 percent of the population adherents of Hinduism, and even smaller Muslim and Christian communities. Liberated from British rule in 1948, Sri Lanka has been a battleground between the majority Sinhalese and the Tamils, an ethnic minority comprising perhaps 18 percent of the island's 17 million inhabitants.

In 1987, Prime Minister Gandhi signed an agreement with the Sri Lankan president designed to put an end to the civil war in Sri Lanka. India committed troops to the island to protect the Tamils during the anticipated end of hostilities. But Indian involvement on the island turned into a fiasco, as the agreement failed and Indian soldiers themselves became numbered among the targets of guerrilla factions. Not only Tamils, but many Sinhalese as well were disillusioned with an agreement that seemed to invite too much involvement from the large nation to the north.

Assassination. By 1987, Rajiv Gandhi's initial popularity had begun to wane. He became another victim of India's political violence in 1991, when he was killed by a bomb while campaigning to return to the office of prime minister he had lost. The assassination was attributed to the Liberation Tigers of Tamil Eelam (LTTE), a military arm of the Tamil separatist movement in Sri Lanka.

Modern India: Some Observations

The rocky road along which India's democracy moved since liberation was beset with difficulties.

ECONOMY AND ENVIRONMENT

Economic gains were often offset by high rates of population growth. Flooding, soil erosion, desertification, and deforestation are ever-present afflictions. Environmental hazards caused by human industry were also tragically manifested in India. In December 1984 an American-owned Union Carbide pesticide plant in Bhopal leaked toxic gas, killing 2,000 people within a few hours and injuring thousands more.

WOMEN

The emancipation of women in India was a slow process. Dominant Hindu traditions placed women in a subservient position. With independence, however, Indian women were given the right to vote. In the 1950s they gained the legal right to divorce and to inherit property on an equal basis with their brothers. The literacy rate for women, on the other hand, is only about half that of men. Despite the high profile of such women as Indira Gandhi and the increasingly important voice of women in electoral politics, full equality is not yet a reality.

DIVERSITY

India in 1991 had a population of over 860 million, with a growth rate of nearly 2 percent. It is a country of great diversity. While the majority of the population are Hindus, there is a sizable Muslim minority (over 11 percent), as well as Christian, Sikh, Buddhist, and other religious communities. Though Hindi is the "national" language, only about 30 percent of India's population claim it as their mother tongue. English is the primary political and commercial language, but there are fourteen official languages besides Hindi and English and numerous other languages spoken by large numbers of people.

OLD AND NEW

India remains a mixture of old and new. Many people adhere to traditional patterns of belief and social behavior. Two-thirds of the labor force is engaged in agriculture, but modern techniques have increased productivity and made India self-sufficient in food grains. Indian industry ranges from handicrafts to modern industrial goods, with the majority of exports going to the United States, Europe, and Japan.

THE MIDDLE EAST IN THE TWENTIETH CENTURY

Independence

The Middle East generally supported the Allied effort during World War II. An uprising among Arab peoples in the Middle East could have seriously hampered British war efforts, and possibly have given Hitler the Suez Canal. The Arabs thus felt that they had helped save Britain from the Germans; the British should now reward them with independence. Indeed, Britain and France were so financially and militarily exhausted by the war that they lacked the resolution and the resources to attempt to maintain their control over the Middle East in the face of serious opposition from the Arabs. Thus, within a few years of the end of World War II, all of the Arab states became independent from European control. For the most part independence was achieved without military conflict. The major exception was in Algeria, where a war from 1954 to 1962 was necessary to expel the French.

RESULTS OF INDEPENDENCE

The Arab nations had an unrealistic view of the results of their independence from Britain and France. Many felt that somehow all their problems would now be resolved. Instead, the departure of the Europeans simply allowed a number of suppressed social and political tensions to come to the surface, creating a new set of problems. Furthermore, although the western Europeans had ceased direct rule, indirect control by outsiders was to continue in a number of forms. Many Arab nations were still dependent on

Western technological and military advisors. Furthermore, a new global conflict was arising which replaced the former European disputes: the Cold War between the Soviet Union and the United States.

COLD WAR IN THE MIDDLE EAST

Strategic Importance of the Middle East. The Cold War had a significant impact on the Middle East. For the superpowers, three basic issues were involved: the spread of communism in the Middle East, control over strategic waterways (Bosporus, Suez and Red Sea, Persian Gulf), and control of access to the region's oil resources. The struggle manifested itself in a number of ways. Turkey became a staunch ally of the West, thereby limiting Soviet land and sea access to the Middle East. Iran, after an unsuccessful flirtation with communism in the 1956 revolution, also became a strong military ally of the United States until the Iranian Islamic revolution of 1979.

Arab-Soviet Alliance. The situation with some Arab states was different, however. U.S. support for Israel greatly antagonized the Arabs, who were also unwilling allies of their former colonial masters. The 1956 Suez crisis, in which British and French troops attempted to take control of the Suez Canal from Egypt, led many Arabs to believe that the West could not be trusted. As military coups overthrew pro-Western monarchies, the new military dictatorships increasingly turned to the Soviet Union as a source for technical and military support. Ultimately, Iraq, Syria, Egypt, and Libya all became heavily armed Soviet clients.

Nonetheless, despite numerous feuds between their respective client states, a major military confrontation in the Middle East between the Soviets and the United States never developed. Both superpowers feared the possibility of escalation to nuclear conflict, and ultimately the Soviets accepted the fact that the Western allies' access to Middle Eastern oil was a vital interest. From a U.S. perspective, the pro-Soviet states were seen as "radicals," while those willing to make accommodation with the United States were termed "moderates." Thus, for two decades the global conflict between the Soviet Union and the United States was in part played out on the stage of the Middle East through the conflicts of client states.

END OF THE COLD WAR

As Soviet power declined in the 1980s, the Soviet Union abandoned its patronage of Middle Eastern states. Radical Middle Eastern states—Syria, Iraq, Libya, and Iran—were all increasingly isolated and left without major military patrons and suppliers. The moderate Arab states have increasingly moved toward accommodation with the United States and Israel, as witnessed by the 1991 Arab-U.S. alliance against Iraq and the Arab-Israeli peace talks. In the long run, the increasing isolation of the radical Arab states may lead to gradual reduction in tensions in the region, and possibly eventual partial demilitarization.

Characteristics of the Modern Middle East

GOVERNMENTS IN THE MIDDLE EAST

The modern Middle East has been the home of a variety of types of government. Here we will briefly consider the most prominent types.

Monarchy. Traditionally, most governments in the Islamic Middle East have been monarchies, although frequently with strong informal consultative elements. The major check on authoritarian power came from Islamic ethical and legal precepts that rulers were expected to obey. The major mechanism for removing intolerable or incompetent rulers was a palace coup or a popular revolt. Following World War I, the Arab governments established by the French and British in the Middle East were all constitutional monarchies. Today monarchies remain in Jordan, Kuwait, the Arab Emirates, Saudi Arabia, and Morocco. For the most part these rulers can be seen as benevolent despots, who provide their people with a wide range of social benefits, while limiting their participation in government. Most of these monarchies have come under increasing criticism from both the Islamic fundamentalist movements and groups attempting to bring about Western-style democratic and liberal reforms.

Military Dictatorship. Throughout the 1950s and early 1960s, a series of military coups took place, removing many Middle Eastern monarchs from their thrones (Egypt, 1952; Yemen, 1962; Libya, 1969; Iran, 1979). Without exception these countries, as well as Syria and Iraq, were ruled by military dictators, although with varying degrees of both popular support and pseudo-democratic institutions. The lack of legitimate mechanisms for dissent and social change, as well as the inability of Middle Eastern governments to defeat Israel and resist Western interference in the region, has created a widespread problem of terrorism.

Democracy. Until recent years in Egypt and Turkey, although fledgling democracies existed in the Middle East, no country in the region could be said to be truly democratic. Nearly all states have parliaments, which for the most part are mere rubber stamps to approve government policy. True freedom of the press is rarely seen. The social tensions in the region seem to be so volatile that free and open debate and elections are widely seen by the ruling elites as extremely dangerous. Nonetheless, slow progress toward establishing human rights and democratic political institutions is being made in some countries.

NATIONALISM IN THE MIDDLE EAST

Traditionally, community loyalties in the Middle East centered around kinship groups (tribes), cities, or religious affiliations. The Ottoman sultans had developed a system of regional government known as the *millet* system.

As long as they paid their taxes and remained loyal to the sultan, tribal, urban, or religious communities were allowed to maintain a large degree of self-government in internal matters.

This social structure began to break down in the mid-nineteenth century when the European idea of nationalism—that each ethnic or linguistic group should form an independent nation—was introduced into the Middle East. The Middle East in the nineteenth century was a patchwork of divergent ethnic groups including Arabs, Turks, Iranians, Kurds, Armenians, and Jews. During the late nineteenth and twentieth centuries each of these groups sought to form their own nation states, independent of both the Ottoman sultans and European overlords. In each case these nationalistic efforts have led to extended wars or conflicts.

Arab Nationalism. Arab nationalism was divided into two conflicting forms. The first, pan-Arabism, was represented by an attempt to unite all Arab-speaking peoples into a single state. Pan-Arabism was manifested during the Arab Revolt of World War I, with its goal of uniting Arabia, Syria, Palestine, and Iraq into a single Arab state. The British and French, however, preferred to keep the Arabs divided into small countries as part of a "divide and conquer" strategy.

Theoretical movement toward the creation of a single Arab state began in 1945 with the creation of the Arab League. Practically, however, the Arabs themselves faced a major problem in attempting to create a single, united Arab state. Although most could agree that such a state was desirable, there was no agreement as to who should be the leader, nor on the principles on which the state would be founded. The most successful advocate of pan-Arabism was Nasser of Egypt, whose charismatic personality and bold rhetoric temporarily created a loose confederation of Egypt, Syria, Yemen, and Libya in the late 1950s and early 1960s. His efforts were doomed to failure, both because of internal tensions between Arab states and because of opposition from the superpowers.

The second form of Arab nationalism centered around the smaller states formed by the Europeans following World War I. Here, Iraqis, Syrians, Palestinians, and Egyptians, although all ethnically Arabs, began to see themselves as separate peoples. The importance of pan-Arabism in the Middle East has thus diminished considerably today.

Turkish Nationalism. For centuries the Ottoman empire was conceived of in non-ethnic terms. The *devshirme* system insured that members of all ethnic groups were included in the military and ruling classes. The unity of the empire was based on Islam, loyalty to the sultan, and on a shared set of cultural values. As the Ottoman empire began to disintegrate in the nineteenth century, many Turks began to view their state as fundamentally Turkish rather than Islamic, as was manifested in Turkish persecution of Armenians, Kurds, and Greeks. After the defeat of the Ottomans in 1918, the sultan was deposed and the Turks were stripped of their non-Turkish provinces. Following an exchange of Greek and Turkish minorities after a war with the Greeks from 1920 to 1923, the modern nation-state of Turkey was born. A related idea was the pan-Turkish movement, aiming at the unification of all Turks in the world into a single state. The fall of the Soviet Union and the independence of Central Eurasian Turkish states such as Azerbaijan, Turkestan, Uzbekistan, and Kazakhstan has again raised the issue of pan-Turkish unity.

Kurds and Armenians. Kurdish Muslim and Armenian Christian minorities also aspired to attain their own nation-states. Both peoples were viewed as a threat to the Ottoman and Iranian states, and their nationalistic movements were ruthlessly suppressed. Hundreds of thousands of Armenians were massacred by the Turks (1905), while it was forbidden to study Kurdish in schools. Although initially crushed, the Armenian and Kurdish nationalistic aspirations have continued until the present. With the breakup of the Soviet Union, a small state of Armenia has been created, while the Kurds have attempted to form their own state in the wake of Iraq's defeat by the United Nations in the Gulf War in 1991.

ZIONISM: JEWISH NATIONALISM

Although the Zionist movement stemmed from intellectual, social, and political developments in Europe, it has been played out in the Middle East, becoming one of the most complex and intractable issues of the region. In the late nineteenth century European Jews, affected by ideas of nationalism and worried by rising European anti-Semitism, increasingly looked for an opportunity to create an independent Jewish state. Although several alternatives were suggested, attention focused on creating a Jewish state in the Ottoman province of Palestine, which had been the Jewish kingdom of Judea under the Roman empire some 2,000 years earlier. For many decades only a trickle of Jews immigrated to their potential new homeland.

Immigration. Following World War I, the British established an ambiguous policy that both encouraged Jewish immigration to Palestine, while at the same time limiting such immigration. Ultimately, the rise of violent anti-Semitism in Europe in the 1920s and 1930s convinced many Jews that their only hope for safety was in the creation of an independent Jewish state. The horrors of the Holocaust confirmed this idea for hundreds of thousands who poured into Palestine during and after World War II.

The State of Israel. Social tensions between the new Jewish immigrants and the local Palestinians steadily mounted throughout the early twentieth century. These tensions culminated in riots and unrest in the 1930s, which led the British to decide to abandon their mandate in Palestine and turn the problem over to the newly formed United Nations. The UN decided that

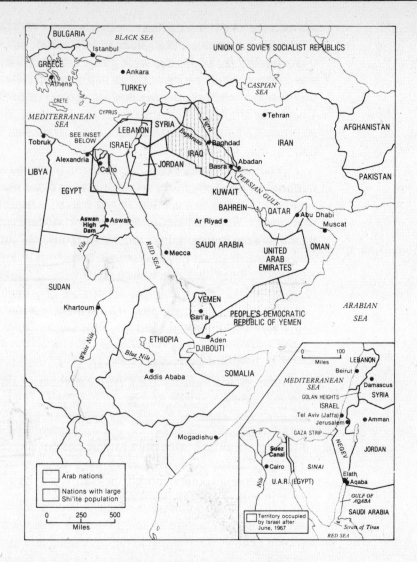

Fig. 20.2   The Modern Middle East

partition of Palestine was the only workable solution; neither side accepted it, and war broke out in 1948 when the state of Israel was officially born.

In the half-century since its creation, Israel has been at the heart of a bloody conflict manifesting itself on many levels: full-scale wars, guerrilla actions, terrorism, riots, oppression, torture, and innumerable violations of human rights. Many Arab states came to the military aid of the Palestinians in the 1967 and 1973 wars but were unable to defeat Israel. Israel's possession of a large nuclear arsenal, however, made it unlikely that the Arabs would achieve their goals through military means. Pragmatists on both sides, though not necessarily in the majority, began to realize that the Arabs and

Israelis needed to create some mechanism by which they could live together. Through the decades, both sides in the conflict had reasonable claims and grievances, and both sides were guilty of horrendous atrocities. The initiation of serious peace negotiations in the early 1990s created an atmosphere of guarded optimism that the Arab-Israeli conflict might eventually reach a solution.

Economic Developments

OIL

The fundamental economic factor in the Middle East in the twentieth century was the discovery and exploitation of oil resources. Exploitation of the oil resources of the Middle East began at the turn of the century as oil became increasingly important, first for modernization of naval engines, then for land transportation, mobile weapons, and aircraft. Initially Western oil companies were giving special concessions in Middle Eastern countries in return for giving the governments a percentage of the revenues. The importance of oil in global economies and military systems expanded exponentially in the early twentieth century, leading to the creation in 1928 of a cartel over Middle Eastern oil production by seven Western oil companies, known as the Seven Sisters. The real oil boom occurred after World War II, when the percentage of world oil production from the Middle East steadily increased, and when Middle Eastern countries began to nationalize the previously Western-owned oil companies. In 1973 a massive oil embargo showed the world the economic and political power of the Middle Eastern states which controlled the oil. Today, nearly two-thirds of the oil used by the Western allies comes from Middle Eastern sources. This dependence on Middle Eastern oil is frequently used as a powerful lever to influence Western foreign policy. Indeed, the Gulf War of 1991 was fought fundamentally to ensure unhindered Western access to Middle Eastern oil.

EFFECTS OF OIL WEALTH

The economic effects of oil have been staggering. Many regions of the Middle East have been transformed in a single generation from agrarian and nomadic tribal societies to some of the wealthiest and most modern urban societies in the world. Middle Eastern oil wealth has become a fundamental factor in the global economy. The economic benefits of improved health care, housing, social services, infrastructure, and education have been enormous. However, there have been several problems related to the rise in oil wealth.

Uneven Distribution. First, oil is unevenly distributed throughout the Middle East. This effectively means that the countries with the largest populations and greatest need for economic benefits from oil have the smallest oil resources. Arabia, with a relatively small indigenous population, has perhaps a quarter of the world's oil resources. Egypt, with nearly 60 million people living in the narrow Nile valley, has little oil. This uneven distribution of oil has led to numerous disputes and occasional wars. Iraq invaded Iran (1980) and Kuwait (1990) in order to conquer oil fields in those countries.

Even within countries possessing abundant oil reserves, however, the benefits from oil have been unevenly distributed. Furthermore, the unstable political situation in the Middle East, both internally and externally, has created a desire for massive militarization. Thus much of the oil wealth of the Middle East has been spent buying arms from the West. The ruling elites tend to enrich themselves from oil revenues; indeed, many ruling families in the Middle East treat the oil resources of their countries as if they were the private wealth of the individual ruling family.

Rich vs. Poor. The uneven distribution of oil wealth among Middle Eastern countries, combined with the concentration of wealth in the hands of a limited few, has created a vast economic imbalance in the Middle East. Kuwait, for example, has one of the highest per capita incomes in the world, while Egypt has one of the lowest. The majority of people in many Middle Eastern countries live lives of marginal or extreme poverty. In recent years the situation seems to be slowly improving with the growth of a middle class of small businessmen and professionals. The educated professional classes in the Middle East are growing but still represent only a small percentage of the population when compared with the mass of unskilled, semi-educated urban laborers and villagers. The huge gap between rich and poor people and countries in the Middle East remains a serious social and political problem.

URBANIZATION

An associated difficulty facing the Middle East has been uncontrolled urbanization. Major cities in the oil-poor Middle Eastern countries have become huge sprawling ghettos. Villagers facing overpopulation and limited agricultural land often flock to the cities seeking work. This massive influx of unskilled laborers creates huge slums of abysmal poverty. Basic resources such as clean water, power, health care, housing, education, and transportation are in short supply or nonexistent. As conditions worsen, the unfulfilled needs and dreams of the urban poor become a major potential social and political problem.

New Ideas in the Middle East

SOCIALISM

A large number of Western philosophical and social ideas have had an impact on Middle Eastern societies. The tremendous impact of the Western idea of nationalism has been discussed above. Although most Middle Eastern states rejected the European idea of communism, socialism played an important role in the post-monarchical military dictatorships. "Arab

Socialism" was widely used to legitimize dictatorial state policies in Iraq, Syria, Egypt, and Libya. These states have recently moderated their previous socialist rhetoric to some extent, while Egypt is increasingly turning to a market economy.

MODERNIZATION

One of the goals of nearly all Middle Eastern countries is modernization—the adoption of Western technology, industry, and some types of social organization. Efforts have been made to adopt Western technologies, modernizing agriculture, manufacturing, industry, trade, banking, communications, the military, transportation, education, government, and medicine. A great deal of success has been achieved, and indeed all types of Western technologies can now be found throughout the Middle East. Unfortunately, the impact of these technologies has often been somewhat superficial, being strongest among the elite and in the large cities. The poor urban dwellers and villagers often see little of the benefits from modernization. Thus, the technological gap between the Middle East and West, as well as between the upper and lower classes within the Middle East, remains significant.

ANTI-WESTERNISM

For many Middle Easterners, the promises of modernization, prosperity, democracy, and civil rights have never been realized. Instead they find an increasing technological dependence on the West, a huge gap between rich and poor, forms of democracy hiding the reality of dictatorship, and the suppression of individual freedom and rights in the name of security. Many Middle Easterners feel that, for them at least, the results of modernization are not an unequivocal good. All accept the benefits of modern technology; many, however, reject the ideological, social, and political elements of modernization. Furthermore, many in the Middle East see the West as being solely concerned with their oil. For all their talk of human rights and democracy, Western powers are seen as being hypocritical in their willingness to deal with any tyrant who will sell them oil.

ISLAMIC FUNDAMENTALISM

Another important issue facing the Middle East is the question of secularization. For thousands of years the fabric of Middle Eastern society has been bound together by religious laws and values. For the West, the separation of church and state has been a mechanism to limit the religious civil strife that plagued Europe during the century of the Reformation and the subsequent wars of religion. Many Muslims, however, believe that Islam cannot be fully lived without the institution of traditional Islamic law, the shari'a; governments must be Islamic, not secular. Those Muslims who seek to establish the shari'a as the official law are often known as Islamic fundamentalists. Their basic goal is that all Middle Eastern societies should be firmly grounded on Islamic ideas and practices, rather than secularized Western concepts and laws. (There is a similar important Jewish fundamentalist movement in Israel, which sees the Jewish Talmud as the basis for a just society in Israel.)

Islamic fundamentalism has been an important part of Middle Eastern society since the coming of Islam. It has witnessed a remarkable rebirth in recent decades, especially following the successful Islamic revolution in Iran in 1979. All Middle Eastern states have strong Islamic fundamentalist movements today, although not all are as radical as the Iranian fundamentalists. Indeed, most are quite willing to see their programs instituted by legal and democratic means. Islam will continue to play an important role in Middle Eastern society for the coming decades. Even the most blatantly secularized despots, such as Saddam Hussein in Iraq, have increasingly been forced to adopt the trappings of religious terminology and practices in an attempt to legitimize their regimes.

Muslim fundamentalists have a natural antipathy to the West, whose ideologies are seen as non-Muslim at best, and often completely secular and anti-Muslim. One of the major challenges facing Western policymakers will be dealing effectively with Islamic states and movements in the Middle East in order to prevent those movements from becoming increasingly radicalized and anti-Western.

Recent Regional Developments

The complex histories of each of the numerous states in the Middle East cannot be discussed in detail. Only brief synopses of the major developments in some of the major countries can be provided here.

EGYPT

Egypt remained a British protectorate from 1882 until 1946. During this period a great deal of modernization occurred, as well as the introduction of some democratic institutions. In 1952 a military coup overthrew King Farouk, leading to the eventual usurpation of power by Gamal Abdel Nasser, who ruled Egypt until his death in 1970. Nasser was the most important Arab leader throughout these two decades, following policies of alliance with the Soviets, socialism, radical modernization, pan-Arabism, and anti-Zionism. Egypt played a leading role in the Arab-Israeli conflict in 1967. Following Nasser's death, Anwar el-Sadat became president, leading Egypt to more liberal social and economic policies and closer ties with the West. Following the 1973 war with Israel, Sadat shifted policies and made a separate peace with Israel in 1979, paving the way for greatly improved relations with the West. Although facing severe and as-yet-unresolved internal problems of poverty and overpopulation, Egypt remained the leading cultural and intellectual center in the Middle East throughout the twentieth century and has become one of the United States' staunchest allies in the region.

SYRIA AND LEBANON

Syria was created as a French mandate territory following World War I. The boundaries of Lebanon were established specifically to create a coastal country in which the pro-French Christians would be in the majority. This has led to numerous factional problems in Lebanon, culminating in the Lebanese civil war from 1975–1990 and the de facto Syrian occupation of much of Lebanon in the late 1980s. Syrians as a whole were not happy with French rule in the 1920s and 1930s. When France fell in World War II, the Free French troops were no longer able to control the situation, and Syria was granted independence. French attempts to maintain influence in the late 1940s were unsuccessful, while Syria itself underwent a decade of political anarchy and coups. The situation was stabilized only in 1964 with the establishment of a military dictatorship by the Baath Party. Since then Syria has remained one of the more radical Middle Eastern states. The military dictatorship of Hafez el-Assad was established in 1970, with a pro-Soviet, and violently anti-Israel policy. Syria's recent isolation from the moderate Arabs, the collapse of their patron, the Soviet Union, and their increasing fear of Iraq has led to some moderation in Syria's policy.

IRAQ

Britain established a pro-British monarchy in Iraq following World War I; Iraq continued on a relatively conservative pro-Western course until 1958, when a military coup overthrew the monarchy, establishing a military dictatorship. The military dictators generally followed nationalistic, pan-Arab, socialistic, and pro-Soviet policies. Their share of oil wealth allowed the Iraqis to build a huge army during the 1960s and 1970s. A coup by the Baath Party in 1968 led to the eventual rise to power of Saddam Hussein, who has followed a policy of military adventurism. Taking advantage of the revolution in Iran in 1979, he invaded Iran in 1980, attempting to annex the Iranian oil fields. The result was an indecisive nine-year war, one of the bloodiest since World War II. Shortly after this war ended, Saddam attempted to annex Kuwait but was expelled by a massive United Nations force in the Gulf War (1990–1991). Although Saddam remains in power in Iraq, Kurdish separatists and Shi'ite rebels, as well as widespread disaffection in the country, make Iraq's future uncertain.

IRAN

Until the 1979 revolution, Iran was seen as one of the more progressive and pro-Western countries in the Middle East. Ruled by a seemingly enlightened monarch, Shah Muhammad Reza Pahlavi (r. 1941–1979), Iran was thought to be a model of economic progress and modernization. However, the thinly veiled tyranny and absolutism of the Shah created widespread disaffection among Iranians, which culminated in the Iranian fundamentalist Islamic revolution of 1979 under the leadership of Ayatollah Khomeini. The sweeping social, governmental, legal, educational, and religious changes brought about by the revolution were accompanied by isolation from Western support because a fundamental Iranian policy has been the export of their Islamic revolution. Pro-Iranian Islamic fundamentalist factions have appeared in Lebanon, Iraq, Afghanistan, and in some portions of Arabia, creating extensive tensions between Iran and its Middle Eastern neighbors. Although the bloody and costly war with Iraq (1980–1989) seriously weakened Iran's economic and military power, Iran's position as the leader of radical Islamic fundamentalism makes it an important player in the current complex political situation in the Middle East.

ISRAEL AND PALESTINE

Since its creation in 1948, Israel has remained at the center of controversy in the Middle East. Having fought a major war with its Arab neighbors each decade, Israel's relations with the Arab states are only now slowly beginning to improve. The most militarized and powerful state in the Middle East, Israel's existence has nonetheless been in part dependent on its strong alliance with the United States. Israel's victories in the 1947 and 1967 wars created a major refugee problem and left hundreds of thousands of Palestinian Arabs living under Israeli military occupation. In the past twenty-five years, the Palestinians have become an increasing source of anguish for Israelis, both because of terrorism and guerrilla attacks on Israel and because of Israel's increasingly tyrannical treatment of the Palestinians. The recent opening of peace talks holds some hope for an eventual solution to the Palestinian question.

ARABIA

The history of the Arabian peninsula in the twentieth century was dominated by two factors: the power of Saudi Arabia and the wealth from oil. The Saudi kingdom in Arabia derives from the fundamentalist Saud bedouin family which ousted the pro-British Hussein clan in 1926. Since then, Saudi Arabia's central position in Arabia and its vast oil resources have made it a major power in the Middle East. A bastion of conservative and monarchical powers, Saudi Arabia has led the coalition of the oil-rich Arab emirates in pragmatic relations with the West. Today Saudi Arabia is a major ally of the United States; it was the staging ground for the U.S.-led war against Iraqi leader Saddam Hussein in 1990 and 1991.

In India, the combination of old religious and social traditions with the new institutions of a democratic republic has produced turbulence and tension. But India remains an extremely important state, not only in South Asia, but for the future of the world. The country's ability to deal with its continuing economic problems and social pressures while still maintaining the viability of its democracy will largely determine its future.

The Middle East has had an increasingly visible impact on the world, largely through its oil production. But oil wealth has also become an added element in the rivalries within the Middle East, exacerbating existing tensions and creating new ones. The added challenges of a revival of Islamic fundamentalism and the continuing antagonism between Arab states and Israel point to an unpredictable future.

Selected Readings

Bickerton, Ian J., and Carla L. Klausner. *A Concise History of the Arab-Israeli Conflict*. Englewood Cliffs, NJ: Prentice-Hall, 1991.

Brown, W. Norman. *The United States and India and Pakistan*. Revised and enlarged edition. Cambridge, MA: Harvard University Press, 1963.

Fisher, Sydney Nettleton, and William Ochsenwald. *The Middle East: A History*. 4th ed. New York: McGraw-Hill, 1990.

Hourani, Albert. *A History of the Arab Peoples*. Cambridge, MA: The Belknap Press of Harvard University Press, 1991.

Lapidus, Ira M. *A History of Islamic Societies*. Cambridge and New York: Cambridge University Press, 1988.

Lapierre, Dominique. *The City of Joy*. Garden City, NY: Doubleday, 1985.

Lenczowski, George. *The Middle East in World Affairs*. 4th ed. Ithaca, NY: Cornell University Press, 1980.

Naipaul, V. S. *India: A Wounded Civilization*. New York: Knopf, 1977.

Vatikiotis, P. J. *The History of Egypt: From Muhammad Ali to Mubarak*. 4th ed. Baltimore: Johns Hopkins University Press, 1991.

Wolpert, Stanley. *A New History of India*. 3rd ed. Oxford: Oxford University Press, 1989.

21

Sub-Saharan Africa

1913	Land Law passed in South Africa
1947	Kwame Nkrumah returns to Ghana
1957	Ghana becomes independent
1958	Charles de Gaulle's "French Commonwealth" proposal
	Guinea votes against French Commonwealth
1960	Sixteen new independent African states
	UN troops sent to Republic of the Congo
1965	Mobutu's coup in Republic of the Congo
1966	Military coup in Ghana; Nkrumah ousted from power
1967–1970	Biafran War
1984	Desmond Tutu of South Africa awarded Nobel Peace Prize
1985–1989	State of emergency in South Africa
1990	Nelson Mandela released from South African prison

Africa in 1990 was a diverse continent of approximately 660 million people. This is 12 percent of the world's population, but Africa accounts for only about 1 percent of the world's industrial production. The economy of Africa is based largely on agriculture. Africa consists of over fifty independent countries, but there are literally hundreds of tribal and cultural groupings throughout the continent, making many national boundaries seem largely artificial. In addition, over 1,000 languages are spoken in Africa (in addition to European languages).

Africa has the highest fertility rate in the world. This, combined with improved health care, has led to a sizable population growth since World War II. But because agricultural production has not experienced a comparable rise, per capita consumption has declined in many areas. It has been estimated that as much as forty percent of Africa's population suffers from some degree of malnutrition and the diseases that result from this affliction.

Three of the most prominent themes of world history since the end of World War II have been decolonization, interdependence, and the development of the so-called Third World. Nowhere are these themes more obvious than in the history of Africa. In this chapter we will only be able to touch on a few aspects of post-war African history, but the problems mentioned here will help illuminate a variety of other problems.

THE END OF COLONIAL RULE

Independence movements in Africa gained momentum after World War II. Among the reasons for this was the sight of European colonial powers fighting against one another with great ferocity during the war, revealing their animosity toward one another. A united colonial front could not be maintained in Africa, nor was there universal agreement on the continued desirability of maintaining colonies. Two countries—Britain and France—held the majority of the colonial possessions in Africa. This chapter will therefore focus on the states that achieved liberation from those two powers.

Programs for Independence

There were many approaches to the question of independence, both in Europe and within individual African states.

LEGISLATIVE REFORMS: SOME EXAMPLES

Before momentum for complete independence reached its full force, for example, a number of reforms affected the status of French African colonies. In 1950, the Second *Loi Lamine Guèye* provided Africans with work and pay opportunities equal with those of Europeans working in the African civil service. Two years later, the Overseas Labor Code expanded labor rights for African workers, again bringing them more in line with privileges enjoyed by European workers.

POLITICAL PARTIES

There were other developments that were more overtly political. In the 1950s, for example, African political parties were created for the first time in French Africa. The *Loi Cadre* (Framework Law), passed in 1956, embodied a new administrative policy for French Africa. The law granted a greater degree of local autonomy, but it was not necessarily designed to be a step on the road to complete independence. This final step was still not official French policy at the time.

BRITISH AFRICA

British Africa moved more consistently in the direction of independence after World War II. In addition to providing funds for improvements in its African possessions, the British government worked to provide more positions within the civil service for Africans and to equalize pay and working conditions between African and European employees.

By the 1950s the British government was generally convinced that the destiny of African territories properly lay in the hands of Africans themselves. The British had both their own experience in India and the experience of other European powers elsewhere (most notably France in Indochina) to provide them with examples of what could happen if they were to continue to force European rule on their colonies. A serious difficulty, however, was the fact that regardless of how convinced European powers might be of the inevitability of independence, colonial rule was essentially authoritarian. In other words, it did not go a long way toward teaching principles of democratic self-rule. This problem would plague African states long after they became independent.

The pace of "Africanization" was the major remaining question for European powers. The agitation of activist political parties, such as Kwame Nkrumah's Convention People's Party in the Gold Coast (later Ghana), accelerated the pace of change. Gradual transference of power from Britain to individual African states generally went smoothly. The primary exceptions were in areas with a significant—though minority—white population. In Kenya, the majority Africans were left in control of the government, but in Northern and Southern Rhodesia the determination of the minority white population caused bitterness and dissension on the part of the African majority. Eventually the former Central African Federation (made up of Nyasaland, Northern Rhodesia, and Southern Rhodesia) gave way to the independent states of Malawi and Zambia in 1964, though white rule remained in Southern Rhodesia until it achieved independence as Zimbabwe in 1980.

Independence, then, proceeded at different rates in different regions, though generally the pace of independence and development was more rapid in British colonies than in French colonies. As was the case in Indochina, the French seemed more determined to hold on to their African possessions, but they also eventually had to acknowledge the irresistible momentum of independence movements and take their leave of Africa. Portugal and

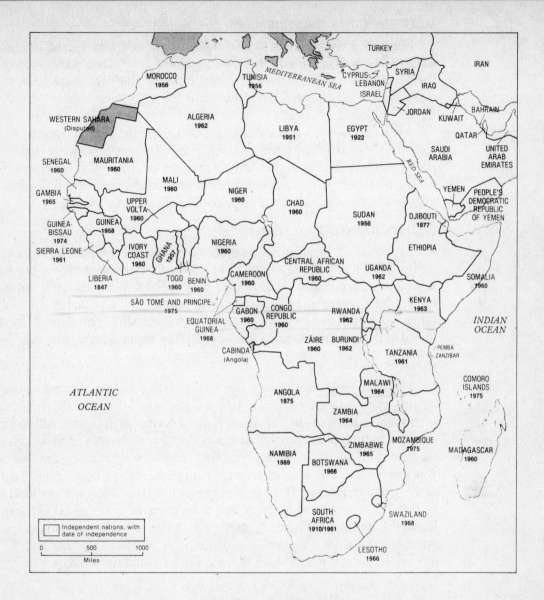

Fig. 21.1   Africa in 1990

Belgium, though they held relatively few colonies in Africa, were the least sympathetic to the desire for independence and also did the least to prepare the native population and economy for the trials of independent statehood.

Problems Facing Emergent Nation-States

Independence was not the cure for all African problems. The states that emerged from postwar decolonization have experienced a number of serious difficulties, some of them the results of colonialism, others inherent in the process of nation building.

MULTIETHNICITY AND TRIBALISM

Multiethnicity continues to be a challenge for many states, and it often stands in the way of the achievement of national unity. Time and resources spent in ethnic wrangling have detracted from the ability of some states to modernize their economies. Ethnic strife has also been used to justify repressive political systems.

Another problem has been tribalism. Whatever the official name of the state, tribal groupings are often more accurate reflections of people's primary political loyalty and cultural identity. Again, the existence of tribal diversity has often been used as an excuse for the elimination of democratic institutions in favor of one or another form of authoritarianism or dictatorship.

ECONOMIC MODERNIZATION

Economic modernization has proceeded at an uneven pace in postwar Africa. This was partly a result of the problems mentioned above, but in some places could also be attributed to a lack of resources, civil strife, inadequate transportation networks, or a lack of training under colonial rulers. And even as economic modernization was slow, populations continued to rise, adding to the difficulties faced by many African states.

LEADERSHIP STYLES

Though specific details vary from state to state, independence in many African states was characterized by the leadership of charismatic figures, such as Jomo Kenyatta in Kenya and Kwame Nkrumah in Ghana. Although attempts to form parliamentary democracies have met with varied success, the demise of such institutions has often been accompanied by the emergence of military rule or other forms of nonrepresentative dictatorship. Two of the most egregious and infamous examples have been Idi Amin in Uganda in the 1970s and Colonel Jean Bedel Bokassa of the Central African Republic, who in 1977 brazenly changed the name of his state to the Central African Empire and crowned himself Emperor Bokassa. Stability and democracy are ideals that African states are still attempting to balance.

INDEPENDENT AFRICA: SOME CASE STUDIES

After the independence of Ghana in 1957 (see below), independence for other African states followed rapidly. Guinea became independent of French control in 1958, but 1960 was the year the floodgates burst open. In that year alone, sixteen former British, French, and Belgian colonies became independent states. During the rest of the 1960s, fourteen more colonies followed the path to independent statehood, leaving only a relatively small number of independence questions to be resolved. Having briefly discussed some of the general issues surrounding African independence, we turn our attention now to a more specific examination of certain aspects of the postwar history of former European colonies in Africa.

French Africa and the Belgian Congo

As was mentioned earlier, the French attempted to hold on to their colonial possessions in Africa and elsewhere for as long as possible after World War II. Though this did not always produce war in Africa, as it did in Indochina, it did mean that in French Africa decolonization was not as smooth as it was in British Africa. And in the case of the former Belgian Congo (now Zaire), the end of colonial rule was an agonizing affair.

DE GAULLE'S "FRENCH COMMONWEALTH" DESIGN

Independence for French Africa picked up speed in 1960, when several former French colonies emerged as independent states. The way for this was paved in 1958, when Charles de Gaulle came to power in France. Knowing that many members of the African educated elite would not favor immediate independence and the severing of their ties with France, and hoping to stem the tide of African nationalism, the French president proposed the creation of a "French Commonwealth" in Africa. Referendums were to be carried out in each French possession to determine whether or not such an arrangement was acceptable.

Sekou Touré. Although many members of French Africa's elite were moderate and willing to continue their ties with France, there was a strong undercurrent of nationalism which came to the surface after 1958 under the leadership of Sekou Touré. Touré had earlier been one of the founders of the *Rassemblement Démocratique Africain*, an African political party with members in several French territories, and in 1952 became the secretary-general of its affiliate, the *Parti Démocratique de Guinée* (PDG). In alliance with the trade union movement in Guinea, Touré propelled the PDG into a position of dominance by the late 1950s and began to agitate against colonialism. When the referendum on de Gaulle's proposed Commonwealth was held in September 1958, the vote in Guinea went against the proposal by a nearly twenty-to-one margin. Fuming French authorities immediately ordered home all their civil servants, professionals, and equipment. But the nation survived, declaring itself independent on October 2, 1958, and naming Touré head of state.

Momentum for Independence. Though Guinea was the only French possession to vote for independence in 1958, other territories were not far behind in demanding their own independence. In 1960 alone, Burkina Faso (then known as Upper Volta), the Central African Republic, Chad, Congo (not to be confused with Belgian Congo), Gabon, Ivory Coast, Madagascar, Mali, Mauritania, Niger, and Senegal all became independent from French rule. They generally maintained ties with France, however, and some of them continued to be economically or militarily dependent on France to one degree or another.

THE BELGIAN CONGO

Belgian Rule. The Belgian Congo (now Zaire) also became independent in 1960, but not easily or smoothly. The Belgian government had been extremely paternalistic and was very slow in integrating native Africans into the colonial political system. Belgian attention was focused almost exclusively on economic exploitation. In addition, the Congo was riddled with tribal hostilities, a problem which the government did little to address. By 1959, Belgium's sole African possession was plagued by unrest, rioting, and calls for independence. In response, the government suddenly announced that a conference on independence would be held in Brussels in January 1960. In surprisingly quick fashion, independence was granted to the Republic of the Congo on June 30, 1960.

The Agony of Tribalism. But creation of a nation out of the mix of tribal groupings that had been the Belgian Congo was more easily said than done. Disorder bordering on anarchy followed formal independence. Tribal disputes and an army mutiny made the early months of independence extraordinarily turbulent. The government of the infant nation was soon forced to call in United Nations forces—numbering over 19,000 by the end of the year—to maintain order. The UN troops left on June 30, 1964—the fourth anniversary of Congolese independence—but the republic was still not secure. In 1965 General Joseph Mobutu took power in a military coup.

British Africa in Transition

THE ADVANTAGES OF BRITAIN'S PROGRAM OF "ENLIGHTENED RULE"

As was mentioned above, Britain generally followed a program of what might be called "enlightened rule" in Africa. To a greater degree than France, Belgium, or Portugal, Britain tended to foster the participation of Africans in colonial administration after World War II. This was part of an overall view that independence for African possessions was the ultimate goal of postwar British administration. The advantage for the soon-to-be-independent states was that there were more Africans in British colonies with Western-style education and administrative experience, though these advantages have not insulated former British colonies from strife and formidable difficulties.

GHANA

In March 1957 Ghana (formerly Gold Coast) became the first British African colony to gain independence. The post-independence history of this West African state illustrates both the promise and the problems of independent Africa.

Kwame Nkrumah. The leader of independence for Ghana was the charismatic Kwame Nkrumah. Educated in the United States, Nkrumah had come under the influence of the personality and writings of such people as Marcus Garvey (the leader of the "Back to Africa" movement), Mahatma Gandhi, Karl Marx, and a variety of socialist and communist thinkers. In 1947, Nkrumah returned to Africa from his time in the United States and Britain. Upon his return, he became general secretary of the United Gold Coast Convention (UGCC), the first real political vehicle for Africans in that country. His efforts to turn the UGCC into a mass political party soon lead to the creation of Nkrumah's Convention People's Party (CPP). Nkrumah began to use this party—of which he was the head—to agitate strongly by means of strikes and other demonstrations for independence from British rule.

The Birth of Ghana. In elections held in 1951 (during which Nkrumah was in jail because of the earlier disturbances), the CPP soundly defeated the rival UGCC. Released from jail, Nkrumah became prime minister of a new government in 1952. Subsequent elections consolidated the CPP's hold on power. Though the Gold Coast was still under British rule, it was clear that independence could not be forestalled much longer. In May 1956 the British government announced that, following elections that year, independence would be granted. Nkrumah's party again won by an overwhelming majority, and Nkrumah announced that on March 6, 1957, the new state—which he renamed Ghana—would be fully independent.

Authoritarianism and Nkrumah's Downfall. Over the next decade, Nkrumah became increasingly authoritarian. The CPP, which had virtually become Nkrumah's personal vehicle for political power, continued to exclude any challengers. There were several attempts on Nkrumah's life during the decade he was in power, none of them successful. But in 1966, while Nkrumah was on an official visit to China, discontented army officers led a revolt that threw the president from power. Despite Nkrumah's promise to return to power, the era of Kwame Nkrumah was over.

Ghana Since Nkrumah. Ghana remained unstable, however, largely due to its massive economic problems. A bloodless military coup in 1972 seemed to offer some stability, but did little to solve Ghana's pressing problems. Inflation soared out of control, reaching an estimated annual rate of 30 percent by 1978, and 200 percent a year later. A new constitution was ratified in 1979 but was suspended two years later by command of Flight Lieutenant Jerry John Rawlings, chairman of the Provisional National Defense Council and de facto head of state. Elections were thus eliminated. After 1983, Rawlings's government embarked on a program to rebuild the economy of Ghana—an economy that relied largely on foreign aid and on exports of cocoa, gold, and timber. But by 1991, the combination of

authoritarian government and inflation still estimated at roughly 50 percent left an uncertain future for Ghana's 16 million inhabitants.

NIGERIA AND THE PAINFUL SEARCH FOR UNITY

The case of Nigeria demonstrates how the granting of independent "nationhood" can mask internal problems that make unity extremely difficult—in fact, even if not in name. Nigeria was one of the flood of nations to gain independence in 1960.

Tribal Conflict. But independence did nothing to resolve longstanding tribal and cultural conflicts. Because their homeland was the center of British rule, the Ibo of the southern and coastal areas generally enjoyed the advantages of British rule to a greater degree than their rivals, the northern Hausa. The 1960s saw continued animosity and fighting between the two groups. In 1967, the Ibo went so far as to declare the area east of the Niger River independent, renaming it Biafra. This was the beginning of a three-year nightmare of civil war, after which Biafra was reincorporated into Nigeria.

Nigeria Today. With its substantial oil reserves, Nigeria has a potential to make significant economic progress not shared by most African countries. But despite the fact that it is Africa's leading oil-producing country, Nigeria is still poor, with a 1990 per capita gross national product estimated at $230. During the oil boom of the 1980s there was a temporary rise in the standard of living, but the standard has continued to fall since then. Politically, Nigeria has fluctuated between civil and military governments. Civil government was restored in 1979, but late in 1983 it was replaced by a military government, which remained into the 1990s. But the diversity of tribal and cultural groups has continued to be one of the biggest obstacles to political and social stability, as Nigeria's population of over 120 million is divided into Hausa, Fulani, Ibo, Yoruba, and at least 250 other tribal groups.

South Africa

African possessions that were not simply ruled by Europeans but in which a sizable (though distinctly minority) white population settled permanently presented a different set of problems after World War II. The Republic of South Africa provides a good example of this.

THE VICTORY OF AFRIKANER NATIONALISM

Before the end of World War II, the real struggle in South Africa was between the Afrikaners—descendants of Dutch settlers who had come as early as the sixteenth century—and later British colonists. The British defeated the Dutch descendants (Boers) in battle, but after the Union of South Africa became a self-governing member of the Commonwealth in

1910, the Afrikaners were able to undercut the British and monopolize political power from that time until the present.

APARTHEID

Having wrested political control from their British rivals, the Afrikaners were not about to allow threats to their position from any other source. They therefore pursued a policy of racial separation known as *apartheid*—one of the most visible symbols of the legacy of European settlement and colonial rule. The black majority was denied political participation and equal economic opportunity. They were excluded from the best land in the country, instead being assigned areas known as "reserves" or, later, "homelands," but these lands were inferior and kept the black majority in a state of poverty and subservience. Though the white majority claimed that such a system would preserve the cultures of all groups and allow them to develop simultaneously but separately, the fact that all political and economic power was in the hands of a small white minority demonstrated that in fact apartheid was the racial manifestation of Afrikaner nationalism.

BLACK RESISTANCE MOVEMENTS

Black resistance to white domination began early in the twentieth century, though many of its early leaders were moderate. The main vehicle for black resistance, the African National Congress (ANC), was originally founded to oppose the Land Act of 1913, which limited black ownership to land in the inferior (and small) reserves. Black opposition became increasingly vocal, with strikes, demonstrations, and other large-scale protests becoming common by the 1950s. The ANC was banned by the South African government and protests were suppressed with increasing harshness, but that did not stop the protests. Rather, resistance began to move from militant nonviolence toward armed struggle. Some resistance leaders left the country to continue their activities abroad, while others stayed in South Africa to continue the underground struggle there. Nelson Mandela, one of the resistance leaders who stayed behind, was arrested and sentenced to life in prison. Another symbol of resistance to white rule, Steven Biko, was arrested in August 1977 for his anti-government activities. He died in custody a month later under suspicious circumstances, and news of his death sparked another wave of protests and violence. This and other incidents focused international attention on South Africa. One expression of opinion in opposition to harsh minority rule came in 1984, when black Anglican Bishop Desmond Tutu was awarded the Nobel Peace Prize for his unswerving but nonviolent opposition to apartheid.

THE 1985 STATE OF EMERGENCY

In response to the rising level of protest and political violence, and in spite of increasing international pressure to carry out political reform that would integrate the black majority into mainstream political and economic life, the South African government in 1985 declared a state of emergency. This made it easier for police to arrest and detain people and gave the police and the army broad powers to suppress dissent. Thousands of people died in political violence over the next five years, as South Africa's international image was increasingly tarnished by the violence and by the severity with which any opposition was suppressed.

THE SLOW DISMANTLING OF APARTHEID

In 1989, Frederik W. de Klerk was elected state president in South Africa. He seemed more inclined than his predecessors to begin reforming apartheid, though still at a slower pace than many black activists would have wished. De Klerk lifted the state of emergency imposed in 1985. He also began discussions with black resistance leaders, including the imprisoned Nelson Mandela. In prison for many years, Mandela had become the leading symbol of black resistance to white rule in South Africa. De Klerk released Mandela from prison in 1990, and Mandela immediately became the chief spokesman—both in South Africa and abroad—for majority rule in his home country.

SOUTH AFRICA TODAY

Whites still monopolize political and economic life in South Africa and benefit disproportionately from South Africa's economy. South Africa has considerable natural resources, two-thirds of its exports coming from minerals such as gold, chromium, platinum, and copper. It is also a major world supplier of diamonds. Roughly 75 percent of its population of 40 million is black, with whites comprising 13 percent and Indians and "coloreds" accounting for 12 percent. South Africa is still racially segregated, but advances toward desegregation have been made in recent years. There are signs—reform legislation, black dissatisfaction, and negative world opinion—that more significant changes may not be far off. But the pace and extent of such changes remain to be seen.

May 31, 1910	South Africa
March 6, 1957	Ghana
October 2, 1958	Guinea
January 1, 1960	Cameroon
April 4, 1960	Senegal
April 27, 1960	Togo

June 26, 1960	Madagascar
June 30, 1960	Zaire
July 1, 1960	Somalia
August 3, 1960	Niger
August 5, 1960	Burkina Faso (formerly Upper Volta)
August 7, 1960	Ivory Coast
August 11, 1960	Chad
August 13, 1960	Central African Republic
August 15, 1960	Congo
August 17, 1960	Gabon
September 22, 1960	Mali
October 1, 1960	Nigeria
November 28, 1960	Mauritania
April 27, 1961	Sierra Leone
December 9, 1961	Tanzania
July 1, 1962	Burundi
July 1, 1962	Rwanda
October 9, 1962	Uganda
December 12, 1963	Kenya
July 6, 1964	Malawi
October 24, 1964	Zambia
February 18, 1965	Gambia
September 30, 1966	Botswana
October 4, 1966	Lesotho
March 12, 1968	Mauritius
September 6, 1968	Swaziland
September 24, 1973	Guinea-Bissau
June 25, 1975	Mozambique
July 6, 1975	Comoros
November 11, 1975	Angola
November 25, 1975	Suriname
June 27, 1977	Djibouti
June 5, 1979	Seychelles
April 18, 1980	Zimbabwe
March 21, 1990	Namibia

Table 21.1   Sub-Saharan Africa: A Chronology of Independence

*T*his *brief survey has only touched on a few of the problems African states have had to face in the modern world. Many others could be cited, including the continuing problem of war (both within and between states) in many regions. Drought and famine have been constant threats in Africa and at times have become so severe that they have been major focuses of world attention. A terrible famine in Somalia in the 1990s, for example, which threatened millions of lives, became the object of a multinational relief effort. Unfortunately, as had happened earlier in other nations, civil war in Somalia prevented many relief supplies from reaching their intended destinations. The people of Somalia therefore suffered from the dual curses of war and famine.*

Africa faces formidable obstacles to modernization: technological and environmental barriers, the continent's disadvantaged position in the world economic structure, and unstable politics. The search for solutions to these problems will continue to challenge Africa's people as well as the world community.

Selected Readings

de St. Jorre, John. *A House Divided*. New York: Carnegie Endowment for International Peace, 1977.

Du Bois, W. E. B. *The World and Africa*. New York: The Viking Press, 1946.

Gailey, Harry A., Jr. *History of Africa. Volume II: From 1800 to Present*. Huntington, NY: Robert E. Krieger, 1981.

Hallett, Robin. *Africa Since 1875: A Modern History*. Ann Arbor: University of Michigan Press, 1974.

July, Robert. *A History of the African People*. 3rd ed. New York: Charles Scribner's Sons, 1980.

Kenyatta, Jomo. *Facing Mount Kenya: The Tribal Life of the Gikuyu*. New York: AMS Press, 1978.

Nkrumah, Kwame. *Ghana*. New York: Thomas Nelson, 1957.

Olaniyan, Richard, ed. *African History and Culture*. Lagos, Nigeria: Longman Nigeria, 1982.

22

Latin America

1910 Mexican Revolution

1929 Institutional Revolutionary Party organized in Mexico

1934 Vargas assumes power in Brazil

1945 Vargas deposed

1946 Peron elected in Argentina

1959 Castro assumes power in Cuba

1970 Allende elected in Chile

1973 Allende overthrown

1976 Peron overthrown

1979 Sandinistas take power in Nicaragua

1990 National elections in Nicaragua replace Sandinistas

*I*t is difficult to make sweeping generalizations about such large areas as Africa, discussed in the previous chapter, or Latin America, discussed below, without being misleading. The histories of individual countries and people were different in many ways, making it essential for students to go beyond the broad textbook summaries presented here if they would truly understand the areas involved. Generalizations are necessary, nevertheless, in order to appreciate the various problems and developments that affected the region as a whole.

The term Latin America refers generally to the Spanish-Portuguese–speaking parts of the Western Hemisphere, i.e., most of Central and South

America and much of the Caribbean. In general, there were several common patterns that characterized the modern history of this region. One was the persistent problem of overpopulation and poverty, which naturally gave rise to continuing and widespread social and economic discontent. This led to regular promises by political leaders of economic and social reform and a variety of efforts in this direction, but little truly fundamental change. The general pattern throughout the twentieth century also included regular and widespread violence in the form of both rebellion and political repression. Behind much, if not most, of the political repression was the military, which was usually attempting to maintain the status quo in the face of threatened social and political change. At times the military was allied with the middle and upper classes, who feared the kind of reform that could undermine their political and economic power. The Latin American economy continued to be characterized, in large part, by neocolonialism as well as by latifundia— the domination of the rural, agricultural population by the owners of large estates. As depressed people continued to search for ways out of poverty, they naturally gave ear to whatever political and economic ideals seemed to promise hope. For that reason many listened to and followed communism, which seemed to offer the best hope for change. To them, history demonstrated that traditional politics simply would not work. This, however, involved them in even broader world struggles as their striving for change caught them up in the Cold War.

THE STRUGGLE AGAINST NEOCOLONIALISM AND LATIFUNDIA

Through most of the twentieth century, Latin American nations continued in a state of economic neocolonialism. Their agrarian economies were largely influenced by investments, and therefore control, from abroad. Even after the economies began to move toward some industrialization, foreign nations became major investors—in some cases owning almost the entire industrial base for particular countries. The major change was simply in the balance. The influence of the United States in the region continued to grow, and that of the Soviet Union increased, both economically and politically. The result was a vastly increasing debt to the United States and other Western nations.

Factors Working Against Change

Several factors made it difficult to change the depressed social and economic conditions that existed in most of the Latin American countries throughout the century.

LATIFUNDIA (GREAT ESTATES)

One was the continuation of latifundia. Even though the portion of population living in rural areas fell below 50 percent, the total number increased. Most remained landless and in poverty. In a way this was ironic. The Latin American economy was built on exports, and in the 1960s over half the total value of these exports came from agriculture, yet the people producing these exports were both landless and in poverty. The best estimates were that 90 percent of the land was owned by 17 percent of the landowners. The most extreme example was Argentina where, in 1950, 2 percent of the landowners owned 60 percent of all the land. At the other extreme, among peasants who held land, some owned plots much too small to sustain themselves. There were other problems, such as highly inefficient agricultural methods and the inherent instability of the agricultural market. The result of all this was not only poverty but also the widespread misery of everything connected with poverty and lack of social response on the part of the wealthy: illiteracy, lack of sanitation, disease of all sorts, and malnutrition. The pattern continued throughout the century and helps to explain why so many peasants were willing to listen to socialist and Marxist schemes for social and economic reform.

Resistance to reform came from politically powerful large landowners, who interpreted all such moves as part of a road toward communism. The rural masses, on the other hand, simply did not have the organization and the power to do anything about the situation. In general, land reform seemed like a good idea to which politicians regularly gave lip service, but few did anything substantial about it.

URBANIZATION

Another factor was an increasing migration to the cities, which quickly swelled urban populations to the point that overcrowding and slums, inhabited by the most poverty-stricken elements of the population, became commonplace. This led to devastating increases in malnutrition and disease in many major cities.

POLITICAL INSTABILITY

Closely connected was continuing political instability and, in fact, a decline in democracy. In some cases socialist governments were established, with the strong support of both the Soviet Union and Cuba and hence with considerable control emanating from those two states. In other cases, as a reaction to communism, authoritarian military regimes took power. In either case, however, there was little economic or social reform that reached down to improve the lives of the poverty-stricken masses. Social and political repression seemed to be the order of the day through most of the late twentieth century. Exceptions included Mexico, Colombia, and Venezuela.

The Mexican Revolution and Subsequent Reform Measures

One nation that made significant strides toward reform was Mexico.

THE REVOLUTION AND THE NEW CONSTITUTION

Reform began with the revolution of 1910 against the dictatorial regime of Porfirio Díaz, who ruled for nearly thirty-five years. The popular uprising finally toppled Díaz in 1911, and its leader, Francisco Madero, assumed the office of president. He was soon overthrown and executed in another military uprising, however, and a new military government was inaugurated under Victorio Huerta. This led to a new round of violence as Pancho Villa and Emiliano Zapata organized dissatisfied peasants and others in an angry uprising against the dictatorship. Among other things, they wanted land redistribution. Huerta was defeated, but then a rich landowner, Venustiano Carranza, took over as president. Carranza had been a part of the revolution, but it was not long before he succeeded in alienating Villa, Zapata, and other leaders. Fighting continued among the revolutionaries themselves until 1917. At that point a new, strongly nationalistic constitution was written. Still another military coup in 1920 overthrew Carranza, but the constitution he promulgated became the permanent basis for the Mexican republic and for reform.

THE PNR

The National Revolutionary Party (PNR) dominated the government in the 1920s. It was ruthless in going about its reform objectives, crushing two military revolts in the process and executing opponents. The party's leader, Plutarco Elias Calles, however, gradually became more conservative in the face of opposition from the church, the military, and labor. His party nevertheless initiated a number of land reforms, though it did not proceed rapidly with land redistribution. It also raised wages for urban workers and increased productivity. With the onset of the Great Depression, however, economic revitalization was clearly threatened.

THE PRI

In 1929 a new party, the Institutional Revolutionary Party (PRI), was organized. It has dominated Mexican politics and government ever since. Beginning in 1934, under newly elected Lazaro Cardenas, the government promoted a more drastic policy of widespread land reform and collective economics. Mexican oil companies (mostly foreign-owned) were nationalized, and Mexican farms became collectives operated by the state.

ECONOMICS: PROGRESS AND PROBLEMS

After 1940 land redistribution was deemphasized, while emphasis was placed on promoting the growth of industry. The result was a rapid rate of economic growth for Mexico, though at the cost of renewing the old pattern of greatly unequal distribution of wealth. The economy went into another decline in the 1960s, but revived in the 1970s as the nation exploited rich oil reserves that had been recently discovered. In the 1980s, however, the decline in the world oil market helped take Mexico into another period of depression. Unfortunately, instead of getting out of debt, and even though in 1985 it signed a fourteen-year debt restructuring agreement, by the end of the decade Mexico's foreign debt was continuing to grow. In addition, its general economy, despite a revival in the oil market, was barely holding its own. Mexico City itself was among the worst examples of the evils of urbanization—pollution, poverty, and living conditions that were often pitiable at best among its teeming lower classes stood in stark contrast to the grand life-style of its wealthy minority. Politically, the significant thing about the second half of the twentieth century is that Mexico was one of the few Latin American nations that carried out its reforms through a democratically elected government. In every case since 1929, however, that government was the PRI.

Reformist Priests and Liberation Theology

The quest for social and economic justice created tension within the Roman Catholic Church as a result of a new movement known as liberation theology. It was inspired partly by the new spirit of brotherhood and ecumenism fostered at the Second Vatican Council (1962–1965), as well as by Pope Paul VI's 1967 encyclical *Populaorum Progressio*. Among other things, this encyclical criticized laissez-faire capitalism and what Paul called the "international imperialism of money." Such sentiment could hardly help but affect reform-minded priests who were all too familiar with the impact of continuing economic imperialism on their parishioners. Their new theology of social reform combined their concerns for the poor with principles of Marxism. The movement was widespread, its leaders including Gustavo Gutierrez of Peru, Leonardo Boff of Brazil, and Juan Luis Segundo of Uruguay. But the church was divided. Some priests objected strongly to Marxism, to liberationists' opposition to traditional church and political institutions, and to their support of revolution. On the other hand, two priests were part of the leftist Sandinista leadership in Nicaragua. All this only illustrates the continuing complexities that have always been involved in mixing religious and political concerns. Well-meaning people attempting to achieve social justice, and even believing in the same religious faith, can often find themselves on opposite sides of the fence even when the conflict turns violent.

The Growth of Industry and Economic Nationalism

During and after the Great Depression, increasing emphasis was placed on industrialization. Economic nationalists (i.e., those who wanted to free their countries from such heavy dependence upon and control by foreign investors) believed that economic diversity was the best way to achieve economic independence, and that industrialization was highly important to that diversity.

FACTORS THAT ABETTED GROWTH

Several factors provided some basis for the growth of industry. One was simply the fact that the depression itself had a powerful enough impact that it helped to diffuse earlier resistance to industrialization. A number of governments began to encourage industry by the same policies invoked by other industrialized nations—tariffs, import quotas, tax incentives, etc., all designed to cut back foreign competition. They also resorted to government ownership and/or control of various economic enterprises.

INDUSTRIAL ADVANCES

In the postwar years, industrial production in several countries began to climb at a much more rapid rate than agriculture. Between 1950 and 1974, for example, industry's share of the gross national product rose from 18 to 24 percent. Though few huge factories were developed, most of the new production was in consumer goods. This, of course, tended to reduce foreign imports.

In their quest for economic independence Latin American countries also developed heavy industries—coal, oil, iron, and steel—after 1940. These industries were usually controlled or owned by the government. In 1946 Brazil began the operation of a huge steel mill. In the same period of time Mexico expanded its steel-producing facilities dramatically, as did Argentina. These three countries—Argentina, Brazil, and Mexico—became the major industrial nations of Latin America, accounting at the end of the 1960s for about 80 percent of Latin America's industrial production.

FOREIGN PENETRATION AND ITS ADVERSE IMPACT

The growth of industrialism, however, had an effect quite different from the one economic nationalists had envisioned. Instead of eliminating dependency upon foreign capital, it actually attracted new foreign investment in industries such as mining, manufacturing, oil, and public utilities. Along with this came more foreign ownership and control. In Argentina, for example, in 1971 foreigners owned eight of the ten major industrial firms (the other two were owned by the government) and over half the private banks. The United States was by far the largest investor, a fact that did little to allay long-standing feelings among Latin Americans that their giant northern neighbor was continuing to engage in economic imperialism.

Latin America continued to face serious economic problems in its quest for economic development at the end of the 1980s. These included the fact that most of its investment capital and technology was imported, so it remained, in effect, in a state of industrial dependency.

THE CYCLICAL PATTERN OF LATIN AMERICAN POLITICS: REVOLUTION, REFORM, AND RETRENCHMENT

A brief overview of the recent history of three selected countries will illustrate some of the political patterns that characterized Latin American history since World War II. There were important exceptions to all these patterns and fundamental differences in the internal histories of individual countries, but the general patterns reflected the larger problems of the area.

These patterns included promises of economic and social reform, continuing political instability characterized by frequent revolutions and coups, and frequent rule by oligarchies or various forms of dictatorships. In the case of two countries, it was soon discovered that dependence on a single export commodity (tin in Bolivia and coffee in Brazil) was an open invitation to economic disaster.

Argentina

In general, Argentina was ruled by powerful conservative forces who represented the interests of landowners, financiers, and the military. At least one regime, nevertheless, that of Juan D. Perón, was immensely popular with the people.

PERÓN

The charismatic Perón's popularity was only enhanced by that of his popular wife, Eva. He dominated the government at the end of World War II. In 1946, having gained the support of the powerful labor unions, he was elected president. He ruled for nine years with virtual dictatorial powers. Through various repressive measures he began a program of economic and social reform that included promotion of industry by the government and various welfare benefits for the poor. By the mid-1950s, however, increased taxes, accompanied by declining agricultural production and exports, had created serious economic problems. Perón was finally ousted by the military in 1955. Even though he went in exile to Spain, however, he continued to have an important influence on Argentine politics through his followers, known as Perónists.

Perón's dictatorship was followed by years of political instability, as military rulers and civilian presidents led the government; however, none of them completed full terms in office. In 1973 Perón returned from Spain and was again elected president, but he died the following year. Meanwhile, his own followers were bitterly divided, his policies were inconsistent, and runaway inflation was destroying the country economically. His new wife, Maria Estela (Isabel), who was his vice-president and therefore succeeded him, was unsuccessful in her efforts to control either the economy or the government (she reorganized her cabinet ten times in twenty-one months). In 1976 she was overthrown by a military coup.

THE POST-PERÓNIST ERA

The army installed four different generals as presidents between 1976 and 1984. They tried to quell political dissent through massive arrests, executions, and even torture, to the extent that the United States cut off military aid. At the same time, they tried various means of restoring economic stability, including higher taxes and a freeze on wages. Nothing seemed to help, however. Then, in 1982, popular discontent reached its peak when Argentine forces invaded the Falkland Islands and were treated to a humiliating defeat by Britain (see chapter 18).

More Instability. The Falkland Islands War led to the resignation of General Leopoldo Galtieri as president. He was succeeded by a retired general, but the popularity and ability to rule of the military government was gone. The following year civilian government returned to Argentina with the election of Raúl Alfonsín, a political liberal. During his administration he attempted to prosecute various people for civil rights abuses during the years of military rule. His effort was frustrated by pressure from the military, but five people, including two ex-presidents, were imprisoned, and Galtieri was convicted of negligence in prosecuting the war.

The Economy. Argentina's economy, meanwhile, was in a shambles. By the time Alfonsín took over inflation was running at an incredible 500 percent, and by the beginning of 1985 it was up to 1,000 percent. He began a program of austerity, borrowed from the International Monetary Fund, and negotiated loans from private American banks. He lowered the inflation rate to 50 percent by mid-1986. However, the continuing economic crisis forced him from office before his six-year term was over. His Perónist successor, Carlos Saul Menem, continued with an austerity program but also failed to solve Argentina's economic problems.

Bolivia

Someone has quipped that Bolivia provided observers of the Latin American scene with a revolution a month. Although they hardly came that often, the characterization of Bolivia as a country of frequent revolutions was well taken.

THE MNR

As in the case of most Latin American countries, the Great Depression wreaked havoc with the economy of Bolivia. Military governments maintained a political and social status quo, though discontent was as widespread beneath the surface in Bolivia as in any country. In 1941 the National Revolutionary Movement (MNR) brought together various left-leaning dissident groups under the leadership of Victor Paz Estenssoro. The new party seized power two years later, but the new president was murdered in 1946. Conservatives were back in power, under a military junta, but in 1951 Estenssoro was elected president even though he was still in exile in Argentina. The army, however, kept him from assuming power. Only in 1953, after another MNR uprising, did he take office.

CONTINUING SEESAW

The almost dizzying seesaw between conservative and liberal revolutions and civilian and military rule continued. Estenssoro was succeeded by his vice-president, reelected in 1960, then overthrown. He was replaced by General Rene Barrientos Ortuno, who was killed in an accident and replaced by Louis Adolfo Siles Salinas in 1969. Before the year was over, however, Salinas was deposed and replaced by a right-wing general who, in turn, was overthrown the following year by a leftist, General Juan Jose Torres Gonzales. Only a year later right-wing General Hugo Banzer Suarez overthrew Torres. The military remained in power until 1979, when the Bolivian congress established an interim civilian government. A new government was elected in 1980, but almost as if it were becoming a tradition, the army refused to let president Siles Zuazo (who was also a former president) take over until 1982. There were no more coups or revolutions through the 1980s, but several internal problems kept the government in a precarious position. On two occasions no presidential candidate won a majority in the election, forcing the congress to choose a president. One of these presidents was Estenssoro, who led his economically and politically troubled nation again from 1985 to 1989.

ECONOMIC PROBLEMS

No matter what government was in power, economic problems continued to plague Bolivia, and little really fundamental social or economic reform was forthcoming. In 1952 the Bolivian government hoped to deal with its economic problems by taking over the tin mines, but a drop in the world price of tin, lasting for fourteen years, destroyed that dream. Later, under Banzer, the government sold its oil and natural gas, as well as other natural resources, to foreign investors. But neither these efforts nor borrowing from foreign banks and the International Monetary Fund did much to alleviate Bolivia's continuing economic crisis.

Brazil

The history of Brazil was also characterized by economic distress and political instability. However it was coffee, Brazil's chief export, that destroyed the long-time republic in 1930. When world coffee prices fell during the Great Depression, they took with them the Brazilian economy as well as the government. A military coup of that year then brought Getulio

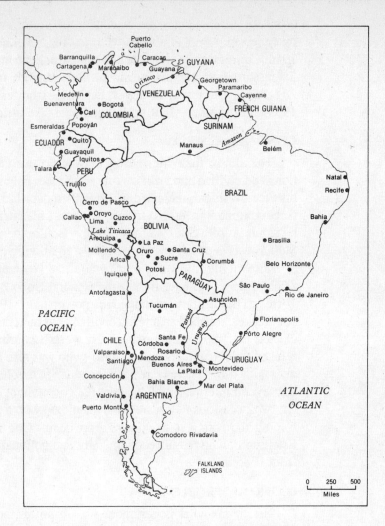

Fig. 22.1   Modern South America

Vargas to the presidency, which he held for the next fifteen years. A new constitution, which defined the responsibilities of the central government much more broadly, was promulgated in 1934. In 1937, reacting to opposition to his program, Vargas assumed dictatorial power.

VARGAS'S EFFORTS AT REFORM

The Vargas government's major challenge was to create some semblance of economic stability. Recognizing the dangers involved in depending almost exclusively on coffee as an export commodity, Vargas attempted to diversify the economy by using the government to promote domestic industry. This was actually the beginning of industrialization for Brazil. The seeming political and economic stability that characterized the war years also brought enough confidence that Vargas was able to obtain foreign loans for further development. In 1945, however, he was deposed by the military, who feared what seemed to be too much of a move toward political liberalism. A democratic regime, still controlled by the military, took his place, though in 1950 Vargas was elected again. In 1954, however, disillusioned by revelations of corruption in his administration and by demands from the army that he resign, he committed suicide. Like other countries, Brazil thereafter swung back and forth between civilian and military rule for the next decade. Then, after a 1964 coup, military governments were in power for the next twenty-one years. As in most military regimes, there was little political freedom, for the press was censored and civil rights were suspended. There was, however, an upswing in the economy.

CIVILIAN GOVERNMENT AGAIN

In 1985 a civilian government was restored, and a new constitution was put into effect in 1988. Fernando Collor de Mello, the first president to be elected under that constitution, took office in 1990. In September 1992, however, the lower house of Brazil's congress voted overwhelmingly to impeach Collor, paving the way for his trial in the Senate on charges of corruption and taking bribes. This was the first impeachment of a president anywhere in the world since World War II. If convicted, Collor would be the first democratically elected president in the history of the Brazilian republic to be removed from office by means other than elections or a military coup. It thus provided a dramatic test of the viability of Brazil's return to constitutional government.

The restoration of civilian government did not immediately solve Brazil's serious economic problems. Its foreign debt was the largest in the world, and inflation was running rampant. Nevertheless, it had developed a diversified export business, including the products of its important steel industry. Brazilians were still optimistic for the future. That optimism was symbolized as early as 1957, when the government commissioned the building of a grand new capital city, Brasilia, in the interior. Though controversial in its inception, Brasilia became a model for some city and government planners in other parts of the world.

THE CHALLENGE FROM THE LEFT

Latin America also became a kind of pawn in the Cold War. Internally, Latin American peoples struggled for greater economic opportunity within a society that continued to be dominated by widespread poverty. Their struggles sometimes led to the rise of strong Marxists movements, encouraged and supported by both the Soviet Union and Cuba. To other Western powers, however, and particularly to the United States, Marxist-oriented revolution was seen as a part of the Cold War. The United States gave both moral and economic support to existing governments or to any group that would fight against the spread of communism anywhere. The result was mixed signals from the United States, so far as many Latin Americans were concerned. On the one hand it called for greater social and economic freedom everywhere, but on the other, in supporting anti-Communist regimes it also seemed to be opposing the very movements that, to Latinos, showed the greatest hope for economic relief.

The Cuban Revolution

THE FALL OF THE BATISTA REGIME

The ruler of Cuba in the 1950s was Fulgencio Batista, a dictator who enjoyed the support of the U.S. government. One of Batista's most active opponents was Fidel Castro, who was sent to prison after leading an ill-fated attempt at revolution in 1953. Released early, Castro went to Mexico in exile, where he planned the 1956 revolution. In December of that year he and eighty-one followers returned to Cuba by boat and began a long guerrilla war against Batista. The dictator's support gradually collapsed and he fled on January 1, 1959. By the middle of the month, Castro was in power.

CASTRO'S MARXIST STATE

Originally Castro was not a Marxist—or, at least, he did not pass himself off as one. His major goal was to get rid of oppression and change the nature of Cuba's society. He was admired and supported by many Americans and was actually aided in his revolution by the fact that the U.S. government did not lend support to Batista. It was not long, however, before Castro began to show totalitarian tendencies of his own. Even though he initially had the support of the masses, his promise to hold elections was not fulfilled. He began a series of socialist reforms and received both military and economic aid from the Soviet Union. His dictatorial regime met opposition with firing squads or political imprisonment. In 1961, Castro announced that he was a committed Marxist. Americans were dismayed, and Cuba became, to them, an element of the Cold War. Diplomatic relations were broken off that year.

At first Castro ruled by fiat, but by the 1970s executive authority was lodged in a council. Castro dominated, however. When elections were finally held, they were typical communist-type, one-party elections, and Castro always won.

Castro's Reforms. Castro's reforms included land redistribution and the establishment of small groups of landowners or large state farms. He also fostered improvement in education, which made Cuba's literacy rate the highest in Latin America, and vastly improved health care, supported by the state. Women became fully equal before the law and were given equal opportunity in education and the professions.

Economically, Castro tried to develop more diversified agriculture. Sugar, however, maintained a central position, and the industry was nationalized. But Castro's grandiose plans were not generally successful. Cuba's economy became partly dependent upon support, in the form of subsidies, from the Soviet Union.

Castro's policies improved the standard of living of many Cubans, but they also alienated many others, particularly the middle classes who were most threatened by economic reform and political oppression. Hundreds of thousands fled the country.

Foreign Relations. Castro's foreign affairs were marked, in large part, by mutual hostility between Cuba and the United States. One result of this was the unsuccessful Bay of Pigs invasion by the United States and Cuban exiles in 1961. A more world-shaking event was the missile crisis the following year (see chapter 18). In addition, much of America's foreign policy was aimed toward keeping Cuba from exporting Marxism to other parts of Latin America—an objective to which Castro was actively committed. With the end of the Cold War, however, these relationships gradually began to change.

Marxism and Reaction in Chile

In contrast to Cuba, the effort to establish Marxism in Chile lasted only fifteen years, after which a reactionary government reversed the previous policies. Neither regime, however, succeeded in bringing about long-lasting economic improvement

THE ALLENDE EXPERIMENT

In the 1960s, Chile's long-standing republican government faced an economic and social crisis. Unemployment skyrocketed, and popular discontent was exacerbated by resentment against U.S. domination of Chile's economy. Finally, in 1970 Salvadore Allende, a Marxist, was elected president—not by a majority but by a plurality. He put together a shaky coalition, however, and began to take drastic action. He nationalized a number of businesses, thus eliminating American control of at least that many. He also redistributed much farmland to peasants and promoted a wide range of health care and social reforms. Nevertheless, by 1973 the real economic situation had improved only slightly, and the nation was still in turmoil. Allende's program, in which he may have tried to do too much too quickly, had plunged the country into massive deficits and runaway inflation. Allende had also lost his base of popular support. In addition, he had alienated the United States, which began to encourage discontented elements within the military. In 1973 Allende was overthrown by an American-supported military coup (dying when a bomb hit his palace).

REACTION UNDER PINOCHET

President of Chile under the new regime was General Augusto Pinochet. He was supported by the United States, even though he was a dictator and used the standard methods of political repression to quiet dissent. His tactics became so blatant that the United States withdrew its support in 1979, though it was restored two years later. Pinochet returned to the original owners many factories, banks, and other businesses, as well as land, that had been appropriated by the Allende regime, but his brand of free enterprise was still one directed by the state. For a time the economy improved, but in the early 1980s it again went into decline. Within a few years it turned around again. Pinochet, however, was rejected at the polls in 1988, even though he was the sole candidate in a plebiscite to determine whether he should remain in office for another four years. He retained the office for two more years, however, and after that still remained as head of the armed forces.

Nicaragua and the Sandinistas

Marxism arose in Nicaragua, too, where it gave rise to a longer period of violence and civil strife than in either of the two countries discussed above. Nicaragua was also the country in which the United States intervened most directly as part of its continuing activity in a Cold War that was, in fact, a hot war in such areas as this.

THE SOMOZA DICTATORSHIP OVERTHROWN

Like other Latin American states, Nicaragua went through a series of revolutions and coups in the twentieth century. In 1936 power was seized by General Anastasia Somoza. When he died his sons took over, and the Somoza family ruled until 1979. It was yet another dictatorship supported by the United States.

The Sandinistas and Ortega. Though the Somoza dictatorship resulted in national economic growth, it was also marked by extensive corruption. Opposition led to the founding of the Sandinista National Liberation Front (FSLN) in 1962. Named for a guerrilla leader who had been assassinated in 1934, the group became known simply as Sandinistas. In 1978 widespread discontent with the Somoza regime resulted in civil war, led by the Sandinistas. In 1979 they took over the government and established a Marxist-oriented regime that began to reorganize the country along socialist lines. Under the leadership of Daniel Ortega, it identified itself as the National Reconstruction Government.

THE SANDINISTA REGIME AND ITS OPPONENTS

In 1984 Ortega was elected president, and the Sandinistas took control of the National Assembly. The new government formed ties with Cuba and the Soviet Union and, of course, alienated the United States.

As elsewhere, the Marxist regime in Nicaragua had is opponents. Many anti-Sandinistas, or "contras," formed themselves into well-organized guerrilla bands and established bases in the neighboring state of Honduras. From there they not only exerted economic pressure on Nicaragua but also conducted raids. They were supported by the United States, openly through military advisors but also covertly through financial and other assistance. Investigation of one American scandal, the "Iran-Contra Affair," revealed that some profits from arms secretly sold to Iran had been diverted to aid the contras, even though the U.S. Congress had specifically prohibited such aid. The United States also imposed an embargo in an effort to weaken the government.

A Central American Settlement. Other nations in Central America were also concerned with the Nicaraguan problem and began to work with the Ortega government to settle it. In August 1987 Ortega and the leaders of four other nations signed a regional peace agreement, and the following year a cease-fire agreement was reached between the contras and the Sandinistas. Later the contras even agreed to dismantle their camps in Honduras, and Ortega agreed to hold a national election in 1990. In that election a coalition opposed to the Sandinistas won a majority, and a woman, Violeta Barrios de Chamorro, was elected president. She began the slow and challenging process of bringing together a people torn apart by years of civil strife and, at the same time, dealing with the economic problems posed by runaway inflation.

OTHER ASPECTS OF RECENT LATIN AMERICAN HISTORY

Drugs and Inter-American Relations

One of the serious problems in inter-American relations was the effort to eliminate drug trafficking. Complicating the problem was the fact that many farmers found it a lucrative source of income. In their depressed economy, it sometimes seemed the only hope for a better life.

DRUG TRAFFICKING

There were several routes by which drugs found their way to the United States and other countries. By the 1980s Honduras had become a chief transshipment center for drugs on their way from Latin America to the United States. It was estimated that some $500 million worth of drugs went through the country every year, often with the knowledge, even the complicity, of the government. Bolivia was also an important source. There was also evidence that Bolivian officials knew of and even encouraged the traffic—for a share of the profits, of course. In some cases the publicity given to efforts to prosecute drug runners even worked to the disadvantage of American bystanders in Bolivia. Unsuspecting tourists would be arrested, after someone had "planted" drugs on them, and thrown in jail. To get out, or even to receive "help" while in prison, they had to pay bribes—sometimes amounting to thousands of dollars during the time of their stay.

AMERICAN PRESSURES

The United States pressured Latin American countries to do something about stopping the illegal trade. It also provided increasing financial and technical assistance in the 1980s in the effort to fight the drug barons who controlled the trade. Peru was among the first countries to provide incentives for farmers to shift from producing cocaine to producing legal crops.

Colombia, too, was an important source. In his 1982 inaugural address as president of Colombia, Julio César Turbay affirmed his commitment to doing everything possible to prevent the drug traffic. He reminded the United States, however, that his job would be much easier if the United States could prevent its "greedy North American traffickers and consumers" from providing so much financial assistance to the criminals in his country.

NORIEGA

The most celebrated case of American intervention was that of Manuel Noriega, chief of staff of the national guard in Panama and the actual political strong man of the country. The United States discovered evidence that he was deeply involved in drug trafficking. In 1989 Noriega was condemned by the Organization of American States. Shortly thereafter Noriega audaciously declared that a state of war existed between Panama and the United States. Sporadic violence broke out in Panama, and an American soldier (part of the contingent guarding the Panama Canal) was killed. On December 20 President George Bush ordered American forces into Panama. In January 1990 Noriega surrendered to American troops. He was then flown to Miami, Florida, where he was arraigned on charges of drug trafficking and finally convicted.

Society, Culture, and Quality of Life

Beyond the cycles of violence, revolution, and reaction, it is important to make a few observations on the nature of Latin American society in the last half of the twentieth century. As may be surmised from what has already been said, democracy, or democratic participation in political life, was not widespread. Religion remained a vital part of Latin American life, and the Roman Catholic Church continued to dominate. In addition, the people of most countries have retained much of their traditional culture, as expressed through folk music, dancing, and skills such as weaving and making pottery. Some Latin American nations have also produced painters, writers, and composers who have become wellknown around the world. Much of their work reflects their own cultural tradition.

Nevertheless, a look at the general quality of life in Latin America reveals a profusion of continuing human problems. As observed by Bradford Burns in his *Latin America: A Concise Interpretive History*, "probably the most terrifying reality is that most of the population is hungry, malnourished, and sick." The evidence is found in every social statistic available, such as the fact that in 1979 100,000 children under the age of five died of malnutrition. Illiteracy rates are high. Income per capita, and hence purchasing power, remains startlingly low. The reasons for all this are multiple but include the continuing unequal distribution of wealth and land ownership—10 percent of all landowners hold 90 percent of the land. Agricultural technology also lags behind other Western nations.

The major continuing challenge facing all Latin American nations is how to deal with such human problems. Conservative political forces, still resistant to schemes for radical change, remain in power. It is still anyone's guess as to whether more land reform, more social welfare legislation, a truly free economic structure, or a combination of these and other schemes will provide an answer.

New Directions

By the 1990s Latin America was involved in a few new directions that seemed to offer hope for the future. These directions are particularly important from the perspective of global history, for they reflect the recognition of the rapidly increasing worldwide interdependence that dominated world economic development in the closing years of the twentieth century. For one thing, some nations, such as Brazil and Argentina, cut back their nuclear arms race as the Cold War ground to a halt. Latin America also looked with hope at efforts to create a free-trade zone in the Americas that would rival or exceed the strength of the European common market.

In a world rife with change, it is somewhat ironic that there was so little change in Latin America in the years since World War II. It is true that those of the upper and middle classes became much better acquainted with the rest of the world and enjoyed all the benefits of modern technology. But most of the people remained among the lower classes and enjoyed a quality of life little improved over that of their parents and grandparents. In the slums of the major cities, in fact, conditions were probably worse. The era was characterized by numerous revolutions, coups, and promises of social reform. There was even considerable real reform—some land redistribution, improved education and health care in places, and governments that took on greater burdens of social legislation. But in general the masses had little say about their political destinies and little hope in the near future for any major improvement in their social and economic life. At least, however, they retain such worthwhile traditions as a rich folk heritage and close family ties.

Selected Readings

Blasier, C. *The Hovering Giant: U.S. Responses to Revolutionary Change in Latin America.* Pittsburgh: University of Pittsburgh Press, 1985.

Burns, E. Bradford. *A History of Brazil.* New York: Columbia University Press, 1971.

————. *Latin America: A Concise Interpretive History.* 3rd ed. Englewood Cliffs, NJ: Prentice-Hall, 1982.

LaFeber, Walter. *Inevitable Revolutions: The United States in Central America.* New York: Norton, 1983.

Meyer, Michael C. *The Course of Mexican History.* 3rd ed. New York: Oxford University Press, 1987.

Ramos, Graciliano. *Barren Lives.* Austin: University of Texas Press, 1969 (a novel about rural life in Brazil).

Wynia, Gary W. *Argentina in the Postwar Era: Politics and Economic Policy Making in a Divided Society.* Albuquerque: University of New Mexico Press, 1978.

————. *The Politics of Latin American Development.* 3rd ed. Cambridge, England; New York: Cambridge University Press, 1990.

23

Contemporary Trends and Portents

In the 500 years covered by this book the world changed dramatically. We will not list all the changes here, but a few are of special significance. Before 1500 there were few national states as we know them today. Rather, there were empires that encompassed many peoples, languages, and ethnic groups. There were also principalities and kingdoms within those empires, but nothing like the division of the world into nearly 200 sovereign states and numerous dependencies that existed toward the end of the twentieth century. Moreover, before 1500 the peoples of these regions lived in relative isolation—Europeans, Asians, Africans, Americans, and Australians knew virtually nothing about each other. By 1500, however, a trend was beginning that would culminate in the phenomenon of almost complete world inter-dependence 500 years later. National states existed in some parts of the world, and some were beginning to appear in Europe. These included England, Portugal, France, and Spain. The trend continued. Each of these European states, however, found their destiny at the time in building world commercial empires. The establishment of colonies and the building of world trade soon brought the peoples of the world closer together, both in knowledge of each other and in economic and political relationships. For that reason, it has sometimes been observed that, symbolically, the year 1500 marked the beginning of global history rather than regional history.

As we have seen, over the next 500 years the world changed drastically. The expanding European empires took over other empires and peoples, but eventually all the regions of the world were divided into national states. These states were sometimes illogical so far as geographical boundaries and ethnic makeup were concerned. By the 1990s many were still characterized by serious internal strife directly related to the same ethnic hostility that had caused civil wars for centuries. Other nations were torn by religious differences, which also continued, especially in the Middle East, to create hostility and threats of war. But from the perspective of global history, one factor stands out: the near completion of the world interdependence that was just beginning to evolve in 1500. In this chapter we will comment on only a handful of the many challenges and problems relating to this interdependence and address the question of where the world may be going.

POPULATION AND POVERTY

A brief insight into the challenges facing the modern world may be gained simply by considering population growth. In 1500 the world was the home of around 425 million people. By 1992 it housed close to 5.5 billion, nearly 40 percent of whom lived in India and the People's Republic of China. Feeding, housing, and caring for the health of the masses, especially in the Third World, was one of the major problems of the world. In extremely poor countries, such as India, Bolivia, and Ethiopia, most of the population consumed less than what was considered the minimal daily requirement of calories. The masses thus suffered from hunger, malnutrition, and related disease. This is graphically illustrated by the fact that some 60,000 people die daily from hunger-related causes. Two-thirds of them are children.

Urbanization

Beginning at least as far back as the nineteenth century, many people began to migrate from rural areas to the cities, where, presumably, they could find work. The pattern continued, but in the late twentieth century it was taking place more rapidly in poor countries that in rich ones. This was partly because in wealthier nations, like the United States, the pattern of movement was toward the suburbs. This gave rise to rapidly growing slums, such as those in Mexico City (which has a population of 20 million), and sometimes even worse problems of malnutrition and disease than in the countryside.

Population Growth

There is much discussion about the reasons for the rise and fall in population as well as about the desirability of population growth at all. In some countries, such as India, the population seems out of hand; it is growing rapidly, yet there is simply not enough food to go around. In other places, such as Austria, the population has leveled out or is even declining, for the number of births is equal to or less than the number of deaths. Austria, therefore, is attempting to encourage population growth by various government programs, such as day-care centers for working mothers.

There is also disagreement over the degree to which the earth can sustain continuing growth, with some authorities suggesting that it will reach an upper limit by the end of the twenty-first century. This raises questions of population control, which are already controversial and promise to become more so. Some countries, such as China, already limit by law the number of children a couple may have without receiving heavy economic penalties. Birth control seems a logical answer to some people, but this is inhibited by many factors. In some areas, such as India, it is related to the unavailability of contraceptives along with lack of knowledge or mere reluctance to use them. In other cases, religious scruples prohibit their use. In addition, abortion as a birth control measure is highly controversial worldwide.

Clearly, the question will remain as to whether the problem is population growth or inefficient use of productive and distributive resources. The answer probably includes elements of both, but the latter is clearly a major factor. Some countries, such as the United States, produce abundant surpluses and have the capacity for producing more. Latin American countries, too, could produce considerably more food with the help of improved agricultural technology and the proper incentives. But even when and if such surpluses are produced, these countries are likely to have large pockets of hunger within their own borders. The question remains as to what it will take to distribute surpluses worldwide, as well as to develop the agricultural potential of the underdeveloped countries of the world. Meanwhile, the growing population, with its accompanying problems of poverty, remains as one of the world's great challenges.

ECONOMIC INTERDEPENDENCE

At the heart of the new world interdependence are certain economic realities. For example, as the peoples of the world demanded more and more energy to feed their growing industries and to raise their own standards of living, many became nearly dependent upon the oil-rich Middle East. This area, in turn, was dependent upon its markets for its own survival. But oil was only one aspect of the new global economic interdependence. The countries of many regions were cooperating in massive trade agreements under which tariffs and other artificial barriers disappeared. Sixteenth-century nations saw mercantilism—regulation of trade through such means as tariffs and quotas—as the way to promote their own economic well-being. The trade agreements based on the new realities of the twentieth century had just the opposite philosophy. No country could produce within its own borders all the goods needed for modern economic life, so the answer was in the law of comparative advantage. Each country produced and marketed what it was most able to, allowing the market itself to ration and distribute goods throughout the region.

European Community

In 1991 the largest such bloc was the European Community, which actually accounted for about 20 percent of the world's trade. But there were also political implications. The European Community had its own budget, revenue sources, and system of ministers. It established firm rules and policies in many areas and by the 1990s was discussing a variety of issues that could affect many internal policies of the member nations. These included such ticklish matters as antitrust legislation, environmental issues, and currency. It also maintained diplomatic ties with over 130 other countries and represented its member nations at talks of the General Agreement on Trade and Tariffs (GATT). This treaty, signed by ninety-six nations, took effect in 1948 and operates under the auspices of the United Nations. By 1991 it had been recognized by most other nations. Although it was by no means the vehicle for solving all world trade problems, it nevertheless provided an effective world forum for discussing the issues. In addition, as a result of a series of agreements known as the Lome Convention (1975–1989), the European Community eliminated tariffs on all goods coming from sixty-nine countries in Africa, the Caribbean, and the Pacific. All this clearly demonstrates the almost total economic interdependence that characterized the world of the 1990s and promised only to become more vital in the decades ahead.

The challenge facing the European Community, of course, was nationalism. People in every country resisted the implications of an organization that would, in effect, subsume them in a new kind of state after having erased national boundaries. The question was whether the clear advantages of greater European unity could be achieved, leading to some kind of "United States of Europe," without destroying the national identities of the people involved.

Other Regions

There were other such regional organizations, such as the Latin American Free Trade Association, though by the 1990s this one had not achieved the unity of the European Community. In the fall of 1992, several years of negotiation were concluded with the signing of the North American Free Trade Agreement. Canada, the United States, and Mexico agreed to eliminate trade barriers. The result, they hoped, would be improved economic activity throughout the region and greater competitiveness with such trading powers as Japan and the European Community.

Other Consequences

The interrelationship between the countries of the world had many other implications. If only for practical reasons, the problems of one part of the world became the problems of another—a crisis in the Middle East affected almost every other nation. But human problems, too, became world problems. No matter where famines, plagues, and other causes of human misery occurred, people worldwide knew of them immediately. Humanitarian impulses as well as practical political necessity gave rise to outpourings of economic and social assistance from diverse corners of the world. Somalia's problems thus became America's problems, and an earthquake in Mexico affected people as far away as Japan.

The political implications of world interdependence were difficult for many, if not most, people to fathom, and therein lay one of the important challenges of the decades ahead. Would the coming world order require nations to give up some degree of their sovereignty, so jealously guarded by all of them, in the cause of maintaining world peace? In the early 1990s the people of Europe were struggling with that question as they considered all of the implications of expanding the scope of the European Community.

THE PROBLEM OF WORLD PEACE

The end of the Cold War seemed to offer new hope for world peace. The arms race between the superpowers came to an end, and Western powers began to cooperate in helping to bring about economic recovery of the states that once formed the Soviet Union and its satellites.

But as the Cold War ended another phenomenon occurred—one that was at best fearsome and at worst as much of a threat as the Cold War itself. Suddenly, especially after the Persian Gulf War, arms merchants from the United States and elsewhere in the world (but especially the United States) began selling weapons of every variety to the Middle Eastern countries—sometimes openly and sometimes as the result of secret negations. Iran, Iraq, Syria, and Saudi Arabia are currently buying millions of dollars' worth of high-tech weapons, with few apparent restraints. It has also been estimated that some of these countries will have biological as well as nuclear weapons within a few short years. How they will use them, if at all, is a question, but the volatile relations between the countries of the Middle East does not bode well for long-term peace. Iran and Iraq, for example, still harbor long-standing animosities toward each other. Weapons and technology are also coming to another potential trouble spot, the Middle East, from such diverse corners of the globe as the United States, China, and North Korea.

RACISM AND HUMAN RIGHTS

Among the greatest impediments to a real sense of world community are the continuing problems of racism and human rights. In some ways these two problems are separate, but they go together in the sense that both reflect the inability of some humans to recognize and promote the moral equality and human dignity of others.

One hopeful sign came in South Africa, where blacks constitute the majority of the population but where apartheid existed for generations. The world community, through the United Nations, imposed sanctions against South Africa. Whether or not these sanctions were the whole reason for the change is not clear, but in the early 1990s many of the racist laws were repealed. President F. W. de Klerk continued to make efforts to provide for full civil rights for all races. He had considerable opposition, however, from conservative white groups, including the vocal (though not large in numbers) neo-Nazis.

Perhaps the most shocking recent example of ethnic hostility came in the Balkans. A civil war in former Yugoslavia resulted in its division into separate states. But it also resulted in the breakout of the same bitter ethnic and religious rivalries that had plagued the region for centuries. In this case, Serbian troops bent on driving Muslims and Croats from the region began a process of "ethnic cleansing." They not only drove over 1 million victims from their homes, but also tortured and killed many. The other nations of the world looked on with horror and debated what could be done to stop the carnage, but they seemed powerless to intervene directly. Beyond such blatant examples of racism, people in many other parts of the world continued to harbor bias and misunderstanding.

In addition, people in many parts of the world continue to be victims of such human rights abuses as torture, suppression of nonviolent political activity, lack of opportunity to participate in the political process, and even, in some cases, abuses that amount to slavery. One of the first activities undertaken by Argentina's government after its return to civilian rule was to investigate years of political kidnapping and extrajudicial executions carried out during the years of military domination. Such activities continue in other military dictatorships and totalitarian regimes.

In 1948 the United Nations adopted a Universal Declaration of Human Rights, but it continues to be ignored by many world governments. Groups such as London-based Amnesty International, the only organization ever to be awarded the Nobel Peace Prize, have regularly drawn attention to human rights abuses around the world and have put pressure on governments to end such polices.

THE ENVIRONMENT

The biosphere, that part of the earth capable of sustaining life, is shared by everyone on the globe—rich and poor. As population increased and as the resources of the earth were exploited with increasing rapidity, the interrelationships and interdependency of the peoples of the world became dramatically clear. The activities of human beings in one part of the world directly affected the quality of life in another, to the extent that by the end of the century the ecological system was becoming dangerously unbalanced. When developers began to destroy the rainforests in Brazil, for example, in order to develop agricultural settlements and various business activities, they did not at first realize that this would affect the climate (and hence the productive capacity) not only of Brazil itself but of much of the rest of the world. Though the immediate threat of nuclear war receded, those who studied the environment observed that the devastation of the environment could be equally catastrophic. Once again, the unity of the world, transcending national boundaries, was illustrated.

By the time the world realized how polluted the globe was, a great deal of damage had already been done. The question has increasingly become one of how much of the damage is irreversible and how much can be solved by greater attention to the environmental impact of human activities. The problem of global environmental pollution is one that cannot be solved simply by refraining from engaging in polluting activities. Positive measures to clean up past damage must go along with changes in the way we live and work.

Though the industrially advanced Northern Hemisphere contains only one-fourth of the world's population, it consumes 80 percent of the world's resources. But the effects of this tremendous use of resources—and the pollution that is one of its byproducts—are hardly limited to the industrial nations. As part of an expedition to Pitcairn Island in 1991, zoologist Tim Benton took a walk on the remote, uninhabited island of Ducie Atoll. This location is about as far away from large population centers as one could go, yet in a mile-and-a-half stretch of beach, the scientist found an incredible array of garbage, most of which probably floated ashore after being tossed overboard from ships. His finds included 268 pieces of plastic, 171 glass bottles, 18 jars, 14 crates, 25 shoes, 6 toy soldiers, 6 light bulbs, 7 aerosol cans, and a variety of other objects—953 in all. "If so much rubbish is washed ashore on these small and extremely isolated islands," Benton observed in the July 11, 1991, issue of *Nature* magazine, "it makes one wonder just how much more is still floating on the surface of the oceans."

Quest for Solutions

Much of the damage done to the environment is the offspring of modern industry, but simply shutting down industrial production is obviously not the solution. The human race has become too dependent on modern industry and other polluting aspects of modern life. Greater awareness of the long-term environmental effects of what we do will go a long way toward creating attitudes of greater respect and care for the environment.

RIO CONFERENCE

In an effort to address global environmental problems and begin to come up with solutions, a worldwide "environmental summit" was held in Rio de Janeiro during the summer of 1992. The policy makers and others gathered there discussed rain forest depletion, damage to the ozone layer, global warming, ocean and air pollution, endangered species, and the relationship between all these problems and world economic development. Although the meeting was short on specific solutions, it did focus world attention, at least for a time, on problems that transcend national boundaries and affect the interests of every nation and individual. It remains to be seen what concrete measures will result from this meeting.

ENVIRONMENTAL ACTIVISTS

Awareness of environmental problems has spawned the creation of a number of environmental lobbying and activist organizations. Their tactics vary, but they are united by a concern for the damage still being done to the environment and by their determination to stem the tide. They range from such lobbying and educational organizations as the Sierra Club and the World Wildlife Fund in the United States to Greenpeace, originally founded in 1969 by Canadian environmentalists but now a worldwide organization that has adopted more directly confrontational tactics in its crusade. Both the potential effectiveness and the potential liabilities of the confrontational approach were demonstrated in 1985, when a Greenpeace ship was sunk by French agents as it protested continued nuclear testing in Polynesia. Environmental concerns have also been the foundation of so-called "green parties" that have become an increasingly visible political presence in some countries, particularly in Europe.

OTHER MAJOR WORLD CONCERNS

Health

Mention has already been made of the problem of malnutrition. But the shrinking of the world has also made other health problems matters of international concern. The most obvious example in the late twentieth century is the spread of Acquired Immune Deficiency Syndrome (AIDS). What seemed in the early 1980s to be a mysterious disease afflicting primarily male homosexuals in the United States was soon found to be communicable to all population groups regardless of age, gender, or sexual orientation. Acquired mainly through sexual contact, tainted blood trans- fusions, and contaminated hypodermic needles (particularly among drug users), the disease has baffled medical researchers. It affects every country of the world and is especially prevalent in Africa. No cure is known for this fatal disease, which thus presents one of the most urgent medical challenges for the future.

Clearly the world faces serious problems in connection with improving the health of its people. One of the agencies leading in this quest is the World Health Organization (WHO), founded in 1948 as an arm of the United Nations. Most UN member nations are also members of WHO, whose mission is to promote "the highest possible level of health" for all the peoples of the world. One of its greatest accomplishments was the virtual elimination of smallpox by the late 1970s through an intensive vaccination program. It continues to promote research, disseminate information, and support nations in their efforts to fight disease and improve health generally.

Growth of Democracy

With the changes in Eastern Europe, it appeared to some people that the world was racing toward democracy. But such images were premature. Democratic experiments got off to a shaky beginning in many areas, and their viability is still not certain. Moreover, the nation that holds the largest population in the world, China, has shown no proclivities to move in this direction, even though it has adopted some elements of capitalism in order to bring about economic recovery. Nor do the semidemocratic regimes in other areas (e.g., Latin America) seem to be moving toward fully democratic political systems. In at least one case, the tiny country of Haiti, a democratic regime was overthrown and a military dictatorship set up in late 1991, but the United States was unable to follow through on its efforts to restore the elected government.

United Nations

The people of the world are still struggling with the implications of interdependency—particularly those of a political nature. World govern- ment is clearly not in the offing, but the United Nations has become tremendously important in many ways. It is the best forum for nations to debate world problems. Although it has not provided a peaceful world, through its intervention in specific areas it has at least helped in resisting aggression. It has also been an effective mediator in some international disputes.

In addition, a variety of UN agencies provide important services that only emphasize the vital interrelationship between all parts of the world.

The Universal Postal Union, the International Civil Aviation Organization, and the International Telecommunication Union, for example, all help facilitate global communication. Other agencies are dedicated to improving the quality of life, both economically and socially. These include the Food and Agricultural Organization, the United Nations Educational, Scientific, and Cultural Organization, the World Bank, the International Monetary Fund, and the Office of the United Nations High Commissioner for Refugees.

Perhaps symbolic of what we have said about global interdependency is the fact that in the 1970s the United Nations began to sponsor a series of conferences to deal with the major challenges confronting the world. The emphasis was on the need for a global approach to all the problems, thus setting the tone for where world history may be headed at the end of the twentieth century.

These are only a few among many contemporary trends and portents that will help shape the world for the rest of the twentieth century and beyond. Increased interaction between regions of the world has created difficult problems, but it is also the source of great opportunities for international cooperation and assistance. There is no reason to believe that all of the world's problems will be solved in the foreseeable future. But at the same time, there is reason for optimism that a greater realization of our common humanity and of our mutual responsibility for the world and its inhabitants will encourage all men and women, regardless of nation, to feel a sense of community and linked destiny.

Index

Maryland, settlement of, 33
Massachusetts Bay Company, 33
Mathematical Principles of Natural Philosophy (Newton), 99
Maurice, F. D., 169
Mauritania, 425, 431
Mauritius, 431
Maximilian (Mexico), 180
Maya, 24
May Fourth Movement, 325–326
Mazarin, Jules, 76–77
McAdam, John, 145
McCarthy, Joseph R., 360
McCartney, George, 232
McDonald, John A., 199
McKinley, William, 253, 267
McMahon Agreement, 332
Medicare, 377
Meiji Restoration, 242–243
Mein Kampf (Hitler), 310, 311
Mendeleev, Dimitri, 154
Menem, Carlos Saul, 440
Mennonites, 10
Mercantilism, 27, 78
Metcalf, John, 145
Metternich, Klemens von, 166, 173
Metternich System, 173–174
Mexico
  Aztecs in, 25–26
  economy in, 436–438
  liberation theology in, 437
  1910 revolution in, 436
  nineteenth century government in, 203–204
  political parties in, 436
  reforms in, 436
  revolution in, 136
  war with United States, 204
Mfecane, 217
Middle East. *See also countries in*
  anti-Westernism in, 415
  Cold War in, 408
  European imperialism in, 331–332
  governments in, 409
  independence movement in, 407–409
  Islamic Fundamentalism in, 415–416
  modernization of, 331–332, 415
  nationalism in, 409–411

Middle East (*cont'd*)
  oil in, 365, 413–414
  regional developments in, 416–418
  socialism in, 414–415
  strategic importance of, 408
  urbanization in, 414
  World War I and its aftermath in, 332–333
  World War II and its aftermath in, 333
Migration, impact of industrialization on, 158–159
Milan decree (1807), 130
Mill, John Stuart, 167, 303
Millet system, 409–410
Ministry of International Trade and Industry (MITI), 384
Minuit, Peter, 35
Miranda, Francisco, 135
Missouri, 350
Mobutu, Joseph, 426
Moldavia, 255
Moluccas, 70
Momoyama period, 54
Monroe, James, 193
Monroe Doctrine, 193, 268–269
Montenegro, 279
Montesquieu, Baron de, 109, 119
Montezuma, 26
More, Thomas, 9
Mormons, 192
Moro, Aldo, 371
Morocco, 220
  crisis in, 278, 279
Mountbatten, Louis, 401, 402
Mozambique, 213, 256, 431
Mozart, Wolfgang Amadeus, 110
Mughal India, 59–61
Muhammad Ali (Egypt), 218–219
Mukden, 266
Mumtaz, Mahal, 61
Mushakoji Saneatsu, 317
Music, in enlightenment, 110
Muslim League, 401
Muslims. *See also* Islam
  European resistance of, 221–222
  relations with Portuguese, 22
  and the jihads, 216

Mussolini, Benito, 308–310, 341, 348
Mwena, Mutapa, 212
Myanmar, 396
Myasaland, 422

N

Nadir, Shah, 61, 63
Nagasaki, 53, 350, 381
Namban paintings, 54
Namibia, 431
Nanking, Treaty of, 234, 262
Napoleon. *See* Bonaparte, Napoleon
Napoleonic Code, 129, 133
Napoleon III (France), 180–182, 185
Nasser, Gamal Abdel, 410, 416
National American Woman Suffrage Association, 273
National Assembly, rise of, in France, 122–123
Nationalism
  in Africa, 335–336, 428–429
  in Eastern Europe, 186–187
  ethnic, 313
  in India, 260, 329–330
  in Italy, 184–185
  in nineteenth century, 167–168
  in the Middle East, 409–411
  and the revolutions of the 1820s and 1830s, 174–175
  in United States, 193–195
National League for Democracy, 396
National Recovery Administration (NRA), 304
National Revolutionary Party (PNR) in Mexico, 436
Nations, Battle of the, 132
Native Americans, 38
  impact of nationalism on, 194–195
NATO, 355–356, 369
Nazi party, 310–311, 312–313
Near East, in the nineteenth century, 217–222
Négritude, 336
Nehru, Jawaharlal, 329, 402, 403

Neoclassicism, 109–110
Neo-Confucianism, 46–47
Netherlands
  colonies of, 34–36
  explorations of, 30
  golden age of, 90–91
  and Japan, 239
  localized power in, 90
  Philip II and revolt of, 15
  rise of the House of Orange, 90
New Amsterdam, 35–36
Newcomen, Thomas, 144
New Deal, 303–305
Newfoundland, 93
New Granada
  rebellion in, 135
  as vice royalty, 27
New Hampshire, settlement of, 33
New Jersey, settlement of, 34
New Spain, as vice royalty, 27
Newton, Sir Isaac, 99, 100
New York, settlement of, 34
New Zealand, self-government in, 306
Nicaragua
  Sandinista regime in, 437, 446–447
  Somoza dictatorship overthrown, 446
Nicholas I (Russia), 179
Nicholas II (Russia), 276, 284, 285
Niger, 425, 431
Nigeria, 428, 431
Niger River, 215
Nile River, 209
Nixon, Richard, 363, 376, 388
Nkrumah, Kwame, 422, 424, 427
Nobel, Alfred, 155
Non-revolutionary socialism, 274
Noriega, Manuel, 448
North America Act (1867), 198–199
North American Free Trade Agreement, 454
North Atlantic Treaty Organization (NATO), 355–356, 369
North Carolina, settlement of, 34
Northern Rhodesia, 422
Northwest Territories, 199
Norway, in 1980s, 371